Rick Steves'®

# EUROPE THROUGH THE BACK DOOR 2007

EUROPE
0
350 mi
0
350 km
NORWAY
Trondheim
Ålesund
Lillehammer
SOGNEFJORD
Bergen
Oslo
Stavanger
Kristiansand
North Sea
DENMARK
Århus
Legoland
Ærøskøbing
Ærø
Lübeck
Hamburg
Inverness
HIGHLANDS
SCOTLAND
NORTHERN IRELAND
Oban
Glasgow
Edinburgh
Derry
Belfast
IRELAND
Aran Islands
Galway
Dublin
AN DAINGEAN (DINGLE) PENINSULA
Cashel
Kinsale
LAKE DISTRICT
Blackpool
York
Conwy
ENGLAND
WALES
COTSWOLDS
Cambridge
Cardiff
Bath
Thames R.
London
CORNWALL
NETHERLANDS
Amsterdam
Haarlem
Arnhem
GERMANY
Bruges
Brussels
BELGIUM
Köln
Rhine R.
Frankfurt
Würzburg
Mosel
St. Goar
Nürnberg
Rothenburg
Atlantic Ocean
Mont St. Michel
Honfleur
Bayeux
Rouen
Reims
NORMANDY
Paris
LUX.
Dinan
BRITTANY
Chartres
Versailles
Seine R.
Strasbourg
Baden-Baden
Danube
LOIRE
ALSACE
Colmar
BLACK FOREST
BAV
Belle-Ile
Loire R.
Amboise
Chinon
Zürich
Füssen
Reutte
BURGUNDY
Beaune
SWITZ.
Bern
Innsbruck
Gimmelwald
FRANCE
Geneva
Beynac
DORDOGNE
Dordogne R.
Chamonix
Aosta
LAKE DISTRICT
Bay of Biscay
Bordeaux
Rhône River
Lyon
Milan
Po
PIEDMONT
Santiago de Compostela
Albi
PROVENCE
Genoa
CINQUE TERRE
St. Jean-de-Luz
GALICIA
Bilbao
San Sebastián
LANGUEDOC
Avignon
Arles
Pisa
BASQUE
Carcassonne
Nice
MONACO
Ligurian Sea
Cassis
Porto
Douro R.
ANDORRA
Collioure
CORSICA (France)
CATALUNYA
Cadaqués
Barcelona
Nazaré
Coimbra
Salamanca
Segovia
PORTUGAL
Madrid
Lisbon
Toledo
CASTILE LA MANCHA
Menorca
SPAIN
SARDINIA (Italy)
Évora
Consuegra
Majorca
Salema
Guadalquivir R.
Ibiza
ALGARVE
Sevilla
Mediterranean
ANDALUCÍA
Granada
Tarifa
COSTA DEL SOL
GIBRALTAR
Tangier
MOROCCO
ALGERIA
TUNISIA

SWEDEN
FINLAND
Savonlinna
Gulf of Bothnia
Turku
Helsinki
St. Petersburg
Volga River
Uppsala
Tallinn
ESTONIA
Stockholm
RUSSIA
Moscow
LATVIA
Riga
Göteborg
Visby
Kalmar
Öland
Växjö
Baltic Sea
Don River
LITHUANIA
Vilnius
Copenhagen
Malmö
købing
RUSSIA
Minsk
Gdańsk
BELARUS
Poznań
Toruń
Warsaw
Berlin
POLAND
Kiev
Elbe R.
Oder River
Dnieper River
Dresden
Vistula R.
L'viv
UKRAINE
Auschwitz
Kraków
Prague
TATRA MTNS
CZECH REPUBLIC
Levoča
Český Krumlov
Brno
SLOVAKIA
MOLDOVA
Chişinău
Odessa
Munich
Melk
Bratislava
Eger
Segesta
Vienna
Salzburg
Budapest
Hallstatt
Sigisoara
AUSTRIA
HUNGARY
ROMANIA
SLOVENIA
Pécs
DOLOMITES
Bled
Bran
Venice
Ljubljana
CROATIA
Zagreb
Bucharest
Black Sea
Plitvice
Belgrade
Danube R.
BOSNIA & HERZ.
Ravenna
SAN MARINO
Sarajevo
SERBIA
BULGARIA
Split
Florence
Ancona
DALMATIAN COAST
Sofia
Siena
Mostar
Podgorica
Plovdiv
Istanbul
Ankara
TUSCANY
KOSOVO
Rila
Assisi
Dubrovnik
MONT.
Adriatic Sea
Skopje
UMBRIA
Civita
MACEDONIA
Rome
Tiranë
Thessaloniki
VATICAN CITY
ITALY
Bari
ALBANIA
Naples
Brindisi
Meteora
TURKEY
Sorrento
Aegean Sea
CAPPADOCIA
GREECE
Paestum
AMALFI COAST
Corfu
Delphi
Ephesus
Sámos
Tyrrhenian Sea
Athens
Bodrum
Mykonos
Ionian Sea
Nafplion
Hydra
Naxos
Paros
Cefalù
Rhodes
Palermo
PELOPONNESE
Santorini
SICILY
Taormina
Finikoundas
Agrigento
Sea
Valletta
MALTA
GORGE OF SAMARIA
CRETE

# Rick Steves'®

# EUROPE THROUGH THE BACK DOOR 2007

Rich Sorensen

# ACKNOWLEDGMENTS

*Danke* to Risa Laib for her travel savvy, editing, and commitment to excellence. *Dank u wel* to Cameron Hewitt, Gene Openshaw, Steve Smith, and Rich Sorensen for research assistance. And *grazie* to the following for help in their fields of travel expertise: Dave Hoerlein (artful maps); Wide World Books & Maps (guidebooks, www.travelbooksandmaps.com); Brooke Burdick (Internet skills and electronics); Joan Robinson and Ann Neel (women's packing tips); Kent Corrick (travel insurance); Elizabeth Holmes (travel agents, overseas flights); Laura Terrenzio and the staff at Rail Europe (train travel); Alfred Celentano at Europe by Car and Gary Koenig at Auto Europe (car rental and leasing); Katherine Widing and Richard Walters (biking); Alan Spira, M.D., and Craig Karpilow, M.D. (health for travelers); Ian Watson (mobile phones); Arlan Blodgett (photography); Deanna Russell and Brad McEwen (tours); Susan Sygall and Ken Plattner (accessible travel); Anne Steves (travel with kids); and Jane Klausen (the European Union). *Merci* for support from my entire well-traveled staff at ETBD and in particular to Anne Kirchner for keeping things in order while I'm both in and out. *Spasiba* also to Pat Larson, Sandie Nisbet, and John Givens at Small World Productions for introducing so many travelers to this book through our original public television series, *Travels in Europe with Rick Steves*. *Muchas gracias* to Simon Griffith for directing and producing our current *Rick Steves' Europe* television series with such passion and artistry. Finally, *tusen takk* to my parents for dragging me to Europe when I didn't want to go, and to my wife, Anne, for making home my favorite place to travel.

# CONTENTS

## PART TWO: BACK DOORS 395

# PREFACE

The average American traveler enters Europe through the front door. This Europe greets you with cash registers cocked, $5 cups of coffee, and service with a purchased smile.

To give your trip an extra, more real dimension, come with me through the back door. Through the back door, a warm, relaxed, personable Europe welcomes us as friends. We're part of the party—not part of the economy.

Traveling this way, we become temporary Europeans, one of the family—approaching Europe on its level, accepting and enjoying its unique ways of life. We'll demand nothing, except that no fuss be made over us.

This "Back Door–style" travel is better because of—not in spite of—your budget. Spending money has little to do with enjoying your trip. In fact, spending less money brings you closer to Europe. A lot of money forces you through Europe's grand front entrance, where people in uniforms greet you with formal smiles. But the back door is what keeps me in my wonderful European rut.

Since 1973, I've spent a hundred days a year exploring Europe. For the first five trips I traveled purely for kicks. Then, it became clear: Each new trip was smoother than the last...I must be learning from my mistakes. And I saw people making the same mistakes I had made—mistakes costly in time, money, and experience. It occurred to me that if I could package the lessons I'd learned into a class or book, others could learn from my mistakes rather than their own. I could help others enjoy a better, smoother trip. (And I'd have a good excuse to go back to Europe every summer to update my material.) Since 1978, I've been doing just that—traveling with my teaching in mind, taking careful notes, making mistakes, ordering a margarita and ending up with pizza, and getting ripped off just to see what happens. This book, which has evolved annually since its first edition in 1980, is my report to you.

My readers (many of whose grandkids warned them, "You shouldn't be doing this") are having great trips and coming home with money in the bank for next summer. I'm careful not to send people to Europe with too much confidence and not enough money, reservations, or skills. If I did, trips would suffer, and I'd hear about it. But judging from the happy gelato-stained postcards my road scholars send me, it's clear that those who equip themselves with good information and expect to travel smart, do.

The first half of this book covers the skills of Back Door European travel—packing, planning an itinerary, finding good hotels, getting around, and so on. The second half gives you keys to my favorite discoveries, places I call "Back Doors," where you can dirty your fingers in pure Europe—feeling its fjords and caressing its castles. So raise your travel dreams to their upright and locked positions, and let this book fly you away. Happy travels!

# Rick Steves' Back Door Travel Philosophy

Travel is intensified living—maximum thrills per minute and one of the last great sources of legal adventure. Travel is freedom. It's recess, and we need it.

Experiencing the real Europe requires catching it by surprise, going casual..."Through the Back Door."

Affording travel is a matter of priorities. (Make do with the old car.) You can eat and sleep—simply, safely, and enjoyably—anywhere in Europe for $100 a day plus transportation costs. In many ways, spending more money only builds a thicker wall between you and what you traveled so far to see. Europe is a cultural carnival, and time after time, you'll find that its best acts are free and the best seats are the cheap ones.

A tight budget forces you to travel close to the ground, meeting and communicating with the people. Never sacrifice sleep, nutrition, safety, or cleanliness in the name of budget. Simply enjoy the local-style alternatives to expensive hotels and restaurants.

Extroverts have more fun. If your trip is low on magic moments, kick yourself and make things happen. If you don't enjoy a place, maybe you don't know enough about it. Seek the truth. Recognize tourist traps. Give a culture the benefit of your open mind. See things as different, but not better or worse. Any culture has much to share.

Of course, travel, like the world, is a series of hills and valleys. Be fanatically positive and militantly optimistic. If something's not to your liking, change your liking.

Travel is addicting. It can make you a happier American, as well as a citizen of the world. Our Earth is home to six and a half billion equally precious people. It's humbling to travel and find that people don't envy Americans. Europeans like us, but with all due respect, they wouldn't trade passports.

Globe-trotting destroys ethnocentricity. It helps you understand and appreciate different cultures. Regrettably, there are forces in our society that want you dumbed down for their convenience. Don't let it happen. Thoughtful travel engages you with the world—more important than ever these days. Travel changes people. It broadens perspectives and teaches new ways to measure quality of life. Rather than fear the diversity on this planet, travelers celebrate it. Many travelers toss aside their hometown blinders. Their prized souvenirs are the strands of different cultures they decide to knit into their own character. The world is a cultural yarn shop, and Back Door travelers are weaving the ultimate tapestry. Join in!

# PART ONE
# **TRAVEL SKILLS**

*In Europe, life's very good—even if you're on a budget.*

EUROPE
500 KM
300 MI
Trondheim
NORWAY
SOGNE-FJORD
Bergen
Oslo
Stockholm
SWEDEN
FINLAND
Helsinki
St. Pete
Turku
Tallinn
ESTONIA
BALTIC SEA
LATVIA
Riga
SCOTLAND
NORTH SEA
Edinburgh
DENMARK
Copenhagen
LITHUANIA
Vilnius
RUSS.
N. IRE.
IRELAND
Dublin
York
ENGLAND
Galway
WALES
Gdańsk
BELA-RUS
GERMANY
POLAND
AN DAINGEAN (DINGLE) PENINSULA
London
Amsterdam
NETH.
Berlin
Warsaw
Bath
Dresden
Bruges
Brussels
BELG.
Mont St. Michel
RHINE
MOSEL
ROM. ROAD
Prague
Kraków
CZECH.
UKRAINE
ATLANTIC
NORMANDY
LUX.
Paris
ALSACE
SLOVAK.
Brat.
BRITTANY
LOIRE
Colmar
Munich
BAVARIA
Vienna
Salzburg
Budapest
OCEAN
FRANCE
Bern
BERN. OBER.
TIROL
AUST.
HUNG.
ROMANIA
SWITZ.
DOLO-MITES
SLOV.
Chamonix
CRO.
Belgrade
Buch.
DORDOGNE
Lyon
Milan
Venice
Zag.
BOSNIA-HERZ.
PROVENCE
CINQUE TERRE
Florence
SERBIA & MONT.
Sofia
Santiago
San Seb.
Carc.
Arles
MONACO
TUSCANY
SAN MARINO
Dubrov.
BULG.
Porto
Sala-manca
ANDORRA
Nice
UMBRIA
ADRIATIC SEA
CORSICA
MAC.
PORTUGAL
Madrid
Barcelona
Rome
ITALY
ALB.
TO TURKEY
Lisbon
Toledo
Naples
GREECE
SPAIN
SARDINIA
AMALFI COAST
CORFU
Athens
Sevilla
Gran.
MEDITERRANEAN
PEL. PEN.
ALGARVE
ANDALUCÍA
SICILY
TO TURKEY
SEA
MOROCCO
ALGERIA
DCH
TUNISIA

# GETTING STARTED

## 1. TAKE A TOUR OR BE YOUR OWN GUIDE?

A European adventure is a major investment of time and money. A well-planned trip is more fun, less expensive, and not necessarily more structured. Planning means understanding your alternatives and choosing what best fits your travel dreams. From the start, you need to decide if you're taking a tour or going on your own.

*Eight and forty tourists baked in a bus*

Do you want the security of knowing that all your rooms are reserved and that a guide will take you smoothly from one hotel to the next? Do you require comfortable, American-style hotels? Will you forgo adventure, independence, and the challenge of doing it on your own in order to take the worry and bother out of traveling? If you don't mind sitting on a bus with the same group of tourists and observing rather than experiencing, a tour may be just the right way for you to scratch your travel bug bites. There's a tour for just about

*Some tours deliver exactly what they promise.*

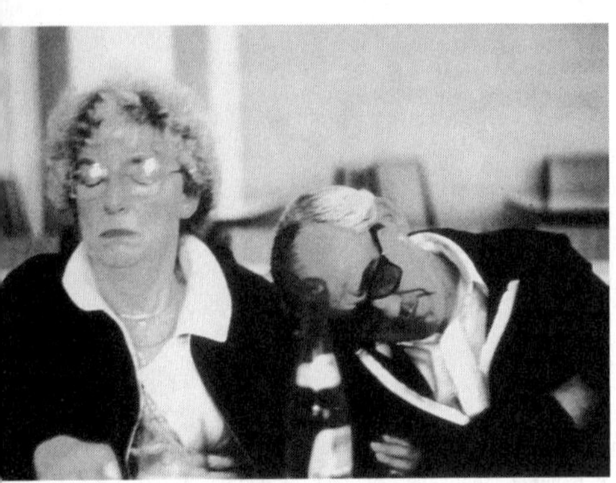

*Not all tours are as exciting as their brochures make them sound.*

every travel dream. Your travel agent can help you.

For many people with limited time and money, tours are the most efficient way to see Europe. Without a tour, restaurant meals and big, modern hotel rooms can be very expensive. Large tour companies book thousands of rooms and meals year-round, and, with their tremendous economic clout, they can get prices that no individual tourist can match. For instance, on a tour with Cosmos (one of the largest and cheapest tour companies in Europe), you will get fine rooms with private baths, some restaurant meals, bus transportation, and the services of a European guide—all for less than $100 a day. Considering that many of the hotel rooms alone cost $100, that all-inclusive tour price is great.

Efficient and "economical" as tours may be, the tour groups that unload on Europe's quaintest towns experience things differently. They are treated as an entity: a mob to be fed, shown around, profited from, and moved out. If money is saved, it's at the cost of real experience. For me, the best travel values in Europe are enjoyed not by gazing through the tinted windows of a tour bus but by traveling independently.

This book focuses on the skills necessary for do-it-yourself European travel. If you're destined for a tour, read on anyway (especially Chapter 28: Bus Tour Self-Defense). Even on a bus with 50 other tourists, you can and should be in control, equipped with a guidebook and thinking as an independent traveler. Your trip is too important for you to blindly trust an overworked, underpaid tour guide.

## Being Your Own Guide

As this book has evolved with my experience as a tour guide, I find myself simply encouraging readers to approach their trip as thoughtfully as I would if you hired me to show you around. As a tour guide, I phone ahead to reconfirm

*Equip yourself with good information, expect yourself to travel smart...and you will.*

reservations, ask at hotel check-in if there's any folk entertainment tonight, and call restaurants to confirm that they're open before I cross town. A good guide reads ahead. Use local entertainment periodicals and talk to other travelers. Ask questions or miss the festival.

Putting together a dream trip requires skills. Consider this book a do-it-yourself manual.

## Traveling Alone

One of your first big decisions is whether to travel alone or with a friend. Consider the pros and cons of solo travel.

You have complete freedom and independence. You never have to wait for your partner to pack up. You never need to consider a partner's wishes when you decide what to see, where to go, how far to travel, how much to spend, or even when to call it a day. You go where you want, when you want, and you can get the heck out of that stuffy museum when all the Monets start to blur together. If ad-libbing, it's easier for one to slip between the cracks than two.

You meet more people when you travel alone because you're more approachable in the eyes of a European, and because loneliness will drive you to reach out and make friends. When you travel with someone, it's easy to focus on your partner and forget about meeting Europeans.

Solo travel is intensely personal. Without the comfortable crutch of a friend, you're more likely to know the joys of self-discovery and the pleasures found in the kindness of strangers. You'll be exploring yourself, as well as a new city or country.

But loneliness can turn hotel rooms into depressing cells. And meals for one are often served in a puddle of silence. Big cities can be cold and ugly when the only person to talk to is yourself. Being sick and alone in a country where no one knows you is, even in retrospect, a sad and miserable experience.

Combating loneliness in Europe is easy. The continent is full of lonely travelers and natural meeting places. You're likely to find vagabuddies in hostels, in museums, on half-day bus tours, and on trains. Eurailers buddy up on the trains. Travel as a student, whatever your age: Students have more fun, make more friends, and spend less money than most travelers. Board the train with a little too much of a picnic—and share it with others. Be bold; if you're lonely, others are, too.

## Traveling with a Partner

Having a buddy overcomes the disadvantages of solo travel. Shared experiences are more fun, and for the rest of your life there will be a special bond between you and your partner. The confident, uninhibited extrovert is better at making things happen and is more likely to run into exciting and memorable events. When I travel with a partner, it's easier for me to be that kind of "wild-and-crazy guy."

*Traveling without a tour, you'll have the locals dancing with you—not for you.*

Traveling with a partner is cheaper. Rarely does a double room cost as much as two singles. If a single room costs $80, a double room will generally be about $100—a savings of $30 per night per person. Virtually everything is cheaper and easier when you share costs: picnicking, guidebooks, banking, maps, magazines, taxis, storage lockers, and much more. Besides expenses, partners can share the burden of time-consuming hassles, such as standing in lines at train stations and post offices.

Remember, traveling together greatly accelerates a relationship—especially a romantic one. You see each other constantly and make endless decisions. The niceties go out the window. Everything becomes very real; you're in an adventure, a struggle, a hot-air balloon for two. The experiences of years are jammed into one summer.

Try a trial weekend together before merging dream trips. A mutual travel experience is a good test of a relationship—often revealing its ultimate course. I'd highly recommend a little premarital travel.

*You can get real close to traditional Europe...sometimes too close.*

Your choice of a travel partner is critical. It can make or break a trip. Traveling with the wrong partner can be like a two-month computer date. I'd rather do it alone. Analyze your travel styles and goals for compatibility. One summer I went to Europe to dive into as many cultures and adventures as possible. I planned to rest when I got home. My partner wanted to slow life down, get away from it all, relax, and escape the pressures of the business world. Our ideas of acceptable hotels and the purpose of eating were quite different. The trip was a near disaster.

Many people already have their partner—for better or for worse. In the case of married couples, minimize the stress of traveling together by recognizing each other's needs for independence. Too many people do Europe as a three-legged race, tied together from start to finish. Have an explicit understanding that there's absolutely nothing selfish, dangerous, insulting, or wrong about splitting up occasionally. This is a freedom too few travel partners allow themselves. Doing your own thing for a few hours or days breathes fresh air into your togetherness.

## Traveling with Three or More Companions

Traveling in a threesome or foursome is usually troublesome. With all the exciting choices Europe has to offer, it's often hard for even a twosome to reach a consensus. Unless there's a clear group leader, the "split and be independent" strategy is particularly valuable.

*Travelers defending Caesar's empire atop Hadrian's Wall in Britain*

To minimize travel-partnership stress, go communal with your money. Separate checks and long lists of petty IOUs are a pain. Pool your resources, noting how much each person contributes, and just assume everything equals out in the long run. Keep track of major individual expenses but don't worry who got an extra postcard or cappuccino. Enjoy treating each other to taxis and dinner out of your "kitty," and after the trip, divvy up the remains. If one person consumed $50 or $60 more, that's a small price to pay for the convenience and economy of communal money.

## If You've Read This Far...

...You've got what it takes intellectually to handle Europe on your own. If you're inclined to figure things out, you'll find Europe well-organized and explained, usually in English. But some people are not inclined to figure things out. They figure things out to earn a living 50 weeks a year, and that's not their idea of a good vacation. These people should travel with a tour...or a spouse. But if you enjoy the challenge of tackling a great new continent—and of being your own guide—you can do it.

# 2. GATHERING INFORMATION

Those who enjoy the planning stage as part of the experience invest wisely and enjoy tremendous returns. Study before you go. This kind of homework is fun. Take advantage of the wealth of material available: guidebooks, classes, videos, libraries, the Internet, and tourist information offices.

## Guidebooks

Guidebooks are $25 tools for $3,000 experiences. Many otherwise smart people base the trip of a lifetime on a borrowed copy of a three-year-old guidebook. The money they save in the bookstore is wasted the first day of their trip, searching for hotels and restaurants long since closed. As a writer of guidebooks, I am a big believer in their worth. When I visit somewhere as a rank beginner—a place like Belize or Sri Lanka—I equip myself with a good, up-to-date guidebook and expect to travel smart. I travel like an old pro, not because I'm a super traveler, but because I have reliable information and I use it. I'm a connoisseur of guidebooks. My trip is my child. I love her. And I give her the best tutors money can buy.

*Never underestimate the value of an up-to-date guidebook.*

Too many people are penny-wise and pound-foolish when it comes to information. I see them every year, stranded on street corners in Paris, hemorrhaging money. It's cascading off of them in €100 notes. These vacations are disasters. Tourists with no information run out of money, fly home early, and hate the French. With a good guidebook, you can come into Paris for your first time, go anywhere in town for less than $2 on the subway, enjoy a memorable bistro lunch for $15, and pay $115 for a double room in a friendly hotel (with a singing maid) on a pedestrian-only street a few blocks from the Eiffel Tower—so French that when you step outside in the morning, you feel you must have been a poodle in a previous life. All you need is a good guidebook that covers your destination.

Before buying a book, study it. How old is the information? The cheapest books are often the oldest—no bargain. Who wrote it? What's the author's experience? Does the book work for you—or for the tourist industry? Does it specialize in hard opinions—or superlatives? For whom is it written? Is it readable? It should have personality without chattiness and information without fluff.

Don't believe everything you read. The power of the printed word is scary. Most books are peppered with information that is flat-out wrong. Incredibly enough, even this book may have an error. Many "writers" succumb to the temptation to write guidebooks based on hearsay, travel brochures, other books, and wishful thinking. A writer met at the airport by an official from the national tourist board learns tips that are handy only for others who are met at the airport by an official from the national tourist board.

While travel information is what keeps you afloat, too much information can sink the ship. I buy several guidebooks for each country I visit, rip them up, and staple the pertinent chapters together into my own personalized hybrid guidebook. To rip a book neatly, bend it over to break the spine, and pull chapters out with the gummy edge intact—or just butcher and staple. Bring only the applicable pages. There's no point in carrying 120 pages of information on Scandinavia to dinner in Barcelona. When I finish seeing a country, I give my stapled-together chapter on that area to another traveler or leave it in my last hotel's lounge.

Bookstores that specialize in travel books have knowledgeable salespeople and a great selection. To find the store nearest you, visit the Independent Travel Stores Association at www.travelstores.org.

### Types of Guidebooks

There are as many types of guidebooks as there are types of travelers. Here are a few general guidelines to help you sort through the options.

Guidebooks differ in how they cover destinations. You'll find guides that specialize in **cities, regions within a single country** (such as Tuscany or the Loire Valley), **individual countries, combinations of two or three neighboring countries** (like Spain and Portugal), and sweeping **multi-country regions** (like Eastern Europe). Shop for guidebooks strategically. For example, if you're visiting only Venice, Florence, and Rome, it can make sense to take three slim, in-depth city guides rather than lugging a hefty all-Italy book that covers far more (and with far less depth) than you need.

Europe is always changing, and guidebooks begin to yellow even before they're printed. It's essential to travel with the most up-to-date information in print. Most guidebooks get an update every two or three years, but a handful of series (like mine) are actually updated in person each year. The rule of thumb: If the year is not printed on the cover, the guidebook is not updated annually (and you'll have to check the copyright information page—usually just inside the front or back cover—to see when it was most recently updated). When I'm choosing a guidebook for a trip, the publication date is usually the single most important factor in which one I buy.

Here are a few of the types of guidebooks you'll encounter:

**Traditional Guidebooks:** This is the industry standard—mostly text, with black-and-white maps for key destinations, generally a few glossy pages of color photos and maps, and sometimes black-and-white photos or illustrations throughout. My guidebooks—and most of those listed under "Guidebook Series," below—follow this model.

**Visual Guides:** These guides feature high-tech, visually super layouts with appealing color photos and illustrations (like cutaway cross-sections of important castles and churches). Visual learners and those who enjoy pretty pictures love this format. But the written information is scant and lacks depth, as it's mostly presented in blurbs short enough to squeeze between the pictures. I don't travel with these (they're printed on glossy paper, so they weigh a ton)—but if I ever need to locate, say, a Caravaggio painting in a church, I seek out a tourist with a copy and ask for a quick peek. **Eyewitness** (published by DK, www.dk.com) and **Knopf** (www.randomhouse.com/knopf/travel) offer gorgeous guides covering London, Paris, Rome, Venice, Florence/Tuscany, Amsterdam, Prague, Budapest, and more, plus several regions and countries ($20–30 each, widely available in Europe). Knopf, the more highbrow of the two, tends to be slimmer, with a more sophisticated layout and more insightful commentary.

**Combination Map-Guidebooks:** These thin guidebooks on individual cities focus on maps, often including a full-size, fold-out map of the destination. Publishers include **Moon Metro, Knopf MapGuides,** and **Fodor's Citypacks.**

**Specialty Books:** If you have a focus, there's a book written just for you—whether you're traveling with toddlers, pets, or grandparents. There are books for vegetarians, galloping gluttons, wine snobs, hedonists, cranky teens, nudists, pilgrims, bird-watchers, gay people, music lovers, potheads, campers, hikers, bikers, and motorcyclists. Some are for the rich and sophisticated; others are for the cheap and earthy. Visit a good travel bookstore and solicit the staff's help.

**eBooks:** Guidebook publishers are trying to figure out how to ride the digital tide. A few years ago many big-name publishers tried selling versions of their best-selling guidebooks to download directly to customers' PDAs (handheld computers). But this trend didn't catch on, and now already-small PDAs are facing new competition in the form of even smaller mobile phones—not too practical for viewing maps or reading long descriptions of sights. These days, if travel information is available for downloading onto PDAs and mobile phones, it tends to be more straightforward (such as translators, currency exchange, and maps with GPS technology). For now, the most practical guidebook format is what you're holding in your hand.

### Guidebook Series

Since most travelers prefer to take a traditional guidebook to Europe, that's what I'll focus on. Each of these series has its own area of specialization. While you'd never read Karen Brown's guides for history, they boast excellent top-end accommodations listings. Let's Go is the hosteler's bible, but you'll be disappointed if you try to use it to find fancy restaurants. If you're into fine cuisine, Michelin Red Guides can't be beat. History nuts seek out Cadogan, Blue Guides, and Rough Guides. Some guidebooks (like mine) are more opinionated and selective, choosing only the most worthwhile destinations in each country and really covering them in depth. These work perfectly for a quick trip to hit the highlights, but it leaves gaps if you're spending a couple of months in a single country. If you're taking a long trip, supplement your information with a more comprehensive guidebook (such as Lonely Planet or Rough Guides) that covers more destinations (though generally in less depth).

Here are some of my favorite series:

**Lonely Planet** (www.lonelyplanet.com): The worldwide standard for a solid, basic guidebook, Lonely Planet guides cover most countries in Europe, Asia, Africa, and the Americas. They offer bricklike editions covering large swathes of Europe (such as Western Europe, Mediterranean Europe, and *Europe on a Shoestring*), as well as books on individual countries, regions, and cities. The Lonely Planet guides offer no-nonsense facts, low- and mid-budget listings, and helpful on-the-ground travel tips. With a recent overhaul to celebrate their 30th anniversary, they're also becoming increasingly opinionated (including an "Author's Choice" section highlighting favorite hotels and restaurants). These guides' biggest strength is that they're as comprehensive as it gets—ideal for spending a long time in one country. Lonely Planet books are widely available in English editions throughout Europe. The drawback is they are not updated annually; before you buy, check the publication date and find out when the new edition is due out.

**Rough Guides** (www.roughguides.com): This fast-growing British series includes books covering just about every country in Europe, as well as a fat all-Europe edition and several regional and city guides. These books are written by Europeans who understand the contemporary and social scene better than American writers. Rough Guides—very similar to Lonely Planet books (see above)—are generally more readable, and particularly strong on historical and cultural information. While the Rough Guides' hotel listings can be skimpy and uninspired, the sightseeing information tends to offer greater depth than Lonely Planet. Like Lonely Planet, Rough Guides are not updated annually—check the copyright date. When deciding between the two series, many travelers simply pick the one that was published more recently.

**Let's Go** (www.letsgo.com): Designed for young train travelers on tight budgets, Let's Go books are written and updated by Harvard students—making them refreshingly youthful and opinionated. As other formerly "budget" series are focusing more and more on mid-range travel (such as my books, Lonely Planet, and Rough Guides), Let's Go has retained its super-low-budget approach and is the best resource for shoestring travelers (in many cities, they list only hostels and student hotels). With a hip student focus, Let's Go offers the best coverage on hosteling and the alternative nightlife scene. The series' biggest drawback is that nearly every young North American traveler uses it, and the flood of backpacker business it generates can overwhelm a formerly cozy village, hotel, or restaurant and give it a whopping Daytona Beach hangover. Titles include the huge *Let's Go Europe,* as well as individual guides on most countries and a few cities in Europe. While most Let's Go books are updated every two or three years, a few editions are updated annually. You can usually find them in Europe for 50 percent more than US prices.

**Frommer's Guides** (www.frommers.com): Arthur Frommer's classic guide, *Europe on $5 a Day,* is now *Europe from $85 a Day.* It's great for the most important big cities but ignores everything else—and there's so much more! It's full of reliable and handy listings of budget hotels, restaurants, and sightseeing ideas originally compiled by the father of independent budget travel himself. But Arthur sold his name, and that's the only thing "Frommer" about the other guides in this series. Those other "Frommer's" guides—covering individual countries, regions, and cities—give good advice on which sights are essential when time is short, and are especially well-attuned to the needs of older travelers, but handle many with unnecessary kid gloves. In addition to the just plain "Frommer's" series, Frommer's publishes piles of other titles, including the "Irreverent," "Unofficial," and "For Dummies" series—many of which, confusingly, have overlapping content on the same destination.

**Karen Brown's Guides** (www.karenbrown.com): Karen's annually updated guides are heavy on frou-frou accommodations, and describe helpful driving routes punctuated by basic sightseeing information. These carefully researched books are ideal for people with extra bucks (most of her doubles run $150–400 a night) and an appetite for doilies under thatch. My splurges are Karen's slums.

**Michelin Green Guides** (www.viamichelin.com): These famous, tall, green books are sort of a hybrid of traditional guidebooks and the newer visual breed: Printed on glossy paper and packed with photos, they offer more written content than most visual guides (such as Eyewitness or Knopf). A French publisher, Michelin has English editions covering several regions of France and most countries of Europe. (The English editions are available in Europe—especially in France—for lower prices than in the United States.) French speakers will find more editions available. Each book includes small but encyclopedic chapters on history, lifestyles, art, culture, customs, and economy. Recent editions also contain information on hotels and restaurants. These practical books are a tour guide's best friend. All over Europe, tour leaders are wowing their busloads by reading from their Green Guides. ("And these are fields of sugar beets. Three-quarters of Austria's beet production lies along the banks of the Danube, which flows through 12 countries, draining an area the size of the Sudan.") A wonderful and unique feature of the Green Guides is their handy "worth a journey/worth a detour" maps. The prominence of a listed place is determined by its importance to you, the traveler, rather than its population. This means that a cute, visit-worthy village (such as Rothenburg) appears bolder than a big, dull city (like Dortmund). These books are filled with fine city maps and are designed for drivers... ideally on Michelin tires. The **Michelin Red Guides** are the hotel and restaurant connoisseur's bibles. But I don't travel with a coat and tie, and my taste buds weren't designed to appreciate $100 meals.

**Blue Guides** (www.blueguides.com): The Blue Guides (which have nothing to do with European brothels) take a dry and scholarly approach to the countries of Europe. They're ideal if you want to learn as much about history, art, architecture, and culture as you possibly can. With the Blue Guide to Greece, I had all the information I needed about any sight in Greece and never needed to hire a guide. Scholarly types actually find a faint but endearing personality hiding between the sheets of their Blue Guides. There are Blue Guides covering many of Europe's countries, cities, and regions. The Blue Guides publisher, Somerset, also produces two other series: the visually oriented **Visible Cities**, and the **art/shop/eat** series, which covers...well, you know.

**Cadogan Guides** (www.cadoganguides.com): Cadogan (rhymes with "toboggan") guides are readable and thought-provoking, giving the curious traveler a cultural insight into many regions. They're similar to Blue Guides, but more accessible to the typical traveler. The series includes country, city, and regional guides for destinations throughout Europe. They're good pre-trip reading. If you're traveling alone and want to understand tomorrow's sightseeing, Cadogan gives you something productive to do in bed.

**Time Out** (www.timeout.com): This popular monthly entertainment guide, which originated in London, has parlayed its wealth of information about the scene in that grand city into a fine series of guidebooks. Time Out Guides now have editions—readily available in Europe—covering 30 European cities and regions from Amsterdam to Vienna. They cover sights, current events, entertainment, eating, and sleeping with an insider's savvy. Written with the English market in mind, they have a hard-hitting, youthful edge and assume readers are looking for the trendy scene.

**Access Guides** (www.accessguides.com): These creatively crafted guides offer sightseeing information on London, Paris, Rome, and Florence/Venice. They're organized by a city's neighborhoods, with text color-coded for sights, hotels, and restaurants.

### Rick Steves' Guidebooks

**Country Guides:** While *Europe Through the Back Door* covers travel skills, my country guides are blueprints for your actual trip. Annually updated, they weave my favorite sights, accommodations, and restaurants into trip strategies designed to give you the most value out of every mile, minute, and dollar. These books cut through the superlatives. Yes, I know you can spend a lifetime in Florence. But you've probably got a day and a half, and I've got a great plan.

These are the most up-to-date books on the market. In order to experience the same Europe that most of my readers do, I insist on doing my research in the peak tourist season—from April through August (for annual editions that come out September through March). Also, my country guides are selective, covering fewer destinations in each country but covering each destination in more depth. It's generally accepted in the travel-publishing world that no one personally updates "annual" guidebooks annually—but, since we have fewer sights to visit, my research partners and I actually do.

My guidebooks will help you explore and enjoy Europe's big cities, small towns, and regions, mixing must-see sights with intimate Back

## Rick Steves' Guidebooks

*Rick Steves' Europe Through the Back Door*
*Rick Steves' Easy Access Europe*
*Rick Steves' Europe 101* (newly revised for 2007)
*Rick Steves' Postcards from Europe*

**Country Guides**
*Rick Steves' Best of Europe*
*Rick Steves' Best of Eastern Europe*
*Rick Steves' Croatia & Slovenia* (new in 2007)
*Rick Steves' England*
*Rick Steves' France*
*Rick Steves' Germany & Austria*
*Rick Steves' Great Britain*
*Rick Steves' Ireland*
*Rick Steves' Italy*
*Rick Steves' Portugal*
*Rick Steves' Scandinavia*
*Rick Steves' Spain*
*Rick Steves' Switzerland*

**City and Regional Guides**
*Rick Steves' Amsterdam, Bruges & Brussels*
*Rick Steves' Florence & Tuscany*
*Rick Steves' Istanbul* (new in 2007)
*Rick Steves' London*
*Rick Steves' Paris*
*Rick Steves' Prague & the Czech Republic*
*Rick Steves' Provence & the French Riviera*
*Rick Steves' Rome*
*Rick Steves' Venice*

(Avalon Travel Publishing)

Door nooks and offbeat crannies. *Rick Steves' Best of Europe,* more than twice the size of the others, thoroughly covers Europe's top destinations—including many of the Back Doors described in the last half of this book. If the table of contents lists all your destinations, this book will serve your trip as well as (and cheaper than) several individual country guides.

**City and Regional Guides:** These annually-updated guides cover Europe's most exciting cities and regions. If you're staying a few days in any of these fascinating places, you'll appreciate the reliable, in-depth information found in these books. You'll also like the engaging, self-guided tours of the top sights, highlighting the great art with photos and commentary.

***Rick Steves' Easy Access Europe:*** This special guidebook, tailored for the needs of slow walkers and wheelchair users, focuses on London, Paris, Amsterdam, Bruges, and the Rhine River.

***Rick Steves' Europe 101: History and Art for the Traveler*** (co-authored with Gene Openshaw) is the only fun travelers' guide to Europe's history and art. The latest edition, published in 2006, is better than ever: updated, expanded, and in full color for the first time. This easily readable manual is full of boiled-down, practical information to carbonate your sightseeing. Written for smart people who were sleeping in their art history classes before they knew they were going to Europe, *101* is the perfect companion to all the other guides...and your passport to goose bumps. After reading *Europe 101,* you can step into a Gothic cathedral, excitedly nudge your partner, and marvel, "Isn't this a great improvement over Romanesque!"

**Rick Steves' Phrase Books** for French, Italian, German, Spanish, Portuguese, and French/Italian/German are the only phrase books on the market designed by a guy who speaks just English. That's why they're so good. They're based on 30 years of experience struggling with other phrase books. These are both fun and practical, with a meet-the-people and stretch-the-budget focus. Mr. Berlitz knew the languages, but he never stayed in a hotel where you need to ask, "When is the water hot?"

***Rick Steves' European Christmas*** covers the joys, traditions, and history of the holiday season in seven European countries. For more

*My phrase books: Spanish, Italian, German, French, Portuguese, and French, Italian & German*

Christmas spirit, pick up the accompanying CD and DVD public-television show, with holiday music and images recorded live in Europe.

In my autobiographical book, ***Rick Steves' Postcards from Europe,*** I take you on a private tour of my favorite 2,000-mile loop through Europe: from Amsterdam through Germany, Italy, and Switzerland, with a grand finale in Paris. Along the way, my European friends offer a wry, contemporary look at Europe and America. My Italian friend Roberto says, "My wife was born in Florida...I know, strange because most people die there." Shuffled among my *Postcards* are stories from my past, including my first trip to Europe—my parents forced me to go. More than three decades later, I can't stop. The reasons are in *Postcards.* I hope you'll distill from it a knack for enjoying Europe as much as I do.

My books are published by Avalon Travel Publishing (www.travelmatters.com).

## Travel Literature

Consider some trip-related recreational reading. A book on the court of Louis XIV brings Versailles to life. Books such as Michener's *Poland* or *Iberia* (for Spain and Portugal), Stone's *The Greek Treasure* for Greece and Turkey, Wordsworth's poems for England's Lake District, and Leon Uris' *Trinity* for Ireland are real trip bonuses. After reading Irving Stone's *The Agony and the Ecstasy,* you'll visit dear friends in Florence—who lived there 500 years ago. Personal accounts are fun and vivid, such as *Notes from a Small Island* by Bill Bryson (on Britain), Peter Mayle's Provence books (on himself), and the Travelers' Tales series (on Ireland, France, Paris, Provence, Italy, Tuscany, Spain, Prague, Greece, and Turkey; www.travelerstales.com).

Here's a distillation of trip-related recreational reading tips from our Road Scholars (for the complete collection, see the Graffiti Wall at www.ricksteves.com):

To glimpse life in Italy, consider Frances Mayes' *Under the Tuscan Sun,* Tim Parks' *Italian Neighbors,* Jan B. Kubik's *Piazzas and Pizzas,* or Christina Björk's *Vendela in Venice* (good for kids).

For the flavor of France, try M. F. K. Fisher's *Two Towns in Provence,* Polly Platt's diplomatic *Savoir-Flair,* Thad Carhart's *The Piano Shop on the Left Bank,* Ernest Hemingway's *A Moveable Feast,* or Adam Gopnik's *Paris to the Moon* (especially if you're taking children). To sample Spain, consider *Driving Over Lemons* by Chris Stewart.

Tony Hawks' *Round Ireland with a Fridge* affords a goofy look at the Irish, *The Emperor's New Kilt* by Jan-Andrew Henderson deconstructs the myths surrounding the tartan-clad Scots, and Susan Allen Toth's *My Love*

*Affair with England* explores the country's charms and eccentricities.

For Germany, consider the travel memoir *The Bells in Their Silence: Travels through Germany,* by Michael Gorra.

To get a sense of Greece, consider Patricia Storace's *Dinner with Persephone* or Gerald Malcolm Durrell's *My Family and Other Animals.* Travelers to Turkey might enjoy Alev Lytle Croutier's novel, *Seven Houses.*

If you're a mystery fan, try the detective series by Anne Perry (Victorian London) or Lindsey Davis (Ancient Rome); Alan Furst's WWII spy novels; or Steven Saylor's Roma Sub Rosa historical mysteries. Dan Brown's popular thrillers, *The Da Vinci Code* and *Angels and Demons,* are set in modern times but deal with real historical figures.

History buffs recommend Ross King's *Brunelleschi's Dome* (on how the stunning dome of Florence's cathedral was built) and his *Michelangelo and the Pope's Ceiling* (the story behind the Sistine Chapel); Jan Morris' and H. V. Morton's books on Italy; Salley Vickers' *Miss Garnet's Angel* (Venice); Colleen McCullough's Masters of Rome series; Edward Rutherfurd's *London* and *Sarum;* Nigel Tranter's trilogies (Scotland); and Ken Follett's *The Pillars of the Earth* (cathedral epic).

*The Diary of Anne Frank* tells the story of a young Jewish girl hiding out from the Nazis in Amsterdam. And Corrie Ten Boom's autobiography, *The Hiding Place,* offers another angle with the story of a Christian family that is caught hiding Jews from the Nazis in Haarlem (near Amsterdam).

For literature lovers, there's Victor Hugo's *The Hunchback of Notre Dame,* set in medieval Paris; Voltaire's 18th-century French satire *Candide;* Czech existentialist Franz Kafka's disturbing *The Metamorphosis;* James Joyce's Irish odyssey, *Ulysses;* and the British classics by Jane Austen, Henry James, the Brontë sisters, D. H. Lawrence, William Shakespeare, C. S. Lewis, and so on.

Your hometown library has a lifetime of valuable reading on European culture. Dewey gave Europe the number 914. Take your travel partner on a date to the library and start your trip early.

Paging through coffee-table books on places you'll be visiting (e.g., *Hill Towns of Tuscany, The French Café*) can give you some great, often untouristy, sightseeing ideas. If travel partners divide up their studying, they can take turns being "guide" and do a better job. Your local travel bookstore stocks good travel literature as well as guidebooks.

## Maps

European travelers have needed good maps since the days of Alexander the Great. But with so many choices, it's hard to know where to start.

Maps and atlases are sold at European gas stations, bookshops, newsstands, and tourist shops. The only reason to buy a map before your trip is for general planning purposes. Once you get to Europe, poke into a book or map store and compare maps side-by-side. Many travelers prefer Michelin maps, but other quality European brands include Hallwag, Freytag Berndt, Marco Polo, and AA (Britain's AAA-type automobile club). The Michelin 705 Europe map provides an excellent overall view of Europe. Many guidebook publishers (including Rough Guides, Lonely Planet, Let's Go, and Rick Steves) are now making maps or combination map-guidebooks. For example, my series of European planning maps are designed to be used with my guidebooks (see www.ricksteves.com).

Here are some tips for choosing and using a map:

**Decide the scope of the map you need.** Your main decision when choosing a map is its purpose. Do you want an overview map or a map of a specific region or city? Are you driving? Bicycling? Walking? Traveling by rail?

**Understand the scale**. European maps indicate their scale with a ratio (such as 1:100,000). The lower the second number on the ratio, the more detailed the map. A 1:100,000 scale means that one centimeter on the map equals 100,000 centimeters (or 1 kilometer) in real life. A basic all-Europe map, such as the Michelin 705, has a scale of 1:3,000,000—perfectly fine for overall route planning. But if you're exploring a specific region by car, you need something more detailed (such as 1:200,000). If you're biking, you could use even more detail (1:100,000 or 1:50,000). Obviously, the more detailed a map is, the more information it can show—but some overachiever maps are so crammed with detail that they become hard to read. Figure out the level of detail you need and purchase accordingly.

**Drivers require first-class maps.** The free maps you sometimes get from your car-rental company usually don't cut it. Drivers need detail, especially when focusing on a specific region. I like Michelin maps (various scales, about $11 each, cheaper in Europe). But the cost for these maps can add up, so consider the popular and relatively inexpensive Michelin road atlases for each country (1:200,000, about $20 each with good city maps and detailed indexes). Though they can be heavy, atlases are compact, a good value, and easier for drivers to use than big fold-out maps. Sometimes the best regional maps are available locally. For example, if you're exploring your roots in the Norwegian fjord country, Cappelens 1:200,000 maps are detailed enough to help you find Grandpa Ole's farm.

**Cyclists and walkers also need highly detailed maps.** Maps at 1:200,000 scale may not show cyclists the off-the-beaten roads. Maps that have even more detail, at 1:100,000 or 1:50,000 (good for walkers), are more helpful but harder to find. Consider OS Ordnance (Britain), Michelin (throughout Europe), IGN's Blue series (good for France), Touring Club Italiano (Italy), and Die Generalkarte (Germany). Elevation gain and loss is a major concern for those traveling by two wheels or two feet. Make sure the map shows general elevation gain with contour lines and/or indicates the steepness of roads (sometimes with small Vs on the road). You'll be outdoors most of the time; maps are rarely waterproof, so keep yours in a plastic pouch.

*Like me, this goat appreciates a good map.*

**Train travelers can get by with less-detailed maps.** By train, you can usually wing it with the map that comes free with your railpass, though some more detailed rail-line maps are available.

**Smart sightseers use city maps.** For an extended stay in a major city, I make a point of buying a good city map immediately upon arrival. While guidebooks come with black-and-white (and sometimes color) maps of big cities, they're generally small, and intended only to give you an overview of the place. A detailed, fold-out map can save you endless time and frustration. You can often get a decent map free at the local tourist office (some TI maps are crisp and durable, while others are fuzzy and fall apart after a few foldings). Many city maps sacrifice important town-center detail by trying to show the entire city (including the suburbs, where you probably won't go). If choosing a city sightseeing map, make sure the city center is detailed enough, since that's where you'll be spending most of your time.

**Look for clarity and durability.** Choose a map that's clear and easy to read. Check to see that the map has crisp lines that don't bleed into one another. Size is another important factor: The bigger the map, the more chance for detail—but the harder it is to use and refold. Also consider durability. A map you plan on using for your entire five-week trip should hold up to constant folding and unfolding (not to mention a few raindrops). A cardboard cover on the map will help it last longer, but it adds weight.

**Learn the legend.** Spend half a traffic jam studying the key. Each map has a legend that indicates navigational as well as sightseeing information, such as types of roads, scenic routes and towns, ruined castles, hostels, mountain huts, viewpoints, and so on. Good maps even include such specific details as tolls and opening schedules of remote mountain roads. When estimating how long a trip will take, figure you'll average 100 kilometers per hour on expressways (about the same as going 60 mph back home). Determining how much ground you can cover off the freeway is a crapshoot. I use a trick an Irish bus driver taught me: Figure a minute for every kilometer (covering 90 km will take you about an hour and a half). Double that for slow, curvy roads (such as in Italy's Dolomites or the Amalfi Coast). Normally the more digits the road number has, the smaller it is. In Britain, M-1 is a freeway, A-34 is a major road, and B-4081 is a secondary road. Roads are labeled on many maps with both national and European designations—for example, the same expressway from Madrid to Sevilla may be labeled N-IV, E-5, or both. As road numbers change, it's often best to navigate by town names.

## Talk with Other Travelers

Both in Europe and here at home, travelers love to share the lessons they've learned. Learn from other tourists. Firsthand, fresh information can be good stuff. Keep in mind, however, that all assessments of a place's touristic merit are a product of that person's personality and time there. It could have rained on her parade, he could have shared an elevator with the town jerk, or she may have been sick in "that lousy, overrated city." Or he might have fallen in love in that "wonderful" village. Every year, I find travelers hell-bent on following miserable travel advice from friends at home. Except for those found in this book, treat opinions as opinions.

Take advantage of every opportunity (such as train or bus rides, or online discussion boards such as the Graffiti Wall at www.ricksteves.com) to swap information with travelers you meet from other parts of the English-speaking world. This is particularly important when traveling beyond Western Europe.

## Good Sources for Travel Information Online

**Accommodations**

**Bed and Breakfast:** www.bedandbreakfast.com
**The Hotel Guide:** www.hotelguide.com

**Blogs and Technology**

**Blogger:** www.blogger.com
**RoadNews (Laptop Advice):** www.roadnews.com
**TeleAdapt:** www.teleadapt.com

**Budget Advice and Resources**

**Backpack Europe:** www.backpackeurope.com
**Eurocheapo:** www.eurocheapo.com
**Eurotrip:** www.eurotrip.com
**Frommer's Budget Travel:** www.frommers.com
**Hostelling International:** www.hihostels.com

**Directories and Newsgroups**

**Google:** www.google.com
**Topica:** http://lists.topica.com/search
**Yahoo! Travel:** http://travel.yahoo.com

**Entertainment**

**Culture Kiosque:** www.culturekiosque.com
**Whatsonwhen.com:** www.whatsonwhen.com

**General European Travel**

**Europe for Visitors:** www.europeforvisitors.com
**The Independent Traveler:** www.independenttraveler.com
**Johnny Jet:** www.johnnyjet.com
**NetTravel.com:** www.nettravel.com
**Practical Nomad:** www.hasbrouck.org
**Rick Steves' Graffiti Wall:** www.ricksteves.com/graffiti
**Tourism Offices Worldwide Directory:** www.towd.com
**Trip Advisor:** www.tripadvisor.com
**Virtual Tourist:** www.virtualtourist.com

### The Internet

The Internet is filled with free online travel talk. Various Web sites offer global weather reports, news, travel advice, visa information, and flight- and hotel-reservation services. Vagabonds between trips hang out in travel forums. I've listed helpful Web sites throughout this book, including the ones that my staff and I use the most when we're planning a trip of our own.

Easy-to-use search engines will help you find what you need. Everyone's heard of **Google,** but **Yahoo! Travel** can also be helpful for

**News, Money, and Weather**

**BBC News Europe:** http://news.bbc.co.uk/europe
**Europeantimes.com:** www.europeantimes.com
**PublicRadioFan.com:** www.publicradiofan.com/statsearch.html
**Newslink:** www.newslink.org
**OANDA Currency Converter:** www.oanda.com/channels/traveler
**Weather.com:** www.weather.com
**Weatherbase:** www.weatherbase.com

**Special Interest**

**Family Adventure Travel:** www.familyadventuretravel.com
**Garden Visit Guide:** www.gardenvisit.com
**Guide to Cooking Schools:** http://cookforfun.shawguides.com
**ISTC (Student Travel):** www.istc.org
**Journeywoman:** www.journeywoman.com
**STA (Student and Youth) Travel:** www.statravel.com
**Seniors Travel Guide:** www.seniorstravelguide.com

**Transportation and Maps**

**A Ferry:** www.aferry.to
**Budget Travel (Europe Transport):** www.budgettravel.com/eurotran.htm
**Deutsche Bahn Trains:** http://bahn.hafas.de/bin/query.exe/en
**Eurolines Bus:** www.eurolines.com
**European Railway Server:** www.railfaneurope.net
**Map24:** www.uk.map24.com
**Maporama:** www.maporama.com
**Michelin:** www.viamichelin.com
**Motoeuropa (Motor Travel):** www.ideamerge.com/motoeuropa
**Subway Navigator:** www.subwaynavigator.com

For more travel tips and links, visit www.ricksteves.com/links

zeroing in on key travel resources.

**Google Groups** and **Topica** are directories of newsgroups and e-mail lists with directions on how to jump into the fray. If you have a particular concern, you can get a world of advice through your Web browser. Use the many discussion lists to contact a European living in the area you want to visit, or a traveler who has just returned. Sometimes travelers can find a place to stay with European residents through these forums.

Several Web sites pull up information according to destination and interest. **Europe for Visitors, Trip Advisor, Johnny Jet, The Independent**

**Traveler,** and **Virtual Tourist** feature travel tips, city maps, and information on cultural sites for most European destinations. **Whatsonwhen .com** and **Culture Kiosque** make it easy to track down live concerts, sporting events, and cultural happenings.

The **Tourism Offices Worldwide Directory** is a searchable directory of tourist information points, including their phone numbers, Web sites, and e-mail addresses.

The books *The Practical Nomad Guide to the Online Travel Marketplace* by Edward Hasbrouck, *The Rough Guide to Travel Online* by Samantha Cook and Greg Ward, and *Internet Travel Planner* by Michael Shapiro include information on how to book a flight, stay online while on the road, and find online travel-planning tips and resources—consult their Web sites for updates. If you're looking for a good guidebook, check out the wide selection at **Amazon.com** and **Books.com.**

*EasyInternetcafé, open 24/7 with big-city branches throughout Europe, is typical of the super Internet cafés available to travelers.*

To keep up with local news, read **Europeantimes.com** or find the local-area newspaper through **Newslink. BBC News Europe** offers some of the best coverage of European news. **PublicRadioFan.com** lets you listen to European public radio (music, commentary, and student-run stations) using a Web browser; to make it work, you'll need to have or install RealPlayer and Windows Media Player, which are both free and downloadable.

Get the latest exchange rates with **OANDA.** For current weather reports, use **Weather.com,** and for climate information, try **Weatherbase.**

Find out about the International Student Identity Card and other student-travel opportunities through **ISTC** or **STA Travel.** Parents will appreciate the interesting activities for kids at **Family Adventure Travel.** Women traveling alone will find **Journeywoman** helpful. Search for senior-friendly travel information through **Seniors Travel Guide.** Gardeners dig the **Garden Visit Guide**, while aspiring chefs feast their eyes upon the **Guide to Cooking Schools** for culinary classes in Europe.

The **Hotel Guide** and **BedandBreakfast.com** list hotels, inns, and

B&Bs in Europe. You can search a destination, choose a hotel, and book your reservation online. For the traveler on a shoestring budget, **Frommer's Budget Travel, Eurotrip, Backpack Europe, EuroCheapo,** and **Hostelling International** offer cheap accommodations and transportation resources on the Internet.

Plan your European train travel with the help of **Deutsche Bahn's** online timetable search service. The **European Railway Server** and **Budget Travel** link you to the Web sites of the European railway and ferry systems. Find your way around underground with **Subway Navigator.** Drivers like **Motoeuropa**. Good map sites include **Maporama, ViaMichelin,** and **Map24. A Ferry** is the top site for ferry information. For information on booking flights online, see page 106.

Travelers can use **Yahoo! Mail** or **Hotmail.com** to pick up and send e-mail at any place with Web access. These sites offer this free service in order to show you a few advertisements. Simply find the sites on the Web, follow their prompts for five minutes, and you'll have your own address with plenty of handy tools for free. Be sure to read the fine print carefully before signing up for these services; for instance, Hotmail will close your account if you don't use it at least once a month and will bounce messages back to senders if you go over your limit—unless you pay an annual fee. Once your e-mail address is set up, tell your friends and you're connected. If you enjoy journaling, write it on **Blogger** and send a link to your travel journal to your friends.

If you're traveling with a laptop, see if your Internet service provider offers local access numbers to get online in Europe. **RoadNews** offers tips on necessary hardware and software and where to find an Internet connection. **TeleAdapt** provides similar know-how as well as information on the adapters and testers you'll need to connect your modem to the various telephone jacks throughout Europe. For more details, see page 53.

## Travel Magazines and Newsletters

Transitions Abroad is the best travel periodical on overseas work and study, as well as thoughtful, responsible travel (6 issues a year, $28/year, www.transitionsabroad.com, tel. 866-760-5340). International Travel News, printed on newsprint in black and white, is packed with down-and-dirty travel news, industry announcements, reports from traveling readers, globetrotting personals, and advertisements from creative small-time travel operators (monthly, $19/year, www.intltravelnews.com, tel. 800-486-4968). National Geographic Traveler offers travel advice, trip ideas, and money-saving tips (8 issues annually, $17.95/year,

## ricksteves.com

With my Web site, www.ricksteves.com, this book becomes just the tip of an informational iceberg sharing the collective travel experience of my 70-person staff (logging well over 2,000 days of European travel each year) and legions of Back Door travelers we call our Road Scholars.

Ricksteves.com is completely free, fast, and user-friendly. You'll find my latest guidebook updates (www.ricksteves.com/update), European country information, a monthly travel e-newsletter (easy and free to sign up), dispatches I send directly from Europe, and scripts for my public-television programs. Look for the most recent version of our railpass guide. Learn the latest about my weekly travel talk show on public radio, and find out how to become a part of the on-air conversation. You can click and listen to dozens of free, information-packed interviews about European culture from our radio show archives. The Press Room includes a sampling of newspaper articles on our work, and our fun and user-friendly online Travel Store covers all the travel gear, guidebooks, videos, railpasses, and tours we offer.

www.nationalgeographic.com/traveler, tel. 800-647-5463). The Nation magazine offers a progressive—and more European—take on American politics (weekly, $52/year, check Web site for better deals, www.thenation.com, tel. 800-333-8536). The Economist, published in Britain, is best for an intellectual look at European contemporary events and politics (weekly, $129/year, www.economist.com).

## Classes

The more you understand a subject, the longer it stays interesting. Those with no background in medieval architecture are the first to get "cathedraled out." Whether you like it or not, you'll be spending lots of time browsing through historic buildings and museums. Those who read or take trip-related classes beforehand have more fun sightseeing in Europe.

There are plenty of worthwhile classes on many aspects of Europe.

Our Graffiti Wall (www.ricksteves.com/graffiti) is one of the most popular corners of our site. It is an immense (yet well-groomed) collection of message boards where our Road Scholars share their experience on the most important or perplexing travel issues of the day. As you read this book, remember that almost every chapter has a corresponding thread growing on our Graffiti Wall with hundreds of postings.

*Scrawl on our Graffiti Wall.*

With more than a hundred topics, there's something for everyone: Room-Finding Tricks, Reservations or Not?, Best European Hostels, Tipping Tips, Drinking the Water, Vegetarian Tips, Shopping Finds, Jet Lag Cures, Marijuana in Europe, Tourist Scam Alert, Staying Healthy, Travel with Disabilities, Leaping Language Barriers, Flying to and within Europe, Driving Europe Crazy, Sleeping on Trains, Tricks for Packing Light, Photography in Europe, Travel with Kids, Women Travelers, Solo Travel, Savvy Seniors, Minority Travelers' Forum, Travel Partners Wanted, and much more.

Although you can get by with English, a foreign language—even a few survival phrases—can only make Europe more fun. A basic modern European history course brings Europe and its "dull" museums to life. A class in Eastern European studies shines some light on that complicated corner of the world.

Art history is probably the most valuable course for the prospective tourist. Don't go to Europe—especially Italy or Greece—without at least having read something on art and architecture.

## Travel DVDs

My series *Rick Steves' Europe* (with 70 episodes now airing on more than 250 public television stations throughout the US) takes a fresh look at well-loved destinations and introduces new favorites. Three of my TV episodes are actually a "how to travel" miniseries. This 90-minute "Travel Skills Special" covers the most important topics featured in this book, filmed on location at my favorite European destinations.

To get in the Christmas spirit, check out *Rick Steves' European Christmas*, a 60-minute look at how seven different European cultures celebrate the holidays.

For more details, see www.ricksteves.com/tv.

### *Travel with Rick Steves* on Public Radio and Podcast

My weekly hour-long show on National Public Radio, *Travel with Rick Steves,* is a great opportunity to hear a wide variety of experts explain what tickles their travel fancy. My guests—who pack their interviews with practical travel tips—include guidebook writers, local tour guides, French philosophers, and even the Princess of Norway. The show also provides a venue for our enthusiastic and well-traveled community of Road Scholars to ask questions and share tips. For all the latest on upcoming topics, and details on how to join in the conversation yourself, see www.ricksteves.com/radio.

On the same Web site, we have two years' worth of shows archived, covering just about any destination or travel topic you can imagine. From France to the Four Corners, from Tuscany to Tanzania, from Dubrovnik to Dubai, from Germany to the Galapagos Islands—plus tips on French food, Italian wine, romance on the road, overcoming the fear of flying, and lots more—there's information that fits any itinerary. Pick and choose from the interviews, download them for free as podcasts, then listen to them on your MP3 player as you prepare for your trip...or as you travel.

### Rick Steves' Audio Tours

At most major European museums, you can rent audioguides that offer a dry headphone commentary on the great works of art (for details, see page 312). If you prefer your art-history information in a light, easy-to-digest style, consider my new free audio tours—just like the ones I give to my tour groups. These guided MP3 walking tours are available at www.ricksteves.com/audiotours. Download the tours to your MP3 player (such as an iPod) before you go, take them with you to France, and let me lead you through the Louvre, Orsay, Versailles, and the historic core of Paris.

### Tourist Information Offices

Tourism is an important part of Europe's economy. Just about every European city has a tourist information office (abbreviated as **TI** in

my books) located downtown and loaded with maps and advice. This is my essential first stop upon arrival in a town. But you don't need to wait until you get to Europe. Each European country has a national tourist office in the United States with a healthy promotional budget. Switzerland, for instance, figures you'll be doing the Alps, but you've yet to decide if they'll be French, Swiss, or Austrian Alps. They are happy to send you a free package of promotional information to put you in a Swiss Alps frame of mind. Just e-mail or call the office of each country you plan to visit. Ask for specific information to get more than the general packet. If you want to sleep in a castle on the Rhine, river-raft in France, or hut-hop across Slovenia, there's a free brochure for you. Ask for an English-language schedule of upcoming events and for maps of the country and various cities you'll be visiting. I find it's best to get answers to specific questions by telephone. Most offices encourage visitors to use their Web sites, so it helps to do some online research before you make the call.

### European National Tourist Offices in the US

**Austrian Tourist Office:** www.austria.info, tel. 212/944-6880. Ask for their "Austria Kit" with map. Fine hikes and city information.

**Belgian Tourist Office:** www.visitbelgium.com, tel. 212/758-8130. Hotel and city guides; brochures for ABC lovers—antiques, beer, and chocolates; map of Brussels; information on WWI and WWII battlefields; and a list of Jewish sights.

**Croatian National Tourist Office:** http://us.croatia.hr, tel. 800-829-4416. Free brochures and maps.

**Czech Tourism Office:** www.czechtourism.com/usa, tel. 212/288-0830. Basic information and map are free; additional materials are $4 (prepaid by check).

**Denmark** (see Scandinavia)

**Estonian Consulate and Tourist Office:** www.visitestonia.com or www.nyc.estemb.org, tel. 212/883-0636.

**Finland** (see Scandinavia)

**French Government Tourist Office:** www.franceguide.com. For questions and brochures (on regions, barging, wine country, etc.), call 514/288-1904 or order online. One brochure and the *France Guide* magazine are free; additional brochures are $0.50 each, with a handling fee of $2 per order. Order will arrive in 2–3 weeks; rush delivery is extra. Some free brochures can also be downloaded from their Web site (read the options carefully to avoid signing up for promotional e-mail).

**German National Tourist Office:** www.cometogermany.com, tel. 800-651-7010. Maps, Rhine schedules, castles, biking, and city and regional information.

**Great Britain Tourist Office:** www.visitbritain.com, tel. 800-462-2748. Free maps of London and Britain. Regional information, garden-tour map, urban cultural-activities brochures.

**Greek National Tourist Organization:** www.gnto.gr (for English, click on British flag in upper right-hand corner), tel. 212/421-5777. General how-to booklet, maps of Athens and Greece, and plenty on the islands.

**Hungarian National Tourist Office:** www.gotohungary.com, tel. 212/695-1221. *Routes to Your Roots* booklet for those of Hungarian descent, *Budapest Guide,* and horseback-riding info.

**Ireland Tourist Office:** www.tourismireland.com, tel. 800-223-6470. Events calendar, golfing, outdoor activities, and historic sights. Tourism Ireland also provides information to travelers who wish to visit Northern Ireland. Learn more about sightseeing opportunities and ask about a vacation-planner packet, maps, walking routes, and horseback riding.

**Italian Government Tourist Board:** www.italiantourism.com, brochure hotline tel. 212/245-4822, general tel. 212/245-5618.

**Luxembourg National Tourist Office:** www.visitluxembourg.com, tel. 212/935-8888. Maps, events calendar, biking, hiking, B&Bs.

**Netherlands Board of Tourism:** www.holland.com, tel. 212/557-3500 or 212/370-7360. They no longer distribute printed material; all information is now available only on the Internet.

**Norway** (see Scandinavia)

**Polish National Tourist Office:** www.polandtour.org, tel. 201/420-9910. Warsaw and Kraków information, regional brochures, and maps.

**Portuguese National Tourist Office:** www.visitportugal.com (general info and to download brochures) or www.orderportugal.com (to order brochures by mail), tel. 800-PORTUGAL (800-767-8842). Maps, regional information, golf, and beach resorts.

**Scandinavian Tourist Board:** www.goscandinavia.com, tel. 212 /885-9700. Good general booklets on all the Scandinavian countries. Ask for specific country info and city maps.

**Slovenian Tourist Office**: www.slovenia.info, tel. 011-386-1/560-8823. *Welcome to Slovenia* brochure, map, information on various regions, hiking, biking, winter travel, and farm stays.

**Spain Tourist Office:** www.okspain.org, www.spain.info, tel. 212/265-8822.

**Sweden** (see Scandinavia)

**Switzerland Tourism:** www.myswitzerland.com, tel. 877-794-8037. Comprehensive brochures, great maps, and hiking material.

**Turkish Tourist Office:** www.tourismturkey.org, tel. 877-367-8875. Numerous maps, hotel guides, and brochures on regions, spas, and outdoor activities.

### Middle Eastern and North African Tourist Offices in the US

**Egyptian Tourist Authority:** www.egypttourism.org, tel. 877-773-4978.

**Israeli Ministry of Tourism:** www.goisrael.com, tel. 888-774-7723. Request the general packet in English. Interesting brochures for Christian and Jewish faiths.

**Moroccan National Tourist Office:** www.visitmorocco.com. You can download a brochure or list of hotels and sign up for an e-mail newsletter.

# 3. PAPER CHASE

While going to Europe isn't all that complex, your trip will be smoother if you consider these documents and details well before your departure date.

## Passports

In most of Europe, the only document a US or Canadian citizen needs is a passport. For most travelers, the only time any customs official will look at you seriously is at the airport as you re-enter the United States. (And those bomb-sniffing dogs keep thinking there's something explosive in my crotch.) You won't even stop as you cross most borders within Western Europe, and even Eastern European border crossings are generally a wave-through for US citizens.

Passports, good for 10 years, cost $97 ($67 to renew). Minors under 16 pay $82 for a passport good for five years (kids under 14 must apply in person with at least one parent and the other parent's notarized permission). You can apply at some courthouses and some post offices. For details and the location of the nearest passport-acceptance facility, see www.travel.state.gov or call 877-487-2778. Although they say applications take six weeks (and you should be prepared for delays), most passports are processed more quickly. If you miss the six-week deadline, tack on an additional $60 speed fee (plus overnight shipping both ways) when you apply at the nearest acceptance facility and you'll get your passport by mail in two to three weeks. If you're in a last-minute emergency situation, call the above number and speak to a customer-service representative. If you can prove that you have to leave within two weeks (by showing a purchased plane ticket or a letter from work requiring you to travel overseas on short notice), you may be able to receive a passport in a day or so. Make an appointment to go in person to the nearest US Passport Agency and pay the additional $60 fee. They'll issue your new passport in 24–72 hours.

Keep an eye on your passport's expiration date. Many European countries require that your passport be valid for three to six months *after* your ticketed date of return to the United Sates. This means that even if your passport doesn't expire for a few months, you may still be denied entry to a country until you get a new passport issued. If necessary, get your passport renewed before you go. Other countries can have surprising entry requirements. For example, the Czech Republic requires visitors to carry proof that they have medical insurance up to $35,000. While it's virtually unheard-of that a border guard would actually request this, it's worth knowing about.

As you travel, take good care of your passport, but relax when it comes to temporarily giving it up. When you sleep on an international night train, the conductor may take your passport so you won't be disturbed when the train crosses the border at 3 a.m. Hotels routinely take your passport "for the night" so they can register you with the police. This bookwork must be done for foreign guests throughout Europe. Receptionists like to gather passports and register them all at the same time when things are quiet. Although it's unreasonable to expect them to drop whatever they're doing to register me immediately, I politely ask if I can pick up my passport in two hours. I just don't like my passport in the top drawer all night long.

A passport works well for collateral in cases when you don't have the cash right now (hefty deposits on bike rentals, audioguides, and so on).

Losing your passport while traveling is a major headache. If you do, contact the police and the nearest US consulate or embassy right away. You can get a short-term replacement, but you'll earn it. A photocopy of your passport (and a couple of passport-type photos you've brought from home or have taken in Europe) can speed the replacement process.

## Visas

A visa is a stamp placed in your passport by a foreign government, allowing you to enter their country. Visas are not required for Americans or Canadians traveling in Western Europe and most of the East (including the Czech Republic, Slovakia, Poland, Hungary, Slovenia, and Croatia).

Both Canadians and Americans need visas to visit **Turkey.** They're easy to get upon arrival at the border or airport—you can pay in US currency or euros (US residents, $26; Canadians, $60—US dollars, not Canadian—or €45). For more information, see www.tourismturkey.org (United States) or www.turkishembassy.com (Canada).

Americans can get a visa in advance by money order through the Turkish embassy (2525 Massachusetts Ave. N.W., Washington, DC 20008, tel. 202/612-6740) or the Turkish consulates in New York (821 United Nations Plaza, New York, NY 10017, tel. 212/949-0160), Chicago (360 N. Michigan Ave. #1405, Chicago, IL 60601, tel. 312/263-0644, ext. 28), Houston (1990 Post Oak Blvd. #1300, Houston, TX 77056, tel. 713/622-5849), or Los Angeles (6300 Wilshire Blvd. #2010, Los Angeles, CA 90048, tel. 323/655-8832).

For Canadians, the Turkish embassy in Ottawa sells single-entry visas for $75 Canadian and multiple-entry visas for $150 Canadian (197 Wurtemburg St., Ottawa, Ontario K1N 8L9, tel. 613/789-4044, www.turkishembassy.com).

Travelers to **Russia** also need visas. The process is expensive and complicated, and you should begin several weeks in advance. Before applying for a visa, you must first get an official "invitation" (generally from a hotel). Then, once you arrive, you must be "registered" (usually by the same hotel that invited you). It's smart to enlist an agency that specializes in steering your application through the red tape (Zierer Visa Service is one of many, www.zvs.com). The costs add up: The visa itself costs $100, visa agencies charge a service fee of about $50–60, and you'll also pay to ship your passport to the embassy and back. Figure about $200 total per person. For more details, see www.russianembassy.org or contact one of the Russian consulates: in Washington (2641 Tunlaw Rd. N.W., Washington, DC 20007, tel. 202/939-8907), in New York (9 East 91st St., New York, NY 10128, tel. 212/348-0926), in San Francisco (2790 Green St., San Francisco, CA 94123, tel. 415/928-6878), in Seattle (2323 Westin Building, 2001 6th Ave., Seattle, WA 98121, tel. 206/728-1910), and in Houston (1333 West Loop S., Ste. 1300, Houston, TX 77027, tel. 713/337-3300).

For **travel beyond Europe,** get up-to-date information on visa requirements from your travel agent or the United States Department of State (www.travel.state.gov/foreignentryreqs.html).

If you do need a visa, it's usually best to get it at home before you leave. If you forget, just about every country has an embassy or consulate (which can issue visas) in the capital of every other European country.

## Shots

At this time, shots are not required for travel in Europe. If you're traveling beyond Europe, check the inoculation requirements with your doctor or a travel-medicine clinic before you leave home. Countries "require" shots in order to protect their citizens from you and "recommend" shots to protect you from them. If any shots are recommended, take that advice seriously. (For more information, see Chapter 22: Staying Healthy.)

## Student Cards and Hostel Memberships

The International Student Identity Card (ISIC), the only internationally recognized student ID card, gets you discounts on transportation, entertainment, and sightseeing throughout Europe, and includes some basic trip insurance. If you are a full-time student (and can prove it), get one. Your ISIC card can also be used as a prepaid phone card (see Chapter 21: Phones, E-mail, and Mail). Be aware that if you're older than 26, you might have trouble using the card in some places. Two other varieties of the card, offering similar discounts, are available, though they're often not honored: for teachers of any age (International Teacher Identification Card, or ITIC) and for non-student travelers under age 26 (International Youth Travel Card, or IYTC). Each of these cards costs $22. Get yours on the ISIC Web site (www.isicus.com), through STA Travel (www.statravel.com), or from your university foreign study office.

Travelers who know they'll be staying at least six nights in official HI hostels should get a hostel membership card from a local hostel or Hostelling International (www.hiusa.org, tel. 301/495-1240; for more information, see Chapter 17: Sleeping).

## Railpasses and Car Rental

Most railpasses are not sold in Europe and must be purchased before you leave home. Car rental is usually cheaper when arranged before your trip through your hometown travel agent. For most, an international driver's permit is not necessary (but if you're getting one, do it at AAA before your departure—for $10 and 2 passport photos). For specifics on driving and train passes, see Chapters 11 and 12.

## Travel Insurance—To Insure or Not to Insure?

Travel insurance is a way to minimize the considerable financial risks of traveling. These risks include accidents, illness, missed flights, canceled tours, lost baggage, emergency evacuation, and getting your body home if you die. Each traveler's risk and potential loss varies, depending on how much of the trip is prepaid, the kind of air ticket purchased, your state of health, the value of your luggage, where you're traveling, what medical coverage you already have, and the financial health of the tour company or airline. For some, insurance is a good deal; for others, it's not.

Travel agents recommend travel insurance because they make a commission on it, they can be held liable for your losses if they don't explain insurance options to you, and sometimes because it's right for you. But the final decision is yours. What are the chances of needing it, how able are you to take the risks, and what's the peace of mind worth to you?

Beta specializes in affordable emergency travel insurance (www.betins.com, tel. 253/238-6374). For more extensive coverage, go with a big-name company (avoid buying insurance from a no-name company on the Web): Consider the package deals sold by Access America (www.accessamerica.com, tel. 800-729-6021), Travelex (www.travelex-insurance.com, tel. 800-228-9792), Travel Guard (www.travelguard.com, tel. 800-826-4919), and Travel Insured International (www.travelinsured.com, tel. 800-243-3174). Insuremytrip.com allows you to compare insurance policies and costs among various providers (they also sell insurance; www.insuremytrip.com, tel. 800-487-4722). The $22 ISIC student identity card (mentioned earlier) includes very minimal travel insurance.

The insurance menu includes five courses: trip cancellation, medical, evacuation, baggage, and flight insurance. The various types are generally sold in some combination—rather than buying just baggage, medical, or cancellation insurance, you'll usually purchase a package that includes all of them. If you want one type of coverage in particular—such as medical—ask for a policy that focuses on that coverage (though it might come with a little cancellation or baggage insurance, too). The most complete version is called "comprehensive insurance."

Insurance costs vary dramatically, but most packages are about 5–12 percent of the total trip cost. Two factors can increase this price: age (rates increase dramatically for every decade over 50) and duration of trip (longer trips cost more to insure).

Note that most travel insurance is reimbursement-only: You'll pay out-of-pocket for your expenses, then submit the paperwork to your insurer to recoup your money. Still, if you have a problem, it's wise to communicate with your insurance company immediately to ask them how to proceed. Many major insurance companies are accessible by phone 24 hours a day—handy if you have problems in Europe.

Policies available vary by state. For example, Washington State strictly regulates insurers, so Washingtonians have fewer options than, say, Ohioans. Furthermore, not all insurance companies are licensed in every state. If you have to make a claim and encounter problems with a company that isn't licensed in your state, you don't have a case.

For each type of insurance below, I've outlined some of the key legalese. But be warned—these guidelines don't apply to every insurer. Policies can differ, even within the same company. Ask a lot of questions, and always read the fine print to see what's covered (e.g., how they define "travel partner" or "family member"—your great-aunt might not qualify).

**Trip cancellation or interruption insurance** covers the non-refundable financial penalties or losses you incur when you cancel a prepaid tour or flight for an acceptable reason. These might include if:

(1) you, your travel partner, or a family member cannot travel due to sickness, death, or a list of other acceptable reasons;

(2) your tour company or airline goes out of business or can't perform as promised;

(3) a family member at home gets sick, causing you to cancel;

(4) for a good reason (such as a car accident, inclement weather, or a strike), you miss a flight or need an emergency flight.

In other words, if you or your travel partner accidentally breaks a leg a few days before your trip, you can both bail out (if you both have travel insurance) without losing all the money you paid for the trip. And if, a day into your tour, you have an accident that prevents you from continuing your trip, you'll be reimbursed for the portion of the tour you haven't used.

This type of insurance can be used by people on an organized tour or cruise, as well as people traveling independently (in which case, only the prepaid expenses—such as their flight and any nonrefundable hotel reservations—are covered). If you're taking a tour, it may come with some cancellation insurance. Understand exactly what's included before you consider buying additional coverage.

Note the difference: Trip *cancellation* is when you don't go on your trip at all, and is fully covered. Trip *interruption* is when you begin a journey but have to cut it short; in this case, your coverage extends only to the portion of the trip that you didn't complete.

Some insurers won't cover certain airlines or tour operators. Many are obvious—such as companies under bankruptcy protection—but others can be surprising (including major airlines). Make sure your carrier is covered.

It's smart to buy your insurance policy within a week of the date you make the first payment on your trip. Policies purchased later than a designated cutoff date—generally 7–21 days, as determined by the insurance company—are less likely to cover default of carrier, pre-existing medical conditions, or terrorist incidents.

These days, jittery travelers are fretful about two big unknowns: terrorist attacks and natural disasters. Ask your company for the details. You'll likely be covered only if a destination on your itinerary actually becomes the target of a terrorist incident within 30 days of your trip. Even then, if your tour operator offers a substitute itinerary, your coverage may become void. As for natural disasters, you're covered only if your destination is uninhabitable (for example, your hotel is flooded or the airport is gone). A terrorist attack or natural disaster in your hometown may or may not be covered—ask. War or disease outbreaks generally aren't covered.

The rugged, healthy, unattached, and gung-ho traveler will probably skip trip cancellation coverage. I have skipped it for more than 70 trips, and my number has yet to come up. But if you're paying out a lot of up-front money for an organized tour (which is expensive to cancel), if you have questionable health, or if you have a loved one at home in frail health, you should probably get this coverage.

**Medical insurance** generally covers only medical emergencies. Before buying a special medical policy for your trip, check with your medical insurer—you might already be covered by your existing health plan. Ask about benefit caps and deductibles (if any), and have them walk you through the procedure. Generally, your expenses are out-of-pocket, and you bring home documentation to be reimbursed. In some cases, you may have to contact your insurer for approval before seeking medical help. While many US insurers cover you overseas, Medicare does not. Most additional coverage you buy is supplemental (or "secondary"), so it covers whatever expenses your primary coverage doesn't.

Many pre-existing conditions are covered by medical and trip-cancellation coverage, depending on when you buy the coverage and how recently you've been treated for the condition. Check with your agent or insurer before you commit.

The US State Department periodically issues warnings about traveling to at-risk countries (see http://travel.state.gov). If you're traveling to one of these countries, your cancellation and medical insurance will likely not be honored—unless you buy supplemental coverage.

**Evacuation insurance** covers the cost of getting you to a place where you can receive appropriate medical treatment in the event of an emergency. (In the worst-case scenario, this can mean a medically equipped—and incredibly expensive—private jet.) This is usually not covered by regular medical insurance. Sometimes this coverage can get you home after an accident, but more often, it'll just get you as far as the nearest major hospital. "Medical repatriation"—that is, getting you all the way home—is likely to be covered only if it's considered medically necessary. Ask your insurer exactly what's covered before *and after* you get to the hospital.

Keep in mind that medical and evacuation insurance may not cover you if you're participating in an activity your insurer considers to be dangerous (such as skydiving, bungee jumping, scuba diving, or even skiing). Some companies sell supplementary adventure sports coverage.

**Baggage insurance** is included in most comprehensive policies, but it's rare to buy it separately. Baggage insurance puts a strict cap on reimbursement for such items as jewelry, eyewear, electronics, and photographic equipment—read the fine print. If you check your baggage for a flight, it's already covered by the airline (generally with a cap of $600–3,000; if you have particularly valuable luggage, you can buy supplemental "excess valuation" insurance directly from the airline). Homeowners' insurance (with the "floater" supplement, if necessary, to cover you out of the country) is cheaper, and you'll have coverage even after your trip. Travelers' baggage insurance will cover the deductibles and items excluded from your homeowners' policy. Double-check the particulars with your agent. If your policy doesn't cover railpasses, consider buying the $10–17 insurance deal sold with the pass.

**Flight insurance** (crash coverage) is a statistical rip-off that heirs love. It's basically a life insurance policy that covers you when you're on the airplane. Since plane crashes are so rare (see "Fear of Flying," page 117), there's little sense in spending money on this insurance.

Another important type of insurance—**collision coverage** for rental cars—is covered on page 148. Collision insurance may be covered in some comprehensive insurance plans.

Your travel agent has insurance brochures. Ask your agent which insurance he or she recommends for your travels and why. Study the information. Consider how insurance fits your travel and personal needs, compare its cost to the likelihood of your using it and your potential loss—and then decide.

# 4. PACK LIGHT PACK LIGHT PACK LIGHT

The importance of packing light cannot be overemphasized, but, for your own good, I'll try. You'll never meet a traveler who, after five trips, brags: "Every year I pack heavier." The measure of a good traveler is how light she travels. You can't travel heavy, happy, and cheap. Pick two.

Limit yourself to 20 pounds in a carry-on–size bag. A 9" x 22" x 14" bag fits under most airplane seats. That's my self-imposed limit. At my company, we've taken tens of thousands of people of all ages and styles on tours through Europe. We allow only one carry-on bag. For many, this is a radical concept: 9" x 22" x 14"? That's my cosmetics kit! But they manage, and they're glad they did. And after you enjoy that sweet mobility and freedom, you'll never go any other way.

*Older people traveling like college kids—light, mobile, footloose, and fancy-free, wearing their convertible suitcase/backpacks—have nothing to be ashamed of.*

You'll walk with your luggage more than you think you will. Before leaving home, give yourself a test. Pack up completely, go into your hometown, and practice being a tourist for an hour. Fully loaded, you should enjoy window-shopping. If you can't, stagger home and thin things out.

When you carry your own luggage, it's less likely to get lost, broken, or stolen. (Some travelers claim that airline employees have stolen items from checked luggage.) Quick, last-minute changes in flight plans become simpler. A small bag sits on your lap or under your seat on the bus, taxi, and airplane. You don't have to worry about it, and, when you arrive, you can hit the ground running. It's a good feeling. When I land in London, I'm on my way downtown while everyone else stares anxiously at the luggage carousel. When I fly home, I'm the first guy the dog sniffs.

Pack light...and pack smart. Since September 11, 2001, you can't bring anything potentially dangerous—such as knives, box cutters, or lighters—in your carry-on bag. Now I leave my Swiss Army knife at home and still carry on my bag as usual. You can take an entire set of knives to Europe if you like—but you'll have to check your bag.

Even before September 11, some airlines were limiting carry-on luggage weight as well as size. For example, British Airways and SAS have a maximum of 13 and 18 pounds, respectively. It's only worth fighting to carry on your bag if you have a tight connection. Call your airline (or read the fine print on your ticket) for details. If you have to check your bag, mark it inside and out with your name, address, and emergency phone number. If you have a lock on your bag, you may be asked to remove it due to increased security checks—or it may be cut off so the bag can be inspected (to avoid this, consider a TSA-approved lock, described in the packing list later in this chapter). I've never locked my bag and never had a problem.

Too much luggage marks you as a typical tourist. It slams the back door shut. Serendipity suffers. Changing locations becomes a major operation. Con artists figure you're helpless. Porters are a problem only to those who need them. With one bag hanging on your back, you're mobile and in control. Take this advice seriously.

## Backpackademia—What to Bring?

How do you fit a whole trip's worth of luggage into a small backpack or suitcase? The answer is simple: Bring very little.

Spread out everything you think you might need on the living-room floor. Pick up each item one at a time and scrutinize it. Ask yourself, "Will I really use this snorkel and these fins enough to justify carrying them around all summer?" Not "Will I use them?" but "Will I use them enough to feel good about carrying them over the Swiss Alps?" Regardless of my budget, I would buy them in Greece and give them away before I would carry that extra weight over the Alps.

*When getting way off the beaten path—like this traveler, who's spending the night at a tiny guest house in Italy's Civita di Bagnoregio—you'll be glad you're packing light.*

Don't pack for the worst scenario. Pack for the best scenario and simply buy yourself out of any jams. Risk shivering for a day rather than taking a heavy coat. Think in terms of what you can do without—not what will be handy on your trip. When in doubt, leave it out. I've seen people pack a whole summer's supply of deodorant, tampons, or razors, thinking they can't get them there. The world's getting really small; you can buy Dial soap, Colgate toothpaste, Tampax tampons, Nivea cream, and Bic razors in Sicily or Slovakia. Tourist shops in major international hotels are a sure bet whenever you have difficulty finding some personal item. If you can't find one of your essentials, ask yourself how 460 million Europeans can live without it.

Whether you're traveling for three weeks or three months, pack exactly the same. Rather than take a whole trip's supply of toiletries, take enough to get started and look forward to running out of toothpaste in Bulgaria. Then you have the perfect excuse to go into a Bulgarian department store, shop around, and pick up something you think might be toothpaste....

## Backpack or Wheeled Bag?

A fundamental packing question is your choice of luggage. Of all the options, I consider only three: 1) a carry-on–size "convertible" bag with zip-away shoulder straps; 2) a carry-on–size wheeled bag; or 3) an internal-frame backpack.

Travelers who want the easy mobility of a backpack but with a more low-key appearance travel with bag #1: a convertible backpack/suitcase with zip-away shoulder straps (see photo on page 39). These bags give you the best of both worlds—a suitcase when in town, and a backpack when you want to be more mobile. I travel with this bag and keep it exclusively in the backpack mode. While these "soft" bags basically hang on your back and are not as comfortable for long hauls as an internal-frame backpack (#3, described below), they work fine for getting from the station to your hotel. And, at 9" x 22" x 14", they fit in the airplane's overhead lockers. live out of this bag for three months each year—and I absolutely love it.

*A 9" x 22" x 14" carry-on bag (with or without wheels) is the ideal size.*

Carry-on–sized wheeled bags (option #2) are well-designed and popular. My wife, daughter, and most of my staff prefer this bag; its tight and compact design makes it roomy while keeping it just small enough to fit in the plane's overhead locker. The advantage of bag #2 over bag #1: You can effortlessly wheel your gear around without getting sweaty. The downside: Wheeled bags cost $20–50 extra, weigh several pounds more, and delude people into thinking they don't need to pack so light. They are cumbersome in places without a smooth surface to roll on (crowded subways, hiking through a series of train cars, walking to your hotel in villages with stepped lanes and dirt paths, and so on)—but they're wonderful in airports (where check-in waits and distances to gates are longer than ever).

Most young-at-heart travelers "backpack" through Europe. They buy an internal-frame backpack (option #3) at REI (www.rei.com) or a similar outdoor store. While these are the most comfortable bags to wear on your back, they can be expensive, and are often built "taller" than carry-on size.

Base your decision on the strength of your back. The day will come when I'll be rolling my bag through Europe with the rest of the gang. But as long as I'm hardy enough to carry my gear on my back, I will. (Bags #1 and #2 are described at the end of this book and on sale at www.ricksteves.com.)

Unless you plan to camp or sleep out a lot, a sleeping bag is a bulky security blanket. Even on a low budget, bedding will be provided. (Hostels provide all bedding free or rent sheets for a small fee, and often don't allow sleeping bags.) Don't pack to camp unless you're going to camp. Without a sleeping bag, a medium-size backpack is plenty big.

Pack your bag only two-thirds full to leave room for picnic food and souvenirs. Sturdy stitching, front and side pouches, padded shoulder straps (for backpacks), and a low-profile color are virtues. I'm not wild about the bags with a zip-off day bag—I take my convertible backpack and supplement it with a separate day bag.

Entire books have been written on how to pack. It's really quite simple: Use stuff bags (one each for toiletries; underwear and socks; and miscellaneous stuff such as a first-aid kit, earplugs, clothesline, sewing kit, and gadgets). Roll clothes and store them in mesh bags or packing cubes to keep them compact—or, to reduce wrinkling, zip them up in airless baggies or a clothes compressor like the one by Pack-Mate (described on page 49).

## Clothing

The bulk of your luggage is clothing. Minimize by bringing less and washing more often. Every few nights you'll spend 10 minutes doing a little wash. This doesn't mean more washing; it just means doing it little by little as you go.

Be careful to choose dark clothes that dry quickly and either don't wrinkle or look good wrinkled. To see how wrinkled shirts will get, give everything a wet rehearsal by hand-washing and drying once at home. You should have no trouble drying clothing overnight in your hotel room. I know this sounds barbaric, but my body dries out a damp pair of socks or shirt in a jiffy. It's fun to buy clothes as you travel—another reason to start with less.

For winter travel, you can pack just about as light. Wear heavier, warmer, high-top, waterproof shoes. Add a down or pile coat, long johns (quick-drying Capilene or super-light silk), scarf, gloves or mittens, hat, and an extra pair of socks and underwear since things dry more slowly. Pack with the help of a climate chart (see the appendix). Layer your clothing for warmth, and assume you'll be outside in the cold for hours at a time.

During the tourist season (April–Sept), the concert halls go casual. I have never felt out of place at symphonies, operas, or plays wearing a decent pair of slacks and a good-looking sweater. Pack with color coordination in mind. Some cultural events require more formal attire, particularly outside of the tourist season, but the casual tourist rarely encounters these.

Many travelers are concerned about appropriate dress. American women, caught up in visions of the super-traditional Old World, wonder whether it's OK to wear pants. But in today's Europe, women are equally comfortable in pants, skirts, and dresses. While you may see elderly women wearing skirts or dresses in some areas (especially southern Europe), you'll attract no unwanted attention if you wear nice dark pants or jeans. Women who prefer to wear pants and don't pack a dress have no regrets.

*In Britain, there's no bad weather...only inappropriate clothing.*

If you're trying to blend in, realize that shorts are uncommon in Europe. They're considered exclusively beachwear, for use in coastal or lakeside resort towns. While most Europeans won't be offended if you wear shorts, you might be on the receiving end of some stares. Shorts are especially uncommon on older women and in big cities, and the cutoff temperature for "hot enough for shorts" is much higher than in the US. Especially in southern Europe, no matter how hot it is, grown adults look goofy in shorts.

Shorts (and other skimpy summer attire) can also put a crimp in your sightseeing plans. Some churches, mostly in southern Europe, have modest dress requirements for men, women, and children: no shorts or bare shoulders. Except at the strict St. Peter's in Rome and St. Mark's in Venice, the dress code is often loosely enforced. If necessary, it's usually easy to improvise some modesty (buy a cheap souvenir T-shirt to cover your shoulders and borrow a nearby tablecloth for a skirt or kilt to cover your legs). At some heavily-touristed churches in southern Europe, people hand out sheets of tissue paper you can wrap around yourself like a shawl or skirt.

But ultimately—so long as you don't wear something that's outrageous or offensive—it's important to dress in a way that makes you comfortable. No matter how carefully you dress, your clothes will probably mark you as an American. Frankly, so what? Europeans will know anyway. I fit in and am culturally sensitive by watching my manners, not the cut of my clothes.

Go casual, simple, and very light. Remember, in your travels you'll meet two kinds of tourists—those who pack light and those who wish they had. Say it once out loud: "PACK LIGHT."

## What to Pack

*Indicates an item you can order online at www.ricksteves.com.

**Shirts.** Bring up to five short-sleeved or long-sleeved shirts in a cotton/polyester blend. Arrange mix according to season.

**Sweater.** Warm and dark is best—for layering and dressing up. It never looks wrinkled and is always dark, no matter how dirty it is.

**Pants.** Bring two pairs: one lightweight cotton and another super-lightweight for hot and muggy big cities and churches with modest dress codes. Jeans can be too hot for summer travel. Linen is great. Many like lightweight pants/shorts with zip-off legs. Button-down wallet pockets are safest.

**Shorts.** Take a pair with pockets—doubles as a swimsuit for men.

**Swimsuit.** Especially for women.

**Underwear and socks.** Bring five sets (lighter dries quicker).

**One pair of shoes.** Take a well-used, light, and cool pair, with Vibram-type soles and good traction. My wife and I like shoes by Ecco. Sturdy, low-profile tennis shoes with a good tread are fine, too. (Some people bring along an extra pair of sandals in case the shoes get wet.) For winter travel, bring heavy shoes (for warmth and to stay dry). See the appendix (page 628) for top reader recommendations on footwear.

**Jacket.** Bring a light and water-resistant windbreaker that has a hood.

## One Carry-on Size Bag

Here's everything I traveled with for two months (photos taken naked in a Copenhagen hotel room): convertible 9" x 22" x 14" suitcase/backpack; lightweight nylon day bag; ripped-up sections of three guidebooks, notes, maps, journal, tiny pocket notepad; wristwatch; money belt (with ATM card, credit card, driver's license, passport, plane ticket, railpass, cash, sheet of phone numbers and addresses); second money belt clipped inside my bag for "semi-precious" documents (e.g., photocopies of the above); toiletries stuff bag (with squeeze bottle of shampoo, soap in a plastic container, shaver, toothbrush and paste, comb, nail clippers, squeeze bottle of liquid soap for clothes); bag with electronic gear (travel alarm clock, mobile phone and charger, PDA, MP3 player, cable for charging batteries, plug adapter); miscellaneous bag with family photos, tiny odds and ends; light rain jacket; long khaki cotton pants (button pockets), super-light long pants, shorts, five pairs of socks and underwear, long-sleeved shirt, two short-sleeved shirts, T-shirt; stuff bag with sweater, plastic laundry bag; a light pair of shoes; and my camera (not pictured).

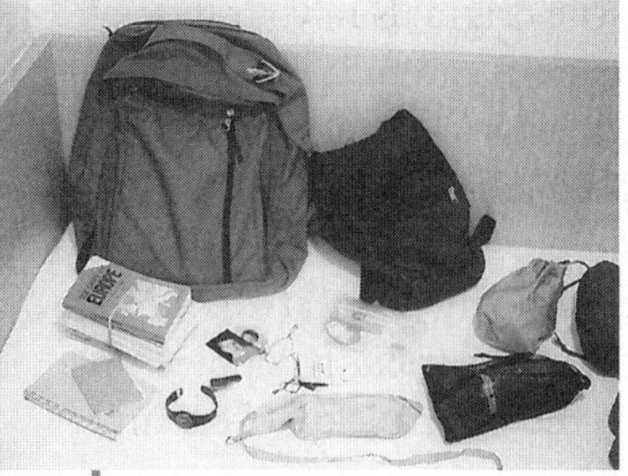

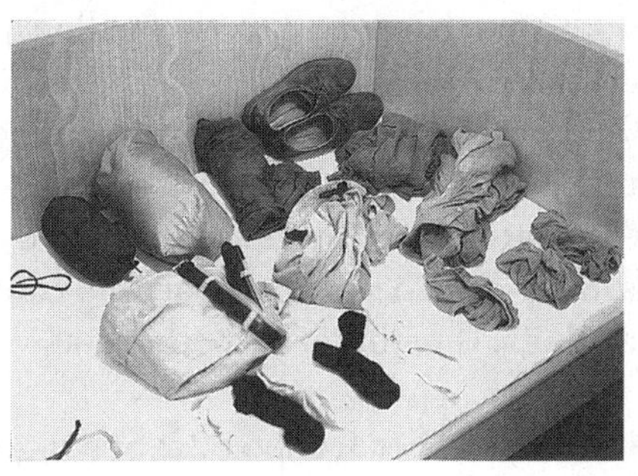

Gore-Tex is good if you expect rain. For summer travel, I wing it without rain gear—but always pack for rain in Britain.

**Tie or scarf.** For instant respectability, bring anything lightweight that can break the monotony and make you look snazzy.

***Money belt.** It's essential for the peace of mind it brings. You could lose everything except your money belt, and the trip could still go on. Lightweight and low-profile beige is best.

**Money.** Bring your preferred mix of a credit card, debit card, an emergency stash of hard cash, and a couple of personal checks. I rely on a debit card for ATM withdrawals, a credit card, and $400 in cash as a backup. (For details, see Chapter 14: Money.)

**Documents and photocopies.** Bring your passport, airline ticket, railpass or car-rental voucher, driver's license, student ID, hostel card, and so on. Photocopies and a couple of passport-type photos can help you get replacements more quickly if the originals are lost or stolen. Carry photocopies separately in your luggage and keep the originals in your money belt. In your luggage, you'll also want to pack a careful record of all reservations (bring the hotels' written confirmations), along with a trip calendar page to keep things up-to-date as your trip evolves.

***Small daypack.** This is great for carrying your sweater, camera, literature, and picnic goodies while you leave your large bag at the hotel or train station. Fanny packs (small bags with thief-friendly zippers on a belt) are a popular alternative, but are magnets for pickpockets and should never be used as money belts.

**Camera.** A digital camera and one high-capacity memory card means no more bulky bags of film. A mini-tripod allows you to take crisp shots in low light with no flash. (For more camera details, see page 316.)

**Sealable plastic baggies.** Get a variety of sizes. They're ideal for packing leftover picnic food, containing wetness, and bagging potential leaks before they happen. The two-gallon jumbo size is handy for packing clothing.

**Water bottle.** The plastic half-liter mineral water bottles sold throughout Europe are reusable and work great.

**Wristwatch.** A built-in alarm is handy. Otherwise, pack a small *travel alarm clock. Cheap-hotel wake-up calls are particularly unreliable.

**Earplugs.** If night noises bother you, you'll love a good set of expandable foam plugs.

**First-aid kit.** See Chapter 22: Staying Healthy.

**Medicine and vitamins.** Keep medicine in original containers, if possible, with legible prescriptions.

**Extra eyeglasses, contact lenses, and prescriptions.** Contact solutions are widely available in Europe. Because of dust and smog, many travelers find their contacts aren't as comfortable in Europe. Bring your glasses just in case.

**Sunscreen and sunglasses.** Depending on the season and your destination.

***Toiletries kit.** Sinks in cheap hotels come with meager countertop space and anonymous hairs. If you have a nylon toiletries kit that can hang on a hook or a towel bar, this is no problem. Put all squeeze bottles in sealable plastic baggies, since pressure changes in flight can cause even good bottles to leak. Consider a vacation from cosmetics. Bring a little toilet paper or tissue packets (sold at all newsstands in Europe).

*With a hangable toiletries kit, you know the hairs on the toothbrush are yours.*

Fingernail clippers and tweezers (for retrieving lost bank cards) are also handy. My Sonicare electric toothbrush holds a charge from home for 30 one-minute brushes.

***Soap.** Not all hotels provide soap. A plastic squeeze bottle of concentrated, multipurpose, biodegradable liquid soap is handy for laundry and more. In the interest of traveling friendlier to our environment, I never use the hotel bathroom "itsy-bitsies," preferring my own bar of soap or bottle of shampoo.

***Clothesline.** Hang it up in your hotel room to dry your clothes. The handy twisted-rubber type needs no clothespins.

***Small towel.** You'll find bath towels at all fancy and moderately priced hotels, and most cheap ones. Although $50-a-day travelers will often need to bring their own towel, $100-a-day folks won't. I bring a thin hand towel for the occasional need. Washcloths are rare in Europe. While I don't use them, many travelers recommend *quick-drying synthetic towels.

**Sewing kit.** Clothes age rapidly while traveling. Take along a few safety pins and buttons.

***Travel information.** Rip out appropriate chapters from guidebooks, staple them together, and store in a sealable plastic baggie. When you're done, give them away.

***Map.** Get a map best suited to your trip's overall needs and pick up maps for specific local areas as you go.

**Address list.** A list of e-mail and mailing addresses will help you keep in touch. You can send mass e-mails as you go (bring a shrunk-down print-out of your e-mail address book in case you can't access it online). Or if you prefer to send postcards, consider printing your mail list onto a sheet of adhesive address labels before you leave. You'll know exactly who you've written to, and the labels will be perfectly legible.

**Postcards from home and photos of your family.** A sealable plastic baggie of show-and-tell pictures is always a great conversation piece with Europeans you meet.

***Small notepad and pen.** A tiny notepad in your back pocket is a great organizer, reminder, and communication aid (for sale in European stationery stores).

### Checklist of Essentials

- ❑ 5 shirts
- ❑ 1 sweater
- ❑ 2 pairs pants
- ❑ 1 pair shorts
- ❑ 1 swimsuit (women only)
- ❑ 5 pairs underwear and socks
- ❑ 1 pair shoes
- ❑ 1 rain-proof jacket
- ❑ Tie or scarf
- ❑ Money belt
- ❑ Money—your mix of:
  - ❑ ATM cash card
  - ❑ Credit card or debit card
  - ❑ Hard cash
  - ❑ Personal checks (optional)
- ❑ Documents plus photocopies
- ❑ Passport
- ❑ Airplane ticket
- ❑ Driver's license
- ❑ Student ID and hostel card
- ❑ Railpass/car rental voucher
- ❑ Insurance details
- ❑ Daypack
- ❑ Sealable plastic baggies
- ❑ Camera and related gear
- ❑ Water bottle
- ❑ Wristwatch and alarm clock
- ❑ Earplugs
- ❑ First-aid kit
- ❑ Medicine
- ❑ Extra glasses/contacts and prescriptions
- ❑ Sunscreen and sunglasses
- ❑ Toiletries kit
- ❑ Soap
- ❑ Laundry soap
- ❑ Clothesline
- ❑ Small towel
- ❑ Sewing kit
- ❑ Travel information
- ❑ Necessary map(s)
- ❑ Address list (e-mail and mailing addresses)
- ❑ Postcards and photos from home
- ❑ Notepad and pen
- ❑ Journal

*Packing light: love it or leave it.*

***Journal.** An empty book to be filled with the experiences of your trip will be your most treasured souvenir. Attach a photocopied calendar page of your itinerary. Use a hardbound type designed to last a lifetime, rather than a spiral notebook. The rugged, black, and simple Moleskine notebooks have a cult following among travel writers (www.moleskine.it).

## Optional Bring-Alongs

*Indicates items you can order online at www.ricksteves.com.

**Picnic supplies.** Bring or buy a small tablecloth to give your meal some extra class (and to wipe the knife on), salt and pepper, a cup, a spoon, a washcloth (to dampen and store in a baggie for cleaning up), and a Swiss Army–type knife with a corkscrew and can opener (or buy the knife in Europe if you want to carry your luggage on the plane). A plastic plate is handy for picnic dinners in your hotel room.

***Packing cubes.** These see-through, zip-up mesh containers keep your clothes tightly packed and well organized.

***Clothes compressor.** This handy invention—I like the one by Pack-Mate—allows you to pack bulky clothes (like sweaters and jackets) without taking up too much space or creating wrinkles. Simply put the item in the bag, roll it up to force the air out through the one-way nozzles, and pack it away.

**Nightshirt.** Especially for women.

**Light warm-up suit.** Use for pajamas, evening lounge outfit, instant modest street wear, smuggling things, and "going" down the hall.

**Spot remover.** Bring Shout wipes or a dab of Goop grease remover in a film canister.

**Sandals or flip-flops.**

**Slippers.** I bring comfy slippers with leather bottoms on winter trips—great for the flight and for getting cozy in my hotel room.

***Inflatable pillow** (or "neck nest"). For snoozing on the plane.

**Pillowcase.** It's cleaner and possibly more comfortable to stuff your own.

**Hair drier.** People with long or thick hair appreciate a travel hair drier in the off-season, when hair takes a long time to dry and it's cold outside (see "Electronics" later in this chapter). These are generally provided in $100-plus hotel rooms.

***Hostel sheet.** Hostels require one. Bring your own (sewn up like a sleeping bag), buy one, or rent a sheet at hostels (about $4 per stay). It doubles as a beach or picnic blanket, comes in handy on overnight train rides, shields you from dirty blankets in mountain huts, and will save you money in other dorm-type accommodations, which often charge extra for linen or don't provide it at all.

***Tiny lock.** Use it to lock your backpack zippers shut. Note that if you check your bag on a flight, the lock may be broken to allow the bag to be inspected. You can improve the odds of your lock's survival by buying one approved by the TSA (Transportation Security Administration, the agency responsible for airport security). While you'll unlock the TSA-approved lock with a combination, security agents will be able to open the lock without damaging it by using a special master key.

***Small flashlight.** Handy for reading under the sheets after "lights out" in the hostel, late-night trips down the hall, exploring castle dungeons, and hypnotizing street thieves. Tiny-but-powerful LED flashlights—about the size of your thumb—are extremely bright, compact, and lightweight.
**Radio, Walkman, MP3 player, or recorder.** Partners can bring a Y-jack for two sets of earphones. Some travelers use micro-cassette or digital recorders to capture pipe organs, tours, or journal entries. Some recorders have radios, adding a new dimension to your experience. For more details, see "Electronics" later in this chapter.
***Adapters.** Electrical plugs (see "Electronics" later in this chapter).
**Stronger light bulbs.** You can buy these in Europe to give your cheap hotel room more brightness than the 40-watt norm.
**Office supplies.** Bring paper, an envelope of envelopes, and some sticky notes (such as Post-Its) to keep your place in your guidebook.
**Small roll of duct tape.**
**Mailing tube.** Great for art lovers, this protects the posters and prints you buy along your trip. You can trim it to fit inside your backpack (though this obviously limits the dimensions of the posters you can carry).
**A good paperback.** There's plenty of empty time on a trip to either be bored or enjoy some good reading. If you're desperate, popular American paperbacks are available in European airports and major train stations (usually for more than double their American price).
**Insect repellent.** Especially for France and Italy.
***Collapsible umbrella.** I like one that's small and compact, but still sturdy and well-constructed enough to withstand strong winds.
**Poncho.** Hard-core vagabonds use a poncho—more versatile than a tarp—as protection in a rainstorm, a ground cloth for sleeping, or a beach or picnic blanket.
**Gifts.** Local hosts appreciate small souvenirs from your hometown (gourmet candy or crafts). Local kids love T-shirts and small toys.

## Packing Tips for Women

Thanks to ETBD tour guides Joan Robinson, Ann Neel, Margaret Cassady, and Kendra Roth for the following tips. At ETBD, Joan teaches classes on packing; her suggested packing list for women is at www.ricksteves.com/plan/tips.

**If you're not going to wear it more than three times, don't pack it!** Every piece of clothing you bring should complement every other item or have at least two uses (e.g., sandals double as slippers, a scarf as a shoulder wrap).

**Shop selectively:** It's worth splurging a little to get just the right clothes for your trip. For durable, lightweight travel clothes, consider Ex Officio (www.exofficio.com, tel. 800-644-7303), TravelSmith (www.travelsmith.com, tel. 800-950-1600), Tilley's (www.tilley.com, tel. 800-363-8737), and REI (www.rei.com). In general, the color black dresses up easily and can be extremely versatile.

**Tops:** Bring two or three T-shirts (or buy overseas), one or two short-sleeved blouses, and one or two long-sleeved shirts. Long-sleeved shirts with sleeves that roll up can double as short-sleeved shirts. Look for a wrinkle-camouflaging pattern or blended fabrics that show a minimum of wrinkles. Cotton/poly T-shirt fabric (such as CoolMax) will often dry overnight. Silk also dries quickly and is lightweight.

**Pants and shorts:** Dark-colored pants don't show dirt or wrinkles. Get a pair with a loose-fitting waistband that accommodates a money belt (and big Italian meals). Try the pants with the zip-off legs that convert to shorts. These are especially functional in Italy, allowing you to cover up inside churches and beat the heat outside.

If you bring shorts, one pair is probably enough, ideal for staying cool in a resort town or your hotel room. Few European women wear shorts. To avoid stares, consider bringing a pair of Capri pants instead.

**Skirts:** Some women bring one or two skirts because they're as cool and breathable as shorts, but dressier. And skirts make life easier than pants when you're faced with a squat toilet! A lightweight skirt made with a blended fabric will pack compactly. Make sure it has a comfy elastic waistband or drawstring. Joan has designed a smart reversible travel skirt that suits most travelers' needs (available at www.ricksteves.com). Tilley's (listed above) makes expensive but great skirts (and other items) from blended fabric that feels like cotton. Skirts go with everything, and can easily be dressed up or down.

**Shoes:** Bring one pair of comfortable walking shoes. Mephisto, Ecco, and Rieker look dressier and more European than sneakers but are still comfortable. For a second pair, consider sandals or Tevas in summer, or dark leather flats in winter (can be worn with opaque hose and a skirt to dress up). Before you leave home, walk several miles in any footwear you'll be taking to be sure they're broken in.

**Socks, underwear, pajamas, and swimsuit:** Cotton/nylon-blend socks dry faster than 100-percent cotton, which loses its softness when air-dried. Sport socks nicely cushion your feet. It's impossible to look stylish when wearing walking shoes and these little white socks, but comfort's more important. Try silk, microfiber, or stretch lace underwear, which dry faster than all-cotton, but breathe more than nylon. Bring at least two bras (what if you leave one hanging over your shower rail by accident?). A sports bra can double as a hiking/sunning top. Shorts or lightweight pajama bottoms with a T-shirt will get you modestly to the bathroom down the hall. You don't need a bikini to try sunbathing topless on European beaches—local women with one-piece bathing suits just roll down the top.

**Jacket:** Neutral colors (black, beige, navy) look more European than bright colors. If your waterproof jacket doesn't have a hood, take a mini-umbrella or buy one in Europe. These are easy to find—vendors often appear with the rain.

**Shoulder- and off-season variations:** Silk long johns are great for layering, weigh next to nothing, and dry quickly. Bring gloves and some kind of warm hat for winter. If you're fair-skinned or prone to sunburn, bring a light, crushable, wide-brimmed hat for sunny days. Wear shoes that are water-resistant or waterproof.

**Toiletries:** All feminine products (even many of the same brands) are sold throughout Europe, but it's easier to figure out how many tampons, pads, or panty shields you'll need and bring them with you rather than having to buy a too-small or too-large box in Europe. If you bring birth control pills (or any timed-dosage prescription), take the time difference into account. If you usually take a pill with breakfast, take it with lunch or dinner in Europe. Remember to carry the pills onto the plane each way to take at your home-dosage time, too.

**Accessorize, accessorize:** Scarves give your limited wardrobe just the color it needs. They dress up your outfit, are lightweight and easy to pack, and, if purchased in Europe, make a great souvenir. Some women bring a towel-size scarf (called a pashmina) to function as a sweater substitute, scarf, head wrap, or even a blanket on a train. Sleeveless vests and button-up cardigans can be worn alone or mixed-and-matched with other clothes to give you several different looks as well as layers for cold weather. Most women feel safe wearing engagement/wedding rings while traveling, but leave other valuable or flashy jewelry at home. A few pairs of inexpensive earrings are fun to bring. Remember that your most important accessory is your hidden money belt.

## Electronics

I used to recommend traveling without electronic gear. But these days, there are just too many cool and handy gadgets to go without. I still pack light...but I also bring a few select electronic items.

*In Europe, two kinds of adapters fit all outlets: Two little round prongs for the Continent, three big rectangular ones for Britain and Ireland.*

Europe's electrical system is different from the United States'—both in the plugs used and the voltage of the current. American appliances run on 110 volts, while European appliances are 220 volts. (These numbers can vary slightly—for example, 120 instead of 110 volts in the US.) You can destroy your American appliance if you plug it directly into a European wall outlet.

There are two different components you'll need to plug in American gear overseas: A **converter** changes the electric current from European to American. A small **adapter** allows American-style plugs (2 flat prongs) to fit into British outlets (which take 3 rectangular prongs) or continental European outlets (which take 2 small, round prongs). While there are some combination converter-adapters, you'll more likely need to deal with each of these issues separately.

Most new electronic travel accessories come with a built-in voltage converter that works in both the US and Europe. These converters "autosense" the voltage from the wall outlet. If you see a range of voltages printed on the item or its plug (such as "110–220"), you're OK in Europe. Older appliances have a voltage switch marked 110 (US) and 220 (Europe). Ask the salesperson when you buy. Often, buying a new travel appliance with a built-in converter can be smarter than buying a separate converter (about $30) to use with your old appliance.

Even if you've got a built-in converter, you'll still need to buy a plug adapter. Remember that British plugs (3 rectangular prongs) are different from continental European plugs (2 round ones). I bring each kind (handy for long layovers in Heathrow Airport). Secure your adapter to your appliance's plug with electrical or duct tape; otherwise it might stay in the outlet (and get left behind) when you pull out the plug. Many sockets in Europe are recessed into the wall; your adapter should be small enough so that the prongs seat properly in the socket. Cheap converters with built-in adapters often have prongs that are the right size but do not seat properly.

Many budget hotel rooms have only one electrical outlet, occupied by the lamp. Hardware stores in Europe sell cheap three-way plug adapters that let you keep the lamp on and your camera battery and MP3 player charged. For more information on plugs and adapters, consult TeleAdapt (www.teleadapt.com).

Well-wired travelers bring reams of personal and travel information. You can store these documents on your laptop or PDA (see below); save them on a USB flash drive (see below); or simply park your details and addresses in a file on your e-mail account for easy access anywhere (though it's not wise to store sensitive information like credit-card numbers or your Social Security number online).

Here's what I bring with me to Europe. Remember that most travelers—going for vacation rather than work—won't need this much gear:

**Laptop computer.** Great for writers, and handy for anyone—but far too heavy and cumbersome for casual use. Consider a PDA instead (see below).

**Laptop gear.** I bring a charger, an extra battery (I get 3 hours out of each; the second is only necessary for long flights or train trips), and a USB flash drive (for backing up all my files; described below).

**Gear to get online in my hotel room.** For details, see page 292.

**Mobile phone and charger.** For details, see page 289.

**MP3 player** (such as an iPod). This convenient, compact device allows you to store and listen to many hours of your favorite music, radio shows, and more. I like to bring a Y-jack for the headphones to share my music with a travel partner or new friend.

**Digital camera.** For details, see page 316.

**PDA** (such as a Pocket PC or Palm Pilot). You can load it with addresses, your calendar, games, music, and any travel information you might need. A PDA is a fine alternative for travelers who need to stay plugged in, but don't want to lug along a heavy laptop. Some travelers even use PDAs for journaling (especially handy with a collapsible keyboard).

**USB flash drive.** A USB flash drive is basically a miniature hard drive, about the size of a pack of gum, that plugs directly into your computer's USB port. If you're taking a laptop with you, this is a convenient and compact way to back up your files in case anything happens to your computer. If you're not taking a laptop, a flash drive allows you to transport files you think you may need once you get to Europe. They plug into a USB port, which is standard on virtually any computer in the United States or Europe. Note, however, that some Internet cafés won't let you use flash drives because they're wary of transferring potentially infected files into their system. If you need to access files in your flash drive, but cafés turn you down, ask your hotelier if you can use the hotel computer.

# PLANNING YOUR ITINERARY

## 5. WHEN TO GO

In travel-industry jargon, the year is divided into three seasons: peak season (roughly late June, July, and August), shoulder season (May, early June, September, early October), and off-season (late October through April). Each has its pros and cons.

### Peak-Season Strategies

Except for the crowds, summer is a great time to travel. The sunny weather, long days, and exuberant nightlife turn Europe into a powerful magnet. I haven't missed a peak season in 30 years. Here are a few crowd-minimizing tips that I've learned:

**Arrange your trip with crowd control in mind.** Consider, for instance, a six-week European trip beginning June 1, half with a Eurailpass to see the famous sights and half visiting relatives in Scotland. It would be wise to do the Eurail section first, enjoying those precious last three weeks of relatively uncrowded shoulder season, and then spend time with the family during the last half of your vacation, when Florence and Salzburg are teeming with tourists. Salzburg on June 10 and Salzburg on July 10 are two very different experiences.

**Seek out places with no promotional budgets.** Keep in mind that accessibility and promotional budgets determine a place's fame and popularity just as much as its worthiness as a tourist attraction. For example, Geneva is big and famous—with nothing special to offer the visitor. The beaches of Greece's Peloponnesian Peninsula enjoy the same weather and water as the highly promoted isles of Santorini and Ios but are out

*St. Mark's Square in July—no wonder Venice is sinking...*

of the way, not promoted, and wonderfully deserted. If you're traveling by car, take advantage of your mobility by leaving the well-worn tourist routes. The Europe away from the train tracks is less expensive and feels more peaceful and relaxed. Overlooked by the Eurail mobs, it's one step behind the modern parade.

**Hit the back streets.** So many people energetically jockey themselves into the most crowded square of the most crowded city in the most crowded month (St. Mark's Square, Venice, July) and complain about the crowds. You could be in Venice in July and walk six blocks behind St. Mark's Basilica, step into a café, and be greeted by Venetians who act as though they've never seen a tourist.

**Spend the night.** Popular day-trip destinations near big cities and resorts such as Toledo (near Madrid), San Marino (near huge Italian beach resorts), and San Gimignano (near Florence) take on a more peaceful and enjoyable atmosphere at night, when the legions of day-trippers retreat to the predictable plumbing of their big-city hotels. Small towns normally lack hotels big enough for tour groups and are often inaccessible to large buses. So they will experience, at worst, midday crowds.

**Be an early bird.** In Germany, walk around Rothenburg's ancient wall at breakfast time, before the tour buses pull in and turn the town into a medieval theme park. Crack-of-dawn joggers and walkers enjoy a special look at wonderfully medieval cities as they yawn and stretch and prepare for the daily onslaught of the 21st century.

*...but anytime of the year, walk a few blocks away and it's just you and Venice.*

**See how the locals live.** Residential neighborhoods rarely see a tourist. Browse through a department store. Buy a copy of the local *Better Homes and Thatches* and use it to explore that particular culture. Get off the map. Consider in Florence, for instance, how the tourists stick to the small section of the city covered by the ubiquitous tourist maps. Wander beyond that, and you'll dance with the locals or play street soccer with the neighborhood gang.

**Plan your museum sightseeing carefully.** Avoid museums on their weekly free days, when they're most crowded. And because many Parisian museums are closed on Tuesday, nearby Versailles, which is open, is predictably crowded—very crowded. And it follows that Parisian museums are especially crowded on Monday and Wednesday. While crowds at the Louvre can't be avoided altogether, leaving home with a thoughtful itinerary can help. (For more tips, see Chapter 24: Museum Strategies.)

*It's Tuesday at Versailles, and these people now have time to read their guidebooks, which warn: "On Tuesday, many of Paris' museums are closed, so Versailles has very long lines."*

**Arrive at the most popular sights early or late in the day to avoid tour groups.** Germany's fairy-tale Neuschwanstein Castle is cool and easy, with relaxed guides and no crowds, at 8:00 in the morning. And very late in the day—when most tourists are long gone, exhausted in their rooms or searching for dinner—I linger alone, taking artistic liberties with some of Europe's greatest art in empty galleries.

**Be aware of the exceptions.** Although Europe's tourist crowds can generally be plotted on a bell-shaped curve peaking in July and August, there are odd glitches. For instance, Paris is relatively empty in July and August but packed full in June (conventions) and September (trade shows). Business-class hotels in Scandinavia are cheapest in the summer, when travel—up there, mostly business travel—is down.

In much of Europe (especially Italy and France), cities are partially shut down in July and August, when local urbanites take their beach break. You'll hear that these are terrible times to travel, but it's really no big deal. You can't get a dentist and many launderettes are shut down, but tourists are basically unaffected by Europe's mass holidays. Just don't get caught on the wrong road on the first or 15th of the month (when vacations often start or finish) or try to compete with all of Europe for a piece of French Riviera beach in August.

## Shoulder Season

For many, "shoulder season"—generally April, May, early June, September, and early October—combines the advantages of both peak-season and off-season travel. In shoulder season, you'll enjoy decent weather, long-enough daylight, fewer crowds, and a local tourist industry that is still eager to please and entertain.

Because fall and spring bring cooler temperatures in Mediterranean Europe, "shoulder season" in much of Italy, southern France, and Spain can actually come with peak-season crowds and prices. For example, except for beach resorts, Italy's peak season is May, June, September, and October rather than July and August. Paris has its own surprising patterns (see above).

If debating the merits of spring versus fall, consider your destination. Mediterranean Europe is generally green in spring, but parched in fall. For hikers, the Alps are better in early fall, because many good hiking trails are covered with snow through the spring.

On a budget note, keep in mind that round-trip airfares are determined by your departure date. Therefore, if you fly over during peak season and return late in the fall (shoulder season), you'll still pay peak-season round-trip fares.

## Off-Season Europe

Each summer, Europe greets a stampede of sightseers and shoppers with eager cash registers. Before jumping into the peak-season pig pile, consider an off-season trip.

*Where are the tourists?*

**The advantages of off-season traveling are many.** Off-season airfares are often hundreds of dollars cheaper. With fewer crowds in Europe, you'll sleep cheaper. Many fine hotels drop their prices, and budget hotels will have plenty of vacancies. And while many of the cheap alternatives to hotels will be closed, those still open are usually empty and, therefore, more comfortable.

Off-season adventurers loiter all alone through Leonardo da Vinci's home, ponder in Rome's Forum undisturbed, kick up sand on virgin beaches, and chat with laid-back guards by log fires in French châteaux. In wintertime Venice, you can be alone atop St. Mark's bell tower, watching the clouds of your breath roll over the Byzantine domes of the church to a horizon of cut-glass Alps. Below, on St. Mark's Square, pigeons fidget and wonder, "Where are the tourists?"

Off-season adventurers enjoy step-right-up service at banks and tourist offices and experience a more European Europe. Although many popular tourist-oriented parks, shows, and tours will be closed, off-season is in-season for the high culture: the Vienna Boys' Choir, opera, and the Spanish Riding School are in their crowd-pleasing glory.

**But winter travel has its drawbacks.** Because much of Europe is at Canadian latitudes, the days are short. It's dark by 5 p.m. The weather can be miserable—cold, windy, and drizzly—and then turn worse. But just as summer can be wet and gray, winter can be crisp and blue, and even into mid-November, hillsides blaze with colorful leaves.

Off-season hours are limited. Some sights close down entirely, and most operate on shorter schedules (such as 10 a.m.–5 p.m. rather than 9 a.m.–7 p.m.), with darkness often determining the closing time. Winter sightseeing is fine in big cities, which bustle year-round, but it's more frustrating in small tourist towns, which often shut down entirely. In December, many beach resorts are shut up as tight as canned hams. While Europe's wonderful outdoor evening ambience survives year-round in the south, wintertime streets are empty in the north after dark. English-language tours, common in the summer, are rare during the off-season, when most visitors are natives. Tourist information offices normally stay open year-round but have shorter hours in the winter. A final disadvantage of winter travel is loneliness. The solo traveler won't have the built-in camaraderie of other travelers that she would find in peak season.

*Italy's Cinque Terre villages are empty in the winter...and the good restaurants take a much-needed extended holiday.*

**To thrive in the winter, you'll need to get the most out of your limited daylight hours.** Start early and eat a quick lunch. Tourist offices close early and opening times are less predictable, so call ahead to double-check hours and confirm your plans. Pack for the cold and wet—layers, rainproof parka, gloves, wool hat, long johns, waterproof shoes, and an umbrella. Dress warmly. Cold weather is colder when you're outdoors trying to enjoy yourself all day long. And cheap hotels are not always adequately heated in the off-season. Use undershirts to limit the washing of slow-drying heavy shirts.

Empty beds abound in the off-season. I used to lead an 18-day November tour of Germany, Italy, and France with 22 people and no room reservations. We'd amble into town around 5 p.m. and always found 22 beds well within our budget.

*In the north, darkness falls early in the winter. This is Oslo at 3:30 p.m.*

Most hotels charge less in the winter. To save some money, arrive late, notice how many empty rooms they have (keys on the rack), let them know you're a hosteler (student, senior, artist, or whatever) with a particular price limit, and bargain from there. The opposite is true of big-city business centers (especially in Berlin, Brussels, and the Scandinavian capitals), which are busiest and most expensive off-season.

Regardless of when you go, if your objective is to "meet the people," you'll find Europe filled with them 365 days a year.

# 6. ITINERARY SKILLS

If you have any goals at all for your trip, make an itinerary. I never start a trip without having every day planned out. Your reaction to an itinerary may be, "Hey, won't my spontaneity and freedom suffer?" Not necessarily. Although I always begin a trip with a well-thought-out plan, I maintain my flexibility and make plenty of changes. An itinerary forces you to see the consequences of any spontaneous change you make while in Europe. For instance, if you spend two extra days in the sunny Alps, you'll see that you won't make it to, say, the Greek Islands. With the help of an itinerary, you can lay out your goals, maximize their potential, avoid regrettable changes...and impress your friends.

## Itinerary Considerations

If you deal thoughtfully with issues such as weather, culture shock, health maintenance, fatigue, and festivals, you'll travel happier.

**Moderate the weather conditions you'll encounter.** Match the coolest month of your trip with the warmest area, and vice versa. For a spring and early summer trip, enjoy comfortable temperatures throughout by starting in the southern countries and working your way north. If possible, avoid the midsummer Mediterranean heat. Spend those weeks in Scandinavia or the Alps. Scandinavia and Britain have miserable weather and none of the crowd problems that plague Italy and France. Ideally, forget crowd concerns and visit Britain and Scandinavia in the peak of summer. (See the climate charts in the appendix.)

**Mix in cities and villages.** Alternate intense big cities with villages and countryside. For example, break a tour of Venice, Florence, and Rome with an easygoing time in the hill towns or on the Italian Riviera. Judging Italy by Rome is like judging America by New York City.

**Join the celebration.** Hit as many festivals, national holidays, and arts seasons as you can. This takes some study (for a starter, go to www.ricksteves.com/festivals). Ask the national tourist office of each country you'll visit (listed in Chapter 2: Gathering Information) for a calendar of events. An effort to hit the right places at the right time will drape your trip with festive tinsel.

**Save your energy for the biggies.** Don't overestimate your powers of absorption. Rare is the tourist who doesn't become somewhat jaded after several weeks of travel. At the start of my trip, I'll seek out every great painting and cathedral I can. After two months, I find myself "seeing" cathedrals with a sweep of my head from the doorway, and I probably wouldn't cross the street for another Rembrandt. Don't burn out on mediocre castles, palaces, and museums. Sightsee selectively.

**Establish a logical flight plan.** It's been years since I flew in to and out of the same city. You can avoid needless travel time and expense by flying "open jaw"—into one port and out of another. You usually pay just half the round-trip fare for each port. Even if your "open jaw" flight plan is more expensive than the cheapest round-trip fare, it may save you lots of time and money when surface connections are figured in. For example, you could fly into London, travel east through whatever interests you in Europe, and fly home from Athens. This would eliminate the costly and time-consuming return to London. Your travel agent will know where flying "open jaw" is economical.

**See countries in order of cultural hairiness.** If you plan to see Britain, the Alps, Greece, and Turkey, do it in that order so you'll grow steadily into the more intense and crazy travel. England, compared to any place but the United States, is pretty dull. Don't get me wrong—it's a great place to travel. But go there first, when cream teas and roundabouts will be exotic. And you're more likely to enjoy Turkey if you work gradually east.

**Save your good health.** Visit countries that may be hazardous to your health (North Africa or the Middle East) at the end of your trip, so you won't needlessly jeopardize your healthy enjoyment of the safer countries. If you're going to get sick, do it at the end of your trip so you can recover at home, missing more work—not vacation.

**Minimize one-night stands.** Even the speediest itinerary should be a series of two-night stands. I'd stretch every other day with long hours on the road or train and hurried sightseeing along the way in order to enjoy the sanity of two nights in the same bed. Minimizing hotel changes saves time and money and gives you the sensation of actually being comfortable in a town on the second night.

**Leave some slack in your itinerary.** Don't schedule yourself too tightly (a common tendency). Everyday chores, small business matters, transportation problems, constipation, and planning mistakes deserve about one day of slack per week in your itinerary.

**Punctuate a long trip with rest periods.** Constant sightseeing is grueling. Schedule a peaceful period every two weeks. If your trip is a long one, schedule a "vacation from your vacation" in the middle of it. Most people need several days in a place where they couldn't see a museum or take a tour even if they wanted to. A stop in the mountains or on an island, in a friendly rural town, or at the home of a relative is a great way to revitalize your tourist spirit.

**Assume you will return.** This Douglas MacArthur approach is a key to touristic happiness. You can't really see Europe in one trip. Don't even try. Enjoy what you're seeing. Forget what you won't get to on this trip. If you worry about things that are just out of reach, you won't appreciate what's in your hand. I've taken dozens of European trips, and I still need more time. I'm happy about what I can't get to. It's a blessing that we can never see all of Europe.

## Your Best Itinerary in Eight Steps

**1. Read up on Europe and talk to travelers.** Get a guidebook or two, take a class, contact the tourist offices. You must have some friends who'd love to show you their pictures or video. What you want to see is determined by what you know (or don't know). Identify your personal interests: WWII buffs study up on battle sites, wine-lovers brainstorm a wish list of wineries, and McGregors locate their clan in Scotland. This is the time to grow a crop of ideas from which you'll harvest the dream trip.

**2. Decide on the places you want to see.** Start by listing everything you'd like to see. Circle your destinations on a map. Have a reason for every stop. Don't go to Casablanca just because you liked the movie.

Minimize redundancy. On a quick trip, focus on only one part of the Alps. England's two best-known university towns, Oxford and

Cambridge, are redundant. Choose one (I prefer Cambridge).

*Example: Places I want to see—London, Alps, Bavaria, Florence, Amsterdam, Paris, the Rhine, Rome, Venice, Greece.*

**Sample Itinerary**

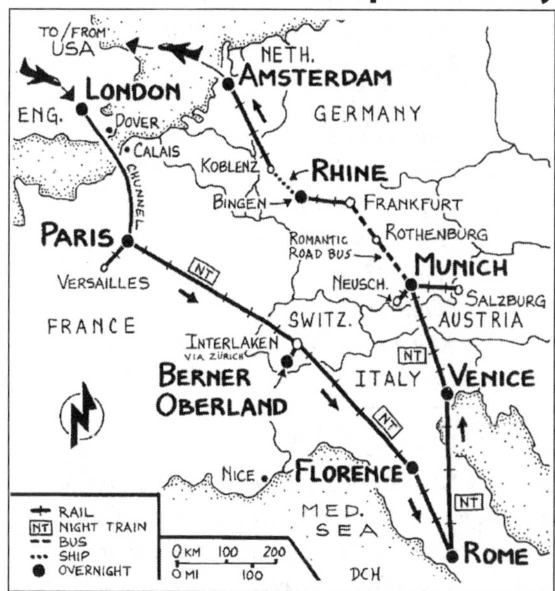


**3. Establish a route and timeline.** Figure out a logical geographical order and length for your trip. Pin down any places that you have to be on a certain date (and ask yourself if it's really worth stifling your flexibility). Once you've settled on a list, be satisfied with your efficient plan, and focus any more study and preparation only on places that fall along your proposed route.

**4. Decide on the cities you'll fly in and out of.** If your route is linear (like London to Athens), fly "open jaw." If it's circular, fly round-trip. An "open jaw" plan is generally most efficient and economical. Take full advantage of "open jaw" when establishing your starting and ending points.

**5. Determine the mode of transportation.** Do this not based solely on economical terms, but by analyzing what is best for the trip you envision.

*Example: Since I'm traveling alone, going so many miles, and spending the majority of my time in big cities, I'd rather not mess with a car. I'll use a railpass.*

**6. Make a rough itinerary.** Taking into account the length of your vacation, write in the number of days you'd like to stay in each place. Carefully consider travel time. Driving, except on expressways, is slower than in the United States. Study Web sites (such as http://bahn.hafas.de/bin/query.exe/en) to get an idea of how long various train journeys will take. Learn which trains are fast, and avoid minor lines in southern countries. Use night trains (NT) or boats (NB) to save time and money whenever possible.

*Example: Logical order and desired number of days in each place:*

*3 London*
*5 Paris (NT)*
*3 Alps (NT)*
*2 Florence*
*3 Rome (NB or flight)*
*7 Greece (NB or flight)*
*2 Venice (NT)*
*3 Munich/Bavaria*
*3 Romantic Road/Rhine Cruise*
*4 Amsterdam*

---

*35 TOTAL DAYS*

*Notes: I have 23 days for my vacation. Greece is time-consuming, even with an "open jaw" flight plan. If I eliminate Greece, I'll still need to cut five days. Flying "open jaw" into London and out of Amsterdam is economical. Logical order may be affected by night-train possibilities.*

**7. Adjust by cutting, streamlining, or adding to fit your timeline or budget.** Minimize travel time. When you must cut something, cut to save the most mileage. For instance, if Amsterdam and Berlin are equally important to you and you don't have time for both, cut the destination that saves the most miles (in this case, Berlin).

Minimize clutter. A so-so sight (Bologna) breaking a convenient night train (Rome–Venice) into two half-day journeys is clutter.

Consider economizing on car rental or a Eurailpass. For instance, try to manage a 23-day trip on a 15-day train pass by seeing London, Paris, and Amsterdam before or after you use the pass.

*Example: Itinerary and number of days adjusted to time limitations:*

*4 London*
*3 Paris (NT)*
*3 Alps (NT)*
*1 Florence*
*2 Rome (NT)*
*2 Venice (NT)*
*3 Munich/Bavaria*
*2 Romantic Road/Rhine Cruise*
*3 Amsterdam*

---

*23 TOTAL DAYS*

*Notes: Get a 15-day Eurailpass (valid from last day in Paris until first day in Amsterdam).*

**8. Fine tune.** Study your guidebook. Maximize festival and market days. Be sure crucial sights are open the day you'll be in town. Remember that most cities close many of their major tourist attractions for one day during the week (usually Mon). It would be a shame to be in Madrid only on a Monday, when the Prado is *cerrado.* Paris closes the Louvre and many other sights on Tuesday. Write out a day-by-day itinerary. Note that when flying from the United States, you arrive in Europe the next day. When returning, you arrive home the same day.

*Example: According to the guidebooks, I must keep these points in mind as I plan my trip. London: Theaters closed on Sunday, Speaker's Corner is Sunday only. Paris: Many museums are closed on Tuesdays. Versailles and the Orsay Museum are closed on Monday. Florence: Museums are closed on Monday. Dachau: Closed on Monday. Note that I'm choosing to pay a little extra on my flight to let my trip stretch over the weekends and minimize lost*

## SAMPLE ITINERARY

### September

| SUN. | MON. | TUE. | WED. | THUR. | FRI. | SAT. |
|---|---|---|---|---|---|---|
| | | | Mom's Birthday! ☺ | | | 1 USA to → London |
| 2 Arrive London (L) | 3 London (L) | 4 London, eve train to Paris (P) | 5 Paris (P) | 6 Paris (P) | 7 S.T. Versailles (N.T.) | 8 Alps (A) |
| 9 Alps (A) | 10 Swiss Lakes (N.T.) | 11 Florence (F) | 12 Early train to Rome (R) | 13 Rome (N.T.) | 14 Venice (V) | 15 Venice (N.T.) |
| 16 Oktoberfest! ☺ Munich (M) | 17 Dachau closed S.T. Neuschwan. Castle (M) | 18 S.T. Salzburg (M) | 19 Romantic Road bus, train to Rhine (RH) | 20 Rhine boat cruise (RH) | 21 To Amst. (A) | 22 Amsterdam (A) |
| 23 Amst. to USA | 24 Back to work ☹ | 25 | 26 | 27 | 28 | 29 |

Initial in the bottom right indicates where to spend each night.

**N.T.** = Night Train **S.T.** = Side Trip

### My Favorite Home-Base Cities and Their Best Day Trips

**Madrid:** Toledo, Segovia, El Escorial, and even Sevilla and Córdoba with the AVE bullet trains

**Amsterdam:** Alkmaar, Enkhuizen's Zuiderzee Museum, Arnhem's Folk Museum and Kröller-Müller Museum, Scheveningen, Delft, and most of the Netherlands

**Copenhagen:** Frederiksborg Castle, Roskilde, Helsingør, Odense, and over the bridge to Malmö (Sweden)

**Paris:** Versailles, Chartres, Vaux-le-Vicomte, Fontainebleau, Chantilly, Giverny, Reims

**London:** Bath, Stonehenge, Stratford-upon-Avon, Cambridge, York, and many others

**Arles:** Pont du Gard, Nîmes, Avignon, and all of Provence

**Florence:** Siena, Pisa, San Gimignano, and many other hill towns

**Venice:** Padua, Vicenza, Verona, and Ravenna

**Munich:** Salzburg, King Ludwig's castles (Neuschwanstein, Linderhof, and Herrenchiemsee), Wies Church, Oberammergau, and other small Bavarian towns

**Sorrento:** Naples, Pompeii, Herculaneum, Mount Vesuvius, Amalfi Coast, Paestum, and Capri

*work time. Yes, I may be a zombie on that first Monday back, but hey, what's more important?*

## The Home-Base Strategy

The home-base strategy is a clever way to make your trip itinerary smoother, simpler, and more efficient. Set yourself up in a central location and use that place as a base for day trips to nearby attractions.

**The home-base approach minimizes set-up time (usually an hour).** Searching for a good hotel can be exhausting, frustrating, and time-consuming. And hotels often give a better price, or at least more smiles, for longer stays. Many private homes don't accept those staying only one night.

**You are freed from your luggage.** Being able to leave your luggage in the hotel lets you travel freely and with the peace of mind that you are set up for the night. Bags are less likely to be lost or stolen in your hotel than en route.

**You feel "at home" in your home-base town.** This comfortable feeling takes more than a day to get, and when you are changing locations every day or two, you may never enjoy this important rootedness. Home-basing allows you to sense the rhythm of daily life.

**Day-trip to a village, enjoy the nightlife in a city.** The home-base approach lets you spend the evening in a city, where there is some exciting nightlife. Most small countryside towns die after 9 p.m. If you're not dead by 9 p.m., you'll enjoy more action in a larger city.

**Transportation is a snap.** Europe's generally frequent and punctual train and bus systems (which often operate out of a hub anyway) make this home-base strategy practical. With a train pass, trips are "free"; otherwise, the transportation is reasonable, often with reductions offered for round-trip tickets (especially for "same-day return").

## High-Speed Town-Hopping

When I tell people that I saw three or four towns in one day, many think, "Insane! Nobody can really see several towns in a day!" Of course, it's folly to go too fast, but many stop-worthy towns take only an hour or two to cover. Don't let feelings of guilt tell you to slow down and stay longer if you really are finished with a town. There's so much more to see in the rest of Europe. Going too slow is as bad as going too fast.

If you're efficient and use the high-speed town-hopping method, you'll amaze yourself with what you can see in a day. Let me explain with an example.

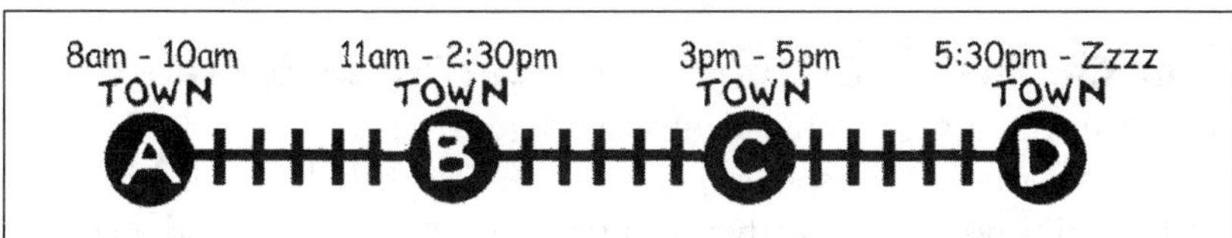


You wake up early in Town A. Checking out of your hotel, you have one sight to cover before your 10 a.m. train. (You checked the train schedule the night before.) After the sightseeing and before getting to the station, you visit the open-air market and buy the ingredients for your brunch and pick up a Town B map and tourist brochure at Town A's tourist office.

From 10 to 11 a.m. you travel by train to Town B. During that hour you have a restful brunch, enjoy the passing scenery, and prepare for Town B by reading your literature and deciding what you want to see. Just before your arrival, you put the items you need (camera, jacket, tourist information) into your small daypack. Then, upon arrival, you check the rest of your luggage in a locker. (Virtually every station has storage lockers or a baggage-check desk.)

Before leaving Town B's station, write down the departure times of the next few trains to Town C. Now you can sightsee as much or as little as you want and still know when to comfortably catch your train.

Town B is great. After a snack in the park, you catch the train at 2:30 p.m. By 3 p.m. you're in Town C, where you repeat the same procedure you followed in Town B. Town C just isn't what it was cracked up to be, so after a walk along the waterfront and a look at the church you catch the first train out.

You arrive in Town D, the last town on the day's agenda, by 5:30 p.m. The man in the station directs you to a good budget pension two blocks down the street. You're checked in and unpacked in no time, and, after a few horizontal moments, it's time to find a good restaurant and eat dinner. After a meal and an evening stroll, you're ready to call it a day. As you write in your journal, it occurs to you: This was a great sightseeing day. You spent it high-speed town-hopping.

# 7. ITINERARY ISSUES

This chapter offers tips on some complicated nuts-and-bolts of itinerary planning: crossing the Channel via the Chunnel; traveling through Belgium, Germany, Eastern Europe, and Italy; long-jumping to Greece; and seeing the best (and missing the worst) of Europe.

### "The Chunnel"—Getting from Great Britain to France

The fastest and most convenient way to get from Big Ben to the Eiffel Tower is by rail. Eurostar, a joint service of the Belgian, British, and French railways, is the speedy passenger train that zips you (and up to 800 others in 18 sleek cars) from downtown London to downtown Paris (12–15/day, 3 hrs) or Brussels (9/day, 3 hrs) faster and easier than flying. The train goes 80 mph in England and 190 mph on the Continent. (When the English segment gets up to speed, the journey time will shrink to 2 hours.) The actual tunnel

**Crossing the English Channel**

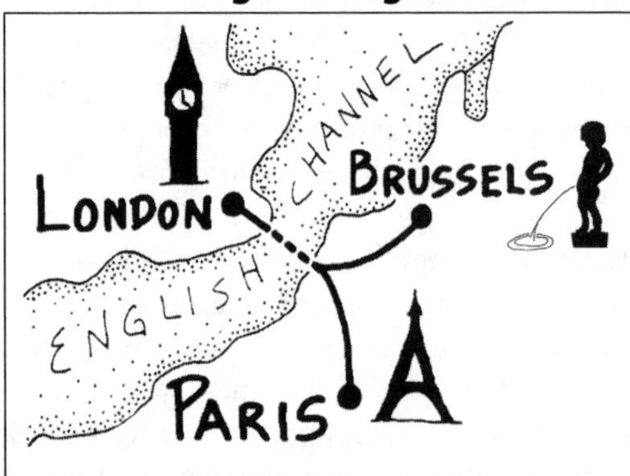

crossing is a 20-minute, black, silent, 100-mile-per-hour nonevent. Your ears won't even pop.

Eurostar fares (essentially the same between London and Paris or Brussels) are reasonable but complicated. Prices vary depending on when you travel, whether you can live with restrictions, and whether you're eligible for any discounts (youth, seniors, and railpass holders all qualify). Rates are lower for round trips and off-peak travel (midday, midweek, low-season, and low-interest). Fares can change without notice. For specifics, visit www.ricksteves.com/eurostar.

As with airfares, the most expensive and flexible option is a **full-fare ticket** with no restrictions on refundability (even refundable after the departure date; for a one-way trip, figure about $375 in first class, $255 second class). A first-class ticket comes with a meal (a dinner departure nets you more grub than breakfast)—but it's not worth the extra expense.

Also like the airlines, **cheaper tickets** come with more restrictions and are limited in number (so they sell out more quickly; for second-class, one-way tickets, figure $90–200). Non-full-fare tickets have severe restrictions on refundability (best-case scenario: you'll get 25 percent back, but with the cheapest options you'll get nothing). But several do allow you to change the specifics of your trip once before departure.

Those traveling with a railpass for Britain, France, or Belgium should look first at the **passholder** fare, an especially good value for one-way Eurostar trips (about $75). In Britain, passholder tickets can be issued only at the Eurostar office in Waterloo Station or the American Express office in Victoria Station—not at any other stations. You can also order them by phone, then pick them up at Waterloo Station.

You can check and book fares by phone or online in the United States (order online at www.ricksteves.com/eurostar; order by phone at US tel. 800-387-6782) or in Britain (British tel. 08705-186-186, www.eurostar.com). These are different companies, often with slightly different prices and discount deals on similar tickets—if you order from the United States, check out both. (If you buy from a US company, you'll pay for ticket delivery in the United States; if you book with the British company, you'll pick up your ticket at Waterloo Station.) In Europe, you can get your Eurostar ticket at any major train station in any country or at any travel agency that handles train tickets (expect a booking fee).

**Bus option:** Crossing the Channel by bus and ferry takes more than twice as long as the Eurostar train at about half the cost (London to Paris by Eurolines bus: about £45 one-way for economy fares booked at least 2 days in advance; 8 hrs, www.eurolines.com, British tel. 08705-143-219).

## Belgium

Anyone taking the four-hour train ride from Paris to Amsterdam will stop in Brussels, but few even consider getting out. Each train on this route stops in Brussels, and there's always another train coming in an hour or so. Leave an hour early, arrive an hour late, and give yourself two hours in one of Europe's underrated cities. Luckily for the rushed tourist, Brussels Central Station has easy baggage storage and puts you two blocks (just walk downhill) from the helpful local tourist office, a colorful pedestrian-only city core, Europe's greatest city square (Grand Place), and its most overrated and tacky sight, the *Manneken-Pis* (a much-photographed statue of a little boy who thinks he's a fountain). Brussels has three stations: Nord, Midi, and Central. Ask if your train stops at Central (middle) Station. If you have to get off at Nord or Midi, there are local subway-like connecting trains every few minutes. You'll have no trouble finding English-speaking help.

*Brussels' Grand Place is the place to kick back with a brew.*

The Paris–Brussels–Amsterdam rail route is virtually monopolized by high-speed Thalys trains that require reservations. Sometimes you can breeze right onto a Thalys train by getting an immediate reservation, but most of the time you can't. Direct Thalys trains also make the whole Paris–Amsterdam trip, but if you plan a stop in Brussels, you can normally catch a non-reserved train for the Brussels–Amsterdam leg. To guarantee yourself a stop in Brussels, reserve both segments of your trip: Amsterdam–Brussels and Brussels–Paris (or vice versa if you're heading north). Note that only railpasses that include France are accepted by Thalys. If your pass does not also cover Benelux, you'll pay more to cover that portion of the trip. While first class includes a meal (reservations about $28 with railpass), go second class (reservations $13) if you're on a budget. Thalys limits the number of seats available to railpass travelers, particularly on popular morning and evening runs, so you may need to reserve your seat a few days in advance.

## The Best of Germany

The most interesting sightseeing route through Germany follows the most prosperous trade route of medieval Germany: down the Rhine, along the "Romantic Road" from Frankfurt to Munich, and through Bavaria near the Austrian border. While this can be done in two days, it's worth taking up to a week.

Many travelers spend too much time cruising the Rhine and not enough time in castles. I'd cruise just the best hour (St. Goar to Bacharach) and get some hands-on castle experience crawling through what was once the Rhine's mightiest fortress, Rheinfels (see Chapter 65).

From the end of this most impressive section of the Rhine, it's a short train ride to Frankfurt, the launching pad for a train or bus ride along the Romantic Road (Chapter 46) through Germany's medieval heartland. From there, the old trading route crossed the Alps (today's Brenner Pass) and headed into Italy, which makes sense for today's travelers as well.

## Eastern Europe

Eastern Europe has opened up quickly to Western travelers. You'll be amazed at how friendly and accessible it's become in a few short years (see Chapter 50). Today's Eastern Europe offers many of the conveniences of Western European travel (many English-speaking locals and ever-present ATMs and Internet cafés), but retains a sense of pioneer excitement (unusual languages, foods, and currencies). And it's substantially less expensive than the West.

Currently the most enjoyable Eastern European countries are the Czech Republic, Slovakia, Poland, Hungary, Slovenia, and Croatia. All of these countries (except Croatia) joined the European Union in 2004. These days, only more adventurous travelers venture farther east (Belarus, Ukraine, Romania, Bulgaria, Bosnia-Herzegovina, Serbia, Russia).

The most logical first foray into the East is Prague—geographically and culturally, it's the most accessible city to the West (see page 499). Beyond that, the best big-city experiences are in Budapest, Hungary (the de facto capital of Eastern Europe), and Kraków, Poland (the spot most deserving of the nickname "the next Prague"; see Chapter 52). To the south, tiny, overlooked Slovenia offers Back Door travelers breathtaking alpine scenery and a breezy Adriatic culture, with surprisingly convenient connections to Western hubs like Munich and Venice. And Croatia's sparkling Dalmatian Coast and undiscovered Plitvice Lakes—feeling perfectly safe and stable just more than a decade after the country's war with Serbia—are rapidly winning back the hearts of travelers.

## How Much Italy?

Italy is Europe's richest cultural brew. Get out of the Venice–Florence–Rome crush and enjoy its hill towns and Riviera ports. Italy intensifies as you go south. If you like Italy as far south as Rome, go farther. It gets better. If Italy is getting on your nerves by the time you get to Rome, don't go farther south. It gets worse. For many first-timers, after a week in Italy, Switzerland starts looking really good.

By train, you might consider seeing everything except Venice on your way south. Enjoy a romantic last night in Rome before catching the overnight train, arriving early in Venice.

## To Greece or Not to Greece?

Many travelers think they can squeeze Greece into a few days at the end of a trip through Europe. But if that's all the time you've got, I question the sanity of investing a lot of time, money, and stress just to spend a couple of days in huge, polluted Athens and a quick trip to an island—especially when you consider that 500 years before Christ, southern Italy was called "Magna Graecia" (Greater Greece). You can find excellent Greek ruins at Paestum, just south of Naples.

But with more time, Greece merits a visit. In the summer, Greece is the most touristed, least explored country in Europe. It seems that nearly all of its tourists are in a few places, while the rest of the country casually goes about its traditional business. For more on Greece, see Chapter 67.

Italy used to be the tourist's launch pad for Greece. But by car or train, it takes two days of solid travel to get from Rome to Athens, and two days to get back. By boat, it's a long overnight trip (Eurail covers Ancona or Bari, Italy, to Patras, Greece, on Superfast Line, www.superfast.com; and gets you a 50 percent discount from Brindisi, Italy, to Patras, Greece, on Hellenic Mediterranean Lines, www.ferries.gr/hml; also see www.youra.com/intlferries).

Ideally, fly to Greece. Popular budget air carriers such as easyJet (www.easyjet.com) offer cheap flights from various European cities. Europe by Air offers $99 one-way tickets connecting Athens to several European destinations on various small airlines, including Aegean Airlines (www.aegeanair.com)—but only if you book at www.europebyair.com. For more on these and other low-cost flight options, see "Flights Within Europe" in Chapter 10: Travel Agents and Flights. If you're beginning or ending your multi-country trip in Greece, it's especially smart to consider an "open jaw" flight plan (described on page 108).

## The Britain/Europe/Greece Plan

Here's an efficient overall plan for a six-week introduction to Europe: Fly into London and spend four days. Rent a car for a week in England (Bath, Cotswolds, Blenheim, Warwick, Ironbridge Gorge, North Wales). Drop the car in North Wales. Catch the boat to Dublin and take a look at West Ireland (Dingle, Galway). Begin your 21-day Eurailpass to catch the discounted 20-hour boat ride from southeast Ireland to France. Spend three weeks touring the heart of Europe (Paris, Benelux, Rhine, Romantic Road, Bavaria, Swiss Alps, Italy). From Italy, fly or take the boat (covered by Eurail) to Greece, where your train pass expires. Relax in the Greek Isles before flying home from Athens.

## The Best and Worst of Europe—With No Apologies

Good travel writers should make hard choices and give the reader solid opinions. Just so nobody will accuse me of gutlessness, I've assembled a pile of spunky opinions. Chances are that you have too many stops on your trip wish list and not enough time. To make your planning a little easier, heed these warnings. These are just my personal feelings after more than 100 months of European travel. And if you disagree with any of them, you obviously haven't been there.

Let's start with the dullest corner of the British Isles, south Scotland. It's so boring the Romans decided to block it off with Hadrian's Wall.

Hadrian's Wall, near the town of Haltwhistle, is far more intriguing than the area beyond it. Like Venice's St. Mark's Square at midnight and Napoleon's tomb in Paris, this sight covers history buffs with goose bumps.

*Kissing the Blarney Stone: Slathered with spit and lipstick, it's a standard stop for typical big-bus tours in Ireland.*

London, York, Bath, and Edinburgh are the most interesting cities in Britain. Belfast, Liverpool, and Glasgow are quirky enough to be called interesting. Oxford pales next to Cambridge, and Stratford-upon-Avon is little more than Shakespeare's house—and that's as dead as he is.

The west coast of Ireland (the Dingle Peninsula), Snowdonia National Park, and the Windermere

Lakes District are the most beautiful natural regions of Great Britain and Ireland. The York Moors disappoint most creatures great and small.

Germany's Berchtesgaden, Ireland's Blarney Stone (slobbered on by countless tourists to get the "gift of gab"), Spain's Costa del Sol, and the French Riviera in July and August are Europe's top tourist traps. The tackiest souvenirs are found next to Pisa's tower and in Lourdes.

Extra caution is merited in southwest England, a minefield of tourist traps. The British are masters at milking every conceivable tourist attraction for all it's worth. Here are some booby traps: the Devil's Toenail (a rock that looks just like...a toenail), Land's End (pay, pay, pay), and cloying Clovelly (a one-street town lined with knickknack shops selling the same goodies—like "clotted cream that you can mail home"). While Tintagel's castle, famous as the legendary birthplace of King Arthur, offers thrilling windswept and wave-beaten ruins, the town of Tintagel does everything in its little power to exploit the profitable Arthurian legend. There's even a pub in town called the Excali Bar.

*England's Land's End...pay, pay, pay.*

Sognefjord is Norway's most spectacular fjord. The Geiranger fjord, while famous as a cruise-ship stop, is a disappointment. The most boring countryside is Sweden's (I am Norwegian), although Scandinavia's best medieval castle is in the Swedish town of Kalmar.

Zürich and Geneva, two of Switzerland's largest and most sterile cities, share the "nice place to live but I wouldn't want to visit" award. Both are pleasantly situated on a lake—like Buffalo and Cleveland. And both are famous, but name familiarity is a rotten reason to go somewhere. If you want a Swiss city, see Bern or Luzern. But it's almost criminal to spend a sunny Swiss day anywhere but high in the Alps.

Les ravages du «fast-travel»

Le Matin

le quotidien romand

Genève dénigrée sur Internet

«Expert» en tourisme, l'Américain Rick Steves n'y va pas de main morte. Son conseil diffusé sur le web: «Evitez Genève et Zurich, deux villes surfaites et ennuyeuses.» Christian Rey (photo), président de Genève Tourisme, prend la chose avec philosophie et répond à ces critiques. Page 2 ▸

*Geneva's newspaper objects to my "denigrating" its dull city on the Internet.*

Bordeaux must mean "boredom" in some ancient language. If I were offered a free trip to that town, I'd stay home and clean the fridge. Connoisseurs visit for the wine, but Bordeaux wine country and Bordeaux city are as different as night and night soil. There's a wine-tourism information bureau in Bordeaux that, for a price, will bus you out of town into the more interesting wine country nearby.

Andorra, a small country in the Pyrénées between France and Spain, is as scenic as any other chunk of those mountains. People from all over Europe flock to Andorra to take advantage of its famous duty-free shopping. As far as Americans are concerned, Andorra is just a big Spanish-speaking Radio Shack. There are no bargains here that you can't get at home. Enjoy the Pyrénées with less traffic elsewhere.

Germany's famous Black Forest disappoints more people than it excites. If that's all Germany offered, it would be worth seeing. For Europeans, any large forest is a popular attraction. But I'd say the average American visitor who's seen more than three trees in one place would prefer Germany's Romantic Road and Bavaria to the east, the Rhine and Mosel country to the north, the Swiss Alps to the south, and France's Alsace region to the west—all high points that cut the Black Forest down to stumps.

Norway's Stavanger, famous for nearby fjords and its status as an oil boomtown, is a large port that's about as exciting as...well, put it this way: Emigrants left it in droves to move to the wilds of Minnesota. Time in western Norway is better spent in and around Bergen.

Kraków, Poland, and Budapest, Hungary, are, after Prague, Eastern Europe's best destinations. Conveniently located Bratislava—the capital of Slovakia, on the Danube between Vienna and Budapest—has not-quite-charming streets filled with dull cafés, mildly interesting museums, and tourists wishing they'd spent more time elsewhere. Likewise, Bucharest, Romania's capital, has little to offer. Its top-selling postcard is of the InterContinental Hotel. If you're heading from Eastern Europe to Greece, skip Thessaloníki, which deserves its place in the Bible but doesn't belong in travel guidebooks.

Europe's most scenic train ride is across southern Switzerland from Chur to Martigny. The most scenic boat ride is from Stockholm to Helsinki—countless islands and blondes. Europe's most underrated sight is Rome's ancient seaport Ostia Antica, and its most misunderstood wine is Portugal's *vinho verde* (green wine).

The best French château is Versailles, near Paris. The best look at Gothic is the Sainte-Chapelle church in Paris. The top two castles are Germany's Burg Eltz on the Mosel River and Italy's Reifenstein near the Brenner Pass border in the north. Lisbon, Oslo, Stockholm, and Brussels are the most underrated big cities. For romance, Varenna on Italy's Lake Como murmurs "honeymoon."

The biggest mistakes that tourists make: packing too heavily, relying on outdated guidebooks, not wearing a money belt, and taking other people's opinions too seriously. Happy travels!

# 8. SAMPLE ROUTES

After years of designing bus tours, brainstorming with my guides, and helping travelers plan their itineraries, I've come up with some fun and efficient three-week plans. These itineraries are fast but realistic if you plan well and travel smart. They're roughly the routes our guided bus tours follow, and are also the routes covered in my various country guidebooks.

## Great Britain in 22 Days

While this three-week itinerary is designed to be done by car, it can be done by train and bus or, better yet, with a rail-and-drive pass (best car days: Cotswolds, North Wales, Lake District, Scottish Highlands, Hadrian's Wall). For three weeks without a car, I'd probably cut back on the recommended sights with the most frustrating public transportation (South and North Wales, Ironbridge Gorge, the Highlands). Lacing together the cities by train is very slick. With more time, everything is workable without a car.

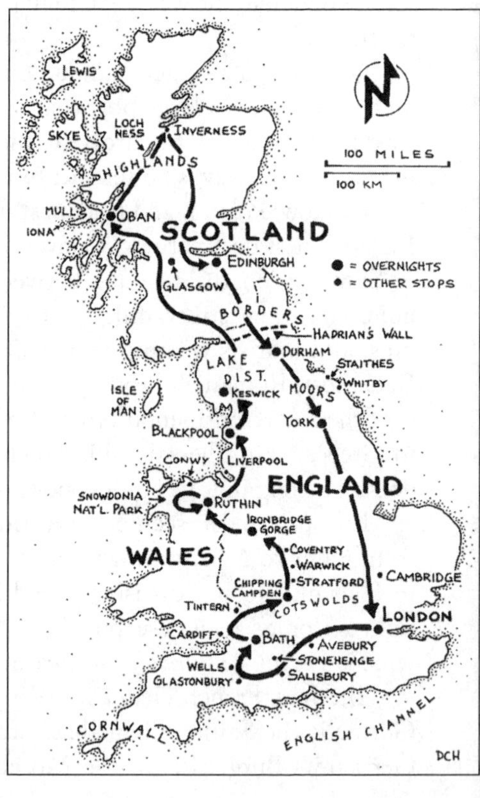


**Day 1:** Arrive in London, catch bus to Bath. Get over your jet lag in Bath (3 nights).

**Day 2:** Enjoy Bath.

**Day 3:** Pick up your rental car and day-trip to the stone circle at Avebury and the towns of Wells and Glastonbury.

**Day 4:** Visit South Wales, including St. Fagans Folk Museum and Tintern Abbey. Head for the Cotswolds and sleep in Chipping Campden (2 nights).

**Day 5:** Explore the Cotswolds and Blenheim Palace.

**Day 6:** Visit Stratford, Warwick Castle, and Coventry. Sleep in Ironbridge Gorge (1 night).

**Day 7:** Explore Ironbridge Gorge, then head to North Wales. If the Welsh medieval banquet is going on at Ruthin Castle, enjoy the banquet and sleep in Ruthin; otherwise, sleep in Conwy (2 nights).

**Day 8:** Enjoy the highlights of North Wales.

**Day 9:** Stop by Liverpool to enjoy Beatles sights, then head to Britain's tacky but fun "Coney Island," Blackpool (1 night).

**Day 10:** Explore the southern Lake District, home-basing in the Keswick area (2 nights).

**Day 11:** Tour the northern Lake District.

**Day 12:** Drive up the west coast of Scotland, overnighting in Oban (1 night).

**Day 13:** Explore the scenic Scottish Highlands, looking for the Loch Ness monster. End your day in Edinburgh (3 nights).

**Day 14:** Another Highlands adventure, or begin touring Edinburgh.

**Day 15:** More time in Edinburgh.

**Day 16:** Visit Hadrian's Wall and the Beamish Folk Museum, arriving in Durham in time for an evensong at the cathedral (1 night).

**Day 17:** Explore the North York Moors, winding up in York. Turn in your car and check into your hotel (2 nights).

**Day 18:** Enjoy York.

**Day 19:** Take an early train to London and begin exploring the city (4 nights).

**Day 20:** Enjoy London.

**Day 21:** More time in London.

**Day 22:** Side-trip to Cambridge or Greenwich.

## Ireland in 22 Days

This three-week itinerary is designed to be done by car, but you can do it by train and bus. For three weeks without a car, spend your first three nights in Dublin using buses and taxis. Cut back on the recommended sights with the most frustrating public transportation (Ring of Kerry, Boyne Valley, County Wexford, Connemara). You can book day tours by bus for parts of these areas through local tourist offices. If there are at least two of you traveling together, don't forget that taxis are affordable if the bus schedule doesn't fit your plans (i.e., Cork to Kinsale, Waterford to New Ross, Dublin to Trim).

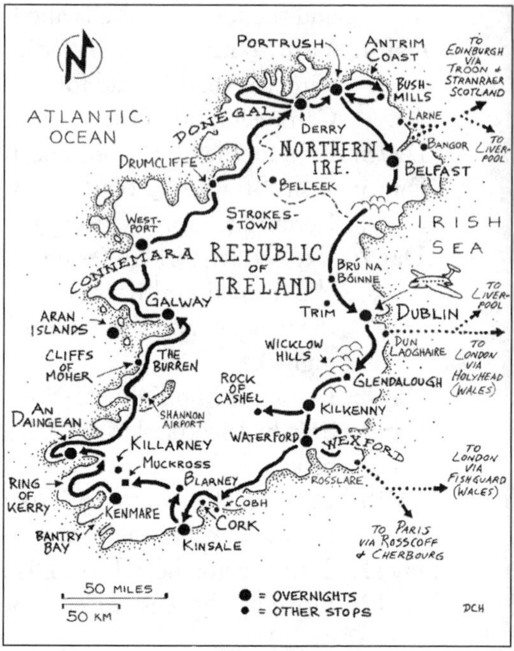

**Day 1:** Fly into Dublin, pick up your rental car, and visit the ancient Glendalough monastic settlement in the Wicklow Mountains. Sleep in Kilkenny (2 nights).

**Day 2:** Explore Kilkenny, with a side-trip to the Rock of Cashel.

**Day 3:** Move on to Waterford, touring the crystal factory. Sleep in Waterford (2 nights).

**Day 4:** Visit County Wexford sights (Hook Head Lighthouse, Kennedy Homestead, *Dunbrody* Famine Ship, Irish National Heritage Park), using Waterford as a home base.

**Day 5:** Drive to Cobh, explore the town, then continue on to Kinsale (2 nights).

**Day 6:** Enjoy Kinsale.

**Day 7:** Visit Muckross House, then move on to Kenmare (1 night).

**Day 8:** Tour the Ring of Kerry, ending in An Daingean/Dingle (3 nights).

**Day 9:** Drive or bike the An Daingean (Dingle) Peninsula loop.

**Day 10:** Make a day trip out to the Blasket Islands or relax in An Daingean/Dingle town (this is a good laundry/rest day).

**Day 11:** Head north to Galway, stopping along the way at the dramatic Cliffs of Moher. Explore the Burren region and enjoy the Dunguaire Castle medieval banquet in Kinvarra before settling down in Galway (2 nights).

**Day 12:** Spend the day in Galway.

**Day 13:** Take a boat out to the Aran Islands, where you'll sleep (1 night).

**Day 14:** Tour the wild Connemara area, winding up in Westport (1 night).
**Day 15:** Drive to Northern Ireland, ending in Derry (1 night).
**Day 16:** Enjoy Derry, then drive to Portrush (2 nights).
**Day 17:** Explore the Antrim Coast as a day trip from Portrush.
**Day 18:** Head into Belfast and explore Northern Ireland's capital (1 night).
**Day 19:** Drive to the Boyne Valley sights, arriving in Dublin. Return your car and check into your hotel or B&B (3 nights).
**Day 20:** Enjoy Dublin.
**Day 21:** More time in Dublin.
**Day 22:** Fly home.

## France in 21 Days

Although this itinerary is designed to be done by car, it can be done by train with a few modifications. A France Flexipass with nine train days works well. For a three-week trip *sans* car, I'd modify it by skipping Honfleur and going straight to Bayeux. Base in Sarlat in the Dordogne, and skip Cahors and Albi on your way to Carcassonne. In Provence, stay in Arles. Take the train from the Riviera to Chamonix (via St. Gervais-les-Bains). Choose Reims or Verdun on your way back to Paris from Colmar, but Verdun is tricky without a car. A France rail-and-drive pass is another good option—a car is especially efficient in Normandy, the Dordogne, and Provence. *Bonne route!*

*Notre-Dame, side view*

**Day 1:** Fly into Paris, pick up your car, visit Giverny and Honfleur, and overnight in Honfleur (1 night). Save Paris sightseeing for the end of your trip.
**Day 2:** Spend today on D-Day sights: Caen World War II Museum, Arromanches, the American cemetery, Pointe du Hoc, dinner and overnight in Bayeux (1 night).
**Day 3:** Bayeux tapestry and church, Mont St. Michel, sleep on Mont St. Michel (1 night).
**Day 4:** Head for châteaux country in the Loire Valley. Tour Chambord, then stay in Amboise (2 nights).

**Day 5:** Do a day trip, touring Chenonceaux and Cheverny or Chaumont. Save time at the end of the day for Amboise and to visit the Château du Clos-Lucé.

**Day 6:** Drive south to the Dordogne region, stopping at Oradour-sur-Glane en route. End in Beynac (2 nights).

**Day 7:** Browse the town and market of Sarlat and tour the Font-de-Gaume cave. Sleep in Beynac.

**Day 8:** Head to the Languedoc region, lunch in Albi, spend evening in Carcassonne (1 night).

**Day 9:** Morning in Carcassonne, then on to Provence with a stop at the Pont du Gard aqueduct. Stay in Arles (2 nights).

**Day 10:** All day for Arles and Les Baux.

**Day 11:** Visit Avignon, then depart for the Riviera, staying in Nice (2 nights).

**Day 12:** Sightsee in Nice and Monaco.

**Day 13:** Head north to the Alps, and sleep in Chamonix (2 nights).

**Day 14:** With clear weather, do the mountain lifts up to Aiguille du Midi.

**Day 15:** A half-day for the Alps. Then head for Burgundy, ending in Beaune for a wine-tasting. Sleep in Beaune (1 night).

**Day 16:** Spend the morning in Beaune, then move on to Colmar (2 nights).

**Day 17:** Enjoy Colmar and the Wine Road villages.

**Day 18:** Return to Paris, visiting Verdun and Reims en route. Collapse in Paris hotel (4 nights).

**Day 19:** Sightsee Paris.

**Day 20:** More time in Paris.

**Day 21:** Finish up your sightseeing in Paris, and consider side-tripping to Versailles.

## Scandinavia in 21 Days

This itinerary, designed to be done by car, can also be done by public transportation (train, bus, and boat). Scandinavia in 21 days by train is

most efficient with a little reworking: I'd go overnight whenever possible on any train ride six or more hours long. Streamline by doing North Zealand, Odense, and Ærø as a three-day side trip from Copenhagen. Take the overnight train from Copenhagen to Stockholm, skipping Växjö and Kalmar. The Bergen/Setesdal/Århus/Copenhagen leg is possible on public transit, but Setesdal (between Bergen and Kristiansand) is not worth the trouble if you don't have a car. Consider flying out of Bergen.

**Day 1:** Arrive in Copenhagen (3 nights).
**Day 2:** Sightsee Copenhagen.
**Day 3:** More time in Copenhagen.
**Day 4:** Head through North Zealand and into Sweden. Spend the night in Växjö (1 night).
**Day 5:** Explore Växjö, then head on to Glass Country and Kalmar, where you'll sleep (1 night).
**Day 6:** Continue on to Stockholm (2 nights).
**Day 7:** Sightsee Stockholm.
**Day 8:** All day in Stockholm, then take the night boat to Helsinki.
**Day 9:** Enjoy the day in Helsinki before returning to Stockholm on the night boat.
**Day 10:** Head to the town of Uppsala, then on to Oslo (3 nights).
**Day 11:** Sightsee Oslo.
**Day 12:** More time for Oslo.
**Day 13:** Go north to Lillehammer, in the Gudbrandsdalen Valley. Sleep in Jotunheimen area (1 night).
**Day 14:** Explore the Jotunheimen Mountains and head for the fjords. Sleep near Lustrafjord (1 night).

**Day 15:** Gawk at the Sognefjord, taking the "Norway in a Nutshell" route to Bergen (2 nights).
**Day 16:** Spend the day in Bergen.
**Day 17:** Take the long drive south through the Setesdal Valley to Kristiansand—where you'll catch a night boat to Denmark.
**Day 18:** Explore Jutland, stopping in Århus and Legoland. Sleep in Århus or near Legoland in Billund (1 night).
**Day 19:** Continue south to the salty island of Ærø, where you'll sleep in the village of Ærøskøbing (2 nights).
**Day 20:** All day to enjoy Ærø.
**Day 21:** Head back north to Copenhagen, via Odense (Hans Christian Andersen House) and Roskilde (Viking ships).

## Spain and Portugal in 22 Days

While this itinerary is designed to be done by car, it works by train and bus (7–8 bus days and 4–5 train days). For three weeks without a car, I'd modify it to start in Barcelona and finish in Lisbon. From Barcelona, fly or take the night train to Madrid (see Toledo, Segovia, and El Escorial as side trips); take the early, direct train from Madrid to Granada (leaving at about 8:10 a.m.); bus along Costa del Sol to Tarifa (day-trip to Morocco); bus to Arcos de la Frontera, Sevilla, and Algarve; and take the train to Lisbon. This skips Coimbra and Salamanca and assumes you'll fly "open jaw" into Barcelona and out of Lisbon. If you're taking the train from Lisbon back to Madrid, you can sightsee your way in three days (via Coimbra and Salamanca) or simply catch the night train to Madrid.

*Granada's Alhambra is a Moorish masterpiece.*

**Day 1:** Arrive in Madrid and check into your hotel (2 nights).
**Day 2:** Sightsee Madrid.
**Day 3:** Pick up your car and drive to El Escorial palace and Franco's monumental Valley of Fallen on your way to Segovia (1 night).
**Day 4:** Enjoy Segovia before driving to Salamanca (1 night).
**Day 5:** See the sights in Salamanca, then cross the Portuguese border and head for Coimbra (2 nights).

**Day 6:** All day for Coimbra.

**Day 7:** Visit Batalha and Fátima on the way to Nazaré, where you'll spend the afternoon and sleep (1 night).

**Day 8:** Enjoy the morning in Nazaré, then visit Alcobaça on the way to Lisbon (3 nights).

**Day 9:** All day to explore Lisbon.

**Day 10:** Using Lisbon as your home base, side-trip to Belém and Sintra.

**Day 11:** Drive early to Évora, then continue to Portugal's south coast, the Algarve. Sleep in Salema (2 nights).

**Day 12:** Enjoy a free day for the beach, and consider a side-trip to Sagres.

**Day 13:** Head east across the Spanish border, winding up in Sevilla (2 nights).

**Day 14:** All day for Sevilla and the night for a flamenco show.

**Day 15:** Follow Andalucía's Route of White Villages to the hill town Arcos de la Frontera (1 night).

**Day 16:** See Arcos, then head south to Jerez (sherry bodegas and horse shows), and on to Tarifa (2 nights).

**Day 17:** Use Tarifa as a home base for a day trip into Morocco.

**Day 18:** Visit Gibraltar (the Rock, views, cave, and ape den) and drive along the Costa del Sol to Nerja (1 night).

**Day 19:** Spend beach time at Nerja, then move on to Granada (2 nights).

**Day 20:** All day to enjoy Granada and visit the Alhambra.

**Day 21:** Drive through La Mancha to Toledo (1–2 nights).

**Day 22:** Spend the day in Toledo. Sleep again in Toledo, or move on to Madrid for another overnight or a late flight home.

## Germany, Austria, and Switzerland in 22 Days

Although this itinerary is designed to be done by car, you can do it by train with minor modifications. For the best three weeks traveling by train, sleep in Füssen rather than Reutte, sleep on the train from Vienna to the Swiss Alps (skipping Hall and Appenzell), skip French Switzerland, skip the Black Forest, and add two days in Berlin, connecting it with night trains.

*Overlooking the Rhine*

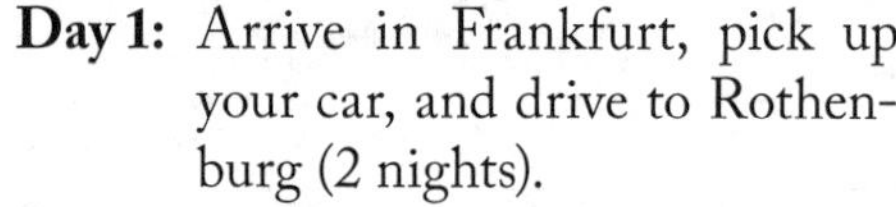

**Day 1:** Arrive in Frankfurt, pick up your car, and drive to Rothenburg (2 nights).

**Day 2:** Sightsee the medieval walled town of Rothenburg.

**Day 3:** Drive along the Romantic Road route to Reutte, Austria (2 nights).

**Day 4:** Using Reutte as a home base, spend the day at castles near Füssen and other Bavaria sights.

**Day 5:** Drive to Munich and begin exploring the city (2 nights).

**Day 6:** All day in Munich.

**Day 7:** Drive over the Austrian border to Salzburg and see the town (1 night).

**Day 8:** Tour the *Sound of Music* country, the Salzkammergut Lake District. Spend the night in tiny Hallstatt (1 night).

**Day 9:** Visit Mauthausen Concentration Camp and follow the Danube into Vienna (3 nights).

**Day 10:** All day to enjoy Vienna.

**Day 11:** Another day for Vienna.

**Day 12:** Make the long drive into Switzerland, ending in the Swiss village of Appenzell. Possibly spend the night in the mountain hut at Ebenalp (1 night).

**Day 13:** Drive west to the Berner Oberland, and stay in the high-altitude village of Gimmelwald (2 nights).
**Day 14:** Enjoy a free day in the Alps. Enjoy the hiking and views.
**Day 15:** Spend some time in Bern, then drive west to Murten (2 nights).
**Day 16:** Using Murten as a home base, day-trip south through the French Swiss countryside to Lake Geneva.
**Day 17:** Drive to the Black Forest, spending the night in the village of Staufen (1 night).
**Day 18:** Tour the Black Forest on your way north to Baden-Baden (2 nights).
**Day 19:** Relax and soak in the baths at Baden-Baden.
**Day 20:** Drive to the Rhine, take a river cruise, and visit some castles. Sleep in the riverside town of Bacharach (1–2 nights).
**Day 21:** Explore the Mosel Valley, including one of Europe's best castles: Burg Eltz. Return to spend the night in Bacharach, or sleep in the cute Mosel village of Beilstein.
**Day 22:** More time on the Rhine, or visit Köln and/or Frankfurt. From here, fly home...or take a night train to Berlin.

## Best of Italy in 22 Days

This trip is best by car, but works fine by rail with a few modifications. An Italy Rail Card (8 days in 1 month) can work well—pay out of pocket for short runs, such as Milan to Varenna or the hops between villages in the Cinque Terre. In the Dolomites, consider basing yourself in Bolzano. From Venice, go directly to the Cinque Terre, then do Florence and Siena. A car is efficient in the hill towns of Tuscany and Umbria, but a headache elsewhere. Sorrento is a good home base for Naples and the Amalfi Coast. Skip Paestum unless you love Greek ruins. To save Venice for last, start in Milan and see everything but Venice on the way south, then sleep through everything you've already seen by catching the night train from Naples or Rome to Venice. This saves you a day and gives you an early arrival in Venice.

**Day 1:** Arrive in Milan, and go directly to Varenna on Lake Como (3 nights).
**Day 2:** Enjoy romantic Lake Como.
**Day 3:** Split your day between Lake Como and Milan.
**Day 4:** Pick up your rental car in Milan, then drive to the Dolomites with a three-hour stop in Verona. Sleep in the alpine town of Castelrotto (2 nights).
**Day 5:** Explore the Dolomites (hikes, lifts, mountain bikes, horseback riding).
**Day 6:** Drive to Venice (2 nights).
**Day 7:** All day for Venice.
**Day 8:** Head to Italy's art capital, Florence (2 nights).
**Day 9:** Spend the day sightseeing in Florence.
**Day 10:** Go to the Cinque Terre, on the Italian Riviera, and set up in the village of Vernazza (2 nights).
**Day 11:** All day to enjoy the Cinque Terre (great beaches and hikes).
**Day 12:** Drive to Siena (2 nights).
**Day 13:** Sightsee Siena.
**Day 14:** Free time to explore Tuscany and Umbria. Sleep in the hill town or *agriturismo* of your choice (2 nights). Assisi and Orvieto are good options.
**Day 15:** More free time in Tuscany and Umbria.
**Day 16:** Drive early to the Amalfi Coast. Sleep in Sorrento (3 nights).
**Day 17:** Spend the day sightseeing in Sorrento, with a side-trip to Pompeii.
**Day 18:** Using Sorrento as a home base, day-trip to the Amalfi Coast.
**Day 19:** Drive to Rome, drop off your rental car, and explore Italy's capital (3 nights).
**Day 20:** Enjoy Rome.
**Day 21:** More time for Rome.
**Day 22:** Finish up your sightseeing in Rome, and fly home.

## The Best of Europe in 22 Days

This far-reaching itinerary makes most sense by train. Taking two night trains avoids two long travel days. The day trips from Munich to Salzburg and from Florence to Siena keep the hotel situation streamlined and take advantage of excellent public transportation services. With your railpass, you can take the Rhine cruise for free. You can also get a big discount on the Romantic Road bus from Rothenburg to Munich (though the train is preferable, entirely covered, and faster). While the route can be done by car (with certain adjustments), this plan is heavy on big cities where cars are worthless and expensive to park.

**Day 1:** Arrive at Amsterdam's Schiphol airport, and stay in the nearby town of Haarlem (2 nights).

**Day 2:** Using Haarlem as a home base, day-trip to Amsterdam.

**Day 3:** Cross the German border to the Rhine River Valley, setting up in the quaint riverside town of Bacharach (2 nights).

**Day 4:** Cruise the best stretch of the Rhine (between Bacharach and St. Goar), then tour St. Goar's Rheinfels Castle. Return to Bacharach by train.

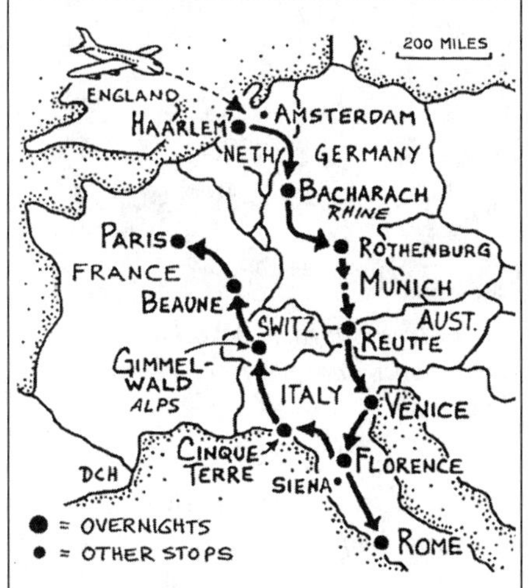


**Day 5:** Take the train to Rothenburg and sightsee (1 night).

**Day 6:** After a morning in Rothenburg, take the Romantic Road bus to Munich (1 night).

**Day 7:** Spend the day in Munich, or consider day trips: a bus tour to "Mad" King Ludwig's fairy-tale castles, or a train from Munich to Salzburg (2 hours each way). Take a night train to Venice.

**Day 8:** All day to enjoy Venice (1 night).

**Day 9:** Head from Venice to Florence (3 nights).

**Day 10:** Spend the day in Florence's museums.

**Day 11:** Using Florence as a home base, side-trip to Siena.
**Day 12:** Head for Rome (3 nights).
**Day 13:** Sightsee Rome.
**Day 14:** More time in Rome.
**Day 15:** Take the train to the Cinque Terre and set up in the village of Vernazza (2 nights).
**Day 16:** Today's a "vacation from your vacation" in the Cinque Terre. Hit the beach or hike the Riviera trails.
**Day 17:** Train into the Swiss Alps, and set up in the mountain town of Gimmelwald (2 nights).
**Day 18:** Alps Appreciation Day: Spend the day enjoying the hiking and high-mountain scenery.
**Day 19:** More time in the Alps, then a night train to Paris.
**Day 20:** Arrive in Paris, check into your hotel (3 nights).
**Day 21:** All day for Paris, maybe with a day trip to Versailles.
**Day 22:** More time in Paris.

## Eastern Europe in 22 Days

This speedy, far-reaching itinerary works best by public transportation. Most of the time, you'll take the train. Exceptions: Bled–Ljubljana and Zagreb–Plitvice Lakes are better connected by bus. The Dalmatian Coast destinations are connected to each other by boat or bus (no trains).

*The massive Hungarian Parliament watches over Budapest from the bank of the Danube.*

By car, this is an exhausting itinerary, with lots of long road days. It makes more sense to connect long-distance destinations by night train (e.g., Prague to Kraków, Kraków to Eger), then strategically rent cars for a day or two in areas that offer inviting day-trip destinations difficult to reach by public transit (e.g., the Czech or Slovenian countrysides).

**Day 1:** Arrive in Prague and begin sightseeing (2 nights).
**Day 2:** All day in Prague.
**Day 3:** All day for more Prague. Take a night train across the Polish border to Kraków.

**Day 4:** Arrive in Kraków and check into your hotel (2 nights). Spend the day sightseeing in Kraków.

**Day 5:** Using Kraków as a home base, side-trip to Auschwitz Concentration Camp.

**Day 6:** More time in Kraków, or consider a day trip to Wieliczka Salt Mine or Warsaw. Take a night train to Eger, in northern Hungary.

**Day 7:** Spend the day enjoying Eger (1 night).

**Day 8:** Take an early train to Budapest, check into your hotel, and begin sightseeing (3 nights).

**Day 9:** All day in Budapest.

**Day 10:** More time in Budapest.

**Day 11:** Catch the early train to Ljubljana, Slovenia, where you'll sleep (2 nights).

**Day 12:** Relax in Ljubljana.

**Day 13:** Go to Lake Bled and explore the lake and surrounding mountains. Sleep in the town of Bled (2 nights).

**Day 14:** Day-trip around the Julian Alps (ideally with a rental car) or relax in Bled.

**Day 15:** Cross the Croatian border to Zagreb, spend time sightseeing in Croatia's capital city, then take an early evening bus to Plitvice Lakes National Park. Sleep in a Plitvice hotel (1 night).

**Day 16:** Spend the morning hiking the waterfall wonderlands of Plitvice, then take an afternoon bus to the Dalmatian Coast. Sleep in Split (2 nights).

**Day 17:** Sightsee Split.

**Day 18:** Take a boat to the island town of Korčula, where you'll sleep (2 nights).
**Day 19:** Spend the day relaxing in Korčula.
**Day 20:** Take the boat to Dubrovnik, and check into your hotel (2 nights).
**Day 21:** All day for exploring Dubrovnik.
**Day 22:** Finish up in Dubrovnik and fly home.

## 9. THE WHIRLWIND TOUR: EUROPE'S BEST TWO-MONTH TRIP

Let's assume you have two months, plenty of energy, and a desire to see as much of Europe as is reasonable. Fly into London and travel around Europe with a two-month Eurailpass. You'll spend two months on the Continent and use any remaining time in Great Britain, before or after you start your railpass (because Eurailpasses don't cover Great Britain). Budgeting for a $900 round-trip ticket to London, about $1,400 for a two-month first-class Eurailpass, and $120 a day for room, board, sightseeing, and entertainment, the entire trip will cost about $9,500. It can be done. Rookies on a budget do it all the time—often for less.

If I were planning my first European trip and wanted to see as much as I comfortably could in two months (and I had the experience I now have to help me plan), this is the trip I'd take. I have to admit, I itch just thinking about this itinerary.

Several of these destinations are included in the "Back Doors" section at the end of this book. In these cases, I've noted which chapter you can turn to for more details and accommodations suggestions. For one fat book covering many of the stops mentioned below, consider this year's *Rick Steves' Best of Europe* guidebook.

### London and Side-Trips—5 days

London is Europe's great entertainer; it's wonderfully historic. Mild compared to anything but the United States, it's the best starting point for a European adventure. The English speak English, but their accents will give you the sensation of understanding a foreign language.

From London's airports, you'll find easy train or subway access to the hotels. To get your bearings, catch a "hop-on, hop-off" orientation bus tour (departs every 20 min) from the park in front of Victoria Station. Give the London Eye Ferris Wheel a spin and tour the spiffed-up British Museum. Every day will be busy and each night filled with a play and a pub. For more on London, see Chapter 53.

**Europe's Best Two-Month Trip**

Spend your remaining time in the English countryside: Bath (see Chapter 54), the Cotswolds (see Chapter 57), York (see Chapter 55), and the university city of Cambridge. But the Continent beckons. Paris is only three hours away by Eurostar train (12–15 trains/day). Cheaper seats can sell fast. To save money, order your tickets from home (www.ricksteves.com/eurostar). If you'll be ending your trip in London, plan for your return: Reserve the accommodations of your choice and get tickets to a hot play.

## Paris—3 days

Ascend the Eiffel Tower to survey a Paris studded with architectural gems and historical one-of-a-kinds. You'll recognize the Louvre, Notre-Dame, the Arc de Triomphe, Sacré-Coeur, and much more.

Take a walk covering Paris' biggies. From the Latin Quarter, head to Notre-Dame, the Deportation Monument to Nazi victims, and Sainte-Chapelle. Cross the Seine over the famous Pont Neuf. Walk by the

*Paris' Eye-ful Tower*

Louvre, through the Tuileries Gardens, and up the avenue des Champs-Elysées to the Arc de Triomphe.

Be sure to experience the Louvre, Orsay Museum (Impressionism), Rodin Museum (*The Thinker* and *The Kiss*), Napoleon's Tomb, a jazz club, and Latin Quarter nightlife. Spend an evening on Montmartre soaking in the spiritual waters of the Sacré-Coeur and browsing among the tacky shops and artists of the place du Tertre. Pick up the *Pariscope* entertainment guide. Most museums are closed on Monday or Tuesday.

Learn the Paris subway—it's fast, easy, and cheap. Ask your hotelier to recommend a small family-owned restaurant for dinner. For more on Paris, see Chapter 41.

Side-trip to Europe's greatest palace, Louis XIV's Versailles (take the RER-C train to the end of the line: Versailles R.G.). Another great side-trip is the city of Chartres, with its great Gothic cathedral (lectures by Malcolm Miller Mon–Sat at noon and 2:45 p.m.).

Start your Eurailpass when you leave Paris. Take the overnight train to Madrid (14 hours), or take a detour....

## Loire Valley—2 days

On the way to Spain, explore the dreamy châteaux of the Loire Valley. Make Amboise your headquarters. Stay at the luxurious Le Manoir les Minimes (34 quai Charles Guinot, tel. 02 47 30 40 40, www.manoirlesminimes.com) or the half-timbered Hôtel le Blason (11 place Richelieu, tel. 02 47 23 22 41, www.leblason.fr), or enjoy bed and breakfast with the engaging Katia Frain (14 quai des Marais, tel. 02 47 30 46 51, vianney.frain@wanadoo.fr). Consider an all-day bus tour of the châteaux. For the simplest approach to château sightseeing, skip the Loire and see Vaux-le-Vicomte, the epitome of a French château, just a 45-minute side-trip from Paris.

## Madrid—2 days

On arrival, reserve your train out. Reservations on long trains are required in Spain, even with Eurail.

Take a taxi or the subway to Puerto del Sol to find a central hotel. Try

Hotel Europa (comfortable, just off Puerta del Sol, Calle del Carmen 4, tel. 915-212-900, www.hoteleuropa.net) or Hostal Acapulco (cheap, Calle de la Salud 13, 4th floor, tel. 915-311-945, hostal_acapulco@yahoo.es).

Bullfights, shopping, and museums will fill your sunny days. Madrid's three essential sights are the Prado Museum (Goya, El Greco, Velázquez, Bosch), Reina Sofía (Picasso's *Guernica*), and the Royal Palace (one of Europe's most lavish interiors). Bullfights are on Sundays throughout the summer (check at hotel, buy tickets at arena). Tourists and pickpockets alike enjoy El Rastro, a huge flea market that sprawls every Sunday.

From Madrid, side-trip to Toledo (35 min by AVE train, or 60 min by bus or shared taxi).

### Toledo—1 day

Save a day for this perfectly preserved historic capital, home of El Greco and his masterpieces. Back in Madrid, take the night train to Lisbon (about 10 hours). Night trains make sense in Iberia—long distances are boring and hot on crowded, slow day trains. But remember, domestic shuttle flights cost less than $100.

*Toledo: Spain's historic capital and El Greco's hometown*

### Lisbon—2 days

Lisbon, Portugal's friendly capital, can keep a visitor busy for days. Its highlight is the Alfama. This salty old sailors' quarter is a photographer's delight. You'll feel rich here in Europe's bargain basement. (See Chapter 37.)

Side-trip to Sintra for its eclectic Pena Palace and mysterious ruined Moorish castle. Circle south for a stop on Portugal's south coast, the Algarve (train from Lisbon to Lagos, about 4 hours).

### Algarve—2 days

Settle down in Salema, the best beach village on the south coast of Portugal. (See Chapter 38.) Cross into Andalucía for flamenco, hill towns, and Sevilla.

### Sevilla and Andalucía—3 days

After strolling the *paseo* of Sevilla, the city of flamenco, sleep at Hotel Amadeus (lovingly decorated with a music motif, Calle Farnesio 6, tel. 954-501-443, www.hotelamadeussevilla.com), or the homey Hostal Córdoba (Farnesio 12, tel. 954-227-498, hostalcordoba@mixmail.com). Then head for the hills and explore Andalucía's Route of the White Villages. Arcos de la Frontera is a good home base. (See Chapter 39.) Ride the speedy AVE train back to Madrid. Fly or catch the night train to Barcelona.

### Barcelona—2 days

Tour the Picasso Museum, relax, shop, and explore the Gothic Quarter. Stay in the simple Hotel Jardi (Plaça Sant Josep Oriol 1, tel. 933-015-900, www.hoteljardi-barcelona.com) or the palatial but affordable Hotel Granvía (Gran Via de les Corts Catalanes 642, tel. 933-181-900, www.nnhotels.es, hgranvia@nnhotels.es). Catch a train to Arles, France (about 7 hours, change in Cerbère and Narbonne).

### Provence or French Riviera—2 days

Your best home base for Provence is Arles (Hôtel Régence, 5 rue Marius Jouveau, tel. 04 90 96 39 85, www.hotel-regence.com). Tour the Papal Palace in Avignon and ramble among Roman ruins in Nîmes (Pont du Gard bridge) and Arles (amphitheater).

Most of the Riviera is crowded, expensive, and stressful, but if you're set on a Riviera beach, Nice is where the jet set lies on rocks. Tour Nice's great Chagall Museum and stay at Hôtel Clémenceau (3 avenue Georges Clémenceau, tel. 04 93 88 61 19, hotel-clemenceau@wanadoo.fr). Then dive into intense Italy.

### Cinque Terre—2 days

The Cinque Terre is the best of Italy's Riviera. You will find pure Italy in these five sleepy, traffic-free little villages between Genoa and Pisa. Unknown to many tourists, it's the ultimate Italian coastal paradise. (See Chapter 32.)

*As you finish a day-long Riviera hike, your home village, Vernazza, comes into view.*

### Florence—1 day

Florence is steeped in history and art. Europe's Renaissance art capital is packed in the summer but worth the headaches. Reserve ahead at the Uffizi Gallery by calling 055-294-883. Stay at Casa Rabatti (cheap, homey, near station, Via San Zanobi 48 black, tel. 055-212-393, casarabatti@inwind.it), Hotel Accademia (elegant, marbled, more expensive, Via Faenza 7, tel. 055-293-451, www.accademiahotel.net), or Soggiorno Battistero (mid-range, next door to the Baptistery, Piazza San Giovanni 1, tel. 055-295-143, www.soggiornobattistero.it).

## Hill Towns of Tuscany and Umbria—2 days

This is where dreams of Italy are fulfilled. Visit Siena and Civita di Bagnoregio. (See Chapter 33.)

## Rome—3 days

Devote your first day to classical Rome: Tour the Colosseum, Forum, Capitol Hill (and its museum), and Pantheon. Linger away the evening at Piazza Navona. Chocolate *tartufo* ice cream is mandatory.

For your second day, visit Vatican City. Tour the Vatican Museum and Sistine Chapel; take the back exit out of the Sistine Chapel to get directly into St. Peter's Basilica (avoiding the line). Climb to the top of the dome for a grand view. Take advantage of the Vatican's post office, which is better than Italy's. Picnickers will find a great open-air produce market three blocks before the Vatican Museum entrance.

Spend your third morning at Ostia Antica, ancient Rome's seaport (like Pompeii, but just a subway ride away from Rome). In downtown Rome, visit Piazza Barberini for its Bernini fountain and Cappuccin crypt (thousands of bones in the first church up Via Veneto). In the early evening, join the locals doing the Dolce Vita stroll from Piazza del Popolo to the Spanish Steps. Have dinner on Campo de' Fiori. Explore Trastevere, where yesterday's Rome lives out a nostalgic retirement.

Stay near the Vatican Museum at Hotel Alimandi (Via Tunisi 8, tel. 06-3972-6300, www.alimandi.it) or near the train station at Hotel Oceania (Via Firenze 38, 3rd floor, tel. 06-482-4696, www.hoteloceania.it). Take a train to Venice (about 4.5 hours, or a 6.5-hour night train).

## Venice—2 days

Cruise the colorful canals of Venice. Grab a front seat on boat #82 for an introductory tour down the Grand Canal. Stay near the Rialto Bridge at Albergo Guerrato (Calle drio la Scimia 240a, tel. 041-528-5927, www.pensioneguerrato.it) or near St. Mark's Square at Hotel Campiello (Castello 4647, tel. 041-520-5764, www.hcampiello.it). The Accademia Gallery showcases the best Venetian art. Tour the Doge's Palace and St. Mark's, and catch the view from the Campanile bell tower. Then wander,

*In Venice, it's fun to get lost.*

leave the tourists, and get as lost as possible. Don't worry, you're on an island and you can't get off. Catch the night train to Vienna (about 7.5 hours).

### Vienna—2 days

Savor the elegance of Hapsburg Vienna, Paris' eastern rival. This grand capital of the mighty Austrian Empire is rich in art history and Old World charm. Stay at tidy Pension Hargita (Andreasgasse 1, tel. 01/526-1928, www.hargita.at) or the classier Hotel-Pension Suzanne (near Opera, Walfischgasse 4, tel. 01/513-2507, www.pension-suzanne.at). Side-trip east for a look at Prague (4.5 hours by train).

### Prague—2 days

Prague, a magnificently preserved city, is a happening place and the easiest first excursion into Eastern Europe. (See Chapter 51.)

### Salzburg—1 day

Mozart's gone, but you'll find his chocolate balls everywhere. Baroque Salzburg, with its music festival and *Sound of Music* delights, is touristy in a way most love. Sleep cheap at Institute St. Sebastian (Linzergasse 41, tel. 0662/871-386, www.st-sebastian-salzburg.at) or pricier at Gasthaus zur Goldenen Ente (Goldgasse 10, tel. 0662/845-622, www.ente.at).

*Surrounded by the Ehrenberg ruins*

### Tirol and Bavaria—2 days

Tour "Mad" King Ludwig's fairy-tale castle at Neuschwanstein and Bavaria's heavenly Wies Church. Visit the Tirolean town of Reutte and its hill-crowning ruined castles. Running along the overgrown ramparts of the Ehrenberg ruins, your imagination works itself loose, and suddenly you're notching up your crossbow and ducking flaming arrows. (See Chapter 65: Dungeons and Dragons.)

## Switzerland—3 days

Pray for sun. For the best of the Swiss Alps, establish a home base in Switzerland's rugged Berner Oberland, south of Interlaken. The traffic-free and quiet village of Gimmelwald above the Lauterbrunnen Valley is everything an Alp-lover could possibly want. (See Chapter 48.)

*King of the Alps, high above Gimmelwald*

Switzerland's best big city is Bern and best small town is Murten. The country is criss-crossed with unforgettably scenic train rides. Be careful: Mixing sunshine and a full dose of alpine beauty can be intoxicating.

## Munich—2 days

Munich, the capital of Bavaria, has a great palace, museums, and the world's best street singers. But they probably won't be good enough to keep you out of the beer halls. You'll find huge mugs of beer, bigger pretzels, and even bigger beer maids! The Hofbräuhaus is the most famous (near Marienplatz in the old town center). Good places to stay include Hotel Schweiz (2 blocks from station at 26 Goethestrasse, tel. 089/543-6960, www.hotel-schweiz.de) and Hotel Münchner Kindl (simple, in old center, Damenstiftstrasse 16, tel. 089/264-349, www.hotel-muenchner-kindl.de). Take the train to Rothenburg.

## Rothenburg and the Romantic Road—1 day

The always-popular queen of quaint German towns, Rothenburg, lies in the heart of medieval Germany. (See Chapter 46.) Then head for the Rhine.

## Rhine/Mosel River Valleys and Köln—2 days

Take a Rhine cruise (free with Eurailpass, Eurail Selectpass, or German railpass) from Bingen to Koblenz to enjoy a parade of old castles. The best hour of the cruise is from Bacharach to St. Goar. In St. Goar, hike up to the Rheinfels castle (see Chapter 65: Dungeons and Dragons). Stay in

### Itinerary Priorities, Country by Country

Use this chart to get ideas on how speedy travelers can prioritize limited sightseeing time in various countries. Add places from left to right as you build plans for the best of that country in 3, 5, 7, 10, or 14 days. (In some cases the plan assumes you'll take a night train.) So, according to this chart, the best week in Britain would be spread between London, Bath, Cambridge, and the Cotswolds.

| Country | 3 days | 5 days | 7 days | 10 days | 14 days |
|---|---|---|---|---|---|
| **Europe** | Forget it | London, Paris | Amsterdam | Rhineland, Swiss Alps | Rome, Venice |
| **Britain** | London | Bath | Cambridge, Cotswolds | York | Edinburgh, N. Wales |
| **Ireland** | Not worth it | Dublin, Dingle Peninsula | Galway, Burren | Kinsale and south coast | Belfast, Antrim Coast, Aran Islands |
| **France** | Paris, Versailles | Loire, Chartres | Normandy | Arles, Nice, Riviera | Chamonix, Burgundy |

Bacharach at Hotel Kranenturm (Langstrasse 30, tel. 06743/1308, www.kranenturm.com) or up at the Castle Youth Hostel (Jugendherberge Stahleck, tel. 06743/1266, bacharach@diejugendherbergen.de, $20 beds) with panoramic Rhine views.

Cruise along the sleepy Mosel Valley and tour Cochem's castle, Trier's Roman ruins, and the impressive medieval castle Burg Eltz (see Chapter 65: Dungeons and Dragons). Then go to Germany's capital, ever-vibrant Berlin (a 4.5-hour train ride from Köln).

## Berlin—2 days

Berlin, capital of a united Germany, with its great art and stunning Reichstag dome, is worth two busy days. For accommodations, try homey Pension Peters (Kantstrasse 146, tel. 030/312-2278, www.pension-peters-berlin.de) or the classy Hotel Astoria (Fasanenstrasse 2, tel. 030/312-4067, www.hotelastoria.de). Take the train from Berlin to

| Country | 3 days | 5 days | 7 days | 10 days | 14 days |
|---|---|---|---|---|---|
| **Germany** | Rhine, Munich | Romantic Road, Rothenburg | Bavarian sights | Berlin | Black Forest, Mosel, Köln |
| **Austria** | Salzburg, Vienna | Danube Valley and slow down | Hallstatt | Innsbruck, Hall, and more Alps | ——— |
| **Switzerland** | Berner Oberland and Bern | French Switzerland, Murten | Luzern, Appenzell | Zermatt and scenic rail trips | Lugano and Zürich |
| **Italy** | Rome | Florence, Venice | Italian Riviera | Siena, hill towns | Milan and Lake Como |
| **Scandinavia** | Copen-hagen, side trips | Oslo | Stockholm | "Norway in a Nutshell," Bergen | Helsinki, Tallinn |
| **Spain & Portugal** | Madrid, Toledo | Lisbon | Barcelona | Andalucía, Sevilla | Algarve |
| **Eastern Europe** | Prague | Budapest | Kraków and Auschwitz | Slovenia and Český Krumlov | Dalmatian Coast with Dubrovnik |

Copenhagen (about 6.5 hours by day; or take the longer night train via Malmö, Sweden).

## Copenhagen—1 day

Finish your continental experience with a blitz tour of the capitals of Scandinavia: Copenhagen, Stockholm, and Oslo. To save money and time, avoid expensive hotels by sleeping on trains and ferries. From Malmö, Sweden (near Copenhagen), you can take overnight trains to Stockholm or Oslo, and from Copenhagen you can also reach Oslo on an overnight cruise.

*Climb Berlin's Reichstag dome.*

### Extras You May Want to Add

More England—Bath, York, Cambridge, and the Cotswolds
Ireland—Dublin, An Daingean (Dingle) Peninsula
Scotland—Edinburgh, the Highlands
French Alps—Chamonix, Aiguille du Midi
Belgium—Bruges, Brussels
Poland—Kraków, Warsaw, Gdańsk
Hungary—Budapest, Eger
Slovenia—Ljubljana, Lake Bled
Croatia—Dubrovnik and the Dalmatian Coast, Plitvice Lakes National Park
Spain's South Coast and Morocco
Southern Italy—Naples and the Amalfi Coast
Greece—Athens, the Peloponnese, the islands
Russia—St. Petersburg and Moscow
A day for showers and laundry
Visiting, resting, and a little necessary slack
Travel days to avoid sleeping on the train

Leave your bags at the Copenhagen train station. Tour the city during the day and spend the evening at Tivoli, just across the street from the train station. Catch the night train to Stockholm (about 8 hours). If you'd like to stay overnight in Copenhagen, try a comfortable B&B (Annette and Rudy Hollender's home, Wildersgade 19, tel. 32 95 96 22, hollender@city.dk).

### Stockholm—2 days

With its ruddy mix of islands, canals, and wooded parks, Stockholm is a charmer studded with fine sights such as the 17th-century *Vasa* warship, Europe's best open-air folk museum at Skansen, and a gas-lamped old town. Sleep in the elegant Norrmalm neighborhood at the Stureparkens Gästvåning (2-night minimum, Sturegatan 58, tel. 08/662-7230, www.stureparkens.nu) or on the centrally located island of Gamla Stan at the Rica Hotel Gamla Stan (Lilla Nygatan 25, tel. 08/723-7250, www.rica.se, info.gamlastan@rica.se). Catch the late-afternoon train to Oslo (5 hours; night train also runs, but sporadically).

## Oslo—1 day

After a busy day wandering through Viking ships, the *Kon-Tiki,* and the Nazi Resistance Museum, and climbing the ski jump for a commanding view of the city and its fjord, you'll be famished. It's red-nosed Rudolph with lingonberries for dinner. (See Chapter 61.)

## Scenic Train, Fjord Country, and Bergen—2 days

For the best look at the mountainous fjord country of west Norway, do "Norway in a Nutshell," a combination of spectacular train, boat, and bus rides (see Chapter 61). Catch the morning train from Oslo over the spine of Norway to Bergen. You can do the Nutshell in a day, but you'll have more fjord fjun if you stay overnight near Flåm in Aurland at the funky Aabelheim Pension or the basic Vangen Motel (same tel. 57 63 35 80, vangsgas@online.no). Enjoy a day in salty Bergen. Stay downtown at the Heskja home (good budget beds, Skivebakken 17, tel. 55 31 30 30, rs@skiven.no) or catch the night train back to Oslo (about 8 hours).

## Oslo—1 day

Take a second day in Oslo. There's plenty to do. Hop an overnight cruise back to Copenhagen (about 16 hours).

## Copenhagen—1 day

Another day in Copenhagen. *Smörgåsbords,* Viking *lur* horns, and healthy, smiling blondes are the memories you'll pack on the night train south to Amsterdam (about 16 hours).

## Amsterdam—2 days

Amsterdam is a study in contrast: Prostitutes shimmy in the Red Light District while marijuana smoke wafts from coffeeshops, all against a backdrop of 17th-century buildings and elegant canals. (See Chapter 45.) If you prefer a small-town home base, consider day-tripping into Amsterdam from nearby Haarlem (Hotel Amadeus, Grote Markt 10, tel. 023/532-4530, www.amadeus-hotel.com; or the homey bed-and-breakfast House de Kiefte, Coornhertstraat 3, tel. 023/532-2980, housedekiefte@gmx.net). You'll

*Go with the flow in Amsterdam.*

discover great side-trips in all directions.

After touring crazy Amsterdam and biking through the tulips, you can get to England via a cheap flight (1 hour), the train (6 hours via the Chunnel), or boat (about 11 hours). Or, easier still, consider avoiding the return to London by flying out of Amsterdam (arrange this "open jaw" flight before you leave home).

## Final Thoughts

This 61-day Whirlwind Tour is just a sampler. There's plenty more to see, but I can't imagine a better first two months in Europe. The itinerary includes opportunities for several nights on trains or ferries. This could save you hundreds of dollars in hotel costs, and also frees up your days for doing more interesting things than sitting on a train or boat.

A Eurailpass is good for two calendar months (e.g., May 15 through midnight July 14). If you validate when you leave Paris and expire (the Eurailpass, not you) on arrival in Amsterdam, you'll spend 53 days, leaving eight days of railpass time to slow down or add options.

Bon voyage!

# TRANSPORTATION

## 10. TRAVEL AGENTS AND FLIGHTS

The travel industry is considered the second biggest industry and employer on the planet (after armaments and the military). To travel, you need to deal with it, so it's good to know how, when, and where. Here are some ideas to help you consume with a little savvy.

### Our Travel Industry

Travel is a huge business. Most of what the industry promotes is decadence: Lie on the beach for two precious weeks of hedonism to make up for the other 50. That's where the money is, and that's where most of the interest is. With the elimination of airline commissions, agents are pushing organized travel more than ever. Obviously they'd prefer you spend your money for Europe here rather than over there. Independent travelers fit the industry like a snowshoe in Mazatlán.

Understand what shapes the information that shapes your travel dreams. As a newspaper travel columnist, I've learned that it takes a bold travel editor to run articles that may upset advertisers. Newspaper travel sections are possible only with the support of travel advertisers. And advertisers are more interested in filling cruise ships or tour buses than in turning people free to travel independently. In fact, when I first started running my weekly travel column, it was called "The Budget Traveler." Within a month of its appearance, that travel section's major advertisers met with the editor and explained they would no longer buy ads if he continued running a column with that name. Hastily, the editor and I found a new name. To save the column, we called it "The Practical

Traveler"—the same subversive information, but with a more palatable title.

Many travel agents don't understand travel "through the Back Door." The typical attitude I get when I hobnob with bigwigs from the industry in Hilton hotel ballrooms is: "If you can't afford to go first class, save up and go next year." I'll never forget the bewilderment I caused when I turned down a free room in Bangkok's most elegant Western-style hotel in favor of a cheap room in a simple Thai-style hotel.

Of course, these comments are generalizations. There are many great travelers in the travel industry. They understand my frustration because they've also dealt with it.

Travel can exploit impoverished local cultures. Or it can promote understanding, bending out our hometown blinders and making our world more comfortable in its smallness. What the industry promotes is up to all of us—writers, editors, agents, and travelers.

## The Advantages of a Travel Agent

I'm not "anti–travel agent." I *am* "anti–*bad* travel agent." My travel agent is my vital ally. I've never gone to Europe without her help. Travel-agency recommendations from other travelers provide excellent leads, but the right agency doesn't guarantee the right agent. You need a particular person—someone whose definition of "good travel" matches yours. Ask for the agency's "independent Europe specialist." Once you find the right agent, nurture your alliance. Be loyal. Send her a postcard.

**Travel agents save you money.** These days it takes a full-time and aggressive travel professional to keep up with the constantly changing airline industry. I don't have time to sort through all the frustrating, generally too-good-to-be-true ads that fill the Sunday travel sections. I rely on the experience of an agent who specializes in budget European travel.

Agents used to earn most of their income from airline commissions, but these are a thing of the past. To stay in business, many agents now charge a $35–100 fee per ticket. Travel agencies have also had to specialize, offering their customers something beyond just plane tickets—a friendly, knowledgeable human being you can call on in a travel-related emergency. In the long run, paying a modest fee is a worthwhile expense to ensure that you have the right—and cheapest—ticket for your trip. Think of it as a consulting cost for your travel agent's expertise.

**You can't save money by buying directly from the airlines.** Most airline representatives barely know what they're charging, much less their competitors' rates and schedules. Only your agent would remind you that leaving two days earlier would get you in on the end of shoulder season or catch a special sale—and save you $200. In many cases, travel agents have access to low consolidator fares that aren't available online or from the airline.

**An agent can get you almost any ticket.** Dumping your agent for a $30 savings from a discount agent down the street is a bad move. These days, many people milk good agents for all they're worth and then buy tickets online. Because of this, it's tough to get good advice over the phone, and "browsers" usually get no respect. As a loyal customer, I enjoy the luxury of sitting down with my agent, explaining my travel plans, getting a briefing on my options, and choosing the best flight. This is especially useful for complicated itineraries, such as flying "open jaw"—into one city and out of another, described in detail below—which can be difficult (or impossible) to book online.

**Use your agent only for arranging transportation.** Although many agents can give you tips on Irish B&Bs and sporadic advice on biking in Holland, assume you'll do better if you use your travel agent only to get you to your destination. After that, rely on a good guidebook. Travel agents handle their clients with kid gloves. Don't let their caution clamp a ball and chain onto your travel dreams. I use an agent for my plane ticket, train pass or car rental, advice on visa and health precautions, and nothing else.

Car rentals are cheaper when arranged before departure through your agent. Eurailpasses and most country railpasses must or should be purchased before you leave home. To get good service on small, tedious items like these, do all your trip business through the agent who charged a fee for booking your air ticket.

**Check student travel agencies—even if you're not a student.** Any city with a university probably has a student travel agency. STA Travel (with more than 100 offices in the US and Canada, www.statravel.com, tel. 800-781-4040) offers budget fares even to nonstudents. Most big West Coast campuses also have a more independent agency that is a member of University and Student Travel Nationwide. These agencies sell STA tickets as well as their own discounted tickets. Note that heavily discounted student tickets often don't count for frequent-flyer miles.

**If your schedule's flexible, consider flying standby.** Air-Tech offers unsold seats at bargain prices (e.g., one-way from Los Angeles to Paris for $249, year-round; www.airtech.com, tel. 212/219-7000). However, a short list of departure cities in the United States (such as Boston, New York, and Washington, D.C.) make arranging these flights tricky. In the summer, prepare to be bumped—two or three times. Finally, it's a gamble: Getting a one-way ticket back home from Europe can be very costly—potentially eating up your initial savings.

## Buying Plane Tickets Online

I'm loyal to my travel agent, but some travelers prefer booking their plane tickets online. Particularly if you have a straightforward itinerary (into and out of the same big city, such as London or Frankfurt), you might save money booking your ticket online instead of using a travel agent. And occasionally you'll find amazing deals on the Web...but usually only after hours of digging. These tips will improve your odds:

**Surf the published-fare Internet travel agencies.** Some Web sites can compare several published fares on a particular route, then sort them by price. Stick with the big names. Travelocity (www.travelocity.com) and Expedia (www.expedia.com) are built upon conventional reservation systems used by travel agents. The Orbitz site (www.orbitz.com), owned by the five largest US airlines, boasts that it offers travelers the lowest fares and the most flights. European-based Opodo (www.opodo.com) is a consortium of nine European airlines. Other Web sites, such as www.kayak.com and www.mobissimo.com, search dozens of other booking sites in one keystroke. These sites are a good place to start, but keep in mind that they don't include all airlines. Some travelers use these sites to find out which airline is cheapest, then go to that airline's own site to see if there's an even better deal. In a few cases, these sites can even beat the carrier's official site. They can sometimes also "mix and match" to connect the legs of a single trip by using different airlines, getting a great price (though these trips can be difficult to rebook in case of a delay or missed leg).

**Check on the airlines' official Web sites for deals.** Often these sites offer special "Web-only" fares that are not published anywhere else. For example, SAS offers incredibly low prices for intercontinental flights each December. Their site (www.scandinavian.net) becomes an Advent calendar, and each day a new European destination is available—but only for one day. (You can sign up for e-mail alerts that tell you today's destination.)

**If you're flexible, consider consolidator sites.** These sites have access to fares that have not yet been published; these low rates were once available only to travel agents. Examples include www.priceline.com, www.hotwire.com, and www.cheaptickets.com. The sites offer many restrictions, inconvenient itineraries, and few possibilities for frequent-flyer miles—but they can help flexible travelers save money. Most provide a list or a grid with multiple flights on various airlines to choose from. Most consolidator sites have serious restrictions; for example, you can't always choose your time of day to fly, or what airline you prefer. But the savings can make it worth considering.

**Consider specialty sites.** Some sites offer discounted, yet-to-be-published fares at discounted rates for people who fit certain criteria, such as students, youth, and teachers. For example, www.statravel.com specializes in student travel.

**Comparison-shop "air plus hotel" promotional deals.** Some major airlines now offer "getaway" deals on their Web site. For one low price, you get a round-trip flight to a European city, as well as a few nights' lodging at a hotel in that city (before moving on to other destinations). The hotels are generally soulless business hotels. But if the cost of the package is considerably less than buying the airfare and booking a hotel separately, go for it. Considering Europe's high accommodations costs—especially in big cities—and the declining dollar, this can be an excellent value.

**Sign up for e-mail alerts.** Most of the above sites can e-mail you updates about low fares for specific routes—a handy way to find out about sales.

**Be aware of extras.** Many airlines award bonus frequent-flier miles if you book on their Web site. Most airlines also let you choose your seat; for pointers, see www.seatguru.com.

**Read the fine print.** The advantage of using a travel agent is that you have an ally who understands the ins and outs of dealing with the airlines. But when you book online, you're on your own. Whichever Web site you use, make sure it lists a phone number—you'll need to speak to a person if you have a problem. Understand the restrictions and additional fees (such as a service charge or delivery fee that shows up only when you're in the final stage of booking).

Personally, I'd rather have my travel agent do the work.

## Flying to Europe

Flying to Europe is a great travel bargain—for the well-informed. The rules and regulations are confusing and always changing, but when you make the right choice, you get the right price.

**Dollars saved = discomfort + restrictions + inflexibility.** There is no great secret to getting to Europe for next to nothing. Assuming you know your options, you get what you pay for. There's no such thing as a free lunch in the airline industry. (In fact, these days, there's usually no lunch at all.) Full fare is very expensive. You get the ultimate in flexibility, but I've never met anyone spending his or her own money who flew that way.

Rather than grab the cheapest ticket to Europe, go with your agent's recommendation for the best combination of reliability, economy, and flexibility for your travel needs. Buy your ticket when you're ready to firmly commit to flight dates and ports. As you delay, dates sell out and prices generally go up. Special fares are generally limited to a few seats to jump-start departures.

**Buy your tickets at the right time.** Book your spring and summer travel in January, February, and March. In general, the sooner the better—but not all of the best fares are available in January, so watch the airfares and ask your travel agent to advise you when to buy your ticket. Fall travel should probably be booked by May or June, because the trend for airfare prices and availability is known by then. If you're traveling in September—a very popular time to fly to Europe (particularly the first half of the month)—start looking even earlier. Again, your travel agent can advise you whether to buy now or hold off for lower fares. Travel during winter—November through March—should be purchased a month or so in advance (with the exception of winter breaks and holidays, which require earlier booking).

**Be aware of surcharges and taxes.** After fuel prices skyrocketed in 2005, most airlines began to levy a hefty "fuel surcharge" of $100–200 round-trip. Combined with airport taxes (which vary by city, but can also exceed $100), this can add a substantial sum to your total ticket price. For example, a "cheap" $300 round-trip off-season flight to London can almost double in price when all the fees are included...not quite such a bargain after all. Most travel agents include all fees in airfare quotes, and many Web sites do not—but it's always smart to figure out the complete price before you decide.

**Consider flying "open jaw."** I routinely fly "open jaw": into one city and out of another. The fare is figured simply by taking half of the round-trip fare for each of those ports. I used to fly into Amsterdam, travel to Istanbul, and (having rejected the "open jaw" plan because flying home from Istanbul costs $200 more than returning from Amsterdam) pay $200 to ride the train for two days back to Amsterdam to catch my "cheap" return flight. Now I see the real

**Flying "Open Jaw"**

economy in spending more for "open jaw." "Open jaw" is cheapest when the same airline covers each segment of the round-trip journey.

**A good agent will check both consolidator and airline fares, then offer you the best deal.** Consolidator tickets are generally cheapest, but sometimes fare wars can make an airline's prices unbeatable. Consolidators (or wholesalers) negotiate with airlines to get deeply discounted fares on a huge number of tickets; they offer these tickets to your travel agent, who then marks them up and still sells you a cheaper flight to Europe than the airline itself can. (Note that some travel agencies *are* consolidators.) An airline's ticket prices in a drawn-out fare war, however, can drop to bargain-basement levels. A good travel agent will offer both consolidator and regular airline fares. If not, specifically ask the agent to check consolidator rates.

With consolidator tickets, you usually have seven days to pay after booking, and credit cards are becoming more acceptable. If, after you buy an airline ticket, the airline's price drops yet again, you can exchange your ticket and save some money—if the discount is greater than the change fee (generally $75–250). Consolidator tickets, however, won't get any cheaper; the price, once established, stays the same. Ask about cancellation policies: What is the fee? Will you receive a refund or credit? Consolidator tickets are usually refundable prior to departure, minus a fee of $200–300.

Consolidator tickets often waive the normal advance-purchase and minimum- and maximum-stay requirements that come with other budget tickets. But consolidator tickets are cheap because they come with disadvantages: They are "nonendorsable," meaning that no other airline is required to honor that ticket if your airline is unable to get you home (though in practice this is rarely a problem). Sometimes you may not get frequent-flyer miles (particularly with British Airways and American Airlines). And, if the airline drops its prices (which often happens), you are stuck with what was, but no longer is, a cheap fare.

**Courier flights usually sound better than they are.** Courier flights can get some travelers to Europe with deeply discounted tickets (30–80 percent off). Couriers, whose luggage is limited to carry-ons, are required to transport shipping documents. Upon landing, they turn the documents over to a courier company representative, who checks the cargo through customs.

For most, these cheap flights are a pipe dream. The number of bargain courier flights to Europe has diminished over the past several years. You need to be able to fly on short notice and live in the key "departure cities" (such as New York, Miami, or San Francisco). Lately, courier

## Know Thy Travel Agent—A Quiz

One way to be sure your travel agent is enthusiastic about European travel and properly suited to helping you with your trip is to ask him or her a few questions. Here's a little quiz—complete with answers.

1. **What is "open jaw"?**
   a) Yet another shark movie sequel.
   b) A tourist in awe of the *Mannekin-Pis.*
   c) A special-interest tour of Romania's dental clinics.
   d) An airline ticket that allows you to fly into one city and out of another.
2. **Which international boat rides are covered by the Eurailpass?**
   a) Poland to Switzerland.
   b) All of them.
   c) Sweden to Finland, Italy to Greece, Germany to Denmark, and Sweden to Denmark.
3. **What's the age limit to sleep in a Hostelling International youth hostel?**
   a) Five.
   b) As high as 30 if you like rap music.
   c) There is none, except in Bavaria, where it's 26.

services have started charging a percentage of the ticket value, making the whole notion less exciting.

If you think courier flights could work for you, do a little research. The International Association of Air Travel Couriers offers free information about air couriers on its Web site ($45/year to join; www.courier.org). But you won't find out much from the Air Courier Association ($39/year, www.aircourier.org, tel. 800-211-5119) or Couriertravel.org ($40/year, www.couriertravel.org) until you pay a membership fee.

**Budget flights are restrictive.** Most are nonchangeable and nonrefundable, but some offer changes on the return dates for a penalty of about $100–200. Even then, you typically need to make changes at least 24 hours before your departure to avoid losing the entire value of the ticket. If you need to change your return date in Europe, telephone your airline's European office. If that fails, I've found airlines become more lenient if you go to their office in person with a good reason for your need to change the return date. If you must get home early, go to the airport.

4. **What is the most economical way to get from London's Heathrow Airport into London?**
   a) Walk.
   b) Ask the queen for a lift.
   c) Don't. Spend your whole vacation at Heathrow.
   d) By subway ("Tube").
5. **What is an ISIC card?**
   a) A universal way to tell foreigners you're not feeling well.
   b) It beats three-of-a-kind.
   c) The International Student Identity Card, good for many discounts at sights and museums.
6. **Is there a problem getting a bed-and-breakfast in England's small towns without a reservation?**
   a) Not if you live there.
   b) Yes. Carry No-Doz in England.
   c) No.
7. **How much does a Hungarian visa cost?**
   a) $45.
   b) You can just charge it on your Visa card.
   c) More than a Greek urn.
   d) It's not required.

*Answers: The last answer to each question is the correct one.*

If you're standing at the airport two days before your ticket says you can go home, and seats are available, regardless of the rules, they may let you fly home early (at no extra cost). They win a happy customer and gain two more days to try to sell an empty seat. Besides, at that point, it's the easiest way to get rid of you.

**Expect to get an electronic ticket.** More and more, airlines are pushing electronic tickets. For years, I've recommended requesting a paper ticket instead. That way, if there's a need to change flights or if computers go down, you have a legal and tangible ticket in your hand. But now the pressure to go electronic is so intense—and the extra fees for getting a paper ticket are so high—that I've given in and accepted the reality that everyone will be flying on e-tickets. While travelers with an e-ticket can fly simply with a photo I.D., it's always smart to also bring the printed receipt with you in case of complications at the airport.

**Review your ticket carefully when you receive it.** Double-check your dates, destinations, and exact spelling of your name. A simple second look as soon as you get your tickets can give you a chance to fix any mistakes...and save you enormous headaches later.

## Flights Within Europe

Flying is now a realistic option for budget travelers. With the deregulation of airlines and the proliferation of many extremely competitive discount carriers, suddenly Europe's vagabonds are jet-setters too. Several new no-frills airlines are taking off, and some well-established carriers continue to offer discounts (or air passes) for flights within Europe to travelers who fly with them from North America. These days, before buying any long-distance train ticket, check with a travel agent (at home or in Europe) or the budget airlines' Web sites (see below).

### Flight vs. Train?

While airfares have dropped, a railpass is still usually a lot cheaper than flying. But if you're short on time or have long distances to cover, flying is worth considering. By taking a quick flight, you can easily visit two countries far apart from each other (say, a week in Norway and a week in Italy). For cities close together, the train is more practical. From London to Paris, the Eurostar Chunnel train can be faster than flying when you consider the train zips you directly from downtown to downtown (www.ricksteves.com/eurostar). While the actual flight between the cities is faster than the train, you must factor in the time it takes to get between downtown and the airports, and the extra time needed for check-in and security. Train and car travel, unlike flights, keep you close to the scenery, to Europe, and to Europeans. Ground transportation is also less likely to be disrupted by bad weather or mechanical problems. But if the distance from Point A to Point B is long, flying can be an attractive, affordable option.

*An affordable flight can beat a long train ride.*

### Budget Flights

Budget airlines offer cheap fares within Europe. While travel agents can book some of these inexpensive flights for you, it's best to do it yourself. Reserve your flight on the Web or by phone, using your credit card to pay. To get the lowest fares, book long in advance. Cheap seats sell out fast, leaving the pricier seats for latecomers.

*Europe's no-frills, smaller airlines offer cut-rate fares and scaled-down services.*

Most budget airlines offer flights between major European cities for about $100, but you can find some incredible, it-must-be-a-typo promotional deals if your timing is right. A tour guide on my staff booked a flight from London to Amsterdam for just £16 ($29) on easyJet. Ryanair sometimes flies from London to any one of dozens of cities for just £0.99 (less than $2). Even after taxes and airport fees, these flights are a great value.

While new budget airlines are continually being launched (see sidebar), a handful of them have been around long enough to be considered old-timers, including easyJet (www.easyjet.com), Ryanair (www.ryanair.com), and Virgin Express (www.virgin-express.com). But there are plenty of other options. The best strategy is generally to select an airline that uses either your starting point or your ending point as a hub. For example, for a trip from Brussels to Nice, I'd look first at Virgin Express, which has a hub in Brussels. Several Britain-based budget airlines specialize in connecting the British Isles to Spain and other popular holiday destinations in southern Europe. If this fits your itinerary, try Monarch (www.flymonarch.com) or Excel Airways (www.xl.com).

Not sure where to start? Some Web sites search routes on multiple (but not necessarily all) cheap airlines: www.skyscanner.net is the best, but you can also try www.mobissimo.com, www.kayak.com, www.wegolo.com, and www.sidestep.com. Because some of these sites focus on budget airlines, they can miss just-as-cheap promotional offers on major carriers. To find the right connection, you may need to search several sites. Other budget-airline information sites—which have destination maps and recent airline news—include www.flycheapo.com, www.flybudget.com, www.attitudetravel.com, and www.flitesite.co.uk. For ratings and reviews of particular airlines, check out www.airlinequality.com.

Europe by Air is another good budget resource (www.europebyair.com, tel. 888-321-4737). They work with more than 20 different European airlines, offering flights between 150 European cities in 30 countries. Using their "flight pass" system, each coupon for a nonstop flight costs $99 plus tax (which can be about $50). Note that if you make

## Budget Airlines within Europe

These are just a few of the many budget airlines taking to the European skies. To discover more, check out www.skyscanner.net, or simply use Google.com to search for "cheap flights" plus the cities you're interested in.

| Airline and Contact Information | Hub(s) |
|---|---|
| **Aer Lingus**<br>www.aerlingus.com<br>US tel. 800-474-7424 | Dublin (and other Irish airports)<br>Irish tel. 0818-365-000 |
| **Air Berlin**<br>www.airberlin.com<br>German tel. 01805/737-800 | Multiple German cities |
| **bmi** (and its subsidiary, **bmi baby**)<br>www.flybmi.com and www.bmibaby.com<br>US tel. 800-788-0555<br>British tel. 0870-607-0555 | London (and other British airports) |
| **Central Wings**<br>www.centralwings.com<br>Polish tel. 022/558-0045 | Warsaw |
| **easyJet**<br>www.easyjet.com<br>British tel. 0870-600-0000 | Multiple cities, including London, Berlin, Paris, Liverpool, Geneva, Basel |
| **Germanwings**<br>www.germanwings.com<br>German tel. 0870/252-1250 | Multiple German cities |
| **Hapag-Lloyd Express**<br>www.hlx.com<br>German tel. 01805/093-509 | Multiple German cities |
| **Ryanair**<br>www.ryanair.com<br>Irish toll tel. 1530-787-787<br>British toll tel. 0906-270-5656 | London, Liverpool, Glasgow, Dublin, Shannon, Brussels, Frankfurt, Milan, Pisa, Rome, Stockholm, Barcelona |

| | |
|---|---|
| **SkyEurope**<br>www.skyeurope.com<br>Slovak tel. 02/4850-4850 | Budapest, Kraków, Warsaw, Bratislava, Prague |
| **SmartWings**<br>www.smartwings.net<br>Czech tel. 255-700-827 | Prague |
| **Snowflake**<br>www.flysnowflake.com<br>Swedish tel. 08/797-4000 | Stockholm, Copenhagen |
| **Spanair**<br>www.spanair.com<br>Spanish tel. 902-929-191 | Madrid, Barcelona |
| **Sterling**<br>www.sterlingticket.com<br>Danish tel. 70 10 84 84 | Multiple Scandinavian cities, including Copenhagen, Oslo |
| **Transavia**<br>www.transavia.com<br>Dutch tel. 020/406-0406 | Amsterdam, Rotterdam |
| **Virgin Express**<br>www.virgin-express.com<br>Belgian tel. 070-353-637 | Brussels |
| **Vueling**<br>www.vueling.com<br>Spanish tel. 902-333-933 | Barcelona, Madrid |
| **Wizz Air**<br>www.wizzair.com<br>Polish tel. 022/351-9499 | Budapest, Warsaw, Katowice (near Kraków) |

More airlines pop up all the time. For other options, consider www.airbaltic.com (Baltic capitals), www.alpieagles.com (Venice), www.blue1.com (Helsinki), www.blueair-web.com (Bucharest), www.estonian-air.com (Tallinn), www.flybaboo.com (Geneva), www.flybe.com (southern England), www.flydba.com (Munich), www.flyme.com (Göteborg), www.flyniki.com (Vienna), www.flynordic.com (Stockholm), www.flyairone.it (Rome, Milan, and Torino), www.flysn.com (Brussels), www.flyvlm.com (London City Airport), www.helvetic.com (Zürich), and www.norwegian.no (Oslo and Bergen).

a connection through one of Europe by Air's many hubs, you pay double—$99 for each flight to and from the hub.

With cheaper airfares come new pitfalls. These budget tickets are usually nonrefundable and nonchangeable. Some airlines take only online bookings, so it can be hard to track down a person to talk to if problems arise. Since they're not making much money on your ticket, these airlines look for other ways to pad their profits—bombarding you with ads, selling you overpriced food and drinks on board (nothing's included), and gouging you with expensive baggage restrictions. For instance, Ryanair charges a $9 fee for each checked bag (less if you pay when you book your ticket). If your checked bag weighs more than 20 kilograms (about 44 pounds), you'll also pay $10 per extra kilo. To avoid unpleasant surprises, read the baggage policy carefully before you book.

Another potential headache: Budget airlines sometimes use obscure airports. For example, Ryanair's England hub is Stansted Airport, the farthest of London's airports from the city center. Ryanair's flights to Frankfurt actually take you to Hahn, 62 miles away. Sometimes you may wind up in a different (though nearby) country: For example, a flight advertised as going to Copenhagen, Denmark, might actually go to Malmö, Sweden, while a flight bound for Vienna, Austria, might land in Bratislava, Slovakia. These are still safe and legal airstrips, but it can take money and time to reach them by public transportation.

When exploring low-cost airlines, be creative. For example, let's say you need to get from Amsterdam to Rome. After a quick search you may not find quite the flight you need, but you discover that a low-budget airline flies to Rome from Brussels for €75 (about $100). It makes good travel sense to take a 2.5-hour train ride from Amsterdam to Brussels ($50 second-class) to catch the 2.5-hour flight to Rome. The train from Amsterdam to Rome would have wasted 20 hours of your valuable vacation time, and cost you $300 (plus another $25 for an overnight berth). The train-plus-flight connection gets you there in a third the time (including transfers) for half the price.

Unlike most US airlines, all of these low-cost European airlines offer one-way flights without a cost increase or penalty. Consider linking cheap flights, either with the same or different airlines. But be very careful to leave plenty of time for the connection—since these airlines generally work alone, you're on your own if the delay of one flight causes you to miss another flight. This is especially risky if that "other flight" is your transatlantic flight back to the US. If you're using a budget carrier to connect to your US-bound flight, allow time to absorb delays—maybe even an overnight.

Major European airlines such as Lufthansa, Air France, Alitalia, SAS, KLM, LOT, and British Airways are getting into the discount airfare game. There's a catch: Often you must buy your transatlantic flight from the airline in order to take advantage of its intra-Europe budget fares. But it can be worth an extra $100 for an overseas flight in order to save on flights within Europe. In some cases, you purchase an "air pass" (for $300–400)—a set of three or more flight coupons, each good for one nonstop flight. Be aware that with any air pass, a flight will "cost" two coupons if you need two connecting flights to reach your destination. Check with your travel agent for details.

## The Fear of Flying

Like many people, I'm afraid to fly. I always think of the little rubber wheels splashing down on a rain-soaked runway and then hydroplaning out of control. Or the spindly landing gear crumbling. Or, if not that, then the plane tilting just a tad, catching a wing tip, and flipping over and bursting into flames.

Despite my fears, I still fly. The chances of being in an airplane crash are minuscule. I remind myself that every day 30,000 planes take off and land safely in the United States alone. While airplanes do crash, entire years go by (like 2002) in which there are no passenger fatalities on any commercial American airline. In 2005, you were statistically more likely to die by being hit in your car by a plane than to die as a passenger in a plane crash. The pilot and crew fly daily, and they don't seem to be terrified. Professional sports teams fly all over the place all the time and never crash.

I guess it's a matter of aerodynamics. Air has mass, and the plane maneuvers itself through that mass. I can understand a boat coming into a dock—maneuvering through the water. That doesn't scare me. So I tell myself that a plane's a boat with an extra dimension to navigate, and its "water" is a lot thinner. Also, the pilot, who's still "flying" the plane after it lands, is as much in control on the ground as in the air. Only when he's good and ready does he allow gravity to take over.

Turbulence scares me, too. A United pilot once told me that he'd have bruises from his seat belt before turbulence really bothered him. Still, every time the plane comes in for a landing, I say a prayer, close my eyes, and take my pen out of my shirt pocket so it won't impale me if something goes wrong. And every time I stick my pen back in my shirt pocket, I feel thankful.

Wondering which airline to choose? For me, it doesn't matter; I have no favorite. If I arrive in Europe safely on the day I had hoped to, it was a great flight.

# 11. TRAIN AND RAILPASS SKILLS

The European train system makes life easy for the visitor. The great trains of Europe shrink what is already a small continent, making the budget whirlwind or far-reaching tour a reasonable and exciting possibility for anyone.

Generally, European trains go where you need them to go and are fast, frequent, and inexpensive. (They're faster and more frequent in the north and less expensive but slower in the south.) You can easily have dinner in Paris, sleep on the train, and have breakfast in Rome, Munich, or Madrid.

You can buy train tickets as you travel or, depending on your trip, save money by buying a railpass.

## Railpasses vs. Point-to-Point Tickets

With a railpass, you can travel virtually anywhere, anytime, generally without reservations. Just step on the right train, sit in an unreserved seat, and, when the uniformed conductor comes, flash your pass. More and more fast trains are requiring reservations, but despite that chore, a railpass is still a joy.

The train-pass scene has become complex. It used to be just Eurail. But digging the English Channel Tunnel, building a bridge between Denmark and Sweden, and adding slick trains all over Europe aren't cheap. Consequently, railpass prices have gone up. The 18-country, consecutive-day Eurailpasses are now harder to afford. Rather than lowering the price, the railpass companies are offering us ways to save money by consuming with more focus. Instead of just a consecutive-day Eurailpass, we now have "flexipasses" allowing us to travel a day here and a day there when we like; a Eurail Selectpass enabling us to choose up to five countries; individual country passes; partner saverpasses (giving 2 or more people traveling together a 15 percent savings); and a slew of rail-and-drive passes.

As an alternative to a railpass, point-to-point tickets can be a good budget option. Many Eurail travelers would save money by simply buying

## A Typical Ticket

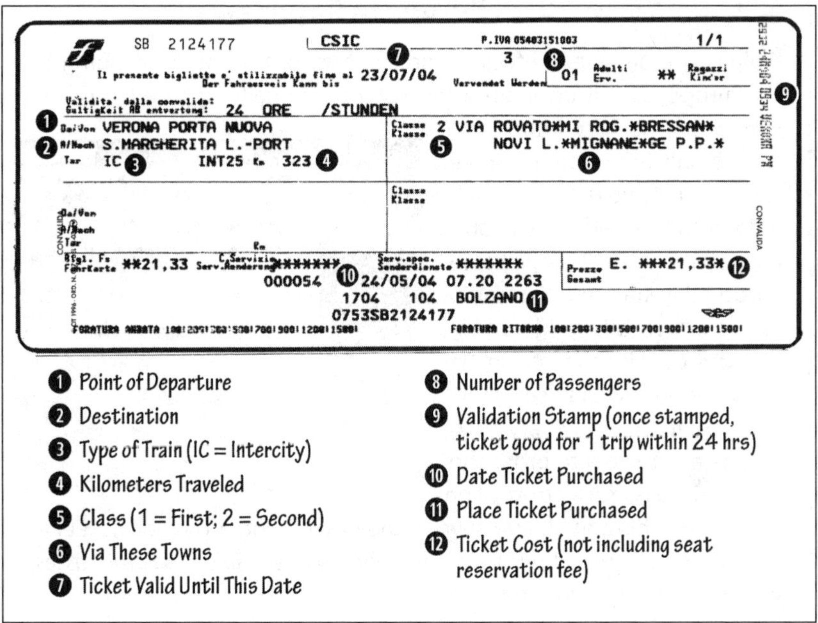


*This is a point-to-point ticket for travel in Italy, but train tickets across Europe have the same kind of information.*

tickets as they go. While you can purchase individual train tickets through your hometown travel agent, tickets are easy to buy—and cheaper—in Europe. You can get tickets in train stations or, more comfortably, in a travel agency near your hotel. Many railpasses push adult travelers into first-class, but travelers of any age can save 33 percent over first-class prices by purchasing second-class point-to-point tickets. Point-to-point tickets are often the best bet in cheaper countries (Italy, Spain, Eastern Europe) or for short travel distances.

You get the most value out of a railpass when you use it for long travel days and more expensive areas. Use the map on page 122 to add up second-class ticket prices for your route. Compare the cost of the tickets to the price of the railpass that best fits your trip. If the costs are close, it makes sense to buy the pass—unless you enjoy standing in lines at ticket windows.

### Comparing Railpasses

Railpasses come in a bewildering array of features and prices. It pays to compare—and to think carefully about which type of pass will best fit your style of travel. For a multi-country trip, the options listed in the

## Guide to European Railpasses

Railpass details are confusing and tedious, but if you're planning to do Europe by rail on limited money, my annually updated *Guide to Eurailpasses* is very important. It's the only information source where you'll find rail deals available in the United States compared with rail deals available in Europe. My staff and I research and produce this guide annually. Our goal is to create smart consumers (as well as sell a few passes). It covers everything you need to know to order the best train pass for your trip, or to order nothing at all and save money by buying a pass or tickets in Europe. To download our free, annually updated *Guide to Eurailpasses*, visit www.ricksteves.com.

**railpass price chart** on page 123 are a fine place to start.

Your most basic decision will be whether to buy a consecutive-day pass or flexipass. Which kind of traveler are you?

**The intense, spontaneous consecutive-day traveler.** If you plan to travel nearly daily and cover a lot of ground, a consecutive-day pass is the right choice for you. You get unlimited train travel for the duration of the pass. If you have a 15-day pass, you can travel 15 consecutive days, hopping on and off trains many times each day. If you have a one-month pass, you can travel, for example, from April 26 through May 25. One-month passes last longer when started in a 31-day month. Eurail, Britrail, Scanrail, and Swiss passes offer this choice.

**The relaxed, organized flexipass traveler.** If you like to linger for a few days at various places, a flexipass is the better choice. You have a certain number of travel days to use within a longer "window" of time (for example, any 10 days within a 2-month period). You can sprinkle these travel days throughout your trip or use them all in a row. You can take as many separate trips as you like within each travel day. A travel day runs from midnight to midnight, but luckily, an overnight train or boat ride uses only one travel day (the day you arrive).

## Eurailpass and Selectpass Coverage

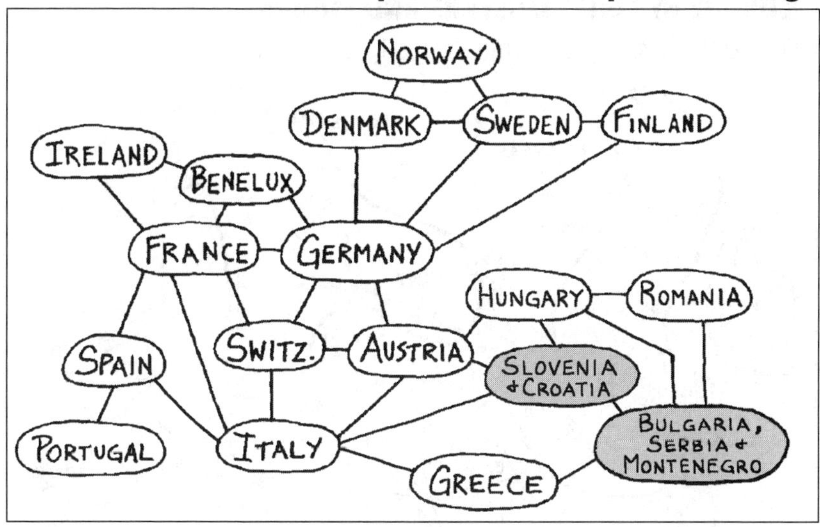


*A* ***Eurailpass*** *covers 18 countries, represented by the white bubbles. (Note that BeNeLux is short for Belgium, Netherlands, and Luxembourg.) In contrast, the* ***Selectpass*** *covers more territory (all the white and gray bubbles), but you select a smaller scope. You design your Selectpass by connecting a "chain" of any three, four, or five countries linked by direct lines in this diagram. Each bubble counts as one country, even though multiple countries can be included (such as Slovenia and Croatia).*

### Eurailpasses

**Eurailpasses** offer you unlimited first-class travel on all public railways in 18 European countries. These popular passes give you Western Europe (except Britain) by the tail. Choose between the consecutive-day pass (ranging from 15 days to three months) or the cheaper flexipass (any 10 or 15 individual days in 2 months). Travel partners (2–5 people traveling together) save 15 percent with Eurail Saverpasses, available in consecutive-day and flexipass versions. Youths under 26 travel cheaper with second-class passes.

For the average independent first-timer planning to see lots of Europe (from Norway to Portugal to Italy, for instance), the Eurailpass is usually the best way to go. In a nutshell, you need to travel from Amsterdam to Rome to Madrid and back to Amsterdam to justify the purchase of a one-month Eurailpass.

**Eurail Selectpasses** give you a selected number of "flexi" travel days in your choice of three, four, or five adjoining countries, whether connected by rail or ferry (for example, Denmark, Germany, and Finland—or Spain, France, Italy, and Greece). You can tailor this flexible pass to your trip instead of trying to make your trip fit a pass—you can, for

## Europe by Rail: Dollars and Hours

Connect the dots, add up the cost, and see if a railpass is right for your trip.

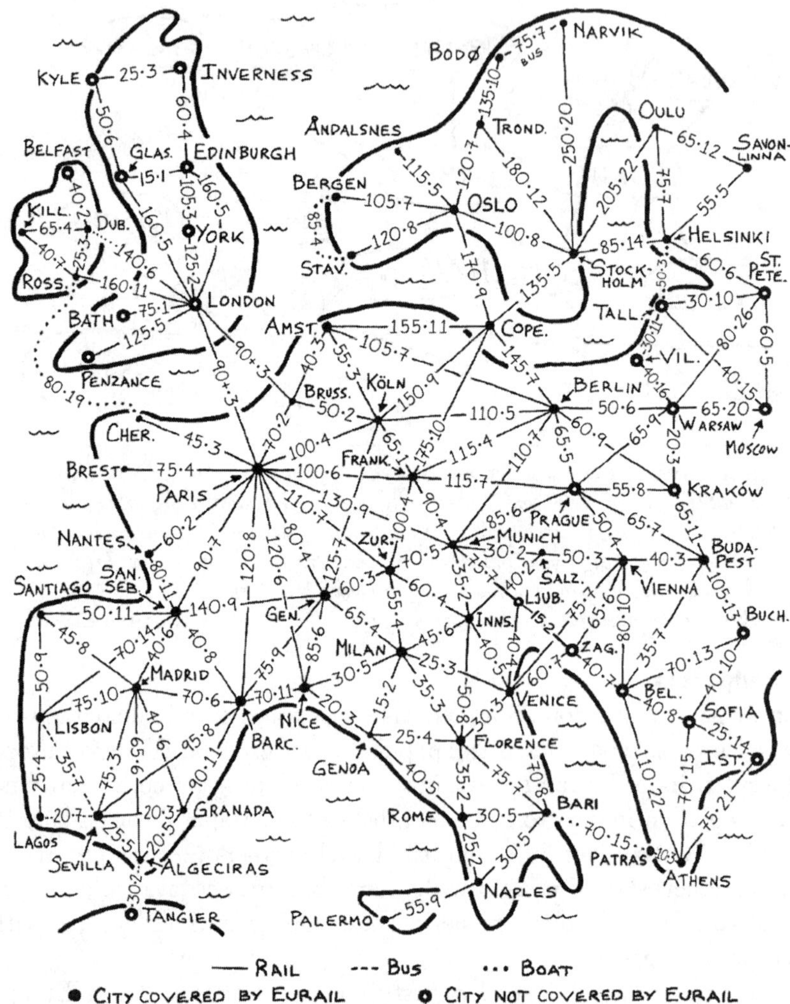


The **first number** between cities = **Approximate cost** in $US for a 1-way, 2nd class ticket.

The **second number** = Number of **hours** the trip takes.

**Important:** These fares and times are based on the Eurail Tariff Guide. Actual prices may vary due to currency fluctuations and local sales. Local competition can cut the actual price of some boat crossings (from Italy to Greece, for example) by 50% or more. For approximate 1st class rail prices, multiply the prices shown by 1½.

### Eurail Consecutive Day Pass

| | 1st Class Individual | 1st Class Saverpass | 2nd Class Youthpass |
|---|---|---|---|
| 15 consec. days | $605 | $513 | $394 |
| 21 consec. days | 785 | 668 | 510 |
| 1 month consec. days | 975 | 828 | 634 |
| 2 months consec. days | 1378 | 1173 | 897 |
| 3 months consec. days | 1703 | 1450 | 1108 |

Saver prices are per person for 2 or more traveling together. Youth passes are for travelers under 26 only, no discounts for companions. Kids 4-11 pay half of 1st class Individual or Saver fare; under 4 free.

### Eurail Flexipass

| | 1st Class Individual | 1st Class Saverpass | 2nd Class Youthpass |
|---|---|---|---|
| 10 days in 2 months flexi | $715 | $608 | $465 |
| 15 days in 2 months flexi | 940 | 800 | 612 |

Saver prices are per person for 2 or more traveling together. Youth passes are for travelers under 26 only, no discounts for companions. Kids 4-11 pay half of 1st class Individual or Saver fare; under 4 free.

### Selectpass

| 1st Class | 3 countries | 4 countries | 5 countries |
|---|---|---|---|
| 5 days in 2 months | $383 | $428 | $473 |
| 6 days in 2 months | 423 | 468 | 513 |
| 8 days in 2 months | 503 | 548 | 593 |
| 10 days in 2 months | 580 | 625 | 670 |
| 15 days in 2 months | | | 850 |

Kids 4-11 half price; under 4 free.

### Selectpass Saver

| 1st Class | 3 countries | 4 countries | 5 countries |
|---|---|---|---|
| 5 days in 2 months | $325 | $363 | $400 |
| 6 days in 2 months | 360 | 398 | 435 |
| 8 days in 2 months | 428 | 465 | 503 |
| 10 days in 2 months | 493 | 530 | 568 |
| 15 days in 2 months | | | 723 |

Prices are per person, based on 2 or more traveling together. Kids 4-11 half price; under 4 free.

### Selectpass Youth

| 2nd Class | 3 countries | 4 countries | 5 countries |
|---|---|---|---|
| 5 days in 2 months | $249 | $278 | $307 |
| 6 days in 2 months | 275 | 304 | 333 |
| 8 days in 2 months | 325 | 354 | 383 |
| 10 days in 2 months | 375 | 404 | 433 |
| 15 days in 2 months | | | 553 |

You must be under age 26 on your first day of railpass travel.

instance, purchase as few as five travel days to use in your selected countries over a period of two months. Discounts are available for youth and traveling companions. Countries and number of days must be selected at the time of purchase and cannot be added in Europe. Note that available countries include some Eastern European destinations not covered by the 18-country Eurailpass (Slovenia/Croatia and Bulgaria/Serbia/Montenegro)—but since point-to-point tickets in these countries are so inexpensive, a railpass probably won't save you much there. Travel in Britain, the Czech Republic, Slovakia, and Poland is not covered by Eurail or Selectpasses.

Be aware of **restrictions.** For instance, passes are good for use only in the countries listed or selected—so if your train passes through a country not on your pass, you must buy a separate ticket for that stretch in advance (or pay a fine for purchasing the ticket on board). For example, if your pass doesn't cover Austria, but you take the Munich–Venice train route that cuts across Austria, it'll cost you about $30 in second class for the Austrian segment. To go from Berlin to Paris by night, you'll pass through Belgium...and pay extra for the privilege. More restrictive exceptions (no partial tickets allowed) include Germany–Austria–Switzerland City Night Line trains. Railpasses do not cover any seat or sleeper reservations, though these extra costs may be required.

Also be aware of **bonuses.** Some boat, bus, and other non-rail rides are either free or discounted with any pass that covers the appropriate country (for international trips, the pass usually has to cover both countries). Free bonuses use a travel day of a flexipass. These include German Rhine boats, Swiss

## A Sample Selectpass

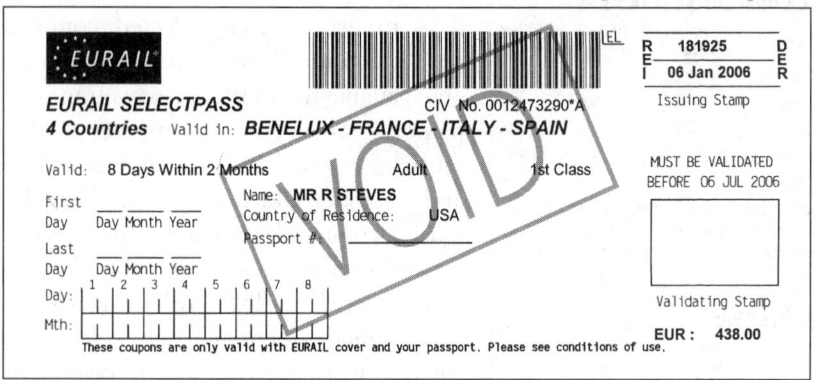
EURAIL

EURAIL SELECTPASS CIV No. 0012473290*A

4 Countries Valid in: BENELUX - FRANCE - ITALY - SPAIN

Valid: 8 Days Within 2 Months Adult 1st Class

First Day: Day Month Year

Last Day: Day Month Year

Name: MR R STEVES

Country of Residence: USA

Passport #:

Day: 1 2 3 4 5 6 7 8

Mth:

These coupons are only valid with EURAIL cover and your passport. Please see conditions of use.

VOID

R E I 181925 06 Jan 2006 D E R

Issuing Stamp

MUST BE VALIDATED BEFORE 06 JUL 2006

Validating Stamp

EUR: 438.00

*Don't write anything on your railpass before it's validated. When you're ready to use it, the ticket agent will fill in validity dates and your passport number, and stamp the validation box on the far right. Each day when you take your seat on the train, write down the date in ink (day first, then month) before the conductor comes around.*

lake boats, and international ferry crossings (including Ancona or Bari, Italy, to Patras, Greece; and Sweden to Finland, Germany, or Denmark). Discounted bonuses usually do not cost you a travel day, but travel must occur within the validity period. These discounts include the Ireland–France international ferry (30 percent off), the Brindisi–Patras international ferry (50 percent off), Germany's Romantic Road Bus or Castle Road Bus (60 percent off), Switzerland's Jungfrau region private railway (25 percent off), and the Eurostar Chunnel train (special discounted fare).

### Other Railpasses

**Country passes** focus on a single country. Virtually every European country has its own pass. These are especially important in Britain, which does not participate in the Eurail or Eurail Selectpass program. If you're limiting your travels to one country, a country pass is your best bet. Because short passes cost much more per day than long passes, a longer Eurail Selectpass is usually a better deal than patching together several country passes. Several two-country passes are available for specific country pairs (e.g., France and Italy).

**Rail-and-drive passes** are popular varieties of many of these passes. Along with a railpass (Eurailpass, Eurail Selectpass, or individual country), you get vouchers for either Hertz or Avis car-rental days (choose the company when you buy the pass; billed at about one-seventh of the economical weekly rate). These allow travelers to do long trips by train and enjoy a car where they need the freedom to explore.

## Money-Saving Railpass Tips

Consecutive-day and flexi railpasses offer a varying number of travel days. Once you've planned a route for your trip, fine-tuning your actual "moving days" will help you zero in on the best pass for your trip—and save you lots of money.

**With careful juggling, a shorter pass can cover a longer trip.** For example, you can take a one-month trip with a 21-day Eurailpass (in first class, that's $190 cheaper than a 1-month pass) by starting and/or ending your trip in a city where you'd like to stay for several days or in a country not covered by your pass. On, say, a London–Rome trip, spend a few days in London, pay separately to take the Eurostar Chunnel train (not covered by any railpass) to Paris, sightsee in Paris for several days, then validate your consecutive-day pass when you leave Paris. Plan for your pass to expire in Rome, where you can easily spend a few days without the use of a railpass.

**It can also make sense to buy a longer pass for a shorter trip.** One long train ride (for example, $210 first-class from Florence to Paris) at the end of a 25-day trip can justify jumping from a 21-day consecutive-day railpass to a one-month pass. Similarly, if you plan to travel for five to seven weeks, consider buying a two-month Eurailpass for $1,378 instead of a one-month Eurailpass for $975. Just a few long rides can justify the $403 you'll pay for the second month.

**Stretch a flexipass by paying out of pocket for shorter trips.** Use your flexipass only for those travel days that involve long hauls or several trips. To determine if a trip is a good use of a travel day, divide the cost of your pass by the number of travel days. For example, a 15-day, five-country Eurail Selectpass for $850 costs about $57 per travel day. If a particular day trip costs significantly less than $57, pay out of pocket (and you'll have saved a flexi travel day for later in your trip).

**Flexipasses are misnamed: They are cheaper, but less flexible.** Let's say you're planning a 21-day trip and choosing between a 21-consecutive-day Eurailpass ($785) and a cheaper 10-days-in-2-months Eurail Flexipass ($715). For $70 more, the consecutive-day pass gives you the option to travel for 11 extra days, allowing you the freedom to hop on any train without wondering if a particular trip justifies the use of a travel day.

**More travel days on a pass = cheaper cost per day.** Compared to shorter passes, longer railpasses are cheaper per travel day. For example, for a 15-consecutive-day Eurailpass at $605, you're paying $40 a day. With a three-month Eurailpass for $1,703, you're paying only $18 a day. Most one-hour train rides cost more than that.

### Class Consciousness: First Class vs. Second Class

*First class—plusher, roomier, and less crowded—costs 50 percent more than second.*

Normally, first class is configured with three plush seats per row (whether in a compartment or open-style seating) and second class has four skinnier, basic seats in the same space. Remember that nearly every train has both first- and second-class cars, each going at precisely the same speed.

If you're on a tight budget, second class is plenty comfortable and makes lots of sense. Back Door travelers know that the nuns and soldiers are partying in second class. If you have the extra money, riding first-class is less crowded and more comfortable (you'll sit with business travelers and railpass holders age 26 or older who had no choice—see facing page). While individual first-class tickets cost 50 percent more

**One railpass can be better than two.** To cover a multiple-country trip, it's usually cheaper to buy one Selectpass or Eurailpass with lots of travel days than to buy several country passes with a few high-cost travel days per pass. If you decide to travel over a border (e.g., France to Germany) using separate France and Germany railpasses, then you will use up a day of each pass.

## Europe's Train Stations

Train stations can be one of the independent traveler's best and most helpful friends. Take advantage of the assistance they can offer.

**Train information:** Every station has a train information office eager (or at least able) to help you with your scheduling. I usually consult the timetables myself first and write down my plan, then confirm this with the information desk. Written communication is easiest and safest. Computer terminals offering all the train schedules are becoming more than second class, first-class railpasses generally bump your price up only 25–40 percent.

Still wrestling with the choice between first and second class? Sometimes the decision is made for you...

**If you're considering a Eurailpass or Selectpass:** If you're age 26 or older, you must buy a first-class railpass. Those under age 26 have the choice of buying either a second- or a first-class pass. For families traveling together, a first-class Saverpass for two costs the same as one first-class adult and one second-class youth.

**If you're considering a country pass:** Most single-country, two-country, and regional passes are available in second-class versions for travelers of any age.

**If you're under 26:** Many passes are discounted for youth traveling second class. To be eligible, you must be under 26 (according to your passport) the day you validate the pass in Europe. Generally, children ages 4 to 11 get passes for half the cost of the adult first-class pass (kids under 4 travel free). Ages vary a bit among different country passes.

**Switching classes:** Those with first-class passes may travel in second-class compartments (although the conductor may give you a puzzled look). Those with second-class passes can pay the 50 percent difference in ticket price to upgrade to first (not possible in Britain).

common. These are multilingual and can be a real time-saver.

**Tourist information and room-finding services:** These are usually either in the station (in the case of major tourist centers) or nearby. Pick up a map with sightseeing information and, if you need it, advice on where to find budget accommodations.

*Train stations often have good long-hours grocery stores. This one in Vienna is open Monday–Sunday, 5:30 a.m.–11 p.m.*

**Money changing:** Most stations have ATMs offering great rates 24 hours a day. Often the station's money-changing office is open long after others have closed (though the rates aren't great). If you're in a jam, you can sometimes change money at ticket windows as well.

### City Name Variations

| American Name | European Name |
|---|---|
| Athens (Gre.) | *Athínai* in Greek, *Athenes* in German |
| Bolzano (Italy) | *Bozen* in German |
| Bratislava (Slovakia) | *Pressburg* in German, *Pozsony* in Hungarian |
| Bruges (Bel.) | *Brugge* in Flemish |
| Brussels (Bel.) | *Bruxelles* in French |
| Cologne (Ger.) | *Köln* (or *Koeln*) |
| Copenhagen (Den.) | *København* |
| Cracow (Pol.) | *Kraków* |
| Florence (Italy) | *Firenze* |
| Geneva (Switz.) | *Genève* in French, *Genf* in German |
| Genoa (Italy) | *Genova* (not Geneva) |
| Gothenburg | *Göteborg* (Swe.) |
| The Hague (Neth.) | *Den Haag, 'S Gravenhage* |
| Helsinki (Fin.) | *Helsingfors* in Swedish |
| Lisbon (Port.) | *Lisboa* |
| London (Brit.) | *Londres* in French |
| Munich (Ger.) | *München* in German, *Monaco di Baviera* in Italian |
| Naples (Italy) | *Napoli* |
| Nuremberg (Ger.) | *Nürnberg* |
| Padua (Italy) | *Padova* |
| Pamplona (Spain) | *Iruña* in Basque |
| Paris (Fr.) | *Parigi* in Italian |
| Prague (Czech.) | *Praha* |
| San Sebastián (Spain) | *Donostia* in Basque |
| Venice (Italy) | *Venezia* |
| Vienna (Aus.) | *Wien* in German, *Bécs* in Hungarian, *Dunaj* in Slovene |
| Warsaw (Pol.) | *Warszawa* |

**Lockers:** Virtually every station has storage lockers and/or a luggage-checking service where, for about $2–5 a day, you can leave your bags. People traveling light can fit two rucksacks into one storage locker, cutting their storage costs in half. In some security-conscious train stations, lockers are no longer in use, and travelers must check their bags at a luggage-deposit desk—often after going through an airport-type security check. This service is expensive; you'll have to pay $5–10 to leave your bag. In some extreme cases, they don't take laptop computers. (I recently spent a day in Marseille carrying around my laptop.)

**Waiting rooms:** Most stations have comfortable waiting rooms. Those with fancy tickets often enjoy fancy business or VIP lounges. The bigger stations are equipped with day hotels for those who want to shower, shave, rest, and so on. If, for one reason or another, I ever need a free, warm, and safe place to spend the night, a train station (or an airport) is my choice. Some stations boot everyone out from about midnight to 6 a.m. Ask before you bed down. Thieves work the stations in the wee hours. Be on guard.

**Bus connections:** Train stations are also major bus stops, so connections from train to bus are generally no more difficult than crossing the street. Buses go from the stations to nearby towns that lack train service. If you have a bus to catch, be quick, since many are for commuters and are scheduled to connect with the train and leave promptly. If there's an airport nearby, you'll find bus or rail shuttle services (usually well marked) at the train station.

## Getting on the Right Track

Armed with a railpass, the independent traveler has Europe as a playground. Most will master the system simply by diving in and learning from their mistakes. To learn more quickly—from someone else's mistakes—here are a few tips:

**Many cities have more than one train station.** Paris has six, Brussels has three, and even Switzerland's little Interlaken has two. Be sure you know whether your train is leaving from Interlaken East or Interlaken West, even if that means asking what might seem like a stupid question. A city's stations are generally connected by train, subway, or bus. When arriving in a city (especially on a milk-run train), you may stop at several suburban stations with signs indicating your destination's name with the name

*Eurail freedom: My idea of good travel is being on this platform in Hamburg. In five minutes, the train on track 7 is going to Berlin. In six minutes, a train will leave from track 8 for Copenhagen. And I've yet to decide which train I'll be on.*

*The train on track 4 will stop at three Berlin stations. It was due to leave 10 minutes ago, but the sign notes it's 20 minutes* später.

of the neighborhood (e.g., Madrid Vallecas or Roma Tiburtina). Don't jump out until you've reached the central station (Madrid Chamartín or Roma Termini). You can also avoid arrival frustrations by finding out if your train stops at a city's main station rather than a suburban one. For instance, several trains to "Venice" leave you at Venice's suburban station (Venezia Mestre), where you'll be stranded without a glimpse of a gondola. (You'll have to catch another train to reach the main Venezia Santa Lucia station.)

**Ask for help and pay attention.** Managing on the trains is largely a matter of asking questions, letting people help you, and assuming things are logical. I always ask someone on the platform if the train is going where I think it is. (Point to the train or track and ask, "Roma?") Uniformed train personnel can answer any question you can communicate. Speak slowly, clearly, and with caveman simplicity. Be observant. If the loudspeaker comes on while you're waiting for your train at track 7, gauge by the reaction of those around you whether the announcement affects you. If, after the babble, everyone dashes over to track 15, assume your train is no longer arriving on track 7.

**Scope out the train ahead of time.** The configuration of many major trains is charted in little display cases on the platform next to where your train will arrive. As you wait, study the display to note where the first-class and sleeping cars are, whether there's a diner, and which cars are going where. Some train schedules will say, in the fine print, "Munich-bound cars in the front, Vienna-bound cars in the rear." Knowing which cars you're eligible for can be especially handy if you'll be competing with a mob for a seat. When expecting a real scramble, I stand on a bench at the far end of the track and study each car as the train rolls by, noting where the most empty places are. First-class cars are marked with a "1" on the outside, second-class cars with a "2." If there are several departures within an hour or so and the first train looks hopeless, I'll wait for the next.

**Never assume the whole train is going where you are.** For long hauls, each car is labeled separately, because cars are usually added and dropped here and there along the journey. I'll never forget one hot afternoon in the middle of Spain. My train stopped in the middle of nowhere. There was some mechanical rattling. Then the train pulled away leaving me alone in my car...in La Mancha. Ten minutes later, another train came along, picked up my car, and I was on my way. To survive all of this juggling easily, be sure that the city on your car's nameplate is your destination. The nameplate lists the final stop and some (but not all) of the stops in between.

*This train started in Istanbul and will end in Wien Südbahnhof—Vienna's South Train Station.*

**Reserve seats if you're traveling in a group.** Even if seat reservations are not required, they can be a good idea if you're traveling with children or a group that wants to sit together. Otherwise, you may end up scattered around the car wherever you can find free seats.

**Every car has plenty of room for luggage.** In 25 years of train travel, I've never checked a bag. Simply carry it on and heave it up onto the racks above the seats. I've seen Turkish families moving all their worldly goods from Germany back to Turkey without checking a thing. People complain about the porters in the European train stations. I think they're great—I've never used one. People with more luggage than they can carry deserve porters.

*Europe's trains are fast—pulling into the station with squashed birds on their windshields. You'd wait all your life to see a bird squashed onto the windshield of a train back home.*

**Luggage is never completely safe.** There is a thief on every train (thieves' union regulations) planning to grab a bag (see Chapter 23: Outsmarting Thieves). Don't be careless. Before leaving my luggage in a compartment, I establish a relationship with everyone there. I'm safe leaving it among mutual guards.

Many train travelers are ripped off while they sleep. A $25 *couchette* (berth in a sleeping compartment—described under "How to Sleep on the Train," later in this chapter) is safer because an attendant monitors who comes and goes. Those sleeping for free in regular cars should exercise extreme caution. Keep your valuables in a money belt or at least securely attached to your body. I clip and fasten my rucksack to the luggage rack. If one tug doesn't take the bag, a thief will usually leave it rather than ask, "*Scusi,* how is your luggage attached?" You'll hear stories of entire train cars being gassed and robbed in Italy, Spain, and Eastern Europe. I think it's a myth—I wouldn't lose sleep over it.

**Women need to be careful on all overnight rides.** Women should use discretion when choosing a compartment. Sleeping in an empty compartment in southern Europe is an open invitation to your own private Casanova. Choose a room with a European granny or nun in it. That way you'll get a little peace, and Don Juan won't even try. A *couchette* (berth) is your best bet.

**Use train time wisely.** Train travelers, especially Eurailers, spend a lot of time on the train. This time can be dull and unproductive, or you can make a point to do whatever you can on the train to free up time off the train. It makes no sense to sit bored on the train and then, upon arrival, sit in the station for an hour reading your information and deciding where to go for hotels and what to do next.

Spend train time productively: studying, reading, writing postcards or journal entries, eating, or organizing. Talk to local people or other travelers. There is so much to be learned. Europeans are often less open and forward than Americans. You could sit across from a silent but fascinating and friendly European for an entire train ride, or you could break the ice by asking a question, quietly offering some candy, or showing your Hometown, USA postcards. This can start the conversation flowing and the friendship growing.

## Train Schedules—Breaking the Code

Learning to decipher train schedules makes life on Europe's rails easier. These list all trains that come to and go from a particular station each day, and are clearly posted in two separate listings: departures (the ones we're concerned with, usually in yellow) and arrivals (normally in white).

You'll also find airport-type departure schedules that flip up and list the next 8 or 10 departures. These often befuddle travelers who don't realize that all over the world the same four easy-to-identify columns are listed: destination, type of train, track number, and departure time. I don't care what language they're in; without much effort you can accurately guess which column is what.

*In this French train station, arrivals and departures are clearly listed. Who says you can't read French? The small schedule in the middle lists trains that are about to depart. The Tabac stand sells candy, phone cards, newspapers, and often subway and bus tickets.*

Train-schedule computers (found across Europc) can save you many long waits in station information lines. Use them to understand all your options. Indicate your language, departure and arrival points, and rough time of departure, and all workable connections will flash on the screen.

If you want to check schedules before you go to Europe, the Internet is your best resource. Try http://bahn.hafas.de/bin/query.exe/en for all of Europe, including tiny towns (if its info on Spain is limited, you can supplement with www.renfe.es/ingles). For more tips on using this site, see page 138. See www.railfaneurope.net for links to each country's rail site.

If you prefer a book format, consider *The Thomas Cook European Timetable.* Published several times a year (because schedules change with the season), it contains times for

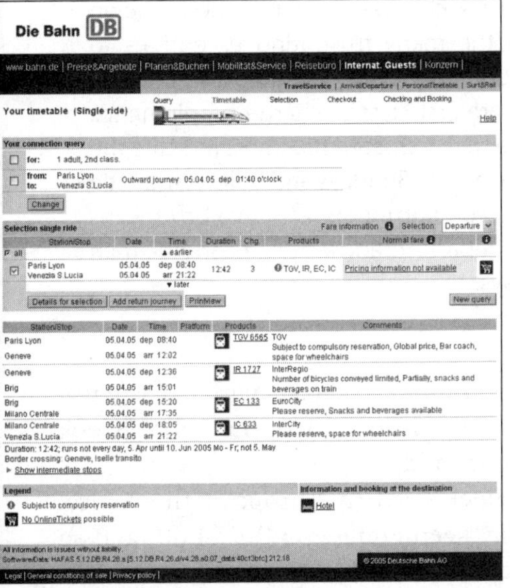


*Deutsche Bahn's Web site is a quick and convenient way to check train schedules in English for all of Europe. This schedule—from Paris to Venice—shows all the changes you'll have to make along the way, how long you'll have at each station, and the types of trains you'll be taking. You'll find this helpful tool at http://bahn.hafas.de/bin/query.exe/en.*

## Scoping Out Schedules

Let's crack the code in the Thomas Cook European Timetable. Find the trip you want to take on the appropriate train map. The number refers you to the proper timetable, which shows the schedule for trains along that route in both directions (a. = arrivals, d. = departures).

As an example, let's go from Turin to Venice (local spellings are always used: Torino and Venezia). This is #350 on the map, so refer to table 350. Locate your starting point, Torino. Reading from left to right, you will see that trains leave Torino for Venezia at 7:08, 9:06, 15:08, 15:50, and 22:50. Those trains arrive in Venezia at 11:55, 13:59, 19:55, 21:25, and 5:08, respectively. Note that Venezia has two stations (Mestre and the more central Santa Lucia). As you can see, not all Torino departures go all the way to Venezia. For example, the 8:50 train only goes to Milan, arriving at 10:40. From there, the 10:50 train will get you to Venezia SL by 13:59. The 15:08 departure stops at Venezia Mestre, not actually in Venice. That's an inconvenience but not a big problem, since you can assume there are frequent connections from outlying stations to downtown. An overnight train is also shown: departing Torino at 22:50, arriving in Venezia by 5:08.

Train schedules are helpful in planning your stopovers. For instance, this table shows a train leaving Torino at 8:50 and arriving in Milan at 10:40. You could spend two hours touring Milan's cathedral, catch the 13:05 train for Verona (arrive at 14:27, see the Roman Arena and Juliet's balcony), and hop on the 19:10 train to arrive in Venezia by 20:35.

Each table has a schedule for each direction (only one is shown here) and a section explaining the many frustrating exceptions to the rules (not shown here). Symbols within the schedule also indicate exceptions, such as which trains are first-class or charge supplements. An X means you'll have to change trains; crossed hammers indicate the train goes only on workdays (daily except Sundays and holidays); a little bed means the train has sleeping compartments; an R in a box means reservations are required for that departure; and a cross means the train goes only on Sundays and holidays.

major stops on nearly every route in Europe, complete with maps (www.thomascooktimetables.com). Although I don't carry the bulky "Cook Book" with me, those who do find it handy.

Learn to use the 24-hour clock used in European timetables. After 12:00 noon, the Europeans keep going—13:00, 14:00, and so on. To convert any time after noon to the 12-hour clock, subtract 12

**Table 350** — **TORINO - MILANO - VENEZIA**

| km | | IC 645 | IR 2007 | IR 2009 | IC 649 | IR 2097 | E 351 | IC 651 | EC 39 | IC 657 | IR 2107 | EC 13 | IR 2019 | IR 2031 | E 869 |
|---|---|---|---|---|---|---|---|---|---|---|---|---|---|---|---|
| | | | | | 🍸 | 🍸 | ✕ ♦ | | ✕ ♦ | 🍸 | | ✕ ♦ | | | ♦ |
| *0* | **Torino Porta Nuova 353** ... d. | 0708 | 0750 | 0850 | 0906 | ... | ... | 1108 | ... | 1508 | ... | ... | 1550 | 2150 | 2250 |
| *6* | **Torino Porta Susa 353** ..... d. | 0718 | 0800 | 0900 | 0915 | ... | ... | 1118 | ... | 1518 | ... | ... | 1600 | 2200 | 2300 |
| *29* | Chivasso **353** .................... d. | \| | 0816 | 0916 | 0933 | ... | ... | \| | ... | \| | ... | ... | 1616 | 2216 | 2316 |
| *60* | Santhia.............................. d. | \| | 0834 | 0934 | \| | ... | ... | \| | ... | \| | ... | ... | 1634 | 2234 | 2334 |
| *79* | Vercelli .............................. d. | 0802 | 0846 | 0946 | 1002 | ... | ... | 1202 | ... | 1602 | ... | ... | 1646 | 2246 | 2346 |
| *101* | Novara ................................ d. | 0818 | 0901 | 1001 | 1018 | ... | ... | 1218 | ... | 1618 | ... | ... | 1701 | 2301 | 0001 |
| *153* | **Milano Centrale** ................ a. | 0850 | 0940 | 1040 | 1050 | ... | ... | 1250 | ... | 1650 | ... | ... | 1740 | 2340 | 0040 |
| | | IC 647 ♦ | | | \| | | | | | \| | | | IR 2109 | | \| |
| *153* | **Milano Centrale** ................ d. | 0905 | ... | ... | 1105 | 1110 | 1210 | .. | 1305 | 1705 | 1710 | .. | 1810 | .. | 0110 |
| *187* | Treviglio ............................ d. | \| | ... | ... | \| | 1135 | 1235 | ... | \| | \| | 1735 | ... | 1835 | ... | 0150 |
| *236* | Brescia............................... d. | 0952 | ... | ... | 1152 | 1206 | 1306 | ... | 1352 | 1752 | 1806 | ... | 1906 | ... | 0239 |
| *263* | Desenzano del Garda ......... d. | \| | ... | ... | \| | 1224 | 1324 | ... | \| | \| | 1824 | ... | 1924 | ... | 0257 |
| *278* | Peschiera del Garda ........... d. | \| | ... | ... | \| | 1235 | 1335 | ... | \| | \| | 1835 | ... | 1935 | ... | 0309 |
| *300* | **Verona Porta Nuova**......... d. | 1027 | ... | ... | 1227 | 1254 | 1354 | ... | 1427 | 1827 | 1854 | 1910 | 1954 | ... | 0331 |
| *325* | San Bonifacio...................... d. | \| | ... | ... | \| | 1311 | 1411 | ... | \| | \| | 1911 | \| | 2011 | ... | 0347 |
| *351* | Vicenza .............................. d. | 1100 | ... | ... | 1300 | 1332 | 1432 | ... | 1500 | 1900 | 1932 | 1945 | 2032 | ... | 0410 |
| *382* | Padova................................ d. | 1122 | ... | ... | 1323 | 1353 | 1453 | ... | 1522 | 1922 | 1953 | 2004 | 2053 | ... | 0433 |
| *411* | **Venezia Mestre** ................ a. | 1140 | ... | ... | 1346 | 1413 | 1513 | ... | 1540 | 1940 | 2013 | 2024 | 2113 | ... | 0454 |
| *411* | **Venezia Mestre** ................ d. | 1155 | ... | ... | 1349 | 1416 | 1516 | ... | 1543 | 1955 | 2016 | 2026 | 2116 | ... | 0459 |
| *420* | **Venezia Santa Lucia**......... a. | \| | ... | ... | 1359 | 1425 | 1525 | ... | 1552 | \| | 2025 | 2035 | 2125 | ... | 0508 |
| | *Trieste Centrale* **376** ... a. | 1345 | ... | ... | ... | ... | ... | ... | ... | 2145 | ... | ... | ... | ... | 0910b |

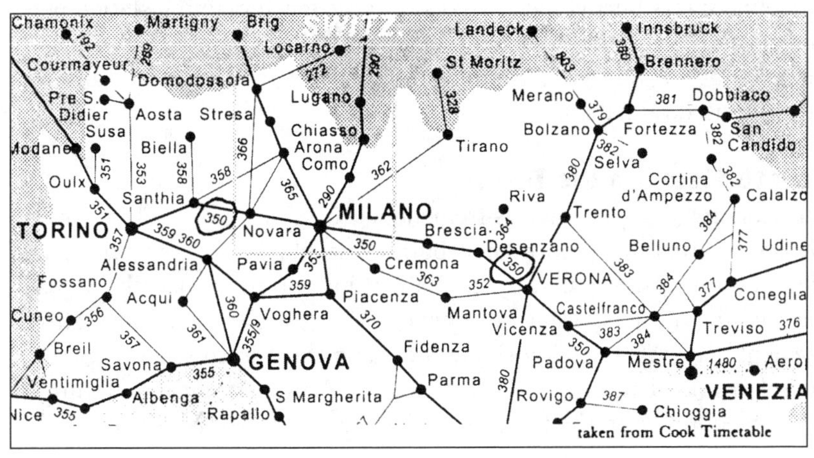


and add p.m. (16:00 is 4 p.m.).

Train schedules are a great help to the traveler—if you can read them. Many rail travelers never take the time to figure them out. In this chapter, you'll find a sample map and schedule to practice on. Understand it. You'll be glad you did.

Confirm your plans at the station. The person who knows for sure what's going on is the one at the train station information window. Let that person help you. He can fix mistakes and save you many hours. Just show your plan on a scrap of paper (e.g., Torino ⟶ Milano, 8:50–10:40; Milano ⟶ Verona, 13:05–14:27) and ask, "OK?" If your plan is good, he'll nod, direct you to your track, and you're on your way. If there's a problem, he'll solve it. Uniformed train employees on the platforms or on board the trains can also help.

*Posted train schedules clearly mark the destination, departure and arrival times, and track numbers.*

Strikes can affect rail service anywhere in Europe (especially in Italy). Most last just a day. Information is usually posted in advance in stations and in local news media. In reality, sporadic trains lumber down main-line tracks during most strikes, and the few remaining station personnel can tell you the expected schedule. While it is usually possible to get a refund for reservations affected by a strike, there is no refund for partially-used railpasses.

## How to Sleep on the Train

The economy of night travel is tremendous. Sleeping while rolling down the tracks saves time and money, both of which, for most travelers, are limited resources. The first concern about night travel is usually, "Aren't you missing a lot of beautiful scenery? You just slept through half of Sweden!" The real question should be, "Did the missed scenery matter, since you gained an extra day for hiking the Alps, biking through tulips, or island-hopping in the Greek seas?" The answer: No. Maximize night trips.

### *Couchettes*

To ensure a safer and uninterrupted night's sleep, you can usually reserve a sleeping berth that's known as a *couchette* (koo-SHET) at least a day in advance from a travel agency, at the station ticket counter, or, if there are any available, from the conductor on the train. For $25—a fraction of the cost of a cheap hotel bed—you'll get sheets, pillow, blankets, a fold-out bunk bed in a compartment with three to five other people, and, hopefully, a good night's sleep.

As you board, you'll give the attendant your *couchette* voucher, railpass or ticket, and passport. He deals with the conductors and customs officials and keeps out the thieves so you can sleep uninterrupted. Some trains have more spacious four-berth *couchettes* (double rather than triple bunks for $45 apiece, requiring first-class ticket on routes through France). Despite this exception, most *couchettes* are the same for both classes. While the top bunk gives you more privacy and luggage space, it can be hotter and stuffier than lower bunks and a couple of inches shorter (a concern if you're 6 feet or taller). While compartments are usually coed, you can request smoking or non-smoking, and top, middle, or bottom berths.

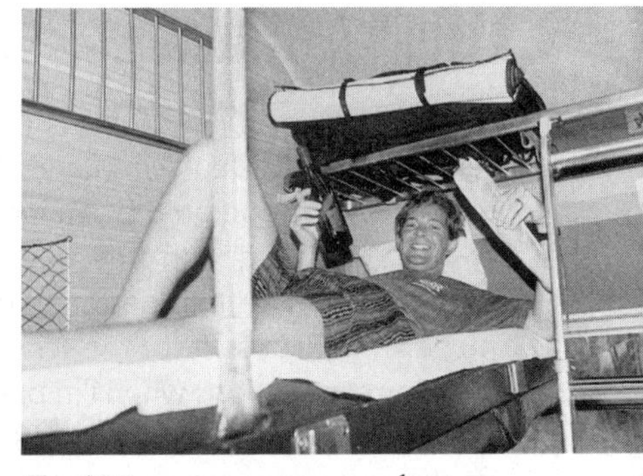

*For $25, you can rent a* couchette *(bunk bed) on your overnight train. Top bunks give you a bit more room and safety—but B.Y.O.B.& B. For much more on night trains in Europe, go to www.seat61.com.*

**Sleepers:** Beds in two-bed or three-bed compartments range from about $50–100 per person. They are ideal though pricey for couples who want privacy. Single-sleeper costs range from $70–190.

*Car #126 from Copenhagen to Paris' North Station is second class (indicated by the large number 2), non-smoking (a crossed-out cigarette), and filled with* couchettes *(the flat bed under the number 2).*

**Hotel Trains:** If you're on a budget, avoid the fancy hotel trains. Increasingly common between Spain and France, Italy, and Switzerland, these overnight hotels-on-wheels are comfortable but expensive (even if discounted with a railpass: $85 per person in a quad, $130 per person in a double, and $200 or more for a single). Cheaper options exist and involve changing trains at the Spanish border.

### Sleeping Free in Compartments

Shoestring travelers avoid a $25 *couchette* and just sack out for free, draping their tired bodies over as many unoccupied seats as possible. But trying to sleep overnight without a bed can be a waking nightmare. And

## Finding Train Schedules on the Deutsche Bahn Web Site

Even though the Deutsche Bahn Web site (http://bahn.hafas.de/bin/query.exe/en) is operated by an individual country (Germany), it offers extensive, detailed, and free train schedule information for most of Europe. While the site is designed for selling tickets, I've never bought one here—I just use it for the schedules. In fact, this Web site is how I check my connections when I'm planning any trip to Europe.

**Begin the search.** Start with a station-to-station search. Enter just the city name, unless you know the name of the specific station you want (explained below). Remember to use European spellings. For example, Cologne is "Köln" in German, but you can spell it as "Koeln" to avoid having to figure out how to type *ö*. Likewise, instead of Munich or München, type "Muenchen." Prague is "Praha," Rome is "Roma," and Florence is "Firenze." (For more European names, see "City Names Variations" earlier in this chapter; your guidebook should also explain these variations.) Also enter the date and time you'd like to travel, as close as you can guess. In the early planning stages, I often do a search for a random date to get a feel for how often the train runs, then plug in my specific dates once my itinerary is set. Schedules change seasonally, around June 10, Sept. 10, and Dec. 10 (though changes are often small); this Web site posts updates as soon as they are available.

**Refine the search.** Many cities have several stations. After you click "Search," you may be asked to specify which station you want. For example, in Venice, you'll want the Santa Lucia station ("Venezia S. Lucia"), which is right on the Grand Canal—rather than the Mestre station on the industrial mainland. In Prague, you'll probably prefer the Main Station ("Praha hl.n."), in Vienna you'll likely use the West Train Station ("Wien Westbahnhof"), and in Rome most people want the Termini station ("Roma Termini"). Your choice of station will probably depend on the specific schedules or the location of your hotel—refer to your guidebook or ask your hotelier. To get the best use out of this site, figure out which station works best and request that station specifically in your search. If you don't specify, the computer may give you several options from different stations, or it may simply select its idea of the "most convenient station" (which may not be yours). Note that for small towns, you may need to choose from several destinations with the same name. For example, there are many Rothenburgs in Germany, but the tourists' target is Rothenburg ob der Tauber. This can apply even to big cities. Frankfurt an der Oder—"Frankfurt (Oder)"—is a grim industrial town on the German–Polish border, while Frankfurt am Main—"Frankfurt (Main)"—is the touristy metropolis in with the big airport. In Germany, your choice is likely to be followed by "Bahnhof" or "Bhf." (train station) or "Hauptbahnhof" or "Hbf." (main train station). You may also have to specify an age to see if you'd be eligible for discounts.

**Review the schedule options.** You'll be given a range of possibilities for your journey. Each one shows the start and end points (with stations specified), the times of departure and arrival, the duration, the number of changes, and the types of trains ("Products"). You can view other times for the connection, if available, by clicking "Earlier" or "Later" at the top and bottom of the "Time" column. Don't be surprised if no fare is listed in the "Fare" column—this site provides ticket prices only within Germany and for some international trips that originate in Germany.

**Get more details.** If you click the connection you're interested in, it'll show you a more detailed version, including the places where you'll have to change trains. If you click "Show intermediate stops," you can actually see each and every stop the train will make.

**Check the fine print.** "Compulsory reservation" means what it says, while "Please reserve" is recommended but optional. "International supplement" notes do not apply with railpasses.

**No luck?** This system shows the most direct and practical routes between two points. To design your own detour, add a "Via" (midpoint) city on the query screen. If, on the other hand, your destination is not covered at all (and if you spelled it correctly), it likely doesn't have train service. Schedules for Spain and Italy may not be complete on this site, so refer to those countries' own rail sites to confirm. For a comprehensive list of each country's railway sites, go to www.railfaneurope.net.

**Some Train Compartments Can Turn into Beds**

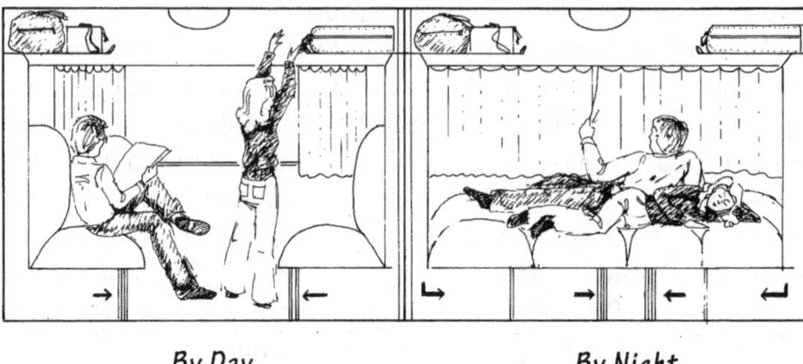


For every night you spend on the train, you gain a day for sightseeing and avoid the cost of a hotel. In some compartments, you can try sleeping for free by pulling out the seats to make a bed...assuming your compartment isn't too full.

even this level of "comfort" is not always free since some night trains now require a $5 seat reservation. One night of endless head-bobbing, very swollen toes, a screaming tailbone, sitting up straight in a dark eternity of steel wheels crashing along rails, trying doggedly—yet hopelessly—to get comfortable, will teach you the importance of finding a spot to stretch out for the night. This is an art that vagabond night travelers cultivate. Those with the greatest skill at this game sleep. Those not so talented will spend the night gnashing their teeth and squirming for relief.

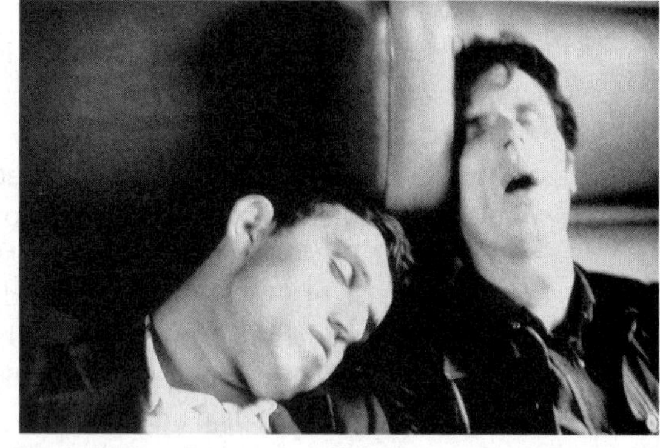

*They didn't rent a* couchette.

A traditional train car has about 10 compartments, each with six or eight seats (three or four facing three or four). Most have seats that pull out and armrests that lift, turning your compartment into a bed on wheels. But this is possible only if you have more seats than people in your compartment. A compartment that seats six can sleep three. So if between 30 and 60 people choose your car, some will sleep and some will sit. Your fate depends on how good you are at encouraging people to sit elsewhere. There are many ways to play this game (which has few rules and encourages creativity). Here are my favorite techniques.

**The Big Sleep:** Arrive 30 minutes before your train leaves. Walk most of the length of the train but not to the last car. Choose a car that is going where you want to go and find an empty compartment. Pull two seats out to make a bed, close the curtains, turn out the lights, and pretend you are sound asleep. It's amazing. At 9 p.m. everyone on that train is snoring away! The first 30 people to get on that car have room to sleep. Number 31 will go into any car with the lights on and people sitting up. The most convincing "sleepers" will be the last to be "woken up."

**The Hare Krishna Approach:** A more interesting way that works equally well and is more fun is to sit cross-legged on the floor and chant religious-sounding, exotically discordant harmonies, with a faraway look on your face. People will open the door, stare in for a few seconds, and leave, determined to sit in the aisle rather than share a compartment with the likes of you. You'll probably sleep alone, or end up chanting the night away with five other religious fanatics.

**Using reservation cards to your advantage:** Each compartment will have a reservation board outside the door. Never sit in a seat that is reserved because you'll be "bumped out" just before the train leaves. Few people realize that you can determine how far the people on a train will travel by reading their reservation tags. Each tag explains which segment of the journey that seat is reserved for. Find a compartment with three or four people traveling for just an hour or two, and for the rest of the night you will probably have that compartment to yourself.

Remember that trains add and lose cars throughout the night. A train could be packed with tourists heading for Milan, and at 1 a.m. an empty Milan-bound car could be added. The difference between being packed like sardines and stretching out in your own fishbowl could be as little as one car away.

These tricks work not to take advantage of others but to equal out the trainload. When all compartments are lightly loaded and people continue to load in, let the air out of your inflatable travel partner and make room for your new roommates. To minimize the misery on a full train, sit opposite your partner, pull out the seats, and share a single bed (and the smell of your feet).

### Bus vs. Train

Except in Ireland, Greece, Turkey, Portugal, and parts of Croatia, Spain, and Morocco, the trains are faster, more comfortable, and have more extensive schedules than buses. Bus trips are usually less expensive (especially in the British Isles) and are occasionally included on your railpass (where operated by the train companies, as many are in Germany, Switzerland, and Belgium).

There are some cheap, long-haul buses, such as Eurolines (www.eurolines.com), and hippie-type "magic buses" such as Busabout (www.busabout.com). These can save you plenty more than train fares. For example, Eurolines' one-way bus fare from Amsterdam to Paris is $50 (compared to $100 second class by train) and from Paris to Rome it's $110 ($185 by train). You get price breaks for round-trips and advance booking.

Use buses mainly to pick up where Europe's great train system leaves off. Buses fan out from the smallest train stations to places too small for the train to cover. For towns with train stations far from the center (e.g., hill towns), buses are often scheduled to meet each arrival and shuttle passengers to the main square (often for no extra cost). Many bus connections to nearby towns not served by train are timed to depart just after the train arrives.

### Taxi Between Cities

While a budget traveler would generally not dream of hiring a taxi for a trip between cities, it can actually be a fairly good value. For example, I paid $50 for the one-hour trip from Madrid to Toledo. Split by two people, it can be worth it, given the time you'll save over public transportation (1 hour of sweat-free, hotel-door-to-hotel-door service versus 3 hours including transfers to and from the train stations). Simply ask any cabbie what they'd charge (it could be off-meter—they know you have a cheap public-transit alternative, and might be willing to deal if they want the work) or ask at your hotel if they have a line on any taxi services that do the trip economically.

## 12. DRIVING IN EUROPE

Behind the wheel you're totally free. You go where you want to, when you want to. You're not limited by tracks and schedules. And driving is great for those who don't believe in packing light...you can even rent a trailer.

Driving can be economical. Solo car travel is expensive, but three or four people sharing a rented car usually travel cheaper than three or four using railpasses.

The super mobility of a car saves you time in locating budget accommodations in small towns and away from the train lines. This savings helps to rationalize the "splurge" of a car rental. You can also play it riskier in peak season, arriving in a town late with no reservation. If the hotels are full, you simply drive to the next town.

Every year, as train prices go up, car rental becomes a better option for budget travelers in Europe. While most travel dreams come with a choo-choo soundtrack, and most first trips are best by rail, you should at least consider the convenience of driving.

*Small car, big scenery*

## Renting a Car

European cars are rented for a 24-hour day, usually with a 59-minute grace period. Cars are economical when rented by the week with unlimited mileage through your travel agent or directly with the rental company in the United States. Daily rates are usually quite high, but there are a few decent three-day deals. There is no way to chart the best car-rental deals. Rates vary from company to company, month to month, and country to country. The cheapest company for rental in one country might be the most expensive in the next. After shopping for half an hour via the toll-free phone numbers listed below, you'll know who has the best deal for your travel plans.

Note that big-name companies (like Avis, Hertz, and Budget) generally charge more than consolidators such as Auto Europe (www.autoeurope.com) and Europe by Car (www.europebycar.com). Consolidators compare rates among various companies (including the big-name firms), find the best deal, and—because they're wholesalers—pass the savings on to you. You pay the consolidator, and they issue you a voucher to pick up your car in Europe. Because consolidators work with several different big companies, they also tend to be more knowledgeable about the practical ins and outs of European car rental.

Rentals arranged from major companies in Europe can be so expensive that you'd save money by having someone arrange your rental for

## Car or Train?

While you should travel the way you like, consider these variables when deciding if your European experience might be better by car or train:

| Concern | By Car | By Train |
|---|---|---|
| • packing heavy? | • no problem | • must go light |
| • scouring one area | • best | • frustrating |
| • all over Europe | • too much driving | • great |
| • big cities | • expensive/worthless | • ideal |
| • camping | • perfect | • more like boot camp |
| • one or two people | • expensive | • probably cheaper |
| • three or more | • probably cheaper | • more expensive |
| • traveling with young kids | • survivable | • miserable |

you back in the United States. Because one-day rates are so high, the various rail-and-drive passes are a good deal (described on page 124). They basically allow you to rent a car one day at a time at one-seventh the cheap weekly rate.

While age limits vary from country to country and company to company, those who are at least 25 years old should have no trouble renting a car. (Younger renters can get stuck with extra costs, like being required to buy CDW insurance or pay a "young driver's surcharge.") Most companies will not rent a car to someone under 21. Only Ireland has a maximum age limit (75), but some car-rental companies enforce age limits of their own. If you're considered too young or too old, look into leasing (see below), which has less stringent age restrictions. STA Travel seeks young renters (www.statravel.com, tel. 800-781-4040).

Rental cars come with the necessary insurance and paperwork to cross borders effortlessly in all of Western Europe. If you plan to drive your rental car from Western to Eastern Europe, keep these tips in mind: State your travel plans up front to the rental company. Some won't allow any of their rental cars to enter Eastern European countries due to the high theft rate in some cities (especially Prague). While these regulations are loosening up, many companies still place limitations for an eastward excursion (for example, you can only take smaller, cheaper cars, and you may have to pay extra fees). The farther east you go, the more restrictions you'll encounter. When you cross an Eastern European border, you'll likely be asked to show proof of insurance (called a "green card"). Ask your car-rental company if you need any other documentation for crossing the borders on your itinerary.

Some rental companies allow you to take a rental car from Britain to the Continent or to Ireland, but be prepared to pay high surcharges and extra drop-off fees (see below). Hertz offers a unique "Le Swap" program—you get a round-trip Chunnel passage and a right-hand-drive car rental for Britain that's swapped for a left-hand-drive rental on the Continent. If you want to drive in Britain, Ireland, and the Continent, it's usually cheaper to rent three separate cars than one, thanks to the high cost of taking cars on ferries (between Ireland and Britain) and crossing under the English Channel via the pricey Eurotunnel (www.eurotunnel.com).

Note that some countries have unfamiliar laws. For example, Austria requires each driver to have a reflective security vest. Your car-rental company should be aware of these concerns—just ask.

You'll generally pay more to pick a car up at the airport than in the center (10–20 percent extra, or a flat fee of $20–100, depending on the destination and the company). When you're calling about prices, rental agents usually quote you this pricier airport pickup rate. Ask if they have a cheaper, downtown-pickup price. Some companies deliver the car to your hotel for free.

When picking up your car, always check the entire vehicle for scratches, dings, and the gas level. If anything is not noted on the rental agreement, return to the counter to make adjustments. When you drop off the car, walk around the car again with the attendant to be sure there are no new problems. Otherwise, unexpected charges might show up on your credit-card statement. They are easier to dispute when the information is documented. On that same note, avoid dropping your car off after hours (at a drop box); it's best to finalize the rental and receive the paperwork in person.

*From sleek German autobahns to windy, cliffside Irish lanes, driving is a fun part of European travel.*

Take advantage of "open jaw" possibilities to save rental days and avoid big-city driving. You can normally pick up and drop off a car at any of your rental company's offices in one country. They don't care if you change your expected drop-off city. (For maximum options, use a bigger company and pick up a list of all their offices in that country.) There's typically a fee (usually $100–300) to drop in another country. You'll find some happy (free) and some outrageous

## Car Rental vs. Train: Comparing Rough Costs

When comparing the costs of renting a car, leasing a car, using a railpass, or buying point-to-point train tickets, consider these factors:

- the **duration** of your trip (this dramatically affects the cost of car rental, but is less important for train tickets or railpasses);
- the **miles** you cover (important for point-to-point train tickets, but irrelevant to railpasses and car leasing—except for gas costs; car rentals also usually come with unlimited mileage); and
- the **countries** you'll be visiting (very important for choosing a railpass, but less important for car rental or leasing—though you'll usually pay more to drop off in a different country than where you picked up).

Here are sample **per-person** prices for three different trips:

| **Means of Transport** | **2,000 miles in 3 wks*** | **4,000 miles in 5 wks**** | **6,000 miles in 8 wks***** |
|---|---|---|---|
| **Railpass** (first class) | $610 | $800 | $1,200 |
| **Train tickets** (second class) | $500 | $750 | $1,400 |
| **Subcompact car rental** (2 people) | $750 | $1,100 | $1,700 |
| **Subcompact car lease** (2 people) | $650 | $900 | $1,200 |
| **Mid-sized car rental** (4 people) | $450 | $675 | $1,075 |
| **Mid-sized car lease** (4 people) | $425 | $575 | $775 |

***Sample Itineraries***

***2,000 miles in 3 weeks (see Best of Europe itinerary on page 87)**

*Amsterdam–Rhine Valley–Munich–Venice–Florence–Rome–Cinque Terre–Swiss Alps–Burgundy–Paris.* The best railpass option for this route is a first-class Eurail Saverpass (10 days in 2 months).

($1,000+) exceptions. The farther the distance between your start and end points, the higher the fee.

Your American driver's license is all you need in most European countries. An international driving permit (IDP) provides a translation of your American license—making it easier for the cop to write out the ticket. Exactly where you need a permit depends on whom you talk to. People who sell them say you should have them almost everywhere. People who rent cars say you need them almost nowhere. People who drive rental cars say the permit is overrated (but it comes in handy as a substitute for a passport at places such as campgrounds and bike-rental

***Sample Itineraries, continued***

****4,000 miles in 5 weeks**
*Same as above, plus Barcelona, Madrid, Lisbon, Rothenburg, Provence, Tuscany.* This trip is best with a first-class Eurail Saverpass (15 days in 2 months).

*****6,000 miles in 8 weeks (see Whirlwind Tour on page 90)**
*Same as above, plus Scandinavia (Copenhagen, Bergen, Oslo, Stockholm), Berlin, Prague, Vienna, and more time along the route.* The best railpass for this itinerary is the first-class Eurail Saverpass (2 consecutive months), plus a Prague Excursion Pass.

***Fine Print***

**Rail:** Second-class train tickets cost about 18 cents per mile in the south and east, 25 cents per mile in the north. We've selected the most economical first-class railpass for each itinerary (since only travelers under 26 are eligible for second-class railpasses). These railpass prices can be higher or lower depending on the specifics of your trip (e.g., how many days of rail travel). Reservation fees (for overnight trains or seats on some high-speed trains) are not included. Assuming two or more people are traveling together, we've listed the "Saverpass" rates for railpasses; individual travelers will pay about 15 percent more.

**Car Rental/Lease:** To get these car-rental and lease rates, I've averaged rates from various consolidators and car-rental companies. Rates can vary dramatically—it pays to check around. These prices are for cars with manual transmission (automatic costs about $100 more per week). The prices in this chart include tax, the cost for dropping the car off in a different country (about $200), and gas costs of about $4–7 per gallon at 30 mpg. Rental-car rates in the chart also include CDW supplements (though not the "super CDW" to buy down the deductible) and fees for picking up at an airport (about 10 percent)—remember that leased cars do not come with these expenses. Costs for parking and tolls are not included (because they depend on the specific route and time spent in each place).

shops that require some kind of photo ID as a security deposit until you pay). Police can get mad—their concern is in finding the expiration date—and fine you if you don't have an international permit. Those driving in Portugal, Spain, Italy, Austria, Germany, Greece, and Eastern Europe are likely to be fined if found without an international driving permit, and should probably get one (at your local AAA office—$10 plus the cost of 2 passport-type photos, www.aaa.com). You have to carry your American driver's license as well as your international permit.

Most rental cars in Europe have manual transmissions. Automatics can tack on an extra $100 per week—or, worse, may only be available if you

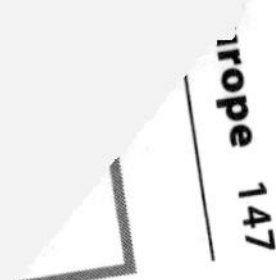

## of Car Rental: About $500 a Week

gh estimate for one week of car rental with unlimited plus collision damage waiver (CDW) insurance. This is the average, ballpark weekly figure for the three-week, 2,000-mile trip listed on page 87.

**Ford Fiesta (including tax):** about $300/week
**CDW:** $15–25/day
**Gas:** $90/week ($4–7/gallon, 30 mpg, 100 miles/day)
**Parking in big cities:** $20/day
**Freeway tolls:** $5–7/hour (France and Italy only)

upgrade to a bigger, more expensive car. Since supplies are limited, if you must have an automatic, you'll need to arrange it farther in advance. Ideally, skip the automatic and brush up on your shifting skills. It's better to lurch through your hometown parking lot than grind your gears over the Alps.

## Car-Rental Expenses

To really compare car costs with train costs, figure your weekly unlimited-mileage rental rate plus:

- **Tax,** clear and consistent within each country, is generally 18–25 percent (less in Spain, Germany, Ireland, and Luxembourg, and only 8 percent in Switzerland—but Swiss rental rates are that much higher)
- **CDW insurance supplement** (figure 25 percent extra, or about $15–25 a day, see below)
- **Gas** ($90 a week, giving you about 700 miles)
- **Tolls** for superfreeways in Italy, France, Spain, Portugal, Croatia, and Slovenia (about $4–7 per hour), $15 to drive in downtown London, $30 for the toll sticker as you enter Switzerland, $10 for Austria, $8 for the Czech Republic, $11 for Hungary, and $4 for Slovakia
- **Parking** ($20 a day in big cities, free otherwise)
- **Theft protection** (required in Italy, about $12–15/day)

### The Collision Damage Waiver (CDW) Racket

When you rent a car, you are liable for a very high deductible, sometimes equal to the entire value of the car. There are various ways you can limit your financial risk in case of an accident.

**Car-Rental Company CDW:** The simplest solution is to buy a collision damage waiver (CDW) supplement from the car-rental company. CDW—which covers everything except the undercarriage, roof, tires, and windshield—costs $15–25 a day, depending on the country, the car, and the company (figure roughly 25 percent extra). Many rental companies have all-inclusive plans that include a more reasonable CDW. Ask your travel agent about this—it's usually cheaper than reserving a basic rental, then adding "super CDW" (described below) when you get to the car-rental desk.

A few years ago, CDW came with a low (or zero) deductible, and was a good value for the peace of mind it provided. But rental rates are so competitive that, to make a reasonable profit, car-rental companies have to make a killing on the CDW. Most car-rental companies have dramatically increased deductibles, with most now hovering at about $1,000–1,500 (this varies by country). When you pick the car up, the counter agent might try to sell you additional coverage (called "super CDW") to buy down the deductible to zero (figure about an additional $10–20 per day).

Most of the major car-rental companies now come with these astronomical deductibles. This added expense has made alternatives to CDW worth considering.

**Credit-Card Coverage:** More and more, credit-card companies are offering their own type of zero-deductible collision coverage (comparable to CDW) to compete with rental companies. Relying on credit-card coverage can be a hassle, but now that rental companies' CDW costs are stacking up, it could be worth it. Basically, if your car is damaged or stolen, your credit card will cover whatever cost you're liable for. Of course, restrictions apply—if you plan to use this coverage, carefully ask your credit-card company what kind of coverage they provide, the maximum number of rental days they'll provide the coverage, and the types of vehicles they cover. Have them explain the worst-case scenario to you.

*Luckily, Bud paid extra for full insurance.*

If you use the coverage offered by your credit card, you'll have to decline the CDW offered by your car-rental company. Therefore, as far as some rental companies are concerned, you're technically liable for the full deductible (which, again, can equal the cost of the car). Because of this, some car-rental companies might put a hold on your credit card for the full value of the car. This is bad news if your credit limit

## Leading Car-Rental Companies

Consolidators work with major companies, comparing rates to find you the best deal. Or you can contact your favorite rental company direct.

### Consolidators

| | | |
|---|---|---|
| Auto Europe | 888-223-5555 | www.autoeurope.com |
| Europe by Car | 800-223-1516 | www.europebycar.com |
| DER/RailEurope | 800-782-2424 | www.raileurope.com |
| Kemwel | 877-820-0668 | www.kemwel.com |
| Renault Eurodrive (leasing only) | 800-221-1052 | www.renaultusa.com |

### Major Car-Rental Companies

| | | |
|---|---|---|
| Avis | 800-230-4898 | www.avis.com |
| Alamo/National | 800-522-9696 | www.alamo.com |
| Budget | 800-527-0700 | www.budget.com |
| Dollar (Thrifty | 800-800-6000 | www.thrifty.com |
| in Europe) | 800-847-4389 | www.dollar.com |
| Hertz | 800-654-3001 | www.hertz.com |

is low—particularly if you plan on using that card for other purchases during your trip. (Consider bringing two credit cards—one for the rental car, the other for everything else.) If you don't have enough credit on your card to cover the car's value, some rental companies require you to purchase CDW insurance.

If you have an accident, the rental company will charge you for the value of the damage (up to the deductible amount), or, if the vehicle is stolen, the value of the deductible associated with theft—which, as noted, could be the full value of the vehicle. You would then seek reimbursement for these charges from your credit-card company when you get home (you'll need to submit the police report and the car-rental company's accident report). Note that big American-based rental companies are easier to work with if you have a problem.

**Before you commit, ask about whatever's applicable to your situation:**

- weekly unlimited mileage rate
- age restrictions
- insurance cost
- CDW options (including "super CDW")
- theft insurance (required in Italy)
- cost of adding another driver
- drop-off costs within a country or in another country
- a listing of offices in the countries you're visiting (consider the most efficient pick-up and drop-off points)
- if it's cheaper to pick up the car at the airport or downtown
- if there is a covered trunk
- availability of automatics and car seats
- any restrictions on driving the car in all countries (particularly in Eastern Europe)
- any additional charges or local taxes such as VAT (value added tax)

**Before you drive away, ask about:**

- the length of the grace period for drop-off (can be 30–59 minutes)
- how to use the wipers, alarm system, lights, radio, etc.
- what type of fuel is best and how to release the gas cap
- location of insurance "green card"
- making repairs and emergency roadside services
- changing a tire

Be warned that if you accept any coverage offered by the car-rental company, you automatically forego any coverage provided by your credit card. (In other words, if you buy CDW that comes with a reduced $1,000 deductible, don't expect your credit card to cover that deductible).

**Travel Guard CDW:** Travel Guard sells renter's collision insurance at very affordable rates ($9/day plus a one-time $3 service fee covers you up to $35,000, $250 deductible, www.travelguard.com, tel. 800-826-4919). It's valid throughout Europe, but some car-rental companies refuse to honor it (especially in Italy and the Republic of Ireland—see more about these exceptions below). If your car-rental company doesn't honor this coverage, and you have to buy other coverage to replace it, Travel Guard will refund your money. Oddly, residents of Washington State aren't allowed to buy this coverage.

Remember that some comprehensive travel insurance policies include collision coverage. For details, see "Travel Insurance—To Insure or Not to Insure?" in Chapter 3: Paper Chase.

**Leasing:** Those renting a car for at least three weeks should look into leasing, which includes zero-deductible collision and theft insurance (see below).

**Exceptions:** There are some exceptions to what I've described. If you rent a car in Italy, you are required to buy theft insurance, and most car-rental companies' rates automatically include CDW coverage (which you sometimes can't decline). It's not unusual to decline CDW when you reserve your Italian car, only to find when you show up at the counter that you must buy it after all.

Car-rental companies in the Republic of Ireland are less amenable to letting renters waive CDW insurance in favor of credit-card coverage. As of this writing, the only credit-card companies that were allowed to provide CDW coverage in Ireland were MasterCard Platinum and Diner's Club—so if you have a Visa or American Express, you're forced to buy CDW. Also unique to Ireland is that you sometimes have the option of buying down the deductible on your CDW at the time of booking (for about $12/day), rather than when you pick up the car.

**Liability Insurance:** It's unusual to purchase additional liability insurance when renting a car in Europe. With most European car-rental companies, any liability coverage you might need is already included in the price. But if you're concerned about this, ask for details when you rent.

**The Final Say:** Buying CDW—and the supplemental insurance to buy down the deductible, if you choose—is the easiest but priciest option. Using the coverage that comes with your credit card is cheaper, but can involve more hassle. If you're taking a short trip (but not in Italy or Ireland), the simplest solution is to buy Travel Guard's very affordable CDW. For longer trips, leasing is the best way to go.

## Leasing and Buying

Leasing (technically, buying the car and selling it back) gets around many tax and insurance costs and is a great deal for people needing a car for three weeks or more. Lease prices include all taxes, as well as zero-deductible theft and collision insurance (comparable to CDW)—and you get to use a new car. Leased cars can most easily be picked up and returned in France, but for an additional fee you can also lease cars in the Netherlands, Belgium, Germany, Spain, Portugal, Italy, and Great Britain. Note that you can't lease a car in Ireland.

Europe by Car, which invented leasing 52 years ago, still offers good deals (for example, you can lease a car in France for as few as 17 days for $829; www.europebycar.com, tel. 800-223-1516). Renault Eurodrive offers similar deals (www.renaultusa.com). The longer you lease the car for, the more you save per day.

Although Americans rarely consider this budget option, Aussies and New Zealanders routinely buy used cars for their trips and sell them when they're done. The most common places to buy cars are Amsterdam, Frankfurt, London, and US military bases. In London, check the used-car market on Market Road (Tube: Caledonian Road) and look in London periodicals such as *TNT* (www.tntmagazine.com), *Loot* (www.loot.com), and *New Zealand News UK* (www.nznewsuk.co.uk), which list used cars as well as jobs, flats, cheap flights, and travel partners.

**Campers:** Consider the advantage of a van or motor home, which gives you the flexibility to drive late and just pull over and camp for free. Fairly cheap to run, these vehicles use diesel—about the cost of gasoline, but with much better mileage (24–30 mpg average).

The 2007 edition of *Europe by Van and Motorhome* contains all the details on renting, buying, and shipping, and includes a free, personal consultation (David Shore and Patty Campbell, 268 pages, $16.95, free shipping for ETBD readers, Odyssey Press, www.roadtripeurope.com, tel. 800-659-5222, shorecam@aol.com).

Campanje, a Dutch company, specializes in long-term rentals of small-size, fully-loaded campervans and RVs (4–7 people) for camping through Europe. Rates run from $780 per week for a four-person camper van up to $1,280 per week for a seven-person RV (minimum 3 weeks), including tax and insurance. Ask about discounts for early booking and off-season (www.campanje.nl, Dutch tel. 030/244-7070, info@campanje.nl).

## Behind the European Wheel

Horror stories about European traffic abound. They're fun to tell, but driving in Europe is really only a problem for those who make it one. Any good American driver can cope with European traffic.

Europe is a continent of frustrated race-car drivers. The most dangerous creature on the road is the timid American. Be aggressive, observe, fit in, avoid big-city driving when you can, and wear your seat belt.

**Drive European.** After a few minutes on the autobahn, you'll learn that you don't cruise in the passing lane. Cruise in the right-hand lane.

**And drive defensively.** Be warned that some Europeans, particularly Italians, make up their own rules of the road. In Rome, my cabbie went through three red lights. White-knuckled, I asked, "*Scusi,* do you see red lights?" He said, "When I come to light, I look. If no cars come, red light *stupido,* I go through. If policeman sees no cars—*no problema.* He agree—red light *stupido.*"

**Learn the signs.** All of Europe uses the same simple set of road symbols. Just take a few minutes to learn them. Many major rest stops have free local driving almanacs (or cheap maps) that explain such signs, roadside facilities, and exits.

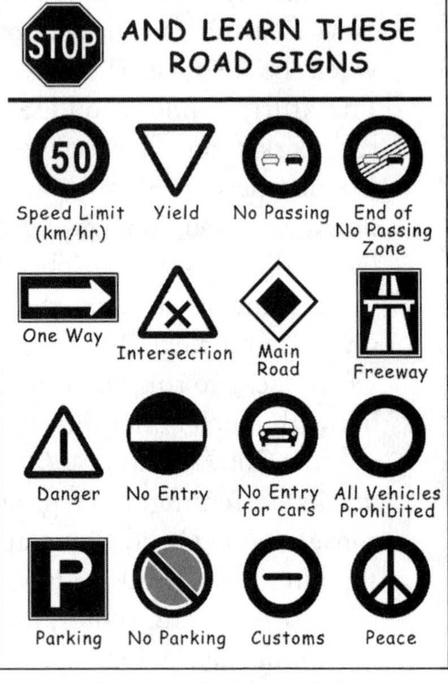


You can drive in and out of strange towns fairly smoothly by following a few basic signs. Most European towns have signs directing you to the "old town" or the center (such as *centrum, centro, centre-ville, Stadtmitte).* The tourist office, normally right downtown, will usually be clearly signposted (*i, turismo, VVV,* or various abbreviations that you'll learn in each country). The tallest spire often marks the center of the old town. Park in its shadow and look for the tourist information office. To leave a city, look for freeway signs (distinctive green or blue, depending on the country) or "all directions" *(toutes directions)* signs. Avoid heavy traffic times. Big cities are great fun and nearly traffic-free for Sunday drives. Mediterranean resort areas are extremely congested on summer weekends.

**To save time, use the expressway.** The shortest distance between any two European points is found on the *autobahn/strada/route.* Some prefer the more scenic and free national highway systems (*route nationale* in France). These small roads can be a breeze, or they can be dreadfully jammed up. To study ahead, consult the excellent route planner at www.viamichelin.com.

**Better roads often come with tolls.** It's free to drive on expressways in some countries—such as most roads in Great Britain, or Germany's famous *Autobahn.* In other countries, you'll pay for the privilege. Sometimes you'll have to buy a toll sticker (sold at border crossings, gas stations, and post offices) to display in your window: You'll pay about $30 for the highway permit decal as you enter Switzerland, $10 for Austria, $8 for the Czech Republic, $11 for Hungary, and $4 for Slovakia. If you don't get the decal, you'll soon meet your first local—in uniform.

In most Mediterranean countries—including Italy, France, Spain, Portugal, Croatia, and Slovenia—you'll periodically encounter toll booths on major expressways ($4–7 per hour). Although tolls can be high in Italy and France ($6/hour in Italy, $50 to get from Paris to the French Riviera—priciest around Monaco), the gas and time saved on European expressways justifies the expense. Note that in all these cases, if you're simply dipping into the country on secondary roads (such as around the town of Reutte, Austria, near Germany's Bavaria), you don't need to buy a toll sticker or otherwise pay for road use. But tolls can pop up in unexpected places. For example, to drive in downtown London, you'll have to pay a $15 "congestion charge" (www.cclondon.com).

*Much of Europe uses cardboard "parking clocks" instead of parking meters. They often come with rental cars or can be bought cheap at gas stations, newsstands, or tobacco shops. Park, set the clock for the current time, and leave it on your dashboard. A street sign indicates how much time you have (according to this sign, parking is limited to 60 min, Mon–Fri, 8 a.m.–6 p.m.). The clock establishes when you arrived. In Germanic countries, where they're widely used, ask for a* Parkscheibe.

**Passing is essential.** Americans are timid about passing. Be bold but careful. On winding, narrow roads, you'll notice a turn-signal sign language from the slower car ahead of you indicating when it's OK to pass. This is used inconsistently. Don't rely on it blindly.

**Don't use a car for city sightseeing.** Park it and use public transportation (or taxis). City parking is a pain. Find a spot as close to the center as possible, grab it, and keep it. For overnight stops, it's crucial to choose a safe, well-traveled, and well-lit spot. A tourist's car parked overnight in a bad urban neighborhood will almost certainly be vandalized. In cities where traffic is worst, look for huge government-sponsored (cheap) parking lots on the outskirts, where a bus or subway will zip you easily into the center. It's often worth parking in a garage ($10–30 a day). Ask your hotel receptionist for advice.

**Consider hiring cabbies.** Even if you've got a rental car, cabbies can be handy when you're driving lost in a big city. Many times I've hired a cab, showed him an elusive address, and followed him in my car to my hotel.

**Go metric.** On the Continent, you'll be dealing with kilometers. To convert kilometers to miles, cut in half and add 10 percent (90 km/hr = 45 + 9 miles = 54 miles—not very fast in Europe). Do the math yourself: 140 km = 84 mph. Or 360 km = 216 miles. Some people prefer to multiply by 6 and drop the last digit (80 km/hr x 6 = 48 miles), though this can be challenging with large numbers (340 miles x 6 = ?). Choose whichever formula works for you.

Ireland is phasing out miles in favor of kilometers. Britain, like us, is stuck on miles.

*A roundabout: take a spin...or two.*

**Explore the roundabouts in Britain and Ireland.** In addition to intersections with stoplights, you'll encounter roundabouts. These work wonderfully if you yield to cars already inside the circle. For many, roundabouts are high-pressure circles that require a snap decision about something you really don't completely understand—your exit. To replace the stress with giggles, make it standard operating procedure to take a 360-degree case-out-your-options exploratory circuit, discuss the exits with your navigator, go around again if necessary, and then confidently wing off on the exit of your choice.

## Gas

The cost of gas in Europe ($4–7 a gallon) sounds worse than it is. Distances are short, the petite cars get great mileage, and, when compared to costly train tickets (for the price of a 2-hour train ride, you can fill your tank), expensive gas is less of a factor. You'll be impressed by how few miles you need to travel to enjoy Europe's diversity. To minimize gas costs, consider renting a car that takes diesel, which costs the same per liter but gets better mileage.

Pumping gas in Europe is as easy as finding a gas station (the word "self-service" is universal), sticking the nozzle in, and pulling the big trigger. Gas prices are listed by the liter (about a quart, 4 to a gallon). Gas is called *petrol* or *benzine*, while diesel is known as *gasoil*. Super is *super*, and normal is *normal* (or *essence*) and increasingly rare. In many countries, the pumps are color-coded to help you find the right kind of gas. When you pick up your rental car, be sure you know what kind of gas (and what color pumps) you need to use, and have them show you how to open the gas cap. As in the United States, most cars take unleaded, but diesel is still widely in use. Freeway gas stations are more expensive than those in towns, but during siesta only freeway stations are open. Giant suburban supermarkets often offer the cheapest gas.

### Joyriding

The British Isles are good for driving—reasonable rentals, no language barrier, exciting rural areas, and fine roads...and after one near head-on collision scares the bloody heck out of you, you'll have no trouble remembering which side of the road to drive on.

Other good driving areas are Scandinavia (call for free reservations to avoid long waits at ferry crossings); Belgium and the Netherlands (yield to bikes—you're outnumbered); Spain and Portugal (explore out-of-the-way villages and hill towns); Germany (enjoy wonderfully engineered freeways much loved by wannabe race-car drivers); Switzerland and Austria (drive down sunny alpine valleys with yodeling on the stereo for auto ecstasy); and Slovenia (a tiny, picturesque country with many diverse sights hard to reach by public transit). The whirlwind, see-Europe-from-top-to-bottom type of trip is best by train.

## 13. BIKING, HITCHING, WALKING, AND HIKING

### Biking in Europe

Biking is big in Europe. Many cities such as Amsterdam, Copenhagen, and Munich are great by bike. Riverside bike paths near Salzburg, Luxor, and along the Rhine have left me with top-notch memories. Within cities, bikes cut transportation times in half, giving you more time to spend at the sights. Wherever it's worth biking, you'll find a bike-rental shop. Bikes are bargains at $10–15 a day.

Bikes are a fun change of pace if you're traveling by car or train. In many countries (especially France, Germany, Austria, Belgium, and the Netherlands), the train stations rent bikes and sometimes have easy "pick up here and drop off there" plans.

Guided bike tours, ranging from two to five hours, are popular in Europe's cities (such as Amsterdam, Bruges, Paris, and Munich). You'll get an entertaining, sometimes informative guide who will show you the back streets and treats of the city or countryside. Tours are fun, reasonable

*Wherever biking is fun, you'll find shops renting bikes and helmets.*

(about $20–30), good exercise, and an easy way to meet other travelers as well as get a fresh angle on an old city.

Some people travel almost exclusively by bike and wouldn't have it any other way. Rich Sorensen and Edwin McCain, who for years have gotten their travel thrills crisscrossing Europe by bike, helped me assemble the following tips on bicycle touring in Europe.

**Bicycle touring is cheap and rewarding.** To see Europe on $30 a day, you don't need a time machine. What you need is a bike, farmers' markets, and campgrounds or hostels. Traveling this way, you'll not only save money and keep fit, but you'll experience a quieter side of Europe that travelers rarely see.

While bicycle touring is one of the cheapest ways to see Europe, most bikers choose to pedal for the sheer joy of it. Imagine low-gearing up a beautiful mountain road on a bike (smell the freshly mown hay), then picture an air-conditioned Mercedes with the windows closed and the stereo on (smell the upholstery). The driver might think, "Masochistic nut!"...but he also might notice the biker's smiling face—the face of a traveler who can see clearly from mountain to village and hear the birds singing, while anticipating a well-earned and glorious downhill run.

**Determine if a bike is the best transportation for your trip.** Define what part of Europe you want to experience, and then ask yourself some basic questions to see whether your bicycle will be your key to freedom or an albatross around your neck. Remember that it takes an entire day to travel the same distance by bicycle that you could cover in a single hour by train or car. Sixty miles per day is a high average. With bakery stops, Rich averages about 40. For example, if you have the entire summer free, you and your bike can cover a lot of ground through, say, France, Germany, Benelux, Switzerland, and Italy. But if you have a month or less, will you be content to focus on a single country or region? Given what you want to see in the time you have, is the slow pace of bicycling a worthwhile trade-off for the benefits? And finally, do you want to spend much more of your time in rural and small-town Europe than in cities?

**Read a biking guidebook.** Lonely Planet publishes cycling guides to

France, Britain, Italy, and Ireland. Katherine Widing has written *Bicycle Touring Holland: With Excursions Into Neighboring Belgium and Germany.* Consider also *Cycle Europe: 20 Tours, 12 Countries,* by Jerry Soverinsky. Cicerone offers biking guides to France, the French Alps, the Loire Valley, the Danube, Spain, and the "Way of St. James" (Camino de Santiago). For Italy, try *Italy by Bike: 105 Tours from the Alps to Sicily,* by the Touring Club of Italy. For Britain, there's *Bike Britain: Cycling from Land's End to John O'Groats,* by Paul Salter. Some titles in The Mountaineers' By Bike series (including Ireland, Germany, England, France, and Europe) haven't been updated in several years.

Adventure Cycling Association's *Cyclists' Yellow Pages* is a good resource directory (available annually in print or online), and their Cyclosource online store contains first-rate books, clothing, maps, and bike gear (www.adventurecycling.org, tel. 800-721-8719).

**Take practice trips.** Make sure you really enjoy taking long rides weighted down with loaded panniers. Try some 60-mile-a-day rides (5 hours at 12 mph) around home. If possible, take a weekend camping trip with everything you'll take to Europe. Know which tools to bring and learn basic repair work (like repairing flat tires, replacing broken spokes, and adjusting brakes and derailleurs). Ask about classes at your local bike shop.

**Decide whether to go solo, with a partner, or with a tour.** You can go it alone, with occasional pick-up pals on the way. As a loner, you'll go where, when, and as far and fast as you want. Traveling with a companion or two is more cost-effective and can be more fun, but make sure your partner's cycling pace and temperament are compatible with yours. Organized tours, which usually have sag wagons to carry gear, average an easy 30–40 miles a day. For information, check out Euro-Bike and Walking Tours (www.eurobike.com, tel. 800-321-6060), Backroads (www.backroads.com, tel. 800-462-2848), Pack & Pedal Europe (www.tripsite.com, tel. 877-965-2064), or Randonnée Tours (self-guided tours only, www.randonneetours.com, tel. 800-242-1825). You can also check the ads in *Bicycling* magazine (www.bicycling.com)

Dominic Bonuccelli

*Mountain biking is permitted on many trails.*

or *Adventure Cyclist* magazine (www.adventurecycling.org/mag).

**When to go depends on where you go.** Ideal biking temperatures are between 50 and 70 degrees Fahrenheit, so May is a good time to bike in the Mediterranean countries. Edwin started his five-week trip in Greece in May before it got too hot and then pedaled up through the Balkans to England. He had good temperatures all the way, but he also had headwinds (the prevailing westerlies). Rich and his wife, Risa, set out from Barcelona on a more leisurely spring-to-fall route that took them through France, England, Germany, Switzerland, Italy, and Greece, and they had not only ideal temperatures but also fewer headwinds.

**Bring your bike from home.** Although you can buy good touring bikes in Europe, they're no cheaper than here, and you're better off bringing a bike that you're sure is the right fit for you, your racks, and your panniers. Cyclists debate whether to tour on a thick-tired mountain bike or a touring bike with skinnier tires. Mountain-bike tires are much more forgiving on the occasional cobblestone street, but they are more durable than necessary for most European roads, and the chunky tread design will slow you down. In addition, straight mountain-bike handlebars will limit your hand positions, increasing fatigue on long riding days. If you already have a mountain bike, go ahead and take it, but add some bolt-on handlebar extensions.

**Airlines have different bike-checking policies.** Call your airline directly. More and more airlines are charging a fee for your bike and for the "bike box" they provide. Some airlines will fly it to Europe free, considering it to be one of your two allotted pieces of checked baggage. Most airlines require that bikes be partially disassembled and boxed. Get a box from your local bike shop, the airline, or from Amtrak (which sells cavernous bike boxes). Reinforce your box with extra cardboard, and be sure to put a plastic spacer between your front forks (any bike shop will give you one). Airlines require that pedals be taken off the bike; never leave them loose in the box. Attach them either to your rear rack or put them in one of your panniers. You can toss in your panniers, tent, and so on for extra padding, as long as you stay under the airline's weight limit. Bring the tools you'll need to get your bike back into riding form so you can ride straight out of the European airport.

**Be prepared.** Expect rain and bring good bikers' rain gear. A Gore-Tex raincoat can double as a cool-weather windbreaker. You'll also be exposed to the sun, so plan on using plenty of sunscreen. A bell is generally required by law in Europe, so you should have one on your bike—for giving a multilingual "Hi!" to other bikers as well as a "Look out, here I come!" Even if you never ride at night, you should at least bring a strobe-type taillight for the many long and unavoidable tunnels. Smaller Presta tire valves are standard in most of Europe, so if your bike has the automotive-type Shraeder valves, take along an adapter. To guard against unsightly road rash (and worse), always wear a helmet and biking gloves.

**Obey Europe's traffic rules.** Bikers generally follow the same rules as drivers. Some countries, such as the Netherlands, have rules and signs just for bikers: A bike in a blue circle indicates a bike route; a bike in a red circle indicates bikes are not allowed. Be alert; if you follow the blue bike signs, these required bike paths will get you through even some of the most complicated highway interchanges. Beware of the silent biker who might be right behind you, and use hand signals before stopping or turning. Stay off the freeways. Little roads are nicer for biking, anyway.

**Use good maps.** Michelin's Europe and individual country maps are fine for overall planning. In Europe, use local maps for day-to-day navigation. Michelin, Touring Club Italiano, and Die Generalkarte 1:200,000 maps reveal all the quiet back roads and even the steepness of hills. Don't be obsessed with following a preplanned route. Delightful and spontaneous side-trips are part of the spirit and joy of biking.

**Taking your bike on a train greatly extends the reach of your trip.** Every hour by rail saves a day that would have been spent in the saddle (and there's nothing so sweet as taking a train away from the rain and into a sunny place). To make sure you and your bike can travel on the same train, look for trains marked in timetables with little bicycle symbols, or ask at the station's information window. In some countries, trains that allow bikes require advance reservations.

**Bike thieves abound in Europe.** Use an improved Kryptonite-style bike lock to secure your bike to something sturdy. Never leave your pump, handlebar bag, panniers, water bottle, or computer on your bike when you can't see it. Keep your bike inside whenever possible. At hostels, ask if there is a locked bike room, and, if not, ask or even plead for a place to put your bike inside overnight. Remember that hotels and many pensions don't really have rules against taking a bike up to your room. Just do it unobtrusively. You can even wheelie it into the elevator. Rich and Risa found campgrounds to be safe, but they always locked their bikes together.

**Travel light...or camp.** Unless you really love camping, staying in hostels or hotels makes more sense, since it frees you from lugging around a tent, sleeping bag, and cooking equipment. European campgrounds tend to be more crowded than American ones, so if you're willing to sacrifice privacy in order to mix with Europeans, camping can add a fun dimension to your trip.

**A bike makes you more approachable.** The most rewarding aspect of bicycling in Europe is meeting people. Europeans love bicycles, and they are often genuinely impressed when they encounter that rare American who rejects the view from the tour-bus window in favor of huffing and puffing through their country on two wheels. Your bike provides an instant conversation piece, the perfect bridge over a maze of cultural and language barriers.

## Hitchhiking—Rules of Thumb

Hitching, sometimes called "auto-stop," is a popular and acceptable means of getting around in Europe. After picking up a Rhine riverboat captain in my rental car and running him back to his home port, I realized that hitchhiking doesn't wear the same hippie hat in Europe that it does in the United States.

Without a doubt, hitching is the cheapest means of transportation. It's also a great way to meet people. Most people who pick you up are genuinely interested in getting to know an American.

The farther you get from our culture's determination to be self-sufficient, the more volunteerism you'll encounter. Bumming a ride is a perfect example. In the Third World—rural Europe in the extreme—anything rolling with room will let you in. You don't hitch, you just flag the vehicle down.

**Hitching is risky.** Although hitching in Europe is safer than hitching in the United States, there is an ever-present danger any time you get into a stranger's car. That, coupled with the overabundance of lawyers in the United States, means I cannot recommend it. Personally, I don't hitchhike at home, and I wouldn't rely solely on my thumb to get me through Europe. But I never sit frustrated in a station for two hours because there isn't a bus or train to take me 15 miles down the road. Riding my thumb out of train and bus schedule problems, I can usually get to my destination in a friendly snap.

**Hitching can be time-consuming.** Some places have 20 or 30 people in a chorus line of thumbs, just waiting their turns. Once I said what I thought was goodbye forever to an Irishman after breakfast. He was heading north. We had dinner together that night, and I learned a lot about wasting a day on the side of a road. You'll find that Germany, Norway, Ireland, and Great Britain offer generally good hitchhiking, while southern countries are less reliable.

**Learn the gestures.** The hitchhiking gesture is not always the outstretched thumb. In some countries, you ring an imaginary bell. In others, you make a downward wave with your hand. Observe and learn.

**Crank up your good judgment.** Feel good about the situation before you commit yourself to it. Keep your luggage on your lap, or at least out of the trunk, so if things turn sour, you can excuse yourself quickly and easily. Women should not sit in the back seat of a two-door car. A fake wedding ring and modest dress are indications that you're interested only in transportation.

**Consider your appearance.** Look like the Cracker Jack boy or his sister—happy, wholesome, and a joy to have aboard. Establish eye contact. Charm the driver. Smile. Stand up. Don't walk and hitch. Pick a good spot on the road, giving the driver plenty of time to see you and a safe spot to pull over. Look respectable and a little gaunt. Arrange your luggage so it looks as small as possible. Those hitching with very little or no luggage enjoy a tremendous advantage.

**A man and a woman make the perfect combination.** A single woman will get picked up quick but takes risks. Two women travel more safely and nearly as fast. A single man with patience will do fine. Two guys go slow, and three or more should split up and rendezvous later. Single men and women are better off traveling together; these alliances are easily made at hostels. A man and a woman traveling together have it easy. If the woman hitches and the guy steps out of view around the corner or into a shop, they should both have a ride in a matter of minutes. (Dirty trick, but it works.)

*Hitchhiking at the Bulgaria–Greece border, or wherever the train and bus schedules leave you stranded.*

**Create pity.** When I'm doing some serious hitching, I walk away from town and find a very lonely stretch of road. It seems that the sparser the traffic, the quicker I get a ride. On a busy road, people will assume that I'll manage without their ride. If only one car passes in five minutes, the driver senses that he may be my only chance.

**Go the distance.** To get the long ride, take a local bus out of town to the open country on the road to your destination. Make a cardboard sign with your destination printed big and bold in the local language, followed by the local "please." At borders, you might decide to choose only a ride that will take you entirely through that country. Use decals and license plates to determine where a car is from (and therefore likely heading). Every car has to have a large decal with a letter or two indicating in which country the car is registered. And in some countries (such as Germany and Italy), hometowns are indicated by the first few letters on the license plate.

**Try to meet the driver directly.** Find a spot where cars stop, and you can encounter the driver face to thumb. A toll booth, border, gas station, or—best of all—a ferry ride gives you that chance to smile and convince him that he needs you in his car or truck. Although it's easy to zoom past a hitchhiker at 60 mph and not feel guilty, it's much more difficult to turn down an in-person request for a ride.

**Share-a-ride organizations match rides and riders.** Start with To Share (particularly active in Spain, France, Italy, and Germany, www.toshare.org), which lists ride possibilities in over a dozen European countries. Look for Mitfahrzentralen in Germany (www.mitfahren.org), FreeWheelers in Britain (www.freewheelers.co.uk) and Taxistop in Belgium (also features deals on ferries, www.taxistop.be). You pay a small amount to join, and you help with gas expenses, but it works well and is much cheaper than train travel. Also ask about rides at student tourist information centers. Informal ride services are posted on college and hostel bulletin boards all over Europe.

**Hitching can become the destination.** With the "hitch when you can't get a bus or train" approach, you'll find yourself walking down lovely rural roads and getting rides from safe and friendly small-town folk. I can recall some "it's great to be alive and on the road" days riding my thumb from tiny town to waterfall to desolate Celtic graveyard to coastal village and remembering each ride as much as the destinations. Especially in Ireland, I've found so much fun in the front seat that I've driven right by my planned destination to carry on with the conversation. In rural Ireland, I'd stand on the most desolate road in Connemara and hitch whichever way the car was coming. As I hopped in the driver would ask, "Where you goin'?" I'd say, "Ireland."

## Walking (and Dodging)

You'll walk a lot in Europe. It's a great way to see cities, towns, and the countryside. Walking tours offer the most intimate look at a city or town. A walker complements the place she walks through by her interest, and will be received warmly. Many areas, from the mountains to the beaches, are best seen on foot.

Travelers who make walking a focus of their trip will find series of books just for them, published by Lonely Planet (on Britain, France,

*Alpine trail signs show where you are, the altitude in meters, and how long in hours and minutes it takes to hike to nearby points.*

Ireland, Italy, Switzerland, Scotland, Spain, and the Alps, www.lonelyplanet.com), Sunflower Books (detailed guides for destinations throughout Europe, www.sunflowerbooks.co.uk), Interlink Books (Independent Walker's guides to France, Italy, Britain, Ireland, and more, www.interlinkbooks.com/Catalogues/Walking_Guides.html), Cicerone Press (trekking guides for many European countries, www.cicerone.co.uk), and Pili Pala Press (*Walking in Portugal* and *Walking the Camino de Santiago*, www.pilipalapress.com).

Be on your toes: Walking in cities can be dangerous. More than 300 pedestrians are run down on the streets of Paris each year. The drivers are crazy, and politeness has no place on the roads of Europe. Cross carefully, but if you wait for a break in the traffic, you may never get a chance to cross the street. Look for a pedestrian underpass or, when all else fails, find a heavyset local person and just follow him like a shadow—one busy lane at a time—across that seemingly impassable street.

Joggers can enjoy a good early morning tour as well as the exercise. Hotel receptionists usually know a good jogging route. Remember to carry identification and your hotel card with you.

## Hiking

Imagine hiking along a ridge high in the Swiss Alps. On one side of you, lakes stretch all the way to Germany. On the other stands the greatest mountain panorama in Europe—the Eiger, Mönch, and Jungfrau. And up ahead you hear the long, legato tones of an alphorn, announcing that a helicopter-stocked mountain hut is open, it's just around the corner... and the coffee schnapps is on.

Hiking in Europe is a joy. Travelers explore entire regions on foot. Switzerland's Jungfrau is an exciting sight from a hotel's terrace café, but those who hike the region enjoy nature's very own striptease as the mountain reveals herself in an endless string of powerful poses.

Romantics commune with nature from Norway's fjords to the English lakes to the Alps to the Dalmatian Coast. Trails are generally well-kept and carefully marked. Very precise maps (scale 1:25,000) are

readily available.

You could walk through the Alps for weeks, sleeping in mountain huts, and never come out of the mountains. You're never more than a day's hike from a mountain village, where you can replenish your food supply or enjoy a hotel bed and a restaurant meal. Most alpine trails are free of snow by July, and lifts take less rugged visitors to the top in a sweat-free flash.

Throughout the Alps, trail markings are both handy and humiliating. Handy, because they show hours to hike rather than miles to walk to various destinations. Humiliating, because these times are clocked by local senior citizens. You'll know what I mean after your first hike.

If you prefer organized walks, look for Volksmarches. These 10-kilometer-or-longer walks are particularly popular in Germanic countries, involve lots of locals, and end with refreshments and socializing. Ask your hotel or the local tourist office for details.

Do some research before you leave. Buy the most appropriate hiking guidebook. Ask for maps and advice from the National Tourist Offices (for a list of tourist offices, see Chapter 2: Gathering Information).

# MONEY

## 14. MONEY

I changed my last traveler's check years ago. And I haven't stepped into a European bank in ages. Now, I get my cash from ATM machines.

### Euros

Fifteen European countries—and about 300 million people—use the same currency. Using euros, tourists and locals can easily compare prices of goods between countries. And we no longer lose money or time changing money at borders.

Not all European countries have switched to euros. As of now, major holdouts include Britain, Denmark, Norway, Sweden, and Switzerland. Each of these countries has its reasons for choosing not to use euros (for example, see the sidebar on Switzerland). Other countries, which have only recently joined the European

*Use euros in €uroland: Austria, Belgium, Finland, France, Germany, Greece, Ireland, Italy, Luxembourg, Netherlands, Portugal, and Spain. Estonia, Lithuania, and Slovenia hope to join in 2007, with more €astern €uropean additions planned in the coming years.*

### Why No Swiss Euros?

You can't help but wonder why the efficient Swiss are stubbornly hanging on to their old franc while surrounded by countries basking in the ease and convenience of the euro. The answer is simple: It's too expensive for the Swiss to change. The Swiss enjoy lower mortgage interest rates and a more stable currency than the rest of Europe. But even more importantly, a huge part of the Swiss economy is based on providing a safe and secret place for wealthy people from around the world to stash their money. When bank fees are figured in, people who "save" in Swiss banks actually earn negative interest—they *pay* the Swiss to keep their money. Compliance with European Union regulations in order to join the euro zone would mean the end of Switzerland's secret banking industry.

Even so, if you're just passing through and don't want to change your euros, you'll find most Swiss businesses in tourist zones are happy to accept euro bills (and often give change in francs).

Union—such as the Czech Republic, Poland, and Hungary—will adopt the euro in the next few years.

But even in some non-Euroland countries, the euro is commonly used. For example, some Swiss ATMs give euros, most prices are listed in both Swiss francs and euros, and travelers can get by in that country with euro cash.

## Cash Machines (ATMs)

Throughout Europe, cash machines (ATMs) are the standard way for travelers to get local currency. European ATMs work like your hometown machine and always have English-language instructions. Using your debit card with an ATM takes dollars directly from your bank account at home and gives you that country's cash. You'll pay fees, but you'll still get a better rate than you would for traveler's checks.

Ideally, use your debit card to take money out of ATMs. You can use a credit card, but you'll pay more (described below). For an explanation of the different cards, see the "Types of Cards" sidebar.

ATM transactions using bank-issued debit cards come with various fees. Your bank may levy a flat $1.50–5 transaction fee each time you use an ATM, and may also charge a percentage for the conversion (1–3 percent); the ATM you use might charge its own fee, too. If your bank charges a flat fee, make fewer visits to the ATM and withdraw

## Types of Cards

You can withdraw money from an ATM with different types of cards.

An **ATM card** is issued by your bank and draws money directly out of your bank account. It does not have a credit-card company logo (such as Visa or MasterCard), which makes it less widely accepted. Most ATM cards have a logo on the back for either Plus (affiliated with Visa) or Cirrus (affiliated with MasterCard). You'll have to look for an ATM with a corresponding logo to be sure it'll work.

A **debit card** (sometimes called a "check card") works the same way (it's issued by your bank, and draws cash from your bank account). However, it's more versatile because it has a credit-card logo (such as Visa or MasterCard), which means it can also be used for making purchases. This is the best option for getting cash in Europe. For more details, see "Cash Machines (ATMs)" on the previous page. In a pinch, debit cards with a Visa or MasterCard logo can be used for over-the-counter cash advances (with a fee) at banks that accept those credit cards. Note that you can also buy prepaid debit cards (described on page 171).

A **credit card** does not draw money from an account; rather, you are billed at the end of each month for any purchases or withdrawals you've made with it. Most credit cards work in ATMs (provided you know the PIN code)—but you're technically getting a cash advance, which is expensive. The second you pull your cash out of the ATM, you're immediately into the high-interest category with your new credit-card debt. If you want to use your credit card for ATM transactions without incurring this interest expense, you can pre-pay the account.

Some European countries are beginning to introduce credit and debit cards with embedded **"smart chips."** You may see signs or keypads referring to this new technology. For example, British cardholders must enter a PIN in order to use new chip-embedded credit cards in retail stores. But non-chip cards, such as those used by most tourists, will still spit out a receipt for you to sign.

larger amounts. (Some major US banks partner with "corresponding" European bank chains, meaning that you can use those ATMs with no fees at all—ask your bank.) Other fees may apply; for all the details, see "The Sleaze of Fees" sidebar later in this chapter. These additional expenses can pile up. Quiz your bank to figure out exactly what you're paying for each withdrawal.

Note that if you use a credit card for ATM transactions, it's technically a "cash advance" rather than a "withdrawal"—and subject to an additional cash-advance fee. If you plan to use a credit card rather than a debit card for ATM transactions, ask your bank about all the associated charges.

Confirm with your bank that your card will work in Europe and alert them that you'll be making withdrawals while traveling—otherwise, the bank might freeze your card if it detects unusual spending patterns. (Some credit-card companies do the same; it can be smart to inform them of your plans as well.) You don't have to give them specific dates you'll be away. Just saying you'll be in France in July is sufficient.

Since European keypads have only numbers, you will need to know your personal identification number (PIN) by number rather than by letter; derive the numbers from your hometown bank's keypad. Plan on being able to withdraw money only from your checking account. You might be able to dip into your savings account or transfer funds between accounts, but don't count on it.

*How to use a European cash machine: Insert card, pull out cash.*

Bringing two different cards provides a backup if one is demagnetized or eaten by a machine. Make sure the validity period of your card won't expire before your trip ends.

Ask your bank how much you can withdraw per 24 hours. Note that foreign ATMs may not let you withdraw your daily limit. Many machines have a small maximum, forcing you to make several withdrawals and incur several fees to get the amount you want. When choosing how much to withdraw from a cash machine, request a big amount on the small chance you'll get it. If you're lucky and the machine complies, you'll save on fees. If you're denied, don't take it personally. Try again, requesting a smaller amount. Few ATM receipts list the exchange rate, and some machines don't dispense receipts at all.

In some less expensive countries (especially in Eastern Europe), an ATM may give you high-denomination bills, which can be difficult to break. My strategy: Request an odd amount of money from the ATM (such as 2,800 Kč instead of 3,000 Kč). If the machine gives you big bills anyway, go immediately to a bank to break them.

If you're looking for an ATM, ask for a *distributeur automatique* in France, a cashpoint in the UK, and a *Bankomat* just about everywhere else. Many European banks have their ATMs in a small entry lobby, which protects users from snoopers and bad weather. When the bank is closed, the door to this lobby may be locked. In this case, look for a credit-card-size slot next to the door. Simply insert or swipe your debit or credit card in this slot, and the door should automatically open.

### Prepaid Debit Cards

Prepaid debit cards are another option for getting funds during your trip. Before you go, load up your card with the money you'll need, then withdraw it as you travel. These cards work in ATMs just like a bank-issued debit card, but provide more security because they aren't connected to your checking account. Let's say you plan instead to finance your trip with a Visa debit card linked to your checking account. If the card is stolen, the thief can use it like a credit card—potentially draining your entire account. But some prepaid cards work only in ATMs, so the thief must also know your PIN to get at the money (unlikely, unless you foolishly write your PIN on your card or keep it in your wallet).

Prepaid cards are convenient for parents, who can send one along with their kids and reload it for them as needed. But the cards also have disadvantages. As with any other card, fees and service charges can add up—for buying the card ($5–15), reloading the card ($5), international transactions ($2–3), overdrawing your account, "cashing out" and canceling the card at the end of your trip, and others. And if the card is lost, it's virtually impossible to get a new one on the road in Europe, so bringing some form of backup is wise.

Many credit-card companies sell prepaid cards (there are links to several at www.mastercard.com), but the best deals are offered by AAA (versatile, with a Visa logo; www.aaa.com/prepaidcards) and American Express (can only be used at ATMs and merchants that accept AmEx, www.americanexpress.com).

If you like the peace of mind that prepaid debit cards offer, go for it. But to me, they seem needlessly complicated—I just take my bank-issued debit card and keep it safe in my money belt.

### Cash-to-Cash Machines

There are 24-hour money munchers in big cities all over Europe. These machines look like ATMs, but you feed in cash instead of a card. At midnight in Florence, you can push in a $20 bill (or any major European currency) and, assuming the president (or royalty) is on the right side, the correct value of local currency will tumble out. They are handy, open all the time, and usually offer bad rates. These are a novelty, useful only

### The Sleaze of Fees

Recently, travelers returning from Europe have opened their mail to discover they paid more for their trip than they thought they had. Over the last couple years, banks have dramatically increased the fees they charge for overseas transactions using credit and debit cards. While these fees are legal, they're basically a slimy way for credit-card companies to wring a few more dollars out of their customers.

There are different types of fees. For years, Visa and MasterCard have levied a 1 percent fee on international transactions. Recently, banks that issue those cards are tacking on an additional 1–2 percent. These are often called "currency-conversion fees" or "foreign-transaction fees." For details on fees associated with using your card for ATM withdrawals, see "Cash Machines (ATMs)" earlier in this chapter.

So, how can a smart traveler avoid (or at least reduce) these fees? Here are a few suggestions:

**Ask about fees.** While fees can sometimes be built into the price on your statement, it's increasingly more common that they're broken out as line items to help the consumer know what they're paying. Even so, it's smart to make a call before your trip to get the whole story: Carefully quiz your bank or credit-card company about what fees come with using their card overseas. Even if your card charged no fees the last time you went to Europe, there's a good chance it does now. Call and ask.

**If you're getting a bad deal, get a new credit card.** Some companies offer far lower international fees than others—and a handful don't charge any fees at all. Capital One has a particularly good reputation for international transactions (www.capitalone.com). If you're going on a long trip, do some research and consider taking out a card just for international purchases.

if you want a new experience or if you're too tired to find a regular cash machine.

## Buying on Plastic

Credit cards work fine throughout Europe (at hotels, shops, travel agencies, and so on), although more and more merchants are establishing a $30 minimum. Visa and MasterCard are the most widely accepted. American Express is less commonly accepted (because it costs merchants more) but is popular with some travelers for its extra services. The Discover card is completely unknown in Europe.

**Avoid "dynamic currency conversion."** Some merchants—capitalizing on the fact that many Americans are intimidated by unusual currencies—cheerfully charge you their prices in dollars. This seems like a nice service, but you'll actually end up paying more. Usually the dollar price is based on a lousy exchange rate (which can be set wherever the merchant likes—generally about 3 percent worse than the prevailing inter-bank rate). To make matters worse, even though you're paying in "dollars," your credit-card company may still levy its 2–3 percent "foreign transaction fee." Some merchants may disagree, but according to Visa, you have the right to decline this service at the store and have your transaction go through using local currency. Your transaction will then be converted by Visa or MasterCard at or near the more favorable inter-bank rate.

**Online purchases can be subject to fees.** If you're buying from an international Web site, you can still get hit with currency conversion fees—even if you make the transaction while in the US. You might be able to bypass the fee if the vendor has a US office (in which case, call the US phone number rather than booking online).

**The bottom line.** Here's the best formula for saving money as you travel: Pay for as much as possible with cash (use a bank that charges low rates for international ATM transactions, and withdraw large amounts at each transaction—keeping the cash safe in your money belt). When using a credit card, try to use a card with the lowest possible international fees, and insist that your transactions be charged in the local currency—not dollars. Then smile and enjoy your trip, feeling very clever for avoiding so much unnecessary expense.

Plastic fans gloat that you get a better exchange rate by using your card. This may be true, if you have the right kind of card. But there are plenty of fees involved (see "The Sleaze of Fees" sidebar, above). Also, realize that you're buying from businesses that have enough slack in their prices to absorb the fees the credit-card company charges the merchant (2–5 percent). In other words, those who travel on their plastic may be getting a better rate, but on a worse price.

As more and more consumers believe they are getting "free use of the bank's money," we're all absorbing the percentage the credit-card companies are making in higher purchase prices. Fully aware of the percentage they lose, merchants and hoteliers—particularly in southern Europe—sometimes give you a better deal if you offer to pay with cash instead of a credit card (cash payments also allow them to avoid reporting—and being taxed on—all their income).

I use my credit card for booking hotel reservations by phone, making major purchases (such as car rentals and plane tickets), and paying for things near the end of my trip to avoid another visit to the ATM. But a dependence on plastic reshapes the Europe you experience. Pedro's Pension, the friendly guide at the cathedral, and most merchants in the market don't take credit cards. Going through the Back Door requires hard local cash.

## Identity Theft

Identity theft—when a criminal steals your personal information and uses it fraudulently—has become aggravatingly common. The most susceptible pieces of information are your Social Security number and birth date. With just these two tidbits plus your full name, someone can grab your identity. Here are some tips you can use, especially while overseas, to protect yourself.

**Protect your credit and debit cards.** Take as few credit and debit cards with you as possible, and keep them safely in your money belt. (For more tips on money belts and foiling pickpockets, see Chapter 23: Outsmarting Thieves.) Don't carry identification that includes your Social Security number unless you absolutely must.

**Safeguard your PIN code.** Memorize your Personal Identification Number; you'd be surprised at how many people write it on their card (which is extremely dangerous). "Shoulder surfing"—a thief watching you as you type your PIN into a keypad—is a common problem. When entering your PIN, carefully block other people's view of the keypad, covering it with your free hand.

**Use your credit card sparingly.** Restaurant servers and shop clerks might try to steal your credit-card information, sometimes by swiping it in a special machine that reads the card (a technique called "skimming"). Pay in cash. Withdraw sizable amounts of local cash from ATMs (stow it in your money belt to protect against pickpockets) so you can pay with paper whenever possible. When you do use your credit card for purchases, check your receipts. If your credit card number is listed on the receipt, tear it up before you toss it.

**Use your debit card even more sparingly.** Use your debit card only for cash-machine withdrawals. To make purchases, pay with cash or your credit card. Because a debit card draws funds directly out of your bank account, charges incurred by a thief are scary—it's *your* money that's gone, not the credit-card company's. You're usually liable for only $50, but it's still worrisome. Talk to your bank about setting a daily withdrawal limit for your ATM or debit card—but note that the limit applies to cash-machine withdrawals, not purchases.

**Make photocopies of your passport and credit cards** (front and back). They'll be easier to replace in case of loss or theft. However, guard these photocopies as carefully as you would the originals. I hide mine in a second money belt clipped into the bottom of my luggage (don't tell anyone). Bring along the phone numbers of your bank and credit-card company.

**Be careful what you e-mail.** Don't send sensitive information (such as your credit-card numbers or Social Security number) in an e-mail message from any Internet terminal, including your personal computer. It's better to call or fax. (Some people e-mail their credit-card number in two chunks, via two separate e-mail messages.) Some forms on the World Wide Web request this type of personal information. Only enter and submit it if you're confident of the Web site's authenticity and if you have a secure connection. (If the Web address begins with *https:* rather than *http:*, it's secure.) Don't store sensitive personal information in your Web-based e-mail account, which can be hacked into.

**Be suspicious, especially on the Internet.** Trust a phone call or e-mail only if you've initiated the communication. For example, if "your bank" sends you an e-mail message claiming they need to confirm details of your account, call the bank to confirm. Sometimes the sender of the message may be "phishing" or "spoofing"—pretending to be a legitimate organization by carefully imitating the look and content of the actual organization.

**Monitor your accounts.** Upon returning home, verify the balance and charges on your debit and credit cards (check this information online from a secure computer, or call to ask). Whether or not you've recently been traveling, it's always smart to periodically check all of your accounts. Get a credit report to be sure that your credit history is accurate. (You can get one free each year—see www.annualcreditreport.com.)

**What to do if your identity is stolen:** If your credit or debit card is stolen, you'll probably know right away. Call immediately to cancel it (see "Damage Control for Lost Cards," on the next page). Other types of identity theft may take a long time—even months—to surface. In the event of any type of identity theft, file a police report (and send copies to creditors). Contact any one of the three major credit-reporting agencies to report the fraud (TransUnion, www.transunion.com, tel. 800-888-4213;

### Damage Control for Lost Cards

If you lose your credit, debit, or ATM card, you can stop people from using your card by reporting the loss immediately to the respective global customer-assistance centers. Call these 24-hour US numbers collect: Visa (410/581-9994), MasterCard (636/722-7111), and American Express (336/393-1111).

Have, at a minimum, the following information ready: the name of the financial institution that issued you the card, along with the type of card (classic, platinum, or whatever). Providing the following information will allow for a quicker cancellation of your missing card: full card number, whether you are the primary or secondary cardholder, the cardholder's name exactly as printed on the card, billing address, home phone number, circumstances of the loss or theft, and identification verification (your birthdate, your mother's maiden name, or your Social Security number—memorize this, don't carry a copy). If you are the secondary cardholder, you'll also need to provide the primary cardholder's identification-verification details. You can generally receive a temporary card within two or three business days in Europe.

If you promptly report your card lost or stolen, you typically won't be responsible for any unauthorized transactions on your account, although many banks charge a liability fee of $50.

Experian, www.experian.com, tel. 888-397-3742; or Equifax, www.equifax.com, tel. 888-766-0008). Also consider filing a report with the Federal Trade Commission (see www.consumer.gov/idtheft) and the Office of the Inspector General (www.ssa.gov/oig/guidelin.htm). Other good resources are the Identity Theft Resource Center (www.idtheftcenter.org) and the Privacy Rights Clearinghouse (www.privacyrights.org).

As with preventing other kinds of theft, the key here is to keep your wits about you to protect your personal information. With a few precautions, you can spend your time in Europe lingering over a gelato instead of stressing over identity theft.

## Traveler's Checks

Ubiquitous ATMs make traveler's checks unnecessary, but some people still prefer them. Traveler's checks function almost like cash but are replaceable if lost or stolen. You need to choose the company, the currency, and denominations.

Use whichever big company's checks (American Express, Visa) you can get without the typical 1.5 percent fee. Buy your checks at a local bank, AAA office (members get Visa checks for no fee), or American Express office (AmEx Gold and Platinum cardholders get checks for no fee). Any legitimate check is good at banks, but it's helpful when you're in a jam to have a well-known check that private parties and small shops will recognize and honor.

Understand the refund policy. Lost or stolen traveler's checks are replaceable only if you keep track of the serial numbers and know exactly which checks you've cashed and lost. Leave a photocopy of all your check numbers (along with photocopies of your passport, plane ticket, and bankcards) with someone at home, in your luggage, and in your wallet. Use checks in numerical order and update your list regularly as you cash them. Get a police report after any theft, and report the loss to your issuing bank within 24 hours. (Travel with their emergency phone numbers.)

For simplicity, buy checks in US dollars. Get a mix of denominations—large checks ($100, $500) save on signing and bulk. Since many banks (especially in Scandinavia) charge a $2–4 fee per check rather than per transaction, cashing large denominations can save money. Also bring a few small checks ($20, $50), which can be easier to cash.

## Cash

**Carry plenty of cash.** American cash in your money belt comes in handy for emergencies, such as when banks go on strike or your ATM card stops working. I carry $400 as a backup. I've been in Greece and Ireland when every bank went on strike, shutting down without warning. But hard cash is cash. People always know roughly what a dollar is worth, and you can always sell it.

**Use local money.** Many Americans exclaim gleefully, "Gee, they accept dollars! There's no need to change money." Without knowing it, they're changing money—at a lousy rate—every time they buy something with their dollars. (Even big corporations engage in this practice—for more details, see the information on "dynamic currency conversion" in "The Sleaze of Fees" sidebar earlier in this chapter.) Anyone on a budget will stretch it by using hard local cash. Local hotels and small businesses—which suffer big bank fees when they take your credit card, dollars, or traveler's checks—prefer local cash.

Figure out the money. To "ugly Americans," foreign money is "funny money." They never figure it out, get no respect from the locals, and are constantly ripped off. Local currencies are all logical. Each system is decimalized just like ours. There are a hundred "little ones" (cents, pence, groszy, stotinki) in every "big one" (euro, pound, złoty, lev). Only the names have been changed—to confuse the tourist. Get a good sampling of coins after you arrive, and in two minutes you'll be comfortable with the "nickels, dimes, and quarters" of each new currency.

A currency-converting calculator isn't worth the trouble. Very roughly figure out what the unit of currency (euros, kroner, Swiss francs, or whatever) is worth in American cents. For example, if there are 1.30 Swiss francs (CHF) in a dollar, each Swiss franc is worth about $0.75. If a strudel costs 5 CHF, then it costs five times $0.75, or about $3.75. Ten Swiss francs is about $7.50 and 250 CHF = roughly $190 (250 x $0.75, or 250 less one-quarter). Quiz yourself. Soon it'll be second nature. Survival on a budget is easier when you're comfortable with the local currency.

**Assume you'll be shortchanged.** In banks, restaurants, at ticket booths, everywhere—assume you'll be shortchanged if you don't do your own figuring. Some people who spend their lives sitting in booths for eight hours a day taking money from strangers have no problem stealing from dumb tourists who don't know the local currency. For 10 minutes I observed a man in the Rome metro shortchanging half of the tourists who went through his turnstile. Half of those shortchanged caught him and got their correct change with apologies. Overall, about 25 percent didn't notice and went home saying, "*Mamma mia,* Italy is really expensive."

**Paper money of any country is good at banks anywhere.** Dollars are not sacred. If you leave Norway with paper money, that 100-kroner note is just as convertible as dollars at any European bank or exchange office. These days, even Polish złoty and Croatian kuna can be converted throughout Europe. Many people change excess local money back to dollars before they leave a country, then change those dollars into the next country's currency (e.g., they change euros to dollars in France, then dollars to pounds in Britain). This double changing is unnecessary and expensive. It can be handy, however, to change your remaining local currency into the next country's currency before leaving a country.

**Coins are generally worthless outside their country.** Since big-value coins are common in Europe, exporting a pocketful of change can be an expensive mistake. Spend them (on postcards, a newspaper, a phone call home, or food or drink for the train ride), change them into bills, or give them away. Otherwise, you've just bought a bunch of souvenirs. Note that while euro coins each have a national side (indicating where they were minted), they are perfectly good in any "euro country."

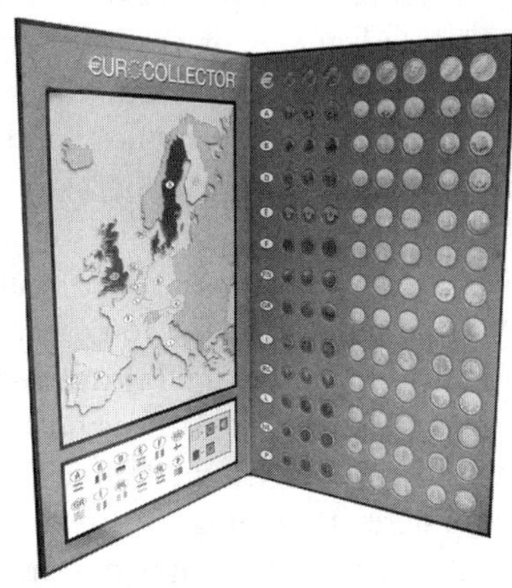


*Avid coin collectors have the joy of filling in coin books, as the eight denominations of euro coins from 12 different countries (and counting) make for a fun frontier in coin collecting. Europhiles can buy these books in Europe and chart their travels by gradually completing the collection.*

**Getting back to dollars at the end of your trip.** At your final European country, gather any leftover bills and change them into that last currency to help fund your trip. If you have any foreign cash left before you fly home, change it into dollars at the European airport or simply spend it at the airport. You might get a few more dollars for that last smattering of foreign bills from your hometown bank, but it's clean and convenient to simply fly home with nothing but dollars in your pocket.

# 15. YOUR BUDGET

Most of today's Europe is more expensive than the United States, and the sloppy traveler can blow a small fortune in a hurry. If you travel like a big shot, you'd better be loaded. You can live well in Europe on a budget, but especially with the value of our dollar so low, it will take some artistry.

I'm cautious about sending people to Europe with too much confidence and not enough money. The tips in this book are tried and tested in the worst circumstances every year. And my feedback from Back Door travelers makes it clear: Enjoying Europe through the Back Door can be done—by you.

## Budget Breakdown

**Airfare:** Flying to Europe is a bargain. Get a good travel agent, understand all your options, and make the best choice. (See Chapter 10: Travel Agents and Flights.) Traveling outside of peak season will save you several hundred dollars.

**Surface Transportation:** Transportation in Europe is reasonable if you take advantage of a railpass or split a car rental between three or four people. (See "Car or Train?" on page 144.) Transportation expenses are generally fixed. People who spend $8,000 for their vacation spend about the same on transportation as do those whose trips cost half as much. Your budget should not dictate how freely you travel in Europe. If you want to go somewhere, do it, but take advantage of whatever money-saving options you can. You came to travel.

**Sightseeing/Entertainment:** Sightseeing costs have risen faster than anything else. Admissions to major attractions are $5–15; smaller sights are $2–5. Concerts, plays, and bus tours cost about $30. Don't skimp here. This category directly powers most of the experiences all the other expenses are designed to make possible.

**Shopping/Miscellany:** Figure about $2 each for bus and subway rides. Shopping can vary in cost from nearly nothing to a small fortune. Good budget travelers find that this category has little to do with assembling a trip full of lifelong and wonderful memories.

**Room and Board:** The area that will make or break your budget—where you have the most control—is in your eating and sleeping expenses. In 2007, smart travelers can thrive on $100 a day for room and board. Figure on $65 per person in a $130 hotel double with breakfast, $10 apiece for lunch, and $20 for dinner. That leaves you $5 for cappuccino or gelato. Remember that these prices are averages; as a general rule, you'll pay less in the countryside and more in big cities.

The key is finding budget alternatives to international-class hotels and restaurants, and consuming only what you want to consume. If you want real tablecloths and black-tie waiters, your tomato salad will cost 20 times what it costs in the market. If you want a suite with fancy room service and chocolate on your pillow, you'll pay in a day what many travelers pay in a week.

My idea of "cheap" is simple but not sleazy. My budget philosophy is to never sacrifice safety, reasonable cleanliness, sleep, or nutrition to save money. I go to safe, central, friendly, local-style hotels, and I shun swimming pools, people in uniforms, and transplanted American niceties in favor of an opportunity to travel as a temporary European. Unfortunately, simple is subversive these days, and the system is bullying even cozy Scottish bed-and-breakfast places into more and more facilities, more and more debt, and higher and higher prices.

I traveled every summer for years on a part-time piano teacher's income (and, boy, was she upset). I ate and slept great by learning and following these guidelines.

## Trip Costs

In 2007, you can travel comfortably for a month for $4,800—not including your airfare ($700–1,000). If you have extra money, it's more fun to spend it in Europe.

Allow:

| | |
|---|---|
| $900 | for a 15-days-in-two-months Eurailpass or split car rental |
| 700 | for sightseeing and entertainment |
| 200 | for shopping and miscellany |
| +3,000 | for room and board ($100 a day) |
| $4,800 | |

Students or rock-bottom budget travelers can enjoy a month of Europe at least as much for about a third less—$2,700 plus airfare.

Allow:

| | |
|---|---|
| $700 | for a one-month youth Eurailpass |
| 400 | for sightseeing and entertainment |
| 100 | for shopping and miscellany |
| +1,500 | for room and board ($50 a day)* |
| $2,700 | |

*$25 for a dorm bed or a bed in a private home with breakfast, $10 for a picnic lunch, $15 for dinner.

## Eating and Sleeping on a Budget

You can get eight good, safe hours of sleep and three square meals in Europe for $50 a day if your budget requires it. If your budget is tight, remember these rules of thumb.

**Minimize the use of hotels and restaurants.** Enjoying the sights and culture of Europe has nothing to do with how much you're spending to eat and sleep. Take advantage of each country's many alternatives to hotels and restaurants. If your budget dictated, you could have a great trip without hotels and restaurants—and probably learn, experience, and enjoy more than most tourists.

**Budget for price variances.** Prices as much as double from south to north. Budget more for the north and get by on less than your daily allowance in Spain, Portugal, and Greece. Exercise those budget alternatives where they'll save you the most money. A hostel saves $10 in

Crete and $50 in Finland. In Scandinavia I picnic, walk, and sleep on trains, but I live like a king in southern Europe, where my splurge dollars go the farthest. And if your trip will last only as long as your money does, travel fast in the north and hang out in the south. On the other hand, be warned that famous places in Italy can be as expensive as the north.

**Swallow pride and save money.** This is a personal matter, depending largely on how much pride and money you have. Many people cringe every time I use the word "cheap"; others appreciate the directness. I'm not talking about begging and groveling around Europe. I'm talking about drinking tap water at restaurants ($4 saved) and choosing a hotel room with a shower down the hall ($30 saved).

*Lunch for $10,* no problema

Find out the complete price before ordering anything, and say "no thanks" if the price isn't right. Expect equal and fair treatment as a tourist. When appropriate, fight the price, set a limit, and search on. Remember, even if the same thing would cost much more at home, the local rate should prevail. If you act like a rich fool, you're likely to be treated as one.

**Avoid the tourist centers.** The best values are not in the places that boast in neon, We Speak English. Find places that earn a loyal local following. You'll get more for your money. If you do follow the tourists, follow the savvy Germans; never follow tour groups.

**Patronize family-run places.** Small family-run places have cheaper labor (Mom, Pop, and the kids) and care more about their customers. For these reasons, they generally offer the best values for eating and sleeping.

**Adapt to European tastes.** Most unhappy people I meet in my travels could find the source of their problems in their own stubborn desire to find the United States in Europe. If you accept and at least try doing things the European way, besides saving money you'll be happier and learn more on your trip. You cannot expect the local people to accept you warmly if you don't accept them. Things are different in Europe—that's why you go. European travel is a package deal. Accept the good with the "bad." If you require the comforts of home, that's where you'll be happiest.

**Be a good guest.** To Europeans, Americans occasionally act as though they "just got off the boat" (putting shoes on the train seats, chilling grapes in the bidet, talking loudly in restaurants, taking flash photos and using camcorders during Mass, hanging wet clothes out the hotel window, and consuming energy like it's cheap and ours to waste). The Europeans you'll deal with can sour or sweeten your experience, depending on how they react to you. When you're in good favor with the receptionist (or whomever), you can make things happen that people who try to let their bucks do all the talking can't.

Each year as I update my books, I hear over and over in my recommended hotels and private homes that my readers are the most considerate and fun-to-have guests. Thank you for traveling sensitive to the culture and as temporary locals. It's fun to follow you in my travels.

# 16. SHOPPING

Gift shopping is getting very expensive. I remember buying a cuckoo clock 20 years ago for $5. Now a Happy Meal at the Munich McDonald's costs that much.

## Souvenir Strategies

**Shop in countries where your dollar stretches farthest.** Shop in Turkey, Morocco, Portugal, Spain, Greece, and Eastern Europe. For the price of a four-inch pewter Viking ship in Norway, you can buy a real boat in Turkey.

**Shop at flea markets.** The most colorful shopping in Europe is at its flea markets. Among the best are Amsterdam's Waterlooplein (daily except Sunday), London's Portobello Market (daily except Sunday, best on Saturday), Madrid's El Rastro (Sunday), and Paris' Puces St. Ouen (Saturday through Monday). Flea markets anywhere have soft prices. Bargain like mad. Pickpockets love flea markets—wear your money belt and watch your day bag.

*Boxloads of* Davids *await busloads of tourists.*

**Check out large department stores.** These often have a souvenir section with standard local knickknacks and postcards at prices way below the cute little tourist shops.

**Stay in control.** Shopping is an important part of the average person's trip, but, all too often, slick marketing and romantic window displays can succeed in shifting the entire focus of your vacation toward things in the tourist shops. (It's a lucrative business. Many souvenir merchants in Italy work through the tourist season, then retire for the rest of the year.) This sort of tourist brainwashing can turn you into one of the many people who set out to see and experience Europe but find themselves wandering in a trancelike search for signs announcing *Duty-Free Shopping.* I've seen half the members of a British Halls of Parliament guided tour skip out to survey an enticing display of plastic "bobby" hats, Big Ben briefs, and Union Jack panties. Even if the sign says, "Keep Italy green, spend dollars," don't let your trip degenerate into a glorified shopping spree.

*Window-shopping the extravagant April Fair dresses in Sevilla can be a sightseeing treat.*

**Ask yourself if your enthusiasm is merited.** More often than not, you can pick up a very similar item of better quality for a cheaper price at home. Unless you're a real romantic, the thrill of where you bought something fades long before the item's usefulness. My life has more room for a functional souvenir than for a useless symbol of a place I visited. Even thoughtful shoppers go overboard. I have several large boxes in my attic labeled "great souvenirs."

**Try to restrict your shopping to a stipulated time.** Most people have an idea of what they want to buy in each country. Set aside one day to shop in each country, and stick to it. This way you avoid drifting through your trip thinking only of souvenirs.

**To pack light, shop at the end of your trip.** Consider enjoying the luxury of not being a shopper for 80 percent of your trip and ending in the best shopping country where you go hog-wild and fly home heavy. One summer I had a 16-pound backpack and nothing more until the last week of my trip when, in Spain and Morocco, I managed to accumulate two medieval chairs, two sets of bongos, a camelhair coat, swords, a mace, and a lace tablecloth.

**Good souvenirs:** My favorites are books (a great value all over Europe, with many editions impossible to find in the US), local crafts (well explained in guidebooks, such as hand-knit sweaters in Portugal or Ireland, glass in Sweden, lace in Belgium), strange stuffed animals (at flea markets), CDs of music I heard live, posters (one sturdy tube stores

8–10 posters safely), clothing, photographs I've taken, and memories whittled carefully into my journal.

## Value-Added Tax (VAT) Refunds

Every year, tourists visiting Europe leave behind millions of dollars of refundable sales taxes. There's a reason why visitors end up donating their dollars to their host countries: VAT refunds often aren't worth the trouble. You could burn a couple hours collecting a few bucks back from a $25 purchase.

But if you're a die-hard shopper who can multitask, you can recover a good chunk of the hefty sales tax. The process isn't difficult; you just have to get the necessary documents from the retailer, carry your purchase with you, and track down the right folks at the airport, port, or border when you leave. These days you've got to check in early at the airport; this will give you something to do while you're hanging around.

Ideally—if you're charming, lucky, and have your passport handy—you can talk a merchant into taking the tax off the price right there at the store. But even so, you'll still need to get the proper documents stamped when you depart Europe.

Europe's Value-Added Tax ranges from 7.6–25 percent per country, averaging about 20 percent overall. Rates change, so you'll want to check with merchants when you're there.

Unlike business travelers, tourists aren't entitled to refunds on the tax they spend on hotels and meals. Still, you can get back most of the tax you paid on merchandise such as clothes, cuckoos, and crystal.

All European countries except Ireland require a minimum purchase for a refund, ranging from about $25 to several hundred dollars. You typically have to ring up the minimum at one retailer—you can't add up your purchases from various shops to reach the required amount—so you benefit from finding one spot where you can buy big. If you'll be on the road for a long time, shop near the end of your trip. You need to collect your refund within three months of your purchase.

Assuming you meet these criteria and you're still game, here's the drill. The details vary per country, but you follow the same basic steps.

**Shop at stores that know the ropes.** Retailers choose whether to participate in the VAT-refund scheme. Most tourist-oriented stores do; often you'll see a sign in the window or by the cash register (if not, ask). It'd be a shame to spend big bucks at a place and not have a chance of getting a refund. You'll also want to know whether the merchant handles refunds directly (which means a potentially bigger refund for you, but more hassle) or uses a service (quicker and easier, but they take a cut).

## VAT Rates and Minimum Purchases Required to Qualify for Refunds

| Country Of Purchase | Vat Standard Rate* | Minimum in Local Currency | Minimum in US Dollars |
|---|---|---|---|
| Austria | 20% | €75.01 | $92 |
| Belgium | 21% | €125.01 | $152 |
| Croatia | 18.5% | 501 HRK | $83 |
| Czech Republic | 19% | 2,000 Kč | $85 |
| Denmark | 25% | 300 DKK | $50 |
| Estonia | 18% | 2,500 EEK | $195 |
| Finland | 22% | €40 | $50 |
| France | 19.6% | €175 | $214 |
| Germany | 16% | €25 | $30.50 |
| Great Britain | 17.5% | £20 (varies) | $35.50 |
| Greece | 18% | €120 | $146 |
| Hungary | 20% | 45,000 HUF | $215 |
| Ireland | 21% | — | — |
| Italy | 20% | €155 | $190 |
| Luxembourg | 15% | €124 | $151 |
| Netherlands | 19% | €137 | $167 |
| Norway | 25% | 315 NOK | $48 |
| Poland | 22% | 200 zł | $63 |
| Portugal | 21% | €57–60 | $70–73 |
| Slovakia | 19% | 5,000 Sk | $163 |
| Slovenia | 20% | 15,001 SIT | $76 |
| Spain | 16% | €90.15 | $110 |
| Sweden | 25% | 200 SEK | $26 |
| Switzerland | 7.6% | 400 SF | $312.50 |
| Turkey | 18% | 118 YTL | $91 |

* The VAT Standard Rates listed above—while listed as exact amounts—are intended to give you an idea of the rates and minimums involved. But VAT rates fluctuate based on many factors, including what kind of item you are buying. Your refund will also likely be less than the above rate, especially if it's subject to processing fees.

**Get the documents.** When you make your purchase, have the merchant fill out the necessary refund document, called a "cheque." You'll need to present your passport. Make sure the paperwork is done before you leave the store so there's nothing important missing. If they leave any blanks for you to fill out, be sure you understand what goes where. Attach your receipt to the form and stash it in a safe place.

What if the store ships your purchase to your home? You can still collect a refund, but the process varies by country. In Italy, the shipper gets your customs stamp for you and sends you the documents. In Germany, you take the documents home and then get a stamp at a German consulate or embassy once you receive the goods. Ask at the shop where you make your purchase how it works in their country.

**Know where to get your refund.** If you buy merchandise in a European Union country and you're bringing the goods home with you, process your documents at your last stop in the EU, regardless of where you made your purchases. So if you buy sweaters in Denmark, pants in France, and shoes in Italy, and you're flying home from Greece, get your documents stamped in Athens. Be aware that if the currencies are different in the country where you made your purchase and where you process your refund—say, pounds and euros—you may have to pay an extra conversion fee. And don't forget—Switzerland, Norway, Croatia, and Turkey are not in the EU, so if you buy in one of those countries, get your documents stamped before you leave that particular country.

**Bring your goods—unused—to the airport or border crossing.** You're not supposed to use your purchased goods before you present them at customs. Some retailers, particularly those in Scandinavia, will staple and seal the shopping bag to keep people from cheating. If you show up at customs wearing your new shoes, officials might look the other way—or deny you a refund.

**Arrive early.** You'll have to wait in a special line at customs and then, if you're collecting your refund right away, at the refund office. In smaller airports, ports, and less-trafficked border crossings, finding the right customs agent can be tough. If you run out of time and have to leave without the stamp, you're probably out of luck. A few countries allow you to try to recover the refund through the embassy in your home country. Regardless, it's a lot of trouble.

**Get your documents stamped.** The customs export officer will stamp your documents after you present your purchased goods to verify that you are, indeed, exporting your purchase (try to keep the goods in your carry-on). Some officials will stamp your documents even if you haven't got your purchase with you, but others are stricter. If you bought something potentially dangerous (such as a set of knives in Spain) that you probably wouldn't even be allowed to carry on a plane, chase down a customs official to have a look before you check your bag.

**Collect the cash—sooner or later.** Once you get your form stamped by customs, you'll need to return it to the retailer or its representative at the airport, port, or border crossing. Many merchants work with a service such as Global Refund or Premier Tax Free, which have offices where you present your stamped document. They'll extract about 4 percent for their services, but it can be worth it—often they'll give you your refund in your currency of choice, right then and there. Otherwise, they'll credit the refund to your card (within one or two billing cycles). If the retailer handles VAT refunds directly, it's up to you to contact the merchant for your refund. You can mail the documents from home, or quicker, from your point of departure (using a stamped, addressed envelope you've prepared or one that's been provided by the merchant)—and then wait. It could be months. If the refund check comes in a foreign currency, you may have to pay $30 or so to get your bank to cash it.

**Don't count on it.** My readers have reported that, even when following all of the instructions carefully, sometimes the VAT refund just doesn't pan out. (For example, they have all the paperwork ready when they get to the airport—but can't find the customs official to process it.) These problems seem most prevalent in Italy. Your best odds are for buying from a merchant who knows how to deal with the red tape for you—but even that is not infallible.

Only you can decide whether VAT refunds are worth the trouble. As for me, my favorite trip souvenirs are my photos, journal, and memories. These are priceless—and exempt from taxes and red tape.

## Customs for American Shoppers

You are allowed to take home $800 in souvenirs per person duty-free, once every 30 days. The next $1,000 is taxed at a flat 3 percent. After that, you pay the individual item's duty rate. You can also bring in duty-free a liter of alcohol (slightly more than a standard-size bottle of wine; you must be at least 21), 200 cigarettes, and up to 100 non-Cuban cigars. As for food, if it's in cans or sealed jars, it's permissible as long as no meat is included. Fresh fruits and vegetables are not allowed. Some, but not all, types of cheese are allowed. To check customs rules and duty rates before you go, visit www.customs.gov. For details about mailing items from Europe to yourself or somebody else, see "Mail," page 293 of the City Skills chapter.

## Successful Bargaining

In much of the Mediterranean world, the price tag is only an excuse to argue. Bargaining is the accepted and expected method of finding a compromise between the wishful thinking of the merchant and the tourist. In Europe, bargaining is common only in the south, but you can fight prices at flea markets and with street vendors anywhere.

While bargaining is good for your budget, it can also become an enjoyable game. Many travelers are addicted hagglers who would gladly skip a tour of a Portuguese palace to get the price down on the black-clad lady's handmade tablecloth.

### The Ten Commandments of the Successful Haggler

**1. Determine if bargaining is appropriate.** It's bad shopping etiquette to "make an offer" for a tweed hat in a London department store. It's foolish not to at a Greek outdoor market. To learn if a price is fixed, show some interest in an item but say, "It's just too much money." You've put the merchant in a position to make the first offer. If he comes down even 2 percent, there's nothing sacred about the price tag. Haggle away.

**2. Shop around and find out what locals pay.** Prices can vary drastically among vendors at the same flea market, and even at the same stall. If prices aren't posted, assume there's a double price standard: One for locals and one for you. If only tourists buy the item you're pricing, see what an Arab, Spanish, or Italian tourist would be charged. I remember thinking I did well in Istanbul's Grand Bazaar, until I learned my Spanish friend bought the same shirt for 30 percent less. Merchants assume American tourists are rich. And they know what we pay for things at home.

*You can troll for quirky souvenirs at flea markets.*

**3. Determine what the item is worth to you.** Price tags can be meaningless and serve to distort your idea of an item's true worth. The merchant is playing a psychological game. Many tourists think that if they can cut the price by 50 percent they are doing great. So the merchant quadruples his prices and the tourist happily pays double the fair value. The best way to deal with crazy price tags is to ignore them. Before you even see the price tag, determine the item's value to you, considering the hassles involved in packing it or shipping it home.

**4. Determine the merchant's lowest price.** Many merchants will settle for a nickel profit rather than lose the sale entirely. Promise yourself that no matter how exciting the price becomes, you won't buy. Then work the cost down to rock bottom. When it seems to have fallen to a record low, walk away. That last price he hollers out as you turn the corner is often the best price you'll get. If the price is right, go back and buy. Prices often drop at the end of the day when merchants are considering packing up.

*When you shop on the street, haggling is half the fun.*

**5. Look indifferent.** As soon as the merchant perceives the "I gotta have that!" in you, you'll never get the best price. He assumes Americans have the money to buy what they really want.

**6. Employ a third person.** Use your friend who is worried about the ever-dwindling budget or who doesn't like the price or who is bored and wants to return to the hotel. This trick can work to bring the price down faster.

**7. Impress the merchant with your knowledge—real or otherwise.** He'll respect you, and you'll be more likely to get good quality. Istanbul has very good leather coats for a fraction of the US cost. Before my trip I talked to some leather-coat sellers and was much better prepared to confidently pick out a good coat in Istanbul for $100.

**8. Obey the rules.** Don't hurry. Bargaining is rarely rushed. Get to know the shopkeeper. Accept his offer for tea, talk with him. He'll know you are serious. Dealing with the owner (no salesman's commission) can lower the price. Bid carefully. If a merchant accepts your price (or vice versa), you must buy the item.

**9. Show the merchant your money.** Physically hold out your money and offer him "all you have" to pay for whatever you are bickering over. He'll be tempted to just grab your money and say, "Oh, OK."

**10. If the price is too much, leave.** Never worry about having taken too much of the merchant's time and tea. They are experts at making the tourist feel guilty for not buying. It's all part of the game. Most merchants, by local standards, are financially well-off.

Remember, you can generally find the same souvenirs in large department stores at fair and firm prices. Department-store shopping is quicker, easier, often cheaper—but not nearly as much fun.

# SLEEPING AND EATING

## 17. SLEEPING

Hotels are the most expensive way to sleep and, of course, the most comfortable. With a reasonable budget, I spend most of my nights in hotels, but they can rip through a tight budget like a grenade in a dollhouse.

I hear people complaining about that "$250 double in Frankfurt" or the "$400-a-night room in London." They come back from their vacations with bruised and battered pocketbooks, telling stories that scare their friends out of international travel and back to Florida or Hawaii one more time. True, you can spend $400 for a double, but I never have. That's three days' accommodations for me.

As far as I'm concerned, spending more for your hotel just builds a bigger wall between you and what you traveled so far to see. If you spend enough, you won't know where you are. Think about it. "In-ter-con-ti-nen-tal." That means the same everywhere—designed for people who deep down inside wish they weren't traveling, people spending someone else's money, people who need a strap over the toilet telling them no one's sat there yet. It's uniform sterility, a lobby full of Stay-Press Americans with tiny wheels on their hard suitcases, English menus, and lamps bolted to the tables.

Europe's small hotels and guest houses may have no room service and offer only a shower down the hall, but their staffs are more interested in seeing pictures of your children and helping you have a great time than in thinning out your wallet.

Europe is full of traditional old hotels—dingy, a bit run-down, central, friendly, safe, and government regulated, offering good-enough-for-the-European-good-enough-for-me beds for $40 a night ($80 doubles). No matter what your favorite newspaper travel writer or travel agent says, this is hardcore Europe: fun, cheap, and easy to find.

## What's a Cheap Room?

In a typical budget European hotel, a double room costs an average of $70 a night. You'll pay about $60 at a pension in Madrid, $70 at a simple guesthouse in rural Germany, and $90 for a two-star hotel in Paris or a private room in a Bergen pension.

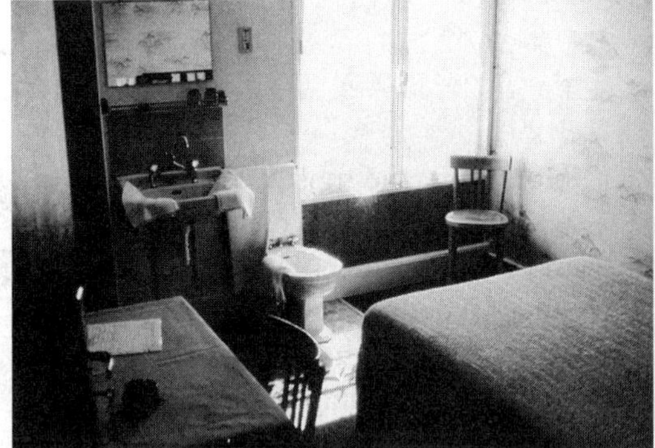

*A typical budget hotel room: tidy, small, affordable*

A typical room in a low-end hotel has a simple bed (occasionally a springy cot, so always check); a rickety, old, wooden (or new, plastic) chair and table; a freestanding closet; a small window; old wallpaper; a good sink under a neon light; a mysterious bidet; a view of another similar room across a tall, thin courtyard; peeling plaster; and a tiled or wood floor. The light fixtures are very simple, often with a weak and sometimes even bare and dangling ceiling light bulb. Some travelers B.Y.O.B. when they travel. A higher wattage kills a lot of dinginess. Naked neon is common in the south. While Britain has many non-smoking places, nearly all rooms on the Continent come with ashtrays. You won't have a TV or telephone. While more and more European hotels are squeezing boat-type prefab showers and toilets into their rooms, the cheapest rooms still offer only a toilet and shower or tub down the hall, which you share with a half-dozen other rooms.

Rooms often come with a continental breakfast (usually served from about 7:30–10:00 a.m. in the breakfast room near the front desk): coffee, tea, or hot chocolate, and a roll that's firmer than your mattress. Breakfasts in northern and eastern Europe can be a bit heartier, with cereal, yogurt, and fruit.

In the lobby, there's nearly always a living room with a TV, a phone, and a person at the desk who's a good information source. You'll climb lots of stairs, as a hotel's lack of an elevator is often the only reason it can't raise its prices. You'll be given a front-door key because the desk is not staffed all night.

*1977: It slowly dawns on Rick that cheap beds aren't always good beds.*

Cheap hotels usually have clean-enough-but-depressing shower rooms, with hot water normally free and constant (but occasionally available only through a coin-op meter or at certain hours). The WC has toilet paper but often has a missing, cracked, or broken lid. In some hotels, you pay $2–5 for a towel and a key to the shower room. The cheapest hotels are run by and filled with people from the Two-Thirds World.

I want to stress that there are places I find unacceptable. I don't mind dingy wallpaper, climbing stairs, and "going down the hall," but the place must be clean, central, friendly, safe, quiet enough for me to sleep well, and equipped with good beds.

The cheap hotel described above is appalling to many Americans; it's charming, colorful, or funky to others. To me, "funky" means spirited and full of character(s): a caged bird in the TV room, grandchildren in the backyard, a dog sleeping in the hall, no uniforms, singing maids, a night-shift man tearing breakfast napkins in two so they'll go farther, a handwritten neighborhood history lesson on the wall, different furniture in each room, and a willingness to buck the system when the local tourist board starts requiring shoeshine machines in the hallways. An extra $40 or $50 per night will buy you into cheerier wallpaper and less funkiness.

As Europe becomes more and more affluent, a powerful force is pushing hotels up in price and comfort. Land in big cities is so expensive that cheap hotels can't survive and are bought out, gutted, and turned into modern hotels. More and more Europeans are expecting what have been considered—until lately—American standards of plumbing and comfort. A great value is often a hardworking family-run place that structurally can't fit showers in every room or an elevator up its spiral staircase. Prices are regulated and, regardless of how comfy and charming it is, with no elevator and a lousy shower-to-room ratio, it is—and will stay—a cheap hotel.

### Making Advance Reservations

Sometimes reserving rooms in advance makes sense. If you know exactly where you want to stay each night, you can systematically set up your accommodations by following these simple steps. Even if you're not a detail person, it pays to be disciplined about this, particularly when you're traveling in high season or visiting popular spots.

1. Using a computer, build a calendar from your itinerary with general notes on top followed by a chart with dates, sights, accommodations, special notes, and reminders to keep track of loose ends. Update your itinerary throughout the process.
2. Decide from guidebook listings or Web research where you want to stay in each destination. Assemble the e-mail addresses or fax numbers of each targeted hotel.
3. Make a template e-mail or fax room-reservation request letter.
4. Go through your list and request rooms.
5. Follow up with telephone calls to places not responding to your e-mail or fax.
6. Slog away until the entire trip is set up.
7. Even with firm reservations ensured by credit card, bring along your written confirmations (in case of a dispute) and call each hotel a day or two before you arrive to reconfirm.

## Making Reservations

I used to travel with absolutely no reservations. A daily chore was checking out several hotels or pensions and choosing one. Europe was ramshackle, things were cheap, and hotel listings were unreliable and unnecessary. Now, like hobos in a Jetsons world, budget travelers need to think one step ahead.

**Use a good guidebook.** Choose a guidebook whose travel philosophy matches yours. These days, those who rely on the tourist office or go potluck are likely to spend $50 more than necessary and get a lousy room. That's why I give hotel listings a very high priority in researching and writing my guidebooks.

**Call ahead.** When traveling off-season or in less crowded places, my standard room-finding tactic (assuming I know where I want to be) is to telephone in the morning to reserve my room for the night. I travel relaxed, knowing a good place is holding a room for me until late afternoon. A simple phone call a little in advance assures me a good-value room. Lately, I've been getting aced out by my own readers. So

## Sample Itinerary

***Notes:***

* Look into renting a car to explore castles in Bavaria/Tirol region, April 29–May 2; compare rates online. Also consider Panorama Tours.
* Find out from store if my mobile phone works in Europe.
* Should I reserve overnight train to Venice on May 3?
* Make reservations for Rome's Borghese Gallery; could visit May 6–9.
* Find out about festivals—check online or call national tourist offices.
* Cancel newspaper, hold mail delivery, put bills on auto-pay.

| Date | Travel and Sights | Sleep | Notes |
|---|---|---|---|
| Sat, April 21 | Arrive Amsterdam 10:30 a.m., take afternoon canal cruise, tour Anne Frank House | Amsterdam, Hotel Brouwer (akita @hotelbrouwer.nl), 2 nights | Reservation confirmed, €90/ night for double. |
| Sun, April 22 | Amsterdam: day-trip to Haarlem and Grote Kerk | Amsterdam, Hotel Brouwer | Confirmed. |
| Mon, April 23 | To Bacharach on the Rhine (nearly hourly trains, allow 4.5 hours) | Bacharach, Hotel Kranenturm (hotel-kranenturm @t-online.de), 2 nights | Confirmed, double with shower for €62/night, request arrival before 16:00. |
| Tue, April 24 | Bacharach: take Rhine cruise, visit St. Goar | Bacharach, Hotel Kranenturm | Confirmed. |
| Wed, April 25 | To Rothenburg (trains nearly hourly, takes 4.25 hrs), see sights, Night Watchman's Tour at 8:00 p.m | Rothenburg, Hotel zur Goldenen Rose (info @thegoldenrose.de), 2 nights | E-mail sent, awaiting response. Backup is pricier Hotel Gerberhaus (gerberhaus@t-online.de). |
| Thu, April 26 | Rothenburg: sights, shop, swimming pool | Rothenburg | |
| Fri, April 27 | To Munich (hourly trains, 3.5 hours), tour Deutsches Museum or Residenz | Munich, Hotel Münchner Kindl (reservierung@hotel -muenchner-kindl.de), 2 nights | E-mail sent, awaiting response. Backup is Hotel Deutsches Theater (info @hoteldeutshcestheater.de). |
| Sat, April 28 | Munich: side-trip to Salzburg (trains twice hourly, 2-hr trip) | Munich | |

when I want to be certain to get my first choice, I call or e-mail several days—or even several weeks—in advance. For peak-season travel and when visiting big, popular cities (such as London, Paris, Madrid, Venice, and so on), I make my reservations as soon as I can pin down a date (see "Making Advance Reservations" sidebar).

A hotelier will usually request your credit-card number as a deposit when you book your reservation. You can be billed for one night if you don't show up. (Be warned that some hotels may charge you if you cancel with too short notice; if your plans are iffy, confirm a hotel's cancellation policy before booking to avoid an unpleasant surprise upon canceling.) Some hotels will hold a room without a deposit if you promise to arrive early. The earlier you promise, the better your chances of being trusted. If you'll be a little late, call again to assure them you're coming. Also, cancel if you won't make it. If someone cancels after 5 p.m. and the room-finding service is closed, the room will probably go unfilled that night. When that happens too often, hotel managers and B&B owners start to get really surly and insist on cash deposits.

**Try to e-mail or fax your long-distance reservations.** European hoteliers prefer reservation requests by e-mail. An e-mail in simple English communicates clearly, minimizes the language barrier (especially helpful in southern Europe, where, because of the language barrier, a phone call may accomplish little), gives your hotel a quick and easy way to respond, and is free for both parties. Whenever possible, reserve by e-mail (you'll find a form online at www.ricksteves.com/reservation).

*Family-run hotels offer the warmest welcome and the best value.*

Hotels, pensions, and B&Bs that lack e-mail likely have a fax number. Photocopy and use the handy fax form included in this chapter. If you don't get a response, assume the hotel received and understood your request and has no room available for you (some hotels get 30–40 faxes a day and would go broke returning them all). You can also make a reservation by telephone.

In your e-mailed or faxed request, always list these items: your dates (with date and expected time of arrival, number of nights you'll stay, and date of departure); your room needs (number of people, the facilities you require); and your budget concerns (of course, a trade-off with facilities).

Once they've offered you a room, accept the reservation and send your credit-card number as a deposit. E-mailing credit-card information poses a security risk. Instead, print a copy of the hotel's confirmation message, write in your card details, and fax it to the hotel. Or simply call them and tell them your credit-card number over the phone. Request a confirmation with the price quoted.

*In France, each hotel has a plaque next to its door telling you its category.*

Ideally your credit-card number will be accepted as a deposit. If a cash deposit is required, you can mail a bank draft or, easier, a signed $100 traveler's check. (Leave the "pay to" line blank and encourage them to avoid bank fees by just holding the check as security until you arrive and can pay in cash.)

**Don't panic.** If, after several tries, it seems that every hotel in town is full, don't worry. Hotels take only so many long-distance advance reservations. They never know how long guests will stay and like to keep a few beds for their regulars. Call between 8 and 10 a.m. the day you plan to arrive. This is when the receptionist knows exactly who's leaving and which rooms he needs to fill. He'll be eager to get a name for every available room. Those who are there in person are more likely to land a room. Many simple hotels don't bother with reservations more than a couple of weeks in advance, and some very cheap hotels take no reservations at all. Just show up and sleep with your money belt on.

## Basic Bed Finding

In more than a thousand unreserved nights in Europe, I've been shut out three times. That's a 99.7 percent bedding average earned in peak season and very often in crowded, touristy, or festive places. What's so traumatic about a night without a bed, anyway? The cost of a wonderfully reservation-free trip is the remote chance you'll end up spending the night on a bench in the train-station waiting room. My survey shows those who have the opportunity to be a refugee for a night have their perspectives broadened and actually enjoy the experience—in retrospect.

While for many trips it makes sense to nail down room reservations long in advance, you can blow like the wind freely through Europe if you want, making reservations as you go. These tricks work for me:

**Travel with a good list of hotels.** I spend more time in Europe finding and checking hotels (for my guidebooks) than anything else. I can spend a day in Amsterdam, scaling the stairs and checking out the rooms of 20 different hotels, all offering double rooms from $80–200 a night. After doing the grand analysis, what's striking to me is how little correlation there is between what you pay and what you get. You are just as likely to spend $150 for a big, impersonal place on a noisy highway as you are to spend $100 for a charming, family-run guest house on a bikes-only stretch of canal.

These days, to sleep well and inexpensively on a big-city bed, you need a good guidebook's listing of hotels and budget alternatives. These lists are reliable and work well (but prices have likely gone up slightly since the book was printed).

**Use room-finding services if necessary.** Popular tourist cities usually have a room-finding service at the train station or tourist information office. They have a listing of that town's "acceptable" available accommodations. For a fee of a few dollars, they'll get you a room in the price range and neighborhood of your choice. Especially in a big city (if you don't have a guidebook's listings), their service can be worth the price when you consider the time and money saved by avoiding the search on foot.

I avoid room-finding services unless I have no listings or information of my own. Their hotel lists normally make no quality judgments, so what you get is potluck. The stakes are too high for this to be acceptable (especially when you consider how readily available good hotel listings are in guidebooks). Also, since many room-finding services profit from taking a "deposit" that they pocket, many managers of the best budget places tell the room-finding service they're full when they aren't. They know they'll fill up with travelers coming direct, allowing them to keep 100 percent of the room cost.

Recently many tourist information offices have lost their government funding and are now privately owned. This creates the absurdity of a profit-seeking tourist information "service." Their previously reliable advice is now colored with a need to make a kickback. Some room-finding services work for a group of supporting hotels. Room-finding services are not above pushing you into their "favored" hotels, and kickbacks are powerful motivators. Only if you insist will you get information on cheap sleep options—dormitories, hostels, and sleep-ins (circus tents, gyms with mattresses on the floor, and other $15-a-night alternatives to the park or station). And beware: Many "tourist information offices" are just travel agencies and room-booking services in disguise.

## Making Your Hotel Reservation

Most hotel managers know basic "hotel English." Faxing or e-m... preferred methods for reserving a room. They're more accurate tha... ing and much faster than writing a letter. Use this handy form for y... or find it online at www.ricksteves.com/reservation. Photocopy and fax away.

**One-Page Fax**

To: ____________________ @ __________________

***hotel*** ***fax***

From: ____________________ @ __________________

***name*** ***fax***

Today's date: _____ /_____ /_____

***day month year***

Dear Hotel , ____________________________________

Please make this reservation for me:

Name: ________________________________________

Total # of people: _______ # of rooms: _______ # of nights: _______

Arriving: ____/_____/_____ My time of arrival (24-hr clock): ______

***day month year*** (I will telephone if I will be late)

Departing: ____/_____/_____

***day month year***

Room(s): Single____ Double ____ Twin ____ Triple ____ Quad ____

With: Toilet____ Shower ____ Bath____ Sink only_____

Special needs: View_____ Quiet ____ Cheapest____ Ground Floor____

Please fax or e-mail confirmation of my reservation, along with the type of room reserved and the price. Please also inform me of your cancellation policy. After I hear from you, I will quickly fax or call you with my credit-card information as a deposit to hold the room. Thank you.

________________________________________

***Signature***

________________________________________

***Name***

________________________________________

***Address***

________________________________________

***City*** ***State*** ***Zip Code*** ***Country***

________________________________________

***E-mail Address***

**Use the telephone.** If you're looking on your own, telephone the places in your guidebook that sound best. Not only will it save the time and money involved in chasing down these places with the risk of finding them full, but you're beating all the other tourists—with the same guidebook—who may be hoofing it as you dial. It's rewarding to arrive at a hotel when people are being turned away and see your name on the reservation list because you called first. If the room or price isn't what you were led to believe it would be, you have every right to say, "No, thank you." In peak times, a guidebook's top hotel listings are likely to be full. Don't hesitate to jump way down the list, where available rooms may abound. Use the tourist office only as a last resort.

**Consider hotel runners.** As you step off the bus or train, you'll sometimes be met by hotel runners wielding pictures of their rooms for rent. My gut reaction is to steer clear, but these people are usually just hardworking entrepreneurs who lack the location or write-up in a popular guidebook that can make life easy for a small hotel owner. If you like the guy and what he promises, and the hotel isn't too far away, follow him to his hotel. You are obliged only to inspect the hotel. If it's good, take it. If it's not, leave. You're probably near other budget hotels anyway. Establish the location very clearly, as many of these people have good places miserably located way out of town. Especially in Eastern Europe, these room hawkers might not be affiliated with a hotel at all, but simply rent out vacant rooms in their own homes. For details, see "Bed-and-Breakfast Places and Pensions," later in this chapter.

*"Welcome! I have rooms."*

**The early bird gets the room.** If you anticipate crowds, go to great lengths to arrive in the morning when the most (and best) rooms are available. If the rooms aren't ready until noon, take one anyway. Leave your luggage behind the desk; they'll move you in later and you're set up—free to relax and enjoy the city. I would leave Florence at 7 a.m. to arrive in popular, crowded Venice early enough to get a decent choice of rooms. Consider the advantage of overnight train rides—you'll arrive, if not bright, at least early.

Your approach to room finding will be determined by the market situation—whether it's a "buyer's market" or a "seller's market." Sometimes you can arrive late, be selective, and even talk down the price. Other times you'll happily accept anything with a pillow and a blanket.

**Leave the trouble zone.** If the room situation is impossible, don't struggle—just leave. An hour by car, train, or bus from the most miserable hotel situation anywhere in Europe is a town—Dullsdorf or Nothingston—with the Dullsdorf Gasthaus or the Nothingston Inn just across the street from the station or right on the main square. It's not full—never has been, never will be. There's a guy sleeping behind the reception desk. Drop in at 11 p.m., ask for 14 beds, and he'll say, "Take the second and third floors—the keys are in the doors." It always works. Oktoberfest, Cannes Film Festival, St-Tropez Running of the Girls, Easter at Lourdes—your bed awaits you in nearby Dullsdorf. If you anticipate trouble, consider staying at the last train stop before the crowded city.

**Follow taxi tips.** A great way to find a place in a tough situation is to let a cabbie take you to his favorite hotel. They are experts.

**Let hotel managers help.** Have your current manager call ahead to make a reservation at your next destination (offer to pay for the call). If you're in a town and having trouble finding a room, remember that nobody knows the hotel scene better than local hotel managers do. If one hotel is full, ask the hotelier for help. Often the manager has a list of neighborhood accommodations or will even telephone a friend's place that rarely fills up and is just around the corner. If the hotel is too expensive, there's nothing wrong with asking where you could find a "not-so-good place." The most expensive hotels have the best city maps (free, often with other hotels listed) and an English-speaking staff that can give advice to the polite traveler in search of a cheap room. I find hotel receptionists understanding and helpful.

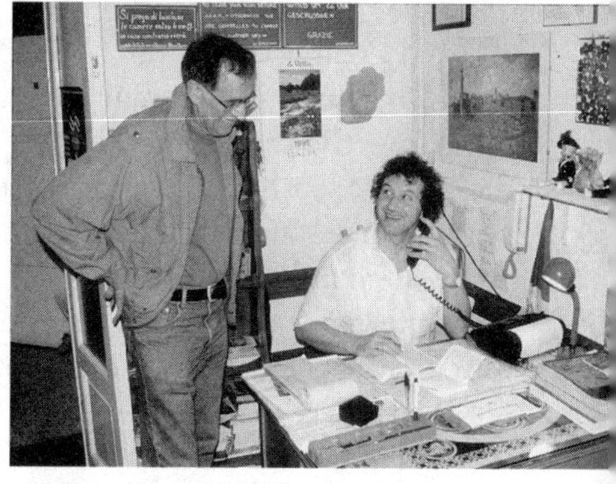

*Ask your friend who runs today's hotel to call tomorrow's hotel to make you a reservation in the local language.*

## To Save Money...

**Think small.** Larger hotels are usually pricier than small hotels or B&Bs, partly because of taxes (e.g., in Britain, once a B&B exceeds a certain revenue level, it's required to pay an extra 15 percent VAT in addition to its other taxes). Hoteliers who pay high taxes pass their costs on to you.

**Consider a cheap chain hotel.** More and more hotel chains—offering cheap or moderately priced rooms—are springing up throughout Europe. The hotels that allow up to four people in a room are great for families. You won't find character at chain hotels, but you'll get predictable, Motel 6–type comfort. The huge Accor chain offers a range of hotels, from the cheap Formule 1 Hotels (mostly in France, www.hotelformule1.com) to the mid-range Ibis Hotels (sterile, throughout Europe, www.ibishotel.com) to the pricier, cushier Mercure and Novotel Hotels (for all Accor Hotels, see www.accorhotels.com, US tel. 800-221-4542). Britain has Travelodge (www.travelodge.co.uk) and Premier Travel Inn (www.premiertravelinn.com). For Ireland, it's Jurys Doyle Hotels (www.jurys.com).

*Europe's cheap, no-character hotels cater to local businessmen interested in going home with some of their per diem still in their pockets.*

**Know the exceptions.** Hotels in northern Europe are pricier than those in the south, but there are exceptions. In Scandinavia, Brussels, and Berlin, fancy "business hotels" are desperate for customers in the summer and year-round on weekends, when their business customers stay away. They offer some amazing deals through the local tourist offices. The later your arrival, the better the discount.

**Be a smart consumer—don't stray above your needs.** Know the government ratings. A three-star hotel is not necessarily a bad value, but if I stay in a three-star hotel, I've spent $70 extra for things I don't need. You can get air-conditioning, elevators, private showers, room service, a 24-hour reception desk, and people in uniforms to carry your bags. But each of those services adds $10 to your room cost, and, before you know it, the simple $80 room is up to $150.

*Throughout southern Europe, even the cheapest hotel rooms come with a bidet. Europeans use them to stay clean without a daily shower.*

### Chill Out

Many hotel rooms in the Mediterranean part of Europe come with air-conditioning that you control—often with a remote control (like for a TV). Various remotes have basically the same features:

- Fan icon (click to toggle through the wind power from light to gale)
- Louver icon (click to choose steady air flow or waves)
- Snowflake and sunshine icons (heat or cold; generally just one or the other is possible: cool in summer, heat in winter)
- Two clock settings (to determine how many hours the air-conditioning will stay on before turning off, or stay off before turning on)
- Temperature control (20 or 21 is a comfortable temperature in degrees Celsius)

**Avoid hotels that require you to buy meals.** Many national governments regulate hotel prices according to class or rating. In order to overcome this price ceiling (especially at resorts in peak season, when demand exceeds supply), hotels often require that you buy dinner in their dining room. Breakfast normally comes with the room, but in some countries it's an expensive, kind-of-optional tack-on. One more meal (called "half board," "half pension," or demi-pension) or all three meals ("full board" or "full pension") is usually uneconomical, since the hotel is skirting the governmental hotel price ceilings to maximize profit. I prefer the freedom to explore and sample the atmosphere of restaurants in other neighborhoods.

**Shop around.** When going door-to-door, rarely is the first place you check the best. It's worth 20 minutes of shopping around to find the going rate before you accept a room. You'll be surprised how prices vary as you walk farther from the station or down a street strewn with B&Bs. Never judge a hotel by its exterior or lobby. Lavish interiors with shabby exteriors (blame the landlord who's stuck with rent control, not the hotel) are a cultural trait of Europe. (If there are two of you, let one watch the bags over a cup of coffee while the other runs around.)

**Check the prices on the room list to find the best value.** Room prices vary tremendously within a hotel according to facilities provided. Most hotels have a room list clearly displayed, showing each room, its bed configuration, facilities, and maximum price for one and for two people. Also read the breakfast, tax, and extra-bed policies. By studying this list you'll see that, in many places, a shower is cheaper than a bath, and a double bed is cheaper than twins. In other words, a sloppy couple that prefers a shower and a double bed can pay $20 more for a bath and twins. In some cases, if you want any room for two and you say "double," they'll think you'll only take a double bed. To keep all my options open (twin and double), I ask for "a room for two people." If you want a cheap room, say it. Many hoteliers have a few unrenovated rooms without a private bathroom; they usually don't even mention these, figuring they'd be unacceptable to Americans.

**See if there's a discount for a longer stay or payment in cash.** If you plan to stay three or more nights at a place, or if you pay in cash rather than by credit card (saving the hotelier the credit-card company's cut and leaving them the option of not declaring the income to avoid taxes), it's worth asking if a discount is available. And if you came direct and point out that the tourist office didn't get their 10 percent, you also have a chance of talking the price down.

**Do a Web search.** If a hotel rents rooms at a discount through a hotel-booking Web site, you can guess they'd take an offer of that same rate from you if you book direct, even if it's lower than the rates posted at the hotel. (Their prices are actually being discounted even further than the cost you see online, since the hotel is paying a substantial commission to the Web service for each booking.)

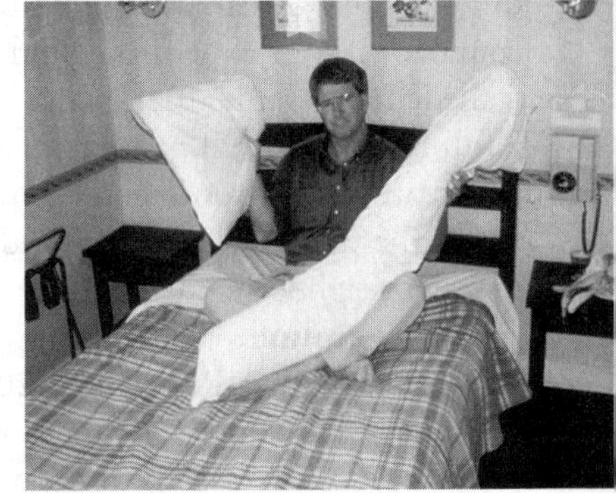

*French hotels often come with Lincoln Log–shaped pillows. To get an American-style pillow, look in the closet or ask at the desk.*

**If it's off-season, bargain.** Prices usually rise with demand during festivals and in July and August. Off-season, try haggling. If the place is too expensive, tell them your limit; they might meet it.

**Put more people in a room.** Family rooms are common, and putting four in a quad is much cheaper than two doubles. Many doubles come with a small double bed and a sliver single. A third person pays very little. A family with two small children can ask for triples and bring a sleeping bag for the stowaway.

**Avoid doing outside business through your hotel.** Go to the bullring and get the ticket yourself. You'll learn more and save money, and you won't sit with other tourists who drown your Spanish fire with Yankee-pankee. So often, tourists are herded together—by a conspiracy of hotel managers and tour organizers—at gimmicky folk evenings featuring a medley of cheesy cultural clichés kept alive only for the tourists.

### The 🔑 to Keys

Tourists spend hours fumbling with old skeleton keys in rickety hotel doors. The haphazard, nothing-square construction of old hotels means the keys need babying. Don't push them in all the way. Lift the door in or up. Try a little in, quarter turn, and farther in for full turn. Always turn the top of the key away from the door to open it. Some locks take two key revolutions to open. Leave the key at the desk before leaving for the day. I've never had my room broken into in Europe. Confirm closing time. Some hotels lock up after their restaurant closes, after midnight, or during their weekly "quiet day" and expect you to keep the key to the outside door with you to get in after hours.

You can't relive your precious Madrid nights. Do them right—on your own.

## Check-In Procedure

**Ask to see the room before accepting.** Then the receptionist knows the room must pass your inspection. He'll have to earn your business. Notice the bellhop is given two keys. You asked for only one room. He's instructed to show the hard-to-sell room first. It's only natural for the hotel receptionist to try to unload the most difficult-to-sell room on the easiest-to-please traveler. Somebody has to sleep in it. If you ask to see both rooms, you'll get the better one. When you check out a room, point out anything that deserves displeasure. The price will come down, or they'll show you a better room. Think about heat and noise. I'll climb a few stairs to reach cheaper rooms higher off the noisy road. Some towns never quiet down. A room in back may lack a view, but it will also lack nighttime noise.

**Establish the complete and final price of a room before accepting.** Know what's included and what taxes and services will be added. More than once I've been given a bill that was double what I expected. Dinners were required, and I was billed whether I ate them or not; so I was told—in very clear Italian.

**When checking in, pick up the hotel's business card.** In the most confusing cities, the cards come with a little map. Even the best pathfinders get lost in a big city, and not knowing where your hotel is can be scary. With the card, you can hop into a cab and be home in minutes.

**If you need help, ask.** Although you don't want to be a pest, remember, hotels are in the business of accommodating people. If you didn't get the kind of room you wanted, ask to switch when possible. If you'd like a room farther from a noisy elevator shaft, ask for it. If you need a different pillow, another blanket, mosquito netting, an electrical adapter, advice on a good restaurant or show, driving instructions for your departure, help telephoning your next hotel, and so on, be sure to ask.

**When you pay is up to the hotel and you.** Normally I pay upon departure. If they want prepayment, that's fine, but unless I'm absolutely certain I'll be staying on, I pay one night at a time. Don't assume your room is yours once you're in. Make it clear when you check in how long you intend to stay, or you may get the boot.

## Bed-and-Breakfast Places and Pensions

Between hotels and hostels in price and style is a special class of accommodations. These are small, warm, and family-run, and offer a personal touch at a budget price. They are the next best thing to staying with a local family, and, even if hotels weren't more expensive, I'd choose this budget alternative.

*Bed-and-breakfasts offer double the cultural experience for half the price of a hotel.*

Each country has these friendly accommodations in varying degrees of abundance, facilities, and service. Some include breakfast, some don't. They have different names from country to country, but all have one thing in common: They satisfy the need for a place to stay that gives you the privacy of a hotel and the comforts of home at a price you can afford.

While information on some of the more established places is available in many budget-travel guidebooks, the best information is often found locally, through tourist information offices, room-finding services, or even from the local man waiting for his bus or selling apples. Especially in the British Isles, each B&B host has a network of favorites and can happily set you up in a good B&B at your next stop.

Many times, the information is brought to you. I'll never forget struggling off the plane on my arrival in Santorini. Fifteen women were begging me to spend the night. Thrilled, I made a snap decision and followed the most attractive offer to a very nice budget accommodation.

The "part of the family" element of a B&B stay is determined entirely by you. Chatty friendliness is not forced on guests. Depending on my mood and workload, I am often very businesslike and private during my stay. On other occasions, I join the children in the barn for the sheep-shearing festivities.

Don't confuse European bed-and-breakfasts with their rich cousins in America. B&Bs in the United States are usually frilly, fancy places, very cozy and colorful but as expensive as hotels. In a European B&B, rather than seven pillows and a basket of jams, you get a warm welcome and a good price.

**Britain:** Britain's B&Bs are the best of all. Very common throughout the British Isles, they are a boon to anyone touring England, Scotland, or Wales. As the name indicates, a breakfast comes with the bed, and (except in London) this is no ordinary breakfast. Most B&B owners take pride in their breakfasts. Their guests sit down to an elegant and very British table setting and feast on cereal, juice, bacon, sausages, eggs, broiled tomatoes, mushrooms, toast, marmalade, and coffee or tea. While you are finishing your coffee, the landlady (who by this time is probably on very friendly terms with you) may present you with her guest book, inviting you to make an entry and pointing out others from your state who have stayed in her house. Your hostess will sometimes cook you a simple dinner for a good price, and, if you have time to chat, you may get in on an evening social hour. When you bid her farewell and thank her for the good sleep and full stomach, it's often difficult to get away. Determined to fill you with as much information as food, she wants you to have the best day of sightseeing possible.

*A special bonus when enjoying Britain's great B&Bs: You get your own temporary local mother.*

If you're going to the normal tourist stops, your guidebook will list some good B&Bs. If you're venturing off the beaten British path, you

## Showers

**To go local, take quick showers.** Americans are notorious (and embarrassing) energy gluttons—wasting hot water and leaving lights on as if electricity were cheap. Who besides us sings in the shower or would even dream of using a special nozzle to take a hot-water massage? European energy costs are shocking, and some hostels and budget hotels have had to put meters in their showers to survive. Fifty cents buys about five minutes of hot water. It's a good idea to have an extra token handy to avoid that lathered look. A "navy shower," using the water only to soap up and rinse off, is a wonderfully conservative method, and those who follow you will more likely enjoy some warm *Wasser* (although starting and stopping the water doesn't start and stop the meter).

**"C" can mean "hot."** Half of all the cold showers Americans take in Europe are cold only because they don't know how to turn the hot on. Study the particular system, and, before you shiver, ask the receptionist for help. There are some very peculiar tricks. In Italy and Spain, "C" is *caldo/caliente,* or hot. In many British places there's a "hot" switch at the base of the shower or even in the hallway. You'll find showers and baths of all kinds. The red knob is hot and the blue one is cold—or vice versa. Unusual showers normally have clear instructions posted.

**If the water stays cold, ask, "When is the best time to take a hot shower?"** Some cheap hotels have water pressure or hot water only during certain times. Hot water 24 hours a day is a luxury many of us take for granted.

**Try a sponge bath.** Nearly every hotel room in Europe comes with a sink, and many have a bidet. Sponge baths are fast, easy, and European. A bidet is that mysterious porcelain (or rickety plastic) thing that looks like an oversized bedpan. Tourists use them as anything from a launderette to a vomitorium to a watermelon rind receptacle to a urinal. They are used by locals to clean the parts of the body that rub together when they walk—in lieu of a shower. Give it the old four S's—straddle, squat, soap up, and swish off.

**Bring soap.** Many dorm-style accommodations don't provide towels or soap. B.Y.O.S. Towels, like breakfast and people, get smaller as you go south. In simple places, you won't get a washcloth, and bath towels are not replaced every day. Hang them up to dry.

Dominic Bonuccelli

*European showers: Each one has its own personality.*

**Use the hall shower.** The cheapest hotels rarely provide a shower or toilet in your room. Each floor shares a toilet and a shower "down the hall." To such a bathoholic people, this sounds terrible. Imagine the congestion in the morning when the entire floor tries to pile into that bathtub! Remember, only Americans "need" a shower every morning. Few Americans stay in these "local" hotels; therefore, you've got a private bath—down the hall. I spend 100 nights a year in Europe—probably shower 80 times—and I typically have to wait four or five times each year. That's the price I pay to take advantage of Europe's simple hotels.

In the last decade, even the simplest places have added lots of private showers. For example, a hotel originally designed with 20 simple rooms sharing two showers will now be retrofitted with private showers in 14 of its rooms. That leaves a more reasonable six rooms rather than 20 to share the two public showers. Those willing to go down the hall for a shower enjoy the same substantial savings with much less inconvenience.

**Try other places to shower.** If you are vagabonding or sleeping several nights in transit, you can buy a shower in "day hotels" at major train stations and airports, at many freeway rest stops, and in public baths or swimming pools. Most Mediterranean beaches have free, freshwater showers all the time.

I have a theory that after four days without a shower, you don't get any worse, but that's another book.

*Never judge a B&B by its name. Like many in Britain, this one is non-smoking and comes with numerous pleasant extras.*

don't need (or want) a listing. The small towns and countryside are littered with places whose quality varies only in degrees of wonderful. I try not to take a B&B until I have checked out three. Styles and atmosphere vary from house to house, and besides, I enjoy looking through European homes.

Britain rates its B&Bs using a diamond system (1–5) that rates cleanliness, furnishings, and decor. But diamond definitions are pretty squishy. Few B&Bs make a big deal of the ratings, and fewer tourists even know the system exists.

**Ireland** has essentially the same system of B&Bs. They are less expensive than England's and, if anything, even more "homely." You can expect a big breakfast and comfortable room, often in the town center.

**Germany, Austria, and Switzerland:** Look for *Zimmer Frei* or *Privat Zimmer.* These are very common in areas popular with travelers (such as Austria's Salzkammergut Lake District and Germany's Rhine, Romantic Road, and southern Bavaria). Signs will clearly indicate whether they have available rooms (green) or not (orange). Especially in Austria, one-night stays are discouraged. Most *Zimmers* cost about $30 per person and include a hearty continental breakfast. *Pension*s and *Gasthaus*es are similarly priced small, family-run hotels. Switzerland has very few *Zimmers.* Don't confuse *Zimmer* with the German *Ferienwohnung,* which is a self-catering apartment rented out by the week or fortnight.

**France:** The French have a growing network of *chambre d'hôte* (CH) accommodations where locals, mainly in the countryside and in small towns, rent double rooms for about the price of a cheap hotel ($70), but they include breakfast. Some CHs post *chambre* signs in their windows, but most are listed only through

*Bed-and-breakfast travelers scramble at the breakfast table.*

### Terms for Private Rooms to Ren

Private rooms throughout Europe cost $20–40 per person and c
breakfast in Great Britain, Ireland, Germany, Austria, and Switzerla

| In... | Look For... |
| --- | --- |
| Great Britain & Ireland | Bed-and-Breakfast |
| Norway/Sweden | *Rom* or *Rum* |
| Denmark | *Værelser* |
| Germany/Austria/Switzerland | *Zimmer* |
| France | *Chambre d'hôte* |
| Italy | *Affitta Camere* |
| Spain | *Casa Particulare* |
| Portugal | *Quarto* |
| Greece | *Dhomatia* |
| Slovenia/Croatia | *Sobe* |
| Poland | *Pokoje* |
| Eastern Europe | *Zimmer* or "Rooms" |

local tourist offices. While your hosts will rarely speak English, they will almost always be enthusiastic and happy to share their home. For longer stays in the countryside, look into France's popular *gîtes* ($300–700/week for 4–6 people). Pick up regional listings at local tourist offices, or try Gîtes de France, an organization that arranges *gîte* rentals (www.gites-de-france.fr).

**Italy:** Check out Italy's good alternatives to its expensive hotels:

locanda, and *pensione.* (While these are technically all bunched ...her now in a hotel system with star ratings, you'll still find these ...ditional names, synonymous with simple, budget beds.) Private rooms, called *camere libere* or *affitta camere,* are fairly common in Italy's small towns. Small-town bars are plugged into the B&B grapevine. While breakfasts are rarely included, you'll sometimes get a kitchenette in the room. Drivers can try *agriturismo,* rooms in farmhouses in the countryside. Weeklong stays are preferred in July and August, but shorter stays are possible off-season. For a sampling, visit www.agriturismoitaly.it.

**Scandinavia:** These usually luxurious B&Bs are called *rom, hus rum,* or, in Denmark, *værelser.* At about $30 per bed, these are incredibly cheap (well, not so incredibly, when you figure it's a common way for the most heavily taxed people in Europe to make a little money under the table). Unfortunately, many Scandinavian B&Bs are advertised only through the local tourist offices, which very often keep them a secret until all the hotels are full. In my *Rick Steves' Scandinavia* guidebook, I list plenty of wonderful money-savers. An evening with a Scandinavian family offers a fascinating look at contemporary Nordic life. If they're serving breakfast, eat it. Even at $15, it's a deal by Nordic standards and can serve as your best big meal of the day.

**Spain and Portugal:** Travelers get an intimate peek into their small-town, whitewashed worlds by renting *camas* and *casas particulares* in Spain and *quartos* in Portugal. In rural Iberia, where there's tourism, you'll find these budget accommodations. Breakfast is rarely included.

**Greece:** You'll find many $30-per-bed *dhomatia.* Especially in touristy coastal and island towns, hardworking entrepreneurs will meet planes, ferries, and buses as they come into town at any hour. In Greek villages with no hotels, ask for *dhomatia* at the town *taverna.* Forget breakfast.

**Croatia and Slovenia:** In these countries—where mass tourism and overpriced, crumbling communist resorts reign—private rooms are often the best deal in town. You'll see signs advertising *sobe* (rooms) everywhere you look, or book one through a travel agency (10–30 percent extra). You'll generally pay extra if you stay less than three nights. Along the Dalmatian Coast, *sobe* skimmers meet every arriving ferry, targeting backpackers and eager to whisk you away to see their room.

## Europe's Hostels

Europe's cheapest beds are in hostels. Several thousand hostels provide beds throughout Europe for $10–30 per night. The buildings are usually in good, easily accessible locations.

As Europe has grown more affluent, hostels have been remodeled to provide more plumbing and smaller rooms. Still, hostels are not hotels—not by a long shot. Many people hate hostels. Others love them and will be hostelers all their lives, regardless of their budgets. Hosteling is a philosophy. A hosteler trades service and privacy for a chance to live simply and communally with people from around the world.

### Official Hostels vs. Independent Hostels

There are two different types of hostels: "official" hostels and "independent" hostels. While official hostels used to be the norm, more and more good independent alternatives are available.

**Official hostels** all belong to the same parent organization (Hostelling International, also known as International Youth Hostel Federation, or IYHF; www.hihostels.com). These hostels are required to adhere to various rules and guidelines. This is both good (you know exactly what you're going to get) and bad (official hostels are more likely to be unimaginative, drab, and institutional).

You technically need to be a member of Hostelling International to stay at an HI hostel, but in practice anyone can stay at one for an extra fee. If you plan to spend at least six nights at official HI hostels, buy a membership card before you go ($28/year, free if you're under 18, $18 if you're over 54; available at your local student-travel office, any HI hostel office, or Hostelling International; www.hiusa.org, tel. 301/495-1240). However, if you think you may not spend six nights at HI hostels—or if you're not certain, and you think you might prefer independent hostels—don't buy the card in advance. Non-members who want to stay at HI hostels can get an "international guest card" at your first hostel. You'll pay a few dollars extra per night for a "welcome stamp" to stick to this card, and once you buy six welcome stamps, you become a member. As independent hostels become a more popular option, this "pay-as-you-go" system for official hostels—rather than buying your membership up front—makes sense for many travelers.

If you're focusing on HI hostels, pick up the *Hostelling International Official Guide* (updated annually, $18, www.hiusa.org; also sold at your local student-travel office and most European hostels). This directory lists all 4,000 HI hostels worldwide, with each one's number of beds, distance from the train station, directions, address, phone number, and day or season (if any) the hostel is closed. Some individual countries have a more accurate and informative directory or handbook (never expensive, often free). England's is especially worthwhile.

**Independent hostels** tend to be more easygoing and colorful, run by people who prefer to avoid the occasionally heavy-handed bureaucracy of HI. These non-HI hostels are looser and more casual, but not as predictably clean or organized as official hostels. Independent hostels don't require a membership card or charge extra for non-members, and generally have fewer rules. Many popular European destinations have wild and cheap student-run hostels that are popular with wild and cheap student travelers, but some independent hostels are tame and mature. Various organizations promote independent hostels, including Hostels .com (www.hostels.com, $2 fee for booking online). Independent Holiday Hostels of Ireland (www.hostels-ireland.com) is a network of more than 100 independent hostels, requiring no membership and welcoming all ages. All IHH hostels are approved by the Irish Tourist Board.

If you're staying at a mix of both official and independent hostels—as most hostelers do—Let's Go guidebooks offer the best all-around listings (www.letsgo.com).

#### Hosteling Tips

Unless noted, these tips apply to both official and independent hostels.

**A youth hostel is not limited to young people.** You may assume hostels aren't for you because, by every other standard, you're older than young. Well, many countries have dropped the word "youth" from their hostels, and for years Hostelling International has given "youths" over the age of 54 a discount on the membership card. If you're alive, you're young enough to hostel anywhere in Europe (except for official hostels in Germany's Bavaria, with a strictly enforced 26-year-old age limit—unless you're traveling with a minor). The average hosteler is 18–26, but every year there are more seniors and families hosteling.

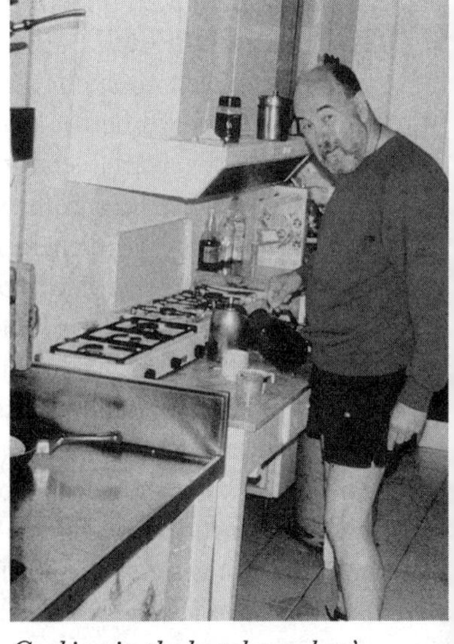

*Cooking in the hostel members' kitchen, this traveler lives in Europe on $15 a day for his bed, plus the price of groceries.*

**Hostels provide "no frills" accommodations in clean dormitories.** Hostels were originally for hikers and bikers, but that isn't the case these days—some newer hostels are downright plush. Still, expect humble conditions. At official hostels, the sexes are segregated, with 4–20 people packed in a room full of bunk beds. Many independent hostels have both segregated and mixed dorms. Hostels often have a few doubles for group leaders and couples, and rooms for families are increasingly common (and affordable). Strong, hot showers (often with coin-op meters) are the norm, but simpler hostels have cold showers or, on rare occasion, none at all.

**Bedding can cost extra.** Pillows and blankets are provided. Sometimes sheets are included in the cost, but often you have to pay extra to rent them (about $4). For about the same price, you can sometimes buy sheets made of paper that last about three nights. Another option is to bring your own "sleep sack"—a sleeping bag–type sack made of lightweight sheet material. You can make your own (fold over a queen-size sheet and sew it up), purchase one before your trip, or buy one at your first hostel in Europe. Because of concerns about bedbugs, some hostels now require you to rent sheets, even if you have your own. Because of this, and because a sleep sack takes up a fair amount of space in your luggage, I wouldn't bring one unless I knew I'd be staying at several hostels.

**Many hostels offer meals and meeting places.** Hearty, super-cheap meals are served, often in family-style settings (usually cost extra, though the price is cheap). A typical dinner is fish sticks and mashed potatoes seasoned by conversation with new friends from Norway to New Zealand. The self-service kitchen, complete with utensils, pots, and pans, is a great budget aid that comes with most hostels. Larger hostels even have a small grocery store. International friendships rise with the bread in hostel kitchens.

*Hostels: Meet, drink, and be merry.*

The hostel's recreation and living rooms are my favorite. People gather, play games, tell stories, share information, marvel at American foreign policy, read, write, and team up for future travels. Solo travelers find a family in every hostel. Hostels are ideal meeting places for those in search of a travel partner. And those with partners do well to occasionally stay in a hostel to meet some new travelers.

**Get to know your host.** The people who live in and run hostels (known as "wardens" in Britain) do their best to strictly enforce rules, quiet hours, and other regulations. Some are loose and laid-back, others are like Marine drill sergeants, but they all work toward the noble goal of enabling travelers to better appreciate and enjoy that town or region.

*One of Europe's hostels—$15 a night, your own kitchen, a million-dollar view of the Jungfrau, and lots of friends. Note the worldwide triangular hostel symbol.*

While they are often overworked and harried, most hostel employees are great people who enjoy a quiet cup of coffee with an American and are happy to give you some local travel tips or recommend a special nearby hostel. Be sensitive to the many demands on their time, and never treat them like hotel servants.

**Hostels have drawbacks.** Many hostels—especially official ones—have strict rules. Some lock up during the day (usually from 10 a.m. to 5 p.m.), and many have a curfew at night (10 p.m., 11 p.m., or midnight), when the doors are locked. Curfew times differ depending on the hostel and destination. In the Swiss Alps, curfew is early because most people are early-rising hikers. In London, the curfew is 11:45 p.m., giving you ample time to return from the theater. Amsterdam, where the sun shines at night, has a 2 a.m. curfew. These curfews are for the greater good—not to make you miserable. In fact, a curfew can be a big advantage—hostels that don't have curfews, especially in big cities, are more likely to have hostelers (often drunk and rowdy) returning at ungodly hours.

The sounds you'll hear just after everyone's turned in remind me of summer camp—giggles, burps, jokes, and strange noises in many languages. Snoring is permitted and practiced openly.

Hostel rooms can be large and packed. Many school groups (especially German) turn hostels upside down (typically weekends during the school year and weekdays in the summer). Try to be understanding (many groups are disadvantaged kids); we were all noisy kids at one time. Get to know the teacher and make it a "cultural experience."

*Stockholm's floating youth hostel, the* af Chapman

Theft is a problem in hostels, but the answer is simple: Wear your money belt (even while sleeping) and don't leave valuables lying around (but no one's going to steal your tennis shoes or journal). Use the storage lockers that are available in most hostels.

In a few hostels in Britain, hostelers are required to do chores (token duties that never take more than a few minutes). It used to be that every hosteler in Europe was assigned a chore. This custom has died out on the Continent, but lives on (barely) in Britain.

**Hostel selectively.** Hostels come in all shapes and sizes, and some are sightseeing ends in themselves. There are castles (Bacharach, Germany), cutter ships (Stockholm), alpine chalets (Gimmelwald, Switzerland), huge modern buildings (Frankfurt), lakefront villas (Lugano), former prisons (Ljubljana, Slovenia), medieval manor houses (Wilderhope Manor, England), former choirboys' dorms (St. Paul's, London), country estates (Loch Lomond, Scotland), and former royal residences (Holland Park, London). Survey other hostelers and hostel employees for suggestions.

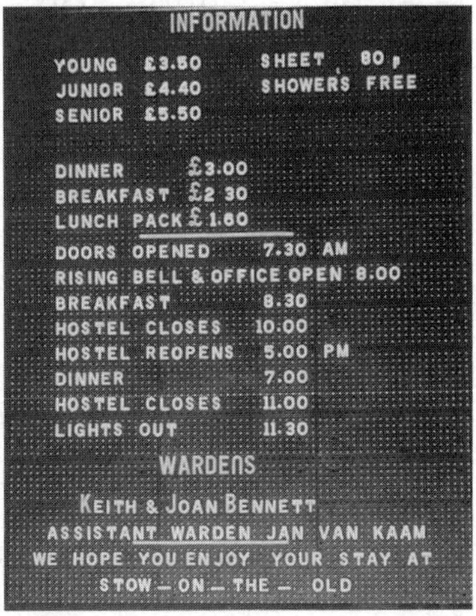

I've hosteled most in the north, where hostels are more comfortable and the savings over hotels more exciting. I rarely hostel in the south, where hostels are less common and two or three people can sleep just as cheaply in a budget hotel.

Big-city hostels are the most overrun by young backpackers. Rural hostels, far from train lines and famous sights, are usually quiet and frequented by a more mature crowd. If you have a car, use that mobility to leave the Eurail zone and enjoy some of Europe's overlooked hostels.

**Getting a hostel bed in peak tourist season can be tricky.** The most popular hostels fill up every day. Most hostels will take telephone or e-mail reservations. I always call or e-mail ahead to try to reserve and at least check on the availability of beds. But don't rely solely on advance reservations, because many hostels hold some beds for drop-ins. Try to arrive early. If the hostel has a lockout period during the day, show up before the office closes in the morning; otherwise, line up with the scruffy gang for the 5 p.m. reopening, when any remaining beds are doled out.

Thankfully, many official hostels are putting out envelopes for each available bed, so you can drop by any time of day, pop your card into the reservation envelope and through the slot, and show up sometime that evening. Also, some hostels have a reservation system where, for a small fee, you can reserve and pay for your next hostel bed before you leave the last one. You can book at official HI hostels from the United States or on the road in Europe online (www.hihostels.com, no extra fee) or by phone (301/495-1240, $5 processing fee per location booked). They accept Visa and MasterCard, restrict their service to hostel members, and sell hostel membership cards. Book at least a day in advance.

*In most hostels, there's a dorm room for boys... and a dorm room for girls.*

Hostel bed availability is unpredictable. Some obscure hostels are booked out on certain days two months in advance. But I stumbled into Oberammergau one night during the jam-packed Passion Play festival and found beds for a group of eight.

## Camping European Style

Relatively few Americans take advantage of Europe's 10,000-plus campgrounds. Camping is the cheapest way to see Europe and the middle-class European family way to travel. Campers give it rave reviews.

"Camping" is the international word for campground. Every town has a camping with enough ground to pitch a tent or park a caravan (trailer), good showers and washing facilities, and often a grocery store and restaurant, all for just a few dollars per person per night. In America, we think of campgrounds as being picturesque, rustic cul-de-sacs near a lake or forest. European campgrounds can range from functional (like spending the night in a park-and-ride) to a vacation extravaganza, with restaurants, mini-water parks, and discos. Campings forbid open fires, and you usually won't find a riverfront lot with a stove, table, and privacy. They rarely fill up, and, if they do, the "Full" sign usually refers to trailers (most Europeans are trailer campers). A small tent can almost always be squeezed in somewhere.

Europe's campgrounds mix well with just about any mode of transportation. And light modern camp gear makes camping without a car easier than ever. Tent and train can be a winning combination, though it can be challenging to find convenient transportation between the train station and the campground. On arrival at the station, stop by the TI and pick up a map with campgrounds marked, local camping leaflets, and bus directions. In some cases, buses shuttle campers from station to campground with ease. Stations generally have lockers in which those with limited energy can leave unneeded baggage.

Hitchhikers find camping just right for their tender budgets. Many campgrounds are located near the major road out of town, where long rides are best snared. Any hitching camper with average social skills can find a friend driving his way with an empty seat. A note on the camp bulletin board can be very effective.

Tents and bikes also mix well. Bikers enjoy the same we-can-squeeze-one-more-in status as hikers and are very rarely turned away.

Camping by car is my favorite combination. A car carries all your camp gear and gets you to any campground quickly and easily. Good road maps always pinpoint campings, and, when you're within a few blocks, the road signs take over. In big cities, the money you save on parking alone will pay for your camping. I usually take the bus downtown, leaving my camper van at the campground.

**Learning about campgrounds:** Each country's national tourist office in the United States can send you information on camping in its country. Consider getting the *Traveler's Guide to European Camping* or *RV and Car Camping Vacations in Europe*, both by Mike and Terri Church (available through www.amazon.com or www.rollinghomes.com). The AA—Britain's AAA-type automobile club—publishes an annual guide called *AA Caravan & Camping Europe.* This excellent resource includes detailed listings for thousands of campgrounds in Western Europe, along with color maps for locating each one. Separate editions focus on France and Britain/Ireland (www.theaa.com/bookshop). The Let's Go guides give good instructions on getting to and from campgrounds. Other resources include *Europe by Van & Motorhome* by David Shore & Patty Campbell (see page 153) and *Camping Europe* by Carol Mickelsen.

*Many campgrounds offer bungalows with kitchenettes and four to six beds. Comfortable and cheaper than hotels, these are particularly popular in Scandinavia.*

Campings are well posted, and local tourist information offices have guides and maps listing nearby campgrounds. Every country has good and bad campgrounds; most of them mirror their surroundings. If the region is overcrowded, dusty, dirty, unkempt, and generally chaotic, you're unlikely to find an oasis behind the campground's gates. A sleepy Austrian valley will most likely offer a sleepy Austrian campground.

European sites called "weekend campings" are rented out on a yearly basis to local urbanites. Too often, weekend sites are full or don't allow what they call "stop-and-go" campers (you). Camping guidebooks indicate which places are the "weekend" types.

**Prices:** Prices vary according to facilities and style—sometimes it's by the tent, sometimes by the person. Expect to spend $5–7 per night per person.

**Registration and regulations:** Camp registration is easy. As with most hotels, you show your passport, fill out a short form, and learn the rules. Checkout time is usually noon. English is the second language of campings throughout Europe, and most managers will understand the monoglot American.

European campgrounds generally require you to leave your passport with the office until you pay your bill. But many campgrounds will accept instead a International Camping Card ($20, also called a Camping Carnet). These cards may get you discounts at some campgrounds. The organization Family Campers and RVers sells the card to members ($25 per family for membership plus $20 for the carnet, www.fcrv.org, tel. 800-245-9755).

Silence usually reigns in European campgrounds beginning at 10 or 11 p.m. Noisemakers are strictly dealt with. Many places close the gates to cars after 11 p.m. If you do arrive after the office closes, set up quietly and register in the morning.

**Campground services:** European campgrounds have great, if sometimes crowded, showers and washing facilities. Hot water, as in many hostels and hotels, is often metered, and you'll learn to carry coins and *douche* quickly. At larger campgrounds, tenters appreciate the in-camp grocery store and café. The store, while high-priced, stays open longer than most, offering latecomers a chance to picnic. The café is a likely camp hangout, and Americans enjoy mixing in this easygoing European social scene. I've scuttled many nights on the town so I wouldn't miss the fun with new friends right in the camp. Camping, like hosteling, is a great way to meet Europeans. If the campground doesn't have a place to eat, you'll find one nearby.

**Camping with kids:** A family sleeps in a tent a lot cheaper than in a hotel. Camping offers plenty to occupy children's attention, including playgrounds that come fully equipped with European kids. And as your kids make European friends, your campground social circle widens.

**Safety:** Campgrounds, unlike hostels, are remarkably theft free. Campings are full of basically honest middle-class European families, and someone's at the gate all day. Most people just leave their gear zipped inside their tents.

**Camping equipment:** Your camping trip deserves first-class equipment. Spend some time and money outfitting yourself before your trip. There are plenty of stores with exciting new gear and expert salespeople to get you up-to-date in a hurry.

For Europe, campers prefer a very lightweight "three-season" sleeping bag (consult the climate chart in the appendix for your probable bedroom temperature) and a closed-cell sleeping pad to insulate and soften the ground.

If you bring a stove from home, it should be the butane Gaz variety (but note that you can't take a Gaz cartridge on the plane—buy it there or lose it here). I keep meals simple, picnicking and enjoying food and fun in the campground café. I'd suggest starting without a stove. If you find out you want one, buy it there. In Europe, it's much easier to find fuel for a European camp stove than for its Yankee counterpart.

Stoves and all other camping gear are cheaper at large superstores (found in Britain, France, Germany, and Spain) than at European backpacking stores. In the US, the cheap chains (Wal-Mart, Target, and Costco) sell cheap equipment. For pricier, fancier gear, consider REI (www.rei.com, tel. 800-426-4840), Campmor (www.campmor.com, tel. 888-226-7667), or L.L. Bean (www.llbean.com, tel. 800-441-5713).

Commit yourself to a camping trip or to a no-camping trip and pack accordingly. Don't carry a sleeping bag and a tent just in case.

**Free camping:** Informal camping, or "camping wild," is legal in most of Europe. Low-profile, pitch-the-tent-after-dark-and-move-on-first-thing-in-the-morning free camping is usually allowed even in countries where it is technically illegal. Use common sense, and don't pitch your tent informally in carefully controlled areas such as cities and resorts. It's a good idea to ask permission when possible. In the countryside, a landowner will rarely refuse a polite request to borrow a patch of land for the night. Formal camping is safer than free camping. Never leave your gear and tent unattended without the gates of a formal campground to discourage thieves.

## Hut-Hopping

Hundreds of alpine huts exist to provide food and shelter for hikers. I know a family who hiked from France to Slovenia, spending every night along the way in a mountain hut. The huts are generally spaced 4–6 hours apart. Most serve hot meals and provide bunk-style lodging. Many alpine huts (like independent hostels) require no linen and wash their blankets annually. I'll never forget getting cozy in my top bunk while a German with a "Rat Patrol" accent in the bottom bunk said, "You're climbing into the germs of centuries." Hut-hoppers hike with their own sheets.

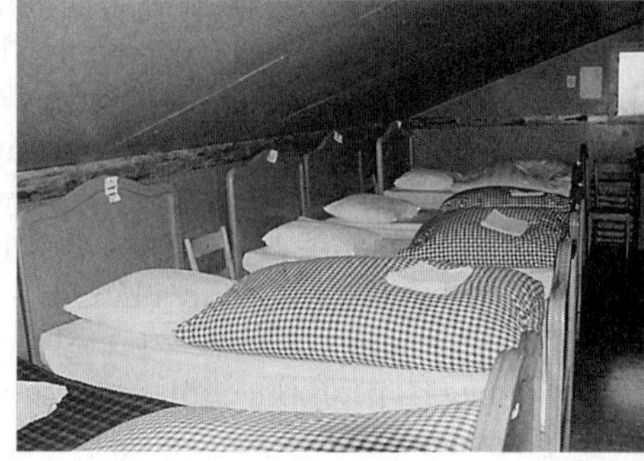

In the Alps, look for the word *Lager,* which means they have a coed loft full of $10-a-night mattresses. Good books on hut-hopping include *Switzerland's Mountain Inns* (Marcia and Philip Lieberman, Countryman Press) and *100 Hut Walks in the Alps* (Kev Reynolds, Cicerone Press). Both are available through www.amazon.com.

## Sleeping Free

There are still people traveling in Europe on $20 a day. The one thing they have in common (apart from B.O.) is that they sleep free. If even cheap pensions and hostels are too expensive for your budget, you too can sleep free. I once went 29 out of 30 nights without paying for a bed. It's not difficult, but it's not always comfortable, convenient, safe, or legal, either. This is not a vagabonding guide, but any traveler may have an occasional free night. Faking it until the sun returns can become, at least in the long run, a good memory.

Europe has plenty of places to roll out your sleeping bag. Some large cities, such as Amsterdam and Athens, are flooded with tourists during peak season, and many spend their nights dangerously in city parks. Some cities enforce their "no sleeping in the parks" laws only selectively. Big, crowded cities such as London, Paris, Munich, Venice, and Copenhagen run safe, legal, and nearly free sleep-ins (tents or huge dorms) during peak season. Away from the cities, in forests or on beaches, you can pretty well sleep where you like. I have found that summer nights in the Mediterranean part of Europe are mild enough that I am comfortable with just my jeans, sweater, and hostel sheet. I no longer lug a sleeping bag around, but if you'll be vagabonding a lot, bring a light bag.

Imaginative vagabonds see Europe as one big free hotel (barns, churches, buildings under construction, ruins, college dorms, etc.). Just keep your passport with you, attach your belongings to you so they don't

*A bench with a view*

get stolen, and use good judgment in your choice of a free bed.

**Sleeping in train stations:** When you have no place to go for the night in a city, you can always retreat to the station (assuming it stays open all night). It's free, warm, safe, and uncomfortable. Most popular tourist cities in Europe have stations whose concrete floors are painted nightly with a long rainbow of sleepy vagabonds. This is allowed, but everyone is cleared out at dawn before the normal rush of travelers converges on the station. In some cases, you'll be asked to show a ticket. Any ticket or train pass entitles you to a free night in a station's waiting room: You are simply waiting for your early train. Whenever possible, avoid the second-class lounges; sleep with a better breed of hobo in first-class lounges. For safety, lock your pack in a station locker or check it at the baggage counter.

**Sleeping on trains:** Success hinges on getting enough room to stretch out, and that can be quite a trick (see Chapter 11: Train and Railpass Skills). It's tempting but quite risky to sleep in a train car that seems to be parked for the night in a station. No awakening is ruder than having your bedroom jolt into motion and roll toward God-knows-where. If you do find a parked train car to sleep in, check to see when it's scheduled to leave. Some Eurailers get a free if disjointed night by riding a train out for four hours and catching one back in for another four hours. Scandinavia, with Europe's most expensive hotels, offers *couchettes* for a reasonable $25.

**Sleeping in airports:** An airport is a large, posh version of a train station, offering a great opportunity to sleep free. After a late landing, I crash on a comfortable sofa rather than waste sleeping time looking for a place that will sell me a bed for the remainder of the night. Many cut-rate inter-European flights leave or arrive at ungodly hours. Frankfurt airport is served conveniently by the train and is great for sleeping free—even if you aren't flying anywhere. Early the next morning you can book into a hotel and only pay for the following night. If your room is still occupied, leave your bag with the receptionist (she'll move it in later) and get out to see the town.

Some large airports have sterile, womblike "rest cabins" which rent for eight hours at the price of a cheap hotel room. (I routinely use these "cocoons" at the Paris and Copenhagen airports.)

## Friends and Relatives

There is no better way to enjoy a new country than as the guest of a local family. And, of course, a night with a friend or relative stretches your budget (usually along with your belly). I've had nothing but good experiences (and good sleep) at my "addresses" in Europe. There are two kinds of addresses: European addresses brought from home and those you pick up while traveling.

*The Europeans you visit don't need to be next-of-kin. This Tirolean is the father of my sister's ski teacher. That's close enough.*

Before you leave, do some research. Dig up some European relatives. No matter how far out on the family tree they are, unless you're a real jerk, they're tickled to have an American visitor in their nest. I send my relatives an e-mail or postcard announcing my visit to their town and telling them when I'll arrive. They answer with "Please come visit us" or "Have a good trip." It is obvious from their response (or lack of one) if I'm invited to stop by.

Follow the same procedure with indirect contacts. I have dear "parents away from home" in Austria and London. My Austrian "parents" are really the parents of my sister's ski instructor. In London, they are friends of my uncle. Neither relationship was terribly close—until I visited. Now we are friends for life.

This is not cultural freeloading. Both parties benefit from such a visit. Never forget that a Greek family is just as curious and interested in you as you are in them (and the same old nightly family meals are probably pretty boring). Equipped with hometown postcards, pictures of my family, and a bag of goodies for the children, I make a point of giving as much from my culture as I am taking from the culture of my host. I insist on no special treatment, telling my host that I am most comfortable when treated simply as part of the family. I try to help with the chores, I don't wear out my welcome, and I follow up each visit with postcards or e-mails to share the rest of my trip with my friends. I pay or reimburse my hosts for their hospitality only with a thank-you letter from home, possibly with photos of all of us together.

The other kind of address is one you pick up during your travels. Exchanging addresses is almost as common as a handshake in Europe. If you have a business or personal card, bring a pile. (Some travelers even print up a batch of personal cards for their trip.) When people meet, they invite each other to visit. I warn my friend that I may very well show up some day at his house, whether it's in Osaka, Auckland, Santa Fe, or Dublin. When I have, it's been a good experience.

## Servas

Servas is a worldwide organization that connects travelers with host families with the noble goal of building world peace through international understanding. International travelers pay $85 to join, plus a refundable $25 deposit for up to five sets of country or regional host lists (additional $25 for 6–10 lists, refunded if you return the lists and complete a travel report when you return). They can stay for two nights (more only if invited) in homes of other members around the world. You'll correspond with your host to make arrangements, and no money changes hands (except to reimburse hosts for telephone calls). This is not a crash-pad exchange. It's cultural sightseeing through a real live-in experience. Plan to hang around to talk and share and learn. Offer to cook a meal or help out around the house. Many travelers swear by Servas as the only way to really travel and build a truly global list of friends. Opening your own home to visitors is not required, but encouraged. For more information, contact Servas (info@usservas.org, tel. 212/267-0252).

A newer, less formal alternative to Servas is CouchSurfing (www.couchsurfing.com).

Friendship Force International offers cultural exchange tours for the purpose of promoting global goodwill (www.friendshipforce.org, 404/522-9490). The London-based Globetrotters Club runs a network of hosts and travelers (annual membership approximately $32, www.globetrotters.co.uk).

## House-Swapping

Many families enjoy a great budget option year after year. They trade houses (sometimes cars, too—but draw the line at pets) with someone at the destination of their choice. Veteran house-swappers offer these tips: Be triple-sure about where to find the key and how to open the door, find out beforehand how to get to the nearest food store, make sure your host family leaves instructions for operating the appliances, make arrangements in advance to handle telephone charges, and ask about any peculiarities with the car you'll be driving.

For information, contact HomeLink (www.homelink.org, tel. 800-638-3841), HomeExchange.com (www.homeexchange.com, tel. 800-877-8723), or Intervac Home Exchange (www.intervacus.com, tel. 800-756-4663).

# 18. EATING

*A fun neighborhood restaurant: no English menus, no credit cards, but good food, good prices, and a friendly staff*

Many vacations revolve around great restaurant meals, and for good reason. Europe serves some of the world's top cuisine at some of the world's top prices. I'm no gourmet, so most of my experience lies in eating well cheaply. Galloping gluttons thrive on $20 a day—by picnicking. Those with a more refined palate and a little more money can mix picnics with atmospheric and enjoyable restaurant meals and eat well for $35 a day.

This $35-a-day budget includes a $10 lunch (cheaper if you picnic or eat fast food), a $20 good and filling restaurant dinner (more with wine or dessert), and $5 for your chocolate, cappuccino, and gelato needs. (This assumes that breakfast is included with your hotel room; if you have to buy breakfast, have a picnic lunch...or eat less gelato.) If your budget requires, you can find a satisfying dinner for $15 anywhere in Europe. If you have more money, of course, it's delightful to spend it dining well.

## Breakfast

The farther north you go in Europe, the heartier the breakfasts. Heaviest are the traditional British fry and Scandinavian buffet breakfasts. Throughout the Netherlands, Belgium, Germany, Austria, Switzerland, and Eastern Europe, expect a more modest buffet—but still plenty of options (rolls, bread, jam, cold cuts, cheeses, fruit, yogurt, and cereal). As you move south and west (France, Italy, Spain, and Portugal), skimpier "continental" breakfasts are the norm. You'll get a roll with marmalade or jam, occasionally a slice of ham or cheese, and coffee or tea.

*The continental breakfast: bread, jam, cheese, and coffee*

If your breakfast is sparse, supplement it with a piece of fruit and a wrapped chunk of cheese from your rucksack stash. Orange juice fans pick up liter boxes in the grocery store and start the day with a glass in their hotel room. If you're a coffee drinker, remember that breakfast is the only cheap time to caffeinate yourself. Some hotels will serve you a bottomless cup of a rich brew only with breakfast. After that, the cups acquire bottoms. Juice is generally available, but in Mediterranean countries, you have to ask...and you'll probably be charged.

Breakfast, normally "included" in your hotel bill, can sometimes be skipped and deducted from the price of your room. Ask what the breakfast includes and costs. In southern Europe, you can usually save money and gain atmosphere by buying coffee and a roll or croissant at the café down the street or by brunching picnic-style in the park. I'm a big-breakfast person at home. But when I feel the urge for a typical American breakfast in Europe, I beat it to death with a hard roll. You can find bacon, eggs, and orange juice, but it's nearly always overpriced and a disappointment.

Few hotel breakfasts are worth waiting around for. If you need to get an early start, skip it.

## Picnics—Spend Like a Pauper, Eat Like a Prince

There is only one way left to feast for $10 anywhere in Europe: picnic. You'll eat better, while spending $15–20 a day less than those who eat exclusively in restaurants.

I am a picnic connoisseur. While I'm the first to admit that restaurant meals are an important aspect of any culture, I picnic almost daily. This is not solely for budgetary reasons. It's fun to dive into a marketplace and actually get a chance to do business. Europe's colorful markets overflow with varied cheeses, meats, fresh fruits, vegetables, and still-warm-out-of-the-bakery-oven bread. Many of my favorite

foods made their debut in a European picnic.

To busy sightseers, restaurants can be time-consuming and frustrating. After waiting to be served, tangling with a menu, and consuming a budget-threatening meal, you walk away feeling unsatisfied, knowing your money could have done much more for your stomach if you had invested it in a picnic. Nutritionally, a picnic is unbeatable. Consider this example: cheese, thinly-sliced ham, fresh bread, peaches, carrots, a cucumber, a half liter of milk, and fruit yogurt or a freshly-baked pastry for dessert.

To bolster your budget, I recommend picnic dinners every few nights. At home, we save time and money by raiding the refrigerator for dinner. In Europe, the equivalent is the corner deli or grocery store. There are plenty of tasty alternatives to sandwiches. Bakeries often sell little pizzas and meat pies. Supermarkets, which hide out in the basements of big-city department stores, are getting very yuppie, offering salads, quiche, fried chicken, and fish, all "to go." "Microwave" is a universal word. When staying several nights, I cozy up a hotel room by borrowing plates, glasses, and silverware from the breakfast room and stocking the closet with my favorite groceries (juice, fruits and vegetables, cheese, and other munchies).

### Picnic Shopping

Every town, large or small, has at least one colorful outdoor or indoor marketplace. Assemble your picnic here. Make an effort to communicate with the merchants. Most markets are not self-service: You point to what you want and let the merchant bag it and weigh it for you. Know what you are buying and what you are spending. Whether you understand the prices or not, act like you do (observing the weighing process closely), and you're more likely to be treated fairly.

*A quick dashboard picnic halfway through a busy day of sightseeing*

**Learn the measurements.** The unit of measure throughout the Continent is a kilo, or 2.2 pounds. A kilo has 1,000 grams. One hundred grams (a common unit of sale) of cheese or meat tucked into a chunk of French bread gives you about a quarter-pounder.

**Food can be priced by the kilo, the 100-gram unit, or the piece.** Watch the scale when your food is being weighed. It'll show grams and kilos. If dried apples are priced at £2 per kilo, that's $3.60 for 2.2 pounds, or about $1.65 per pound. If the scale says 400 grams, that means 40 percent of £2 (or 80 pence), which is about $1.45.

Specialty foods are sometimes priced by 100 grams. If the pâté seems too cheap to be true, look at the sign closely. The posted price is probably followed by "100 gr." Chunky items like cucumbers will be priced by the piece (Stück in Germany or pezzo in Italy).

**If no prices are posted, be wary.** Tourists are routinely ripped off by market merchants in tourist centers. Find places that print the prices. Assume any market with no printed prices has a double price standard: one for locals and a more expensive one for tourists.

I'll never forget a friend of mine who bought two bananas for our London picnic. He grabbed the fruit, held out a handful of change, and said, "How much?" The merchant took two pounds (worth $3.60). My friend turned to me and said, "Wow, London really is expensive." Anytime you hold out a handful of money to a banana salesman, you're just asking for trouble.

**If you want only a small amount...**You'll likely want only one or two pieces of fruit, and many merchants refuse to deal in such small quantities. The way to get what you want and no more is to estimate what it would cost if the merchant were to weigh it and then just hold out a coin worth about that much in one hand and the apple, or whatever, in the other. Have a Forrest Gump look on your face that says, "If you take this coin, I'll go away." Rarely will he refuse the deal.

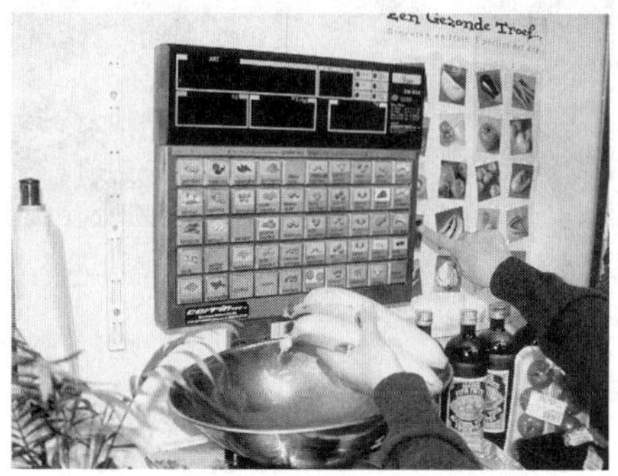
*Put your banana in the bin, push the banana button, rip off the price sticker, and stick it on your banana.*

In supermarkets, it's a cinch to buy a tiny amount of fruit or vegetables. Most have an easy push-button pricing system: Put the banana on the scale, push the picture of a banana (or enter the banana bin number), and a sticky price tag prints out. You could weigh and sticker a single grape.

## Picnic Drinks

There are plenty of cheap ways to wash down a picnic. Milk is always cheap and available in quarter, half, or whole liters. Be sure it's normal drinking milk. Strange white liquid dairy products in look-alike milk cartons abound, ruining the milk-and-cookie dreams of careless tourists. Look for local words for "whole" or "light," such as *voll* or *lett*. Nutritionally, half a liter provides about 25 percent of your daily protein needs. Get refrigerated, fresh milk. You will often find a "long life" kind of milk that needs no refrigeration. This milk will never go bad—or taste good.

*This happy gang is living simply and well on the cheap: enjoying a picnic in the hometown of St. Francis, Assisi.*

European yogurt is delicious and can usually be drunk right out of its container. Fruit juice comes in handy liter boxes (look for "100% juice" or "no sugar" to avoid Kool-Aid clones). Buy

*Picnic on the train—quick, hearty, scenic*

cheap by the liter, and use a reusable half-liter plastic mineral-water bottle (sold next to the Coke all over) to store what you can't comfortably drink in one sitting. Liter bottles of Coke are cheap, as is wine in most countries. Local wine gives your picnic a nice touch. Any place that serves coffee has free boiling water. Those who have more nerve than pride get their plastic water bottle (a sturdy plastic bottle will not melt) filled with free boiling water at a café, then add their own instant coffee or tea bag later. Many hotels or cafés will fill a thermos with coffee for about the price of two cups.

### Picnic Atmosphere

There is nothing second-class about a picnic. A few special touches will even make your budget meal a first-class affair. Proper site selection can make the difference between just another meal and *le pique-nique extraordinaire.* Since you've decided to skip the restaurant, it's up to you to create the atmosphere.

Try to incorporate a picnic brunch, lunch, or dinner into the day's sightseeing plans. For example, I start the day by scouring the thriving market with my senses and my camera. Then I fill up my shopping bag and have breakfast on a riverbank. After sightseeing, I combine lunch and a siesta in a cool park to fill my stomach, rest my body, and escape the early afternoon heat. It's fun to eat dinner on a castle wall enjoying a commanding view and the setting sun. Some of my all-time best picnics have been lazy dinners accompanied by medieval fantasies in the quiet of after-hours Europe.

Mountain hikes are punctuated nicely by picnics. Food tastes even better on top of a mountain. Europeans are great picnickers. Many picnics become potlucks, resulting in new friends as well as full stomachs.

### Table Scraps and Tips

**Bring picnic supplies.** Pack resealable plastic baggies (large and small, hard to find in Europe). Buy a good knife with a can opener and corkscrew

*Kick back and munch a picnic dinner in your hotel room.*

in Europe (or bring it from home, if you plan to check your luggage on the plane). In addition to being a handy plate, fan, and lousy Frisbee, a plastic coffee-can lid makes an easy-to-clean cutting board with a juice-containing lip. A dishtowel doubles as a small tablecloth, and a washcloth helps with clean-up. A fancy hotel shower cap contains messy food nicely on your picnic cloth. Bring an airline-type coffee cup and spoon for cereal, and a fork for take-out salad and chicken. Some travelers get immersion heaters (buy in Europe for a compatible plug) to make hot drinks to go with munchies in their hotel room.

**Stretch your money.** Bread has always been cheap in Europe. (Leaders have learned from history that when stomachs rumble, so do the mobs in the streets.) Cheese is a specialty nearly everywhere and is, along with milk, one of the Continent's cheapest sources of protein. The standard low-risk option anywhere in Europe is Emmentaler cheese (the kind with holes, which we call "Swiss"). In season, tomatoes, cucumbers, and watermelons are good deals in Italy. Slovenia and Croatia have some of the best, cheapest ice cream anywhere. Wine is a great buy in France and Spain. Anything American is usually expensive and rarely satisfying. Cultural chameleons eat and drink better and cheaper.

*For restaurant food at halfway-to-picnic prices, visit the local* rosticceria *or take-out deli.*

**Make your big meal of the day a picnic lunch or dinner.** Only a glutton can spend more than $15 for a picnic feast. In a park in Paris, on a Norwegian ferry, high in the Alps, on your dashboard at an autobahn rest stop, on your convent rooftop, or in your hotel room, picnicking is the budget traveler's key to cheap and good eating.

## Fast Food, Cafeterias, and Mensas

**McEurope:** Fast-food restaurants are everywhere. Yes, the hamburgerization of the world is a shame, but face it—the busiest and biggest McDonald's in the world are in Tokyo, Rome, and Moscow. The burger has become a global thing. You'll find Big Macs in every language—not exciting (and more than the American price), but at least at McDonald's you know exactly what you're getting, and it's fast. A hamburger, fries, and shake are fun halfway through your trip.

American fast-food joints are kid-friendly and satisfy the need for a cheap salad bar and a tall orange juice. They've grabbed prime bits of real estate in every big European city. Since there's no cover, this is an opportunity to savor a low-class paper cup of coffee while enjoying some high-class people-watching.

Each country has its equivalent of the hamburger stand (I saw a "McCheaper" in Switzerland). Whatever their origin, they're a hit with the young locals and a handy place for a quick, cheap bite to eat.

**Cafeterias:** "Self-service" is an international word. You'll find self-service restaurants in big cities everywhere, offering low-price, low-risk, low-stress, what-you-see-is-what-you-get meals. A sure value for your euro is a department-store cafeteria. These places are designed for the shopping housewife who has a sharp eye for a good value. At a salad bar, grab the small (cheap) plate and stack it like the locals—high.

*Cafeteria leftovers: even cheaper than picnics...*

**Mensas:** If your wallet is as empty as your stomach, find a "mensa." Mensa is the pan-European word for a government-subsidized institutional (university, fire station, union of gondoliers, etc.) cafeteria. If the place welcomes tourists, you can fill yourself with a plate of dull but nourishing food for an unbeatable price in the company of local students or workers.

University cafeterias (often closed during summer holidays) offer a surefire way to meet educated English-speaking young locals with open and stimulating minds. They're often eager to practice their politics and economics, as well as their English, on a foreign friend. This is especially handy as you travel beyond Europe.

## Cafés and Bars

From top to bottom, Europe is into café-sitting, coffee-sipping, and people-watching. Tourists are often stung by not understanding the rules of the game. You'll pay less to stand and more to sit. In general, if you simply want to slam down a cup of coffee, order and drink it at the bar. If you want to sit awhile and absorb that last museum while checking out the two-legged art, grab a table with a view and a waiter will take your order. This will cost you about double. If you're on a budget, always confirm the price for a sit-down drink. While it's never high profile, there's always a price list posted somewhere inside with the two-tiered price system clearly labeled (e.g., cheap at the bar, more at the table). If you pay for a seat in a café with an expensive drink, that seat's yours for the entire afternoon if you like. Lingering with your bar-priced drink on a nearby public bench or across the street on the beach is usually OK—just ask first.

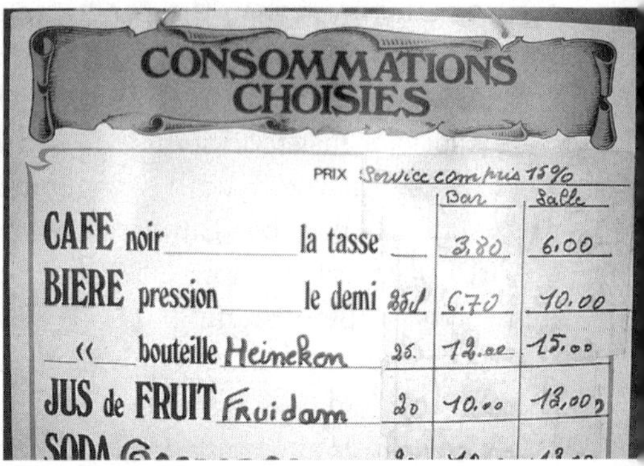

*In European cafés, menus are two-tiered: cheaper at the bar, more at a table.*

In some coffee bars (especially in Italy), you pay for your drink (or whatever) at the cash register, then take your receipt to the bar, where you'll be served.

## Restaurants

Restaurants are the most expensive way to eat. They can pillage and plunder a tight budget, but it would be criminal to pass through Europe without sampling the local specialties served in good restaurants. A country's high cuisine is just as culturally important as its museums. Experience it.

European restaurants are no more expensive than American restaurants. The cost of eating is determined not by the local standard but by your personal standard. Many Americans can't find an edible meal for less than $30 in their hometown. Their neighbors enjoy eating out for half that. If you can enjoy a $15 meal in Boston, Detroit, or Seattle, you'll eat well in London, Rome, or Helsinki for the same price. Last year I ate 100 dinners in Europe. My budget target was $15 for a simple, fill-the-tank meal; $20 for a good restaurant dinner; and $40 for a splurge feast.

Forget the scare stories. People who spend $50 on dinner in Dublin and then complain either enjoy complaining or are fools. Let me fill you in on filling up in Europe.

Average tourists are attracted—like moths to a light bulb—to the biggest neon sign that boasts, *We speak English and accept credit cards.* Wrong! I look for a handwritten menu in the local language only, with a very small selection. This means they're cooking what was fresh in the market this morning to a loyal, local clientele (and not targeting tourists). Find a restaurant filled with local customers enjoying themselves. Be snoopy. Look at what people are eating—just don't ask for a taste. After a few days in Europe, you'll have no trouble telling a local hangout from a tourist trap.

Restaurants listed in your guidebook are usually fine, but too often when a place becomes famous this way, it goes downhill. You don't need those listings to find your own good restaurant. Leave the tourist center and stroll around until you find a restaurant with a happy crowd of locals. Ask your hotel receptionist, or even someone on the street, for a good place—not a good place for tourists, but a place they'd take a local guest.

The key challenge of budget eating is ordering just enough to fill you, while leaving nothing on your plate. If a single main dish is enough for 1.5 people (as many are), split it between you and your travel partner, and add a bowl of soup or something small to supplement it. With the recent euro-related inflation, prices are high for Europeans, too. Waiters are generally understanding and accommodating.

### Deciphering the Menu

European restaurants post their menus outside. Check the price and selection before entering. If the menu's not posted, ask to see one.

Finding the right restaurant is only half the battle. Then you need to order a good meal. Ordering in a foreign language can be fun, or it can be an ordeal. Ask for an English menu—if nothing else, you might get the waiter who speaks the *goodest* English. Most waiters can give at least a very basic translation—"cheekin, bunny, zuppa, green salat,"

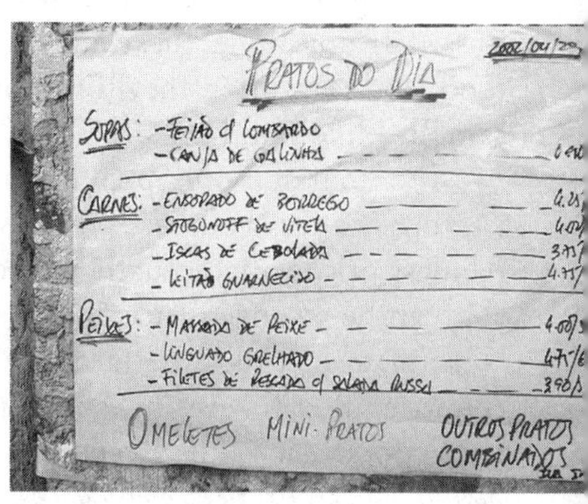


*A small, handwritten menu in the local language is a good sign. Here you see a Portuguese restaurant's "plates of the day"...soups, meats, and fish.*

and so on. A phrase book or menu reader (especially one of Altarinda Publishing's useful-but-hard-to-find *Marling Menu Masters* for France, Germany, Italy, and Spain) is very helpful for those who want to avoid ordering sheep stomach when all they want is a lamb chop.

*Young taste buds having their horizons gently stretched*

If you don't know what to order, go with the waiter's recommendation or look for your dream meal on another table and order by pointing. People are usually helpful and understanding to the poor and hungry monoglot tourist. If they aren't, you probably picked a place that sees too many of them. Europeans with the most patience with tourists are the ones who rarely deal with them.

People who agonize over each word on the menu season the whole experience with stress. If you're in a good place, the food's good. Get a basic idea of what's cooking, have some fun with the waiter, be loose and adventurous, and just order something.

To max out culturally, my partner and I order two different meals: one high risk and one low risk. We share, sampling twice as many dishes. At worst, we learn what we don't like and split the chicken and fries. My tour groups cut every dish into bits, and our table becomes a lazy Susan. If anything, the waiters are impressed by our interest in their food, and very often they'll run over with a special treat for all of us to sample—like squid eggs.

The "tourist *menu*," popular in restaurants throughout Europe's tourist zones, offers confused visitors a no-stress, three-course meal for a painless price which usually includes service, bread, and a drink. While this can be a convenience, locals rarely order it. They consider the local "blue plate special" a better value—and so do I. Small eateries in most countries offer this fresh, economical "*menu* of the day" to those looking for a good basic value. Recognize the local word (*dagens rett* in Sweden, *plat du jour* in France, *menù del giorno* in Italy). These are often limited to early seatings (with the time—usually before 7:30 p.m.—posted on the door and in the menu).

The best values in entrées are usually chicken, fish, and veal. Lately my travel partner and I, rather than getting entrées, have shared a

### Tap Water in guages

Italian: *acqua del rubinetto*
French: *l'eau du robinet*
German: *Leitungswasser*
Spanish: *agua del grifo*
Portuguese: *água da torneira*

In all other languages, just do the international charade: Hold an imaginary glass in one hand, turn on the tap with the other, and make the sound of a faucet. Stop it with a click of your tongue and drink it with a smile.

memorable little buffet of appetizers—they're plenty filling, less expensive, and more typically local than entrées. Drinks (except for wine in southern Europe) and desserts are the worst value. Skipping those, you can enjoy some surprisingly good $15 meals.

**Restaurant Drinks**

In restaurants, Europeans generally drink bottled water (for taste, not health). You can normally get free tap water, but you may need to be polite, patient, inventive, and know the correct phrase. There's nothing wrong with ordering tap water, and waiters are accustomed to this request. Availability of (and willingness to serve) tap water varies from country to country. It's sometimes considered a special favor, and while your glass or carafe of tap water is normally served politely, occasionally it just isn't worth the trouble, and it's best to just put up with the bottle of Perrier or order a drink from the menu.

Bottled water is served crisp and cold, either with or without carbonation, usually by happier waiters. Most tourists don't like the bubbly stuff. Learn the phrase *con/avec/mit/con/*with gas or *senza/sans/ohne/sin/* without gas (in Italian, French, German, and Spanish, respectively), and you will get the message across. Acquire a taste for *acqua con gas.* It's a lot more fun (and read on the label what it'll do for your rheumatism).

If your budget is tight and you want to save $5–10 a day, never buy a restaurant drink. Scoff if you have the money, but drinks can sink a tight budget. While water is jokingly called the "American champagne" by the waiters of Europe, with the cost of living going up for locals lately, these days it's not only tourists going with tap water. Last year in an Oslo restaurant, I counted 17 of 20 diners drinking tap water. (They were charged $1 a glass—but it was still a substantial savings over a $5 Coke.)

Drink like a European. Cold milk, ice cubes, and coffee with (rather than after) your meal are American habits. Insisting on any of these in Europe will get you nothing but strange looks and a reputation as the ugly—if not downright crazy—American. Order local drinks, not just to save money but to experience the culture and to get the best quality and service. The timid can always order the "American waters" (Coke, Fanta, and 7-Up), sold everywhere.

*German pubs don't serve minors beer—but many locals do.*

Buying local alcohol is cheaper than your favorite import. A shot of the local hard drink in Portugal will cost a dollar, while an American drink would cost more than the American price. Drink the local stuff with local people in local bars; it's a better experience than having a Manhattan in your hotel with a guy from Los Angeles. Drink wine in wine countries and beer in beer countries. Sample the regional specialties. Let a local person order you her favorite. You may hate it, but you'll never forget it.

### Getting the Bill

In Europe, the meal is routinely the event of the evening. At good restaurants, service will seem slow. Meals won't always come simultaneously—it's fine to start eating when served. Europeans will spend at least two hours enjoying a good dinner, and, for the full experience, so should you. Fast service is rude service. If you need to eat and run, make your time limits very clear as you order.

To get the bill, you'll have to ask for it (catch the waiter's eye and, with raised hands, scribble with an imaginary pencil on your palm). Before it comes, make a mental tally of roughly how much your meal should cost. The bill should vaguely resemble the figure you expected. It should have the same number of digits. If the total is a surprise, ask to have it itemized and explained. Some waiters make the same "innocent" mistakes repeatedly, knowing most tourists are so befuddled by the money and menu that they'll pay whatever number lies at the bottom of the bill.

## Tipping

Restaurant tips are more modest in Europe than in America. In Europe, 10 percent is a good tip. If your bucks talk at home, muzzle them on your travels. As a matter of principle, if not economy, the local price should prevail.

Tipping is an issue only at restaurants that have waiters and waitresses. If you order your food at a counter (in a pub, for example), don't tip.

Menus in any country will usually state—at the bottom of the menu—if service is included (e.g., in Italy: *servizio incluso*). In this case, a service charge of about 15 percent is included in the menu price or added automatically to your bill. When the service is included, you don't need to tip beyond that, but if you like to tip and you're pleased with the service, you can round up a few euros.

If the menu states that the service is not included (e.g., in France: *service non compris* or *s.n.c.*), tip 5–10 percent by rounding up or leaving the change from your bill. Typically, it's better to hand the tip to the waiter when you're paying your bill than to leave it on the table, particularly in busy places where the wrong party might pocket the change. In Germanic countries, rather than physically leaving a tip on the table, it's considered discreet and classy to say the total number of euros you'd like the waiter to keep (including his tip) when paying. So, if the bill is €78, hand him €100 while saying, "85." You'll get €15 back and feel pretty European. In some places, such as Italy, it's best to tip in cash even if you pay with your credit card. Otherwise the tip may never reach your waitress.

## Vegetarians

Vegetarians find life a little frustrating in Europe. Very often, Europeans think "vegetarian" means "no red meat" or "not much meat." If you are a strict vegetarian, you'll have to make things very clear. Write the appropriate phrase (see below), keep it handy, and show it to each waiter before ordering your meal:

German: *Wir sind (Ich bin) Vegetarier. Wir essen (Ich esse) kein Fleisch, Fisch, oder Geflügel. Eier und Käse OK.*

French: *Nous sommes (Je suis) végétarien. Nous ne mangons (Je ne mange) pas*

*Salad bars are abundant and great for vegetarians.*

*de viande, poisson, ou poulet. Oeufs et fromage OK.*

Italian: *Siamo vegetariani (Sono vegetariano/a). Non mangiamo (mangio) nè carne, nè pesce, nè polli. Uova e formaggio OK.*

Dutch: We are (I am) vegetarian. We (I) do not eat meat, fish, or chicken. Eggs and cheese are OK. (Most Dutch people speak English.)

*A big plate of veggies makes for an energizing lunch...even if you're not a vegetarian.*

Vegetarians have no problem with continental breakfasts, which are normally meatless anyway. Meat-free picnic lunches are delicious, since bread, cheese, and yogurt are wonderful throughout Europe. It's in restaurants that your patience may be minced. Big-city tourist office brochures list restaurants by category. In any language, look under "V." Italy seems to sprinkle a little meat in just about everything. German cooking normally keeps the meat separate from the vegetables. Hearty German salads, with beets, cheese, and eggs, are a vegetarian's delight. Vegetarians enjoy *antipasti* buffets, salad bars, and ethnic restaurants throughout Europe.

## Local Specialties, One Country at a Time

Eating in Europe is sightseeing for your taste buds. Every country has local specialties that are good, memorable, or both. At least once, seek out and eat or drink the notorious "gross" specialties: ouzo, horse meat, snails, raw herring, blood sausage, tripe stew, octopus, and so on. All your life you'll hear references to them, and you'll have actually experienced what everyone's talking about. Here are some tips to help you eat, drink, and be merry in Europe. For more on the delicious and diverse flavors of Europe—especially France and Italy—see Chapter 64.

### Belgium

Belgians boast that they eat as heartily as the Germans and as well as the French. This tiny country is into big steaks and designer chocolates. While Godiva's chocolate is considered the finest, most locals enjoy triple the dose for the same investment by getting their fix at a local place.

Seafood—fish, eel, oysters, and shrimp—is especially well-prepared in Belgium. Mussels are served everywhere. You get a big-enough-for-two bucket and a pile of fries. Go local by using one empty shell to tweeze out the rest of the *moules.*

Belgian fries (*Vlaamse frites,* or "Flemish fries") taste so good because they're deep-fried twice—once to cook, and once to brown. The natives dunk them in mayonnaise...especially delicious if the mayo is flavored with garlic.

Belgium has about 120 different varieties of beer and 580 different brands, more than any other country—and the locals take their beers as seriously as the French regard their wines.

*According to Belgians, the best part of the crab is the guts.*

**Britain and Ireland**

The British Isles' reputation for miserable food is now dated, and today's cuisine scene is lively, trendy, and pleasantly surprising. (Unfortunately, it can also be expensive.)

While you can seek out fine cuisine in Britain and Ireland, it's cheaper and easier to enjoy decent cuisine in great atmosphere. That means pub grub. For $10–15, you'll get a basic, budget, hot lunch or dinner in friendly surroundings.

British pubs generally serve traditional dishes, like fish-and-chips, roast beef, and meat pies. "Crisps" are potato chips. Irish pubs often serve Irish stew (mutton), chowders, pork dishes, and lots of potatoes. Try boxty, a potato pancake filled with fish, meat, or vegetables.

Pub meals are usually served from 12:00–14:00 and from 18:00–20:00, not throughout the day. There's usually no table service. Order at the bar, then take a seat and they'll bring the food when it's ready (or sometimes you pick it up at the bar). Pay at the bar (sometimes when you order, sometimes after you eat). Don't tip unless it's a place with full table service. Pubs that advertise their food and are crowded with locals are less likely to be the kinds that serve only lousy microwaved snacks.

Of course, there are alternatives to pub grub. At classier restaurants, look for early-bird specials, allowing you to eat well and affordably, but early (at about 17:30–19:00, last order by 19:00). A top-end restaurant often serves the same quality two-course lunch deals for a third the price.

Ethnic restaurants from all over the world add spice to England's cuisine scene. Eating Indian or Chinese is cheap (even cheaper if you take it out). Middle Eastern stands sell gyros sandwiches and *shwarmas* (lamb in pita bread).

The British take great pride in their beer. Many Brits think that drinking beer cold and carbonated, as Americans do, ruins the taste. At pubs, long-handled pulls are used to pull the traditional, rich-flavored "real ales" up from the cellar. Short-hand pulls at the bar mean colder, fizzier, mass-produced, and less interesting keg beers. Try the draft cider (sweet or dry)...carefully.

If you're in Scotland and want a nonalcoholic drink, try Irn-Bru, which has the flavor of orange bubblegum, the color of a traffic cone, and this warning on the label: "If it spills, it *will* stain."

When you say "a beer, please" in an Irish pub, you'll get a pint of Guinness (the black beauty with a blonde head). If you want a small beer, ask for a glass or a half pint. Never rush your bartender when he's pouring a Guinness.

For a distinctive local flavor in Britain, sample Marmite—a brown yeasty-salty spread that's every young Brit's peanut butter. But beware... a little Marmite goes a long way. For an unforgettable experience in Scotland, try haggis—liver and suet boiled in a sheep's stomach.

### Eastern Europe

Eastern Europe offers good food for very little money—especially if you venture off the main tourist trail. The cuisine here is generally heavy, hearty, and tasty. Expect lots of meat, potatoes, and cabbage. Still, there's more variety in the East than you might expect.

Czech food is heavy on pork and kraut, but more modern eateries are serving up pasta and salads. Czechs are among the world's most enthusiastic beer *(pivo)* drinkers. The pub is a place to have fun, complain, discuss art and politics, talk hockey, and chat with locals and visitors alike.

In Poland, try the hearty soups, tasty sauerkraut stew, and pierogi (ravioli-like dumplings with various fillings). Take advantage of Poland's amazingly cheap, government-subsidized milk bars *(bar mleczny)*, which usually offer tasty traditional specialties. And be sure to sample the national drink, *wódka*.

The quintessential ingredient in Hungarian cuisine is spicy paprika, which appears in red shakers alongside salt and pepper on tables. Meat of all kinds (especially goose liver) is popular. Seek out the sweet, creamy cold fruit soup *(hideg gyümölcs leves)*.

Slovenia and Croatia offer more variety. Choosing between strudel and baklava on the same menu, you're constantly reminded that this is a land where the Germanic world meets the Mediterranean. Slovenia has good, hearty German-style food, with lots of sausage and buckwheat. In Croatia, the seafood is succulent and plentiful. Both countries have been influenced by Italian cuisine, with excellent pastas and pizzas.

### France

France is famous for its cuisine—and rightly so. Dining in France can be surprisingly easy on a budget, especially in the countryside. Small restaurants throughout the country love their regional cuisine and take great pride in serving it.

The *plat du jour* (daily special), salad plate, and *menu* (fixed-price, three- to six-course meal) are often good deals. To get a complete list of what's cooking, ask for the *carte* (not the *menu*). The cheese boards that come with multi-course meals offer the average American a new adventure in eating. When it comes, ask for "a little of each, please" *(un peu de chaque, s'il vous plaît)*. Wine is the cheapest drink, and every region has its own wine and cheese. Order the house wine *(vin du pays)*. Classy restaurants are easiest to afford at lunchtime, when meal prices are usually reduced. France is known for particularly slow (as in polite) service. If you need to eat and run, make it clear from the start. Bars

*Cheers!*

serve reasonable omelets, salads, and the *croque-monsieur*—your standard grilled cheese and ham sandwich.

French food, while delicious, at times stretches your culinary horizons. A few words to look out for: *cervelle* (brains), *ris de veau* (calf pancreas), *viande de cheval* (horse meat), *andouillette* (intestines), *langue* (tongue)...and, of course, *escargot* (snails) and *cuisses de grenouilles* (frog's legs).

*Degustation gratuite* is not a laxative, but an invitation to sample the wine. You'll find *D/G* signs throughout France's wine-growing regions.

When buying cheese, be sure to ask for samples of the local specialties. Croissants are served warm with breakfast, and baguettes (long, skinny loaves of French bread) are great for budget munching.

Regardless of your budget, picnic for a royal tour of French delicacies. Make a point of visiting the small specialty shops and picking up the finest (most expensive) pâtés, cheeses, and hors d'oeuvres. As you spread out your tablecloth, passersby will wish you a cheery *"Bon appétit!"*

### Germany

Germany is ideal for the "meat-and-potatoes" person. With straightforward, no-nonsense food at budget prices, Deutschland feeds me very well. Small-town restaurants serve up wonderful plates of hearty local specialties for $10.

Ein *Beer,* ein *Pretzel,* und *Thou*

Germany's *Wurst* is the best anywhere, and *Kraut* is not as *sauer* as the stuff you hate at home. Only a tourist puts the sausage in a bun like a hot dog. Munch alternately between the meat and the bread (that's why you have two hands), and you'll look like a local. Generally, the darker the weenie, the spicier it is.

Potatoes are the standard vegetable, but *Spargel* (giant white asparagus) is a must in-season. The bread and pretzels in the basket on your table often cost extra.

When I need a break from pork, I order the *Salatteller* (big, varied dinner-size salad). For budget (and palate) relief in big-city Germany, find a Greek, Turkish, or Italian restaurant. Fast-food stands are called *Schnell Imbiss.*

German wine (85 percent white) is particularly good from the Mosel and Rhine River Valleys. The Germans enjoy a tremendous variety and quantity of great beer. The average German drinks 40 gallons of beer a year.

Browse through supermarkets and see what Germany eats when there's no more beer and pretzels. Try Gummi Bears, the bear-shaped jelly bean with a cult following, and Nutella, a sensuous chocolate-hazelnut spread that turns anything into a first-class dessert.

A few unusual German flavors are worth sampling. *Handkäse* is an especially pungent cheese, sometimes pickled in vinegar. Tourists flock to Rothenburg to buy, sample, and immediately throw away the notorious *Schneeballs*—made of balled-up strips of dough. *Schmalz,* a popular spread, is pure lard...literally. And at Bavarian beer halls, you're likely to see people munching on *Steckerlfisch*—an entire mackerel fish on a stick, roasted over a fire.

### Greece

While the menus are all Greek to most tourists, it's common and acceptable to go into the kitchen and point to the dish you want. This is a good way to make some friends, sample from each kettle, get what you want (or at least know what you're getting), and have a truly memorable meal. (The same is true in Turkey.) Be brave.

*The best snack deal in Europe—a Greek souvlaki*

My favorite Greek snack is a tasty shish kebab wrapped in flat bread called a souvlaki pita. Souvlaki stands, offering $2 take-out pita sandwiches, are all over Greece. On the islands, eat fresh seafood and dunk bread into *tzatziki*, a refreshing cucumber and yogurt dip. Don't miss the creamy yogurt with honey. The feta (goat) cheese salads and the flaky nut 'n' honey dessert baklava are two other tasty treats. If possible, go to a wine festival. Retsina is a pine resin–flavored wine that is a dangerous taste to acquire. Ouzo is a powerful, love-it-or-hate-it, licorice-flavored aperitif. For American-style coffee, order "Nescafé"...but try the potent, grainy Greek coffee for a real kick. Eat when the locals do—late.

### Italy

Italians eat huge meals consisting of a first course of pasta, a second plate of meat, plus a salad, fruit, and wine. The pasta course alone is usually enough to fill the average tourist. You'll save money by ordering pasta as your main course. Some fancier restaurants won't serve just pasta; find one that will, and you'll enjoy a reasonably priced meal of lasagna or minestrone and a salad.

Veggie lovers will enjoy the restaurants that have self-serve antipasti buffets. These offer a variety of cooked appetizers spread out like a salad bar (pay per plate, not weight). A plate of antipasti combined with a pasta dish makes a healthy, affordable, interesting meal for two. Note that anytime you eat or drink at a table, you'll be charged a cover *(coperto)* of a couple dollars. That, plus service *(servizio)*, makes even a cheap, one-course restaurant meal cost $10.

For inexpensive Italian eateries, look for the term *osteria, tavola calda, rosticceria, trattoria, pizzeria,* or "self-service." A meal-size pizza (sold everywhere for less than $7) and a cold beer is my idea of a good, fast, cheap Italian dinner. For a stand-up super-bargain meal, look for a *Pizza Rustica* shop, which sells pizza by weight. Just point to the best-looking pizza and tell them how much you want (200 grams is a filling meal). They weigh, you pay. They heat it, you eat it.

Three important phrases to know are *menù del giorno* (menu of the day, usually a good deal), *pane e coperto* (charge for bread and cover), and *servizio incluso* (service included). But the most important words in your Italian vocabulary are *corposo* (full-bodied—as in wine) and gelato—probably the best ice cream you'll ever taste. A big cone or cup containing a variety of flavors costs about $2.

Cappuccino, rich coffee with a frothy head of steamed milk, is very popular, and it should be. Tiny coffee shops are tucked away on just about every street. All have a price list, and most require you to pay the cashier first and then take the receipt to the man who makes the drinks. Experiment. Try coffee or tea *freddo* (cold) or *frappé* (blended with ice). Discover a new specialty each day. Bars sell large bottles of cold mineral water, with or without gas, for about $2. *Panini* (sandwiches)—*calda* (toasted) if you ask—are cheap and widely available.

Bar-hopping is fun. A carafe of house wine serves four or five people for $5. Many bars have delicious *cicchetti* (cheh-KET-tee), local toothpick munchies. A

*Two fine reasons to savor Italy: gelato and the Riviera*

*cicchetteria* is a great place for an entire meal of these pint-size taste treats. In big cities, many bars offer these munchies free during happy hour.

**The Netherlands**

Traditional Dutch food is basic and hearty, with lots of bread, cheese, soup, and fish. Dutch treats include pancakes, "syrup waffles," and cheese. An experience you owe your tongue in Holland: slurping down raw herring at an outdoor herring stand.

My favorite Dutch food is Indonesian. Indonesia, a former colony of the Netherlands, fled the nest, leaving behind plenty of great Indonesian restaurants. The cheapest meals, as well as some of the best splurges, are found in these "Indisch" or "Chinese-Indisch" restaurants. The famous rijsttafel (rice table) is the ultimate Indonesian meal, with as many as 36 delightfully exotic courses, all eaten with rice. One meal is plenty for two, so order carefully. In a small-town restaurant, a rijsttafel can be a great bargain—two can split 12 exotic courses with rice for $25. *Bami* or *nasi goreng* are smaller and cheaper but still filling versions of a rijsttafel.

Order a beer, and you'll get a *pils,* a light lager. *Jenever* is Dutch gin made from juniper berries. While cheese gets harder and sharper with age, *jenever* grows smooth and soft. Old *jenever* is best.

**Portugal**

Portugal has some of the most enjoyable and cheapest eating I've found in Europe. Find a local sailors' hangout and fill up on fresh seafood, especially clams, cockles, and the fish soup. While Portuguese restaurants are not expensive, food stands in the fairs and amusement parks are even cheaper. The young *vinho verde* is an addictive local specialty and a favorite of visiting wine buffs. In fishing towns you'll find boiled barnacles *(percebes)* sold on the street and as the Portuguese answer to beer nuts in the bars. Let a local show you how to strip and eat one. A fun excuse to visit the fine bakeries is to go on a quest for the best *pastel de nata.* These delightful mini–cream pies are sold

everywhere but originated near Lisbon in Belém, where you can visit the famous Casa Pasties de Belém and try the original.

Be warned that in restaurants, pricey little appetizers might be placed at your table as if they're free. These are fun and tasty, but if you nibble even one you'll be charged for the entire lot. To clear out the temptation, ask to have them taken away.

### Scandinavia

Most Scandinavians avoid their highly taxed and very expensive restaurants. The cost of alcohol alone is a sobering experience. The key to budget eating in Nordic Europe is to take advantage of the *smörgåsbord.* For about $15 (cheap in Scandinavia), breakfast *smörgåsbords* will fill you with plenty of hearty food. Since both meals are, by definition, all-you-can-eat, I opt for the budget breakfast meal over the fancier, more expensive ($25) *middag,* or midday, *smörgåsbords.* Many train stations and ferries serve *smörgåsbords.*

*Enough food to sink a Viking ship:* smörgåsbord

For a budget lunch in Denmark, find a *smörrebrød* (open-face sandwich) shop. These places make artistic and delicious sandwich picnics to go. Or munch on a *pølse,* the Danish version of a hot dog.

All over Scandinavia, keep your eyes peeled for daily lunch specials called *dagens rett.* You can normally have all the vegetables (usually potatoes) you want when you order a restaurant's entrée. Just ask for seconds. Many Scandinavian pizzerias offer amazing all-you-can-eat deals and hearty salad bars. (Your bill will double if you order a beer.) The cheapest cafeterias often close at about 5 or 6 p.m.

Fresh produce, colorful markets, and efficient supermarkets abound in Europe's most expensive corner. Liver paste is curiously cheap but tastes powerfully nutritious. The rock-bottom, bilge-of-a-Viking-ship-cheap meal is a package of cracker bread and a tube of sandwich spread. Handy tubes of cheese, shrimp, and even caviar spread are popular throughout Scandinavia. To save money and enjoy the great Nordic outdoors—picnic.

Licorice is a popular Scandinavian snack. Finland's distinctive *salmiakki* is a salty licorice, popularized after World War II when sugar was carefully rationed.

Iceland is home to perhaps the most unusual culinary specialty in Europe: "buried" or "rotted" shark, called *hákarl.* A shark is buried raw, then dug up several months later and eaten (still frozen), washed down with *brennevin,* a powerfully bitter schnapps nicknamed "Black Death." Try it if you like...but most visitors prefer to stick with the raw herring.

### Spain

Spaniards eat to live, not vice versa. The Spanish diet—heavy on ham, deep-fried foods, more ham, weird seafood, and ham again—can be brutal on Americans more accustomed to salads, fruit, and grains. But it's cheap—you can eat well in restaurants for $10.

*At Spanish bars, tapas easily add up to a meal.*

The Spanish eating schedule—lunch from 1 p.m.–4 p.m., dinner after 9 p.m.—frustrates many visitors. Most Spaniards eat one major meal of the day: lunch *(almuerzo)* at 2 p.m., when stores close, schools let out, and people gather with their friends and family for the so-called "siesta." Because most Spaniards work until 7:30 p.m., a light supper *(cena)* is usually served at about 9 p.m. or 10 p.m.

To get by in Spain, either adapt yourself to the Spanish schedule and diet, or do the tapa tango. Bars and coffee spots serve tapas (hors d'oeuvres), sandwiches, and *tortillas* (omelets, great for a hearty breakfast). On my last trip, I ate at least one easy, quick, and very cheap tapas meal a day (see sidebar on next page).

Two famous Spanish dishes are gazpacho (chilled tomato soup) and paella (saffron-flavored rice with seafood, chicken, and sausage). *Platos combinados* (combination plates of three or more items) are a reasonable way to sample Spanish cuisine. For a more unusual Spanish taste, seek out *pulpo* (octopus)—especially popular in the northwest region of Galicia.

Spain is one of the world's leading producers of grapes, and that means lots of excellent wine. Sherry is the fortified wine from the Jerez region and *cava* is Spain's answer to champagne. Rioja is a full-bodied wine from the Basque region. Sangria (red wine mixed with fruit juice) is popular and refreshing.

## Tapas Tips

Any time of day or night, you'll see Spaniards enjoying small plates of tapas (appetizers) in bars. For me, tapas are the best thing about Spanish cuisine. They're small $1–10 portions of seafood, salads, meat-filled pastries, deep-fried tasties, and on and on—normally displayed under glass at the bar. But don't limit yourself to what you see on the bar. A huge variety of interesting plates are being thrown together in a little backroom kitchen. Get a menu and explore. Several plates can easily make a meal. With these tips you can eat cheaply, well, and memorably anywhere in Spain.

Chasing down a particular bar for tapas nearly defeats the purpose and spirit of these snacks. Tapas are impromptu. Just drop in at any lively place. Don't expect "My name is Alan and I'll be your waiter tonight" cheery service. Service is not friendly or unfriendly...just proficient. *Por favor* is a key phrase—it grabs a guy's attention. Be assertive or you'll never be served. Don't worry about paying until you're ready to leave (he's keeping track of your tab). To get the bill, ask: *"¿La cuenta?"*

Eating and drinking at a bar is usually cheapest. You may pay a little more to eat sitting at a table *(mesa)* and still more for an outdoor table *(terraza)*. Locate the price list (often posted in fine type on a wall somewhere) to know the menu options and price tiers.

When searching for a good bar, look for the noisy places with lots of locals, a blaring TV, and piles of napkins and food debris on the floor ("go local" and toss your trash, too). Popular television shows include bullfights and soccer games, American sitcoms, Spanish soaps, and silly game shows.

### Switzerland

Here at a crossroads of Europe, the food has a wonderful diversity: heavy *Wurst-und-Kraut* Germanic fare; delicate, subtle French cuisine; and pasta dishes *all' Italiana*. But Swiss restaurant prices can ruin your appetite and send you running to a grocery store. Even locals find their restaurants expensive. The Migros and Co-op grocery stores sell groceries for about the same prices you find in American stores—reasonable by Swiss standards.

Aside from clocks, banks, and knives, Switzerland is known for its cheeses: strong-flavored Gruyère, mild Emmentaler, and pungent Appenzeller, with a smell that verges on nauseating... until you taste it.

Two of Switzerland's best-known specialties are cheese-based: fondue and raclette. You eat fondue with a long fork, dipping cubes of bread into it. Raclette is melted cheese over potatoes, pickled onions, and gherkins.

Another must-try dish, most typical in the mountains of the German-speaking areas, is *Rösti*: traditional hash browns with alpine cheese, often served with an egg cracked over it...yum.

And, of course, there's chocolate. The Swiss changed the world in 1875 with their invention of milk chocolate. Stroll the chocolate aisle of a grocery store and take your pick.

### Turkey

Bring an appetite and order high on the menu in nice restaurants. Eating's cheap in Turkey. The typical eatery is a user-friendly cafeteria with giant bins of lots of delicacies you always thought were Greek. Kebabs are a standard meaty snack. *Pide*, fresh out of the oven, is Turkish pizza. *Sutlac* (rice pudding) and baklava will satisfy your sweet tooth. Munch pistachios by the pocketful. Tea in tiny hourglass-shaped glasses is served constantly everywhere. A refreshing, milky yogurt drink called *ayran*, cheap boxes of cherry juice, and fresh-squeezed orange juice make it fun to quench your Turkish thirst. Or try the *raki* (Turkish ouzo). Let a local show you how to carefully create a two-layered *raki* drink by slowly dribbling in the water. For breakfast, get ready for cucumbers, olives, tomatoes, and lots of goat cheese and bread.

# CITY SKILLS

## 19. GETTING ORIENTED

Many Americans are overwhelmed by European big-city shock. Struggling with the Chicagos, New Yorks, and L.A.s of Europe is easier if you take advantage of the local tourist information office, catch some kind of orientation tour, and learn the public-transportation system. You can't Magoo Europe's large cities. Plan ahead. Have a guidebook for wherever you're traveling. As you approach by train or plane, spend the last hour reading and planning. Know what you want to see. To save time and energy, plan your sightseeing strategy to cover the city systematically and efficiently, one neighborhood at a time.

### Tourist Information Offices

No matter how well I know a town, my first stop is the tourist information office (abbreviated **TI** in this book). Any place with a tourist industry has an information service for visitors on the main square, in the city hall, or at the train station, airport, or freeway entrance. You don't need the address—just follow the signs. A busy but normally

*Your first stop in a new town: the tourist information office*

friendly and multilingual staff gives out sightseeing information, reserves hotel rooms, sells concert or play tickets, and answers questions.

Prepare a list of questions ahead of time. Write up a proposed sightseeing schedule. Find out if it's workable or if you've left out any important sights. Confirm closed days and free-admission days.

*At the Oslo tourist office, you can pick up a monthly entertainment guide, list of sights, 24-hour bus pass, telephone card, and city map.*

Ask for a city map, public-transit information, and a list of sights with current hours. Find out about special events and pick up any local entertainment guides. See if walking tours or self-guided walking-tour brochures are available. Check on any miscellaneous concerns (such as safety, laundry, Internet access, bike rental, parking, camping, transportation tips for your departure, maps of nearby towns, or help with booking a room for your next destination). If you feel the first person you talk to is rushed or uninterested, browse around for a few minutes and talk to another.

Europe is amazingly well organized. For instance, tourist offices in some major cities (particularly Scandinavian capitals) sell a "tourist card" for about $30, which includes 24 hours of free entrance to all the sights; free use of all the subways, buses, and boats; a booklet explaining everything; and a map.

If necessary, get ideas on where to eat and sleep. But remember, most tourist information offices aren't services—they're businesses that sell things and work on fees and commissions. They don't volunteer information on cheap alternatives to hotels, and they pocket any "deposits" collected on big "front door" places they recommend.

If you'll be arriving late, call ahead before the tourist office closes. Good information (in English) is worth a long-distance phone call. Guidebooks list the phone numbers.

## Cruising the Web as You Travel

With the abundance and ease of Internet cafés in Europe, I often get online as I travel—to check my e-mail and sports scores back home, but also to travel smarter. Most city tourist offices, museums, hotels, and other tourist services have extensive Web sites these days, making it easy to confirm events schedules, hotel directions, museum hours, train timetables, and other crucial info on the fly, without picking up a phone.

## More Information Sources

Big-hotel information desks, hostel employees, other travelers, and guidebooks are helpful. To find guidebooks in English, check newsstands and English sections in large bookstores. All big cities have English bookstores, and most general bookstores have guidebooks in English (especially of that city or region). If you find yourself in a town with no information and the tourist office is closed, a glance through a postcard rack will quickly show you the town's most famous sights.

**Youth centers:** Many cities, especially in the north, have industrious youth travel-aid offices. Copenhagen and Oslo have great youth centers called Use It, and several cities publish very practical youth-oriented budget-travel magazines (available at the tourist office).

**Entertainment guides:** Big European cities bubble with entertainment, festivities, and nightlife. But they won't come to you. New in town and unable to speak the local language, travelers can be oblivious to a once-in-a-lifetime event erupting just across the bridge. A periodical entertainment guide is the ticket. Every big city has one, either in English (such as *What's On in Oslo*) or in the local language but easy to decipher (such as the *Pariscope* weekly). Buy one at a newsstand (if it's not free from the tourist office). In Florence and Rome, entertainment guides are published monthly by the big, fancy hotels and are available for free at their desks (look like a hotel guest and help yourself). Ask at your hotel about entertainment. Events are posted on city walls everywhere. Read posters. They are in a foreign language, but that really doesn't matter when it reads: *Weinfest, Música Folklórica, 9 Juni, 21:00, Piazza Majore, Entre Libre,* and so on. Figure out the signs—or miss the party.

## Maps

The best and cheapest map is often the public-transit map. Try to get one that shows bus and tram lines, subway stops, and major sights. Many tourist offices and big-city hotels (along with the McDonald's in some cities) give out free city maps. Study the map to understand the city's layout. Relate the location of landmarks—your hotel, major sights, the river, main streets, and the train station—to each other. Use any viewpoint—such as a church spire, tower, hilltop, or top story of a skyscraper—to understand the lay of the land. Retrace where you've been, see where you're going. Back on the ground, you won't be in such constant need of your map.

*Guides bring museums and castles to life.*

## Walking Tours and Local Guides

Walking tours are my favorite introduction to a city. Since they focus on just a small part of a city (generally the old town center), they are thorough. The tours are usually conducted in English by well-trained local people who are sharing their town for the noble purpose of giving you an appreciation of the city's history, people, and culture—not to make a lot of money. Walking tours are personal, inexpensive, and a valuable education. I can't recall a bad one.

Many tourist offices also rent audioguides you can take for a walk or provide do-it-yourself walking-tour leaflets. The avid walker should consider purchasing one of the many "turn right at the fountain"–type guidebooks that are carefully written collections of self-guided walks through major cities. My city guides include these types of walking tours.

For the price of three seats on a forgettable quadrilingual tape-recorded city bus tour, you can often hire your own private guide for a personalized city tour (most cost-effective if you're traveling with a group). Every city has a long list of English-speaking professional guides who earn their living giving tours any way they can. They hire out by the day or half day and generally follow a national guide service fee schedule (about $100 per half-day). In my research, I've grown accustomed to relying heavily upon these local experts and generally find them well worth the investment. You can find and book guides by calling the local tourist information office (or

*Audioguides...for all the hair-raising details on Europe's historic sights*

visiting their Web site) in advance, or even by dropping by and arranging a guide upon arrival in a town. Although you get the contact information from the tourist office, you typically book the guide by calling or e-mailing the person directly. When I meet particularly good independent local guides, I include their contact information in my guidebooks.

Hiring a private guide is an especially good value in Eastern Europe and Russia, where guides tend to be young, intelligent, and enthusiastic... and charge half as much. The best guides are often those whose tours you can pick up at a specific sight. They usually really know their museum, castle, or cathedral.

## Bus Orientation Tours

Many cities have fast-orientation bus tours like London's famous tours that take you around the city on a double-decker bus. You'll get a feel for the urban lay of the land as you see the major sights (from the bus window) and hear a live or recorded narration. The innovative "hop-on, hop-off" bus tours give tourists an all-day pass to hop on and off buses making a circular route through the city's top sights. These buses come by several times an hour and generally include a live or tape-recorded narration. Since guide quality varies, if I find myself enjoying a particularly good guide, I'll stay on that bus for the entire route. They cost about $30, and, if you've got the money and not much time, they provide a good orientation. If I had only one day in a big city, I might spend half of it on one of these tours. Along with London, you'll find bus tours in Bath, York, Edinburgh, Copenhagen, Helsinki, Paris, Berlin, Munich, Vienna, Budapest, Prague, Madrid, Barcelona, Sevilla, Milan, Rome, and more.

*A minibus tour of Bruges—name your language*

As a popular trend, many cities now offer a public bus (e.g., Berlin's bus #100) or boat route (e.g., Amsterdam's museum boat) that connects all of the city's major sightseeing attractions. Tourists buy the one-day pass and make the circuit at their leisure.

Bus tours can be worthwhile solely for the ride. Some sights are awkward to reach by public transportation, such as the châteaux of France's Loire, King Ludwig's castles in Bavaria, the Sound of Music sights outside Salzburg, and the pilgrimage site of Međugorje near

Dubrovnik. An organized tour not only whisks you effortlessly from one hard-to-reach-without-a-car sight to the next, but gives you lots of information as you go.

If you're about to spend $60 anyway for a train ticket—let's say, from London to Bath—why not spend $90 for a one-day tour from London that visits Stonehenge and Bath? You can leave the tour in Bath before it returns to London and enjoy a day of transportation, admissions, and information for not much more than a two-hour train ticket.

Fancy coach tours—the kind that leave from the big international hotels—are expensive. Some are great. Others are boring and so depersonalized, sometimes to the point of multilingual taped messages, that you may find the Chinese soundtrack more interesting than the English. These tours can, however, be of value to the budget-minded do-it-yourselfer: Pick up the brochure for a well-thought-out tour itinerary and do it on your own. Take local buses at your own pace and tour every sight for a fraction of the cost.

## Public Transportation

Shrink and tame big cities by mastering their subway and bus systems. Europe's public-transit systems are so good that many Europeans go through life never learning to drive. Their wheels are trains, buses, and subways.

**Save time, money, and energy.** Too many timid tourists avoid buses or subways and waste time walking or money on taxis. Subways are speedy and comfortable, never slowed by traffic jams. And with the proper attitude, a subway ride can be an aesthetic experience, plunging you into the people- and advertisement-filled river of local workaday life.

*Public transit—the European treat*

**Get a transit map.** With a map, anyone can decipher the code to cheap and easy urban transportation. Paris and London have the most extensive—and the most needed—subway systems. Both cities come with plenty of subway maps and expert subway tutors. Paris even has maps that plan your route for you. Just push your destination's button, and the proper route lights up.

*If you take advantage of public transportation, you can zip quickly, effortlessly, and inexpensively under Europe's most congested cities.*

**Find out about specials.** Some cities offer deals, such as tourist passes allowing unlimited travel on all public transport for a day or several days. These "go as you please" passes may seem expensive, but, if you do any amount of running around, they can be a convenient money-saver. They can also save time—with a transit pass, you go directly to the track, avoiding long ticket lines.

**Ask for help.** Europe's buses and subways are run by people who are happy to help lost tourists locate themselves. Confirm with a local that you're at the right platform or bus stop. If a ticket seems expensive, ask what it covers—$2 may seem like a lot until you learn it's good for a round-trip, two hours, or several transfers. And if you tell them where you're going, bus drivers and passengers sitting around you will gladly tell you where to get off.

**Be cautious.** While public transportation feels safe, be constantly on guard. Wear your money belt. Thieves—often dressed as successful professionals or other tourists—thrive underground. Buses that are particularly popular with tourists are equally popular with pickpockets. (See Chapter 23: Outsmarting Thieves.)

## Taxis

Taxis are underrated, scenic time-savers that zip you effortlessly from one sight to the next. Especially for couples and small groups who value their time, a taxi ride can be a good investment.

Taxis are especially cheap in Mediterranean and Eastern Europe. While expensive for the lone budget traveler, a group of three or four people can often travel cheaper by taxi than by buying three or four bus tickets. (You can go anywhere in downtown Lisbon, Prague, or Athens for $5.)

*These cabbies hire by the hour and would love to show you around.*

Don't be bullied by cabbie con men (common in the south and east). Insist on the meter, agree on a price up front, or know the going rate. Taxi drivers intimidate too many tourists. If I'm charged a ridiculous price for a ride, I put a reasonable sum on the seat and say good-bye. But don't be too mistrusting. Many tourists wrongly accuse their cabbies of taking the long way around or adding unfair extras. Cabbies are generally honest. There are lots of legitimate supplements (nights, weekends, baggage, extra person, airport ride, etc.), and winding through medieval street plans with lots of one-ways is rarely even close to direct.

A taxi ride can be a smart intercity bet. Recently I rode a taxi from Florence to Siena (50 miles, $100). This convenient time-saver was an affordable splurge. Taxis also have hourly rates and can be hired to simply show you the town (offering a scant commentary and stops here and there along the way). While this seems expensive, when the cost is split by two people, and the ease and time saved is figured in, an intercity taxi ride becomes a good investment.

To tip the cabbie, round up. For a typical ride, round up to the next euro on the fare (to pay a €13 fare, give €14); for a long ride, to the nearest 10 (for a €75 fare, give €80). If the cabbie hauls your bags and zips you to the airport to help you catch your flight, you might want to toss in a little more. But if you feel like you're being driven in circles or otherwise ripped off, skip the tip.

You or your hotel receptionist can always call for a cab, but the meter may be well under way by the time you get in. In Western Europe, it's usually cheaper and easier just to flag one down or ask a local to direct you to the nearest taxi stand. Taxi stands are often listed as prominently as subway stations on city maps; look for the little *T*s.

In Eastern Europe, where crooked cabbies are a major problem, locals always recommend calling for a taxi (or having your hotel or restaurant call one for you). It'll dramatically decrease your odds of getting ripped off. If you do hail a cab on the street or find one at a taxi stand, choose one marked with a big, prominent taxi-company logo and telephone number. Always ask for a rough estimate up front.

## Tipping

Tipping in Europe isn't as automatic and generous as it is in the United States, but in many countries, tips are appreciated, if not expected. As in the US, the proper amount depends on your resources, tipping philosophy, and the circumstance. That said, there are big tippers and misers the world around.

Tipping varies widely by country, but some general guidelines apply.

At restaurants, check the menu to see if service is included; if it isn't, a tip of 5–10 percent is normal (for details, see page 239). For taxis, round up the fare (see above).

Tipping for special service is optional. It's thoughtful to tip a couple of euros to someone who shows you a special sight and who is paid in no other way (such as the man who shows you an Etruscan tomb in his backyard). Guides who give talks at public sites or on bus or boat tours often hold out their hands for tips after they give their spiel. If I've already paid for the tour, I don't tip extra (if you feel you must tip, a euro or two is enough for a job well done). I don't tip at hotels, but if you do, give the porter a euro for carrying bags and leave a couple of euros in your room at the end of your stay for the maid if the room was kept clean. In general, if someone in the service industry does a super job for you, a tip of a couple of euros is appropriate...but not required.

When in doubt, ask. The French and British generally tip hairdressers, the Dutch and Swedish usually don't. If you're not sure whether (or how much) to tip for a service, ask your hotelier or the TI; they'll fill you in on how it's done on their turf.

## Traveler's Toilet Trauma

Every traveler has one or two great toilet stories. Foreign toilets can be traumatic, but they are one of those little things that can make travel so much more interesting than staying at home. If you plan to venture away from the international-style hotels in your Mediterranean travels and become a temporary resident, "going local" may take on a very real meaning.

Most European toilets are reasonably similar to our own, but some consist simply of porcelain footprints and a squat-and-aim hole. Those of us who need a throne to sit on are in the minority. Most humans sit on their haunches and nothing more.

*One of Europe's many unforgettable experiences is the squat-and-aim toilet.*

Toilet paper (like a spoon or a fork) is another Western "essential" that most people on our planet do not use. What they use varies. I won't get too graphic here, but remember that a billion people in south Asia never eat with their left hand. Some countries, such as Turkey, have very frail plumbing, and toilet paper will jam up the WCs. If wastebaskets are full of dirty paper, leave yours there, too.

The WC scene has improved markedly in Europe in the last few years, but it still makes sense to carry pocket-size tissue packs (easy to buy in Europe) for WCs sans TP.

### Finding a Toilet

Finding a decent public toilet can be frustrating. I once dropped a tour group off in a town for a potty stop, and when I picked them up 20 minutes later, none had found relief. Most countries have few public rest rooms. With a few tips, you can sniff out a biffy in a jiffy.

*Going local*

**Restaurants:** Any place that serves food or drinks has a rest room. No restaurateur would label his WC so those on the street can see, but you can walk into nearly any restaurant or café, politely and confidently, and find a bathroom. Assume it's somewhere in the back, either upstairs or downstairs. It's easiest in large places that have outdoor seating, because waiters will think you're a customer just making a quick trip inside. Some call it rude—I call it survival. If you feel like it, ask permission. Just smile, "Toilet?" I'm rarely turned down. American-type fast-food places are very common these days and always have a decent and fairly "public" rest room. Timid people buy a drink they don't want in order to use one. That's unnecessary.

**Public buildings:** When nature beckons and there's no restaurant or bar handy, look in train stations, government buildings, and upper floors of department stores. Parks often have rest rooms, sometimes of the gag-a-maggot variety. Never leave a museum without taking advantage of its rest rooms—free, clean, and decorated with artistic graffiti. Large, classy, old hotel lobbies are as impressive as many palaces you'll pay to see. You can always find a royal retreat here, and plenty of soft TP.

**Coin-op toilets on the street:** Some large cities, such as Paris, London, and Amsterdam, are dotted with coin-operated telephone booth–type WCs on street corners. Insert a coin, the door opens, and you have 15 minutes of toilet use accompanied by Sinatra Muzak. When you leave, it even disinfects itself.

**Trains:** Use the free toilets on the train rather than in the station to save time and money. Toilets on first-class cars are a cut above second-class toilets. I "go" first class even with a second-class ticket. Train toilets are located on the ends of cars, where it's most jiggly. A trip to the train's john always reminds me of the rodeo. Toilets empty directly on the tracks. Never use a train's WC while stopped in a station (unless you didn't like that particular town). A train's WC cleanliness deteriorates as the journey progresses.

**The flush:** After you've found and used a toilet, you're down to your last challenge—flushing it. Rarely will you encounter a familiar handle. Find some protuberance and push, pull, twist, squeeze, stomp, or pray to it until the water starts. Automatic sinks and urinals with "electric eyes" are increasingly common.

**The tip:** Paying to use a public WC is a European custom that irks many Americans. But isn't it really worth a quarter, considering the cost of water, maintenance, and cleanliness? And you're probably in no state to argue, anyway. Sometimes the toilet is free, but the woman in the corner sells sheets of toilet paper. Most common is the tip dish by the entry. The local equivalent of about 25 cents is plenty. Caution: Many attendant ladies leave only bills and too-big coins in the tray to bewilder the full-bladdered tourist. The keepers of Europe's public toilets have earned a reputation for crabbiness. You'd be crabby, too, if you lived under the street in a room full of public toilets. Humor them, understand them, and carry some change so you can leave them a coin or two.

**Men:** The women who seem to inhabit Europe's WCs are a popular topic of conversation among Yankee males. Sooner or later you'll be minding your own business at the urinal and the lady will bring you your change or sweep under your feet. Yes, it is distracting, but you'll just have to get used to it—she has.

Getting comfortable in foreign rest rooms takes a little adjusting, but that's travel. When in Rome, do as the Romans do—and before you know it...Euro-peein'.

## Travel Laundry

I met a woman in Italy who wore her T-shirt frontward, backward, inside-out frontward, and inside-out backward to delay the laundry day. A guy in Germany showed me his take-it-into-the-tub-with-you-and-make-waves method of washing his troublesome jeans. And some travelers just ignore their laundry needs...and stink.

One of my domestic chores while on the road is washing my laundry in the hotel room sink. I bring a quick-dry travel wardrobe that either looks OK wrinkled or doesn't wrinkle. I test wash and dry my shirts in the sink at home once before I let them come to Europe with me. Some shirts are fine, others prune up.

*Whistler's laundry*

**Pack a self-service laundry kit.** Bring a stretchable "travel clothesline." The cord is double stranded and twisted, so clothespins are unnecessary. Stretch it over your bathtub or across the back of your car, and you're on the road to dry clothes. Pack a concentrated liquid detergent in a small, sturdy, plastic squeeze bottle wrapped in a zip-lock baggie to contain leakage. A large plastic bag with a drawstring is handy for dirty laundry.

**Wash clothes in the sink in your room.** Every real hotel room in Europe has a sink, usually equipped with a multilingual "no washing clothes in the room" sign. This (after "eat your peas") may be the most ignored rule on earth. Interpret this as "I have lots of good furniture and a fine carpet in this room, and I don't want your drippy laundry ruining things." In other words, you can wash clothes carefully, wring them nearly dry, and hang them in a low-profile, nondestructive way. Do not hang your clothes out the window. The maid hardly notices my laundry. It's hanging quietly in the bathroom or shuffled among my dry clothes in the closet. Occasionally a hotel will keep the stoppers in an attempt to discourage washing. You can try using a wadded-up sock or a film canister cap, or line the sink with your plastic laundry bag and wash in it. Some create their own washing machine with a large, two-gallon zip-lock baggie: soak in suds for an hour, agitate, drain, rinse.

Wring wet laundry as dry as possible. Rolling it in a towel and twisting or stomping on it can be helpful, but many places don't provide new towels every day. Always separate the back and front of hanging clothes to speed drying. Some travelers pack an inflatable hanger. Laid-back hotels will let your laundry join theirs on the lines out back or on the rooftop.

Smooth out your wet clothes, button shirts, set collars, and "hand iron" to encourage wrinkle-free drying. If your shirt or dress dries wrinkled, hang it in a steamy bathroom. A piece of tape is a good ad-lib lint brush. In very hot climates, I wash my shirt several times a day, wring it, and put it on wet. It's clean and refreshing, and (sadly) in 15 minutes it's dry.

**Use a launderette occasionally.** For a thorough washing, ask your hotel to direct you to the nearest launderette. Nearly every neighborhood has one. It takes about $10 and an hour if there's no line. (Many hostels have coin-op washers and dryers or heated drying rooms.) Better launderettes have coin-op soap dispensers, change machines, and helpful attendants. Others can be very frustrating. Use the time to picnic, catch up on postcards and your journal, or chat with the local crowd. Launderettes throughout the world seem to give people the gift of gab. Full-service places are quicker—just drop it off and come back in the afternoon—but much more expensive. Also pricey, but handiest of all: You can hire your hotel to do your laundry. Regardless of the price, every time I slip into a fresh pair of jeans, I figure it was worth the hassle and expense.

## 20. HURDLING THE LANGUAGE BARRIER

### Confessions of a Monoglot

For English-speakers, that notorious language barrier is about two feet tall. It keeps many people out of Europe, but, with a few communication tricks and a polite approach, the English-only traveler can step right over it.

I've been saying this for 30 years, and during that time an entire generation of Europeans has grown up speaking more English than ever. English really has arrived as Europe's second language. Historically, many European signs and menus were printed in four languages: German, French, English, and—depending on where you were—Italian or Spanish. In the last few years, there's been a shift. In the interest of free trade and efficiency, the European Union has established English as Europe's standard language of commerce. Now most signs are printed in just two languages: The local language for locals, and English for everyone else. In some airports, signs are now actually in English only.

*As English triumphs, new signs in Amsterdam's airport don't even bother with the Dutch.*

While it's nothing to brag about, I speak only English. Of course, if I spoke more languages, I could enjoy a much deeper understanding of the people and cultures I visit. But even with English only, I have no problems getting transportation and rooms, eating, and seeing the sights. While you can manage fine with the blunt weapon of English, you'll get along with Europe better if you learn and use a few basic phrases and polite words.

Having an interest in the local language wins the respect of those you'll meet. Get an English–German (or whatever) phrase book and start your practical vocabulary growing right off the bat. You're surrounded by expert, native-speaking tutors in every country. Let them teach you. Spend bus and train rides learning. Start learning the language when you arrive. Psychologically, it's hard to start later because you'll be leaving so soon. I try to learn five new words a day. You'd be surprised how handy a working vocabulary of 50 words is. A phrase book with a dictionary is ideal. Pocket-size two-language dictionaries are cheap and sold throughout Europe.

While Americans are notorious monoglots, Europeans are very good with languages. Make communication easier by choosing a multilingual person to speak with. Business people, urbanites, well-dressed young people, students, and anyone in the tourist trade are most likely to speak English. Most Swiss grow up trilingual. Many young Scandinavians and Eastern Europeans speak several languages. People speaking minor languages (Dutch, Belgians, Norwegians, Czechs, Hungarians, Slovenes) have more reason to learn English, German, or French since their linguistic world is so small. All Croatians begin learning English in elementary school, and—since their TV programming is subtitled—they listen to Americans talk for hours each day. Scandinavian students of our language actually decide between English and "American." My Norwegian cousin speaks with a touch of Texas and knows more slang than I do.

We English speakers are the one linguistic group that can afford to be lazy. English is the world's linguistic common denominator. When a Greek meets a Norwegian, they speak English. (You'd be hard-pressed to find a Greek speaking Norwegian.)

Imagine if each of our states spoke its own language. That's the European situation. They've done a great job of minimizing the communication problems you'd expect to find on a small continent with such a Babel of tongues. Most information that the traveler must understand (such as road signs, menus, telephone instructions, and safety warnings) are printed either in English or in universal symbols. Europe's uniform road-sign system (see page 154) enables drivers to roll right over the language barrier. And rest assured that any place trying to separate tourists

## Europeans: Babel of Tongues

Europe's many languages can be arranged into a family tree. Most of them have the same grandparents and resemble each other more or less like you resemble your brothers, sisters, and cousins. (Occasionally, an oddball uncle sneaks in whom no one can explain.) An understanding of how these languages relate to one another can help boost you over the language barrier.

**Romance Countries: Italy, France, Spain, and Portugal**

The Romance family evolved out of Latin, the language of the Roman Empire ("Romance" comes from "Roman"). Few of us know Latin, but knowing any of the modern Romance languages helps with the others. For example, your high school Spanish will help you learn some Italian.

**Germanic Countries: The British Isles, Germany, the Netherlands, and Scandinavia**

The Germanic languages, though influenced by Latin, are a product of the tribes of northern Europe (including the Angles and Saxons)—people the ancient Romans called "barbarians" because they didn't speak Latin. German is spoken by all Germans and Austrians, and by most Swiss. The people of Holland and northern Belgium speak Dutch (called Flemish in Belgium), which is very closely related to German. While Dutch is not Deutsch, a Hamburger or Frankfurter can almost read an Amsterdam newspaper. The Scandinavians (except the Finns) can read each other's magazines and enjoy their neighbors' TV shows.

**Multilingual Regions**

The people of Switzerland speak four languages: 64 percent of the people speak Swiss German, 20 percent French, 7 percent Italian, and half of 1 percent Romansch (a language related to ancient Latin). Most Swiss are at least bilingual.

from their money will explain how to spend it in whatever languages are necessary. English always makes it.

Dominant as English may be, it's just good style to start every conversation by politely asking, "Do you speak English?", *"Parlez-vous anglais?"*, *"Sprechen Sie Englisch?"*, or whatever. If they say "No," then I do the best I can in their language. Normally, after a few sentences they'll say, "Actually, I do speak some English." One thing Americans do well

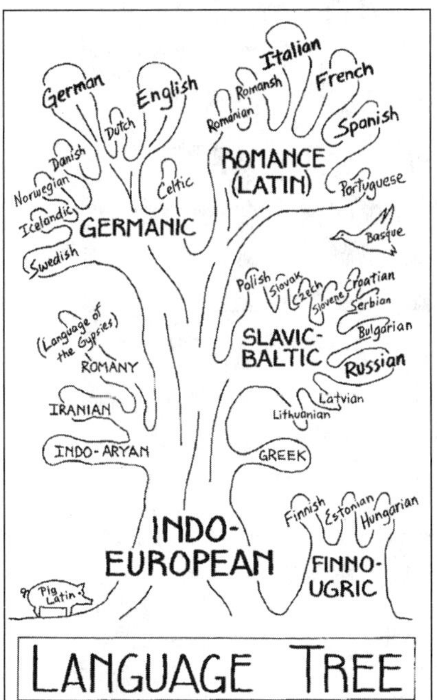


Alsace is on the French–German border. Its people have been dragged through the mud during several French–German tugs-of-war. For the time being, it's a part of France—but most locals also speak German.

Belgium waffles (linguistically), with the southern half (the Walloons) speaking French and the rest speaking Flemish. The French in Belgium, like those in Switzerland and Canada, often feel linguistically abused.

**Endangered Tongues**

The Basques, struggling to survive in the area where Spain, France, and the Atlantic all touch, are well aware that every year five languages die on our planet and that the cards are stacked against isolated groups like theirs.

England is surrounded by a "Celtic Crescent." In Wales, Scotland, Ireland, and Brittany (northwestern France), the old Celtic language survives. Seek out these die-hard remnants in militant bookstores (fronts for the autonomy movement in Brittany), Gaelic pubs, and the Gaeltachts (districts, mostly in Western Ireland, where the old culture is preserved by the government).

Small linguistic groups, such as those who speak Flemish, Slovene, or Norwegian, are quicker to jump on the English bandwagon. These cultures are melting into the English sphere of linguistic influence, while large groups such as the Spanish, French, and Germans can get by without embracing English so readily.

linguistically is put others at ease with their linguistic shortcomings. Your European friend is doing you a favor by speaking your language. The least we can do is make our English simple and clear.

## Using Simple English

English may be Europe's lingua franca, but communicating does require some skill. If you have a trip coming up and don't speak French yet,

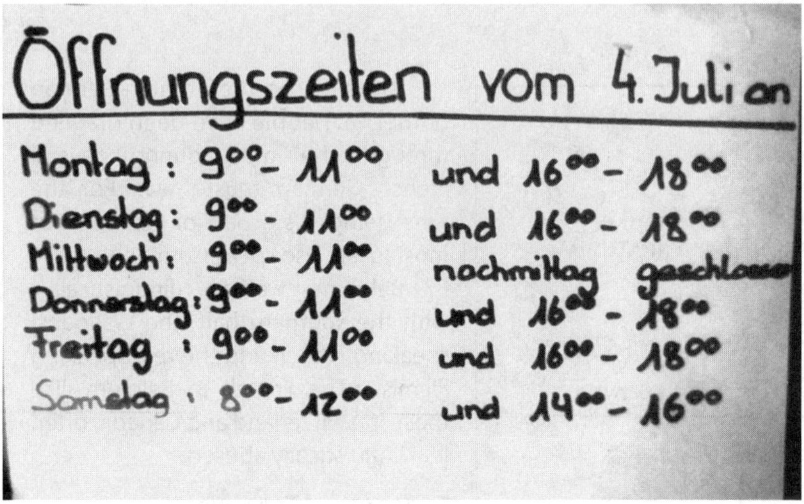

*Hurdle the language barrier by thinking of things as multiple-choice questions and making educated guesses. This is a sign on a shop in Germany. It lists times. The top word can only mean "open times" or "closed times." I'd guess it lists hours open from* (vom = *from, if it rhymes, I go for it) the Fourth of July. Those six words on the left, most of which end in* tag, *must be days of the week. Things are open from 9:00–11:00* und *from 16:00–18:00 (24-hour clock). On* Mittwoch *(midweek) afternoon... something different happens. Since it can only be open or closed, and everything else is open, you can guess that on Wednesdays,* nach Mittag, *this shop is* geschlossen!

forget it. It's hopeless. Rather than learning a few more French verbs, the best way to increase your ability to communicate is to master what the Voice of America calls "simple English."

**Speak slowly, clearly, and with carefully chosen words.** Assume you're dealing with someone who learned English out of a book—reading British words, not hearing American ones. They are reading your lips, wishing it were written down, hoping to see every letter as it tumbles out of your mouth. Choose easy words and clearly pronounce each letter. (Crispy po-ta-to chips.) Use no contractions. When they aren't understood, many Americans speak louder and toss in a few extra words. Listen to other tourists, and you'll hear your own shortcomings. If you want to be understood, talk like a Dick and Jane primer. For several months out of every year, I speak with simple words, pronouncing every letter. When I return home, my friends say (very deliberately), "Rick, you can relax now, we speak English fluently."

**Can the slang.** Our American dialect has become a super-deluxe slang pizza not found on any European menu. The sentence "Can the slang," for example, would baffle the average European. If you learned

## International Words

As our world shrinks, more and more words leap their linguistic boundaries and become international. Sensitive travelers develop a knack for choosing words most likely to be universally understood ("auto" instead of "car;" "kaput" rather than "broken;" "photo," not "picture"). They also internationalize their pronunciation. "University," if you play around with its sound (oo-nee-vehr-see-tay), can be understood anywhere. The average American really flunks out in this area. Be creative.

Analogy communication is effective. Anywhere in Europe (except in Hungary), "Attila" means "crude bully." When a bulky Italian crowds in front of you, say, "Scusi, Ah-tee-la" and retake your place. If you like your haircut and want to compliment your Venetian barber, put your hand sensually on your hair and say "Casanova." Nickname the hairstylist "Michelangelo" or "Rambo."

Here are a few internationally understood words. Remember, cut out the Yankee accent and give each word a pan-European sound.

| | | |
|---|---|---|
| Stop | Kaput | Vino |
| Restaurant | Ciao | Bank |
| Hotel | Bye-bye | Rock 'n' roll |
| Post | Camping | OK |
| Auto | Picnic | Amigo |
| Autobus (booos) | Nuclear | English (Engleesh) |
| Yankee, Americano | Tourist | Mamma mia |
| Michelangelo (artistic) | Beer | Oo la la |
| Casanova (romantic) | Coffee | Moment |
| Disneyland (wonderland) | Tea | Hercules (strong) |
| Coke, Coca-Cola | No problem | Attila (mean, crude) |
| Sex/Sexy | Europa | Self-service |
| Toilet | Police | Super |
| Taxi | Telephone | Photo |
| Photocopy | Central | Information |
| Mañana | University | Passport |
| Chocolate | Pardon | Fascist |
| Rambo | Communist | Hello |
| Elephant (a big clod) | No | Bon voyage |
| Bill Gates | McDonald's | Michael Jackson |
| Disco | Computer | Sport |
| Internet | America's favorite four-letter words | |

English in school for two years, how would you respond to the American who exclaims, "What a day!" or asks, "Howzit goin'?"

**Keep your messages grunt-simple.** Make single nouns work as entire sentences. When asking for something, a one-word question ("Photo?") is more effective than an attempt at something more grammatically correct ("May I take your picture, sir?"). Be a Neanderthal. Strip your message naked and drag it by the hair into the other person's mind. But even Neandertourists will find things go easier if they begin each request with the local "please" (e.g., "*Bitte,* toilet?").

**Use internationally understood words.** Some spend an entire trip telling people they're on *vacation,* draw only blank stares, and slowly find themselves in a soundproof, culture-resistant cell. The sensitive communicator notices that Europeans understand the word *holiday,* probably because that's what the English say. Then she plugs that word into her simple English vocabulary, makes herself understood, and enjoys a much closer contact with Europe. If you say rest room or bathroom, you'll get no room. *Toilet* is direct, simple, and understood. If my car is broken in Portugal, I don't say, "Excuse me, my car is broken." I point to the vehicle and say, "Auto kaput."

## Tips on Creative Communication

Even if you have no real language in common, you can have some fun communicating. Consider this profound conversation I had with a cobbler in Sicily:

"Spaghetti," I said, with a very saucy Italian accent.

"Marilyn Monroe," was the old man's reply.

*"Mamma mia!"* I said, tossing my hands and head into the air.

"Yes, no, one, two, tree," he returned, slowly and proudly.

By now we'd grown fond of each other, and I whispered, secretively, "*Molto buono,* ravioli."

He spat, "Be sexy, drink Pepsi!"

Waving good-bye, I hollered, *"No problema."*

*"Ciao,"* he said, smiling.

**Risk looking goofy.** Even with no common language, rudimentary communication is easy. Butcher the language if you must, but communicate. I'll never forget the lady in the French post office who flapped her arms and asked, "Tweet, tweet, tweet?" I understood immediately, answered with a nod, and she gave me the airmail stamps I needed. At the risk of getting birdseed, I communicated successfully. If you're hungry, clutch your stomach and growl. If you want milk, "moo" and pull two imaginary udders. If the liquor was too strong, simulate an atomic

## Happy Talk

| English | French | Italian | German | Spanish |
|---|---|---|---|---|
| Good day. | *Bonjour.* | *Buon giorno.* | *Guten tag.* | *Buenos dias.* |
| How are you? | *Comment allez-vous?* | *Come sta?* | *Wie geht's?* | *¿Cómo está?* |
| Very good. | *Très bien.* | *Molto bene.* | *Sehr gut.* | *Muy bien.* |
| Thank you. | *Merci.* | *Grazie.* | *Danke.* | *Gracias.* |
| Please. | *S'il vous plaît.* | *Per favore.* | *Bitte.* | *Por favor.* |
| Do you speak English? | *Parlez vous anglais?* | *Parla inglese?* | *Sprechen Sie Englisch?* | *¿Habla usted inglés?* |
| Yes./No. | *Oui./Non.* | *Si./No.* | *Ja./Nein.* | *Sí./No.* |
| My name is... | *Je m'appelle...* | *Mi chiamo...* | *Ich heiße...* | *Me llamo...* |
| What's your name? | *Quel est votre nom?* | *Come si chiama?* | *Wie heißen Sie?* | *¿Cómo se llama?* |
| See you later. | *Á bientôt.* | *A più tardi.* | *Bis später.* | *Hasta luego.* |
| Goodbye. | *Au revoir.* | *Arrivederci.* | *Auf Wiedersehen.* | *Adiós.* |
| Good luck! | *Bonne chance!* | *Buona fortuna!* | *Viel Glück!* | *¡Buena suerte!* |
| Have a good trip! | *Bon voyage!* | *Buon viaggio!* | *Gute Reise!* | *¡Buen viaje!* |
| OK. | *D'accord.* | *Va bene.* | *OK.* | *De acuerdo.* |
| No problem. | *Pas de problème.* | *Non c'è problema.* | *Kein Problem.* | *No hay problema.* |
| Everything was great. | *C'était super.* | *Tutto magnifico.* | *Alles war gut.* | *Todo estuvo muy bien.* |
| Enjoy your meal! | *Bon appétit!* | *Buon appetito!* | *Guten Appetit!* | *¡Qué aproveche!* |
| Delicious! | *Délicieux!* | *Delizioso!* | *Lecker!* | *¡Delicioso!* |
| Magnificent! | *Magnifique!* | *Magnifico!* | *Wunderbar!* | *¡Magnifico!* |
| Bless you (after sneeze) | *À vos souhaits!* | *Salute!* | *Gesundheit!* | *¡Salud!* |
| You are very kind. | *Vous êtes très gentil.* | *Lei è molto gentile.* | *Sie sind sehr freundlich.* | *Usted es muy amable.* |
| Cheers! | *Santé!* | *Salute!* | *Prost!* | *¡Salud!* |
| I love you. | *Je t'aime.* | *Ti amo.* | *Ich liebe dich.* | *Te quiero.* |

## Tongue Twisters

These are a great way to practice a language—and break the ice with the Europeans you meet. Here are some that are sure to challenge you and amuse your new friends.

|  |  |  |
|---|---|---|
| German | **Fischer's Fritze fischt frische Fische, frische Fische fischt Fischer's Fritze.** | Fritz Fischer catches fresh fish, fresh fish Fritz Fischer catches. |
| German | **Ich komme über Oberammergau, oder komme ich über Unterammergau?** | I am coming via Oberammergau, or am I coming via Unterammergau? |
| Italian | **Sopra la panca la capra canta, sotto la panca la capra crepa.** | On the bench the goat sings, under the bench the goat dies. |
| Italian | **Chi fù quel barbaro barbiere che barberò così barbar-amente a Piazza Barberini quel povero barbaro di Barbarossa?** | Who was that barbarian barber in Barberini Square who shaved that poor barbarian Barbarossa? |
| French | **Si ces saucissons-ci sont six sous, ces six saucissons-ci sont trop chers.** | If these sausages are six cents, these six sausages are too expensive. |
| French | **Ce sont seize cents jacinthes sèches dans seize cent sachets secs.** | There are 1,600 dry hyacinths in 1,600 dry sachets. |
| Spanish | **Un tigre, dos tigres, tres tigres comían trigo en un trigal. Un tigre, dos tigres, tres tigres.** | One tiger, two tigers, three tigers ate wheat in a wheatfield. One tiger, two tigers, three tigers. |
| Spanish | **Pablito clavó un clavito. ¿Qué clavito clavó Pablito?** | Paul stuck in a stick. What stick did Paul stick in? |
| Portuguese | **O rato roeu a roupa do rei de Roma.** | The mouse nibbled the clothes of the king of Rome. |
| Portuguese | **Se cá nevasse fazia-se cá ski, mas como cá não neva não se faz cá ski.** | If the snow would fall, we'd ski, but since it doesn't, we don't. |

*Excerpted from* Rick Steves' Phrase Books*—full of practical phrases, spiked with humor, and designed for budget travelers who like to connect with locals.*

explosion starting from your stomach and mushrooming to your head. If you're attracted to someone, pant.

**Be melodramatic.** Exaggerate the local accent. In France, you'll communicate more effectively (and have more fun) by sounding like Maurice Chevalier or Inspector Clouseau. The locals won't be insulted; they'll be impressed. Use whatever French you know. But even English spoken with a sexy French accent makes more sense to the French ear. In Italy, be melodic and exuberant, and wave those hands. Go ahead, try it: *Mamma mia!* No. Do it again. *MAMMA MIA!* You've got to be uninhibited. Self-consciousness kills communication.

**Figure things out.** Most major European languages are related, coming from (or at least being influenced by) Latin. Knowing that, words become meaningful. The French word for Monday (our "day of the moon") is *lundi* (lunar day). The Germans say the same thing—*Montag. Sonne* is sun, so *Sonntag* is Sunday. If *buon giorno* means good day, *zuppa del giorno* is soup of the day. If *Tiergarten* is zoo (literally "animal garden") in German, then *Stinktier* is skunk and *Kindergarten* is children's garden. Think of *Vater, Mutter, trink, gross, gut, Nacht, rapide, grand, económico, delicioso,* and you can *comprender mucho.*

*Make an educated guess and go for it. Can you read the Norwegian: "Central Sick House"? Too many Americans would bleed to death on the street corner looking for the word "hospital."*

Many letters travel predictable courses (determined by the physical way a sound is made) as related languages drift apart over the centuries. For instance, p often becomes v or b in the neighboring country's language. Italian menus always have a charge for *coperto*—a "cover" charge.

Practice your understanding. Read time schedules, posters, multilingual signs (and graffiti) in bathrooms, and newspaper headlines. Develop your ear for foreign languages by tuning in to the other languages on a multilingual tour. It's a puzzle. The more you play, the better you get.

**A notepad can work wonders.** Words and numbers are much easier to understand when they're written rather than spoken—and mispronounced. (My back-pocket notepad is my constant travel buddy.) To repeatedly communicate something difficult and important (such as

## Polite Paris

The "mean Parisian" problem is a holdover from Charles de Gaulle days. It's definitely fading, but France's lingering reputation of rudeness can create a self-fulfilling expectation. If you want to enjoy the French, you can. Make it your goal.

The French, as a culture, are pouting. They used to be the crème de la crème, *the* definition of high class. Their language was the lingua franca—everyone wanted to speak French. There was a time when the czar of Russia and his family actually spoke better French than Russian. A US passport even has French on it—leftovers from those French glory days.

*Enjoy the French.*

Modern French culture is reeling—humiliated by two world wars, lashed by Levi's, and crushed by the Big Mac of American culture. And our two cultures aren't natural buddies. The French enjoy subtleties and sophistication. American culture sneers at these fine points. We're proud, brash, and like to think we're rugged individualists. We are a smiley-face culture whose bank tellers are fined if they forget to say, "Have a nice day." The French don't find slap-on-the-back niceness terribly sincere.

Typically, Americans evaluate the French by the Parisians they meet. Big cities anywhere are colder than small towns. And, remember, most of us see Paris at the height of the hot, busy summer, when those Parisians who can't escape on vacation see their hometown flooded with insensitive foreigners who butcher their language and put ketchup on their meat. That's tough to take smiling, and if you're looking for coldness, this is a good place to start.

To make the Parisians suddenly 40 percent friendlier, learn and liberally use these four phrases: *bonjour, s'il vous plaît, merci,* and *pardon.* And to really revel in French friendliness, visit an untouristy part of the countryside and use those four phrases. Oh, and *vive la différence*—celebrate the differences.

medical instructions, "I'm a strict vegetarian," "boiled water," "well-done meat," "your finest ice cream," or "I am rich and single"), have it written in the local language on your notepad.

**Assume you understand and go with your educated guess.** My master key to communication is to see most communication problems as multiple-choice questions, make an educated guess at the meaning of a message (verbal or written), and proceed confidently as if I understood it correctly. At the breakfast table the waitress asks me a question. I don't understand a word she says but I tell her my room number. Faking it like this applies to rudimentary things like instructions on customs forms, museum hours, and menus. With this approach I find that 80 percent of the time I'm correct. Half the time I'm wrong I never know it, so it doesn't really matter. So 10 percent of the time I really blow it. My trip becomes easier—and occasionally much more interesting.

## European Gestures

In Europe, gestures can contribute to the language barrier. Here are a few common gestures, their meanings, and where you're likely to see them:

**Fingertips kiss:** Gently bring the fingers and thumb of your right hand together, raise to your lips, kiss lightly, and joyfully toss your fingers and thumb into the air. This gesture is used commonly in France, Spain, Greece, and Germany as a form of praise. It can mean sexy, delicious, divine, or wonderful. Be careful—tourists look silly when they overemphasize this subtle action.

**Hand purse:** Straighten the fingers and thumb of one hand, bringing them all together and making an upward point about a foot in front of your face. Your hand can be held still or moved a little up and down at the wrist. This is a common and very Italian gesture for a query. It is used to say "What do you want?" or "What are you doing?" or "What is it?" or "What's new?" It can also be used as an insult to say "You fool." The hand purse can also mean "fear" (France), "a lot" (Spain), and "good" (Greece and Turkey).

**Cheek screw:** Make a fist, stick out your forefinger, and (without piercing the skin) screw it into your cheek. The cheek screw is used widely and almost exclusively in Italy to mean good, lovely, beautiful. Many Italians also use it to mean clever. Be careful: In

Dominic Bonuccelli

*Very delicious!*

southern Spain, the cheek screw is used to call a man effeminate.

**Eyelid pull:** Place your extended forefinger below the center of your eye and pull the skin downward. In France and Greece this means "I am alert. I'm looking. You can't fool me." In Italy and Spain, it's a friendlier warning, meaning "Be alert, that guy is clever."

**Forearm jerk:** Clench your right fist and jerk your forearm up as you slap your right bicep with your left palm. This is a rude phallic gesture that men throughout southern Europe often use the way many Americans "give someone the finger." This jumbo version of "flipping the bird" says "I'm superior" (it's an action some monkeys actually do with their penises to insult their peers). This "get lost" or "up yours" gesture is occasionally used by rude men in Britain and Germany as more of an "I want you" gesture about (but never to) a sexy woman.

*This is Danish for "tour bus." These days most come with air-conditioning.*

**Chin flick:** Tilt your head back slightly and flick the back of your fingers forward in an arc from under your chin. In Italy and France, this means "I'm not interested, you bore me," or "You bother me." In southern Italy it can mean "No."

**"Thumbs up," "V for Victory," and more:** The "thumbs up" sign popular in the United States is used widely in France and Germany to say "OK." (Note that it also represents the number one when counting throughout Europe.) The "V for victory" sign is used in most of Europe as in the United States. (Beware—the V with your palm toward you is the rudest of gestures in England.) "Expensive" is often shown by shaking your hand and sucking in like you just burned yourself. In Greece and Turkey, you signal "no" by jerking your eyebrows and head upward. In Bulgaria and Albania, "OK" is indicated by happily bouncing your head back and forth as if you were a bobblehead doll and someone slapped you.

To beckon someone, remember that in northern Europe you bring your palm up, and in the south you wave it down. While most people greet each other by waving with their palm out, you'll find many Italians wave "at themselves" as infants do, with their palm towards their face. *Ciao-ciao.*

## European Numbers and Stumblers

Europeans do many things differently from the way we do. Simple as these things are, they can be frustrating barriers and cause needless, occasionally serious problems.

**Numbers:** A European's handwritten numbers look different from ours. The 1s have an upswing ( 1 ). The number 4 often looks like a short lightning bolt ( 4 ). If you don't cross your 7 ( 7 ), it may be mistaken as a sloppy 1, and you could miss your train (and be mad at the French for "refusing to speak English"). Avoid using "#" for "number"—it's not common in Europe.

**Counting:** When counting with your fingers, start with your thumb. If you hold up your first finger, you'll probably get two; and making a "peace" sign to indicate the number two may get you three—or a punch in the nose in parts of Britain, where it's an obscene gesture.

**Dates and decimals:** Europeans reverse the day and month in numbered dates. Christmas is 25-12-07 instead of 12-25-07, as we would write it. Commas are decimal points and decimals commas, so a dollar and a half is 1,50 and there are 5.280 feet in a mile.

**Time:** The 24-hour clock is used in any official timetable. This includes bus, train, and tour schedules. Learn to use it quickly and easily. Everything is the same until 12:00 noon. Then, instead of starting over again at 1:00 p.m., the Europeans keep on going—13:00, 14:00, and so on. 18:00 is 6:00 p.m. (subtract 12 and add p.m.). Remember that European time is six/nine hours ahead of the East/West Coasts of the US. (British, Irish, and Portuguese time is five/eight hours ahead.)

**Metric:** European countries (except Great Britain) use kilometers instead of miles. A kilometer is six-tenths of a mile. To quickly translate kilometers to miles, cut the kilometer figure in half and add 10 percent of the original figure (e.g., 420 km = 210 + 42 = 252 miles). Some people prefer to drop the last digit and multiply by six: Quick, what's 150 km? (15 x 6 = 90 miles.) "36-26-36" means nothing to a European (or metric) girl watcher. But a "90-60-90" is a real pistachio.

**Temperatures:** Europeans measure temperatures in degrees Celsius. Zero degrees C = 32 degrees Fahrenheit. You can use a formula to convert temperatures in Celsius to Fahrenheit (divide C by 5, multiply by 9, and add 32 to get F), or easier and nearly as accurate, double the Celsius temperature and add 30. (To convert Fahrenheit to Celsius, subtract 32 from F, divide by 9, then multiply by 5.) A memory aid: 28° C = 82° F—darn hot. And a poem: 30 is hot, 20 is nice, 10 is cold, 0 is ice.

**Addresses:** House numbers often have no correlation to what's across the street. While odd is normally on one side and even is on the other,

## A Yankee–English Phrase Book

Oscar Wilde said, "The English have everything in common with the Americans—except, of course, language." On your first trip to England, you'll find plenty of linguistic surprises. I'll never forget checking into a small-town bed-and-breakfast, a teenager on my first solo European adventure. The landlady cheerily asked me, "And what time would you like to be knocked up in the morning?" I looked over at her husband, who winked, "Would a fry at half-eight be suitable?" The next morning I got a rap on the door at 8:00 and a huge British breakfast a half hour later.

Traveling through England is an adventure in accents and idioms. Every day you'll see babies in prams and pushchairs, sucking dummies as mothers change wet nappies. Soon the kids can trade in their nappies for smalls and spend a penny on their own. "Spend a penny" is British for a visit to the loo (bathroom). Older British kids enjoy candy floss (cotton candy), naughts and crosses (tic tac toe), big dippers (roller coasters), and iced lollies (popsicles), and are constantly in need of an Elastoplast or sticking plaster (Band-Aid).

It's fun to browse through an ironmonger's (hardware store), chemist's shop (pharmacy), or Woolworth's, noticing the many familiar items with unfamiliar names. The school-supplies section includes sticky tape or Sellotape (adhesive tape), rubbers (erasers), and scribbling blocks (scratch pads). Those with green fingers (a green thumb) might pick up some courgette (zucchini), swede (rutabaga), or aubergine (eggplant) seeds.

In England, chips are fries and crisps are potato chips. A beefburger, made with mince (hamburger meat), comes on a toasted bap (bun). Wipe your fingers with a serviette—never a napkin (sanitary pad).

The English have a great way with names. You'll find towns with names like Upper and Lower Piddle, Once Brewed, and Itching Field. This cute coziness comes through in their language as well. Your car is built with a bonnet and a boot rather than a hood and trunk. You drive on motorways, and when the freeway divides, it becomes a dual carriageway. And never go anticlockwise (counterclockwise) in a roundabout. Gas is petrol, a truck is a lorry, and when you hit a traffic jam, don't get your knickers in a twist (make a fuss), just queue up (line up) and study your American–English phrase book.

A two-week vacation in England is unheard of, but many locals holiday for a fortnight in a homely (pleasant) rural cottage, possibly on the Continent (continental Europe). They might pack a face flannel (washcloth), torch (flashlight), and hair grips (bobby pins) in their bum bag (never a fanny pack!) before leaving their flat (apartment). On a cold evening it's best to wear the warmest mackintosh (raincoat) you can find or an anorak (parka) with press studs (snaps). You can post letters in the pillar box and give your girlfriend a trunk (long-distance) call. If you reverse the charges (call collect), she'll say you're tight as a fish's bum. If she witters on (gabs and gabs), tell her you're knackered (exhausted) and it's been donkey's years (ages) since you've slept. After washing up (doing the dishes) and cleaning up with a hoover (vacuum), you can go up to the first floor (second floor) with a neat (straight) whisky and a plate of biscuits (sweet cookies) and get goose pimples (goose bumps) just enjoying the view. Too much of that whisky will get you sloshed, paralytic, bevvied, wellied, popped up, ratted, or even pissed as a newt.

*Don't take British road signs personally.*

All across the British Isles, you'll find new words, crazy local humor, and colorful accents. Pubs are colloquial treasure chests. Church services, sporting events, the Houses of Parliament, live plays featuring local comedy, the streets of Liverpool, the docks of London, and children in parks are playgrounds for the American ear. One of the beauties of touring the British Isles is the illusion of hearing a foreign language and actually understanding it—most of the time.

#27 may be directly across from #2.

**Floors:** Floors of buildings are numbered differently. The bottom floor is called the ground floor. What we would call the second floor is a European's first floor. So if your room is on the second floor (European), bad news—you're on the third floor (American). On the elevator, push whatever's below "1" to get to the ground floor. On an escalator, keep the left lane open for passing. Stand to the right.

## 21. PHONES, E-MAIL, AND MAIL

Communication for travelers in Europe has never been easier. Not only are more and more people speaking English, but telephoning is a cinch, whether you're making local, long-distance, or international calls. E-mail communication is so standard (and preferred) that some hotels are actually retiring their fax machines. Internet cafés are everywhere. Oh, yes, and each country still has a postal system.

### Smart Travelers Use the Telephone

Travel goes most smoothly for those who use the telephone. Call tourist offices to check sightseeing plans, train stations to check travel plans, museums to see if an English tour is scheduled, restaurants to see if they're open, hotels to confirm reservations, and so on.

I get earnest letters from readers asking me to drop a hotel from my listings because they made a reservation, got a written confirmation, and still arrived to find no room available. Hotels make mistakes. Call a day or two in advance to double-check reservations. I even call again on the day of arrival to tell them what time I expect to get there (especially for a small hotel or B&B that may not have a 24-hour reception desk). As we were filming my public television show in Ireland, I took a minute to call Avis in England to reconfirm our car pickup the next day at the ferry dock in North Wales. The man at Avis said, "Right-tee-o, Mr. Steves, we will have your car waiting for you, noon tomorrow, at Heathrow Airport." No, at North Wales! "Oh, sorry, Mr. Steves. It's good you called ahead." I didn't think, "Boy, Avis sure screwed up." I thought, "You can't travel smart without double-checking things by telephone." The more I travel, the more I use the telephone.

Each country's phone system is different, but each one works—logically. The key to figuring out a foreign phone is to approach it without comparing it to yours back home. It works for the locals, and it can work for you. Many people flee in terror when a British phone starts its infamous "rapid pips." (That's just the British way of telling you to pop in a few coins.)

Each country has phone booths with multilingual instructions. If you follow these step by step, the phone will work—usually. Operators generally speak some English and are helpful. International codes, instructions, and international assistance numbers are usually on the wall (printed in several languages) or in the front of the phone book. If I can't manage in a strange phone booth, I ask a nearby local person for help.

*Most European phone booths use phone cards rather than coins.*

## Types of Phones

Here are the different kinds of phones you'll encounter in Europe. Note that while European phones generally have keypads, you can't count on being able to access your stateside voice mail from Europe (particularly in Italy).

**Card phones:** Most public phones in Europe work with insertable phone cards that you buy locally. While some card phones also accept coins, most don't. Great Britain doesn't have insertable phone cards, but their pay phones accept coins (see below) or major credit cards. For more on using an insertable phone card, see "Making Calls," below.

**Coin-operated phones:** Coin-op phones are being phased out in most European countries (except Britain), but you'll still encounter a few. Have enough small coins to complete your call. Only entirely unused coins will be returned—so don't plug in large coins until it's clear that you'll be having a long conversation. The digital meter warns you when you're about to be cut off. Many phones allow run-on calls, so you won't lose your big-coin credit (if you need to make another call). Look for this (usually black) button and push it rather than hanging up. In countries such as Britain, where you hear tourists in phone booths yelling, "Hello... Hello...HELLO," your voice won't be heard until you push a button to engage the call.

**Metered phones:** Phone offices and some post offices have metered phone booths. The clerk assigns you a booth and can help you with your long-distance prefixes. You sit in your private sweatbox, make the call, and pay the bill when you're done (same cost as a public phone). Beware of a popular new rip-off: small businesses on main tourist streets that look like telephone-company long-distance services but actually charge like hotels. Ask the price per minute (or per unit on the clicking meter) before you take a metered phone booth.

**Hotel phones:** Telephoning through your hotel's phone system is fine for local calls or calls using cheap international phone cards (described below), but it's an almost-criminal rip-off for long-distance calls. I do this only when I'm feeling flush and lazy, for a quick "Call me in Stockholm at this number" message. Many hotels charge a fee for local and "toll-free" as well as long-distance or international calls—always ask the rates before you dial. You'll never be charged for receiving calls, so having someone from the US call you in your room can be a very cheap way to stay in touch. First, get a long-distance plan or a prepaid card that offers good rates on calls from the US to Europe. Give your family a list of your hotels' phone numbers before you leave, and while you're on the road set up calling times by e-mail or quick pay-phone calls. Then relax in your room and wait for the ring.

**Mobile phones:** For the ins and outs of mobile phones in Europe, see page 289.

## Making Calls

There's a dizzying array of ways to pay for your phone calls. The best deals are available only in Europe. For each country I enter, I buy a low-denomination phone card for domestic calls (from phone booths) and an international calling card for calling home (from phone booths or my hotel room).

**Insertable phone cards:** Insertable phone cards are common throughout Europe (except Britain). They are easy to use and sold conveniently at post offices, newsstands, street kiosks, tobacco shops, and train stations. Since they must be inserted into the telephone, these prepaid cards can be used only in phone booths. Simply take the phone off the hook, insert the card, wait for a dial tone, and dial away. The price of the call (local or international) is automatically deducted while you talk. Domestic rates are cheap, and international rates (including to the US) rarely exceed $1 per minute. Each European country has its own phone card—so your German card won't work in an Austrian phone. The only drawback is that the cheapest cards can cost $5—more phone time than you may need in that country. If you're as frugal as I am, you'll lie awake at night wondering how to productively use it up before you cross the next border. You can always blow the remaining telephone time by calling home.

**International phone cards:** Calling the United States from Europe now costs as little as a nickel a minute with handy international phone cards available throughout Europe. These prepaid cards come with a toll-free number and a scratch-to-reveal PIN code (similar to cheap calling cards widely available in the US). The back of the card often contains information in English on how to make calls.

International phone cards are not inserted into the phone. Instead, you dial the toll-free number, reaching an automated operator. When prompted, you punch in your PIN code, then the number you want to dial. A voice tells you how much is left in your account and connects you. The prompts are nearly always in English, but if they aren't, experiment: Dial your code, followed by the pound sign (#), then the phone number, then pound again, and so on, until it works.

If you're making lots of calls, you can avoid redialing the access number and PIN code by pressing whatever key (usually the pound sign) allows you to launch directly into your next call (just follow the instructions on the card).

Since you don't insert international phone cards into the phone, you can use them to make inexpensive calls from most phones, including the one in your hotel room (avoiding pricey hotel rates—but ask the front desk whether there's a surcharge for dialing a toll-free number). Calls to the US generally cost 5–10 cents per minute, and you can also use the card to call within the same country or to another European country.

Look for international phone cards at small newsstand kiosks, hole-in-the-wall long-distance phone shops, youth hostels, and Internet cafés. Because there are so many brand names, simply ask for an international phone card and tell the vendor where you'll be making most calls ("to America"), and he'll select the brand with the best deal. Some international phone cards work in multiple countries—if traveling to Norway, Denmark, and Sweden, look for a card that you can use in all three places. Because cards are occasionally duds, avoid the high denominations.

International phone cards are such a good deal that the German telecom company has cracked down. Using such a card in Germany is very expensive if used from a pay phone, but it works fine from a fixed line (such as in a hotel room).

Be warned that you can only buy these cards in Europe—the big-name American calling cards that you buy in the US are a horrendous value (see page 286).

**Collect calls:** Calling collect is more complicated and always more expensive. It's cheaper and easier if you have your friend call you back,

## European Calling Chart

Just smile and dial, using this key:
AC = Area Code, LN = Local Number.

| European Country | Calling long distance within... | Calling from the US/ Canada to... | Calling from a European country to... |
|---|---|---|---|
| Austria | AC + LN | 011 + 43 + AC (without the initial zero) + LN | 00 + 43 + AC (without the initial zero) + LN |
| Belgium | LN | 011 + 32 + LN (without initial zero) | 00 + 32 + LN (without initial zero) |
| Britain | AC + LN | 011 + 44 + AC (without initial zero) + LN | 00 + 44 + AC (without initial zero) + LN |
| Croatia | AC + LN | 011 + 385 + AC (without initial zero) + LN | 00 + 385 + AC (without initial zero) + LN |
| Czech Republic | LN | 011 + 420 + LN | 00 + 420 + LN |
| Denmark | LN | 011 + 45 + LN | 00 + 45 + LN |
| Finland | AC + LN | 011 + 358 + AC (without initial zero) + LN | 00 + 358 + AC (without initial zero) + LN |
| France | LN | 011 + 33 + LN (without initial zero) | 00 + 33 + LN (without initial zero) |
| Germany | AC + LN | 011 + 49 + AC (without initial zero) + LN | 00 + 49 + AC (without initial zero) + LN |
| Greece | LN | 011 + 30 + LN | 00 + 30 + LN |
| Hungary | 06 + AC + LN | 011 + 36 + AC + LN | 00 + 36 + AC + LN |
| Ireland | AC + LN | 011 + 353 + AC (without initial zero) + LN | 00 + 353 + AC (without initial zero) + LN |
| Italy | LN | 011 + 39 + LN | 00 + 39 + LN |
| Netherlands | AC + LN | 011 + 31 + AC (without initial zero) + LN | 00 + 31 + AC (without initial zero) + LN |
| Norway | LN | 011 + 47 + LN | 00 + 47 + LN |

| European Country | Calling long distance within... | Calling from the US/ Canada to... | Calling from a European country to... |
|---|---|---|---|
| Poland | AC + LN | 011 + 48 + AC (without initial zero) + LN | 00 + 48 + AC (without initial zero) + LN |
| Portugal | LN | 011 + 351 + LN | 00 + 351 + LN |
| Slovakia | AC + LN | 011 + 421 + AC (without initial zero) + LN | 00 + 421 + AC (without initial zero) + LN |
| Slovenia | AC + LN | 011 + 386 + AC (without initial zero) + LN | 00 + 386 + AC (without initial zero) + LN |
| Spain | LN | 011 + 34 + LN | 00 + 34 + LN |
| Sweden | AC + LN | 011 + 46 + AC (without initial zero) + LN | 00 + 46 + AC (without initial zero) + LN |
| Switzerland | LN | 011 + 41 + LN (without initial zero) | 00 + 41 + LN (without initial zero) |
| Turkey | AC (if no initial zero is included, add one) + LN | 011 + 90 + AC (without initial zero) + LN | 00 + 90 + AC (without initial zero) + LN |

- The instructions above apply whether you're calling a fixed phone or mobile phone.
- The international access codes (the first numbers you dial when making an international call) are 011 if you're calling from the US/ Canada, or 00 if you're calling from anywhere in Europe.
- To call the US or Canada from Europe, dial 00, then 1 (the country code for the US and Canada), then the area code and number. In short, 00 + 1 + AC + LN = Hi, Mom!

dialing direct from the States. Call cheap and fast from a phone booth and ask your friend to call you back at your hotel.

**Student and hostel phone cards:** Many travel cards—such as the ISIC student identity card (see page 34) or the HI hostel membership card (see page 213)—also double as prepaid calling cards. Ask for details when you buy your card.

**US calling cards:** Calling-card services offered by American companies such as Sprint, AT&T, and MCI are a terrible value (figure at least $3/min from Europe to the US). If you're calling home, you'll almost always save money dialing direct—whether from a phone booth or your hotel phone—rather than use your US calling card.

## How to Dial

Many Americans are intimidated by dialing European phone numbers. You needn't be. It's simple, once you crack the code.

**Making calls within a European country:** About half of all European countries use area codes (like we do); the other half uses a direct-dial system without area codes.

To make calls within a country that uses a direct-dial system (Belgium, the Czech Republic, Denmark, France, Greece, Italy, Norway, Portugal, Spain, and Switzerland), you dial the same number whether you're calling across the country or across the street.

In countries that use area codes (such as Austria, Croatia, Britain, Finland, Germany, Hungary, Ireland, the Netherlands, Poland, Slovakia, Slovenia, Sweden, and Turkey), you dial the local number when calling within a city, and you add the area code if calling long-distance within the country. Example: To call a Munich hotel (tel. 089/264-349) within Munich, dial 264-349; to call it from Frankfurt, dial 089/264-349.

Note that some countries, particularly those with area codes, can have phone numbers of varying lengths. For instance, a hotel might have a seven-digit phone number and an eight-digit fax number.

**Making international calls:** You always start with the international access code (011 if you're calling from America or Canada, 00 from anywhere in Europe), then dial the country code of the country you're calling (see chart on page 284).

What you dial next depends on the phone system of the country you're calling. If the country uses area codes, drop the initial zero of the area code, then dial the rest of the number. Example: To call the Munich hotel (tel. 089/264-349) from Italy, dial 00, then 49 (Germany's country code), then 89/264-349.

Countries that use direct-dial systems vary in how they're accessed

## Phone Codes

### International Access Codes

When dialing direct, first dial the international access code of the country you're calling from. For all European countries, it's "00." From the United States and Canada, it's "011."

### Country Codes

After you've dialed the international access code, dial the code of the country you're calling.

|  |  |  |  |
|---|---|---|---|
| Austria: | 43 | Italy: | 39 |
| Belgium: | 32 | Morocco: | 212 |
| Britain: | 44 | Netherlands: | 31 |
| Canada: | 1 | Norway: | 47 |
| Croatia: | 385 | Poland: | 48 |
| Czech Rep: | 420 | Portugal: | 351 |
| Denmark: | 45 | Slovakia: | 421 |
| Estonia: | 372 | Slovenia: | 386 |
| Finland: | 358 | Spain: | 34 |
| France: | 33 | Sweden: | 46 |
| Germany: | 49 | Switzerland: | 41 |
| Greece: | 30 | Turkey: | 90 |
| Hungary: | 36 | US: | 1 |
| Ireland: | 353 | | |

internationally by phone. For instance, if you're making an international call to Denmark, the Czech Republic, Italy, Norway, Portugal, or Spain, simply dial the international access code, country code, and phone number. Example: To call a Madrid hotel (tel. 915-212-900) from Germany, dial 00, 34 (Spain's country code), then 915-212-900. But if you're calling Belgium, France, or Switzerland, drop the initial zero of the phone number. Example: To call a Paris hotel (tel. 01 47 05 49 15) from London, dial 00, then 33 (France's country code), then 1 47 05 49 15 (phone number without initial zero).

**Calling home:** You can call the United States directly from Europe for a nickel a minute—a fraction the cost of a postcard stamp (see "International phone cards," above). Rather than write postcards or send e-mails, just call in your "scenery's here, wish you were beautiful" messages. Remember, from most of Europe, it's six hours earlier in New York and nine hours earlier in California. To dial direct, first enter the

## Desperate Telephone Communication

Let me illustrate with a hypothetical telephone conversation. I'm calling a hotel in Barcelona from a phone booth in the train station. I just arrived, read my guidebook's list of budget accommodations, and I like Pedro's Hotel. Here's what happens:

Pedro answers, "Hotel Pedro, grabdaboodogalaysk."

I ask, "Hotel Pedro?" (Question marks are created melodically.)

He affirms, already a bit impatient, "*Sí*, Hotel Pedro."

I ask, "*Habla* Eng-leesh?"

He says, "No, dees ees Ehspain." (Actually, he probably would speak a little English or would say *"momento"* and get someone who did. But we'll make this particularly challenging. Not only does he not speak English, he doesn't want to...for patriotic reasons.)

Remembering not to overcommunicate, you don't need to tell him you're a tourist looking for a bed. Who else calls a hotel speaking in a foreign language? Also, you can assume he's got a room available. If he's full, he's very busy and he'd say "complete" or "no hotel" and hang up. If he's still talking to you, he wants your business. Now you must communicate just a few things, like how many beds you need and who you are.

I say, "OK." (OK is international for, "Roger, prepare for the next transmission.") "Two people"—he doesn't understand. I get fancy, "*Dos* people"—he still doesn't get it. Internationalize, "*Dos* pehr-son"—*no comprende. "Dos hombre"*—nope. Digging deep into my bag of international linguistic tricks, I say, "*Dos* Yankees."

"OK!" He understands that you want beds for two Americans. He says, "*Sí*," and I say, "Very good" or *"Muy bien."*

Now I need to tell him who I am. If I say, "My name is Mr. Steves, and I'll be over promptly," I'll lose him. I say, "My name Ricardo (Ree-KAR-do)." In Italy I say, "My name Luigi." Your name really doesn't matter; you're communicating just a password so you can identify yourself when you walk through the door. Say anything to be understood.

He says, "OK."

You repeat slowly, "Hotel, *dos* Yankees, Ricardo, coming *pronto*, OK?"

He says, "OK."

You say, "*Gracias, adiós*!"

Twenty minutes later you walk up to the reception desk, and Pedro greets you with a robust, "Eh, Ricardo!"

international access code (00 from Europe), then the country code of the US (1), then the area code and the seven-digit number. To call me from France, dial 00-1-425/771-8303. Every country has its quirks. Try pausing between codes if you're having trouble, or dial the English-speaking international operator for help. Off-hour calls are cheaper.

**Communication tips:** Once you've made the connection, the real challenge begins. With no visual aids, getting the message across in a language you don't speak requires some artistry. Speak slowly and clearly, pronouncing every letter. Keep it very simple—don't clutter your message with anything more than what's essential. Don't overcommunicate—many things are already understood and don't need to be said (those last 6 words didn't need to be written). Use international or carefully chosen English words. When all else fails, let a local person on your end (such as a hotel receptionist) do the talking after you explain to him, with visual help, the message.

## Mobile Phones

A mobile phone can come in handy while traveling. Imagine the efficiency of getting driving instructions from your hotel as you approach; or letting your friend know that your train is late but you're on your way; or being reachable day or night by loved ones back home (or a lost travel partner).

Mobile phones aren't for everybody. They're expensive, and often not worth the cost or hassle. If you're on a tight budget, if your trip is short, if you'll be visiting several countries in a relatively short period of time, or if you just really want to be on vacation, you can easily get by with phone cards you buy in Europe (described above). But if you're willing to pay more for the convenience of calling from wherever you are, a mobile phone may be a reasonable choice.

*Mobile phones give B&B owners the freedom to run errands and their business at the same time.*

You have two basic mobile-phone options: Take your American phone (if it works in Europe), or buy one in Europe.

### American Phones

Some American mobile phones work in Europe. This option is pricey (figure $1–2 per minute), but it can be a good, low-hassle option if you use it very sparingly.

The standard phone network in Europe is called GSM. Nokia, Motorola, Samsung, and Sony Ericsson all make GSM-enabled phones. If you'd like to roam with your current mobile phone, check to see if it will work internationally—it must be "GSM enabled." If you're thinking of buying a new mobile phone and would like to use it in Europe, look for anything labeled "tri-band" or "quad-band" to get the "world phone" option. ("Dual-band" phones sometimes work in Europe, but not as well.)

Once you have a GSM-enabled phone, you'll also need a calling plan that allows for international calls. T-Mobile has a good international phone plan, charging about $1–2 per minute with no additional fees. Cingular's international rates are similar. Ask your carrier for details.

Before you leave, confirm with your provider that you're cleared for using the phone in Europe. You may have to go into your phone's menu and manually switch it from the American band to the European one, but most phones automatically detect the change. As you cross each border, you'll usually get a text message welcoming you to the new country's network, and explaining how to take advantage of their services.

### European Phones

If your American phone doesn't have an international option, consider buying a cheap European mobile phone instead. You'll usually need to get two separate components: the mobile phone itself, and the card that makes it work.

You can buy European phones in America (try www.mobal.com or www.telestial.com), but it's generally smarter and cheaper to shop for a phone in Europe at the ubiquitous corner phone marts or at mobile-phone counters in big department stores. The cheapest new phones run about $75 and work fine. (You probably don't need the latest and best model.) Buying or borrowing a used phone is fine, too. A few hotels offer you the option to borrow or rent a mobile phone for the duration of your visit.

The "identity" of a GSM mobile phone—your phone number and account information—is stored on a removable fingernail-sized chip, called a SIM card, which fits into the back of the phone. The phone won't work without a SIM card. Some phones are "locked" so that you can't switch SIM cards, but this lock can be removed by the service provider (confirm that the phone is unlocked before leaving the store). Buying a locked phone, which can save you a little money, makes sense only if you will always be using the phone in a single country.

## Buying a Mobile Phone SIM Card in Europe

Here's a checklist of things to ask when you buy a European SIM card:

1. What is the cost per minute for domestic and international calls and for SMSs (text messages)?
2. Are there different calling plans with different per-minute costs? Which one is right for me?
3. What are my code (PIN) numbers and when do I need them?
4. How do I get a tally of the remaining credit on my chip?
5. How can I get more credit when I run out? Is there a way to get more credit when I'm in another country?
6. What are the extra costs for calls and SMSs when I'm roaming in another country?

Before leaving the shop, turn off your phone, put the SIM card in it, and go through the entire process, from turning the phone on through actually making a call—to the store, or, for fun, to the salesperson's personal phone.

SIM cards usually cost $20–50, which gives you a phone number and starter credit. Making a domestic call usually costs 10–20 cents per minute. International calls are expensive ($1 per minute or more to other European countries and the US). Unlike in America, incoming domestic calls to European mobile phones cost the phone owner nothing; instead, callers pay more to reach a European mobile phone than a fixed line. Top up your credit by buying refill cards at newsstands and gas stations. There is no monthly fee. These prepaid SIM cards, while more expensive, are much more convenient for travelers than being tied down to an American-style monthly contract (though contracts are available if you're planning a long stay).

SIM cards work best in the country where you bought them. When you use the same SIM card in another country, you are "roaming." Call prices go way up ($1 per minute or more), and you also pay international rates to receive incoming calls. While this might be tolerable for a quick call or two, you should get a local SIM card if you want to use your phone a lot in a new country. You can usually choose between two or three telephone companies in each country.

Europeans (and, increasingly, American teens) are really into SMSs, or text messages, which usually cost 5–10 cents to send and nothing to receive. Any GSM phone can send and receive text messages. Communicating by SMS is much cheaper than voice calls when you're roaming outside your chip's home country—only about 35 cents per message.

Mobile phones aren't for everybody. In fact, for the majority of travelers, phone booths are the best way to make calls in Europe—they're cheap and easy to find. But if you travel frequently, a mobile phone is a great convenience. I bought my cheap one in Italy four years ago and have used it in more than a dozen different countries. No more noisy, urine-perfumed phone booths for me...I travel Europe with a mobile phone.

## Calling over the Internet

More and more Europeans—and many tech-savvy Americans—are using the Internet to save money on otherwise-expensive international phone calls. This technology is called Voice over Internet Protocol (VoIP; sometimes also known as Internet telephony or broadband phone).

The major providers of this service are Skype (www.skype.com) and Google Talk (www.google.com/talk). At either of these Web sites, you can download the application and register for free. Once you're signed up, you can talk via your computer (using the computer's built-in speakers and microphone, or through an operator-type headset) to any other computer running the program. These calls are free, no matter where you are, and the sound quality is generally as good as a standard phone connection. Of course, the service only works well if both parties have a high-speed Internet connection.

You can also call from a computer to a traditional telephone number (or vice versa), but the calls are not free, and the quality can be bad on the telephone end (aggravating voice delays, scratchy sound). Other companies, such as Vonage (www.vonage.com), allow you to place calls over the Internet using a fixed-line phone (rather than a computer), with cheaper rates to Europe than those offered by most old-fashioned long-distance companies.

While VoIP is not yet a practical tool for the casual American tourist (unless you're carrying a laptop with a speedy Internet connection), it's worth knowing about because of its increasing popularity in Europe. It's only a matter of time before a new European friend who wants to keep in touch asks you, "Do you use Skype?"

## E-Mail

Cybercafés, along with the many shops that offer Internet access without the coffee, are popular throughout Europe. Large European chains such as easyInternetcafé (www.easyinternetcafe.com) offer inexpensive access in big cities. In small towns, you can usually get online in libraries and youth hostels, and sometimes at bookstores, copy shops, post offices, and video stores. Ask the TI, your hotelier, a young person, or another traveler for the nearest place to access the Internet.

You can send and receive e-mail using free services such as Yahoo! Mail (mail.yahoo.com) or Hotmail (www.hotmail.com). Although you can set up your e-mail account from anywhere, it's easier to figure it out at home than in Europe.

Be patient with foreign-letter keyboards. It takes time to find the right keys. If you can't locate a special character (such as the @ symbol), simply copy it from a Web page and paste into your e-mail message. Or you can ask the clerk for help. Often with a simple keystroke or a click of the mouse, you can turn the keyboard into an American one.

Avoid storing personal information (such as passport and credit-card numbers) online. If you need important documents, e-mail or phone home and have them sent by fax.

*Sending e-mail is e-zee.*

If you're going to Europe as a tourist, I recommend leaving your laptop at home. E-mail is cheap and easy at the Internet cafés that you'll see everywhere. If you do bring a laptop, you have two options for getting online in Europe. If your laptop has wireless Internet access ("Wi-Fi" for short), you should be able to get on a network at a café or your hotel, sometimes for a small fee—look for signs. Another option is to access a dial-up Internet service provider (such as MCI) from your hotel room. The company can give you local or toll-free access numbers for each country you'll visit. I also bring a phone-line tester to check line polarity and current. (My dial-up modem works fine with an older analog phone system, but newer digital phones could fry it.)

Although you can buy plug adapters for European phone outlets, I have nearly always gotten by without one. While phone outlets in the wall are different in every country, you will find the standard US-style (RJ-45) connection in the back of almost every phone. Sometimes I've had to change my dial-up network settings for pulse or tone.

## Mail

**Sending packages home:** Shoppers lighten their load by sending packages home by surface mail. Postage is expensive. A box the size of a small fruit crate costs about $40 by slow boat. Books are much cheaper if they are sent separately.

Customs regulations amount to 10 or 15 frustrating minutes of filling out forms with the normally unhelpful postal clerk's semi-assistance. Be realistic in your service expectations. Remember, European postal clerks are every bit as friendly, speedy, and multilingual as American postal clerks.

You can mail one package per day to yourself worth up to $200 duty-free from Europe to the US (mark it "personal purchases"). (If you mail an item home valued at $250, you pay duty on the full $250, not $50.) When you fill out the customs form, keep it simple and include the item's value (contents: clothing, books, souvenirs, poster, value $50). For alcohol, perfume containing alcohol, and tobacco valued at more than $5, you will pay a duty. You can also mail home all the "American Goods Returned" you like (e.g., clothes you packed but no longer need) with no customs concerns—but note that these goods really must be American (not Bohemian crystal or a German cuckoo clock), or you'll be charged a duty. If it's a gift for someone else, they are liable to pay customs if it's worth more than $100 (mark it "unsolicited gift").

Post offices usually sell boxes and string or tape for about $2. Service is best north of the Alps. (The fastest way to get a package home from Italy is to use the Vatican post office...or take it home in your suitcase.) Small-town post offices can be less crowded and more user-friendly. Every box I've ever mailed has arrived—bruised and battered but all there—within six weeks. To send precious things home fast, I use DHL (e.g., to send the tapes shot for my TV series, it cost me $100 for 2-day service). DHL has offices in any big city, listed in local phone books and online at www.dhl.com.

**Receiving mail:** Now that telephoning and e-mailing are so cheap and easy, I see little need to receive mail in Europe. But if you still want to get snail mail on the road, minimize mail pickups to maximize your flexibility. Arrange your mail stops before you leave. Every city has a general delivery service. Pick a small town with only one post office and no crowds. Have letters sent to you in care of "Poste Restante." Tell your friends to print your last name in capitals, underline it, and omit your middle name. If possible, avoid the Italian male...I mean, mail.

Friends or relatives in Europe are fine for mail stops. Or, to avoid mail pickup commitments on a long trip, have mail sent to a friend or relative at home. When you know where you'll be, you can telephone them from Europe with instructions on where to mail your letters. Second-day US–Europe services are reliable and reasonable, but allow up to four days for a delivery to a small town.

# 22. STAYING HEALTHY

## Get a Checkup

Just as you'd give your car a good checkup before a long journey, it's smart to meet with your doctor before your trip. Get a general checkup and ask for advice on maintaining your health on the road. Obtain recommended immunizations and discuss proper care for any preexisting medical conditions while traveling. Bring along a letter from your doctor describing any special health problems and a copy of any pertinent prescriptions. If you have any heart concerns, pack a copy of a recent EKG.

**Travel-medicine specialists:** While I consider Europe as safe as the US, those traveling to more exotic destinations should consult a travel-medicine physician. Only these specialists keep entirely up-to-date on health conditions for travelers around the world. Tell the doctor about every place you plan to visit and anyplace you may go. Then you can have the flexibility to take that impulsive swing through Turkey or Morocco knowing that you're prepared medically and have the required shots. Ask the doctor about Havrix (a vaccine that protects against hepatitis A—see www.havrix.com), Twinrix (protects against both hepatitis A and B—see www.twinrix.com), antidiarrheal medicines, and any extra precautions. The Centers for Disease Control offers updated information on every country (www.cdc.gov/travel).

**Dental checkup:** Get a dental checkup well before your trip. (If you get a crown right before you leave, it's timed to fall out on the plane.) Emergency dental care during your trip is time- and money-consuming, and can be hazardous and painful. I once had a tooth crowned by a German dentist who knew only one word in English, which he used in question form—"Pain?"

## Jet Lag and the First Day of Your Trip

Anyone who flies through time zones has to grapple with the biorhythmic confusion known as jet lag. When you switch your wristwatch six to nine hours forward, your body says, "Hey, what's going on?" Body clocks don't reset so easily. All your life you've done things on a 24-hour cycle. Now, after crossing the Atlantic, your body wants to eat when you tell it to sleep and sleep when you tell it to enjoy a museum.

Too many people assume their first day will be made worthless by jet lag. Don't prematurely condemn yourself to zombiedom. Most people I've traveled with, of all ages, have enjoyed productive—even hyper—first days. You can't avoid jet lag, but with a few tips you can minimize the symptoms.

*Jet lag hits even the very young.*

**Leave home well-rested.** Flying halfway around the world is stressful. If you leave frazzled after a hectic last night and a wild bon-voyage party, there's a good chance you won't be healthy for the first part of your trip. An early-trip cold used to be a regular part of my vacation until I learned this very important trick: Plan from the start as if you're leaving two days before you really are. Keep that last 48-hour period sacred (apart from your normal work schedule), even if it means being hectic before your false departure date. Then you have two orderly, peaceful days after you've packed so that you are physically ready to fly. Mentally, you'll be comfortable about leaving home and starting this adventure. You'll fly away well-rested and 100 percent capable of enjoying the bombardment of your senses that will follow.

**On the flight, drink plenty of liquids, eat lightly, and rest.** Long flights are dehydrating. I ask for "two orange juices with no ice" every chance I get. Help yourself to the juice pitchers in the galley area. Eat lightly and have no coffee and only minimal sugar until the flight's almost over. Alcohol will stress your body and aggravate jet lag. The in-flight movies are good for one thing—nap time. With two or three hours' sleep during the transatlantic flight, you will be functional the day you land.

**Reset your mind to local time.** When the pilot announces the local European time, reset your mind along with your wristwatch. Don't prolong jet lag by reminding yourself what time it is back home. Be in Europe.

**On arrival, stay awake until an early local bedtime.** If you doze off at 4 p.m. and wake up at midnight, you've accomplished nothing. Plan a good walk until early evening. Jet lag hates fresh air, daylight, and exercise. Your body may beg for sleep, but stand firm: Refuse. Force your body's transition to the local time. You'll probably awaken very early on your first morning. Trying to sleep later is normally futile. Get out and enjoy a "pinch me, I'm in Europe" walk, as merchants set up in the marketplace and the town slowly comes to life. This will probably be the only sunrise you'll see in Europe.

You'll read about many jet-lag cures. Some travelers rave about melatonin, but I tackle jet lag without drugs. Just leave unfrazzled, minimize jet lag's symptoms, force yourself into European time, and give yourself a chance to enjoy your trip from the moment you step off the plane.

## Traveling Healthy

Europe is generally safe. All the talk of treating water with purification tablets is applicable only south and east of Europe. Using discretion and common sense, I eat and drink whatever I like in Europe. As our world becomes more chemical, reasons for concern and caution will increase on both sides of the Atlantic.

I was able to stay healthy throughout a six-week trip traveling from Europe to India. By following these basic guidelines, I never once suffered from Tehran Tummy or Delhi Belly.

**Eat nutritiously.** The longer your trip, the more you'll be affected by an inadequate diet. Budget travelers often eat more carbohydrates and less protein to stretch their travel dollar. This is the root of many nutritional problems. Protein helps you resist infection and rebuilds muscles. Get the most nutritional mileage from your protein by eating it with the day's largest meal (in the presence of all those essential amino acids). Supplemental super-vitamins, taken regularly, help me to at least feel healthy. If you have a serious dietary restriction, have a multilingual friend write it in the local language on the back of a business card and use it to order in restaurants.

**Use good judgment.** Avoid unhealthy-looking restaurants. Meat should be well cooked and, in some places, avoided altogether. Have "well done" written on a piece of paper in the local language and use it when ordering. Pre-prepared foods gather germs (a common cause of diarrhea). Outside of Europe, be especially cautious. When in serious doubt, eat only thick-skinned fruit...peeled.

**Keep clean.** Wash your hands often, keep your nails clean, and avoid

*Good news for your health: Europe is getting enthusiastic about not smoking. Cigarette packages make it really clear: "Smoking kills"; and Berlin's subway—like much of Europe—is now smoke-free.*

touching your eyes, nose, and mouth.

**Practice safe sex.** Sexually transmitted diseases are widespread. Obviously, the best way to prevent acquiring an STD is to avoid exposure. Condoms (readily available at pharmacies and from rest-room vending machines) are fairly effective in preventing transmission. AIDS is also a risk, especially among prostitutes.

**Exercise.** Physically, travel is great living—healthy food, lots of activity, fresh air, and all those stairs! If you're a couch potato, try to get in shape before your trip by taking long walks. To keep in shape, you may want to work out during your trip. Jogging, while not as widespread in Europe as it is in the US, is not considered weird. Traveling joggers can enjoy Europe from a special perspective—at dawn. Swimmers will find that Europe has plenty of good, inexpensive public swimming pools. Whatever your racket, if you want to badly enough, you'll find ways to keep in practice as you travel. Most big-city private tennis and swim clubs welcome foreign guests for a small fee, which is a good way to make friends as well as stay fit.

**Give yourself psychological pep talks.** Europe can do to certain travelers what southern France did to Vincent van Gogh. Romantics can get the sensory bends, patriots can get their flags burned, and anyone can suffer from culture shock.

Europe is crowded, smoky, and not particularly impressed by America or Americans. It will challenge givens that you always assumed were above the test of reason, and most of Europe on the street doesn't really care that much about what you, the historical and cultural pilgrim, have waited so long to see.

Take a break: a long, dark, air-conditioned trip back to California in a movie theater; a pleasant sit in an American embassy reading room surrounded by eagles, photos of presidents, *Time* magazines, and other Yankees; or a visit to the lobby of a world-class hotel, where any hint of the local culture has been lost under a big-business bucket of intercontinental whitewash. It can do wonders to refresh the struggling traveler's spirit.

## European Water

I drink European tap water and any water served in restaurants. Read signs carefully, however: Some taps, including those on trains and airplanes, are not for drinking. If there's any hint of nonpotability—a decal showing a glass with a red "X" over it, or a skull and crossbones—don't drink it. Many fountains in German-speaking countries are for drinking, but others are just for show. Look for *Trinkwasser* ("drinking water")

*The water at many European public fountains is safe to drink...unless your travel partner has dirty hands.*

or *Kein Trinkwasser* ("not drinking water").

The water (or, just as likely, the general stress of travel on your immune system) may, sooner or later, make you sick. It's not necessarily dirty. The bacteria in European water are different from those in American water. Our bodily systems—raised proudly on bread that rips in a straight line—are the most pampered on earth. We are capable of handling American bacteria with no problem at all, but some people can go to London and get sick. Some French people visit Boston and get sick. Some Americans travel around the world, eating and drinking everything in sight, and don't get sick, while others spend weeks on the toilet. It all depends on the person.

East of Bulgaria and south of the Mediterranean, do not drink untreated water. Water can be treated by boiling it for 10 minutes or by using purifying tablets or a filter. Bottled water, beer, wine, boiled coffee and tea, and bottled soft drinks are safe as long as you skip the ice cubes. Coca-Cola products are as safe in Syria as they are at home.

## Traveler's First-Aid Kit

You can buy anything you need in Europe, but it's handy to bring along:

- Band-Aids
- soap or alcohol preps (antiseptic Handi-Wipes)
- antibiotic cream (in Europe, you may need a prescription to buy skin ointments with antibiotics)
- moleskin
- tweezers
- thermometer in a hard case
- non-aspirin pain reliever
- medication for colds and diarrhea
- prescriptions and medications (in labeled, original containers)

Particularly if you'll be hiking in isolated areas, bring a first-aid booklet, Ace bandage, space blanket, and tape and bandages.

**For eye care:** Those with corrected vision should carry the lens prescription as well as extra glasses in a solid protective case. Contact lenses are used all over Europe, and the required solutions for their care are easy to find.

## Basic First Aid

Travel is much more fun when you're healthy. Be proactive to stay well. If you do get sick, take action to regain your health.

**Headaches and other aches:** Tylenol (or any other non-aspirin pain reliever) soothes headaches, sore feet, sprains, bruises, Italian traffic, hangovers, and many other minor problems.

**Abrasions:** Clean abrasions thoroughly with soap to prevent or control infection. Bandages help keep wounds clean but are not a substitute for cleaning. A piece of clean cloth can be sterilized by boiling for 10 minutes or by scorching with a match.

**Blisters:** Moleskin, bandages, tape, or two pairs of socks can prevent or retard problems with your feet. Cover any irritated area before it blisters.

**Motion sickness:** To be effective, medication for motion sickness (Bonine or Dramamine) should be taken one hour before you think you'll need it. This medication (or Tylenol PM) can also serve as a mild sleeping pill.

**Swelling:** Often accompanying a physical injury, swelling is painful and delays healing. Ice and elevate any sprain periodically for 48 hours. A package of frozen veggies works as a cheap ice pack. Use an Ace bandage to immobilize, stop swelling, and, later, provide support. It is not helpful to "work out" a sprain.

**Fever:** A high fever merits medical attention. A normal temperature of 98.6° Fahrenheit equals 37° Celsius. If your thermometer reads 40°C, you're boiling at 104°F.

**Colds:** Haste can make waste when it comes to gathering travel memories. Keep yourself healthy and hygienic. If you're feeling rundown, check into a good hotel, sleep well, and force fluids. (My trick during the hectic scramble of TV production is to suck on vitamin C tablets.) Stock each place you stay with boxes of juice upon arrival. Sudafed (pseudoephedrine) and other cold capsules are available nearly everywhere.

**Diarrhea:** Get used to the fact that you might have diarrhea for a day. (Practice that thought in front of the mirror tonight.) If you get the runs, take it in stride. It's simply not worth taking eight Pepto-Bismol tablets a day or brushing your teeth in Coca-Cola all summer long to avoid a day of the trots. I take my health seriously, and, for me, traveling in India or Mexico is a major health concern. But I find Europe no more threatening to my health than the US.

## Converting Temperatures

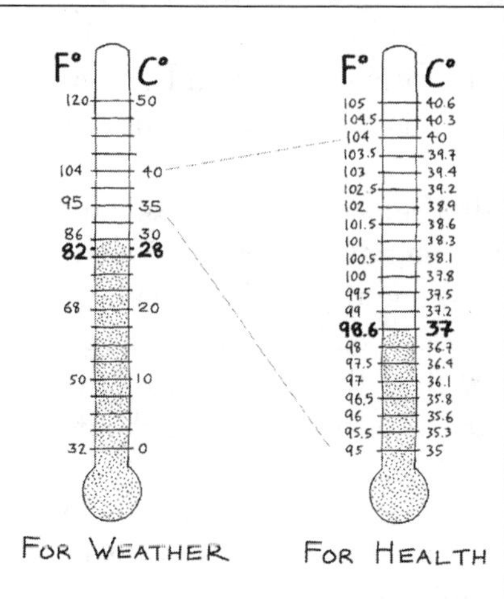


*Europe takes its temperature using the Celsius scale, while we opt for Fahrenheit. For weather, remember that 28°C is 82°F—perfect. For health, 37°C is just right.*

I've routinely taken groups of 24 Americans through Turkey for two weeks. With adequate discretion, we eat everything in sight. At the end of the trip, my loose-stool survey typically shows that five or six travelers coped with a day of the Big D and one person was stuck with an extended weeklong bout.

To avoid getting diarrhea, eat yogurt. Its helpful enzymes ease your system into the local cuisine.

If you get diarrhea, it will run its course. Revise your diet, don't panic, and take it easy for a day. Make your diet as bland and boring as possible for a day or so (bread, rice, boiled potatoes, clear soup, toast, weak tea). Keep telling yourself that tomorrow you'll feel much better. You will. Most conditions are self-limiting.

If loose stools persist, drink lots of water to replenish lost liquids and minerals. Bananas are effective in replacing potassium, which is lost during a bout with diarrhea.

Do not take antidiarrheals if you have blood in your stools or a fever greater than 101°F (38°C). You need a doctor's exam and antibiotics. A child (especially an infant) who suffers a prolonged case of diarrhea also needs prompt medical attention.

I visited the Red Cross in Athens after a miserable three-week tour of the toilets of Syria, Jordan, and Israel. My intestinal commotion was finally stilled by its recommended strict diet of boiled rice and plain tea. As a matter of fact, after five days on that dull diet, I was constipated.

**Constipation:** With all the bread you'll be eating, constipation, the other side of the intestinal pendulum, is (according to my surveys) as prevalent as diarrhea. Get exercise, eat lots of roughage (raw fruits, leafy vegetables, prunes, or bran tablets from home), and everything will come out all right in the end.

## Pharmacies and Doctors

Throughout Europe, people with a health problem go first to the local pharmacy, not to their doctor. European pharmacists diagnose and prescribe remedies for most simple problems. They are usually friendly and speak English, and some medications that are by prescription only in the US are available over the counter (and surprisingly cheap) in Europe. If necessary, the pharmacist will send you to a doctor or the local health clinic.

A visit to a clinic (or the emergency drop-in section of a hospital), while time-consuming, is actually an interesting travel experience. You'll sign in with the receptionist and answer a few questions, take a seat, and eventually meet your nurse or doctor. Every year I end up in a European clinic for one reason or another, and every time I'm impressed by the efficiency, effectiveness, and price. (Visits to the doctor at the neighborhood clinic are generally free—even for a traveler.)

If you're sick in your hotel and would rather not go out, the hotel receptionist can generally call a doctor who will make a house call. In this case, you'll be diagnosed, billed, and have to pay on the spot. Prescription in hand, you'll trudge off to the local 24-hour pharmacy, pick up the necessary medicine, and be on the mend pronto.

For traveling beyond Europe, getting an English-speaking and Western-trained doctor is a reasonable concern. In that case, consider joining **IAMAT,** the International Association for Medical Assistance to Travelers. You'll get a list of English-speaking doctors in member countries who charge affordable, standardized fees for medical visits (membership is free but a donation is requested, www.iamat.org, tel. 716/754-4883). Those needing IAMAT-type services, but who don't have a membership, can get referrals for medical help from other agencies that deal with Americans on the road (such as embassies, consulates, tourist offices, large hotels, and American Express offices).

## 23. OUTSMARTING THIEVES

Europe is safe when it comes to violent crime. But it's a very dangerous place from a petty purse-snatching, pickpocketing point of view. Thieves target Americans—not because they're mean, but because they're smart. Loaded down with valuables in a strange new environment, we stick out like jeweled thumbs. If I were a European street thief, I'd specialize in Americans. My card would say "Yanks Я Us." Americans are known as the ones with all the good stuff in their bags and wallets. Recently I met an American woman whose purse was stolen, and in her purse was her money belt. That juicy little anecdote was featured in every street-thief newsletter.

If you're not constantly on guard, you'll have something stolen. One summer, four out of five of my traveling companions lost cameras in one way or another. (Don't look at me.) In more than 30 summers of travel, I've been mugged once (in a part of London where only fools and thieves tread), had my car broken into six times (broken locks and shattered wing windows, lots of nonessential stuff taken), and had my car hot-wired once (it was abandoned a few blocks away after the thief found nothing to take). But I've never had my room rifled and never had any money belt–worthy valuables stolen.

Remember, nearly all crimes suffered by tourists are nonviolent and avoidable. Be aware of the pitfalls of traveling, but relax and have fun. Limit your vulnerability rather than your travels. Leave precious valuables at home and wear your money belt on the road. Most people in every country are on your side. If you exercise adequate discretion, aren't overly trusting, and don't put yourself into risky situations, your travels should be about as dangerous as hometown grocery shopping. Don't travel afraid–travel carefully.

## Money Belts

**Money belts are your key to peace of mind.** I never travel without one. A money belt is a small, nylon-zippered pouch that fastens around the waist under your pants or skirt. You wear it completely hidden from sight, tucked in like a shirttail—over your shirt and under your pants. (If you find it uncomfortable to wear a money belt in front—as many women do—slide it around and wear it in the small of your back.)

With a money belt, all your essential documents are on you as securely and thoughtlessly as your underpants. Have you ever thought about that? Every morning you put on your underpants. You don't even think about them all day long. And every night when you undress, sure enough, there they are, exactly where you put them. When I travel, my valuables are just as securely out of sight and out of mind, around my waist in a money belt. It's luxurious peace of mind. I'm uncomfortable only when I'm not wearing it.

**Operate with a day's spending money in your pocket.** You don't need to get at your money belt for every euro. Your money belt is your deep storage—for select deposits and withdrawals. Lately, I haven't even carried a wallet. A few bills in my shirt pocket—no keys, no wallet—I'm on vacation!

**Precautions:** Never leave a money belt "hidden" on the beach while you swim. It's safer left in your hotel room. In hostel or dorm situations where your money belt shouldn't be left alone in your room, you can shower with it (hang it—maybe in a plastic bag—from the nozzle).

## Tour of a Money Belt

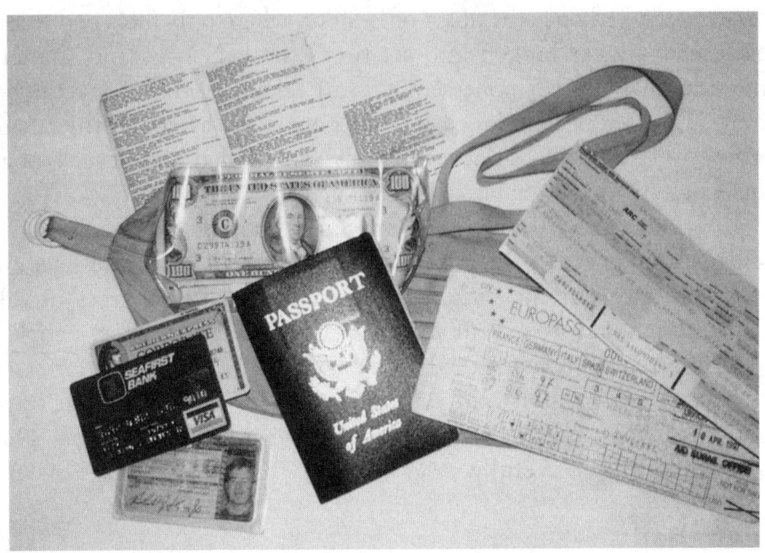


Packing light applies to your money belt as well as your luggage. Here's what to pack in your money belt:

**Passport.** You're legally supposed to have it with you at all times.

**Plane ticket.** Put essential pages in your money belt, nonessential pages (like the receipt) in your luggage.

**Railpass.** This is as valuable as cash.

**Driver's license.** This works just about anywhere in Europe and is necessary if you want to rent a car on the spur of the moment.

**Credit card.** It's required for car rental and handy to have if your cash runs low.

**Debit card.** A Visa debit card is the most versatile for ATM withdrawals. (I no longer use traveler's checks.)

**Cash.** Keep only major bills in your money belt.

**Plastic sheath.** Money belts easily get slimy and sweaty. Damp plane tickets and railpasses can be disgusting and sometimes worthless. Even a plain old baggie helps keep things dry.

**Contact list.** Print small, and include every phone number or e-mail address of importance in your life.

**Trip calendar page.** Include your hotel list and all necessary details from your itinerary (see sample itinerary, page 65).

*Tourists are often the targets of thieves at major sights in Italy, especially around Rome's Forum and the Florence train station. Some will pose as beggars—using babies or newspapers to distract you while they rip you off.*

Keep your money-belt contents dry (sweat-free) with a plastic sheath or a resealable plastic baggie.

Purses and wallets are handy for odds and ends and a day's spending money, but plan on losing them. A button-down flap or a Velcro strip sewn into your front or back pocket slows down fast fingers. Those with nothing worth stealing (cars, video cameras, jewelry, and so on) except what's in their money belt are virtually invulnerable.

## Tips on Avoiding Theft

Thieves thrive on confusion, crowds, and tourist traps. Here's some advice given to me by a thief who won the lotto.

**Keep a low profile:** Never leave your camera lying around where hotel workers and others can see it and be tempted. Keep it either around your neck or zipped safely out of sight. Luxurious luggage lures thieves. The thief chooses the most impressive suitcase in the pile—never mine. Things are much safer in your room than with you in a day bag on the streets. Hotels are a relative haven from thieves and a good resource for advice on personal safety.

**On trains and at the station:** On the train, be alert at stops, when thieves can dash on and off—with your bag. When sleeping on a train (or at an airport, or anywhere in public), clip or fasten your pack or suitcase to the seat, luggage rack, or yourself. Even the slight inconvenience of undoing a clip foils most thieves. Women shouldn't sleep in an empty train compartment. You're safer sharing a compartment with a family. Be on guard in train stations, especially upon arrival, when you may be overburdened by luggage and overwhelmed by a new location. If you check your luggage, keep the claim ticket or key in your money belt—thieves know just where to go if they snare one of these.

**Public transit and flea markets:** Crowding through big-city subway turnstiles is a popular way to rip off the unsuspecting tourist. Imaginative artful-dodger thief teams create a fight or commotion to distract their victims. Crowded flea markets and city buses that cover the tourist sights (like Rome's notorious #64) are also happy hunting grounds. Thief teams will often block a bus or subway entry, causing the person behind you to "bump" into you. While I don't lock my zippers, most zippers are lockable, and even a wire twisty or key ring is helpful to keep your bag zipped up tight. Don't use a waist (or "fanny") pack as a money belt. Thieves assume this is where you keep your goodies.

**Your rental car:** Thieves target tourists' cars—especially at night. Don't leave anything even hinting of value in view in your parked car. Put anything worth stealing in the trunk (or, better yet, in your hotel room). Leave your glove compartment open so the thief can look in without breaking in. Choose your parking place carefully. Your hotel receptionist knows what's safe and what precautions are necessary.

Make your car look local. Take off or cover the rental-company decals. Leave no tourist information lying around. Put a local newspaper under the rear window. More than half of the work that European automobile glass shops get is repairing wings broken by thieves. Before I choose where to park my car, I check if the parking lot's asphalt glitters. If you have a hatchback, leave the trunk covered during the day. At night take the cover off the trunk and lay it on the back seat so the thief thinks you're savvy and can see there's nothing stored in the back of your car. Many police advise leaving your car unlocked at night. Worthless but irreplaceable things (journal, spent film, etc.) are stolen only if left in a bag. Lay these things loose in the trunk. In major cities in Spain, crude thieves reach into windows or even smash the windows of occupied cars at stoplights to grab a purse or camera. In Rome my

*You can judge the safety of a European parking lot by how it glitters.*

favorite pension is next to a large police station—a safe place to park, if you're legal.

## Scams

Many of the most successful scams require a naive and trusting tourist. Be wary of any unusual contact or commotion in crowded public (especially touristy) places. If you're alert and aren't overly trusting, you should have no problem. Here are some clever ways European thieves bolster their cash flow. (For more examples, look in the appendix for excerpts from my Graffiti Wall message board.)

*Thieving moms with their babies are hard at work. Be careful. The wrap—not her left arm—is holding the baby...freeing that hand to pick your pocket.*

**Slow count:** Cashiers who deal with lots of tourists thrive on the "slow count." Even in banks, they'll count your change back with odd pauses in hopes the rushed tourist will gather up the money early and say *"Grazie."* Also be careful when you pay with too large a bill. Waiters seem to be arithmetically challenged. If giving a large bill for a small payment, clearly state the value of the bill as you hand it over. Some cabbies or waiters will pretend to drop a large bill and pick up a hidden small one in order to shortchange a tourist. In Italy, the now-worthless 500-lire coin looks like a €2 coin—be alert when accepting change.

*Don't confuse the €2 coin (left, value $2.40) with the old 500-lira coin (right, value $0).*

**Oops!** You're jostled in a crowd as someone spills ketchup or fake pigeon poop on your shirt. The thief offers profuse apologies while dabbing it up—and pawing your pockets. There are variations: Someone drops something, you kindly pick it up, and you lose your wallet. Or, even worse, someone throws a baby into your arms as your pockets are picked.

*In Berlin, the police teach the public the latest shell-game scam. On the streets of Europe, anything that seems too good to be true...is.*

Assume beggars are pickpockets. Treat any commotion (a scuffle breaking out, a beggar in your face) as fake—designed to distract unknowing victims. If an elderly woman falls down an escalator, stand back and guard your valuables, then...carefully... move in to help.

**The "helpful" local:** Thieves posing as concerned locals will warn you to store your wallet safely—and then steal it after they see where you stash it. If someone wants to help you use an ATM, politely refuse (they're just after your PIN code). If a bank machine eats your ATM card, see if there's a thin plastic insert with a tongue hanging out that crooks use to extract it. (A similar scam is to put something sticky in the slot.) Some thieves put out tacks and ambush drivers with their "assistance" in changing the tire. Others hang out at subway ticket machines eager to "help" you, the bewildered tourist, buy tickets with a pile of your quickly disappearing foreign cash. If using a station locker, beware of the "hood samaritan" who may have his own key to a locker he'd like you to use.

**Fake police:** Two thieves in uniform—posing as "Tourist Police"—stop you on the street, flash their bogus badges, and ask to check your wallet for counterfeit bills or "drug money." You will not even notice some bills are missing until they leave. Never give your wallet to anyone.

*Groups of teenagers, using newspapers to distract their prey, pickpocket tourists strolling the beach promenade in Nice. Not nice.*

**Young thief gangs:** These are common all over urban southern Europe, especially in the touristy areas of Milan, Florence, and Rome. Groups of boys or girls with big eyes, troubled expressions, and colorful raggedy clothes play a game where they politely mob the unsuspecting tourist, beggar-style. As their pleading eyes grab yours and they hold up their pathetic message scrawled on cardboard, you're fooled into thinking that they're beggars. All the while, your purse, fanny pack, or backpack is being expertly rifled. If you're wearing a money belt and you understand what's going on here, there's nothing to fear. In fact, having a street thief's hand slip slowly into your pocket becomes just one more interesting cultural experience.

### If You are Ripped Off...

Even the most careful traveler can get ripped off. If it happens, don't let it ruin your trip. Many trips start with a major rip-off, recover, and with the right attitude and very light bags, finish wonderfully.

Immediately after a theft, get a police report if you intend to make an insurance claim. Traveler's check thefts must be reported within 24 hours. If you lose your credit, debit, or ATM card, follow the damage control tips on page 176 (also printed in all my city and country guidebooks). For tips on what to do in case of identity theft, see page 175.

Before you leave on your trip, make two sets of photocopies of your valuable documents and tickets. Pack a copy and leave a copy at home. It's easier to replace a lost or stolen plane ticket, passport, railpass, or car-rental voucher if you have a photocopy proving that you really owned what you lost. A couple of passport-type pictures you've brought from home can speed up the process of replacing a passport.

American embassies or consulates are located in major European cities. They're there to help American citizens in trouble, but don't fancy themselves as travelers' aid offices. They will inform those at home that you need help, assist in replacing lost or stolen passports, and arrange for emergency funds to be sent from home (or, in rare cases, loan it to you directly).

## 24. MUSEUM STRATEGIES

### Culture Beyond the Petri Dish

Europe is a treasure chest of great art. You'll see many of the world's greatest museums. These tips will help you make the most out of your visit.

**Study your guidebook.** Some museums now require reservations, such as the Alhambra (in Granada, Spain), the church that houses Leonardo da Vinci's *Last Supper* (Milan), Giotto's Scrovegni Chapel (Padua), and the Borghese Gallery (Rome). If you don't reserve in advance, you'll likely miss out.

At Florence's famous galleries—the Accademia (Michelangelo's

*At many great galleries, such as the Uffizi in Florence, you can wait in line for two hours...or call ahead for an appointment and walk right in. Remember: Lines like this are not for the entry turnstile, but for the ticket booth.*

*David*) and the Uffizi (the showcase for Italian Renaissance art)—it's smart to book ahead. While hundreds of tourists are sweating in the long lines, you can just show up at your reserved entry time and spend your time in the museums instead of the lines.

Know the closed days. Most museums are closed one day during the week (usually Mon or Tue). If you've got only one day for the Sistine Chapel, avoid Sunday. It's either closed, or—on the last Sunday of the month—free and terribly crowded, when it feels more like the Sardine Chapel. It can be worth paying the entrance fee to avoid the rampaging hordes on a museum's free day.

Arrive early (or late) at popular sights. If you show up by 8:00 in the morning at Neuschwanstein, Bavaria's famous fairy-tale castle, you'll get a ticket. Come an hour later and you'll either wait a long time or find that tickets are sold out—or worse, both.

Some museums are open late one or two nights a week. For instance, London's Tate Modern stays open Friday and Saturday evenings—when the crowds disappear and you're glad you came.

Museum passes (such as the Paris Museum Pass) and combo-tickets allow you to bypass the long admission lines and walk right in. More and more, Europe's most popular sights are being paired in combo-tickets with sights few people pay to see. The bad news: You have to pay for both to visit one. The good news: You can avoid the line at the congested sight by buying your ticket at the less popular sister sight. You can wait up to an hour to get into

*In Europe, there are two kinds of travelers: smart ones...and those who wait in lines. Good guidebooks offer crowd-beating tips. For Rome's Colosseum, buy your ticket 200 yards away at the Palatine Hill—which never has a line—and skip directly past the not-so-smart travelers pictured here.*

Rome's Colosseum or Venice's Doge's Palace—or buy a combo-ticket (at another participating yet less-crowded site) and just scoot inside.

*A victim of the Louvre*

Note that many museums stop selling tickets and start shutting down rooms 30 to 60 minutes before closing. My favorite time in museums is the cool, lazy, last hour. But I'm careful to get to the far end early, see the rooms that are first to shut down, and work my way back toward the entry.

These tricks aren't secrets. They're in any good, up-to-date guidebook. Just read ahead.

**Learn about art.** If the art's not fun, you don't know enough about it. I remember touring the National Museum of Archaeology in Athens as an obligation. My mom said it would be a crime to miss it. It was boring. I was convinced that the people who looked like they were enjoying it were actually just faking it—trying to look sophisticated. Two years later, after a class in classical art history, that same museum was a fascinating trip into the world of Pericles and Socrates, all because of some background knowledge. Some pre-trip study makes the art more fun. When you understand the context in which it was made, art becomes the closest thing to a time-tunnel machine Europe offers.

*Cleverly avoid the crowds. The Palace of Versailles can be a mob scene. But arrive an hour before closing any day but Tuesday or Sunday, and you'll be waltzing in a deserted Hall of Mirrors with your favorite travel partner.*

**Be selective.** A common misconception is that a great museum has only great art. A museum such as the Louvre in Paris is so big (the building itself was at one time the largest in Europe), you can't possibly cover everything—so don't try. Only a fraction of a museum's pieces are really masterpieces.

With the help of a tour guide or guidebook, focus on just the museum's top two hours. Some of Europe's great museums provide brief pamphlets recommending the best basic visit. With this selective strategy, you'll appreciate the highlights when you're fresh. If you have any energy left afterward, you can explore other areas of specific interest to you. For me, museum-going is the hardest work I do in Europe, and I'm rarely good for more than two or three hours at a time. If you're determined to cover a large museum thoroughly, try to tackle one section a day for several days.

*With a good guidebook, you stand a chance of finding Michelangelo's* Slaves *in the Louvre.*

**Try to get a tour.** Phone ahead. Some museums offer regularly scheduled tours in English. If the tour is in the local language only, politely let the guide know at the beginning that there are several English-speaking people in the group who'd love some information.

Audioguide tours are getting more and more popular at museums (sometimes included in the entry cost, sometimes a few dollars extra). These portable devices allow you to dial up generally worthwhile information in English on particular pieces of art. If you're traveling with an MP3 player (such as an iPod), consider taking along one of my audio tours (described on page 28).

*Stroll with a chatty curator through Europe's greatest art galleries, thanks to digital audioguides.*

**Eavesdrop.** If you are especially interested in one piece of art, spend half an hour studying it and listening to each passing tour guide tell his or her story about *David* or the *Mona Lisa* or whatever. They each do their own research and come up with different information to share. Much of it is true. There's nothing wrong with this sort of tour freeloading. Just don't stand in the front and ask a lot of questions.

**Make sure you don't miss your favorites.** On arrival, look through the museum's guidebook index or the gift shop's postcards to make sure you won't miss anything of importance to you. For instance, I love Salvador Dalí's work. One time I thought I was finished with a museum, but as I browsed through the postcards...Hello, Dalí. A museum guide was happy to show me where this Dalí painting was hiding. I saved myself the disappointment of discovering too late that I'd missed it.

More and more museums offer a greatest-hits plan or brochure. Some (such as London's National Gallery) even have a computer study room where you can input your interests and print out a tailored museum tour.

**Miscellaneous tips:** Particularly at huge museums, ask if your ticket allows in-and-out privileges. Check the museum map or brochure at the entrance for the location of particular kinds of art, the café, and bathrooms (usually free and clean). Also, note any special tours or events or early closings of rooms or wings. Get comfortable: Check your bag and coat. (If you want to try to keep your bag with you, carry it low and under your arms like a purse, not on your back.) Cameras are usually allowed if you don't use a flash or tripod; look for signs or ask. If your camera has an automatic flash, know how to turn it off.

## Open-Air Folk Museums

Many people travel in search of the old life and traditional culture in action. While we book a round-trip ticket into the romantic past, those we photograph with the Old World balanced on their heads are struggling to dump that load and climb into the modern world. In Europe, most are succeeding.

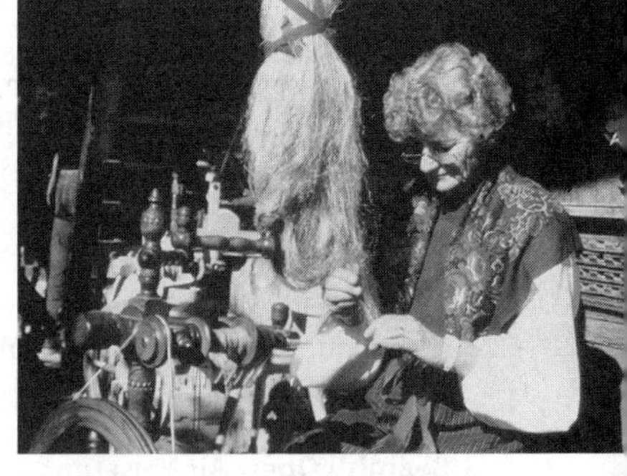

*Traditional culture is kept alive in Europe's open-air folk museums.*

The easiest way, and more than ever the only way, to see the "real local culture" is by exploring the open-air folk museums. True, it's culture on a lazy Susan, but the future is becoming the past faster and faster, and in many places it's the only "Old World" you're going to find.

An open-air folk museum is a collection of traditional buildings from every corner of a country or region, carefully reassembled in a park, usually near the capital or a major city. These sprawling museums are the best bet for the hurried (or tired) tourist craving a magic-carpet ride

## Some of Europe's Best Open-Air Folk Museums

***Benelux***

- **Zaanse Schans,** near Zaandijk, 30 miles north of Amsterdam. Windmills, wooden shoes, etc.
- **Dutch Open-Air Folk Museum,** in Arnhem, Netherlands. Holland's first and biggest.
- **Zuiderzee Open-Air Museum,** in Enkhuizen, Netherlands. Lively setting, lots of craftspeople.
- **Bokrijk Open-Air Museum,** between Hasselt and Genk, in Belgium. Old Flemish buildings and culture in a natural setting.

***Denmark***

- **Funen Village (Den Fynske Landsby),** just south of Odense. Life in the 18th century.
- **Old Town,** Århus. Sixty houses and shops show Danish town life from 1580–1850.

***Finland***

- **Seurasaari Island,** near Helsinki. Reconstructed buildings from all over Finland.
- **Handicraft Museum,** Turku. The life and work of 19th-century craftspeople.

***Germany***

- **Black Forest Open-Air Museum,** in Gutach. A collection of farms filled with exhibits on the local dress and lifestyles.

***Great Britain***

- **Blists Hill Victorian Town,** Ironbridge Gorge. Shows life from the early days of the Industrial Revolution.
- **Beamish Open-Air Museum,** northwest of Durham. Life in northeast England in 1900.
- **Welsh Folk Museum,** at St. Fagans, near Cardiff. Old buildings and craftspeople illustrate traditional Welsh ways.

***Hungary***

- **Skanzen,** in Szentendre, near Budapest. Traditional architecture from around Hungary.

***Ireland***

- **Bunratty Folk Park,** near Limerick. Buildings from the Shannon area and artisans at work.
- **Irish Open-Air Folk Museum,** at Cultra, near Belfast. Traditional Irish lifestyles and buildings from all over Ireland.
- **Glencolumbcille Folk Museum,** Donegal. Thatched cottages show life from 1700–1900. A Gaelic-speaking cooperative runs the folk village and a traditional-crafts industry.

***Norway***

- **Norwegian Folk Museum,** at Bygdøy, near Oslo. Norway's first, with 150 old buildings from all over Norway and a 12th-century stave church.
- **Maihaugen Folk Museum,** at Lillehammer. Folk culture of the Gudbrandsdal Valley. Norway's best.

***Sweden***

- **Skansen,** Stockholm. One of the best museums, with more than 100 buildings from all over Sweden, craftspeople at work, live entertainment, and a Lapp camp with reindeer.
- **Kulturen,** Lund. Features southern Sweden and Viking exhibits.

***Switzerland***

- **Ballenberg Swiss Open-Air Museum,** just northeast of Lake Brienz. A fine collection of old Swiss buildings with furnished interiors.

through that country's past. Log cabins, thatched cottages, mills, old schoolhouses, shops, and farms come complete with original furnishings and usually a local person dressed in the traditional costume who's happy to answer any of your questions about life then and there.

To get the most out of your visit, start by picking up a list of that day's special exhibits, events, and activities at the information center, and take advantage of any walking tours. In the summer, folk museums buzz with colorful folk dances, live music performances, and young craftspeople specializing in old crafts. Many traditional arts and crafts are dying, and these artisans do what they can to keep the cuckoo clock from going the way of the dodo bird. Some of my favorite souvenirs are those I watched being dyed, woven, or carved by folk-museum artists.

Popularized in Scandinavia, these sightseeing centers of the future are now found all over the world. The best folk museums are still in the Nordic capitals. Oslo's, with 150 historic buildings and a 12th-century stave church, is just a boat ride across the harbor from the city hall. Skansen, in Stockholm, gets my first-place ribbon for its guided tours, feisty folk entertainment, and Arctic camp complete with reindeer and Lapp dancing.

*At Stockholm's open-air folk museum, you may be entertained by this rare band of left-handed fiddlers.*

Switzerland's Ballenberg Open-Air Museum, near Interlaken, is a good alternative when the Alps hide behind clouds.

There is no shortage of folk museums in the British Isles. For an unrivaled look at the Industrial Revolution, spend a day at Blists Hill Victorian Town in Ironbridge Gorge, northwest of Stratford-upon-Avon. You can cross the world's first iron bridge to see the factories that lit the fuse of our modern age.

Folk museums teach traditional lifestyles better than any other kind of museum. As our world hurtles past 200 billion McDonald's hamburgers served, these museums will become even more important. Of course, they're as realistic as Santa's Village, but how else will you see the elves?

# 25. TRAVEL PHOTOGRAPHY

Every year I ask myself whether it's worth the worry and expense of mixing photography with my travels. After I return home and I relive my trip through those pictures, the answer is always "Yes!" Here are some tips and lessons that I've learned from the photographic school of hard knocks.

Good shots are made by the photographer, not the camera. For most people, a very expensive camera is a bad idea. Your camera is more likely to be lost, broken, or stolen than anything else you'll travel with. An expensive model may not be worth the risks and headaches that accompany it.

When buying a camera, get one that will do what you want and a little bit more. You are buying one not only for the trip, but also for use later.

Don't buy a camera a day or two before you fly. Not every camera works perfectly right out of the box. Practice shooting indoors and outdoors before you leave and study the results. Check your pictures for good exposure and sharp focus. If they're not right, take it back. Do the same checks with the replacement camera. Do your learning on hometown Main Street—before you're standing at the base of the Eiffel Tower, wondering how to zoom out.

## Digital Cameras

As technology has improved and prices have plummeted, digital cameras have become the standard. I haven't taken a film camera to Europe in years. Most of the photos in this book were taken with a digital camera.

*A good eye is more important than an extra lens.*

The advantages of "going digital" are many. You can view and delete photos immediately, allowing you to take several shots of a subject, then keep only the best one. You're free to experiment with artsy angles, tricky lighting, and nighttime shots without wasting film. Digital photos are also easier to share: Post your favorites on a Web site, e-mail them directly to your family and friends, or print them to create an old-fashioned scrapbook. Printing digital images is getting more common and cheaper (most photo labs charge about 10–20 cents per print)—and, since you can choose only the very best pictures to print, you know they'll all be keepers.

Most digital cameras come with conventional-camera features such as a zoom lens, flash, and auto and manual focus. They also feature a handy liquid crystal display (LCD) screen, which functions as a viewfinder and allows you to review photos you've already taken. Most cameras also come with a traditional squint-through viewfinder. (The LCD screen drains batteries more quickly, but shows you a more accurate version of what the final photo will look like.) Models with a pivoting viewfinder let you sneak candid shots while looking the other way (periscope-style).

### Buying a Digital Camera

There's a wide range of digital cameras available. How to choose? Narrow down your options based on the criteria below. Ask your friends what they recommend and why. Flip through sales fliers to see which models are hot right now. (Today's bestseller will be obsolete in 6 months, so you might as well get the most up-to-date model.) Then read reviews and compare specs on your likely choices. You'll find extremely detailed technical information, in-depth professional reviews, and informal consumer reviews at www.steves-digicams.com, www.dpreview.com, and www.cnet.com (more informal reviews are at www.epinions.com).

Once you've gotten an overview, head to a store to test-drive the likely candidates. Most stores that sell digital cameras have floor models that you can try out. While camera specialty shops can be more knowledgeable than the big electronics stores, they're also more likely to work on commission (which might color their advice).

These factors will help you zoom in on your ideal camera:

**Resolution:** Digital cameras are classified by resolution—that is, by how many megapixels make up each image. (A pixel is a tiny building-block of an image, and one megapixel equals one million pixels.) Any camera that's three megapixels or more will produce crisp images and suitable 4" x 6" prints. The more megapixels, the sharper the image—and the better it'll look when printed (especially for larger prints). As camera prices drop, and high-quality four- and five-megapixel cameras become affordable, it's hard to justify buying a three-megapixel model just to save a few bucks—and buying anything smaller than three megapixels just doesn't make sense.

**Brand-name:** Digital cameras are available from most traditional camera makers (such as Nikon, Olympus, Canon, and Minolta), as well as from electronics or computer companies (such as Sony and Hewlett-Packard). Many avid photographers already have a favorite brand, but anyone who wants decent images should pay a little extra for a big name–brand, rather than the no-name cheapos you'll see advertised.

**Size:** If you travel a lot, you might prefer a camera that's as lightweight as possible. Several models—often called "compact" or "ultracompact"—are almost as small as a deck of cards but can still take high-resolution pictures. I used to have a bigger camera, but found that I was inclined to use it less—it was just too bulky to hassle with. Now that I have a pocket-size camera, I take it with me just about everywhere, and can pop it out anytime something catches my eye. There are trade-offs—smaller cameras have, by definition, smaller lenses, and the image quality can suffer slightly. Serious photographers who prefer SLR film cameras can consider more elaborate SLR-type digital cameras (with interchangeable lenses and a satisfying, old-fashioned shutter click). These cameras—which are available only in high-resolution versions—are expensive and bulky, but produce beautiful, professional-looking images.

**Ease of use:** Some cameras are made for first-time users, with only a few bells and whistles to negotiate. Other types appeal to semi-pro photographers, requiring you to sit down with a manual to figure out how to use the flash. If you're buying a new camera, ask lots of questions in the store and get a good demo on everything you'll need to do (zoom in, delete bad photos, transfer pictures to a computer's hard drive, turn the viewfinder on and off to save battery power, etc.).

When talking to friends and reading reviews, keep in mind these other important features: the ability to take pictures indoors and in low light (make sure it has a good light-metering system), a simple control that turns off the flash (since flash photos are prohibited in most museums), a good wide-angle lens (and/or a panoramic option), and the ability to switch "compression settings" (how many pixels make up your image—and how much room those images take up on your memory card). Also, see how long the camera takes to "boot up" once you turn it on and between photos. Some high-megapixel cameras take a while to go from shot to shot—and can cost you spontaneity as you try to capture a fleeting moment.

### Digital Camera Accessories

Though you can forego the film, there are several other accessories and add-ons to consider for your digital camera.

**Memory:** Digital cameras store photos on a memory card. You can choose how high-resolution you want your images to be; the higher the resolution, the more memory each image takes up. There are different types of memory cards (including CompactFlash, Secure Digital, and Sony's Memory Stick, depending on your camera), and different sizes of memory cards (ranging from 16 megabytes to 1 gigabyte). Most cameras come with a chart explaining how many images will fit on different sizes of memory card, depending on the resolution that you choose. For example, I travel with a five-megapixel camera and a 512-megabyte Memory Stick (which cost me about $90). Taking photos at high resolution, I can fit about 200 photos onto my memory card. For more tips on storing your images—especially on a long trip—see below.

**Batteries:** Some digital cameras come with a battery that can be recharged; others take AA batteries (which the camera will burn through amazingly quickly). Rechargeable AA batteries last much longer than disposable alkalines, and are significantly cheaper in the long run—you can buy a good set of rechargeable nickel–metal hydride (NiMH) batteries and a charger for about $20. Before you buy, make sure the charger will work in Europe (look for the voltage numbers "110V" and "220V"—see "Electronics," page 52), and take an adapter to plug it in.

**TV adapter cable:** Many cameras come with a cable that allows you to plug directly into a TV set. If you're staying at a hotel in Europe with a modern TV, you can enjoy a big-screen digital slideshow while you're still on the road.

For other accessories that work with both digital and non-digital cameras, see "Gadgets," on page 321.

### Storing Digital Images

The biggest disadvantage of a digital camera is the dilemma of how to store all of your photos when you're on a lengthy trip. The easiest solution is to edit your images ruthlessly and often, keeping only the very best shots. (The people who wind up watching your slideshow will thank you for it.) But even the most selective shutterbug will start to run out of room after a week or so on the road.

**Upload to a laptop.** Since I usually travel with a laptop, I can simply upload my photos to my computer every so often. But it's not practical for most travelers to carry a laptop, so you'll have to consider other options.

**Don't skimp on memory.** Buy the biggest memory card you can afford. While it may seem excessive to spend as much as a third of the price of the camera on memory, having a massive memory card gives you flexibility when it comes to how many shots you can keep. Consider investing in a second memory card to increase your capacity (these are available in Europe, but they're more expensive).

**Consider lower resolution.** If you plan to use your photos only for e-mailing or posting to a Web site—and if you're certain you won't want to print any of your photos—you can get by with taking photos at a lower resolution, and fit more on your card. In order to get double the shots on my memory card, I sometimes shoot at the grainier "basic" level rather than the memory-gobbling fine-resolution level. But I've sometimes regretted taking lower-resolution images—such as when I've taken a really great shot, but the resolution is too low to make a satisfactory print.

**Empty your memory card as you go.** Many European photo stores and Internet cafés can now burn your images to a CD, allowing you to free up space on your camera's memory card. This costs only about $5–10 per CD, and it's well worth the expense to allow you to keep snapping away. A backup CD can also provide peace of mind; if anything happens to your camera, your images are safe on a CD in your suitcase.

High-capacity portable hard drives are another place to dump your pictures. But for most travelers, these expensive and heavy devices simply aren't practical.

## Non-Digital Cameras

If you prefer film, here are the options.

**Disposables:** The simple choice for an amateur photographer is a disposable or "single-use" camera. Disposables cost as little as $7 for 24 exposures of 400-speed film. A cheap panorama camera, with a very wide-angle lens for 180-degree shots, can be a fun supplement ($15).

**Point-and-shoot:** Compact little "focus-free" cameras ($25–50) allow minimal creative control but take decent pictures. They're inexpensive, fragile, and, when broken, usually just tossed out.

The more expensive point-and-shoot cameras ($50–350) have autofocus and a wide-angle 38 mm lens. Models more than $100 come with a few helpful bells and whistles and a small adjustable zoom lens of 38–70 mm. The pricier cameras have lenses that zoom from 28 to 105 mm.

If you spend less than $100, you'll get a cheap camera that might not last much longer than the trip.

**Single-lens reflex (SLR):** Those shooting slides should stick with a good SLR ($200–1,000). Regardless of advertising claims, there's no real difference between the mind of Minolta and the mind of Pentax, Nikon, or Canon. The trend in SLRs is toward autofocus lenses, but most of these units have a manual focus–override switch. For traveling, the quick and accurate autofocus is handy, but creative photographers will also want the manual capabilities.

**Lenses:** Your best all-around lens is an f/3.5 28–70 mm or 80 mm "midrange" zoom lens, which ranges between $120 and $300. No, it's not as fast as an f/1.7, but with the fine-grain ASA-400 films on the market today, it's almost like having an f/1.7 lens.

**Filters:** Make sure all your lenses have a haze or UV filter ($15). It's better to bang and smudge up your filter than your lens. The only other filter you might use is a polarizer, which eliminates reflections and enhances color separation, but you can lose up to two stops in speed with it. Never use more than one filter at a time.

**Batteries:** Remember to leave home with fresh batteries in your camera (and it doesn't hurt to bring a spare).

**Gadget bag:** The most functional and economical is simply a small nylon stuff bag made for hikers. When I'm taking a lot of pictures, I like to wear a nylon belt pouch (designed to carry a canteen). This is a handy way to have your different lenses and filters readily accessible, allowing you to make necessary changes quickly and easily. A formal camera bag is unnecessary and attracts thieves.

**Film:** When choosing film, go with 400-speed film in 36-exposure rolls. Print films are all about the same. You'll see more difference between the print processors than between the films. With slide film, stick with the films that are known as E-6 developing (Ektachrome, Fujichrome, and so on). They can be developed overnight in most large cities, and usually cost less, too. Kodak film is cheapest in the United States. In Europe, buy film in department stores or camera shops rather than for rip-off prices at the sights. Fuji and Konica are reasonable in Europe.

If you're concerned about your film being damaged by airport X-ray scanners, you have several choices: 1) ask the security personnel to hand-check your film (no guarantee that they'll consent); 2) buy slow film (slower than ASA-400), which is less likely to get fogged by X-rays; 3) buy and develop your film abroad (more expensive than at home); or 4) switch to digital.

## Gadgets

Like many hobbies, photography allows you to spend endless amounts of money on accessories. The following are particularly useful to the traveling photographer:

**Mini-tripod:** About five inches high, this great little gadget screws into most cameras, sprouts three legs, and holds the camera perfectly still for slow shutter speeds, timed exposures, and automatic shutter-release shots. (It looks like a small lunar-landing module.) Because the flash on

Dominic Bonuccelli

*The Vatican Museum staircase: Have fun with composition and find creative new angles.*

my digital camera gives a harsh image, I prefer to use existing light—which often requires a tripod. A conventional tripod is too large to lug around Europe. Those without a mini-tripod use a tiny beanbag (or sock filled with rice) or get good at balancing their camera on anything solid and adjusting the tilt with the lens cap or strap.

**Tissue, cleaner, and lens cap:** A lens-cleaning tissue and a small bottle of cleaning solution are wise additions to any gadget bag. You can leave your protective camera case at home and protect your lens with a cap that dangles on its string when you're shooting.

## Tricks for a Good Shot

The principles of good photography apply to both digital and film cameras. Most people are limited by their skills, not by their camera. Understand your camera. Devour the manual. Shoot experimental shots, take notes, and see what happens. If you don't understand f-stops or depth of field, find a photography class or book and learn (for tips on taking pictures, visit www.photosecrets.com and www.betterphoto.com). Camera stores sell good books on photography in general and travel photography in particular. I shutter to think how many people are underexposed and lacking depth in this field.

A sharp eye connected to a wild imagination will be your most valuable piece of equipment. Develop a knack for what will look good and be interesting after the trip. The skilled photographer's eye sees striking

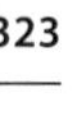

*Back lighting "puts an edge" on ice-cream lickers.*

light, shade, form, lines, patterns, texture, and colors. With a digital camera, you have unlimited freedom to experiment, without worrying about paying for film and developing.

**Look for a new slant to an old sight.** Postcard-type shots are boring. Everyone knows what the Eiffel Tower looks like. Find a unique or different approach to sights that everyone has seen. Shoot the bell tower through the horse's legs or lay your camera on the floor to shoot the Gothic ceiling.

**Capture the personal and intimate details of your trip.** Show how you lived, who you met, and what made each day an adventure (a close-up of a picnic, your leech bite, laundry day, or a local schoolboy playing games with his nose).

**Vary your perspective.** You can shoot close, far, low, high, during the day, and at night. Don't fall into the rut of always centering a shot. Use foregrounds to add color, depth, and interest to landscapes.

**Be bold and break rules.** For instance, we are told never to shoot into the sun. But some into-the-sun shots bring surprising results. Try to use bad weather to your advantage. Experiment with strange or difficult light situations. Buy a handbook on shooting photos in existing light.

**Maximize good lighting.** Real photographers get single-minded at the magic hours—early morning and late afternoon—when the sun is very low and the colors glow. Plan for these times. Grab bright colors. Develop an eye for great lighting; any time of day you may luck into a perfectly lit scene.

**Get close.** Notice details. Get closer, real close. Eliminate distractions. Get so close that you show only one thing. Don't try to show it all in one shot. For any potentially great shot, I invest several exposures.

*The best people shots are up close and well lit, with a soft background.*

**People are the most interesting subjects.** It takes nerve to walk up to people and take their picture. It can be difficult, but if you want some great shots, be nervy. Ask for permission. (In any language, point at your camera and ask, "Photo?") Your subject will probably be delighted. Try to show action. A candid is better than a posed shot. Even a "posed candid" shot is better than a posed one. Give your subject something to do. Challenge the kid in the market to juggle oranges. Many photographers take a second shot immediately after the first portrait to capture a looser, warmer subject. If the portrait isn't good, you probably weren't close enough. My best portraits are so close that the entire head can't fit into the frame.

*Vary your perspective—give extra depth with a foreground.*

Buildings, in general, are not interesting. It does not matter if Karl Marx or Beethoven was born there—a house is as dead as its former resident. As travel photographers gain experience, they take more people shots and fewer buildings or general landscapes.

**Expose for your subject.** Even if your camera is automatic, your subject can turn out a silhouette. Meter without the sky. Get those faces in the sun or lit from the side.

**Don't be afraid to handhold a slow shot.** At most major museums, you're not allowed to use a flash (which ages paintings) or a tripod. Tripods enable you to take professional (profitable) shots that could compete with those at the museum gift shop. (Nearly every important museum has a good selection of top-quality slides, cards, and prints at reasonable prices.)

*Fill the lens with your subject.*

Despite these restrictions, you can take good shots by holding your camera as still as possible. If you can lean against a wall, for instance, you become a tripod instead of a bipod. Use a self-timer, which clicks the shutter more smoothly than your finger can. With these tricks, I get good pictures inside

*Capture the magic with just the right light.*

a museum at 1/30 of a second.

**Bracket shots when the lighting is tricky.** The best way to get good shots in difficult lighting situations is to bracket your shots by trying several different exposures of the same scene. With a digital camera, you can simply delete the unsuccessful attempts, but this approach is even worthwhile with a film camera. You'll have to throw out a few slides, but one good shot is worth several in the garbage can. Automatic cameras usually meter properly up to 8 or 10 seconds, which makes night shots easy, though bracketing may still be necessary.

**You could make a scrapbook on the flight home.** Buy a book and get your prints developed at your last stop in Europe. Then happily pass the hours on the long flight home putting together a vacation scrapbook.

**Limit your slideshow.** Nothing is worse than suffering through an endless parade of lackluster and look-alike shots. If putting together a slideshow (digital or otherwise), set a limit and prune your show down until it bleeds. Keep it tight. Keep it moving. Leave the audience crying for more...or at least awake.

## Traveling with a Video Camera

With video cameras getting better, smaller, and more affordable, more and more Americans are compromising a potentially footloose and fancy-free vacation to get a memory on videotape. To me, a still camera is trouble enough. But thousands of amateur videographers happily seeing Europe through their viewfinders can't all be wrong.

## Stow that Camera

When not using your camera or camcorder, stow it in your day bag. Many go through their entire trip with a camera bouncing on their belly. That's a tourist's badge that puts a psychological wall between you and Europe. To locals, it just screams, "Yodel."

# SPECIAL CONCERNS

## 26. THE WOMAN TRAVELING ALONE

*In my classes, women often ask, "Is it safe for a woman to travel alone through Europe?" This is a question best answered by a woman. Europe Through the Back Door researcher Risa Laib wrote this chapter based on her solo experience and tips contributed from other travelers: Gail Morse, Peggy Roberts, Suzanne Hogsett, Bharti Kirchner, Kendra Roth, Gretchen Strauch, Ann Neel, and Heidi Sewell. Collectively, these women have more than a decade of solo travel experience in dozens of countries.*

Every year, thousands of women, young and old, travel to Europe on their own. You're part of a grand group of adventurers. Traveling alone, you'll have the chance to make your own discoveries and the freedom to do what you like. It becomes habit-forming.

As a solo woman, you're more approachable than a couple or a solo man. You'll make friends from all over the world, and you'll have experiences that others can only envy. When you travel with a partner, you need to compromise, your focus narrows, and doors close. When you're on your own, you're open to the moment.

Your friends and family may try to talk you out of solo travel, worrying for your safety and regaling you with horror stories. Remind them—and yourself—that millions of women have traveled alone, and will continue to do so time and time again.

Solo travel is fun, challenging, vivid, and exhilarating. It's a gift from you to you. Prepared with good information and a positive attitude, you'll thrive in Europe. And you'll come home stronger and more confident than ever before. Here's how to make it happen.

*Phrasebook + big smile = plenty of friends*

## Getting Inspired

Read exciting books written by solo women travelers about their experiences (try Dervla Murphy's outrageous adventures). For practical advice, read "how-to" travel guidebooks written by and for women. (See sidebar, page 332.)

Seek out other women travelers. Invite them out for dinner and pepper them with questions. Visit online forums for your destination and send e-mail to other women for advice.

Take classes. A foreign-language course is ideal. Consider a class in European history, art history, or travel skills.

Keep up on international news so you can discuss local politics. Study a map of Europe—get to know your neighbors.

Pretend you're traveling alone before you ever leave America. Practice reaching out. Strike up conversations with people in the grocery line. Consciously become more adaptable. If it rains, marvel at the miracle.

Think hard about what you want to see and do. Create the vacation of your dreams.

## Facing the Challenges

These are probably your biggest fears: vulnerability to theft, harassment, and loneliness. Take heart. You can tackle each of these concerns head-on. If you've traveled alone in America, you're more than prepared for Europe. In America, theft and harassment are especially scary because of their connection with assault. In Europe, you'll rarely, if ever, hear of violence. Theft is past tense (as in, "Where did my wallet go?"). As for experiencing harassment, you're far more likely to think, "I'm going to ditch this guy A.S.A.P." than "This guy is going to hurt me."

Loneliness is often the most common fear. But, remember, if you get lonely, you can do something about it.

## Traveling Alone Without Feeling Lonely

Here are some tips on meeting people, eating out, and enjoying your evenings.

**Meeting people:** Stay in hostels and you'll have a built-in family (hostels are open to all ages, except for HI hostels in Bavaria, where the age limit is 26). Or choose small pensions and B&Bs, where the owners have time to talk with you. Join Servas (see page 225) and stay with local families. Camping is also a good, safe way to meet Europeans.

At most tourist sites, you'll meet more people in an hour than you would at home in a day. If you're feeling shy, cameras are good icebreakers; offer to take someone's picture with their camera.

Talk to other solo women travelers and share advice.

Take your laundry and a deck of cards to a launderette and turn solitaire into gin rummy. You'll end up with a stack of clean clothes and conversations.

If traveling with an MP3 player (such as an iPod) with your favorite tunes, bring along a Y-jack and a second set of headphones to share your music.

Take a walking tour of a city (ask at the tourist information office). You'll learn about the town and meet other travelers, too. If you're staying in a hostel, check their boards—some also arrange tours.

It's easy to meet local people on buses and trains. You're always welcome at a church service; stay for the coffee hour. When you meet locals who speak English, find out what they think—about anything.

Play with kids. Learn how to say "pretty baby" in the local language. If you play peek-a-boo with a baby or fold an origami bird for a kid, you'll make friends with the parents as well as the children.

Call the English department at a university. See if they have an English conversation club you can visit. Or ask if you can hire a student to be your guide (you'll see the city from a local's perspective, give a student a job, and possibly make a friend).

Try pairing up with another solo traveler. Stay for a while in a small town or return to a city you enjoyed. The locals will remember you, you'll know the neighborhood, and it'll feel like home.

**Eating out:** Consider quick and cheap alternatives to formal dining. Try a self-service café, a local-style fast-food restaurant, or a small ethnic eatery. Visit a supermarket deli and get a picnic to eat in the square or a park (local families often frequent parks). Get a slice of pizza from a take-out shop and munch it as you walk along, people-watching and window-shopping. Eat in the members' kitchen of a hostel; you'll always have companions. Make it a potluck.

A restaurant feels cheerier at noon than at night. Have lunch as your main meal. If you like company, eat in places so crowded and popular that you have to share a table or ask other single travelers if they'd like to join you.

If you eat alone, be busy. Use the time to learn more of the language.

Practice your verbal skills with the waiter or waitress (when I asked a French waiter if he had kids, he proudly showed me a picture of his twin girls). Read a guidebook, a novel, or the *International Herald Tribune.* Do trip-planning, draw in your journal, or scrawl a few postcards to the folks back home.

An afternoon at a café is a great way to get some writing done; for the cost of a beverage and a snack, you'll be granted more peace and privacy than at a public fountain or other open space.

Most countries have a type of dish or restaurant that's fun to experience with a group. When you run into tourists during the day, make plans for dinner. Invite them to join you for, say, a rijsttafel dinner in the Netherlands, a *smörgåsbord* in Scandinavia, a fondue in Switzerland, a paella feast in Spain, or a spaghetti feed in an Italian trattoria.

**At night:** Experience the magic of European cities at night. Go for a walk along well-lit streets. With gelato in hand, enjoy the parade of people, busy shops, and illuminated monuments. Night or day, you're invariably safe when lots of people are around. Take advantage of the wealth of evening entertainment: concerts, movies, puppet shows, and folk dancing. Some cities offer tours after dark. You can see Paris by night on a river cruise.

During the evening, visit an Internet café. Send travel news to your friends and family. You'll find friendly answers in your inbox the next time you have the opportunity to go online.

If you like to stay in at night, get a room with a balcony overlooking a square. You'll have a front-row seat to the best show in town. Bring along a small radio to brighten your room; pull in local music, a friendly voice, maybe even the BBC. An MP3 player loaded with familiar tunes can also help cheer you. Call home, a friend, your family. With cheap international phone cards, it's actually inexpensive (as little as a nickel a minute). Read novels set in the country you're visiting. Learn to treasure solitude. Go early to bed, be early to rise. Shop at a lively morning market for fresh rolls and join the locals for coffee.

## Protecting Yourself from Theft

As a woman, you're often perceived as being more vulnerable to theft than a man. Here are tips that'll help keep you safe:

Carry a daypack instead of a purse. Leave expensive-looking jewelry at home. Keep your valuables in your money belt and tuck your wallet (containing only a day's worth of cash) in your front pocket. Keep your camera zipped up in your daypack. In crowded places (buses, subways, street markets), carry your daypack over your chest or firmly under one arm. Ask at your hotel or the tourist office if there's a neighborhood you should avoid, and mark it on your map.

Avoid tempting people into theft. Make sure valuables in your hotel room are kept out of sight. Wear your money belt when you sleep in hostels. When you're sightseeing, never set down anything of value (such as a camera, wallet, or railpass). Either have it in your hand or keep it zipped away. If you're sitting down to rest, eat, or check your e-mail, loop a strap of your daypack around your arm, leg, or chair leg. Remember, you're unlikely ever to be hurt by thieves. They want to separate you from your valuables efficiently and painlessly without alerting you.

## Dealing with Men

In small towns in continental Europe, men are often more likely to speak English than women. If you never talk to men, you could miss out on a chance to learn about the country. So, by all means, talk to men. Just choose the men and choose the setting.

In northern Europe, you won't draw any more attention from men than you do in America. In southern Europe, particularly in Italy, you'll get more attention than you're used to, but it's usually in the form of the "long look"—nothing you can't handle.

Be aware of cultural differences. In the Mediterranean world, when you smile and look a man in the eyes, it's often considered an invitation. Wear dark sunglasses and you can stare all you want.

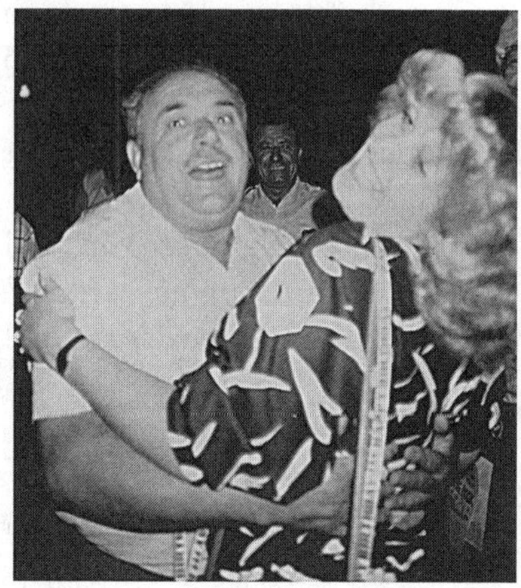

*In Italy, sometimes blondes have more trouble.*

Dress modestly to minimize attention from men. Take your cue from what the local women wear. In Italy, slacks and skirts (even short ones) are considered more proper than shorts.

Wear a real or fake wedding ring and carry a picture of a real or fake husband. There's no need to tell men that you're traveling alone, or whether you're actually married or single. Lie unhesitatingly. You're traveling with your husband. He's waiting for you at the hotel. He's a professional wrestler who retired from the sport for psychological reasons.

If you'd like to date a local man, meet him at a public place. Tell him you're staying at a hostel—you have a 10 p.m. curfew and 29 roommates. Better yet, bring a couple of your roommates along to meet him.

After the introductions, let everyone know where you're going and when you'll return.

## Handling Harassment

The way you handle harassment at home works in Europe, too.

In southern Europe, men may think that if you're alone, you're available. Keep your stride confident and look away from men trying to attract your attention. If a man comes too close to you, say "no" firmly in the local language. That's usually all it takes. Tell a slow learner that you want to be alone. Then ignore him. (Some women like to pretend they don't understand English by shrugging and mumbling a phrase in another language.)

If he's obnoxious, solicit the help of others. Ask people at a café or on the beach if you can join them for a while.

If he's well-meaning but too persistent, talk openly to him. Turn him into an ally. If he's a northern Italian, ask him about southern Italian men. Get advice from him on how you can avoid harassment when you travel farther south. After you elicit his "help," he'll be more like a brother than a bother to you.

Usually men are just seeing if you're interested. Only a few are difficult. If a man makes a lewd gesture, look away and leave the scene. Harassers don't want public attention drawn to their behavior. I went out for a walk in Madrid one evening, and a man came up much too close to me, scaring me. I shouted, "Get!" And he was gone. I think I scared him as much as he scared me. Ask a local woman for just the right thing to say to embarrass jerks. Learn how to say it, loudly. (The Rick Steves' Phrase Books have a whole section on phrases handy for women.)

If you feel like you're being followed, trust your instincts. Don't worry about overreacting or seeming foolish. Forget ladylike behavior—start screaming and acting crazy if the situation warrants it. Or head to the nearest hotel and chat up the person behind the desk until your would-be admirer moves on. Ask them to call you a cab to take you to your hotel, hostel, or B&B.

If you feel the need to carry mace, take a self-defense class instead. Mace will be confiscated at the airport, but knowledge and confidence are yours to keep. And, remember, the best self-defense is common sense.

## Keeping Healthy

You can find whatever medications you need in Europe, but you already know what works for you in the United States. It's easiest to B.Y.O. pills,

### Resources for the Woman Traveling Alone

Travel books for women fall into three camps: practical advice, tales from the road, and stories to inspire you. While there are hundreds of women-travel books, here are some classics and bestsellers get you started.

Thalia Zepatos' *A Journey of One's Own: Uncommon Advice for the Independent Woman Traveler* delivers recommendations on everything from how to trek in Nepal to how to handle sexual harassment. *Safety and Security for Women Who Travel,* by Sheila Swan and Peter Laufer, offers tips on self-protection. *Traveling Solo: Advice and Ideas for More than 250 Great Vacations,* by Eleanor Berman, has advice on specific destinations for solo travelers.

If reading travelogues will inspire you to make your solo trip a reality, consider *A Woman's World: True Stories of Life on the Road; Gutsy Women: Travel Tips and Wisdom for the Road*; and *A Woman's Europe: True Stories,* all edited by Marybeth Bond. *Expat: Women's True Tales of Life Abroad* gives readers a glimpse of what it means to head to a new country for more than just a vacation. Rough Guides' *Women Travel: First-Hand Accounts from More Than 60 Countries* has essays on travel in exotic locations, as does *A Woman Alone: Travel Tales from Around the Globe.* For humorous tales about traveling as a woman, try *The Unsavvy Traveler: Women's Comic Tales of Catastrophe; Sand in My Bra and Other Misadventures: Funny Women Write from the Road;* and its sequels, *Whose*

whether for cramps, yeast infections, or birth control. Some health-insurance companies issue only a month's supply of birth control pills at a time; ask for a larger supply for a longer trip. Condoms are as easy to buy in Europe as in America from pharmacies and vending machines in some women's rest rooms.

Tampons and pads, widely available in Europe, are sold—for more than the US price—at supermarkets and pharmacies. You'll rarely see a big display of the brands and sizes typical in American supermarkets. If you're used to a particular brand and absorbency, it's simpler and cheaper to bring what you'll need from home.

Women prone to yeast infections should bring their own over-the-counter medicine (or know the name and its key ingredient to show a pharmacist in Europe). Some women get a prescription for Diflucan, a powerful pill that cures yeast infections quicker and tidier than creams and suppositories. If you get a yeast infection in Europe and lack

*Panties Are These? More Misadventures from Funny Women on the Road* and *The Thong Also Rises: Further Misadventures from Funny Women on the Road.*

There's an entire cottage industry of travel memoirs by women describing a journey that changed their lives forever. These titles, unlike the collections of essays above, follow one person's story throughout the length of the book. The most famous of these is probably Frances Mayes' *Under the Tuscan Sun*, which is so popular that she wrote a sequel, *Bella Tuscany: The Sweet Life in Italy.* Mayes writes about other European destinations in *A Year in the World: Journeys of a Passionate Traveller.* Other reader favorites include *Long Ago In France: The Years In Dijon* (M.F.K. Fisher); *Tales of a Female Nomad: Living at Large in the World* (Rita Golden Gelman); *Almost French: Love and a New Life in Paris* (Sarah Turnbull); *Without Reservations: The Travels of an Independent Woman* and *Educating Alice: Adventures of a Curious Woman* (both by Alice Steinbach); and *A Thousand Days in Venice* and *A Thousand Days in Tuscany* (both by Marlena De Blasi).

For a Web resource, consider Journeywoman, a site where women share travel tips (www.journeywoman.com). And don't forget about the 2002 film *Bread and Tulips*, an inspiring story of a woman who heads to Venice—solo—and finds her destiny.

medication, go to a pharmacy. Most pharmacists speak English. If you encounter the rare one who doesn't, find an English-speaking local woman to write out "yeast infection" for you in the country's language to avoid the embarrassing charade.

You can treat minor urinary tract infections with unsweetened cranberry juice (available in northern Europe) or with cranberry pills (made from cranberry juice concentrate) sold at health food stores. If you often get urinary tract infections, bring antibiotics and a prescription from your doctor.

**Traveling When Pregnant:** Some couples want to time conception to occur in Europe so they can name their child Paris or Siena or wherever. If that's your plan, consider bringing a pregnancy test from home to help you find out when you can celebrate.

If you'll be traveling during your first pregnancy, rip out a few chapters from a book on pregnancy to bring along. It's hard to find basic information on pregnancy in English in much of Europe. If you want certain tests done (such as amniocentesis), ask your doctor when you need to be home.

In the first trimester, climbing all the stairs can be exhausting—packing light is more essential than ever. You might find it easier to travel in the second trimester, when your body's used to being pregnant and you're not too big to be uncomfortable. Note that no airline really wants you on board when you're eight months pregnant.

Wear comfortable shoes that have arch supports. If you'll be traveling a long time, bring loose clothing (with elastic waistbands) and shoes a half size larger to accommodate your body's changes. Keep your valuables (cash, passport, etc.) in a neck pouch rather than a constricting money belt.

Pace yourself and allow plenty of time for rest. Contact an English-speaking doctor if you become ill; medical care in most European countries is reassuringly good.

Seek out nutritious food (though some of it may make you nauseated, just as in America). Picnics, with drinkable yogurt, are often healthier than restaurant meals. Pack along baggies for carrying snacks. Bring prenatal vitamins from home, plus a calcium supplement if you're not a milk drinker.

It's actually pleasant to be pregnant in Europe. People are particularly kind. And when your child is old enough to understand, she'll enjoy knowing she's already been to Europe—especially if you promise to take her again.

## Traveling Smart

Create conditions that are likely to turn out in your favor. By following these tips, you'll have a safer, smoother, more enjoyable trip.

Be self-reliant so that you don't need to depend on anybody unless you want to. Always carry local cash, food, water, a map, a guidebook, and a phrase book. When you need help, ask another woman or a family.

When you use cash machines, withdraw cash during the day on a busy street, not at night when it's dark with too few people around.

Walk purposefully with your head up. Look like you know where you're going. Use landmarks (such as church steeples) to navigate. If you get lost in an unfriendly neighborhood, go into a restaurant or store to ask for directions or to study your map.

Learn enough of the language to get by. With a few hours' work you'll know more than most tourists and be better prepared to deal with whatever situation arises. At a bus station in Turkey, I witnessed a female tourist repeatedly asking in English, louder and louder, "When does the bus leave?" The frustrated ticket clerk kept answering her in Turkish, "Now, now, now!" If you know even just a little of the language, you'll make it much easier on yourself and those around you.

Before you leave a city, consider visiting the train or bus station you're going to leave from, so you can learn where it is, how long it takes to reach it, and what services it has. Reconfirm your departure time.

On a bus, if you're faced with a choice between an empty double seat and a seat next to a woman, sit with the woman. You've selected your seat partner. Ask her (or the driver) for help if you need it. They will make sure you get off at the right stop.

Skip hitchhiking. But if you absolutely have to hitch, choose people to ask, instead of being chosen. Try your luck at a gas station, restaurant, on a ferry, or in the parking lot of a tourist attraction. Ideally, pair up with another traveler.

When taking the train, avoid staying in empty compartments, especially at night. Rent a *couchette* for overnight trains. For about $20, you'll stay with like-minded roommates in a compartment you can lock, in a car monitored by an attendant. You'll wake reasonably rested with your belongings intact.

Ask for a female roommate on overnight trains. (You'll have better luck if the train isn't crowded.) Some countries, such as Spain, are better about accommodating these requests than others. In France, they set aside a one-bed compartment closest to the conductor for women, but it's the most expensive type of accommodation. In general, ask what the options are, make the request to bunk with other women, and hope for the best—but don't count on it.

Try to arrive at your destination during the day. Daylight feels safer than night. For peace of mind, reserve a room, particularly if you can't avoid a late-night arrival. If you're departing late at night, ask your B&B owner if you can hang out in their breakfast room—generally untouched in the evening—until you need to leave for your train. Cafés, including busy Internet cafés such as the late-night easyInternetcafé chain, can be a better spot to kill time than the train station waiting room. (If you arrive at a train station you'll later be departing from, note if the station seems clean, well-lit, and safe—or not.)

If you're not fluent in the language, accept the fact that you won't always know what's going on. There's a reason why the Greek bus driver drops you off in the middle of nowhere. It's a transfer point, and another bus will come along in a few minutes. You'll discover that often the locals are looking out for you.

The same good judgment you use at home applies to Europe. Start out cautious and figure out as you travel what feels safe to you.

Treat yourself right—get enough rest, healthy food, and exercise. Walking is a great way to combine exercise and sightseeing. I've jogged alone in cities and parks throughout Europe without any problems. If a neighborhood looks seedy, head off in another direction.

Relax. There are other trains, other buses, other cities, other people. If one thing doesn't work out, something else will. Thrive on optimism.

Have a grand adventure!

# 27. FAMILIES, SENIORS, AND TRAVELERS WITH DISABILITIES

## Family Travel—From Toddlers to Teens

*By Rick and Anne Steves*

### Travels with Baby Andy—Leashes and Valium?

My wife (Anne), seven-year-old (Andy), and VW van (Vinnie) took seven one-month trips with me, traveling from Norway to Naples and Dublin to Dubrovnik. It wasn't hell, but it wasn't terrific travel, either. Still, when Andy was a baby, it was more fun to change diapers in Paris than Seattle.

Young European families, like their American counterparts, are traveling, babies and all. You'll find more and more kids' menus, hotel playrooms, and kids-go-crazy zones at freeway rest stops all over Europe. And Europeans love babies. Your baby will be your ticket to countless conversations.

You'll need the proper documents. Even babies need passports. If you're traveling with a child who isn't yours (say, a niece or grandson), bring along a signed, notarized document from the parent(s) to prove to authorities that you have permission to take the child on a trip.

An international adventure is a great foundation for a mountain of memories. Here are some of the lessons we learned whining and giggling through Europe with baby, toddler, and little boy, Andy.

### Baby Gear

Since a baby on the road requires a lot of gear, the key to happiness is a rental car or a long stay in one place. Of course, pack as light as you can, but if you figure you'll need it, trust your judgment.

Bring a car seat, buy one in Europe, or see if your car rental company can provide one. (Pack along a car-seat clip to help secure the car seat to

a shoulder-strap seat belt.) If you're visiting friends, with enough notice they can often borrow a car seat and a stroller for you. If you'll be driving long hours while the baby sleeps, try to get a car seat that reclines.

A stroller is essential. Umbrella models are lightest, but we found a heavy-duty model with a reclining back worth bringing for the baby. Andy could nap in it, and it served as a luggage cart for the Bataan Death March parts of our trip when we had to use public transportation. Carry the stroller onto the plane—you'll need it in the airport. Big wheels handle cobblestones best.

A small travel crib was a godsend. No matter what kind of hotel, pension, or hostel we ended up in, as long as we could clear a four-by-four-foot space on the floor, we'd have a safe, clean, and familiar home for Andy to sleep and play in. During the day we'd salvage a little space by flipping it up on its side and shoving it against the wall.

If a baby backpack works for you at home, bring it to Europe. (I just use my shoulders.) Backpacks in general are great for parents who need to keep their hands free. Prepare to tote more than a tot. A combo purse/diaper bag with shoulder straps is ideal. Be on guard: Purse snatchers target mothers (especially while busy and off-guard, as when changing diapers). In most of Europe, a mother with a small child is given great respect. You'll generally be offered a seat on crowded buses and allowed to go to the front of the line at museums.

There's lots more to pack. Encourage bonding to a blanket or stuffed critter and take it along. We used a lot of Heinz dehydrated food dumped into plastic baggies. Sippy cups cut down on spills. Tiny Tupperware containers with lids were great for crackers, raisins, and snacks. You'll find plenty of disposable diapers, wipes, baby food, and so on in Europe, so don't take the whole works from home. Before you fly away, be sure you've packed a decongestant, acetaminophen, and a thermometer. For a toddler, bring a few favorite books and a soft ball (easier on hotel rooms), and buy little European toys as you go. As Andy got older, activity books and a handheld video game kept him occupied for what might have been countless boring hours. Also, a daily holiday allowance as a reward for

## Resources for Traveling with Kids in Europe

Common sense and lessons learned from day trips at home are your best sources of information. *Take Your Kids to Europe* is full of practical, concrete lessons from firsthand family-travel experience, and the only good book I've seen for those traveling with kids ages 6–16 (by Cynthia Harriman, Globe Pequot Press, 7th ed., 2005). The best book we found on traveling with infants is Lonely Planet's *Travel with Children* by Cathy Lanigan (4th edition, Lonely Planet Publications), which covers travel worldwide, including Europe. For families interested in hiking, biking, and sailing abroad, pick up *Adventuring With Children: An Inspirational Guide to World Travel and the Outdoors* (by Nan Jeffrey). Cadogan offers many worthwhile books in its Take the Kids series, including books on London, Paris, Ireland, and more. Also consider Fodor's guides *Around London with Kids, Around Paris with Kids, Around Rome with Kids,* and *Family Adventures.* For single parents, there's Brenda Elwell's *Single Parent Travel Handbook.*

*What's more fun: A museum or Disneyland Paris?*

assembling a first-class daily picture journal gave our seven-year-old reasons to be enthusiastic about every travel day. (As an older child, his journal projects have grown.)

In case Andy got lost, he wore a metal Medic Alert bracelet that listed his name, address, home phone, an emergency phone number (of our relatives), and any allergies.

### Parenting at 32,000 Feet

Gurgling junior might become an airborne Antichrist as soon as the seat-belt light goes off. You'll pay 10 percent of the ticket cost to take a child under the age of two on an international flight. The child doesn't get a seat, but many airlines have baby perks for moms and dads who ask for them in advance—roomier bulkhead seats, hang-from-the-ceiling bassinets, and baby meals. After age two, a toddler's ticket typically costs 75–80 percent of the adult fare—a major financial owie (some sale fares do not allow any discounts for kids). From age 12 on, kids pay full fare. (Railpasses and train tickets are free for kids under age four. Those under 12 ride the rails for half price.)

*Siena? We love Siena!*

Ask your pediatrician about sedating your baby for a 10-hour intercontinental flight. We think it's only merciful (for the entire family). Dimetapp, Tylenol, or PediaCare have also worked well for us.

Prepare to be 100 percent self-sufficient throughout the flight. Expect cramped seating and busy attendants. Bring extra clothes (for you and the baby), special toys, and familiar food. Those colored links are handy for attaching toys to the seat, crib, high chairs, jail cells, and so on. The in-flight headphones (or an MP3 player loaded with favorite tunes) are great entertainment for flying toddlers.

*With a little imagination—and a suit of armor—any kid can storm a castle.*

Landings and takeoffs can be painful for ears of all ages. A bottle, a pacifier, or anything to suck helps equalize the baby's middle-ear pressure. For this reason, nursing moms will be glad they do when it comes to flying. If your kid cries, remember: Crying is a great pressure equalizer.

Once on foreign soil, you'll find that your footloose and see-it-all days of travel are over for a while. Go easy. Traveling with a tyke is tiring, wet, sticky, and smelly. Your mobility plummets. You accomplish far less sightseeing.

Be warned—jet lag is nursery purgatory. On his first night in Europe, baby Andy was furious that darkness had bullied daylight out of his up-until-then-reliable 24-hour body-clock cycle. Luckily, we were settled in a good hotel (and most of the guests were able to stay elsewhere).

## Accommodations

We slept in rooms of all kinds, from hostels (many have family rooms) to hotels. Until he was five, we were never charged for Andy, and while we always use our own bedding, many doubles have a sofa or extra bed that can be barricaded with chairs and used instead of the crib.

Childproof the room immediately on arrival. A roll of masking tape makes quick work of electrical outlets. Anything breakable goes on top of the free-standing closet. Proprietors are generally helpful to considerate and undemanding parents. We'd often store our bottles and milk cartons in their fridge, ask (and pay) for babysitting, and so on.

Every room had a sink where baby Andy could pose for cute pictures, have a little fun, make smelly bubbles, and get clean. With a toddler, budget extra to get a bath in your room—a practical need and a fun diversion. (Many showers have a 6-inch-tall "drain extension," enabling you to create a kid-friendly bathing puddle.) Toddlers and campgrounds—with swings, slides, and plenty of friends—mix wonderfully.

Self-catering flats rented by the week or two-week period, such as *gîtes* in France and villas in Italy, give a family a home on the road. Many families prefer settling down this way and side-tripping from a home base.

## Food

We found European restaurants and their customers cool to noisy babies. High chairs are rare. We ate happily at places with outdoor seating; at the many McDonald's-type, baby-friendly fast-food places; or picnicking. In restaurants (or anywhere), if your infant is making a disruptive fuss, apologetically say the local word for "teeth" (*dientes* in Spanish, *dents* in French, *denti* in Italian, *Zähne* in German), and annoyed locals will become sympathetic.

Nursing babies are easiest to feed and travel with. Remember, some cultures are uncomfortable with public breast-feeding. Be sensitive.

We stocked up on munchies (fruit, pretzels, and tiny boxes of juice—which double as squirt guns). A 7 a.m. banana worked wonders, and a 5 p.m. snack made late European dinners workable. In restaurants, we ordered an extra plate for Andy, who just nibbled from our meals. We'd order "fizzy" (but not sticky) mineral water, call it "pop," and the many spills were no problem. With all the candy and sweet temptations at toddler-eye level in Europe, you can forget a low-sugar diet. While *gelati* and pastries are expensive, Andy's favorite suckers, Popsicles, and hollow, toy-filled chocolate eggs were cheap and available everywhere.

Plan to spend more money. Use taxis rather than buses and subways.

Hotels can get babysitters, usually from professional agencies. The service is expensive but worth the splurge when you crave a leisurely, peaceful evening sans bibs and cribs.

With a baby, we arranged our schedule around naps and sleep time. A well-rested child is worth the limitation. Driving while Andy siesta'd worked well. As a toddler, however, Andy was up very late, playing soccer with his new Italian friends on the piazza or eating huge ice creams in the hotel kitchen with the manager's kids. We gave up on a rigid naptime or bedtime, and we enjoyed Europe's evening ambience as a family.

OK, you're there—watered, fed, and only a little bleary. Europe is your cultural playpen, a living fairy tale, a sandbox of family fun and adventure. Grab your kid and dive in.

### A Decade Later: Traveling with Teens in Europe

When our kids were still in their single digits, our family travel was consumed with basic survival issues, such as eating and sleeping. Now that Andy is 19 and Jackie is 16, the big challenges are making our trips educational and fun. Our kids are at the age when traveling with Mom and Dad isn't cool, friends at home are the preferred vacation partners, and being told to "get in the car, we're going on an airplane today" no longer works.

High schoolers and college students feel that summer break is a vacation they've earned. If this European trip is not their trip, then you become the enemy. Ask for their help. Kids can even get excited about a vacation if they're involved in the planning stages. Consider your child's suggestions and make real concessions. "Europe's greatest collection of white-knuckle rides" in Blackpool might be more fun than another ruined abbey. Remember to take it easy at the beginning of your trip, allowing a couple of low-impact days to get over jet lag.

Pre-trip study helps get children tuned into and prepared for upcoming experiences. Read books such as *The Diary of Anne Frank* for Amsterdam. Watch movies together such as *The Sound of Music* for Salzburg, and *Brother Sun, Sister Moon* for Assisi. Get a jump on the phrases, learning the top 20 or so before you leave home.

### Our Kids Vote on Britain's Best and Worst

Imagine being a teenager forced to spend a big part of your summer vacation with that fortysomething robo-tourist, Rick Steves (alias Dad). Jackie and Andy did just that, and yes, they're glad to be home. What were the highlights? Here are the results of our family's post-trip interview:

**Best city:** Blackpool—England's white-knuckle ride capital! The Pepsi Max Big One (one of the world's fastest and highest roller coasters) is still the best. A tip: Avoid the old wooden-framed rides. They're too jerky for parents.

**Best nature experience:** A horse ride through the Cotswolds (about $30 per hour with a guide who'll teach you to trot). But wear long pants. One hour is plenty.

**Types of tours:** Open-deck bus tours are good for picnic lunches with a moving view. Audioguide tours (now available at most sights) are nice because you can pick and choose what you want to learn about.

**Fun museums:** Camera Obscura, Edinburgh's primitive 1830s spy camera from a tower. It comes with a funny demonstration and three floors of fun illusions and early 3-D photographs. Warwick Castle, with Madame Tussaud's wax people having a garden party in 1900.

**Worst food:** The "black pudding" that so many B&B people want you to try for breakfast...it's a gooey sausage made of curdled blood.

**Best new food:** Chocolate-covered digestive biscuits and vinegar on chips (that's British for French fries).

Since a trip is a splurge for the parents, the kids should enjoy a larger allowance, too. Provide ample money and ask your kids to buy their own treats, *gelati*, batteries, and trinkets within that daily budget. In exchange for the extra allowance, require them to keep a daily journal or scrapbook.

Help your kids collect and process their observations. Bring tape, a glue stick, and scissors (in your checked baggage) from home. But if you buy the actual journal at your first stop, it becomes a fun souvenir in itself. Kids like cool books—pay for a nice one. The journal is important, and it

**Most boring tour:** The Beatles tour in Liverpool—most kids couldn't care less about where Paul McCartney went to grade school or a place called Strawberry Fields.

**Funniest activity:** Bizarre Bath's walking tour is two hours of jokes and not a bit of history. It's irreverent and dirty—but in a way that parents think is OK.

**Best activities:** Leisure (LEZH-ur) Centres in almost every town have good swimming pools. Some B&Bs have video libraries, and others have VCRs and a video-rental place nearby that rents to guests of that B&B. Checking e-mail and surfing the Web at Internet cafés—London's easyInternetcafé is huge, cheap, and fast.

**Best theater:** Shakespeare's Globe. First tour the theater to learn about how and why it was built like the original from 1600. Then buy cheap ($9) "groundling" tickets to see the actual play right up front, with your elbows on the stage. The actors involve the audience...especially the groundlings.

**Most interesting demonstrations:** The precision slate-splitting demonstration at the slate mines in North Wales. The medieval knight at the Tower of London who explained his armor and then demonstrated medieval sword fighting tactics—nearly killing his squire.

should feel that way. Encourage the kids to record more than just a trip log...collect feelings, smells, reactions to cultural differences, and so on.

With older kids, Mom and Dad have much more freedom. Kids can go to the breakfast room early or late. If they don't want to go out for the evening, they can stay in the hotel. Nearly all rooms have TVs (although be careful—many have pornography channels). To pass the time, our kids each pack a handheld video game and an MP3 player.

Review the day's plan at breakfast. It should always include a kid-friendly activity. Hands-on tours, from cheesemaking to chocolate factories, keep kids engaged. Go to sports or cultural events, but don't insist on staying for the entire event.

Kids need plenty of exercise. Allow time for a few extra runs on the luge. Small towns often have great public swimming pools. And mountain bikes are easily rentable (with helmets), suddenly making the Alps cool.

*Picking green peppers off their pizzas, our kids discover that in Italy,* peperoni *doesn't mean spicy sausage.*

Help your kids connect with children their own age. Staying in B&Bs or small guest houses, you'll find it's easy to hook up with other traveling families. When visiting with Europeans, be careful to work your children into the conversation (easier if meeting other families). In hot climates, kids hang out on the squares when it's cooler, until late in the evening. Take your children to the European nightspots to observe—if not actually make—the scene (such as the rollerbladers at Trocadero in Paris or the crowd at Rome's Trevi Fountain). Small-town pubs in Britain and Ireland welcome kids and are filled with family-friendly social opportunities. Many times our children have enjoyed playing pool or throwing darts with new friends in a pub.

Internet cafés and e-mail allow kids to keep in touch with friends at home and European pals they meet on their trip. While Anne and I lingered over a glass of wine or dessert, our kids would run across the street to an Internet café and spend their dessert money for 20 minutes online.

Make the consequences of packing heavy perfectly clear—they carry all their stuff all the time. Help your kids pack layers for warmth, clothes that don't show dirt, and sturdy, well-broken-in shoes. Each person should have a day bag for ready access in the car (it keeps down clutter). Make the car trunk a pantry of snacks, water, and picnics.

While the train is workable with older kids, we still prefer family vacations by car. With a car, we enjoy doorstep-to-doorstep service with our luggage and can be a little bolder about coming into town without a reserved room. I delegate navigating responsibilities to our kids. Following a map to help Dad drive through a new town or leading the family back to the hotel on the Paris Métro is a great confidence builder.

An occasional Big Mac or Whopper between all the bratwurst and kraut helps keep our family happy. In a village, we let the kids find dinner on their own. We were in Austria the first time we did this—our kids couldn't believe we'd actually abandon them this way. After Anne and I gave them enough money for pizza and a drink, we took off for a romantic adults-only dinner under the floodlit abbey with a view of the Danube. Our children had no choice but to use their few German words and a phrase book, sort through a menu on their own, deal with the waiter, and be careful they understood the bill and had enough money. They did wonderfully and used their spare change to buy ice cream down the street.

In a crowded situation, having a unique family noise (a whistle or call, such as a "woo-woop" sound) enables you to easily get each other's attention. Consider buying cheap walkie-talkies in Europe to help you relax when the kids roam (don't bring them from home, as ours use a different bandwidth and are illegal in Europe). Older children can wear money belts with photocopies of their passport and hotel information.

Most hotels have large family rooms. You need to know the necessary phrases to communicate your needs. When our children were younger, we requested a triple room plus a small extra child's bed. Now we get two rooms for our family of four: A double (one big bed) and a twin (a room with two single beds). In much of Europe, a "double" bed is actually two twins put together. These can easily be separated.

Families can hostel very cheaply. Family membership cards are inexpensive, and there's no age limit except a maximum of 26 in Bavaria (waived for adults traveling with their children). Many hostels have "members' kitchens" where the family can cook and eat for the price of groceries.

When parents tell me they're going to Europe and ask me where to take their kids, I'm tempted to answer, "to Grandma and Grandpa's on your way to the airport." While we've enjoyed our family time in Europe, it's easy to make the case against taking the kids. Traveling with kids is expensive. (They fly for full fare. And, out of exhaustion and

*Getting goofy on the Alps*

frustration, you may opt for pricey conveniences like taxis and the first restaurant you find with a kid-friendly menu.) And two adults with kids spend twice as much to experience about half the magic of Europe per day that they might without. Also, older kids would very often rather stay home to enjoy their school break with friends. If you and your partner have 20 days for a family vacation, are on a budget, and are dreaming of an adult time in Europe, consider this plan: Go for 10 days without the kids and really enjoy Europe as adults rather than parents—the savings from leaving them at home will easily cover top-notch child care. Then fly home and spend the other 10 days with your kids—camping, at a water park, or just playing with them at home. (If your kids have a "cool" but responsible young-adult relative somewhere else in the US who they'd enjoy getting to know better, pay to fly them in and watch your kids while you're gone.)

Our two best family trips have been in Italy and the Alps. Our Italy trip featured five days in Venice (in an apartment in the town center), followed by four days in the Cinque Terre (a Riviera wonderland for kids). Our 20-day trip across the Alps—by car from Vienna to Zürich—included a few museums and lots of outdoor fun. For a range of perspectives on parenting in Europe, see the Travel with Kids board on the Graffiti Wall at www.ricksteves.com/graffiti.

Living on the road far from their favorite TV shows and neighborhood friends has broadened our children's outlook. They've learned what all travelers know: The size of your backyard is up to you.

My kids' love of travel didn't end with family trips. Two summers ago, my son Andy joined his best buddy Alex for a six-week high-school graduation trip. His wonderfully candid (and politically incorrect) journal is available at www.ricksteves.com/andyblog. The good news: Europe on $50 a day plus a Eurailpass is still possible. The better news: The same magic I enjoyed on my "Europe through the gutter" trip in 1973 can still be had by vagabonds today. Any 18-year-old (or parent with an 18-year-old) pondering a European adventure on a shoestring will enjoy reading the account Andy and Alex share in their journal.

*Free from parents, but remembering the lessons he learned on those many family trips, Andy Steves discovers that Europe is his playground.*

## Savvy Seniors

More people than ever are hocking their rockers and buying plane tickets. Many senior adventurers are proclaiming, "Age matters only if you're a cheese." Travel is their fountain of youth.

*Their fountain of youth is Europe!*

I'm not a senior—yet—so I put an appeal on the Graffiti Wall of my Web site (www.ricksteves.com/graffiti) asking seniors to share their advice. Thanks to the many who responded, here's a summary of top tips from seniors who believe it's never too late to have a happy childhood.

**Packing:** Bring a backpack with wheels or a rolling suitcase. One of my readers wrote, "Retired travelers with rolling suitcases in hand would do well to bring a short bungee cord, so that you can secure a smaller carry-on bag on top to the suitcase upright handle and roll the whole thing along." Whichever you use, pack light. When you pack light, you're younger. Two tops, a pair of lightweight pants, good shoes, a couple of changes of underwear and socks, and you're set. It's easier to wash out your clothes in your hotel room at night than to carry a big backpack all day.

**When to Go:** Consider traveling in shoulder season (April, May, Sept, Oct). The most exhausting things about European travel are the crowds and heat of summer.

**Airports:** If you're not flying direct, check your bag—because if you have to transfer to a connecting flight at a huge, busy airport, your carry-on bag will become a lug-around drag. If you're a slow walker, ask the airline or flight attendant to arrange transportation so you can easily make your next flight.

**Accommodations:** Request a ground-floor room if stairs are a problem. Different locations and types of accommodations offer different advantages. If you stay near the train station, you'll minimize carrying your bag. If you stay outside the big cities and travel in for the day, your hotel room (in the suburbs or nearby small town) will likely be quieter, bigger, and cheaper, with fewer stairs and more ground-floor options. To save money, try hostels, which offer the bonus of ready-made friends. To really relax, rent a cottage, condo, or flat for a week or more. You can settle down and stay awhile, doing side-trips if you choose.

## Resources for Seniors

Good books include *Unbelievably Good Deals and Great Adventures That You Absolutely Can't Get Unless You're Over 50,* by Joan Rattner Heilman (McGraw-Hill); *Travel Unlimited: Uncommon Adventures for the Mature Traveler,* by Alison Gardner (Avalon); and *The Grown-Up's Guide to Running Away from Home* and *The Grown-Up's Guide to Retiring Abroad,* both by Roseanne Knorr (Ten Speed Press).

Elderhostel, which offers study programs around the world for those over 55, will send you a free catalog listing their educational curriculum, varying in length from one to four weeks (www.elderhostel.org, tel. 877-426-8056).

Also consider *Rick Steves' Easy Access Europe,* a guide for people with limited mobility (see page 353).

**Senior Discounts:** Just showing your gray hair or passport can snare you a discount on many sights and even some events such as concerts. (The British term for a senior discount is "concessions.") Note that some sights may offer discounts for seniors, but not always to seniors from the US. That's because the United States is notorious for not reciprocating.

You can get deals on point-to-point rail tickets in Scandinavia, Austria, France, and more (including the Eurostar Chunnel crossing between Britain and France). To get rail discounts in some countries, such as Britain, you need to purchase a senior card at a minimal cost at a local train station (don't be put off if these cards are valid for a year—you can save money even on a short trip). Railpasses for Britain and Scandinavia give seniors a discount. Many airlines offer a discount to seniors and companions of any age. Always ask.

**City Transportation:** Subways involve a lot of walking and stairs (and are a pain with luggage). Consider using city buses or taxis instead. With lots of luggage, definitely take a taxi (better yet, pack light).

**Sightseeing:** Many museums have elevators, and even if these are freight elevators not open to the public, people bend the rules for older travelers. Take advantage of the benches in museums; sit down frequently to enjoy the art and rest your feet. Go late in the day for no crowds and cooler temperatures. Take bus tours (usually 2 hours long) for a painless overview of the highlights. Boat tours—of the harbor, river, lake, or fjord—are a pleasure. Hire an English-speaking cabbie to take you on a tour of a city or region (if it's hot, spring for an air-conditioned taxi). If you're traveling with others but need a rest break, set up a rendezvous point. For easy sightseeing, grab a table at a sidewalk café for a drink and people-watching.

**Keep a Record:** As you travel, record your experiences on a micro-cassette recorder to transcribe when you get home. A journal helps capture your trip. Reread, relive, recharge—plan your next trip!

*Pilgrims of all ages hike from France to Santiago de Compostela in northwest Spain.*

**Excerpts from "Senior Savvy" on the Graffiti Wall at www.ricksteves.com**

"London is a very good deal for the over-60 crowd. Ask for the senior rate at museums, theaters, and so on. In quite a few places, we got reduced rates and, in several, admission was free. You will have to show proof of age."

"On our last trip to Europe, we smiled and politely asked if the establishment offered a senior discount, even when it was not posted that one was available. In nearly every instance we got one. Sometimes it saved us as much as half price. Don't be afraid to ask, but remember to smile."

"We just returned from a wonderful trip to Germany with my 79-year-old mother-in-law. It soon became apparent that she was having trouble realizing the fact that we 'weren't in Kansas anymore.' My tip to seniors: Please keep an open mind. Your hotel accommodations may not provide washcloths, Kleenex, or more than one wastebasket. If you don't expect things to be like they are in the States, you'll have a much better time and so will your traveling companions."

"My wife and I, both seniors, took a tour of Spain, Morocco, and Portugal. After the long transatlantic flight and a day of riding in the bus, my wife's ankles swelled up appreciably. According to the tour guide, this is not unusual. She had my wife keep her legs high the next two nights (by putting a bolster pillow under the foot end of the mattress) and drinking lots of water both days. The swelling was gone by the second day. Moral: Drink lots of water on the way over and during each day!"

"For peace of mind, compile a checklist of all the things you need to do to get your house ready before leaving on vacation. Then, check off the items and take the list with you. This way there is no worrying, 'Did I turn off the stove?'"

"People who wear hearing aids should bring spare batteries along and not plan to purchase them in Europe. I thought I had taken enough batteries, but my hearing aids quit near the end of our trip. I went to pharmacies but no one had what I needed, nor did they know where I might purchase that particular size. Finally I discovered the last set in the bottom of my toiletries bag. Otherwise I would have missed lots of sounds our last week."

"Carry a small notebook to write down things to remember: train reservations to be made, events you want to record later in your journal, and so on."

"Those of us over-60s traveling by train in Great Britain can take advantage of their Senior Railcard obtainable from the station agent for £20 (valid for one year, www.senior-railcard.co.uk). The 33 percent savings on most rail fares quickly justifies the cost."

"I took my 82-year-old mother to London for Christmas. I got excellent help on accessible hotels and sights in the UK from the Holiday Care Service in London (www.holidaycare.org.uk)."

"At 65+ with bad backs, we hired a taxi in Sorrento to take us sightseeing in Positano, Amalfi, and Ravello, a $150 splurge that was worth every cent."

"My partner and I stayed in a 'youth' hostel for the first time by Lake Como and thought we'd be the oldest people there. Not so! This was the wonderful La Primula hostel near Menaggio, Italy, which offers a spectacular view of the lake while you're dining on great food on their outdoor patio. At our table was a 60-ish couple from Sydney and a 79-year-old British woman who was backpacking alone through Europe! All three were a delight, but especially the backpacker, who said she stays in hostels for the evening company."

"Most major museums have loaner wheelchairs available, and you'll find this information on their Web sites. (If they don't mention it, call or e-mail to ask them.) Also, be sure to request, in advance, assistance at the airport. This is a free service that airlines are happy to provide."

"We have found that many museums in Europe do have elevators even though they have no sign telling about them. Just ask! You will be taken to a small, carefully hidden elevator, and most often escorted to your floor."

"I just returned from a wonderful week in Belgium. Seniors (over 65 and departing after 9 a.m.) get a huge discount on train fares. For instance, the 90-minute ride from Bruges to Louven cost only €3.50."

"Seniors, before traveling outside the US, make sure your travel insurance covers air-ambulance evacuation. I traveled with my 92-year-old father and he became very ill. We had to evacuate him by air ambulance and it cost me $10,000. Thankfully he's fine now. But we could have saved so much anguish if we had been prepared."

"I traveled for a month in Italy with my 65-year-old mother. We stayed in hotels located as centrally as possible to the sights we wanted to see, and broke most of our days into two parts (with at least an hour of feet-up time after lunch). We were happy to splurge on cabs from the train station to the hotel (easier than hauling your own luggage up and down stairs in the metro or bus, and not terribly expensive). We had an extremely enjoyable trip by not trying to fit too much into each day and enjoying people-watching from cafés when our feet were tired."

"I went on a trip with a piece of small luggage that also converts into a backpack. I'm in good shape, walk every day, and watch what I eat, but I'm 64 and the backpack eventually made my shoulders ache. The pain lasted for several months. I will use wheeled luggage from now on. I know Rick doesn't like the rolling suitcases, but he isn't 65 yet, so he will learn."

## Travelers with Disabilities Take on the World

*Thanks to Susan Sygall and staff from Mobility International USA for this article.*

More and more people with disabilities are heading to Europe, and more of us are looking for the Back Door routes. We, like so many of our non-disabled peers, want to get off the tourist track and experience the real France, Italy, or Portugal. Yes, that includes those of us who use wheelchairs. I've been traveling the "Rick Steves way" since about 1973—and here are some of my best tips.

*Susan Sygall, on Italy's Cinque Terre*

I use a lightweight manual wheelchair with pop-off tires. I take a backpack that fits on the back of my chair and store my daypack underneath my chair in a net bag. Since I usually travel alone, if I can't carry it myself, I don't take it. I keep a bungee cord with me for the times I can't get my chair into a car and need to strap it in the trunk or when I need to secure it on a train. I always insist on keeping *my own* wheelchair up to the airline gate, where I then check it at the gate. When I have a connecting flight, I again insist that I use my own chair.

Bathrooms are often a hassle, so I have learned to use creative ways to transfer into narrow spaces. To be blatantly honest, when there are no accessible bathrooms in sight, I have found ways to pee discreetly just about anywhere (outside the Eiffel Tower or on a glacier in a national park). You gotta do what you gotta do, and hopefully one day the access will improve, but in the meantime there is a world out there to be discovered. Bring along an extra pair of pants and a great sense of humor.

I always try to learn some of the language of the country I'm in, because it cuts through the barriers when people stare at you (and they will) and also comes in handy when you need assistance in going up a curb or a flight of steps. Don't accept other people's notions of what is possible—I have climbed Masada in Israel and made it to the top of the Acropolis in Greece.

If a museum lacks elevators for visitors, be sure to ask about freight

## Easy Access Europe

Since my first guidebook in 1980, my mission has been to make Europe accessible. Until now my books have focused on *economic* accessibility—travel needn't be a rich person's hobby. With my book *Rick Steves' Easy Access Europe,* I've broadened that passion to include *physical* accessibility.

I teamed up with a committed band of researchers—led by Dr. Ken Plattner—who care about travelers with limited mobility. Together we've written *Easy Access Europe* to help guide slow walkers and wheelchair users through Europe.

I picked a handful of Europe's best and most accessible destinations: London, Paris, Bruges, Amsterdam, and Germany's Rhine River. Using core material from my existing guidebooks, Ken and his team researched it a second and third time for accessibility. Like an additional fermentation turns a good wine into fine champagne, these additional research trips were designed to bring our Easy Access travelers a smooth and bubbly experience.

For a taste of the travel tips and inspirational feedback from our readers, check out www.ricksteves.com/access.

elevators. Almost all have them somewhere, and that can be your ticket to seeing a world-class treasure.

I always get information about disability groups where I am going. See the resources listed at the end of this article for a number of organizations to try. They will have the best access information, and many times they will become your new traveling partners and friends. They can show you the best spots. Remember that you are part of a global family of disabled people.

It can be helpful to contact tourism offices and local transit providers before you travel. Some even include information about accessibility for people with disabilities on their Web sites.

Each person with a disability has unique needs and interests. Many of my friends use power wheelchairs, or are blind or deaf, or have other disabilities—they all have their own travel tips. People who have difficulty walking long distances might want to think of taking or borrowing a sports wheelchair when needed. Whether you travel alone, with friends, or with an assistant, you're in for a great adventure.

Don't confuse being flexible and having a positive attitude with settling for less than your rights. I expect equal access and constantly let people know about the possibility of providing access through ramps or other modifications. When I believe my rights have been violated, I do whatever is necessary to remedy the situation so that the next traveler, or disabled people in that country, won't have the same frustrations.

Know your rights as a traveler with a disability. If, under the Americans with Disabilities Act, you feel you have been discriminated against (such as not being allowed on a US tour company's tour of Europe), call the US Department of Justice ADA Information Line at 800-514-0301. The US Department of Transportation's Aviation Consumer Protection Division (ACPD) handles complaints regarding the Air Carrier Access Act (tel. 202/366-2220, http://airconsumer.ost.dot.gov).

Keep in mind that accessibility can mean different things in different countries. In some countries people rely more on human-support systems than on physical or technological solutions. People may tell you their building is accessible because they're willing to lift you and your wheelchair over the steps at the entryway. Be open to trying new ways of doing things, but also ask questions to make sure you are comfortable with the access provided.

If you are interested in short-term work, study, research, or volunteering abroad, contact the National Clearinghouse on Disability and Exchange at Mobility International USA for free information and referrals (see listing below). Get online and do some investigating. Search for "travel" and "disability."

Hopefully more books like Rick's *Easy Access Europe* will include accessibility information—which will allow everyone to see Europe through the Back Door. Let's work toward making that door accessible so we can all be there together.

## Additional Resources

**Mobility International USA** (MIUSA) is a nonprofit organization whose mission is to empower people with disabilities around the world through international exchange and international development to achieve their human rights. MIUSA periodically sponsors international exchange programs for people with disabilities. They also sell helpful resources, such as the book *Survival Strategies for Going Abroad: A Guide* *for People with Disabilities,* in which more than 20 experienced travelers with disabilities share stories, tips, and resources related to participating in international programs. This easy-to-use guide addresses the disability-related aspects of participating in international exchange programs, including choosing a program, applying, preparing to travel, adjusting to life in a new country, and returning home (www.miusa.org, tel. 541/343-1284, info@miusa.org).

The **National Clearinghouse on Disability and Exchange (NCDE)** provides information about work, study, volunteer, and research opportunities abroad for people with disabilities. The NDCE offers many resources, including a Peer-to-Peer Network connecting people with disabilities who have been abroad with those planning to go abroad; an online database with information about exchanges and disability organizations worldwide; the free publication *Preparing for an International Career: Pathways for People with Disabilities*; Web resources for parents and youth; and the free journal *A World Awaits You,* with tips and stories about a wide range of exchange opportunities. NCDE is a project sponsored by the Bureau of Educational and Cultural Affairs of the US State Department and administered by MIUSA (same contact as above; www.miusa.org/ncde).

**Access-Able Travel Source** sponsors a useful Web site (www.access-able.com) that has access information and resources for travelers with disabilities, and offers a free e-mail newsletter. They have information about guidebooks, accessible transportation, wheelchair travel, scooter rental, disabled-travel forums, accessible transportation, and more (tel. 303/232-2979, carol@access-able.com, Bill and Carol Randall).

The **Society for Accessible Travel and Hospitality (SATH),** an educational nonprofit membership organization, publishes a travel magazine *(Open World)* and offers travel advice ($45 membership, $30 for students and seniors, includes magazine; $13 for magazine subscription only; www.sath.org, tel. 212/447-7284, fax 212/725-8253, info@sath.org).

Several organizations specialize in **health** issues: The **International Association for Medical Assistance to Travelers (IAMAT)** provides a directory of English-speaking doctors around the world (described on page 302, www.iamat.org, tel. 716/754-4883). The **Centers for Disease Control and Prevention (CDC)** maintain health-related information online, including travel preparation and health information for travel worldwide (www.cdc.gov/travel). **PersonalMD.com** provides information on a wide variety of health topics. The main feature is the PersonalMD

Emergency Card, a free service that allows users to enter their medical information into a secure database that can be accessed anywhere in the world via the Internet, in case of an emergency. **Shoreland's Travel Health Online** offers health tips, a planning guide, and country information (www.tripprep.com).

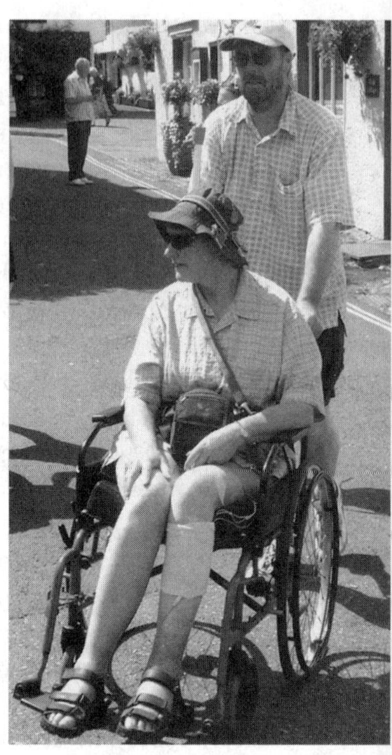

*There's no reason why travelers with disabilities can't explore the Old World.*

**Additional Web Sites:** In addition to the organizations listed above, you can find helpful resources and links pages on the Web sites for **Emerging Horizons** (www.emerginghorizons.com), **Gimp on the Go** (www.gimponthego.com), **Disabled Peoples' International** (www.dpi.org), and **MossRehab ResourceNet** (www.mossresourcenet.org/travel.htm). **AARP**'s Web site features articles written for seniors and slow walkers (www.aarp.org/destinations). **Access Abroad** is a good resource for students with disabilities planning to study abroad (www.umabroad.umn.edu/access). **Wheelchair Accessible Europe** lists hotels throughout Europe offering accessible rooms (www.wheelchairaccessibleeurope.com).

**Tours:** If you'd rather not go it alone, you'll find a selection of groups that run accessible tours to Europe, including **Accessible Journeys** (wheelchair trips to Britain, France, and Holland, www.disabilitytravel.com, tel. 800-846-4537), **Flying Wheels Travel** (escorted tours to Great Britain and France, plus custom itineraries, www.flyingwheelstravel.com, tel. 507/451-5005), and **Nautilus Tours and Cruises** (tours to France, Belgium, and the Netherlands, plus cruises to other destinations, www.nautilustours.com, tel. outside California 800-797-6004, tel. in California 818/591-3159). **Access/Abilities** offers information and custom searches on accessible-travel opportunities (tel. 415/388-3250). **Accessible Europe** is a collection of European travel agents and tour operators who specialize in disabled travel (www.accessibleurope.com). **Accessible City Breaks,** based in Britain, runs trips to several European cities and has a Web site with travel tips and some destination information (www.accessiblecitybreaks.co.uk).

# 28. BUS TOUR SELF-DEFENSE

Many American tourists see Europe on an organized bus tour and don't even consider using a guidebook. Rather than wander around without direction, they pay a company to organize their trip and provide a professional guide. For some people, having someone else do the driving, arrange the hotels, and make the decisions takes the stress and work out of travel. In this case, tours can be a great option. The key is finding the right one.

When considering tours, remember that some of the bestsellers are those that promise more sightseeing than is reasonable in a given amount of time. No tour can give you more than 24 hours in a day or seven days in a week. What the "blitz" tour can do is give you more hours on the bus. Choose carefully among the itineraries available. Do you really want a series of one-night stands? Bus drivers call tours with ridiculous itineraries "pajama tours." You're in the bus from 8 a.m. until after dark, so why even get dressed?

A typical big bus tour has a professional, multilingual European guide and 40–50 people sharing 50 seats. The tour company is probably very big, booking rooms by the thousand and often even owning the hotels it uses. Typically, the bus is luxurious and fairly new, with a high, quiet ride, comfy seats, air-conditioning, and a toilet on board.

*Many who take an organized bus tour could have managed fine on their own.*

Tour hotels fit American standards—large, not too personal, and offering mass-produced comfort, good plumbing, and double rooms. Your hotel's location is important. It can make the difference between a fair trip and a great trip. Beware: Some tour companies save money by parking you in the middle of nowhere. If the tour brochure says you'll be sleeping in the "Florence area," that could be halfway to Bologna (and you'll spend half your sightseeing time on transportation to and from the city center). Centrally located hotels maximize your sightseeing efficiency. Get explicit locations in writing before your trip.

Big, cheap bus-tour meals can be a lowlight. Included meals can often be forgettable buffets that hotel restaurants require large groups to

## Cheap Trick Bus Tours

The cheapest bus tours are impossibly cheap. There's literally no profit in their retail price. They can give you bus transportation and hotels for about what the tourist-off-the-street would pay for just the hotels alone. An independent (but lazy) traveler on a tight budget can think of the tour as a tailored bus pass with hotels tossed in, and it can actually be a cheap trick. Skip out of the shopping, don't buy any of the optional tours, and every day you can do your own sightseeing. Simply apply the skills of independent travel to the efficient, economical trip shell an organized coach tour provides.

take. The prices are driven to almost inedible lows by the tour company. A common complaint among tourists is that hotel meals don't match the local cuisine. While this generally isn't true at smaller, family-run hotels and pensions, meals can be a big disappointment in the larger, impersonal tourist hotels.

Guides generally prefer to spoon-feed Europe to you—from their menu. Sights may be chosen for their convenience rather than merit. Many tours seem to make a big deal out of a statue in Luzern called the *Lion Monument.* When the guide declares this mediocre sight great, obedient tourists ooh and awe in unison. What makes it "great" for the guide is that Luzern (which has a hotel owned by the tour company, but not a lot of interesting sights) was given too much time in the itinerary, and the *Lion Monument* has easy tour-bus parking. However, Leonardo da Vinci's *Last Supper* in Milan may be passed over, because it's expensive to visit and its mandatory reservation system is inconvenient.

Remember, when 50 tourists drop into a "cozy" pub, coziness sneaks out the back door. A good stop for a guide is one with great freeway accessibility and bus parking; where guides and drivers are buttered up with free coffee and cakes (or even free meals); where they speak English and accept credit cards; and where 50 people can go to the bathroom at the same time. *Arrivederci, Roma.*

Empathize with your guide. Leading a tour is a demanding job with lots of responsibility, paperwork, babysitting, and miserable hours. Very often, guides are tired. They're away from home and family, often for months on end, and are surrounded by foreigners having an extended party that they're probably not in the mood for. Most guides treasure their time alone and, except for romantic adventures, keep their distance from the group socially. Each tourist has personal demands, and a big group can amount to one big pain in the bus for the guide.

To most guides, the best group is one that lets him do the thinking and is happy to be herded around. As long as people on board don't think too much or try to deviate from the plan, things go smoothly and reliably, and you really will see (but not necessarily experience) a lot.

Tour companies often put guides in a difficult position. Many companies pay their guides little (or even no) wage. The guide then earns his living from: 1) commissions on the optional daily sightseeing excursions he sells; 2) kickbacks on the souvenirs his group buys from retailers the tour patronizes; and 3) trip-end tips. An experienced and aggressive guide can make $300–500 a day. A guide who's also good can make tour members happy.

## How to Enjoy a Bus Tour

**Keep your guide happy.** Independent-type tourists tend to threaten guides. Maintain your independence without alienating your guide. Don't insist on individual attention when the guide is hounded by countless others. Wait for a quiet moment to ask for advice or offer feedback. If a guide wants to, he can give his entire group a lot of extras—but when he pouts, everyone loses. Your objective, which requires some artistry, is to keep the guide on your side without letting him take advantage of you.

*A well-chosen tour can be a fine value, giving you a great trip and a breakfast table filled with new friends.*

**Discriminate among optional excursions.** While some activities may be included (such as the half-day city sightseeing tours), each day one or two special excursions or evening activities, called "options," are offered for $30–50 a day. Each person decides which options to take and pay for. To make sure you're not being ripped off on excursion prices, ask your hotelier the going rate for a gondola ride, Seine River cruise, or whatever.

Some options are great, others are not worth the time or money. While illuminated night tours of Rome and Paris are marvelous, I'd skip most "nights on the town." On the worst kind of big-bus-tour evening, several bus tours come together for the "evening of local color." Three hundred Australian, Japanese, and American tourists drinking watered-down sangria and watching flamenco dancing onstage to the rhythm of

## Questions to Ask Tour Companies

When calling tour companies, here are questions to ask:

***Nail down the price.***

- What does the price actually include? (How many nights and days? How many meals? Admission to sights? Exactly what kind of transportation?)
- If the dollar drops, will the tour price stay the same or will a supplement be charged?
- If the tour doesn't fill up, will the price increase? Are prices lower for off-season tours?
- Do you take credit cards? (If you're dealing with a tour company that's not well established, pay by credit card. A credit-card company can be a strong ally in resolving disputes.)
- Do singles pay a supplement? Can singles save money by sharing rooms?
- Are optional excursions offered? Daily? Average cost?
- Is trip interruption/cancellation insurance included?
- Will the guide and driver expect to be tipped? How much? How often?
- Are there any other costs?
- Do customers receive any freebies for signing up?

***Find out how much the guide guides.***

- Is the guide also the driver?
- Does the guide give talks on the cities, history, and art?
- What are the guide's qualifications (education, experience, fluency in languages)?

their automatic rewinds is big-bus tourism at its grotesque worst.

Your guide promotes excursions because she profits from them. Don't be pressured. Compare. Some options are cheaper through your tour than from the hotel concierge. Some meals are actually a better value with the group. Keep an open mind. While you are capable of doing plenty on your own, optional excursions can be a decent value—especially when you factor in the value of your time.

But don't let bus tour priorities keep you from what you've traveled all the way to Europe to see. In Amsterdam, some tour companies instruct their guides to spend time in the diamond-polishing place instead of the Van Gogh Museum (no kickbacks on Van Gogh). Skip out if you like.

***Run a reality check on your dream trip.***

- How many tour members will be on the tour?
- Roughly what is the average age and singles-to-couples ratio?
- Are children allowed? What is the minimum age?
- How many seats on the bus? Is there a bathroom on the bus? How much time is spent on the bus each day?
- Is smoking allowed?
- Roughly how many hours a day are spent shopping and watching product demonstrations?
- How much free time is usually allotted at each sight, museum, and city?
- Are all the hotels located downtown or are they on the outskirts?
- What's the average length of stay at hotels? One night? Two?
- Does each room have a private bathroom? Air-conditioning?
- What percentage of included meals are eaten at the hotel?

***Let's get personal.***

- How many years have you been in business?
- Roughly how many tours do you run a year?
- What is your policy if you have to cancel a tour?
- What are your refund policies before and during the tour?

***Request:***

- The detailed itinerary and location of hotels.
- The names and phone numbers of satisfied customers, though these aren't always given out.
- Written tour evaluations, if available (may be posted on their Web site).

Your guide may warn you that you'll get lost and the bus won't wait. Keep your independence (and the hotel address in your money belt).

**Be informed.** Tour guides call the dreaded tourist with a guidebook an "informed passenger." But a guidebook is your key to travel freedom. Get maps and tourist information from your (or another) hotel desk or a tourist information office. Tour hotels are often located outside the city, where they cost the tour company less and where they figure you are more likely to book the options just to get into town. Ask the person behind the desk how to catch the bus downtown. Taxis are always a possibility, and, with three or four people sharing, they're affordable. Team up with others on your tour to explore on your own. No city is dead after

## Comparing Tours

When you're selecting a tour, the cost you're quoted isn't the only factor to consider. Investigate how many people you'll be traveling with as well as what extras you'll be expected to cover. Most tour companies include customer feedback on their Web sites—look around and see what previous tour members have to say.

Here is a summary of information we gathered from the Web sites of eight popular European tour companies (Abercrombie & Kent, Cosmos, Globus, Insight, Maupintour, Perillo, Tauck, and Trafalgar). All are advertised as fully-guided. Prices per day do not include airfare.

| | Higher-end Tours | Rick Steves' Tours | Lower-end Tours |
|---|---|---|---|
| **Price per day** | $300–1,000 | $190–240 | $90–190 |
| **Maximum Group Size** | 20–40 | 24–28 | 40–50 |
| **Meals Included** | 50–75% | 50% | 35–50% |
| **Sightseeing Included** | All included | All included | Most costs extra |
| **Tips Included** | All except guide | All included | None included |

the shops are closed. Go downtown and stroll.

**If you shop...shop around.** Many people make their European holiday one long shopping spree. This suits your guide and the local tourist industry just fine. Guides are quick to say, "If you haven't bought a Rolex, you haven't really been to Switzerland," or "You can't say you've experienced Florence if you haven't bargained for and bought a leather coat." Any tour guide in Europe knows that if she's got Americans on board, she's carting around a busload of stark raving shoppers. In Venice, as I orient my groups, merchants are tugging at my arm and whispering, "Bring your groups to our glassworks next time. We'll give you 15 percent back on whatever they spend—and a free glass 'orse!"

Don't necessarily reject your guide's shopping tips; just keep in mind that the prices you see often include a 10–20 percent kickback. Tour guides are clever at dominating your time, making it difficult for shoppers to get out and discover the going rate for big purchases. Don't let them rush you. Never swallow the line, "This is a special price available only to your tour, but you must buy now."

Remember, as your cruise ship docks in Turkey, that some cruise companies don't even hire a guide. They actually rent their groups out to the highest bidder. That "scholar" who meets you at the dock is actually a carpet salesman in disguise. He'll take you to the obligatory ancient site and then to the carpet shop. The demonstrations (by carpet sellers, glass merchants, and so on) are usually interesting. Use your newfound knowledge from the demonstration to shop around; you may find an item of equal quality for less elsewhere. Bargain.

**Spend time with locals who never deal with tourists.** The only locals most tour groups encounter are hardened business people who know how to make money off tour groups. Going through Tuscany in a flock of 50 Americans following your tour guide's umbrella, you'll meet all the wrong Italians. Break away. One summer night in Regensburg, I skipped out. While my tour was still piling off the bus, I enjoyed a beer—while overlooking the Danube and under shooting stars—with the great-great-great-grandson of the astronomer Johannes Kepler.

# PERSPECTIVES

## 29. TERRORISM, POLITICAL UNREST, AND YOUR TRAVEL DREAMS

### Terrorism

Since the events of September 11, 2001, and the latest war with Iraq, our media has been filled with reports of Americans feeling jittery about travel.

But the travelers I talk to seem unfazed. While mindful that war is serious business, they continue to pursue their travel plans. Maybe it's just the kind of travelers we're dealing with, but our guidebooks and tours have never sold better. The fact is that 12 million Americans go to Europe every year, and for the last several years, not a single one has been killed by terrorists.

Terrorism is not a new consideration for Americans heading to Europe. In the 1970s, we worried about Italy's Red Brigades, Basque separatists, and the Irish Republican Army. In the '90s, we feared widespread retaliation for the first round of American bombs dropped on Baghdad. Then there were threats to Americans by Muslim extremists. Now there's potential fallout from the war in Iraq.

## Relative Risks: Fly or Drive?

You may die this year from a number of causes. Here are a few of your odds:

|  |  |
|---|---|
| Heart disease | 1 in 300 |
| Cancer | 1 in 500 |
| Gunshot | 1 in 9,000 |
| Car accident | 1 in 18,000 |
| Hit by a car while walking | 1 in 45,000 |
| Drowning | 1 in 200,000 |
| Lightning | 1 in 4 million |
| Airline accident | 1 in 8 million |
| Terrorist attack | 1 in 9 million |

Afraid of flying these days? Worldwide, more than a million people die each year in road accidents—about the same as if a fully-loaded 747 crashed every four hours. Out of every 1,000 transportation deaths, 720 are by car and two are by airplane. If a plane blows up tomorrow, America will likely freak out—but it has no effect on the fact that flying is by far the safest way to travel. Drive or fly? You make the call.

Here are some thoughts on keeping the risk in perspective and traveling safely:

Don't plan your trip thinking you can slip over there and back while there's a lull in the action. It's in your interest, psychologically, to plan your trip assuming there will be a terrorist event somewhere in the world sometime between now and your departure date. It will be all over the news, and your loved ones will leap into action trying to get you to cancel your trip.

Your loved ones' hearts are in the right place, but your trip's too important for sensationalism and hysteria to get in the way. The fact remains (according to the US State Department) that of the 200 million overseas trips made by Americans in the last 10 years, fewer than 90 Americans were killed by terrorists while traveling abroad. While the Iraq war begun in the spring of 2003 likely increased the risk of terrorist attacks on Americans, I believe that risk is no greater for an American in Milan or Paris than at home in Miami or Pittsburgh.

It's human nature to feel anxious about some things, even when our brains tell us it's unfounded. I know that 30,000 commercial planes took off and landed safely in the United States every day, and entire years go by—such as in 2002—without a single fatality in the US airline industry.

Even so, I'm still edgy on take-off. After 9/11, I was nervous in a stadium filled with 50,000 potential terrorism victims. But the twinges of anxiety haven't kept me, or most other folks, at home.

While many travelers may feel fine about their physical safety, many grumble about airport security headaches. Europe, the acknowledged world leader in quality security, has been on "orange alert" since the 1980s. Be grateful for and patient with security procedures. I also expect a 30-minute delay for extra security when I leave and enter the US (for which I am thankful). I use the extra time to meditate on the thought, "How has America's place in our world changed...and why?"

*Paris' new see-through garbage cans give terrorists one less place to hide a bomb.*

If you want to worry about something, worry about this: Each year, more than 10,000 Americans are shot to death in the United States by handguns (compared to fewer than 400 in Britain, France, or Germany).

Meanwhile, as America continues to be at odds with most of our planet on everything from birth control to bad regimes to oil to the environment, some people will put their travel dreams on hold and decide to stay home. That's OK. I'm still bringing home TV shows that they can watch from the safety of their living room sofas.

*Security on Europe's trains is tighter than ever these days. Here at London's Waterloo Station, the police keep a close eye on who boards the Eurostar for Paris.*

Most of us would rather enjoy the fun and wonders of Europe firsthand. Travel is a springboard for experiencing the beauty of our world, and this is a great time to dive in.

## Practical Tips for Safe and Smooth Travel

All of us want to travel as safely as possible. Here are some tips:

**Consider State Department travel advisories** (http://travel.state.gov)...**but don't trust them blindly.** A threat against the embassy in Rome doesn't affect my sightseeing at the Pantheon. While I travel right through many advisories (which can seem politically motivated), other warnings (for example, about civil unrest in a country that's falling apart) are grounds to scrub my mission. Keep in mind that in recent years, Canada and many European countries have issued travel advisories to their citizens for a land they consider more dangerous than their own: the US. For other perspectives, check the British (www.fco.gov.uk) and Canadian (www.voyage.gc.ca) government travel warnings.

**Be patient.** Be thankful for security measures that may delay you. Call airports to confirm flight schedules before heading out. And allow plenty of time to catch your flight.

**Pack lighter than ever to minimize airport frustrations.** New conditions at airports will favor those with carry-on–size luggage. The basic limits have not changed (one 9" x 22" x 14" bag plus a day bag). But those checking bags will incur longer waits and less flexibility. Nimble ones with carry-on bags do better in the scramble to get through the flight-schedule shuffling that follows any major disaster or scare.

**Avoid being a target by melting into Europe.** Fancy luggage and jewelry impresses only thieves and gives you a needlessly high profile. Travel and look like a local. This is smart travel anytime. Likely targets are icons of American culture—towering American corporations, fancy high-profile American tour groups, military and diplomatic locations, and luxury hotels. Stay in local-style places. Terrorists don't bomb Pedro's Pension. That's where they sleep.

Two weeks after the World Trade Center was destroyed, I was in Padua, the town where Copernicus studied and Galileo taught. The square was filled with college students sharing drinks and discussing America's response to "our new reality." As we talked, I kept dipping little strips of bread into a puddle of olive oil on my plate, tiptoe-style. Watching me do this, my new friend said, "You make the *scarpetta*... little shoes."

My Italian wasn't good enough to tell him my thoughts: Travel is a celebration of life and freedom. Terrorists will not take that away from me. My mission in life is to inspire Americans to travel, one by one—"making the little shoes"—to absorb and savor the wonders of Europe.

## Political Unrest

Political turmoil is part of life these days, and security in Europe has never been tighter. Countries from Britain to Italy continue to deal with internal discord, from separatists to religious extremists. An awareness of current social and political problems is as important to smart travel as a listing of top sights. As some popular destinations are entertaining tourists with "sound and light" shows in the old town, they're quelling angry demonstrations in the new.

*The only real difference for Americans exploring Europe in our post-9/11 world is that you'll be interviewed by these guys before boarding your plane back into the US.*

Travel broadens our perspective, enabling us to rise above the 6 p.m. advertiser-driven entertainment we call news—and see things as citizens of our world. By plugging directly into the present and getting the European take on things, a traveler gets beyond traditional sightseeing and learns "today's history."

There are many peoples fighting the same thrilling battles for political rights we Americans won 200 years ago. And while your globe may paint Greece orange and Bulgaria green, racial, religious, and linguistic groups rarely color within the lines.

Understand a country's linguistic divisions. It's next to impossible to keep everyone happy in a multilingual country. Switzerland has four languages, but *Deutsch ist über alles.* In Belgium, there's tension between the Dutch- and French-speaking halves. And Hungarians living in Slovakia had to rely on European Court intervention to get road signs in their native language. Like many French Canadians, Europe's linguistic underdogs will tell you their language receives equal treatment only on cornflakes boxes, and many are working toward change.

Look beyond the pretty pictures in your tourist brochures for background on how your destination's demographic makeup may be causing problems today or tomorrow. If you're planning a trip to Poland, for example, start clipping newspaper articles and surfing the Web a few months in advance to gather political news on what's happening (information you'll seldom find in guidebooks).

With this foundation and awareness, you can get the most out of the nearly unavoidable opportunities to talk with involved locals about complex current situations. At any pub on the Emerald Isle, you'll get an

earful of someone's passionate feelings about "the Troubles." In Russia and Eastern Europe, whenever you want some political or economic gossip, sit alone in a café. After a few minutes and some eye contact, you'll have company and a fascinating chat. Young, well-dressed people are most likely to speak (and want to practice) English. Universities can be the perfect place to solve the world's problems with a liberal, open-minded foreigner over a cafeteria lunch.

But be prepared for a challenge when the topic shifts to American foreign policy. Among deaf people, the international sign-language symbol for "American" is the "fat cat"—holding your arms around an imaginary big belly. Like it or not, people around the world look at America as the kingpin of a global and ruthless game of Monopoly. As a person who loves his country, I see travel as a patriotic exercise in helping my country fit better into this ever-smaller planet.

# 30. ATTITUDE ADJUSTMENT

## The Ugly American

Many Americans' trips suffer because they are treated like ugly Americans. Those who are treated like ugly Americans are treated that way because they *are* ugly Americans. They aren't bad people, just ethnocentric.

Even if you believe American ways are better, your trip will go better if you don't compare. Enjoy doing things the European way during your trip, and you'll experience a more welcoming Europe.

Europe sees two kinds of travelers: Those who view Europe through air-conditioned bus windows, socializing with their noisy American friends, and those who are taking a vacation from America, immersing themselves in different cultures, experiencing different people and lifestyles, and broadening their perspectives.

Europeans judge you as an individual, not by your government. A Greek fisherman told me, "For me, Bush is big problem—but I like you." I have never been treated like the ugly American. My Americanness in Europe, if anything, has been an asset.

You'll see plenty of ugly Americans slogging through a sour Europe, mired in a swamp of complaints. Ugly Americanism is a disease, but fortunately there is a cure: A change in attitude. The best over-the-counter medicine is a mirror. Here are the symptoms. The ugly American:

- criticizes "strange" customs and cultural differences. She doesn't try to understand that only a Hindu knows the value of India's sacred cows, and only a devout Spanish Catholic appreciates the true worth of his town's patron saint.
- demands to find America in Europe. He throws a fit if the air-conditioning breaks down in a hotel. He insists on orange juice and eggs (sunny-side up) for breakfast, long beds, English menus, ice in drinks, punctuality in Italy, and cold beer in England. He measures Europe with an American yardstick.
- invades a country while making no effort to communicate with the "natives." Traveling in packs, he talks at and about Europeans in a condescending manner.

## The Thoughtful American

The thoughtful American celebrates the similarities and differences in cultures. You:

- seek out European styles of living. You are genuinely interested in the people and cultures you visit.
- want to learn by trying things. You forget your discomfort if you're the only one in a group who feels it.
- accept and try to understand differences. Paying for your Italian coffee at one counter and then picking it up at another may seem inefficient, until you realize it's more sanitary: The person handling the food handles no money.
- are observant and sensitive. If 60 people are eating quietly with hushed conversation in a Belgian restaurant, you know it's not the place to yuk it up.
- maintain humility and don't flash signs of affluence. You don't joke about the local money or overtip. Your bucks don't talk.
- are positive and optimistic in the extreme. You discipline yourself to focus on the good points of each country. You don't dwell on problems or compare things to "back home."
- make an effort to bridge that flimsy language barrier. Rudimentary communication in any language is fun and simple with a few basic words. On the train to Budapest, you might think that a debate with a Hungarian over the merits of a common European currency would be frustrating with a 20-word vocabulary, but you'll surprise yourself at how well you communicate by just breaking the ice and trying. Don't worry about making mistakes—communicate!

### Thank You

| | | | |
|---|---|---|---|
| Arabic | **shukran** | Hebrew | **todah** |
| Bulgarian | **blagodarya** | Hungarian | **köszönöm** |
| Croatian | **hvala** | Iraqi | **shukran** |
| Czech | **děkuji** | Italian | **grazie** |
| Danish | **tak** | Polish | **dziękuję** |
| Dutch | **dank u wel** | Portuguese | **obrigado** |
| English | **thank you** | Russian | **spasiba** |
| Estonian | **tänan** | Slovak | **d'akujem** |
| Finnish | **kiitos** | Slovene | **hvala** |
| French | **merci** | Spanish | **gracias** |
| German | **danke** | Turkish | **teşekkür ederim** |
| Greek | **efharisto** | | |

I've been accepted as an American friend throughout Europe, Russia, the Middle East, and North Africa. I've been hugged by Bulgarian workers on a Balkan mountaintop; discussed the Olympics over dinner in the home of a Greek family; explained to a young, frustrated Irishman that California girls take their pants off one leg at a time, just like the rest of us; and hiked through the Alps with a Swiss schoolteacher, learning German and teaching English.

Go as a guest; act like one, and you'll be treated like one. In travel, too, you reap what you sow.

## Responsible Tourism

As we learn more about the problems that confront the Earth and humankind, more and more people are recognizing the need for the world's industries, such as tourism, to function as tools for peace. Tourism is a $2 trillion-a-year industry that employs more than 60 million people. As travelers become more sophisticated and gain a global perspective, the demand for socially, environmentally, and economically responsible means of travel will grow. Peace is more than the absence of war, and if we are to enjoy the good things of life—such as travel—the serious issues that confront humankind must be addressed now.

Although the most obvious problems relate specifically to travel in the Third World, European travel also offers some exciting socially responsible opportunities. In this chapter are a few sources of information for the budding "green" traveler.

Consume responsibly in your travels—do your part to conserve

## Resources for Socially Responsible European Travel

**Global Volunteers,** a nonprofit organization, offers useful "travel with a purpose" trips throughout the world (www.globalvolunteers.org, tel. 800-487-1074, email@globalvolunteers.org). The work varies per country, but if Europe's your goal, you'll likely work with vulnerable children in Romania, help with a renovation project at the peace center in Ireland, work at a home for disabled youth in Greece, or teach conversational English in Italy, Hungary, Poland, Ukraine, or Romania.

**Volunteers for Peace,** a nonprofit organization, runs international work camps to promote goodwill through friendship and community service. European options include historical preservation, festival event planning, conservation projects, AIDS awareness instruction, and social work with disabled or elderly people (www.vfp.org, tel. 802/259-2759, vfp@vfp.org).

**SCI-International Voluntary Service** runs work camps with projects involving children, the elderly, the environment, or local culture and history (www.sci-ivs.org, sciinfo@sci-ivs.org).

The **Center for Global Education** (at Augsburg College in Minneapolis) organizes powerfully educational tours to Central America and South Africa. The three trips of theirs in which I participated gave me the most vivid and perspective-stretching travel experiences I've ever enjoyed. (For trip journals of my CFGE experiences in El Salvador and Nicaragua—including my latest 2005 adventure—see www.ricksteves.com/centam). For their latest "reality tour" schedule, visit www.augsburg.edu/global or call 800-299-8889.

The book *Volunteer Vacations: Short-Term Adventures That Will Benefit You and Others* (9th edition), by Bill McMillon, Doug Cutchins, and Anne Geissinger, lists 500 options for one- to six-week domestic and foreign volunteer programs. Get a copy of this book if you'd like to restore medieval ruins, work in wildlife reserves, or care for refugee children in camps and orphanages (order from www.amazon.com or through the Independent Publishers Group, www.ipgbook.com, tel. 800-888-4741).

Other good books (all available through www.amazon.com) include *Vacation Work's International Directory of Voluntary Work* (9th edition), by Victoria Pybus (Vacation Work); *How to Live Your Dream of Volunteering Overseas,* by Joseph Collins, Stefano DeZerega, and Zahara Heckscher (Penguin USA); and *Green Volunteers: The World Guide to Voluntary Work in Nature Conservation,* by Fabio Ausenda (Universe).

energy. If your hotel overstocks your room with towels, use just one. Carry your own bar of soap and bottle of shampoo rather than rip open all those little soaps and shampoo packets. Bring a lightweight plastic cup instead of using and tossing a plastic glass at every hotel. Turn the light off when you leave your room. Limit showers to five minutes. Return unused travel information (booklets, brochures) to the tourist information office or pass it on to another traveler rather than toss it into a European landfill. In little ways, we can make a difference.

Understand your power to shape the marketplace by what you decide to buy, whether in the grocery store or in your choice of hotels. In my travels (and in my writing), whenever possible, I patronize and support small, family-run, locally owned businesses (hotels, restaurants, shops, tour guides). I choose people who invest their creativity and resources in giving me simple, friendly, sustainable, and honest travel experiences—people with ideals. Back Door places don't rely on slick advertising and marketing gimmicks, and they don't target the created needs of people whose values are shaped by capitalism gone wild. Consuming responsibly means buying as if your choice is a vote for the kind of world we could have.

## Making the Most of Your Trip

**Accept that today's Europe is changing.** Among the palaces, quaint folk dancers, and museums, you'll find a living civilization grasping for the future while we romantic tourists grope for its past. This presents us with a sometimes painful dose of truth.

Today's Europe is a complex, mixed bag of tricks. It can rudely slap you in the face if you aren't prepared to accept it with open eyes and an open mind. Europe is getting crowded, tense, seedy, polluted, industrialized, hamburgerized, and far from the everything-in-its-place, fairy-tale land it may have once been.

If you're not mentally braced for some shocks, local trends can tinge your travels. Hans Christian Andersen's statue has four-letter words scrawled across its base. Amsterdam's sex shops and McDonald's share the same streetlamp. In Paris, armies of Sudanese salesmen bait tourists with ivory bracelets and crocodile purses. Many a Mediterranean hotel keeper would consider himself a disgrace to his sex if he didn't follow a single woman to her room. Drunk punks do their best to repulse you as you climb to St. Patrick's grave in Ireland, and Greek ferryboats dump mountains of trash into their dying Aegean Sea. A 12-year-old boy in Denmark smokes a cigarette like he was born with it in his mouth, and in a Munich beer hall, an old drunk spits *Sieg heil*s all over you. The

## Anti-Americanism and Weapons of Mass Unfriendliness

Four years after America's invasion of Iraq, Europeans are still steamed at George W. Bush. The unilateral decision to wage war in Iraq when the community of nations sought other solutions seemed so typically American. Europeans label it the "cowboy" mentality—an insult meaning reckless, unthinking, violent, and naive. Even now that the US has begun to mend relations with European governments, polls of ordinary Europeans show an overwhelmingly negative view towards American foreign policy.

Europeans—who generally dislike President Bush—were further frustrated by Bush's re-election in 2004. This time around, Europeans figure that America understood the agenda of the Bush administration when they voted for him, and many now seem to hold the American electorate responsible for its decision. Europeans marvel that we have an administration whose policies are shaped by people who believe that our world was actually created in six days, AIDS can be spread by tears, and this planet is not warming up.

What does that mean for Americans traveling abroad? Reading scores of e-mails, I've learned that travelers who've been outspoken in their support of President Bush have been treated rudely, Bush-bashers have felt they're among friends—and those showing no interest in politics have encountered no anti-Americanism. They've enjoyed great trips through Europe. The bottom line is that most Europeans recognize that you, the traveler, do not represent your government, and they'll treat you as an individual.

But if our government continues to isolate our country, first from Islam and now from Europe, Americans may find future welcomes conditional—much like the welcome that a lot of very nice travelers from apartheid-era South Africa found in Europe during the 1980s. (I remember meeting many white South Africans back then...and trying my best not to assume they were racist.)

Having said all that, do I think anti-American sentiment in Europe will be a negative on our next trip? Absolutely not. Is it an opportunity to learn more about the planet we share? Absolutely yes.

Barcelona shoeshine man will triple-charge you, and people everywhere eat strange and wondrous things. They eat next to nothing for breakfast, mud for coffee, mussels in Brussels, and snails in Paris, and dinner's at 10 p.m. in Spain. Beer is room-temperature here and flat there, coffee isn't served with dinner, and ice cubes are only a dream. Roman cars stay in their lanes like rocks in an avalanche, and beer maids with huge pretzels pull mustard packets from their cleavage.

Contemporary Europe is alive and groping. Today's problems will fill tomorrow's museums. Feel privileged to walk the vibrant streets of Europe as a sponge—not as a judge. Be open-minded. Absorb, accept, and learn.

**Don't be a creative worrier.** Travelers tend to sit at home before their trip—all alone, just thinking of reasons to be stressed. Travel problems are always there; you just notice them when they're yours. Every year there are air-controller strikes, train wrecks, terrorist attacks, new problems, and deciduous problems sprouting new leaves.

Travel is ad-libbing while incurring and conquering surprise challenges. Make an art out of taking the unexpected in stride. Relax—you're on the other side of the world playing games in a continental backyard. Be a good sport, enjoy the uncertainty, and frolic in the pits.

Many of my readers' richest travel experiences were the result of seemingly terrible mishaps: the lost passport in Slovenia, having to find a doctor in Ireland, the blowout in Portugal, or the moped accident on Corfu.

Expect problems, tackle them creatively. You'll miss a museum or two and maybe blow your budget for the week. But you'll make some local friends and stack up some memories. And this is the essence of travel that you'll enjoy long after the journal is shelved and your trip is stored neatly in the photo album of your mind.

**KISS: "Keep it simple, stupid!"** Don't complicate your trip. Simplify! Travelers get stressed and cluttered over the silliest things, which, in their niggling ways, can suffocate a happy holiday: registering your camera with customs before leaving home, standing in a long line at the post office on a sunny day in the Alps, worrying about the correct answers to meaningless bureaucratic forms, making a long-distance hotel reservation in a strange language and then trying to settle on what's served for breakfast, having a picnic in pants that make you worry about grass stains, and sending away for Swedish hotel vouchers. Time-shares, frequent-flyer incentives, VAT refunds...concerns like these are outlawed in my travels.

People can complicate their trips with video cameras, lead-lined

*When I see a bunch of cute guys on a bench, I ask 'em to scoot over...*

*...and 30 years later, I'm still one of the gang.*

film bags, special tickets for free entry to all the sights they won't see in England, inflatable hangers, immersion heaters, instant coffee, 65 Handi-Wipes, and a special calculator that figures the value of the euro to the third decimal. They ask for a toilet in 17 words or more, steal artificial sweeteners and plastic silverware off the plane, and take notes on facts that don't matter. Travel more like Gandhi—with simple clothes, open eyes, and an uncluttered mind.

**Ask questions.** If you are too proud to ask questions, your trip will be dignified but dull. Many tourists are actually afraid or too timid to ask questions. The meek may inherit the earth, but they make lousy travelers. Local sources are a wealth of information. People are happy to help a traveler. Hurdle the language barrier. Use a paper and pencil, charades, or whatever it takes to be understood. Don't be afraid to butcher the language.

Ask questions—or be lost. If you are lost, take out a map and look lost. You'll get help. If you're lonely or in need of contact with a local person, take out a map and look lost. Perceive friendliness and you'll find it.

**Be militantly humble—Attila had a lousy trip.** All summer long I'm pushing for a bargain, often for groups. It's the hottest, toughest time of year. Tourists and locals clash. Many tourists leave soured.

When I catch a Spanish merchant shortchanging me, I correct the bill and smile, *"Adiós."* When a French hotel owner blows up at me for no legitimate reason, I wait, smile, and try again. I usually see the irate ranter come to his senses, forget the problem, and work things out.

"Turn the other cheek" applies perfectly to those riding Europe's magic carousel. If you fight the slaps, the ride is over. The militantly humble and hopelessly optimistic can spin forever.

**Make yourself an extrovert, even if you're not.** Be a catalyst for adventure and excitement. Meet people. Make things happen or often they won't. The American casual-and-friendly social style is charming to Europeans who are raised to respect social formalities. While our "slap-on-the-back" friendliness can be overplayed and obnoxious, it can also be a great asset for the American interested in meeting Europeans. Consider that cultural trait a plus. Enjoy it. Take advantage of it.

*If people stare...sing cowboy songs.*

I'm not naturally a wild-and-crazy kind of guy. But when I'm shy and quiet, things don't happen, and that's a bad rut to travel in. It's not easy, but this special awareness can really pay off. Let me describe the same evening twice—first with the mild-and-lazy me, and then with the wild-and-crazy me.

*The traffic held me up, so by the time I got to that great historical building I've always wanted to see, it was six minutes before closing. No one was allowed to enter. Disappointed, I walked to a restaurant and couldn't make heads or tails out of the menu. I recognized "steak-frites" and settled for a meat patty and French fries. On the way home I looked into a colorful local pub but it seemed kind of exclusive, so I walked on. A couple waved at me from their balcony, but I didn't know what to say, so I ignored them. I returned to my room and did some laundry.*

That's not a night to be proud of. A better traveler's journal entry would read like this:

*I got to the museum only six minutes before closing. The guard said no one could go in now, but I begged, joked, and pleaded with him. I had traveled all the way to see this place, and I would be leaving early in the morning. I assured him that I'd be out by six o'clock, and he gave me a glorious six minutes in that building. You can do a lot with a Botticelli in six minutes when that's all you've got. Across the street at a restaurant that the same guard recommended, I couldn't make heads or tails out of the menu. Inviting myself into the kitchen, I met the cooks and got a firsthand look at "what's cookin'." Now I could order an exciting local dish and know just what I was getting.* Delizioso! *On the way home, I passed a local pub, and, while it seemed dark and uninviting, I stepped in and was met by the only guy in the place who spoke any English. He proudly befriended me and told me, in very broken English, of his salty past and his six kids, while treating me to his favorite local brew. As I headed home, a couple waved at me from their balcony, and I waved back, saying* "Buon giorno!" *I knew it didn't mean "Good evening," but they understood. They invited me up to their apartment. We joked around—not understanding a lot of what we were saying to each other—and they invited me to their summer cottage tomorrow. What a lucky break! There's no better way to learn about this country than to spend an afternoon with a local family. And to think that I could be back in my room doing the laundry.*

Pledge every morning to do something entirely different today. Meet people and create adventure—or bring home a boring journal.

## Becoming a Temporary European

Most travelers tramp through Europe like they're visiting the cultural zoo. "Ooo, that guy in lederhosen yodeled! Excuse me, could you do that again in the sunshine with my wife next to you so I can take a snapshot?" This is fun. It's a part of travel. But a camera bouncing on your belly tells locals you're hunting cultural peacocks. When I'm in Europe, I'm the best German or Spaniard or Italian I can be. While I never drink tea at home, after a long day of sightseeing in England, "a spot of tea" really does feel right. I drink wine in France and beer in Germany. In Italy, I eat small breakfasts. Find ways to really be there. For ideas on connecting, consider these (and also see the Graffiti Wall tips in the appendix):

**Go to church.** Many regular churchgoers never even consider a European worship service. Any church would welcome a traveling American. And an hour in a small-town church provides an unbeatable peek into the local community, especially if you join them for coffee and cookies afterwards. I'll never forget going to a small church on the south coast of Portugal one Easter. A tourist stood at the door videotaping the "colorful natives" (including me) shaking hands with the priest after the service. You can experience St. Peter's by taking photographs...or taking a seat at Mass.

*Mass with the sun's rays, daily at 5 p.m. in St. Peter's*

**Root for your team.** For many Europeans, the top religion is soccer. Getting caught up in a sporting event is going local. Whether enjoying soccer in small-town Italy, or hurling in Ireland, you'll be surrounded by a stadium crammed with devout locals.

**Play where the locals play.** A city's popular fairgrounds and parks are filled with local families, lovers, and old-timers enjoying a cheap afternoon or evening out. European communities provide their heavily taxed citizens with wonderful athletic facilities. Check out a swimming center, called a "leisure center" in Britain. While tourists outnumber locals five to one at the world-famous Tivoli Gardens, Copenhagen's other amusement park, Bakken, is enjoyed purely by Danes. Disneyland Paris is great. But Paris' Parc Astérix is more French.

**Experiment.** Some cafés in the Netherlands (those with plants in the windows or Rastafarian colors on the wall) have menus that look like the inventory of a drug bust back in the United States. Marijuana is less controversial in Holland than tobacco (which was recently banned in public spaces). For a casual toke of local life without the risk that comes with smoking in the United States, drop into one of these cafés and roll a joint. (See Chapter 45: Amsterdam's Counter-Culture.)

**Take a stroll.** Across southern Europe, communities have a *paseo,* or stroll, in the early evening. Stroll along. Join a *Volksmarch* in Bavaria to spend a day on the trails with people singing "I love to go a-wandering" in its original language. Remember, hostels are the American target, while mountain huts and "nature's friends huts" across Europe are filled mostly with local hikers. Most hiking centers have alpine clubs that welcome foreigners and offer organized hikes.

**Get off the tourist track.** Choose destinations busy with local holiday-goers but not on the international tourist map. Campgrounds are filled with Europeans in the mood to toss a Frisbee with a new American friend (bring a nylon "Whoosh" Frisbee). Be accessible. Accept invitations. Assume you're interesting and do Europeans a favor by finding ways to connect.

*Connect with the locals. Greeks and Turks love a revealing game of backgammon.*

**Challenge a local to the national pastime.** In Greece or Turkey, drop into a local teahouse or *taverna* and challenge a local to a game of backgammon. You're instantly a part (even a star) of the local café or bar scene.

Normally the gang will gather around, and what starts out as a simple game becomes a fun duel of international significance.

**Contact the local version of your club.** If you're a member of a service club, bridge club, professional association, or international organization, make a point to connect with your foreign mates.

**Search out residential neighborhoods.** Ride a city bus or subway into the suburbs. Wander through a neighborhood to see how the locals live when they're not wearing lederhosen and yodeling. Visit a supermarket. Make friends at the launderette.

**Drop by a school or university.** Mill around a university and check out the announcement boards. Eat at the school cafeteria. Ask at the English-language department if there's a student learning English whom you could hire to be your private guide. Be alert and even a little bit snoopy. If you stumble onto a grade-school talent show—sit down and watch it.

**Truly become a local.** The ultimate way of becoming a temporary local is to actually become one—by moving to Europe. For ideas on how to do this, see the "Overseas Work and Study" sidebar, page 382.

**Join in.** When you visit the town market in the morning, you're just another hungry local, picking up your daily produce. You can snap photos of the pilgrims at Lourdes—or volunteer to help wheel the chairs of those who've come in hope of a cure. Traveling through the wine country

*Blend into Europe: Shop with the locals at the town market.*

of France during harvest time, you can be a tourist taking photos—or you can pitch in and become a local grape picker. Get more than a photo op. Get dirty. That night at the festival, it's just grape pickers dancing—and you're one of them.

If you're hunting cultural peacocks, remember they spread their tails best for people...not cameras. When you take Europe out of your viewfinder, you're more likely to find it in your lap.

## Innocence Abroad

As a kid, my image of travel was clear. It was hardworking people vacationing on big white ships in the Caribbean. They'd stand on the deck, toss coins overboard, and photograph what they called "little dark kids" jumping for them.

*What a difference perspective makes. When I bragged about how many gold medals our American athletes were winning, my Dutch friend replied, "Yes, you have many medals, but per capita, we Dutch are doing five times as well."*

As an idealistic student, I wondered if I should make teaching travel my life's work. I questioned whether promoting travel in a hungry world was a good thing. Even today, travel remains a hedonistic flaunting of affluence for many—see if you can eat five meals a day and still snorkel when you get into port.

I was raised thinking the world was a pyramid with the US on top and everyone else trying to get there. I believed our role in the world was to help other people get it right...American-style. If they didn't understand that, we'd get them a government that did.

But travel changed my perspective.

My egocentrism took a big hit in 1969. I was a pimply kid in an Oslo city park filled with parents doting over their adorable little children. I realized those parents loved their kids as much as my parents loved me. And then it hit me: This world was home to billions of equally precious children of God. From that day on, my personal problems and struggles had to live in a global setting. I was blessed...and cursed...with a broader perspective.

That same year, travel also undermined my ethnocentrism. Sitting

### Overseas Work and Study

If you're interested in becoming a full-time European, consider these helpful resources:

Vacation Work publishes Susan Griffith's *Work Your Way Around the World* and *Summer Jobs Abroad,* edited by David Woodworth and Victoria Pybus. Also consider the *Directory of Jobs & Careers Abroad,* edited by Deborah Penrith; *The Expert Expatriate: Your Guide to Successful Relocation Abroad,* by Melissa Brayer Hess and Patricia Linderman; and *GenXpat: The Young Professional's Guide To Making A Successful Life Abroad,* by Margaret Malewski. All of these titles are available at www.amazon.com.

The Council on International Educational Exchange offers undergrads study-abroad programs (for credit) in 20 European countries (www.ciee.org/isp, tel. 800-407-8839).

For information online, www.expatexchange.com offers postings from expats in virtually every European country.

on a living room carpet with Norwegian cousins, I watched the Apollo moon landing. Neil Armstrong took *"ett lite skritt for et menneske, ett stort skritt for menneskeheten."* While I waved an American flag in my mind, I saw this was a human triumph even more than an American one.

In later years, I met intelligent people—nowhere near as rich, free, or blessed with opportunity as I was—who wouldn't trade passports. They were thankful to be Nepali, Estonian, Turkish, Nicaraguan, or whatever...and I was perplexed. I witnessed stirring struggles in lands that found other truths to be self-evident and God-given. I learned of Nathan Hales and Patrick Henrys from other nations who only wished they had more than one life to give for their country.

I saw national pride that wasn't American. When I bragged about the many gold medals our American athletes were winning, my Dutch friend replied, "Yes, you have many medals, but per capita, we Dutch are doing five times as well."

Travel shows me exciting struggles those without passports never see. Stepping into a high school stadium in Turkey, I saw 500 teenagers thrusting their fists in the air and screaming in unison, "We are a secular nation." I asked my guide, "What's the deal...don't they like God?" She said, "Sure, they love God. But here in Turkey, we treasure the separation of mosque and state as much as you value the separation of church and state. And, with Iran just to our east, we're concerned about the rising tide of Islamic fundamentalism."

Good travel is thoughtful travel—being aware of these national struggles. In Berlin, I helped celebrate the opening of Germany's new national parliament building, the Reichstag. For a generation, it was a bombed-out hulk stranded in the no-man's-land separating East and West Berlin. But today the building is newly restored and crowned by a gleaming glass dome. The dome—free and open long hours—has an inviting ramp spiraling to its top. The architecture makes a powerful point: German citizens will keep an eye on their government—they can now literally look over the shoulders of their legislators at work.

Standing on the top of this great new capitol building on its opening day, I was surrounded by teary-eyed Germans. Any time you're surrounded by teary-eyed Germans, something extraordinary is going on. Traveling thoughtfully, I was engaged...not just another tourist snapping photos, but a traveler witnessing an important moment as a great nation was symbolically closing the door on a terrible chapter in its history. After so much war, fascism, communism, and division, a wiser Germany was entering a new century united and free, and filled with hope.

Travel teaches the beauty of human fulfillment. I believe God created each of us to be fulfilled. And that doesn't necessarily mean to become doctors and lawyers. As you travel, you find people who make crêpes like they invented them...and will make them that way all their lives. Being poured a glass of wine by a vintner whose family name has been on the bottle for more than a century, you feel the glow of a person fulfilled. Sitting above the congregation with an organist whose name is at the bottom of a 300-year-long list of musicians who've powered that cathedral with music, you know you're in the presence of an artist who's found his loft.

*Happiness in the developing world is a thatched roof over your head, a bike, enough land to plant your rice and beans, healthy children, peace, and political stability. These people don't have the American Dream—they have the Sri Lankan Dream.*

From the border of pre-war Iraq, I have vivid memories of another lesson in fulfillment. A weather-beaten old Kurd held his chisel high in the sky. He was the region's much-loved carver of prayer niches for village mosques. The world was brown and blue—his face, his robe, the parched earth, and the sky. The blade gleamed as he declared, "A man and his chisel...the greatest factory on earth." The pride in a simple man, carving for the glory of God, was inspirational. He was fulfilled. When I asked the price of a piece he'd carved, he gave it to me—explaining that for a man his age, to know a piece of his work would be enjoyed in America was payment enough.

*Throughout the developing world, scruffy kids have fun chasing tourists like dogs chase cars. They beg while their parents labor in the fields for $2 a day.*

Travel helps us celebrate differences and overcome misunderstandings—big and little—between people. Recently in Germany, a pre-schooler stared at me. Finally his mother said, "Excuse my son. He stares at Americans." She went on to explain that last time they went to McDonald's, the boy (munching the fluffy hamburger bun) asked why Americans have such soft bread. She explained that it's because Americans have no teeth. Giving the child a smiley growl, I did my part to dispel that misunderstanding.

I grew up thinking cheese was orange and the shape of a slice of bread. Travel changed that in a hurry. Following a restaurateur friend through her Parisian neighborhood market taught me about the love of fine food from a woman who serves it daily. Stepping into a cheese shop—a festival of mold—she picked up a gross wad of the stinkiest cheese imaginable. Holding it close to her nose, she took a long, sensual whiff. Then she offered it to me, saying, "Oh Rick, smell this cheese...it smells like zee feet of angels." Travel shows me how in life, there's much to be passionate about.

On another trip I was in Afghanistan. Eating lunch in a Kabul cafeteria, my meal came with a lesson in pride and diversity. An older man joined me with his lunch, intent on making one strong point. He said, "I am a professor here in Afghanistan. In this world, one third of the people use a spoon and fork like you, one third use chopsticks, and one third use fingers—like me. And we are all civilized the same."

On another trip—this time in Egypt, in a field across the Nile from the Temple of Luxor—children mugged in front of my camera. I took photo after photo while parents looked on, knowing that two clicks of my shutter cost me what they make in a day. Even though my camera's worth a year's wages, they smiled and waved graciously before returning to their crops.

My travels—whether in Egypt, Afghanistan, Turkey, or Holland—teach me more about my country as well as the rest of our world. Travel has sharpened both my love of what America stands for and my connection with our world. And lessons I've learned far from home combined with passion for America have heightened my drive to challenge my countrymen to higher ideals. Crass materialism and a global perspective don't mix. We can enjoy the fruits of our hard work and still be a loved and respected nation. While I've found no simple answers, I spend more time than ever searching. The world needs America the beautiful. But lately, the world sees America as more aggressive and materialistic than beautiful. As our eagle soars, much of humanity wishes it were house-trained.

Like America, Europe is wealthy. But it gives capitalism a compassionate twist—a safety net for the losers—even if it weakens the much-vaunted incentives of pure capitalism. It's tough to get really rich in Europe. Belgians like it when their queen does her own shopping. Norwegians unilaterally forgave the debt owed them by the poor world.

Travel in Europe puts you in touch with societies who believe in good government. In Scandinavia, you sip your coffee on town squares where the city hall rather than a church is the centerpiece. The city hall bell tower stands like a steeple...an exclamation mark declaring communities can work together and care for all. Inside the city hall, you enter what feels like the nave of a church and are surrounded with murals extolling the beauties of good government and the sorry consequences of bad government. Citizens pay high taxes in expectation of a high-service government. (For much more on this topic, visit www.ricksteves.com/dream for an article entitled "A United Europe in the 21st Century: Eclipsing the American Dream.")

*Scandinavians place their city hall on the main square like a temple to good government. Oslo's is wallpapered with murals celebrating how a society can work together for the benefit of all.*

Europeans have a different take on the social contract. America gives it a Locke spin: rugged individualism, don't fence me in, do what you want as long as it doesn't hurt others. And Europeans go with Rousseau's version: If we all give a little more than our share, society can live together nicely. To Locke, the government restricts freedom. To Rousseau, the government *is* us and serves our needs.

My European friends amaze me with their willingness to pay huge taxes and live with regulations I would chafe at. And, with all the regulations, expenses, and safeguards for society and workers in Europe, it's not a place I'd want to run my small business. But it is a place that challenges me to see how a society can build compassion into its affluence.

*When I shudder at Switzerland's high taxes, Ollie asks, "What's it worth to live in a country with no hunger, no homelessness, and where everyone has access to good health care and a top-quality education?"*

Hiking high in the Alps, I asked my Swiss friend Ollie why they are so docile when it comes to paying high taxes. Without missing a beat, he replied, "What's it worth to live in a country with no hunger, no homelessness, and where everyone has access to good health care and a top-quality education?" While America is embracing the "Texas model" (low tax, low service), Europe believes government can be both big *and* good.

Europe is investing in its infrastructure. And travelers know the results are breathtaking. With the English Channel tunnel, trains speed from Big Ben to the Eiffel Tower in 3 hours. You zip under the English Channel in 17 minutes...looking out the window for fish. More travelers now connect London and Paris by train than by air.

Exciting as the Chunnel is, that's just the tip of the infrastructure iceberg. Norway is drilling the longest tunnels on earth—lacing together its fjord communities by highways. Denmark and Sweden are now connected by a massive bridge. With the opening of that bridge, Malmö and Copenhagen became the biggest metropolis in Scandinavia. And every year it seems new autobahns, tunnels, and bridges lop a couple hours off the time it takes to lace together Europe's great sights by car.

European money is making this happen. The European Union—a vast free-trade zone—is investing in its weakest partners. On my last visit, the roads in Portugal were constantly messing up my itinerary. Every day I'd arrive at my destination hours *before* I thought I would. There are freeways in Portugal now! And just recently, Ireland surpassed England in per capita income...thanks again to EU investments. (For more on the European Union, see below.)

While America (which spends as much as the rest of the world combined on its war machine) is pressuring its European allies to spend more on their militaries, Europeans are sticking stubbornly to their budget priorities—roads, public transportation, health care, education, and social programs.

*Europeans love their fuel-efficient "Smart Cars." Oil-friendly American politicians laugh at them.*

European governments are also progressive on the environment. Entire communities (with government encouragement) are racing to see who will become the first in Europe to be 100 percent wind-powered. London has a "congestion charge" that costs drivers about $15 to enter the city center. This has lessened traffic congestion and enabled buses to get around faster. The money raised subsidizes cheaper public-transit fares and more frequent service.

Public transportation is so good that many Europeans never get around to learning how to drive. They're not making any kind of political or environmental statement. If you live in a city, you simply don't need a car.

Europeans may not have the opportunities to get rich that Americans do. And those with lots of money are highly taxed. But Europeans—who consume about a third of what Americans do—claim they live better. Most Europeans like their system and believe they spend less time working, have less stress, enjoy longer life spans, take longer vacations, and savor more leisurely (and tastier) meals. They experience less violence and enjoy a stronger sense of community.

Through travel, we learn how the world views America. Most of the Europeans I meet who support the American war in Iraq are old enough to remember World War II. They seem to have made a personal pact to forever support America in thanks for our heroic rescue of Europe from Hitler. But the majority of Europeans see American foreign policy as driven by corporate interests, oil, and baffling electoral needs. They believe America's Cuban policy is designed to win the votes of Castro's enemies in Florida, our Israel policy is driven by the demands of Jewish voters, and our passion for democracy in Iraq is actually a thirst for oil.

Twenty years ago, it was the USSR against the world in UN votes.

*These 13-year-old Salvadoran girls, whose parents eke a living from scavenging off a garbage dump, have the same pride and dignity as my teenage daughter.*

Today it's the US. No other nation is routinely outvoted in the United Nations 140 to 4. And Europeans find it amazing that when we lose a vote so thoroughly, we think we (along with our voting bloc: Israel, Micronesia, and the Marshall Islands) have it right and everyone else has it wrong.

Like anyone who loves his country, homeland security is a big issue for me. I like Europe's approach to "homeland security": a well-educated electorate, a healthy environment, and the maintenance of civil liberties. It considers quality housing, nutrition, health care, and education a birthright. It expects a government to work for corporations only by working for people first. And Europeans take a multilateral approach to world problems.

By connecting me with so many people, travel has heightened my concern for people issues. It hasn't given me any easy solutions. But it has shown me that the men running our government have a bigger impact on the lives of the poor overseas that they do on me. And I know that suffering across the sea is as real as suffering across the street. I've learned to treasure—rather than fear—the world's rich diversity. I've learned that people around the world want to like Americans. And I believe that America—with all its power, wisdom, and goodness—can do a better job of making our world a better place.

I will promote thoughtful travel more energetically than ever because of my belief that if Americans had to travel before they could vote, our country would fit more comfortably into this ever-smaller planet.

# 31. UNDERSTANDING THE EUROPEAN UNION

A desire for peace and prosperity is powering some sweeping changes that are taking place in today's Europe. Over the last generation, many European countries have gone from being bitter rivals to member states in one of the world's strongest economies: the European Union. Bringing together such a diverse collection of separate nations—with different languages, cultures, and soccer teams—is almost unprecedented.

Today, the 25-nation European Union includes most of Western Europe (except Switzerland and Norway) and a large part of Eastern Europe. (Two more members, Romania and Bulgaria, are due to join in 2007.) The EU is a free-trade zone with its own currency (the euro, used in about half the member countries). But it's much more than that: The EU is increasingly a political unit that looks, acts, and quacks like a single unified nation-state. While not a "United States of Europe," the EU has an elected Europe-wide Parliament that passes laws on economic policy and some social and foreign policy issues.

As you travel in Europe today, you can't avoid hearing about the EU. Everyone has an opinion. "Eurocrats" and other optimists see it as a bold and idealistic experiment in unity, mutual understanding, and shared priorities. On the other hand, "Euroskeptics" view it as a bloated, overly bureaucratic monster that's threatening to wring the diversity and charm out of the Old World. Here's a snapshot of the EU to help you navigate the many interesting conversations you'll have about it with your new European friends.

## The History of the EU

World War II left 40 million dead and a continent in ruins, and convinced Europeans that they must work together to maintain peace. Wedged between competing superpowers (the US and the USSR), they also needed to cooperate economically to survive in an increasingly global economy. Just after the war ended, visionary Eurocrats began convincing

**US vs. EU—By the Numbers**

| | US | EU |
|---|---|---|
| **Population** | 296 million | 487 million |
| **Land area** | 3.7 million sq. miles | 1.4 million sq. miles |
| **Gross Domestic Product** | $12.4 trillion | $12.3 trillion |
| **Life expectancy** | 77.43 years | 78.1 years |
| **Infant mortality rate** | 6.63 deaths/1,000 | 5.3 deaths/1,000 |
| **Internet users** | 159 million | 206 million |
| **Annual military spending** | $440 billion* | $150 billion |

*Does not include Iraq War

*Statistics from the CIA's* World Factbook, *2006*

reluctant European nations to relinquish elements of their sovereignty and merge into a united body.

The transition towards unity happened very gradually, bit by bit. It started in 1948, when Belgium, the Netherlands, and Luxembourg—jointly called "BeNeLux"—established a free trade zone. Then, in 1951, the former archenemies Germany and France joined with Italy and the BeNeLux countries to form the European Coal and Steel Union. They relaxed trade barriers, shared resources, subsidized private business, and maximized profits. Based on their success, the same group of countries established the European Economic Community (the EEC, also called the "Common Market") in 1957, expanding economic cooperation to include all industries.

Progress came in fits and starts, but over the following 30 years the number of member states in the Common Market doubled. As trade between member countries increased in the 1970s and 1980s, they recognized the need for closer cooperation on currency and money. The result was the establishment of the European Currency Unit (the ECU, precursor to the euro). While the ECU was not a paper currency, it enabled member countries to trade and conduct financial transactions without worrying about currency fluctuations and exchange fees.

In 1992, with the Treaty of Maastricht, the 12 member countries of the Common Market made a leap of faith: They decided to try to create a "European Union" that would have free movement of capital, goods, services, and labor. The by-product would be a common currency, continued removal of trade barriers, introduction of EU passports, and elimination of border checks between member countries. In 2002, most EU members adopted a single currency (the euro), and for all practical purposes economic unity was a reality. Ten new member states joined in 2004, with two more due to join in 2007—creating the world's seventh largest "country" (1.4 million square miles), with the third largest population (487 million), and an economy that rivals the US's as the world's biggest ($12.3 trillion GDP).

## The EU Today

The European Union is governed from Brussels, the unofficial capital of Europe (though some EU institutions meet in Strasbourg, Frankfurt, Luxembourg, and other cities). The EU does not have checks and balances like America's executive/legislative/judicial branches of government. While it does have a Parliament, it is primarily governed by the European Commission (with Commissioners appointed by individual member governments) and the Council of Ministers. Daily business is conducted by an army of bureaucrats and policy wonks.

*The EU headquarters—a vast and shiny complex of skyscrapers in Brussels—welcomes visitors on guided tours to take a peek at Europe at work.*

While there is a movement to streamline EU responses to international conflicts and issues, there's no unified foreign policy among the member countries. The European response to the Balkan wars in the early 1990s and the recent war in Iraq has demonstrated that Europe isn't always prepared to speak with a single voice. Likewise, the EU has no single chief executive with powers similar to America's president—the presidency of the EU rotates every six months among the member countries. And unlike America's federation of 50 states, Europe's member states retain the right to opt out of (but not veto) EU policies. Britain, for example, belongs to the EU but chose not to adopt the euro as its currency. Having many different departments with overlapping responsibilities helps ensure that final decisions are acceptable to most member states.

The EU cannot levy taxes (that's still done through national governments, which then fund the EU), and cannot deploy troops without each nation's approval. For practical purposes, the military and major foreign policy decisions are still largely the domain of individual countries. It's a delicate balance trying to develop laws and policies for all Europeans while respecting the rights of nations, regions, and individuals. An oft-quoted EU slogan is: promoting unity (economic and political) while preserving diversity (cultural).

*As Europe unites, downtrodden peoples are enjoying more autonomy. The Scottish Parliament originated in 1293, was dissolved by England in 1707, and returned in 2000. Their extravagant, and therefore controversial, new Edinburgh digs opened in 2004.*

The scope of the EU grows with each year, as they try to establish standards for taxes, laws, environmental practices, goods, and services. They also coordinate local police and security forces.

The EU is currently financing—with an initial investment of $500 billion—an ambitious 21st-century infrastructure of roads, high-speed trains, high-tech industries, and communication networks. The goal is to create a competitive, sustainable, environmentally friendly economy that improves the quality of life for all Europeans. This involves government and private industry working hand in hand—a kind of "socialism" with a global perspective. Their success so far is making some elements of the more competitive American-style free-market capitalism seem outmoded and short-sighted.

Still, Europe has its problems, and many ordinary Europeans remain skeptical. Some chafe at the overly-regulated business environment and high taxes. They complain about the bureaucracy and worry that their unique national cultures will be swallowed up and Eurofied. But the French and Germans still mix like wine and sauerkraut. Brits still tell insulting jokes about Italians, and vice versa. Nations still duke it out for world domination... on the soccer field. And while the EU's economy is

*New roads (like this one, in Ireland) are bringing the infrastructure in Europe up to speed. These EU-funded projects come with a billboard and EU flag reminding locals where the funding came from.*

booming and the euro is strong, high prices make the Continent's famed *dolce vita* more expensive than ever for ordinary Europeans—as well as for American travelers.

But despite the problems facing Europe, virtually no one wants to go back to the way it used to be; most recognize that a strong and unified Europe is necessary to compete in a global economy.

The next step for the EU is further expansion: After Romania and Bulgaria join, Croatia and Turkey are next in line to become members. Most Eastern European members will adopt the euro by 2010. And current member states are debating and trying to ratify a European Constitution. If successful, the constitution will make Europe more unified and powerful than ever.

*Europe is enthusiastic about civil rights. Catalans celebrate a double dose of liberty with this statue at Cadaqués, the hometown of Salvador Dalí.*

## Highlights of Europe

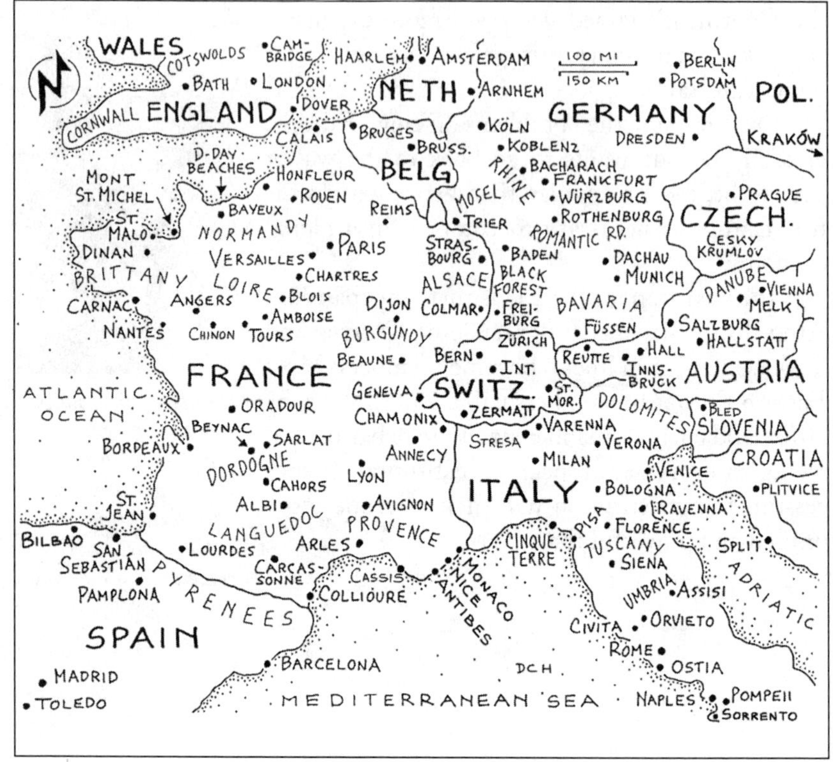

# PART TWO
# BACK DOORS

*Europe, here you come!*

# CONTENTS

## Europe's Back Doors

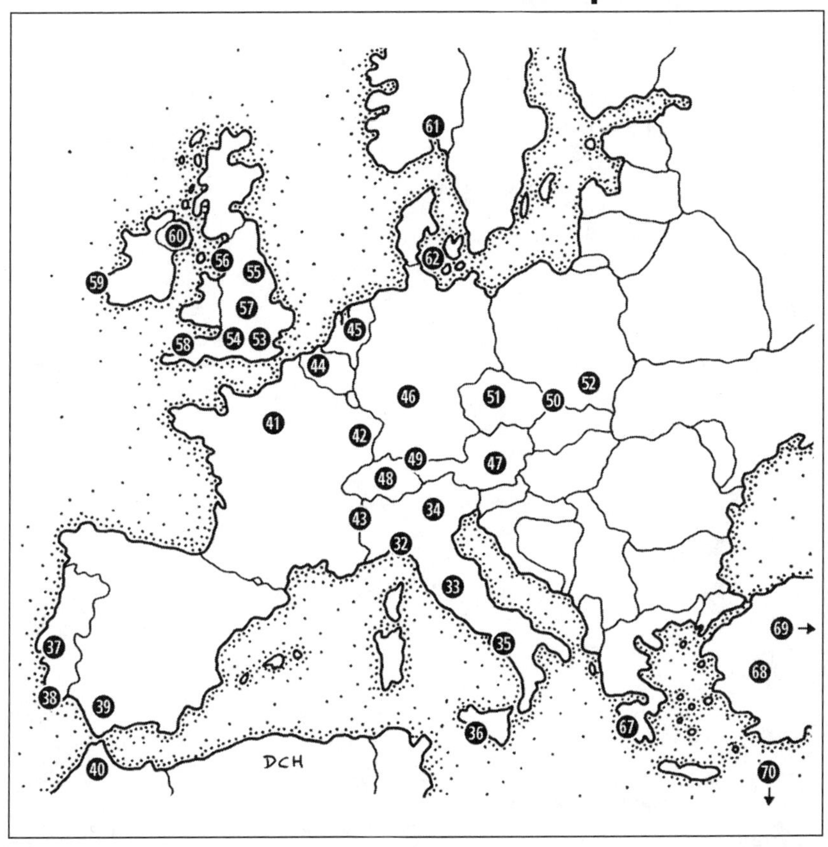

# What Is a Back Door, and How Can I Find One of My Own?

The travel skills covered in the first half of this book enable you to open doors most travelers don't even know exist. Now I'd like you to meet my "Back Doors." I'm the matchmaker, and you and the travel bug are about to get intimate. By traveling vicariously with me through these chapters, you'll get a peek at my favorite places. And, just as important, by internalizing this lifetime of magic travel moments, you'll develop a knack for finding your own.

Europe is a bubbling multicultural fondue. A Back Door is a steaming forkful. It could be an all-day walk on an alpine ridge, a sword-fern fantasy in a ruined castle, or a friendly swing with a bell-ringer in a church spire. You could jam your camera with Turkish delights or uncover the village warmth hiding in a cold metropolis. By learning where to jab your fork, you'll put together a travel feast that exceeds your wildest dreams.

Some of my Back Doors are undiscovered towns that have, for various reasons, missed the modern parade. With no promotional budgets to attract travelers, they're ignored as they quietly make their traditional way through just another century. Many of these places won't hit you with their cultural razzle-dazzle. Their charms are too subtle to be enjoyed by the tour-bus crowd. But, learning from the experiences described in the last half of this book, Back Door travelers make their own fun.

We'll also explore natural nooks and undeveloped crannies. These are rare opportunities to enjoy Europe's sun, beaches, mountains, and natural wonders, without the glitz. While Europeans love nature and are fanatic sun worshippers, they have an impressive knack for enjoying themselves in hellish crowds. Our goal is to experience Europe's quiet alternatives: lonesome stone circles, desolate castles, breezy bike rides, and snippets of the Riviera not snapped up by entrepreneurs.

With a Back Door angle on a big city, you can slip your fingers under its staged culture and actually find a pulse. Even London has a warm underbelly, where you'll rumble with a heart that's been beating for 2,000 years.

And finally, to squeeze the most travel experience out of every mile, minute, and dollar, look beyond Europe. Europe is exciting, but a dip into Turkey, Morocco, or Egypt is well worth the diarrhea.

The promotion of a tender place that has so far avoided the tourist industry reminds me of the whaler who screams, "Quick, harpoon it before it's extinct!" These places are this Europhile's cupids. Publicizing them gnaws at what makes them so great. But what kind of a travel writer can keep his favorite discoveries under wraps? Great finds are too hard to come by to just sit on. I keep no secrets.

With ever-more-sophisticated travelers armed with ever-better guidebooks, places I "discovered" 10 or 15 years ago are undeveloped and uncommercial only in a relative sense. And certain places that I really rave about suffer from Back Door congestion. Every year or so, I revisit my poster-child village discoveries (Gimmelwald, An Daingean/Dingle, Ærø, Salema, and the Cinque Terre) and, while more crowded now, they are still great. At least from my experience, Back Door readers are pleasant people to share Europe with.

People recommended in this book tell me that Back Door readers are good guests who undo the "ugly" image created by the more demanding and ethnocentric American tourists. By traveling sensitively, you're doing a favor for yourself, as well as for the Europeans you'll meet, travelers who'll follow...and me. Thank you.

These Back Doors combine to give you a chorus line of travel thrills. I've written these chapters to give you the flavor of the place, not for you to navigate by. For a handy list of hotels at these destinations, visit my Web site at www.ricksteves.com/update. Better yet, my various country guidebooks provide you with all the details necessary to splice your chosen Back Doors into a smooth trip. *Bon voyage!*

# ITALY

## 32. THE CINQUE TERRE: ITALY'S FIAT-FREE RIVIERA

"A sleepy, romantic, and inexpensive town on the Riviera without a tourist in sight." That's the mirage travelers chase around busy Nice and Cannes. Pssst! The most dream-worthy stretch of the Riviera sleeps in Italy just across the border, between Genoa and Pisa. It's Italy's Cinque Terre.

Leaving the nearest big city, La Spezia, your train takes you into a mountain. Ten minutes later, you burst into the sunlight. Your train nips in and out of the hills, teasing you with a series of Mediterranean views. Each scene is grander than the last: azure blue tinseled in sunbeams, carbonated waves hitting desolate rocks, and the occasional topless human camped out like a lone limpet.

The Cinque Terre (pronounced CHINK-weh TAY-reh), which means "five lands," is five villages clinging to this most inaccessible bit of Riviera coastline. Each is a variation on the same theme: a well-whittled pastel jumble of homes filling a gully like crusty sea creatures in a tide pool. Like a gangly clump of oysters, the houses grow on each other. Locals are the barnacles—hungry, but patient. And we travelers are like algae, coming in with the tide.

The rugged villages of the Cinque Terre, founded by Dark Age locals hiding out from marauding pirates, were long cut off from the modern world. Only with the coming of the train was access made easy. Today, the villages draw hordes of hikers and the castles protect only glorious views. To preserve this land, the government has declared the Cinque Terre a national park. Visitors now pay a small entrance fee (of a few

**The Cinque Terre's Five Towns**

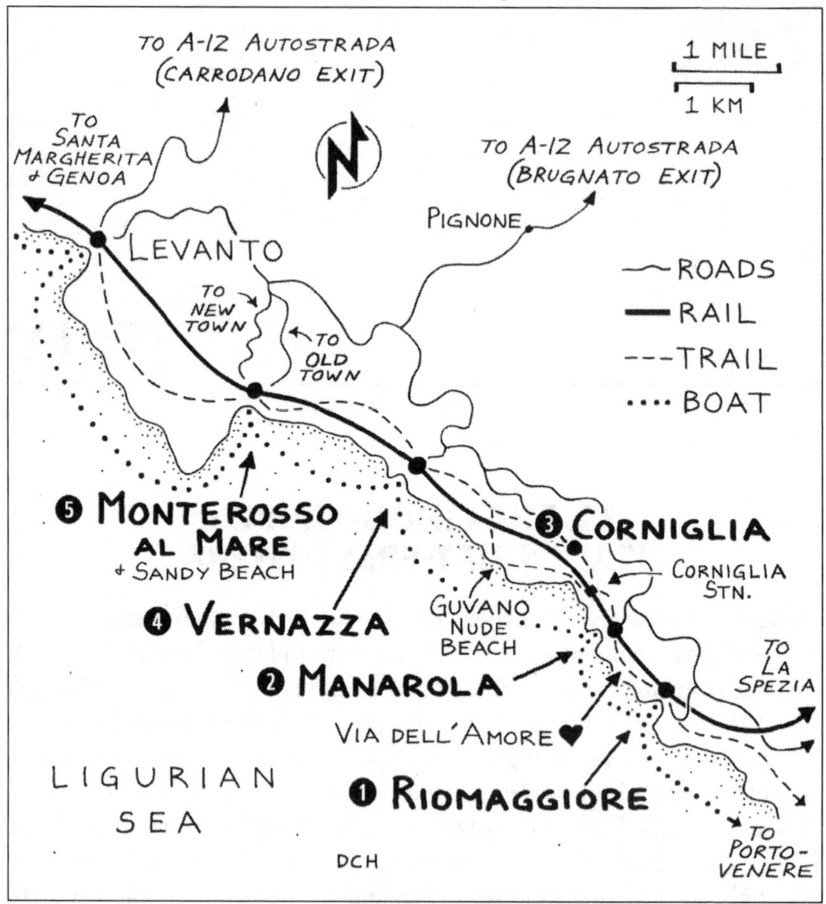


dollars), which stokes a fund designed to protect the flora and fauna and keep the trails clean and well-maintained.

The government, recognizing how wonderfully preserved these towns are, has long prohibited anyone from building any modern buildings. For that reason, today there are no big, comfortable hotels in the area—great news for Back Door travelers because it keeps away the most obnoxious slice of the traveling public: those who need big, comfortable hotels. But rugged travelers, content to rent a room in a private home or simple *pensione,* enjoy a land where the villagers have almost no choice but to go about their business as if the surrounding vineyards are the very edges of the earth.

*Vernazza, my home base in the Cinque Terre*

## Vernazza

Overseen by a ruined castle, with the closest thing to a natural harbor, Vernazza is my Cinque Terre home base. Only the occasional noisy slurping up of the train by the mountain reminds you there's a modern world out there somewhere.

From Vernazza's harbor, wander through the jumble of a tough community living off the sea...or living off travelers who love the sea. The church bells dictate a relaxed tempo. Yellow webs of fishing nets, tables bedecked with umbrellas, kids with plastic shovels, and a flotilla of gritty little boats tethered to buoys provide splashes of color. And accompanying the scene is the soundtrack of a dream...a celebrate-the-moment white noise of children, dogs, and waves.

Vernazza's one street connects the harbor with the train station before melting into the vineyards. Like veins on a grape leaf, paths and stairways reach from Main Street into this watercolor huddle of houses. All of life is summer reruns in this hive of lazy human activity. A rainbow of laundry flaps as if to keep the flies off the fat grandmothers who clog ancient doorways.

Locals spend early evenings doing their *vasca* (laps), strolling between the station and the breakwater. Sit on a bench and study this slow-motion parade.

Sailors who suckle at salty taverns brag that while Portofino sold out, "Vernazza is locally owned." Years ago, fearing the change it would bring, they stopped the construction of a major road into the town and region.

Today, at the top end of town, Vernazza's cruel little road hits a post. No cars enter this village of 600 people. Like the breakwater keeps out the waves at the bottom of the town, the post keeps out the modern storm at the top. But Vernazza's ruined castle no longer says "stay away." And

### Vernazza: View from a Vineyard

It's a sunny afternoon a thousand years ago in the Cinque Terre, long before it became the Italian Riviera. This string of humble villages, surrounded by terraced vineyards, is a two-day sail from Genoa.

The leathery old farmer, taking a break from tending his grape vines, picks a cactus fruit to quench his thirst. Suddenly, howls come from the crude, stony tower crowning a bluff that marks his village of Vernazza. Turkish pirates are attacking.

Avoiding powerhouse cities like nearby Genoa and Pisa, pirates delight in the villages. These Cinque Terre towns, famous since Roman times for their white wine, are like snack time for rampaging pirates. Villagers run for cover down corridors buried deep in the clutter of homes that clog Vernazza's ravine.

Nine centuries pass. Another leathery grape-picker is startled by the roar of a smoke-billowing train. Emerging from the newly built tunnel, it flies a red, white, and green flag. It's 1870, and the feudal and fragmented land of Italy is finally united. This first Italian train line, an engineering triumph of fledgling Italy, laces together Turin, Genoa, Rome...and, by chance, tiny Vernazza.

Decades later, in the 1930s, an Italian dictator teams up with a German tyrant. The war they started is going badly. In 1943, the German Führer calls on Vernazza's teenage boys to report for duty. The boys, who are told they'll only work in German farms and factories, know they'll end up as fodder on the front. Rather than dying for Hitler, they become resistance fighters. Running through the night, they climb the ancient terraces into the hills high above the village cemetery.

The 1970s bring on a different battle scene. Hippies exercise their right to lie naked on the Cinque Terre's remote Guvano beach. Outraged, an angry armada of villagers—fully clothed and accompanied by a raft of reporters—converge on the rat pack of sunburned urbanite hedonists.

its breakwater—a broad, inviting sidewalk edged with seaside boulders—sticks into the sea like a finger beckoning the distant excursion boats.

## The Five-Village Cinque Terre Hike

Follow the fragrant trail through sunny vistas from Riomaggiore to Monterosso al Mare. Since my mind goes on vacation with the rest of me when I'm here, I think of the towns by number for easy orientation. They go—east to west—from one (Riomaggiore) to five (Monterosso).

Next, the age of tourism arrives. In 1978, a college-aged American backpacker, stumbling onto the region, finds the traditions vivid, the wine cheap, and the welcome warm. Inspired by the Cinque Terre and similar places throughout the Continent, he declares the region a "Back Door" and writes what will become a top-selling guidebook on Europe.

By the 1990s, word of this paradise is out. More and more travelers visit, staying in local apartments rather than in hotels. One day, at the crack of dawn, another invasion comes...this time by land. A platoon of Italian tax inspectors blitzes the sleepy town, rousting out the tourists and cornering locals renting unlicensed rooms. B&B income in Vernazza is suddenly no longer tax-free.

Today, gnarled old men still tend their grapevines. Now Vernazza's castle, named "Belforte" centuries ago for the screams of its watchmen, watches over tourists. And the screams ringing out are of delight from children playing on the beach below.

But the local economy has changed. The poor village is now a rich village, living well in its rustic and government-protected shell. Tourism drives the economy as the less-calloused locals feed and house travelers. While the private rooms rented are basic, the cuisine—super-charged by a passion for pasta, pesto, and seafood—is some of Italy's best. The sunny scene is a happy collaboration between locals, travelers, a long past, a lazy present...and no thought of tomorrow.

For a great day, catch the early train to Riomaggiore, hike from towns one through four, and catch the boat from Vernazza to the resort town of Monterosso for some beach time. From there, a five-minute train ride takes you home to Vernazza for the sunset and a seafood dinner.

The first town of the Cinque Terre, Riomaggiore (#1), has seduced famed artists into becoming residents. The biggest non-resort town of the five, Riomaggiore is a disappointment from the station. But the tunnel next to the train tracks takes you to a fascinating tangle of colorful homes leaning on each other as if someone stole their crutches. There's homemade gelato at Bar Central. And Riomaggiore's beach, an uncrowded cove, is a two-minute walk from town.

From Riomaggiore, the Via dell'Amore (walkway of love) leads to Manarola (#2). This photogenic 15-minute promenade is wide enough for baby strollers. While you'll find no beach here, stairways lead to remote rocks for sunbathing. Uppity little Manarola rules its ravine and drinks its wine while its sun-bleached walls slumber on. Buy a picnic before walking to the beaches of Corniglia.

Corniglia (#3)—the only Cinque Terre town not directly on the water—sits smugly on its hilltop, a proud and victorious king of the mountain. Most visitors—lured to Corniglia by its scrawny, stony beach and the Cinque Terre's best swimming—never tackle the 370 stairs that zigzag up to the actual town. Those who make the Corniglian climb are rewarded by the Cinque Terre's finest wine and most staggering view. Corniglia has cooler temperatures, a windy belvedere, a few restaurants, and more than enough private rooms for rent.

The village was originally settled by a Roman farmer who named it for his mother, Cornelia. Since ancient times, when Corniglian wine was so famous that vases found at Pompeii touted its virtues, wine has been this town's lifeblood. Follow the pungent smell of ripe grapes into an alley cellar and get a local to let you dip a straw into her keg.

Just out of Corniglia on the high trail to Vernazza, you'll see the well-hung Guvano beach far below. This nude beach made headlines in Italy in the 1970s, as clothed locals in a makeshift armada of dinghies and fishing boats retook their town beach. But big-city nudists still work on all-around tans in this remote setting.

The crowd is Italian counterculture: pierced nipples, tattooed punks, hippie drummers in dreads, and nude exhibitionist men. The ratio of men to women is about three to two. About half the people on the pebbly beach keep their swimsuits on.

A steep trail leads to Guvano from the Corniglia–Vernazza trail. Or, from the Corniglia train station (below the tracks), an old, unused train tunnel provides access to the beach. Buzz the intercom and the hydraulic *Get Smart*–type door opens. After a spooky, cool, and moist 15-minute hike, you pop out at the beach—and get charged $6.

The 90-minute hike from Corniglia (#3) to Vernazza (#4) is the wildest and greenest of the coast. The trail is as rugged as the people who've worked the terraced vineyards that blanket the region. Flowers and an ever-changing view entertain you at every step. As you make your sweaty way high above the glistening beaches, you'll ponder paying for your trip with the photos you've shot. The trail descends scenically into Vernazza, from where you can take the train, the boat, or a hike to town #5.

Monterosso al Mare (#5), happy to be appreciated, boasts the area's only sandy beach. This is a resort with cars, hotels, paddleboats, and crowds under rentable beach umbrellas. Adventurers in search of no-tan-line coves, refreshing waterfalls, and natural (and dangerous) high dives find them tucked away along the coast between towns #4 and #5.

Regardless of which town you call home, getting around is easy. While these towns are barely accessible by car, the nearly hourly milk-run train connects all five towns for about $1.50. A ferry provides a more relaxed and scenic town-hopping option.

Traditions ring through the Cinque Terre as persistently as the church bells—which remind locals of the days before tourism. The fishermen out at sea could hear the bells. The men in the vineyards high on the mountain could hear them, too. In one village, the hotel keepers tried to stop the bells for the tourists who couldn't sleep. But the people of the village nearly revolted, and the bells ring on.

You'll eat well in the Cinque Terre. This is the home of pesto. Basil—which loves the region's temperate climate—is mixed with cheese (half parmigiano cow cheese and half pecorino sheep cheese), garlic, olive oil, and pine nuts, then poured over pasta. If you become addicted, small jars of pesto are sold in the local grocery stores.

And the *vino delle Cinque Terre,* famous throughout Italy, flows cheap and easy throughout the region. If you like sweet, sherrylike wine, try the local Sciacchetrà wine—served with a cookie. While 10 kilos of grapes yield seven liters of local wine, 10 kilos of grapes make only 1.5 liters of Sciacchetrà, which is made from near-raisins. If your room is up a lot of steps, be warned: Sciacchetrà comes with 50 percent more alcohol than regular wine.

In the cool, calm early evening, sit on the Vernazza breakwater nursing a glass of wine. Paint a dream in vineyard greens and Mediterranean blues. Nowhere else does the lure of the Mediterranean, Italy, and village life combine so potently to shipwreck a speedy itinerary.

*For good-value accommodations in Vernazza, try Trattoria Gianni (sea views, near castle, Piazza Marconi 5, tel. 0187-821-003, tel. & fax 0187-812-228, www.giannifranzi.it) or Albergo Barbara (sea views, on harbor square, Piazza Marconi 30, tel. & fax 0187-812-398, mobile 338-793-3261, www.albergobarbara.it). For more hotels, visit www.ricksteves.com/update, and for all the travel specifics, see this year's edition of* Rick Steves' Italy.

## 33. HILL TOWNS OF CENTRAL ITALY

Too many people connect Venice, Florence, and Rome with straight lines. Break out of this syndrome, and you'll lick a little Italy that the splash of Venice, the finesse of Florence, and the grandeur of Rome were built upon.

The hill towns of central Italy hold their crumbling heads proudly above the noisy flood of the 21st century and offer a peaceful taste of what eludes so many tourists. Sitting on a timeless rampart high above the traffic and trains, hearing only children in the market as the rustling wind ages the weary red-tile patchwork that surrounds me, I find the essence of Italy.

There are a dozen great touristy towns and countless ignored communities casually doing time and drinking wine. See some of each.

### The Big-Name Hill Towns

**Siena,** unlike its rival, Florence, is a city to be seen as a whole rather than as a collection of sights. While memories of Florence consist of dodging Vespas and pickpockets between museums, Siena has an easy-to-enjoy Gothic soul: Courtyards sport flower-decked wells, churches modestly hoard their art, and alleys dead-end into red-tiled rooftop panoramas. Climb to the dizzy top of the 100-yard-tall bell tower and reign over urban harmony at its best. At twilight, first-time poets savor that magic moment when the sky is a rich blue dome no brighter than the medieval towers that seem to hold it high.

*Siena turns tourists into poets.*

Il Campo, Siena's great central piazza, with its gently tilted floor fanning out from the city hall tower, is like a people-friendly stage set. It offers the perfect invitation to loiter. Think of it as a trip to the beach without sand or water. Wander among lovers stroking guitars and each others' hair. Il Campo immerses you in a troubadour's world where bellies become pillows. For a picnic dessert on the Campo, try *panforte,* Siena's claim to caloric fame. This

## Hill Towns of Central Italy

rich, chewy concoction of nuts, honey, and candied fruits impresses even fruitcake-haters.

The *panforte* of medieval churches is Siena's cathedral. Its striped facade is piled with statues and ornamentation. And the chewy interior, decorated from top to bottom, comes with the heads of 172 popes peering down from the ceiling over the fine inlaid art on the floor. This is as Baroque as Gothic gets.

For those who dream of a city with a traffic-free core, Siena is it. Take time to savor the first European square to go pedestrian (1966), and then, just to be silly, wonder what would happen if they did it in your town.

**Assisi,** a worthy hometown for St. Francis, is battling a commercial cancer of tourist clutter. In summer, the town bursts with flash-in-the-pan St. Francis fans and monastic knickknacks. But those able to see past the tacky monk mementos can actually have a "travel on purpose" experience.

*A perch of Franciscan splendor, overlooking Assisi*

In the early 1200s, a simple friar from Assisi challenged the decadence of church government and society in general with a powerful message of simplicity, non-materialism, service to the community, and a "slow down and smell God's roses" lifestyle. Like Jesus, Francis taught by example. A huge monastic order grew out of his teachings, which were gradually embraced by the church. In 1939, Italy made Francis its patron saint.

The Basilica of St. Francis, built upon his grave, is one of the artistic highlights of medieval Europe. Open again, restored, and safe after being damaged by the earthquakes of 1997, it's covered with precious frescoes by Giotto, Cimabue, Simone Martini, and other leading artists of the day.

With a quiet hour in the awesome basilica, some reflective reading (there's a great bookstore on the main square), and a meditative stroll through the back streets, you can dissolve the tour buses and melt into the magic of Assisi. Grab a picnic and hike to the ruined castle, surrounded by the same Tuscan views and serenaded by the same birdsong Francis enjoyed.

Most visitors are day-trippers. Assisi after dark is closer to a place Francis could call home.

*So often photography—and a little wine—bring out the warmth in Italian women.*

**San Gimignano** bristles with towers and bustles with tourists. A thrilling silhouette from a distance, Italy's best-preserved medieval skyline gets better as you approach. With 14 towers still standing (out of an original 72!), it's a fun and easy stop. In the 13th century, back in the days of Romeo and Juliet, towns were run by feuding noble families who would periodically battle things out from the protective bases of their respective family towers. Sunset's the right time to conquer San Gimignano's castle. Climb high above the crowds, sit on the castle's summit, and imagine the battles Tuscany's porcupine has endured.

**Orvieto,** the tourist's token hill town, sits majestically on its tufa throne, offering those on the train or *autostrada* to Rome its impressive hill-capping profile. Its cathedral, with some fascinating Signorelli frescoes, is surrounded by an excellent tourist information office, a fine Etruscan museum, a world-class gelato shop, and Italy's most un-Italian public toilets. With three popular gimmicks (ceramics, cathedral, and Classico wine), Orvieto is loaded with tourists by day and quiet by night. Drinking a shot of wine in a ceramic cup as you gaze up at the cathedral lets you experience the essence of Orvieto all at once. Buses go regularly from Orvieto to the queen of hill towns, Civita di Bagnoregio.

## Civita di Bagnoregio

Of all the Italian hill towns, Civita di Bagnoregio is my favorite. Less known than the famous hill towns mentioned above, it deserves more description.

People who've been here say "Civita" (chee-VEE-tah) with warmth and love. This precious chip of Italy, a traffic-free community with a grow-it-in-the-valley economy, has so far escaped the ravages of modernity. Please approach it with the same respect and sensitivity you would a dying relative, because—in a sense—that's Civita.

Civita teeters atop a pinnacle in a vast canyon ruled by wind and erosion. But, while its population has dropped to 15, the town survives (and even has a Web site: www.civitadibagnoregio.it).

*The perfect hill town, Civita di Bagnoregio*

## Civita di Bagnoregio

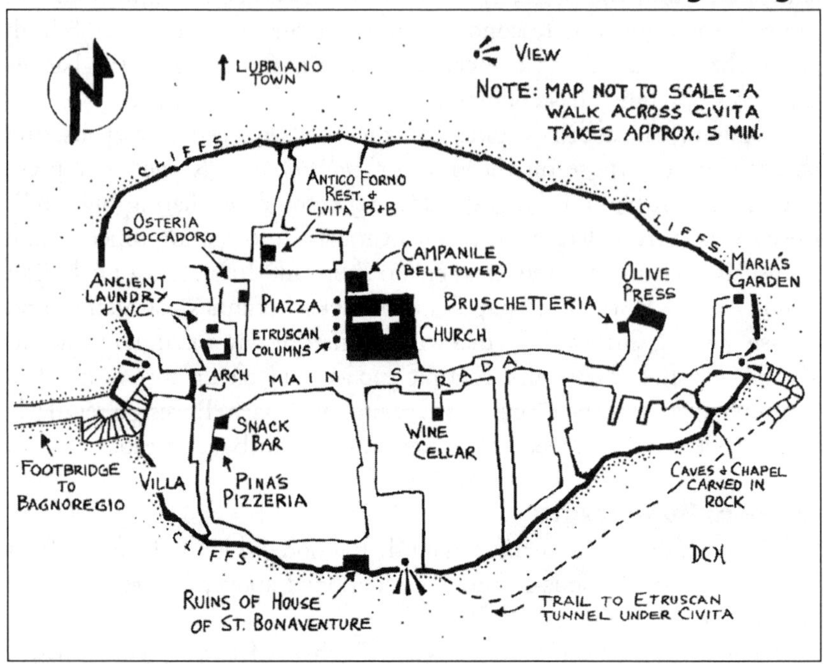


The saddle that once connected Civita to its bigger and busier sister town, Bagnoregio, eroded away. Today a bridge connects the two towns. A man with a Vespa does the same work his father did with a donkey—ferrying the town's goods up and down the umbilical bridge that connects Civita with a small, distant parking lot and the rest of Italy. Rome, just 60 miles to the south, is a world away.

Entering the town through a cut in the rock made by Etruscans 2,500 years ago, and heading under a 12th-century Romanesque arch, you feel history in the huge, smooth cobblestones. This was once the main Etruscan road leading to the Tiber Valley and Rome.

Inside the gate, the charms of Civita are subtle. Those searching for arcade tourism wouldn't know where to look. There are no lists of attractions, orientation tours, or museum hours. It's just Italy. Civita is an artist's dream, a town in the nude. Each lane and footpath holds a surprise. The warm stone walls glow, and each stairway is dessert to a sketch pad or camera.

Sit in the piazza. Smile and nod at each local who passes by. It's a social jigsaw puzzle, and each person fits. The old woman hanging out in the window monitors gossip. A tiny hunchback lady is everyone's daughter. And cats, the fastest-growing segment of the population, scratch their itches on ancient pillars.

Civita's young people are gone, lured away by the dazzle of today to grab their place in Italy's cosmopolitan parade. And as old people become frail, they move into apartments in nearby Bagnoregio.

Today, Civita's social pie has two slices: the aging, full-time residents; and rich, big-city Italians who are slowly buying up the place for their country escape (the Ferrari family owns the house next to the town gate—and Civita's only Jacuzzi). Buoyed by my writing and recent exposure in German and French travel magazines, Civita can see up to 200 tourists a day on summer weekends. In summer, visit on a weekday.

Explore the village. The basic grid street plan of the ancient town survives—but its centerpiece, a holy place of worship, rotates with the cultures: first an Etruscan temple, then a Roman temple, and today a church. The pillars that stand like bar stools in the square once decorated the pre-Christian temple.

Step into the church. The heartbeat and pride of the village, this is where festivals and processions start, visitors are escorted, and the town's past is honored. Enjoy paintings by students of famous artists; relics of the hometown-boy Saint Bonaventure; a dried floral decoration spread across the floor; and a cool, quiet moment in a pew.

Just around the corner from the church, on the main street, is Rossana and Antonio's cool and friendly wine cellar. Pull up a stump and let them or their children, Arianna and Antonella, serve you *panini* (sandwiches), *bruschetta* (garlic toast with tomato), wine, and a local cake called *ciambella*. The white wine has a taste reminiscent of dirty socks. But it's made right here. Climb down into their cellar. Note the traditional wine-making gear and the provisions for rolling huge kegs up the stairs. Grab the stick and thunk on the kegs to measure their fullness.

The ground below Civita is honeycombed with ancient cellars (for keeping wine at the same temperature all year) and cisterns (for collecting rainwater, since there was no well in town). Many of these date from Etruscan times.

Explore further through town, but remember nothing is abandoned. Everything is still privately owned. Vittoria, numb to her eye-boggling view of the valley, shows off the latest in a 2,000-year line of olive presses that have filled her ancient Etruscan cave. Buy a postcard in Italian.

On weekends, Vittoria's sons Sandro, Maurizio, and Felice, and her grandson Fabrizio, run the local equivalent of a lemonade stand, selling *bruschetta* to visitors. Bread toasted on an open fire, drizzled with the finest oil, rubbed with pungent garlic, and topped with chopped tomatoes—these edible souvenirs stay on your breath for hours and in your memory forever.

Further down, Maria introduces you to a baby donkey as if it were her child and then shows you through her garden with a grand view (small donation accepted).

At the end of town, the main drag shrivels into a trail that leads past a chapel (once a jail) and down to a tunnel that has cut through the hill under the town since Etruscan times. It was widened in the 1930s so farmers could get between their scattered fields more easily.

Civita has only a few restaurants, which cluster near the piazza. At Trattoria Antico Forno ("Antique Oven"), you eat what's cooking. Owner Franco slices and dices happily through the day. Spaghetti, salad, and wine on the Antico Forno patio, cuddled by Civita—I wouldn't trade it for all-you-can-eat at Maxim's.

Spend the evening. After dinner, sit on the church steps with people who've done exactly that for 60 years. Children play on the piazza until midnight. As you walk back to your car—that scourge of the modern world that enabled you to get here—stop under a lamp on the donkey path, listen to the canyon...distant voices...fortissimo crickets.

Towering above its moat, Civita seems to be fortified against change. But the modern world is a persistent battering ram. Civita will be great for years, but never as great as today.

## Virgin Hill Towns

Italy is spiked with similar hill towns. Gubbio, Todi, Volterra, and Arezzo are discovered but rarely visited. Cortona (with its fine youth hostel), Pienza (a Renaissance-planned town), and Montepulciano (with its dramatic setting) are touristy but also worth the hill-town lover's energy and time.

Any guidebook lists popular hill towns. But if you want to dance at noon with a toothless lady while your pizza cooks, press a good-luck coin into the moldy ceiling of an Etruscan wine cellar, or be introduced to a mediocre altar piece as proudly as if it were a Michelangelo, then stow your guidebook, buy the best local map you can find, and explore.

Many bigger hill towns have a train station nearby (with a shuttle bus beginning its winding climb to the old town center shortly after your train arrives). But to find your own gem, you'll need to leave the train lines. Take the bus, hitch, or rent a car for a few days. If you're using a rail-and-drive pass, this is car country.

Hill towns, like the Greek Islands, come in two basic varieties: discovered...and virgin. The difference, touristically speaking, is that "discovered" towns know what tourism is and have an appetite for the money that comes with it. "Virgin" towns are simply pleased you dropped in.

Sorano, Pitigliano, Poppi, Trevi, and Bagnaia (near Viterbo) have almost no tourism. Bevagna (near Assisi) is as dazed as its town fool, who stands between the twin dark Romanesque churches on its main square.

Perfect Back Door villages, like hidden pharaohs' tombs, are worth uncovering. Photographers delight in hill towns. Their pictorial collections (such as *Italian Hilltowns,* by Norman F. Carver) are a fine source of information. Study these, circling the most intriguing towns on your map. Talk to travelers who have studied or lived in Italy. Ask locals for their favorites. Scan the horizon for fortified towers. Drive down dead-end roads far from the nearest promotional budget.

Hill towns are a vital slice of the Italian pizza—crumbly crust with a thick, gooey culture. Don't just chase down my favorites or your guidebook's recommendations. Somewhere in the slumber of Umbria and the texture of Tuscany, the ultimate hill town awaits your discovery.

*For good-value accommodations in Siena, try Alma Domus (convent-run hotel, request view room, Via Camporegio 37, tel. 0577-44177, fax 0577-47601); in Assisi, Hotel Ideale (Piazza Matteotti 1, tel. 075-813-570, fax 075-813-020, www.hotelideale.it, info@hotelideale.it); and in Orvieto, Hotel Corso (Via Cavour 343, tel. & fax 0763-342-020, www.hotelcorso.net). In Civita, try Franco Sala's Civita B&B (rooms on town square, tel. 0761-760-016, mobile 347-611-5426, www.civitadibagnoregio.it, fsala@pelagus.it); or, in nearby Bagnoregio, Romantica Pucci B&B (Piazza Cavour 1, tel. 0761-792-121, www.hotelromanticapucci.it, hotelromanticapucci@libero.it). For more hotels, visit www.ricksteves.com/update, and for all the travel specifics, see this year's edition of* Rick Steves' Italy.

## 34. NORTH ITALY CHOICES: MILAN, LAKES, OR MOUNTAINS

Italy intensifies as you plunge deeper. If you like it as far south as Rome, go farther—it gets better. But if Italy's wearing you down, you'll enjoy a milder Italy in the north, complete with the same great cappuccino, gelato, and people-watching you need.

North Italy's charms come in three packages: urban Milan, romantic lakes, and alpine Dolomites. All are within three hours of Venice, Florence, and each other.

## Milan

Milan is today's Italy. The economic success of modern Italy (which now has a higher per-capita income than Britain) can be blamed on cities like Milan. As the saying goes, for every church in Rome, there's a bank in Milan. Italy's second city has a hardworking, fashion-conscious population of more than 1.3 million. From publicists to pasta power lunches, Milan is Italy's industrial, banking, TV, publishing, and convention capital.

Much of Milan is ugly, with a recently bombed-out feeling (World War II). Its huge financial buildings are as manicured as its parks are shaggy. As if to make up for its harsh concrete shell, its people and windows are works of art. Milan is an international fashion capital. Cigarettes are still chic, and even the cheese is gift-wrapped.

Milan's cathedral, the city's centerpiece, is the fourth-largest church in Europe. At 480 feet long and 280 feet wide, forested with 52 sequoia-sized pillars and more than 2,000 statues, the place can seat 10,000 worshippers. Hike up to the rooftop—a fancy crown of spires—for great views of the city, the square, and, on clear days, the Swiss Alps.

*Milan's cathedral dominates the main square.*

The cathedral square, Piazza Duomo, is a classic European scene. Professionals scurry, label-conscious kids loiter, and young thieves peruse. Facing the square, the Galleria Vittorio Emanuele, Milan's great four-story-high, glass-domed arcade, invites you in to shop or just sip a slow latte. Some of Europe's hottest people-watching turns that pricey cup into a good value. Enjoy the parade. For good luck, locals step on the testicles of the Taurus in the floor's zodiac mosaic. Two local girls explained that it's even better if you twirl.

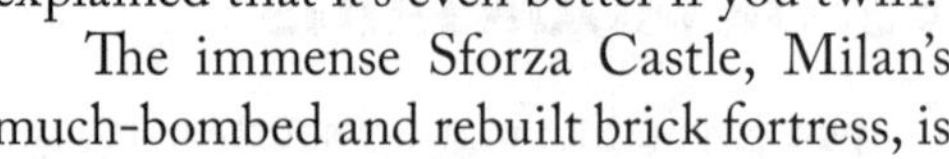

The immense Sforza Castle, Milan's much-bombed and rebuilt brick fortress, is overwhelming at first sight. But its courtyard has a great lawn for picnics and siestas. Its museum features interesting medieval armor, furniture, Lombard art, and a Michelangelo statue with no crowds—his unfinished *Rondanini Pietà*. The Brera Art Gallery, Milan's top collection of paintings, is world-class (although you'll see better in Rome and Florence).

La Scala is possibly the world's most prestigious opera house. Opera

## Northern Italy: Milan, Lakes, and Mountains

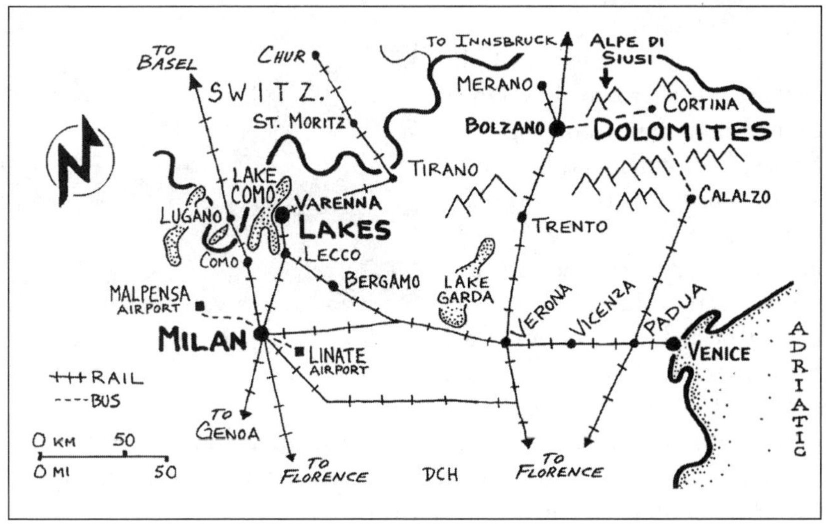


buffs will love the museum's extensive collection of things that would mean absolutely nothing to the MTV crowd: Verdi's top hat, Rossini's eyeglasses, Toscanini's baton, Fettucini's pesto, and the original scores, busts, portraits, and death masks of great composers and musicians.

Leonardo's ill-fated *Last Supper* is flecking off the refectory wall of the church of Santa Maria delle Grazie. The fresco suffers from Leonardo's experimental use of oil. Decay began within six years of its completion. It's undergone more restoration work than Cher and is now viewable only with a reservation (call 02-8942-1146 in Italy, or, from the US, dial 011-39-02-8942-1146; the number is often busy, keep trying; book at least a month ahead). Most of the original paint is gone, but tourists still enjoy paying $10 to see what's left.

More of Leonardo's spirit survives in Italy's answer to the Smithsonian, the National Leonardo da Vinci Science and Technology Museum. While most tourists visit for the hall of Leonardo's designs illustrated in wooden models, the rest of this vast collection of industrial cleverness is just as fascinating. Plenty of push-button action displays the development of trains, radios, old musical instruments, computers, batteries, and telephones, alongside chunks of the first transatlantic cable.

### Italy's Lakes

The Italian Lakes, at the base of Italy's Alps, are a romantic and popular destination for Italians and their European neighbors. The million-euro question is: "Which lake?" For a complete dose of Italian-lakes wonder and aristocratic old-days romance, visit Lake Como.

*On Lake Como, ferries hop from town to town.*

Lined with elegant 19th-century villas, crowned by snow-capped mountains, buzzing with ferries, hydrofoils, and little passenger ships, this is a good place to take a break from the intensity and obligatory turnstile culture of central Italy. Handy, accessible, and offbeat, Lake Como is Italy for beginners. It seems that half the travelers you'll meet on Lago di Como have tossed their itineraries overboard and are actually relaxing. The area's isolation and flat economy have left it pretty much the way the 19th-century romantic poets described it.

While you can circle the lake by car, the road is narrow, congested, and lined by privacy-seeking walls, hedges, and tall fences. This is train-and-boat country. Trains whisk you from intense Milan into the serenity of Lago di Como in an hour. Then, happy-go-lucky ferries sail scenically from port to port.

The town of Bellagio, "the Pearl of the Lake," is a classy combination of tidiness and Old World elegance. If you don't mind that tramp-in-a-palace feeling, it's a fine place to surround yourself with the more adventurous of the soft travelers and shop for umbrellas and ties. The heavy curtains between the arcades keep the tourists and their poodles from sweating. While Johnnie Walker and jewelry sell best at lake level, the locals shop up the hill.

Menaggio, directly across the lake from Bellagio and just eight miles from Lugano in Switzerland, feels more like a real town than its neighbors. Since the lake is too dirty for swimming, consider its fine public pool.

One hop from Menaggio or Bellagio by ferry, the town of Varenna offers the best of all lake worlds. On the quieter side of the lake, with a romantic promenade, a tiny harbor, narrow lanes, and its own villa, Varenna is the right place to munch a peach and ponder the place where Italy is welded to the Alps. Varenna's volume goes down with the sun. After dark, the *passerella* (lakeside walk) is adorned with lovers pressing silently against each other in the shadows.

## The Dolomites

The Dolomites, Italy's dramatic limestone rooftop, serve alpine thrills with Italian sunshine. The famous valleys and towns of the well-developed Dolomites suffer from an après-ski fever, but the bold, snow-dusted mountains and green meadows offer great hikes. The cost for reliably good weather is a drained-reservoir feeling. Lovers of the Alps may miss the lushness that comes with the unpredictable weather farther north.

*Don't forget Italy's Alps, the Dolomites.*

A hard-fought history has left this part of Italy bicultural and bilingual, with *der* emphasis on the *Deutsch*. Locals speak German first. Many wish they were still Austrian. In the Middle Ages, the region faced north, part of the Holy Roman Empire. Later it was firmly in the Austrian Hapsburg realm. After Austria lost World War I, its South Tirol (Südtirol) became Italy's Alto Adige. Mussolini did what he could to Italianize the region, including giving each town an Italian name. The government has wooed cranky German-speaking locals with economic breaks that make this one of Italy's richest areas (as local prices attest). Today, signs and literature in the autonomous province of Südtirol/Alto Adige are in both languages.

In spite of all the glamorous ski resorts and busy construction cranes, local color survives in a blue-aproned, ruddy-faced, long-white-bearded way. There's yogurt and yodeling for breakfast. Culturally as much as geographically, the area feels Austrian. (The western part of Austria is named after Tirol, a village that is now actually in Italy.)

*Treating the Alps like a beach, in Italy's Dolomites*

Lifts, good trails, outdoor activity–oriented tourist offices, and a decent bus system make the region especially accessible. But it's expensive. Most towns have no alternative to $100 doubles in hotels, or $60 doubles in private homes. Beds usually come with a hearty breakfast, a rarity in Italy.

The seasons are brutal. The best time to visit—when everything is open and booming, but also at full-price and crowded—is from mid-July through September. After a dreary November, the snow hits, and it's busy with skiers until April. May and early June are dead (though the sedentary sort will enjoy the views and tranquility). The most exciting trails are still under snow, and the mountain lifts are shut down. Most mountain huts and budget accommodations are closed, as the locals are more concerned with preparing for another boom season than catering to the stray off-season tourist.

By car, circle north from Venice and drive the breathtaking Grande Strada delle Dolomiti, or Great Dolomite Road (65 miles: Cortina d'Ampezzo–Pordoi Pass–Sella Pass–Val di Fassa–Bolzano; $6 toll possible). In the spring and early summer, passes labeled "Closed" are often bare, dry, and, as far as local drivers are concerned, wide open. Conveniently for Italian tour operators, no direct public-transportation route covers the Great Dolomite Road.

With limited time and no car, maximize mountain thrills and minimize transportation headaches by taking the train to Bolzano, then catching a public bus into the mountains.

If Bolzano (or "Bozen" to its German-speaking locals) weren't so sunny, you could be in Innsbruck. This arcaded old town of 100,000, with a great open-air market on Piazza Erbe, is worth a Tirolean stroll and a stop at its Dolomite information center. To chill out, see Bolzano's Ice Man, a 5,000-year-old body found frozen with his gear a few years ago.

Tourist offices in any Dolomite town are a wealth of information. Before choosing a hike, get their advice. Ideally, pick a hike with an overnight in a mountain hut and make a telephone reservation. Most huts, called *refugios,* offer reasonable doubles, cheaper dorm *(Lager)* beds, and good inexpensive meals.

*I wouldn't steer you wrong: Hiking through Dolomite meadows is an udderly heifer-vescent experience.*

Many are tempted to wimp out on the Dolomites and admire the spires from a distance. They take the cable car into the hills above Bolzano, to the cute but very touristy village of Oberbozen. Don't. Bus into the Dolomites instead.

Europe's largest high-alpine meadow, Alpe di Siusi, spreads high above Bolzano, separating two of the most famous Dolomite ski-resort valleys (Val di Fassa and Val Gardena). Measuring three miles by seven and a half miles, and soaring 6,500 feet high, Alpe di Siusi is dotted by farm huts and wildflowers and surrounded by dramatic (if distant) Dolomite peaks and cliffs.

The Sasso Lungo mountains at the head of the meadow provide a storybook Dolomite backdrop, while the bold, spooky Mount Schlern stands gazing into the haze of the Italian peninsula. Not surprisingly, the Schlern, looking like a devilish *Winged Victory*, gave ancient peoples enough willies to spawn legends of supernatural forces. Fear of the Schlern witch, today's tourist-brochure mascot, was the cause of many a broom-riding medieval townswoman's fiery death.

A natural preserve, the alpine meadow is virtually car-free. A gondola whisks visitors up to the park from the valley below. Within the park, buses take hikers to and from key points along the tiny road all the way to the foot of the postcard-dramatic Sasso peaks. Meadow walks are ideal for flower lovers and strollers, while chairlifts provide springboards for more dramatic and demanding hikes.

The Alpe di Siusi is my recommended one-stop look at the Dolomites because of its easy accessibility to those with or without cars, the variety of walks and hikes, the quintessential Dolomite views, and the charm of neighboring Castelrotto as a home base.

*Castelrotto/Kastelruth: Your home base in the Dolomites*

The town of Castelrotto (population: 2,000; German name: Kastelruth) was built for farmers rather than skiers. It has good bus connections, fine and friendly hotels, and more village character than any town around. Pop into the church to hear the choir practice. And be on the town square at 2:45 p.m. as the bells peal and the moms bring home their preschoolers.

At Europe Through the Back Door, where I work, Italy is considered the greatest country in Europe. If all you have is 10 days, then do Venice, Florence, Rome, the hill towns, and the Riviera. If you have more time and seek intensity, head south. But to round out your itinerary with all the best of Italy and none of the chaos, splice in a little of the Dolomites, the lakes, and Milan.

*For good-value accommodations in Milan, try Hotel Speronari (Via Speronari 4, a block off main square, tel. 02-8646-1125, fax 02-7200-3178, hotelsperonari@inwind.it); in Varenna, Albergo Olivedo (at ferry dock, tel. & fax 0341-830-115, www.olivedo.it) or Albergo Milano (splurge, Via XX Settembre 29, tel. & fax 0341-830-298, www.varenna.net); and in Castelrotto/Kastelruth, Albergo Torre/Gasthof zum Turm (Kofelgasse 8, tel. 0471-706-349, fax 0471-707-268, www.zumturm.com). For more hotels, visit www.ricksteves.com/update, and for all the travel specifics, see this year's edition of* Rick Steves' Italy.

## 35. NAPLES, THE AMALFI COAST, AND A STEAMY VOLCANO

Naples Bay rounds out any trip to Italy with an *antipasto misto* of travel thrills. Serene Sorrento, an hour south of Naples' urban intensity, is a great home base and the gateway to the much-drooled-over Amalfi Coast. From the jet-setting island of Capri to the stunning Amalfi Coast towns, from ancient Pompeii to even more ancient Paestum, this is Italy's coast with the most. Naples is Italy intensified, from its best (birthplace of pizza and Sophia Loren) to its worst (home of the Camorra, Naples' "family" of organized crime).

On a quick trip, give the area three days. With Sorrento as your sunny springboard, spend a day exploring the Amalfi Coast, a day split between Pompeii and the town of Sorrento, and a day dodging Vespas in Naples. Paestum, the crater of Vesuvius, Herculaneum, and the island of Capri are all good reasons to give the area a few more days.

For a blitz day trip from Rome, you could have breakfast on the early Rome–Naples express (about 7–9 a.m.), do Naples and Pompeii in a day, and be back at your hotel in time for *Letterman*. That's exhausting but more interesting than a third day in Rome. (In the heat of the afternoon, Naples' street life slows and many sights close. Things pick up again in the early evening.)

**Sorrento,** wedged on a ledge between the mountains and the Mediterranean, is an attractive resort of 20,000 residents and—in the summer—as many tourists. It's as well-located for regional sightseeing as it is a pleasant place to stay and stroll. The Sorrentines have gone out of their way to create a completely safe and relaxed place for tourists to spend money. Everyone seems to speak fluent English and work for the Chamber of Commerce. Spritzed by lemon and olive groves, this gateway to the Amalfi Coast has an unspoiled old quarter, a lively main shopping street, a spectacular cliffside setting, and easy public

## From Naples to Paestum

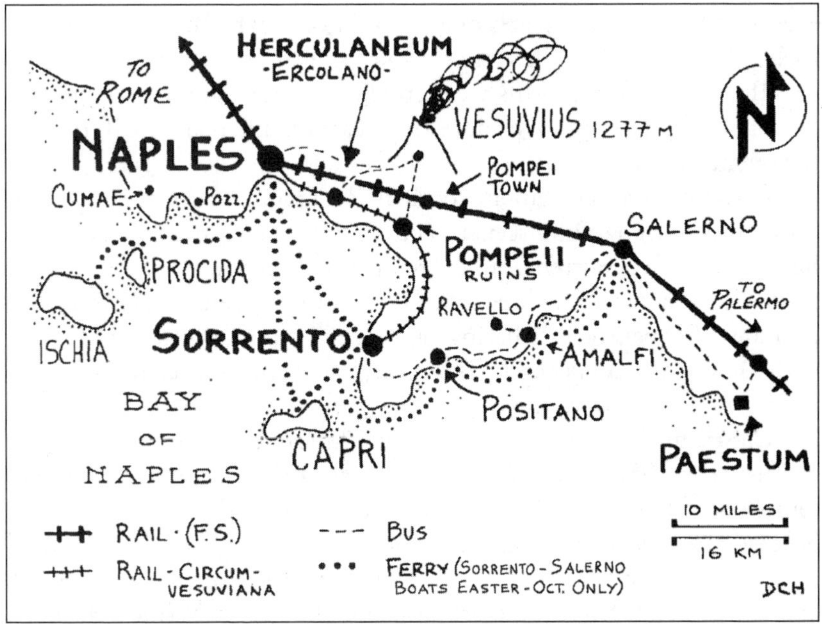


transportation (Circumvesuviana trains run twice hourly to Naples, stopping at Pompeii and Herculaneum en route; and blue or green-and-white SITA buses depart nearly hourly from the Sorrento train station to the Amalfi Coast).

The **Amalfi Coast** offers one of the world's great bus rides: The coastal trip from Sorrento to Salerno will leave your mouth open and your camera smokin'. You'll gain respect for the Italian engineers who built the road—and even more respect for the bus drivers who drive it. As you hyperventilate, notice how the Mediterranean, a sheer 500-foot drop below, twinkles.

*The breathtaking Amalfi Coast*

Cantilevered garages, hotels, and villas cling to the vertical terrain. Beautiful sandy coves tease from far below and out of reach. Gasp from the right side of the bus as you head toward Salerno, and the left on the way back to Sorrento. Traffic is so heavy that in the summer local cars are allowed to drive only every other day—even-numbered license plates one day, odd the next. (Buses and tourists foolish enough to drive here are exempt from this system.)

The Amalfi Coast towns are pretty but generally touristy, congested, overpriced, and a long hike above tiny beaches. The real Amalfi thrill is the scenic drive.

If you need a destination, consider Positano, an easy day trip from Sorrento. Specializing in scenery and sand, the town of Positano hangs halfway between Sorrento and Amalfi town on the most spectacular stretch of the coast. A three-star sight from a distance, Positano is a pleasant (if expensive) gathering of women's clothing stores and cafés, with a good but pebbly beach. There's little to do here but enjoy the beach and views and window-shop.

**Capri,** made famous as the vacation hideaway of Roman emperors Augustus and Tiberius, is today a world-class tourist trap where gawky tourists search for the rich and famous but find only their prices. A quick boat ride from Sorrento, this four-mile-by-two-mile "Island of Dreams" is a zoo in July and August. At other times of year, it provides a relaxing and scenic break from the cultural gauntlet of Italy. While Capri has some Roman ruins and an interesting 14th-century Carthusian monastery, its chief attraction is its famous Blue Grotto and its best activity is a scenic hike.

**Pompeii,** stopped in its tracks by the eruption of Mount Vesuvius in A.D. 79, offers the best look anywhere at what life in Rome must have been like nearly 2,000 years ago. An entire city of well-preserved ruins is yours to explore. Once a thriving commercial port of 20,000, Pompeii grew from Greek and Etruscan roots to become an important Roman city. Then Pompeii was buried under 30 feet of hot mud and volcanic ash. For archaeologists, this was a shake 'n' bake windfall, teaching them volumes about daily Roman life.

When touring Pompeii, remember this was a booming trading city. Most streets would have been lined with stalls and jammed with customers from sunup to sundown. Chariots vied for street space with shoppers, and many streets were off-limits to chariots during shopping hours (you'll still see street signs with pictures of men carrying vases—this meant pedestrians only). Pompeii's best art is in the Naples Archaeological Museum (described below).

**Herculaneum**—smaller, less ruined, and less crowded than its famous sister, Pompeii—offers a closer look at ancient Roman life. Caked and baked by the same eruption in A.D. 79, Herculaneum is a small community of intact buildings with plenty of surviving detail.

**Vesuvius,** mainland Europe's only active volcano, has been sleeping restlessly since 1944. Complete your Pompeii or Herculaneum experience by scaling the volcano that made them famous. The 4,000-foot summit of Vesuvius is accessible by car, Vesuviana Mobilità shuttle bus ($10 round-trip, leaves from the Herculaneum station), or taxi (about $100 round-trip). From the Vesuvius parking lot, pay $8 and hike 30 minutes to the top for a sweeping Bay of Naples view, desolate lunar-like surroundings, and hot rocks. On the top, walk the entire crater lip for the most interesting views. The far end overlooks Pompeii. Be still and alone to hear the wind and tumbling rocks in the crater. Any steam? Vesuvius is closed when erupting.

**Paestum** is one of the best collections of Greek temples anywhere—and certainly the most accessible to Western Europe. Serenely situated, it's surrounded by fields and wildflowers and a modest commercial strip. Founded by the Greeks in the sixth century B.C., it was a key stop on an important trade route. It was conquered first by Romans in the third century B.C. and later by malaria-carrying mosquitoes that kept the site wonderfully desolate for almost a thousand years. Rediscovered in the 18th century, Paestum today offers the only well-preserved Greek ruins north of Sicily.

**Naples,** a thriving Greek commercial center 2,500 years ago, remains southern Italy's leading city, offering a fascinating collection of museums, churches, eclectic architecture, and crazy traffic. The pulse of Italy throbs in this urban jungle. Like Cairo or Bombay, it's appalling and captivating at the same time, the closest thing to "reality travel" you'll find in Western Europe. But this tangled mess still somehow manages to breathe, laugh, and sing—with a captivating Italian accent.

Overcome your fear of being run down or ripped off long enough to talk with people: Enjoy a few smiles and jokes with the man running the neighborhood tripe shop or the woman taking her day-care class on a walk through the traffic.

For a quick visit, start with the Archaeological Museum, explore a few streets, and celebrate your survival with pizza.

Naples' Archaeological Museum offers the closest possible peek into the artistic jewelry boxes of Pompeii and Herculaneum. The actual sights, while impressive, are barren. The best frescoes and mosaics ended up here. The Secret Room (for which you need to reserve an entry time at the ticket desk) displays R-rated Roman "bedroom" art. A museum highlight is the Farnese Collection—a giant hall of huge, bright, and wonderfully restored statues excavated from Rome's Baths of Caracalla. You can almost hear the *Toro Farnese* snorting. This largest intact statue from antiquity (a third-century copy of a Hellenistic original) was carved out of one piece of marble and restored by Michelangelo.

*Naples: an urban jungle with straight streets and friendly cops.*

Marble lovers chisel out time for the Cappella Sansevero, six blocks southeast of the Archaeological Museum. This small chapel is a Baroque explosion mourning the body of Christ, lying on a soft pillow under an incredibly realistic veil—all carved out of marble (by Giuseppe "Howdeedoodat" Sammartino, 1750). Loving statues, each carved from a single piece of marble, adorn the altar. *Despair* (by Francesco Queirolo, 1759) struggles with a marble rope net, while *Modesty* poses coyly under her full-length marble veil (by Antonio Corradini, 1752). For your inner ghoul, descend into the crypt for a creepy look at two 200-year-old studies in varicose veins. Was one decapitated? Was one pregnant?

Take time to explore Naples. This living medieval city is its own best sight. Couples artfully make love on Vespas, while surrounded by more fights and smiles per cobblestone than anywhere else in Italy.

Paint a picture with these thoughts: Naples has the most intact ancient Roman street plan anywhere. Imagine life here in the days of Caesar (retain these images as you visit Pompeii), with street-side shop fronts that close up to form private homes after dark. Today is just one more page in a 2,000-year-old story of city activity: all kinds of meetings, beatings, and cheatings; kisses, near misses, and little-boy pisses.

The only thing predictable about this Neapolitan mix is the friendliness of its shopkeepers and the boldness of its mopeds. Concerned locals will tug on their lower eyelid, warning you to be wary. Pop into a grocery shop and ask the man to make you his best ham-and-mozzarella sandwich.

For a peek behind the scenes in the shade of wet laundry, venture down a few narrow streets lined by tall apartment buildings. Black-and-

*A Naples balcony greeting*

white death announcements add to the clutter on the walls. Widows sell cigarettes from plastic buckets. Buy two carrots as a gift for the woman on the fifth floor if she'll lower her bucket down to pick them up. One wave works wonders as six floors of balconies fill up, each with its own waving family. Walking around, craning my neck upward, I feel like a victorious politician among hordes of supporters. It's a *Laugh-In* wall with each window and balcony vying for a photo: Mothers hold up babies, sisters pose arm in arm, a wild pregnant woman stands on a fruit crate holding her bulging stomach, and an old, wrinkled woman fills her paint-starved window frame with a toothy grin. A contagious energy fills the air. It hurts to say *arrivederci.*

*For good-value accommodations in Sorrento, try Hotel Loreley (request view room, Via Califano 2, tel. 081-807-3187, fax 081-532-9001, www.sorrentohotelmignon.com/loreley.htm) or Hotel Minerva (cliff-hanging views, Via Capo 30, tel. 081-878-1011, fax 081-878-1949, www.minervasorrento.com). For more hotels, visit www.ricksteves.com/update, and for all the travel specifics, see this year's edition of* Rick Steves' Italy.

## 36. SASSY, SPICY SICILY

Jabbing his pole like a one-pronged pitchfork into the slow red river of molten rock, the ashtray salesman pulled out a wad of lava. I scrambled back as he swung it by me and plopped it into a mold. His partner snipped it off with big iron clippers and rammed it into shape. The now shapely mass was dropped into a bucket of water that did a wild jig. Cooling on a crispy black ledge were a dozen more lava ashtrays, each with the words "Mount Etna, Sicily" molded into it.

As the red lava poured out of its horribly hot trap door, I unzipped the ski parka I'd rented for $1 at the lift. At 11,000 feet, even on a sunny day, it's cold on top of Mount Etna...unless you're three feet from a lava flow.

At the edge of the volcano, I surveyed the island that I had just explored on my scriptwriting mission for a TV show on Sicily. Old lava

*Auntie Pasta says, "It's* ciao *time!"*

flows rumbled like buffalo toward teeming Catania. The island's sprawling second city butted up against a crescent beach that stretched all the way to Taormina, the Santorini of Sicily, popular with Italians who dress up to travel. And to my right was the hazy, high, and harsh interior. Two hours later, I had dropped my rental car at the Catania airport and was flying back to Rome, a rough script unfolding on my laptop screen.

Sicily sights are hard to grasp. Its historic and artistic big shots just don't ring a bell. The folkloric traditions, such as marionette theaters promoted by tourist brochures, seem to play out only for tour groups. And the place must lead Europe in litter. But there's a workaday charm here. If you like Italy for its people, tempo, and joy of living—rather than for its Botticellis, Guccis, and touristic icons—you'll dig Sicily.

Sicily, standing midway between Africa and Europe, really is a world unto itself. While part of Italy, it's not quite that simple. Even though (with government encouragement) the siesta is fading out of Italian life, it thrives in Sicily. As European safety regulations take hold in the north, with laws requiring helmets on motorbikers, hair continues to fly in the Sicilian wind.

**Palermo** is the Rome of Sicily, with lavish art, boisterous markets, and holy cannoli. In the market, animals hang like anatomy lessons, sliced perfectly in half. *Fichi di India,* the fist-size cactus fruit that tastes like a cousin of the kiwi, are peeled and yours for less than a buck.

*Even in death, Italians know how to look cool.*

Palermo offers a great bone experience—skull and shoulders above anything else you'll find in Europe. Its Cappuccin crypt is a subterranean gallery filled with 8,000 "bodies without souls" howling silently at their mortality. For centuries, people would thoughtfully choose their niche before they died, and even linger there, getting to know

## Sicily

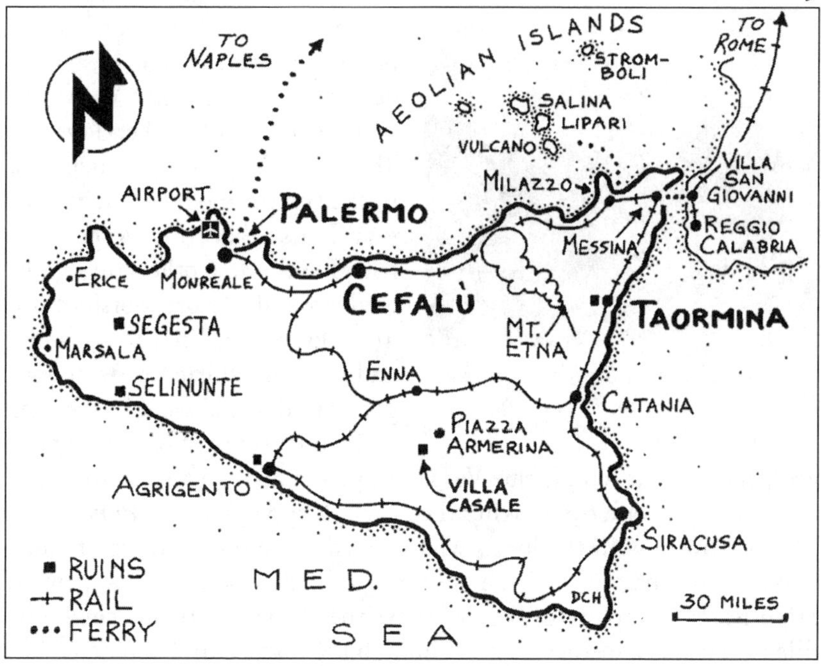


their macabre neighborhood. Then, after death, dressed in their Sunday best, they'd be hung up to dry. The entrepreneurial monk at the door said that for $125 we could take our TV camera inside for an hour. For $2, a tourist can spend all day.

Sicily's slick *autostrada* seems out of place (and way too wide), cutting a nearly deserted swath through the heart of the island. For the tourist, it zips you to some of the best Roman mosaics ever excavated. An emperor's hunting villa at Casale (near the town of Piazza Armerina) shows off 50 lavishly decorated mosaic floors. With the help of a guidebook (Giuseppe di Giovanni's is the best), the duck-driven chariots, bikini-clad triathletes, and amorous love scenes make more sense.

**Cefalù** was my favorite stop. Steeped in history and bustling with color, it's dramatically set with a fine beach on a craggy coast under a pagan mountain. I dutifully toured Cefalù's museum and cathedral. But the real attraction is on the streets. As the sun grew red and heavy, the old women—still in bathrobes, it seemed—filled their balconies as the young people (and Vespas) clogged the main drag. Tsk-tsking at the age-old flirting scene, the women gossiped about the girls below.

My friend—ignoring the boy-toy girls—told me of the motorbike he lusted after. It was a classic Vespa from the '70s...with a body that's

*The Greek theater at Sicily's Taormina: With a view like this, no play is a tragedy.*

"round like a woman's." Just then, another guy galloped up on his very round, very blue, classic Vespa. He declared, "It's the only Vespa I've ever owned. I got it when I was 14. That was in 1969. The year man first walked on the moon—that was the year I first rode this Vespa." My friend and a few other guys gathered around almost worshipfully. The old women in the balconies and the mini-skirted flirts no longer existed. Cefalù and its teeming main drag were just Mediterranean wallpaper as that round, blue Vespa dripped in Sicilian testosterone.

Later, at a café overlooking the beach, I sipped my *latte di mandorla* (almond milk) with the locals who seemed to be posted there on duty, making sure that big, red sun goes down. Little wooden boats, painted brightly, sat plump on the beach. Above them, the fisherman's clubhouse filled what was a medieval entry through the town wall. I wandered in.

I was greeted warmly by the senior member, "Il Presidente." The men go by nicknames and often don't even know their friends' real names. Since 1944, Il Presidente has spent his nights fishing, gathering anchovies under the beam of his gas-powered *lampara*. When he took the pre-Coleman vintage lamp off its rusty wall hook, I saw tales of a lifetime at sea in his face. As he showed me the ropes he wove from local straw and complained that the new ropes just aren't the same, I lashed him to my budding script.

*For the TV script, see www.ricksteves.com/tv. For good-value accommodations in Palermo, try Grande Albergo Sole (splurge, Corso Vittorio Emanuele 291, tel. 091-604-1111, www.ghshotels.it) or Hotel Moderno (budget, Via Roma 276, tel. 091-588-683); in Cefalù, Hotel Riva del Sole (Via Lungomare 25, tel. 092-142-1230, www.rivadelsole.com); in Taormina, Hotel Continental (Via Dionisio 2a, tel. 094-223-805, www.continentaltaormina.com).*

*Travel smart in Sicily: Pay your respects to the Big Cheese.*

# PORTUGAL, SPAIN, AND MOROCCO

## 37. LISBON'S GOLD STILL SHINES

Barely elegant outdoor cafés, glittering art, and the saltiest sailors' quarter in Europe, all at bargain-basement prices, make Lisbon an Iberian highlight. Portugal's capital is a wonderful mix of now and then. Old wooden trolleys shiver up its hills, bird-stained statues guard grand squares, and people sip coffee in Art Nouveau cafés.

*A lazy viewpoint overlooking Lisbon's Alfama*

Present-day Lisbon is explained by its past. Her glory days were the 15th and 16th centuries, when explorers such as Vasco da Gama opened up new trade routes, making Lisbon the queen of Europe. Later, the riches of Brazil boosted Lisbon even higher. Then, in 1755, an earthquake leveled the city, killing nearly a quarter of its people.

Lisbon was rebuilt on a strict grid plan, symmetrically, with broad boulevards and square squares. The grandeur of pre-earthquake Lisbon survives in only three neighborhoods: Belém, the Alfama, and the Bairro Alto.

While the earthquake flattened a lot of buildings, and its colonial empire is long gone, Lisbon's heritage survives. Follow me through a day in Lisbon.

## Lisbon

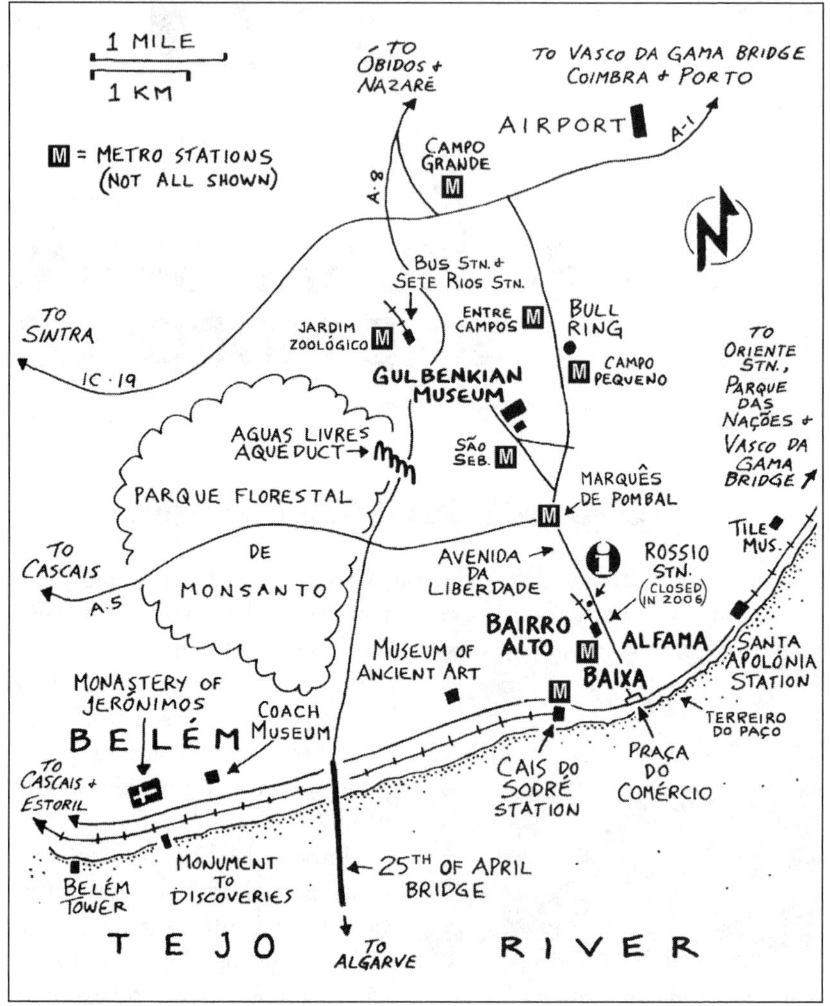


After breakfast, grab a trolley or taxi to Torre de Belém (Belém Tower). The Belém District, four miles from downtown, is a pincushion of important sights from Portugal's Golden Age, when Vasco da Gama and company made her Europe's richest power.

The Belém Tower, built in Manueline style (ornate Portuguese late Gothic), has guarded Lisbon's harbor since 1555. Today, it symbolizes the voyages that made her powerful. This was the last sight sailors saw as they left—and the first one they'd see when they returned, loaded down with gold, diamonds, and venereal diseases.

Nearby, the giant Monument to the Discoverers honors Portugal's

Prince Henry the Navigator and the country's leading explorers. Across the street, the Monastery of Jerónimos is Portugal's most exciting building—with my favorite cloister in Europe. King Manuel had this giant church and its cloisters built—using "pepper money," a 5 percent tax on spices brought back from India—as a thanks for the discoveries. Sailors would spend their last night here in prayer before embarking on their frightening voyages. The Manueline style of this giant church and cloister combines late Gothic and early Renaissance features with motifs from the sea, the source of the wealth that made this art possible.

*Enjoying the peace of Lisbon's Monastery of Jerónimos, Europe's finest cloister.*

Before leaving Belém, take your taste buds sightseeing at a famous pastry shop, Casa Pasties de Belém (a block from the monastery at Rua de Belém 88). This is the birthplace of the wonderful cream tart called *pastel de nata* throughout Portugal. But in Lisbon, they're called *pastel de Belém.* Since 1837, locals have come here to get them warm out of the oven. Sprinkle on the cinnamon and powdered sugar, get a *café com leite,* and linger.

Spend the early afternoon in your choice of Lisbon's fine museums waiting for the setting sun to rekindle the action in the Alfama. A colorful sailors' quarter, this was the center of the Visigothic town, a rich district during the Arabic period and now the shiver-me-timbers home of Lisbon's fisherfolk. One of the few areas to survive the 1755 earthquake, the Alfama is a cobbled cornucopia of Old World color.

Wander deep. This urban jungle's roads are squeezed into tangled stairways and confused alleys. Bent houses comfort each other in their romantic shabbiness, and the air drips with laundry and the smell of clams and raw fish. Get lost. Poke aimlessly, sample ample grapes, avoid rabid-looking dogs, peek through windows. Make a friend, pet a chicken. Taste the *branco seco*—the local dry wine.

Gradually zigzag your way up the castle-crowned hill until you reach a viewpoint, the little green square called Miradouro de Santa Luzia. Rest here and survey the cluttered Alfama rooftops below you. A block away is Largo Rodrigues Freitas, a square with several scruffy, cheap, very local eateries. Treat yourself to the special—a plate of boiled clams.

If you climb a few more blocks to the top of the hill, you'll find the ruins of Castelo de São Jorge. From this fortress, which has dominated the city for more than 1,000 years, enjoy the roaming peacocks and a commanding view of Portugal's capital city.

In the late afternoon, for a quintessential Lisbon drink, duck into one of the funky hole-in-the-wall shops throughout town and ask for a *ginginha* (zheen-zheen-yah). Sold for about a buck a shot, it's a sweet liquor made from the sour cherry–like ginja berry, sugar, and schnapps. The only choices are: With or without berries (*com* or *sem fruta*), and *gelada* if you want it from a chilled bottle out of the fridge—very nice. In Portugal, when someone is impressed by the taste of something, they say, *"Sabe melhor que nem ginjas"* (It tastes even better than ginja).

Spend the evening at a Portuguese bullfight. It's a brutal sport, but the bull lives through it and so will you. The fight starts with an equestrian duel—a fast bull against a graceful horse and rider. Then the fun starts. A colorfully clad eight-man team enters the ring strung out in a line as if to play leapfrog. The leader taunts *O Touro* noisily and, with testosterone sloshing everywhere, the bull and the man charge each other. The speeding bull plows into the leader head-on. Then—thud, thud, thud—the raging bull skewers the entire charging crew. The horns are wrapped so no one gets gored—just mashed.

*In a Portuguese bullfight, the matador is brutalized, too.*

The crew wrestles the bull to a standstill, and one man grabs the bull's tail. Victory is complete when the team leaps off the bull and the man still hanging onto the tail "water-skis" behind the enraged animal. This thrilling display of insanity is repeated with six bulls. After each round, the bruised and battered leader limps a victory lap around the ring.

Portugal's top bullring is Lisbon's Campo Pequeno (fights generally on Thu and Sun, mid-June–Sept, may be closed for renovation; other arenas offer fights most Sun, Easter–Oct). Half the fights are simply Spanish-type *corridas* without the killing. For the real slam-bam

Portuguese-style fight, confirm that there will be *grupo de forcados.*

For a good lowbrow Lisbon evening out, visit the Feira Popular (open nightly until late, May–Sept, Avenida da Republica at the Entrecampos metro stop). On summer evenings, this popular fair bustles with Portuguese families at play. I ate dinner surrounded by chattering locals ignoring the ever-present TVs, while great platters of fish, meat, fries, salad, and lots of wine paraded frantically in every direction. A seven-year-old boy stood on a chair and sang hauntingly emotional folk songs. With his own dogged clapping, he dragged applause out of the less-than-interested crowd and then passed his shabby hat. All the while, fried ducks dripped, barbecues spat, dogs squirted the legs of chairs, and somehow local lovers ignored everything but each other's eyes.

*For good-value accommodations in Lisbon, try Hotel Lisboa Tejo (Condes de Monsanto 2, tel. 218-866-182, fax 218-865-163, www.evidenciahoteis.com) or the cheaper Pensão Residencial Gerês (Calçada do Garcia 6, tel. 218-810-497, fax 218-882-006, www.pensaogeres.com). For more hotels, visit www.ricksteves.com/update, and for all the travel specifics, see this year's edition of* Rick Steves' Portugal.

## 38. SALEMA, ON PORTUGAL'S SUNNY SOUTH COAST

"Let's get the *cataplanas,*" said my wife Anne, urging me to try the fish stew at Ze's Carioca Restaurant in Salema.

Overhearing her, Ze came to our table and said, "I have developed a secret recipe for this specialty. If you don't like it, you don't pay."

"What if we don't like anything else we order?" I asked.

*Salema: Catch the Algarve before it's gone.*

## Portugal's Algarve Coast

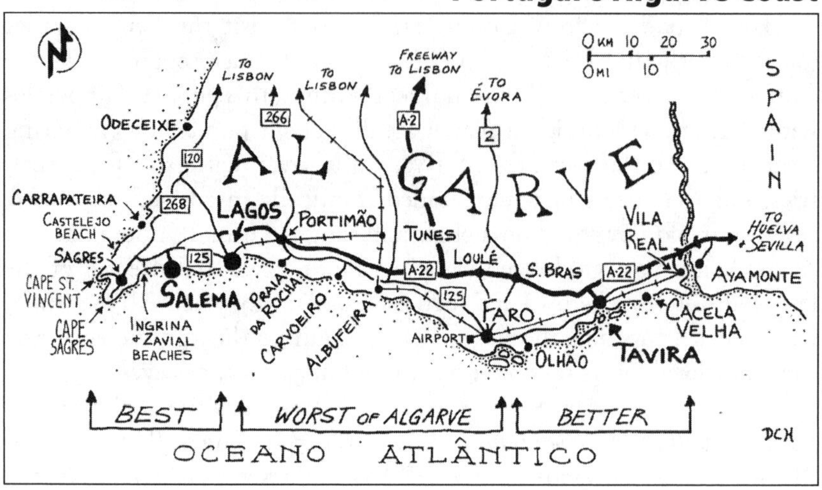


"If you don't pay, I break your fingers," Ze said cheerfully.

We ordered the *cataplanas.* Savoring our meal, we savored one of the last true villages on the Algarve—Salema.

Any place famous as a "last undiscovered tourist frontier" no longer is. But the Algarve of your dreams survives—just barely. To catch it before it goes, find a fringe. It took me three tries. West of Lagos, I tried Lux and Burgano, both offering only a corpse of a fishing village, bikini-strangled and Nivea-creamed. Then, just as darkness turned couples into peaceful silhouettes, I found Salema.

Any Algarve town with a beach will have tourism, but few mix tourism and realism as well as little Salema. It's my kind of resort—an inviting beach with four hotels, lots of *quartos* (Portuguese bed-and-breakfasts), and four restaurants specializing in fresh fish and *vinho verde* (green wine). Tucked away where a dirt road hits the beach on Portugal's southwestern tip, Salema is an easy 15-mile bus ride or hitch from the closest train station in Lagos. Don't let the ladies hawking rooms in Lagos waylay you into staying in their city by telling you Salema is full.

Salema has a split personality. Half is a whitewashed old town of scruffy dogs, wide-eyed kids, and fishermen who've seen it all. The other half was built for tourists. With the horn-tooting arrival of the trucks, the parking lot that separates the jogging shorts from the black shawls becomes a morning market. The *1812 Overture* horn of the fish truck wakes you at 8 a.m. Then the bakery trailer rolls in steaming with fresh bread, followed by a fruit-and-vegetables truck, and a five-and-dime truck for clothing and odds and ends. And, most afternoons, the red mobile post office stops by.

Salema is still a fishing village. Unwritten tradition allocates different chunks of undersea territory to each Salema family. While the fishermen's hut on the beach no longer hosts a fish auction, it provides shade for the old-timers arm-wrestling octopi out of their traps. The pottery jars stacked everywhere are traps. The traps are tied about a yard apart in long lines and dropped offshore. Octopi, looking for a cozy place to set an ambush, climb inside—making their final mistake.

Fishing is important, but Salema's tourist-based economy sits on a foundation of sand. Locals hope and pray that their sandy beach returns after being washed away each winter.

In Portugal, restaurateurs are allowed to build a temporary, summer-only beachside restaurant if they provide a lifeguard for swimmers and run a green/yellow/red warning-flag system. The Atlântico Restaurant, which dominates Salema's beach, takes its responsibility seriously—providing lifeguards and flags through the summer...and fresh seafood by candlelight all year long.

Locals and tourists pursue a policy of peaceful coexistence at the beach. Tractors pull in and push out the fishing boats, two-year-olds toddle in the waves, topless women read German fashion mags, and old men really do mend the nets. British, German, and Back Door connoisseurs of lethargy laze in the sun, while locals grab the shade.

On the west end of the beach, you can climb over the rocks to Figueira Beach. While the days of black widows chasing topless Nordic women off the beach are gone, nudity is still risqué today. Over the rocks and beyond the view of prying eyes, Germans grin and bare it.

So often, tourism chases the sun and quaint folksiness. And the quaint folks can survive only with the help of tourist dollars. Fishermen boost their income by renting spare bedrooms to the ever-growing stream of tan fans from the drizzly North. One year I arrived at 7 p.m. with a group of eight people and no reservations. I asked some locals, "*Quartos?*" Eyes perked, heads nodded, and I got nine beds in three homes at $15 per person. *Quartos* line Salema's main residential street offering simple rooms with showers, springy beds, and glorious Atlantic views.

If you need to do some touring, drive 15 minutes to the best romantic, secluded beach in the region: Praia do Castelejo, complete with a good restaurant, just north of Cape Sagres.

Closer to home, you could take a two-hour cruise from Salema halfway to Cape Sagres and back with Sebastián, a local English-speaking guide. You'll enjoy a light commentary on the geology and plant and bird life (morning trips are best for bird-watching) and then nip into some cool blue natural caves. Kicking back and watching the cliffs glide by, I felt like I was scanning a super-relaxing gallery of natural art. Consider being dropped at the (nude) Figueira Beach just before returning to Salema (a 50-min walk away—bring shoes, a picnic, and extra water). Easygoing and gentle Sebastián charges little more than what it costs to run his small boat (about $25 per person); ask for him at the beachside fishermen's hut or at Pensión Maré.

But Salema's sleepy beauty kidnaps our momentum, and Anne and I go nowhere. Leaving Ze's restaurant with stomachs full and fingers intact, we take a glass of wine from the Atlântico's waterfront bar and sip it with the sunset in a beached paddleboat. Nearby, a dark, withered granny shells almonds with a railroad spike, dogs roam the beach like they own it, and a man catches short fish with a long pole. Beyond him is Cape Sagres—the edge of the world 500 years ago. As far as the gang sipping port and piling olive pits in the beachside bar is concerned, it still is.

*For good-value accommodations in Salema, try Pensión Maré (Praia de Salema, tel. 282-695-165, www.algarve.co.uk) or Casa Duarte (tel. 282-695-206 or 282-695-307). For more hotels, visit www.ricksteves.com/update, and for all the travel specifics, see this year's edition of* Rick Steves' Portugal.

## 39. ANDALUCÍA'S ARCOS DE LA FRONTERA AND THE ROUTE OF THE WHITE VILLAGES

When tourists head south from Madrid, it's generally for Granada, Córdoba, Sevilla, or the Costa del Sol. The big cities have their urban charms, but the Costa del Sol is a concrete nightmare, worthwhile only as a bad example. The most Spanish thing about the south coast is the

*In Arcos, locals brag that only they see the backs of the birds as they fly.*

## Spain's White Villages

sunshine—but that's everywhere. For something different and more authentic, try exploring the interior of Andalucía along the "Route of the White Villages." The Ruta de Pueblos Blancos, Andalucía's charm bracelet of cute towns, gives you wonderfully untouched Spanish culture.

Spend a night in the romantic queen of the white towns, Arcos de la Frontera. Towns with "de la Frontera" in their names were established on the front line of the Christians' centuries-long fight to recapture Spain from the Moors, who were slowly pushed back into Africa. Today, these hill towns—no longer strategic or on any frontier—are just passing time peacefully.

**Arcos** smothers its hilltop, tumbling down all sides like an oversized blanket. While larger than the other Andalusian hill towns, it's equally atmospheric. The labyrinthine old center is a photographer's feast. Viewpoint-hop through town. Feel the wind funnel through the narrow streets as drivers pull in car mirrors to fit around tight corners.

Locals brag that only they see the backs of the birds as they fly. To see why, climb to the viewpoint at the main square high in the old town. Belly up to the railing—the town's suicide jumping-off point—and look down. Ponder the fancy cliffside hotel's erosion concerns, orderly orange groves, flower-filled greenhouses, fine views toward Morocco...and the backs of the birds.

The thoughtful traveler's challenge is to find meaning in the generally overlooked tiny details of historic towns such as Arcos. On a recent visit, I discovered that a short walk from Arcos' church of Santa María to the church of San Pedro (St. Peter) is littered with fun glimpses into the town's past.

The church of Santa María faces the main square. After Arcos was reconquered from the Moors in the 13th century, this church was built—atop a mosque. In the pavement is a 15th-century magic circle: 12 red and 12 white stones—the white ones with various constellations marked. When a child came to the church to be baptized, the parents would stop here first for a good Christian exorcism. The exorcist would stand inside the protective circle and cleanse the baby of any evil spirits. This was also a holy place back in Muslim times. While locals no longer use it, Islamic Sufis still come here in pilgrimage.

In 1699, an earthquake cracked the church's foundation. Arches were added to prop it against neighboring buildings. Thanks to these, the church survived the bigger earthquake of 1755 (which destroyed much of Lisbon). All over town, arches support earthquake-damaged structures.

Lately the town rumbles only when the bulls run. Señor González Oca's tiny barbershop (behind the church) is plastered with posters of bulls running Pamplona-style through the streets of Arcos during Holy Week. A brave (but not particularly bright) American from the nearby Navy base at Rota was killed here by a bull in 1994.

Small towns like Arcos come with lively markets. On my last visit, I was encouraged by the pickle woman to try a *banderilla,* named for the bangled spear that a matador sticks into the bull. As I gingerly slid an onion off the tiny skewer of pickled olives, onions, and carrots, she told me to eat it all at once. Explosive!

An important part of any Spanish market is the meat stall—the *salchichonería.* Since Roman times in Spain, December has been the season to slaughter pigs and cure (salt and dry) every possible bit of meat into various hams and sausages. By late spring, the now-salty meat is cured and able to withstand the heat.

Near the market is a convent. The spiky security grill over the window protects cloistered nuns. Tiny peepholes allow the sisters to look out unseen. I stepped into the lobby to find a one-way mirror and a blind spinning lazy Susan–type cupboard. I pushed the buzzer, and a sister spun out some boxes of freshly baked cookies for sale. When I spun back the cookies with a *"No, gracias,"* a Monty Python–esque voice countered, "We have cupcakes as well." I bought a bag of these *magdalenas,* both to support their church work and to give to kids on my walk. Feeling like a religious Peeping Tom, I actually saw—through the not-quite one-way mirror—the sister in her flowing robe and habit momentarily appear and disappear.

Walking on toward St. Peter's, I passed Roman columns plastered into street corners—protection from reckless donkey carts. The walls are scooped out on either side of the windows, a reminder of the days when women stayed inside but wanted the best possible view of any people-action in the streets.

Arcos' second church, St. Peter's, really is the second church. It lost an extended battle with Santa María for papal recognition as the leading church in Arcos. When the pope finally recognized Santa María, pouting parishioners from St. Peter's even changed their prayers. Rather than say "María, mother of God," they prayed "St. Peter, mother of God."

The tiny square in front of the church—about the only flat piece of pavement around—serves as the old-town soccer field for neighborhood kids. I joined the game and shared my cupcakes.

Until a few years ago, this church also had a resident bellman who lived in the spire. He was a basket-maker and a colorful character—famous for bringing in a donkey, which grew too big to get back out. Finally, there was no choice but to kill and eat him (the donkey).

Exploring on, I entered a cool, dark bar filled with very short, old guys. In Spain, any man in his 70s spent his growth-spurt years trying to survive the brutal Civil War (1936–1939). Those who did, generally did so just barely. That generation is a head shorter than the people of the next.

In the bar, the gang—side-lit like a Rembrandt portrait—was fixed on the TV, watching the finale of a long series of bullfights. El Córdobes was fighting. His father, also called El Córdobes, was the Babe Ruth of bullfighting. El Córdobes uses his dad's name even though his dad sued him not to. Today, this generation's El Córdobes is the Ichiro of bullfighting.

Marveling at the bar's fun and cheap list of wines and hard drinks, I ordered a Cuba Libre for $2. The drink came tall and stiff, with a dish of peanuts. Suddenly everyone gasped—all eyes on the TV. El Córdobes had been hooked and did a cartwheel over the angry bull's head. The gang roared as El Córdobes buried his head in his arms and the bull trampled and tried to gore him. The TV repeated the scene many times.

El Córdobes survived and—no surprise—eventually killed the bull. But as he made his victory lap and picked up adoring bouquets, the camera zoomed in on the rip exposing his hip and a 10-inch-long bloody wound. The short men around me would remember and talk about this moment for years.

*Zahara reigns in Spain, rising mainly above the plain.*

That evening, I caught the sunset from the viewpoint, then took in dinner at Restaurante El Convento, surrounded by the plants and arches of another old convent—this one long replaced by the best restaurant in town. The proud owner is María Moreno Moreno. (Spanish children take the name of both parents—who in María's case must have been distant cousins.) The walls are decorated with bronzed newspaper pages heralding MMM's many culinary awards. As church bells clanged, I poured a *vino tinto con mucho cuerpo* (full-bodied red wine) from the Rioja region, and ordered up the best-quality ham, *jamón ibérico,* from acorn-fed pigs with black feet.

I told María the man at the next table looked like El Córdobes. One glance and she said, "El Córdobes is much more handsome." When I mentioned his recent drama, she said, "It's been a difficult year for matadors."

From Arcos, the back road to Ronda is spiked with plenty of undiscovered and interesting hill towns. About half the towns I visited were memorable. Only Arcos (by bus) and Ronda (by train) are easily accessible by public transportation. Other towns are best seen by car. Good information on the area is rare but not necessary. Pick up the tourist brochure on the white towns at a nearby big-city tourist office, get a good map, and crank your spirit of adventure to high.

Along with Arcos, here are my favorite white villages:

**Zahara,** a tiny town with a tingly setting under a Moorish castle, has a spectacular view. During Moorish times, Zahara was contained within the fortified castle walls above today's town. It was considered the gateway to Granada and a strategic stronghold for the Moors by the Spanish Christian forces of the *Reconquista.*

Today, the castle is little more than an evocative ruin with a commanding view (always open, free, and worth the climb). And Zahara is a fine overnight stop for those who want to hear only the sounds of birds, wind, and elderly footsteps on ancient cobbles.

**Grazalema,** another postcard-pretty hill town, offers a royal balcony for a memorable picnic, a square where you can watch old-timers playing cards, and plenty of quiet, whitewashed streets to explore. Plaza de Andalucía, a block off the view terrace, has several decent little bars, restaurants, and a popular candy store busy with local kids. Grazalema, situated on a west-facing slope of the mountains, catches clouds and is famous as the rainiest place in Spain—but I've had only blue skies on every visit.

**Estepa,** spilling over a hill crowned with a castle and convent, is a freshly washed, happy town that fits my dreams of southern Spain. It's situated halfway between Córdoba and Málaga, but it's light years away from either. Atop Estepa's hill is the convent of Santa Clara, worth three stars in any guidebook but found in none. Enjoy the territorial view from the summit, then step into the quiet, spiritual perfection of the church.

In any of these towns, evening is prime time. The promenade begins as everyone gravitates to the central square. The spotless streets are polished nightly by the feet of families licking ice cream. The whole town strolls—it's like "cruising" without cars. Buy an ice-cream sandwich and join the parade.

*For good-value accommodations in Arcos, try Hotel Restaurant El Convento (Maldonado 2, tel. 956-702-333, fax 956-704-128, www.webdearcos.com/elconvento) or Hotel los Olivos (Paseo de los Boliches 30, tel. 956-700-811, fax 956-702-018, www.hotelolivosarcos.com). For more hotels, visit www.ricksteves.com/update, and for all the travel specifics, see this year's edition of* Rick Steves' Spain.

## 40. MOROCCO: PLUNGE DEEP

Walking through the various souks of the labyrinthine medina, I found sights you could only dream of in America. Dodging blind men and clubfeet, I was stoned by smells, sounds, sights, and feelings. People came in all colors, sizes, temperaments, and varieties of deformities. Milky eyes, charismatic beggars, stumps of limbs, sticks of children, tattooed women, walking mummies, grabbing salesmen, teasing craftsmen, seductive scents, half-bald dogs, and little boys on rooftops were reaching out from all directions.

Oooh! Morocco! Slices of Morocco make the *Star Wars* cantina

## Morocco

scene look bland. And it's just a quick cruise from Spain. You can't, however, experience Morocco in a day trip from the Costa del Sol. Plunge deep and your journal will read like a Dalí painting. While Morocco is not easy traveling, it gets rave reviews from those who plug this Islamic detour into their European vacation.

You can catch a boat to Tangier, Morocco, from Tarifa, Gibraltar, or Algeciras. As you step off the boat in Tangier, you realize that the crossing has taken you further culturally than did the trip from the US to Iberia.

Once in Morocco, don't linger in Tangier and Tétouan, the Tijuanas of the north coast. Tangier is not really Morocco—it's a city full of con men who thrive on green tourists. Find the quickest connections south to Rabat. At Tangier, power your way off the boat and hop a taxi to the train station. They'll tell you there's no train until tomorrow, or "Rabat is closed on Thursdays"—anything to get you to stay in Tangier. Believe nothing. Be rude if you have to. Tangier can give you only grief, while the real Morocco lies to the south. Try to make friends with a Moroccan traveler on the boat. He won't be a con man, and he'll usually be happy to help you slip through his embarrassingly stressful port of entry.

Rabat, Morocco's capital, is a good first stop. This comfortable, most-European city in Morocco lacks the high-pressure tourism of the towns on the north coast. Or, for a pleasant break on the beach and a relaxing way to break into Morocco, spend a day at Asilah, between Tangier and Larache.

Taxis are cheap and a real bargain when you consider the comfort, speed, and convenience they provide in these hot, dusty, and confusing cities. Eat and drink carefully in Morocco. Bottled water and bottled soft drinks are safe. The extra-cautious have "well-cooked" written in Arabic on a scrap of paper and flash it when they order meat. I found the couscous, *tajine*, and omelets uniformly good. The Arabs use different number symbols. Learn them. You can practice on license plates, which list the number twice (using their numbers and "ours"). Morocco was a French colony, so French is more widely understood than English. A French phrase book is handy. Travel very light in Morocco. You can leave most of your luggage at your last Spanish hotel for free if you plan to spend a night there on your return from Africa.

| | | |
|---|---|---|
| 0 | ٠ | Sifr |
| 1 | ١ | Waahid |
| 2 | ٢ | Itneen |
| 3 | ٣ | Talaata |
| 4 | ٤ | Arba'a |
| 5 | ٥ | Khamsa |
| 6 | ٦ | Sitta |
| 7 | ٧ | Sab'a |
| 8 | ٨ | Tamanya |
| 9 | ٩ | Tis'a |
| 10 | ١٠ | 'Ashra |

After Rabat, pass through Casablanca (great movie, dull city) and catch the Marrakech Express south. You'll hang your head out the window of that romantic old train and sing to the passing desert.

Marrakech is the epitome of exotic. Take a horse-drawn carriage from the station to downtown and find a hotel near the Djemaa el Fna, the central square of Marrakech, where the action is. Desert musicians, magicians, storytellers, acrobats, snake charmers, gamblers, and tricksters gather crowds of tribespeople who have come to Marrakech to do their market chores. As a tourist, you'll fit in like a clown at a funeral. Be very careful, don't gamble, and hang onto your wallet. You're in another world, and you're not clever here. Spend an entire day in the colorful medina wandering aimlessly from souk to souk. There's a souk for each trade, such as the dyers' souk, the leather souk, and the carpet souk.

In the medina, you'll be badgered—or "guided"—by small boys all claiming to be "a friend who wants to practice English." They are after

*Moroccan road signs: Beware of toboggans.*

money, nothing else. If you don't want their services, make two things crystal clear: You have no money for them, and you want no guide. Then completely ignore them. Remember that while you're with a guide, he'll get commissions for anything you buy. Throughout Morocco, you'll be pestered by these obnoxious hustler-guides.

I often hire a young and easy-to-control boy who speaks enough English to serve as my interpreter. It seems that if I'm "taken," the other guides leave me alone. And that in itself is worth the small price of a guide.

The market is a shopper's delight. Bargain hard, shop around, and you'll come home with some great souvenirs. Government emporiums usually have the same items you find in the market, but priced fairly. If you get sick of souks, shop there and you'll get the fair price, haggle-free.

From Marrakech, consider getting to Fès indirectly by taking an exciting seven-day loop to the south. While buses are reliable and efficient throughout Morocco, this tour is best by car, and it's easy to rent a car in Marrakech and drop it off in Fès. (Car rentals are cheaper when arranged from the U.S.)

Drive or catch the bus south over the rugged Atlas Mountains to Saharan Morocco. Explore the isolated oasis towns of Ouarzazate, Tinerhir, and Er-Rachidia. If time permits, the trip from Ouarzazate to Zagora is an exotic mud-brick pie. These towns each have a weekly "market day," when the tribespeople gather to do their shopping. This is your chance to stock up on honeydew melons and goats' heads. Stay in Tinerhir and climb to the roof of your hotel for a great view of the busy marketplace.

Venture out of town into the lush fields, where you'll tumble into an almost biblical world. Sit on a rock and dissect the silence.

*What century is it?*

A weary donkey, carrying a bearded old man in a white robe and turban, clip-clops slowly past you. Suddenly, six Botticelli maidens flit like watercolor confetti across your trail and giggle out of sight. Stay tuned. The show goes on.

Bus rides in this part of Morocco are intriguing. I could write pages about experiences I've had on Moroccan buses—good and bad—but I don't want to spoil the surprise. Just ride them with a spirit of adventure, cross your fingers, and keep your bag off the rooftop.

## Saharan Adventure

Heading south from Er-Rachidia, a series of mud-brick villages bunny-hop down a lush river valley and into the Sahara. Finally the road melts into the sand, and the next stop is, literally, Timbuktu.

*Leave Europe and a warm Islamic welcome awaits.*

The strangeness of this Alice-in-a-sandy-Wonderland world, untempered, can be overwhelming—even frightening. The finest hotel in Erfoud, the region's major town, will provide a much-needed refuge, keeping out the sand, heat waves, and street kids and providing safe-to-eat and tasty local food, reliable information, and a good and affordable bed.

But the hotel is only your canteen and springboard. Explore! If you plan to go deep into the desert, hire a guide. Choose one you can understand and tolerate, set a price for his services, and before dawn head for the dunes.

You'll drive to the last town, Rissani, and then farther south over 15 miles of natural asphalt to the oasis village of Merzouga. There's plenty of tourist traffic at sunrise and in the early evening, so hitching is fairly easy. A couple of places in Merzouga rent spots on their terrace for those who spend the night.

Before you glows a chain of sand-dune mountains. Climb one. It's not easy. I seemed to slide farther backward with each step. Hike along a cool and crusty ridge. Observe bugs and their tracks. Watch small sand avalanches you started all by yourself. From the great virgin summit, savor the Sahara view orchestrated by a powerful silence. Your life sticks out like a lone star in a black sky. Try tumbling, rolling, and sloshing down your dune. Look back and see the temporary damage one person can inflict on a formerly perfect slope. Then get back in your car before the summer sun turns the sand into a steaming griddle and you into an omelet. Off-season, the midday desert sun is surprisingly mild.

Merzouga is full of very poor people. The village children hang out at the ruins of an old palace. A ragtag percussion group gave us an impromptu concert. The children gathered around us tighter and tighter, as the musicians picked up the tempo. We shared smiles, warmth, and sadness. A little Moroccan Judy Garland saw out of one eye, the other cloudy as rice pudding. One gleaming six-year-old carried a tiny sleeping brother slung on her back. His crusty little fly-covered face was too tired to flinch. We had a bag of candy to share and tried to get 40 kids into an orderly line to march past one by one. Impossible. The line degenerated into a free-for-all, and our bag became a piñata.

Only through the mercy of our guide did we find our way back to Rissani. Camels loitered nonchalantly, looking very lost and not caring. Cool lakes flirted, a distant mirage, and the black hardpan road stretched endlessly in all directions.

Then, with a sigh, we were back in Rissani, where the road starts up again. For us, it was breakfast time, and Rissani offered little more than some very thought-provoking irony. My friends and I could find no "acceptable" place to eat. Awkwardly, we drank germ-free Cokes with pursed lips, balanced bread on upturned bottle caps, and swatted laughing legions of flies. We were by far the wealthiest people in the valley—and the only ones unable to enjoy an abundant variety of good but strange food.

Observing the scene from our humble rusted table, we saw a busy girl rhythmically smashing date seeds; three stoic, robed elders with horseshoe beards; and a prophet wandering through with a message for all that he was telling to nobody.

Our Er-Rachidia hotel was Western-style—as dull and comforting as home. We listened to music and enjoyed the pool, resting and recharging before our next Saharan plunge.

## Saharan Nightlife

Desert dwellers and smart tourists know the value of a siesta during the hottest part of the day. But a Saharan evening is the perfect time for a traveler to get out and experience the vibrancy of North African village life. We drove 10 miles north of Erfoud to a fortified mud-brick oasis village. There was no paint, no electricity, no cars—only people, adobe walls, and palm trees. Absolutely nothing other than the nearby two-lane highway hinted of the modern world.

We entered like Lewis and Clark without Sacagawea, knowing instantly we were in for a rich experience. A wedding feast was erupting, and the whole town buzzed with excitement, all decked out in colorful robes and their best smiles. We felt very welcome.

The teeming street emptied through the medieval gate onto the field, where a band was playing squawky, oboe-like instruments and drums. A circle of 20 ornately dressed women made siren noises with tongues flapping like party favors. Rising dust diffused the lantern light, giving everything the grainy feel of an old photo. The darkness focused our attention on a relay of seductively beautiful, snake-thin dancers. A flirtatious atmosphere raged, cloaked safely in the impossibility of anything transpiring beyond coy smiles and teasing twists.

Then the village's leading family summoned us for dinner. Pillows, blankets, a lantern, and a large, round filigreed table turned a stone cave into a warm lounge. The men of this family had traveled to Europe and spoke some English. For more than two hours, the women prepared dinner and the men proudly entertained their New World guests. First was the ritualistic tea ceremony. Like a mad chemist, the tea specialist mixed it just right. With a thirsty gleam in his eye and a large spike in his hand, he hacked off a chunk of sugar from a coffee-can–size lump and watched it melt into Morocco's basic beverage. He sipped it, as if testing a fine wine, added more sugar, and offered me a taste. When no more sugar could be absorbed, we drank it with cookies and dates. Then, with the fanfare of a pack of Juicy Fruit, the men passed around a hashish pipe. Our shocked look was curious to them. Next, a tape deck brought a tiny clutter of music, from Arab and tribal Berber music to James Brown, reggae, and twangy Moroccan pop. The men danced splendidly.

Finally the meal came. Fourteen people sat on the floor, circling two round tables. Nearby, a child silently waved a palm-branch fan, keeping the flies away. A portable washbasin and towel were passed around to start and finish the meal. With our fingers and gravy-soaked slabs of bread, we grabbed spicy meat and vegetables. Everyone dipped eagerly into the delicious central bowl of couscous.

So far, the Moroccan men dominated. Young girls took turns peeking around the corner and dashing off—much like teenyboppers anywhere. Two older women in striking, black-jeweled outfits were squatting attentively in the corner, keeping their distance and a very low profile. Then one pointed to me and motioned in charades, indicating long hair, a backpack, and a smaller partner. I had been in this same village years earlier. I had longer hair and a backpack and was traveling with a short partner. She remembered my 20-minute stay so long ago!

People in remote lands enjoy a visiting tourist and find the occasion at least as memorable as we do. So many more doors open to the traveler who knocks.

After a proud tour of their schoolhouse, we were escorted across the field back to our car, which had been guarded by a silent, white-robed man. We drove away, reeling with the feeling that the memories of this evening would be the prize souvenir of our trip.

# FRANCE

## 41. PARIS: A GRAND BOULEVARD AND A PETITE LANE

Paris is the epitome of elegance, a cultural touchstone for art, fashion, food, literature, and good living. Come ready to be charmed by that Parisian *je ne sais quoi*. For me, the true magic of Paris is in the sweeping boulevards and intimate lanes. Start at the Arc de Triomphe, saunter down the grand avenue des Champs-Elysées, then disappear down rue Cler.

### The Grand Boulevard

My cabbie plunges into the grand traffic circle where a dozen boulevards converge on the Arc de Triomphe. Like referees at gladiator camp, traffic cops are stationed at each entrance to this traffic circus and let in bursts of eager cars.

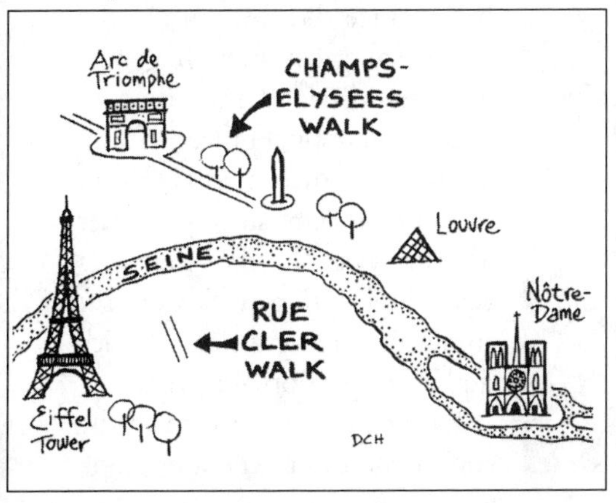


As marble Lady Liberties scramble up Napoleon's arch, heroically thrusting their swords and shrieking at the traffic, all of Paris seems drawn into this whirlpool.

I say to the cabbie, "There must be an accident every few minutes here."

He responds, "In Paris, a good driver gets only

scratches, not dents. But bad drivers...If there is an accident here, each driver is considered equally at fault. This is the only place in Paris where the accidents are not judged. No matter what the circumstances, insurance companies split the costs fifty-fifty."

It's a game of fender-bender chicken. This circle is the great equalizer. Tippy little Citroën 2CVs, their rooftops cranked open like sardine lids, bring lumbering buses to a sudden, cussing halt.

While we're momentarily stalled on the inside lane, I pay and hop out. The cabbie drives away, leaving me under Europe's grandest arch and at the top of its ultimate boulevard. My plan is to stroll the length of the Champs-Elysées (literally "Elysian Fields"). But first, the flame of France's unknown soldier—flickering silently in the eye of this urban storm—seems to invite me to savor this grandiose monument to French nationalism.

The Arc de Triomphe affords a great Paris view, but only to those who earn it. There are 284 steps. Begun in 1806, the arch was intended to honor Napoleon's soldiers, who, in spite of being vastly outnumbered by the Austrians, scored a remarkable victory at the battle of Austerlitz. Napoleon died long before the arch was completed. But it was finished in time for his posthumous homecoming in 1840. Nineteen years after he died in exile on St. Helena, his remains were carried in a grand parade underneath his grand arch.

The Arc de Triomphe is dedicated to the glory of all French armies. Like its Roman ancestors, this arch has served as a parade gateway for triumphal armies (French or foe) and important ceremonies. From 1940 to 1944, a large swastika flew from here as Nazis goose-stepped daily down the Champs-Elysées. Allied troops marched triumphantly under this arch in August 1944.

Standing under the arch, you're surrounded by names of French victories since the Revolution, the names of great French generals (underlined if they died in battle), and by France's Tomb of the Unknown Soldier. Every day at 6:30 p.m. since just after World War I, the flame is rekindled and new flowers set in place, but any time of day it's a place of patriotic reverence.

Once you've climbed to the top of the top of the arch, look

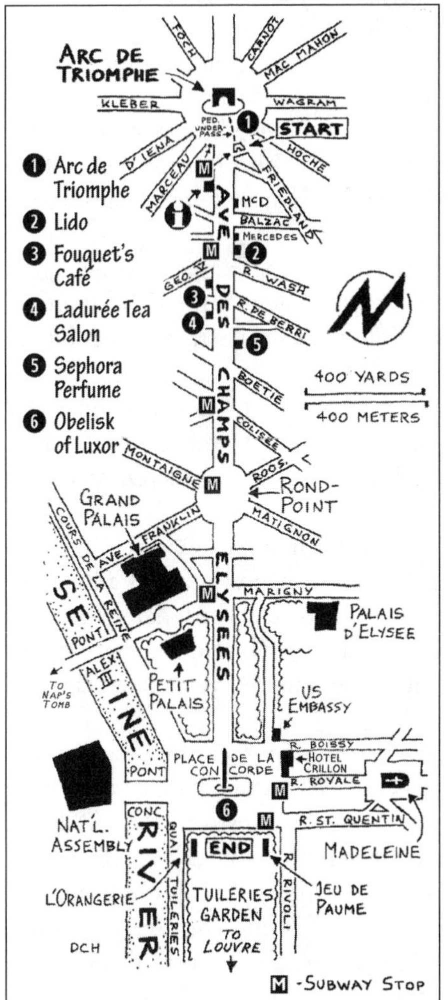


down along the huge axis that shoots like an arrow all the way from the Louvre, up the Champs-Elysées, through the arch, then straight down the avenue de la Grande-Armée to a forest of distant skyscrapers around an even bigger modern arch in suburban La Défense. Notice the contrast between the skyscrapers in the suburbs and the uniformly low-slung buildings downtown. The beauty of Paris—basically a flat basin with a river running through it—is man-made. The key to this beauty is the harmonious relationship between the width of its grand boulevards and the height and design of the buildings. This elegant skyline is broken only by venerable historic domes and spires—and the rude and lonely Montparnasse Tower, which stands like the box the Eiffel Tower came in. The appearance of this tower served as a wake-up call in the early 1970s to preserve the historic skyline of downtown Paris.

In the mid-19th century, Baron Georges-Eugène Haussmann set out to make Paris the grandest city in Europe. The 12 arterials that radiate from the Arc de Triomphe were part of his master plan: the creation of a series of major boulevards, intersecting at diagonals with monuments (such as the Arc de Triomphe) as centerpieces.

His plan did not anticipate the automobile, which is obvious when you study what appears to be a chaotic traffic mess around the arch. But watch how smoothly it actually functions. Cars entering the circle have the right-of-way; those in the circle must yield. (It's the only roundabout in France that works this way.) Parisian drivers navigate the circle like a comet circling the sun—making a parabola. They quickly arc toward the smoothly-flowing center. Then, a couple of avenues before their desired exit, they begin working their way back out.

A stroll down the Champs-Elysées will give you Paris at its most Parisian: sprawling sidewalks, stylish shops, grand cafés, and glimmering showrooms. Europe's characteristic love of strolling (a stately paced triathlon of walking, window shopping, and high-profile sipping) dates from the booming 19th century, with its abundance of upper-class leisure time and cash.

So, don an aristocratic air. From the Arc de Triomphe, amble gently downhill to the immense and historic square called the place de la Concorde. But before you stroll, you must master the name. Say it: shahn-zay-lee-zay.

Even small-town French kids who haven't traveled beyond a TV screen know that this is their country's ultimate parade ground, where major events all unfold: the Tour de France finale, Bastille Day parades, New Year's festivities.

In 1667, Louis XIV opened the first stretch of the Champs-Elysées: a short extension of the Tuileries Gardens leading to Versailles Palace. This date is considered the birth of Paris as a grand city. The Champs-Elysées soon became *the* place to cruise in your carriage. (It still is today—traffic can be jammed up even at midnight.) One hundred years later, the café scene arrived.

The grand café scene survives today, amid pop clothing outlets and music megastores. Two cafés, Fouquet's and Ladurée (a block apart on the quiet side of the boulevard), are among the most venerable in Paris. Even elegant cafés like these often have humble roots. (Fouquet's started as a coachman's bistro.) Today, Parisians keep 12,000 cafés in business.

Fouquet's gained fame as the hangout of French biplane pilots during World War I (Paris was just a few nervous miles from the Western Front). It also served as James Joyce's dining room. Today, it's pretty stuffy—unless you're a film star. The golden plaques at the entry are from winners of France's version of our Oscars, the Césars. While the intimidating interior is impressive, the outdoor setting is great for people-watching—and you can pay $6 for the most expensive shot of espresso I found in Paris.

You're more likely to see me hanging out at Ladurée, munching on a macaroon. This classic 19th-century tea salon/restaurant/pastry shop has an interior right out of the 1860s. Wander around and peek into the cozy rooms upstairs. The bakery makes traditional little cakes and gift-wrapped finger sandwiches. The traditional macaroons—with a pastel palette of flavors from mint to raspberry to rose—really are worth the

## Making Scents of it All

Strolling the Champs-Elysées, you'll come to Sephora, the incredible flagship store (at #72) of the huge perfume chain. Glide down Sephora's ramp into a vast hall of cosmetics and perfumes. It's well laid out: The entry hall is lined with the new products, all open with disposable white "sniff strips" inviting you to take a whiff.

Women's perfumes are on the left wall, and the men's line is on the (shorter) right wall. All are organized alphabetically by company, from Armani to Versace.

The mesmerizing music, chosen just for Sephora, actually made me crave cosmetics. A stock exchange–type board fills one wall. The red flashing numbers are the current prices of perfumes in cities throughout the world—allowing jet-setters to scents-ibly comparison shop.

journey. Get a frilly little gift box to go, or pay the *rançon* and sit down for a *très elegant* coffee and enjoy the Champs-Elysées show.

From the 1920s through the 1960s, this was a street of top-end hotels, cafés, and residences—pure elegance. Locals actually dressed up to stroll here. Then, in 1963, the government, wanting to pump up the neighborhood's commercial metabolism, brought in the RER (underground light rail). Suddenly, suburbanites had easy access. *Bam*—there went the neighborhood.

The coming of McDonald's was a shock. At first it was allowed only white arches painted on the window. Today, the hamburger joint spills out onto the sidewalk with café-quality chairs and flower boxes.

As fast food and pop culture invaded and grand old buildings began to fall, Paris realized what it was losing. In 1985, a law prohibited the demolition of the elegant building fronts that once gave the boulevard a uniform grace. Consequently, many of today's modern businesses hide behind preserved facades. As you stroll, imagine the boulevard pre-'63, with only the finest structures lining both sides all the way to the palace gardens.

The *nouvelle* Champs-Elysées, revitalized in 1994, has new street benches, lamps, and an army of green-suited workers armed with high-tech pooper scoopers. Two lanes of traffic were traded away to make broader sidewalks. And plane trees (a kind of sycamore that thrives despite big-city pollution) provide a leafy ambience.

As you stroll, you'll notice the French appetite for good living. The foyer of the famous Lido, Paris' largest cabaret, comes with leggy photos and a perky R-rated promo video. Movie-going on the Champs-Elysées is popular. Showings *(séances)* with a "v.o." *(version originale)* next to the time indicate the film will be in its original language.

The Club Med building is a reminder of the French commitment to the vacation. Since 1936, the French, by law, have enjoyed one month of paid vacation. In the swinging sixties, Club Med made hedonism accessible to France's middle class. And, as today's French enjoy their 35-hour work week and standard six weeks of paid vacation, there's plenty of time for fun.

Luxury-car dealerships show off their futuristic "concept cars" alongside their current and classic models. Buying a new Mercedes here is like a fashion makeover—you pick out a leather jacket and purse to match.

That new-car smell is a far cry from the 19th century, when this block carried the aroma of horse stables (which evolved into upper-crust limousine garages en route to today's dealerships).

Cross the boulevard at least once to pause at one of the midstream pedestrian islands and enjoy the view. Look up at the Arc de Triomphe, with its rooftop bristling with tourists. Notice three kinds of architecture: old and elegant, new, and new behind old facades.

On the Champs-Elysées, the shopping ends and the park begins at a big traffic circle called Rond-Point des Champs-Elysées M. Dassault. This leafy circle is always colorful, lined with flowers or festive seasonal decorations (thousands of pumpkins at Halloween, hundreds of decorated trees at Christmas). Nearby a statue of General Charles de Gaulle strides out toward the boulevard as he did on the day Paris was liberated in 1944 (6' 4" tall, walking proudly for the length of the Champs-Elysées, as others around him ducked during sporadic gunfire).

From here, it's a straight shot down the last stretch of the boulevard to the sprawling 21-acre square called the place de la Concorde. Its centerpiece is the 3,300-year-old Obelisk of Luxor. It was carted here from Egypt in the 1830s, a gift to the French king. The gold-leaf diagrams on the obelisk tell the story of its laborious journey.

During the French Revolution, this was named "place de la Revolution." A guillotine stood where the obelisk now stands. A bronze plaque memorializes the place where Louis XVI, Marie-Antoinette, and nearly 3,000 others were made "a foot shorter on top." Invented as a humane alternative to the poorly aimed executioner's axe, the guillotine's efficiency was breathtaking. It took a crew of three: one to manage the blade, one to hold the blood bucket, and one to catch the head and raise it high to the roaring crowd.

Standing in the shadow of that obelisk with your back to the Louvre while you look up the grandest boulevard in Europe, you can't help but think of the sweep of history...and those great macaroons.

## The Petite Lane

After taking a turn along Paris' showcase of a boulevard, tune into the rhythm of real life—hop in a cab and say, *"Rue Cler, s'il vous plaît."*

The rue Cler, lined with little food shops, captures the art of Parisian living. Shopping for groceries is an integral part of daily life here for three good reasons: Refrigerators are small (tiny kitchens), produce must be fresh, and it's an important social event. Shopping is a chance to hear about the butcher's vacation plans, see photos of the florist's new grandchild, relax over *un café,* and kiss the cheeks of friends (the French standard is twice for regular acquaintances, three times for friends you haven't seen in a while).

Rue Cler—traffic-free since 1984—offers plenty of space for tiny stores and their shops to spill into the street. It's an ideal environment for this ritual to survive and for you to explore. Along with all the necessary shops—wine, cheese, chocolate, bread—there's a bank and a post office. The shops of this community are run by people who've found their niche: boys who grew up on quiche, girls who know a good wine. If you see anyone in uniform, they're likely from the Ecole Militaire (military school, Napoleon's alma mater two blocks away).

There's no better place to assemble the ultimate French picnic. Visit when the market is open and lively, in the morning or early evening (dead on Sunday evening and all day Monday). Remember that these shops are busy serving regular customers. Be polite and careful not to get in the way.

Have the cabbie drop you off at the intersection of rue Cler and rue

## Rue Cler Walk

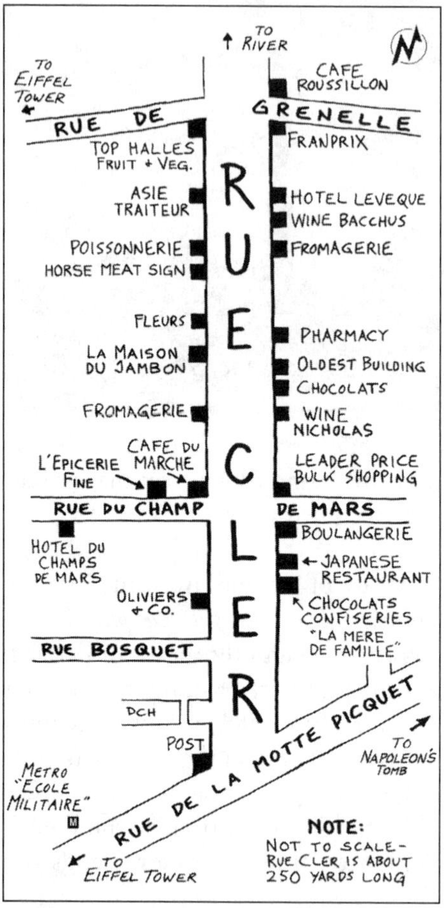

de Grenelle, so you can start your walk where the pedestrian section of rue Cler does.

Café Roussillon is a neighborhood fixture. Drinks at the always-active bar *(comptoir)* are about half the price of drinks at the tables. Notice the list of wines sold by the little (7 cl.) glass on the blackboard. The *cheque déjeuner* decals on the door advertise that this café accepts lunch "checks." In France, an employee lunch subsidy program is an expected perk. Employers issue these checks (worth about $6) for the number of days an employee works in a month. Sack lunches are rare. A good lunch is sacred. This place recently dumped its old-fashioned, characteristic look for the latest café style—warm, natural wood tones, a back-to-basics move with easy lighting and music.

Each morning, Top Halles fruits and vegetables receives fresh produce that has been trucked in from farmers to Paris' huge Rungis market near Orly Airport, then out to merchants with FedEx speed and precision. Locals generally shop with a trolley rather than use bags needlessly. Also notice how the French resist unnecessary packaging and go with what's in season.

Parisians, who insist on quality, shop with their noses. Try it. Smell the cheap foreign strawberries. Then smell the torpedo-shaped French ones *(gariguettes)*. Find the herbs in the back. Is today's delivery in? Look at the price of those melons. What's the country of origin? It must be posted. If they're out of season, they come from Guadeloupe. Many people buy only French products.

The Franprix across the street is a small Safeway-type store. Opposite the Grand Hôtel Lévêque is Asie Traiteur. Fast Asian food to go is popular in Paris; these shops—about as common as bakeries now—are

making an impact on Parisian eating habits.

Drop into the fish shop *(poissonerie).* Fresh fish is brought in daily from ports on the English Channel, 110 miles away. In fact, fish in Paris is likely fresher than in many towns closer to the sea because Paris is a commerce hub and it's shipped from here to outlying towns. Anything wiggling? This shop, like all such shops, has been recently upgraded to meet the new European-wide standards of hygiene.

Across the street is a wine shop. Shoppers often save this stop for last, after they have assembled their meal and are able to pick the appropriate wine. The wine is classified by region. Most "Parisians" have an affinity to their home region, which affects their selection. Notice the great prices. Wines of the month—in the center—sell for about $6. You can get a fine bottle for $12. The salesperson will help you work with your needs and budget. And notice the beer. Since this is a quality shop, there's nothing French—only Belgian specialty beers.

Smell the *fromagerie* next door. A long, narrow, canopied cheese table brings the *fromagerie* into the street. Wedges, cylinders, balls, and miniature hockey pucks all powdered white, gray, and burnt marshmallow—it's a festival of mold. Much of the street cart is devoted only to the goat cheeses. "Ooh la la" means you're impressed. If you really like cheese, show greater excitement with more las: "Ooh la la la la."

Step inside and browse through some of the 400 different types of French cheese. A cheese shop (like a section at the supermarket) is known as BOF *(beurre, oeuf, fromage)* and is where people go for butter, egg, and cheese products. In the back room are *les meules,* the big, 170-pound wheels of cheese (250 gallons of milk go into each wheel). The "hard" cheeses are cut from these. Don't eat the skin of these big ones...they roll them on the floor. But the skin on most smaller cheeses—the

*The cheese shop—known as BOF* (beurre, oeuf, fromage)*—sells butter, eggs, and cheese.*

Brie, the Camembert—is part of the taste. It completes the package.

At dinner tonight, you can take the cheese course just before or as the dessert. On a good cheese plate you have a hard cheese (like Emmentaler, a.k.a. "Swiss cheese"), a flowery cheese (maybe Brie or Camembert), a blue cheese, and a goat cheese—ideally from different regions. Because it's strongest, the goat cheese is usually eaten last.

Across the street is a cheap Greek eatery. Its classy old storefront is a work of art that survives from the previous occupant. The inset stones and glass advertise horse meat: *Boucherie Chevaline.* The decorated front, from the '30s and signed by the artist, would fit in a museum. But it belongs right here. And everyone knows this is a place for a souvlaki and crêpes, not horse meat.

Wander on past the flower shop, pharmacy (in France, the first diagnosis and prescription are made by the pharmacist; if it's out of his league, he'll recommend a doctor), rotisserie (quarter of a roasted chicken with a salad and a drink to go?), and another wine shop. Notice the oldest and shortest building. It's from the early 1800s, when this street was part of a village near Paris and lined with buildings like this. Of course, over the years Paris engulfed these surrounding villages—and the street is a mishmash of architectural styles.

La Maison du Jambon, a charcuterie, sells mouthwatering deli food to go. Because kitchens are so small, these gourmet delis are handy, allowing hosts to concentrate on the main course and buy beautifully prepared side dishes to complete a fine dinner. Notice the system: Order, take your ticket to the cashier to pay, and return with the receipt to pick up your food.

The Café du Marché, on the corner, is *the* place to sit and enjoy the rue Cler action. For a reasonable meal, grab a chair and check the chalky menu listing the *plat du jour* (blue plate special).

The shiny, sterile Leader Price grocery store (across the street, on the corner) is a French Costco, selling bulk items. Because storage space is so limited in most Parisian apartments, bulk purchases are unlikely to become a big deal here. The trend for Parisians lately is to purchase non-perishables via the Internet, pick up their produce three times a week, and get their bread daily.

A short side trip west to 8 rue du Champ de Mars takes you to L'Epicerie Fine, where helpful Pascal tempts visitors with fine gourmet treats. His mission in life is to explain to travelers, in fluent English, what the French fuss over food is all about. Say *bonjour* and let him educate you with generous tastes (balsamic vinegar, olive oil, and caramel). Ask about his gourmet picnic basket—maybe tonight by the Eiffel Tower?

Back on the Rue Cler, you'll come upon a *boulangerie*, diagonally across from Café du Marché. Locals debate the merits of *boulangeries*. It's said that a baker cannot be good at both bread and pastry. At cooking school, they major in one or the other. Here, the baker does good bread. He has a man who does the tasty little pastries for him.

Next door is a strangely out-of-place Japanese restaurant. Sushi is mysteriously for sale everywhere in Paris these days. Locals explain that the phenomenon is the same as when Chinese restaurants were spreading like gastronomic weeds. Real French restaurants were unable to compete, as the cheap Chinese places were actually just crime "fronts," whose real profits came from laundering "black money." In many districts, local authorities actually forbid business permits to Chinese restaurants. Some figure today's countless Japanese restaurants are mostly Chinese-owned and thriving for similar reasons.

Nearby, Oliviers & Co Olive Oils, a shop typical of a ritzy neighborhood like this, sells fine gourmet goodies from the south of France and olive oil from around the Mediterranean. They are happy to give visitors a taste test including tiny spoons of three distinct oils.

Across the street, La Mère de Famille Gourmand Chocolats Confiseries has been in the neighborhood for 30 years. The owner was courted by wholesalers wanting her to take new products, but she kept the old traditional candies, too. "The old ladies, they want the same sweets that made them so happy 80 years ago," she says. Until a few years ago, chocolate was dipped and decorated in the back, where the merchants used to live. As was the tradition in rue Cler shops, the merchants resided and produced in the back and sold in the front.

Rue Cler ends at the post office. The Ecole Militaire Métro stop is just around the corner. If you bought a rue Cler picnic, you'll find benches and gardens nearby. From the post office, avenue de la Motte-Picquet leads to two fine parks: Turn left for Les Invalides or right for the Eiffel Tower.

Settle in and enjoy your Parisian feast. *Bon appétit!*

*To sleep in the rue Cler neighborhood, consider the Grand Hôtel Lévêque (29 rue Cler, tel. 01 47 05 49 15, fax 01 45 50 49 36, www.hotel-leveque.com) or Hôtel du Champ de Mars (7 rue du Champ de Mars, tel. 01 45 51 52 30, fax 01 45 51 64 36, www.hotelduchampdemars.com). In the Marais neighborhood, try the Grand Hôtel Jeanne-d'Arc (3 rue de Jarente, tel. 01 48 87 62 11, www.hoteljeannedarc.com) or Hôtel Castex (5 rue Castex, tel. 01 42 72 31 52, www.castexhotel.com). For more hotels, visit www.ricksteves.com/update, and for all the particulars on Paris, see this year's edition of* Rick Steves' Paris.

# 42. ALSACE AND COLMAR: VINTAGE FRANCE

The French province of Alsace stands like a flower-child referee between Germany and France. Bounded by the Rhine River on the east and the well-worn Vosges Mountains on the west, this is a lush land of villages, vineyards, ruined castles, 20th-century war memorials, and an almost naive cheeriness.

Because of its location, natural wealth, naked vulnerability, and the fact that Germany thinks the mountains are the natural border and France thinks the Rhine River is, nearly every Alsatian generation has weathered an invasion. Centuries as a political pawn between Germany and France have given the Alsace a hybrid culture. Alsatian French is peppered with German words. On doorways of homes, you'll see names like Jacques Schmidt or Dietrich Le Beau. Most locals can swear bilingually. Half-timbered restaurants serve sauerkraut and escargot.

Wine is the primary industry, topic of conversation, dominant mouthwash, perfect excuse for countless festivals, and a tradition providing the foundation for Alsatian folk culture.

Alsace's wine road, the Route du Vin, is an asphalt ribbon tying 90 miles of vineyards, villages, and feudal fortresses into an understandably popular tourist package. The dry and sunny climate has produced good wine and happy tourists since Roman days.

During the October harvest season, all Alsace erupts into a carnival of colorful folk costumes, traditional good-time music, and Dionysian smiles. I felt as welcome as a local grape picker, and my tight sightseeing plans became as hard to follow as a straight line.

If you can pick grapes, you might land a job in October. For a hard day in the vineyards, you'll get room and board, a modest wage, and an intimate Alsatian social experience lubricated liberally, logically, by plenty of local wine.

Wine tasting is popular throughout the year. Roadside *dégustation* signs invite you into wine *caves,* where a local producer will serve you all seven Alsatian wines from dry to sweet, with educational commentary (probably in French) if requested. Try Cremant, the Alsatian champagne. *Cave*-hopping is a great way to spend an afternoon on the Route du Vin. With free samples and fine $6 bottles, French wine-tasting can be an affordable sport.

The small *caves* are fun, but be sure to tour a larger wine co-op. Beer-drinking Germans completely flattened many Alsatian towns in 1944. The small family-run vineyards of these villages sprang back as large, modern, and efficient cooperatives. In the village of Bennwihr, a co-op of 211 people is proud to show you its facilities, which can crush 600 tons of grapes a day and turn out 14,000 bottles an hour. No tour ends without taking full advantage of the tasting room. Bennwihr has a wine tradition going back to Roman times. Its name is from the Latin *Benonis Villare,* or "Beno's estate"—and Beno served up a great Riesling.

There's more to Alsace than meets the palate. Centuries of successful wine production built prosperous, colorful villages. Countless castles capped hilltops to defend the much-invaded plain, and wine wasn't the only art form loved and patronized by local connoisseurs.

Alsatian towns are historic mosaics of gables, fountains, medieval bell towers and gateways, ancient ramparts, churches, and cheery old inns. More than anywhere in France, you'll find plenty of budget beds in private homes ($40–50 doubles, ask at village tourist offices or look for *chambre d'hôte* signs). While Colmar is the best home-base city, petite Eguisheim, with plenty of small hotels, a minimum of tour crowds, and maximum village charm, is the ideal small-town home. Nearby Riquewihr and Kaysersberg are two more crackerjack villages. A scenic path—one of countless in the Alsace—connects these two towns. Take a hike or rent a bike. Drop by a castle or two. Climb the tallest tower and survey Alsace, looking as it has for centuries—a valley of endless vineyards along the Route du Vin.

## Colmar

Colmar, my favorite city in Alsace, sees few American tourists but is popular with Germans and the French. This well-preserved old town of 70,000 is a handy springboard for Alsatian explorations.

Historic beauty, usually a poor excuse to be spared the ravages of World War II, saved Colmar. The American and British military were careful not to bomb the burghers' old half-timbered houses, characteristic red-and-green-tiled roofs, and the cobbled lanes of Alsace's most beautiful city.

Today, Colmar not only survives, it thrives—with historic buildings, impressive art treasures, and a cuisine that attracts eager taste buds from all over Europe. And Colmar has that special French talent of being great but cozy at the same time. Antique shops welcome browsers, and hotel s run down the sleepy streets to pick up fresh croissants in time for breakfast. Schoolgirls park their rickety horse-drawn carriages in front of the city hall, ready to give visitors a clip-clop tour of the old town.

**Colmar Area**

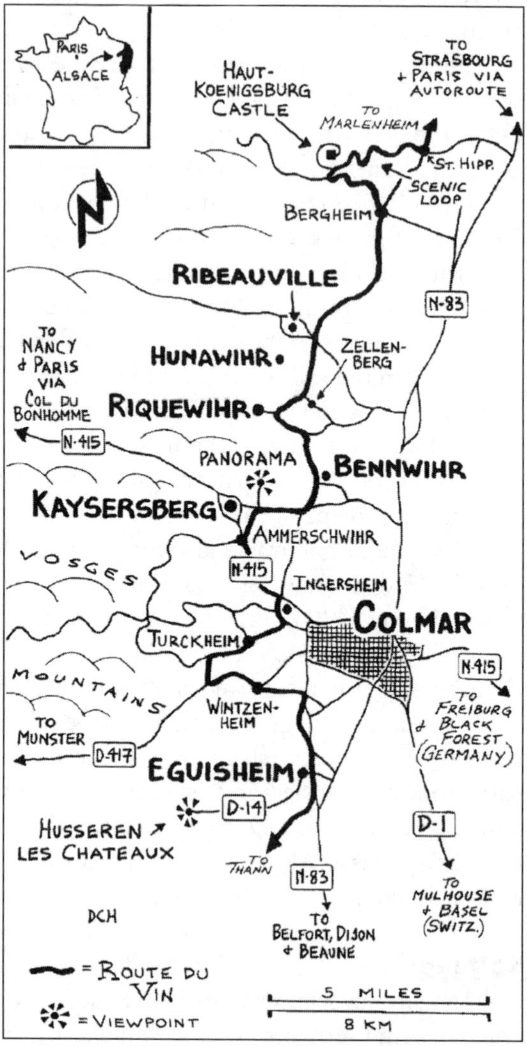

Colmar offers heavyweight sights in a warm, small-town package. By the end of the Middle Ages, the walled town was a thriving trade center filled with rich old houses. The wonderfully restored tanners' quarters is a quiver of tall, narrow, half-timbered buildings. Its confused rooftops struggle erratically to get enough sun to dry their animal skins. Nearby you'll find "La Petite Venise," complete with canals and a pizzeria.

Colmar combines its abundance of art with a knack for showing it off. The artistic geniuses Grünewald, Schongauer, and Bartholdi all called Colmar home.

Frédéric-Auguste Bartholdi, who created our Statue of Liberty a century ago, adorned his hometown with many fine, if smaller, statues. Don't miss the little Bartholdi museum, offering a good look at the artist's life and some fun Statue of Liberty trivia.

Four hundred years earlier, Martin Schongauer was the leading local artist. His *Virgin of the Rose Garden* could give a state trooper goose bumps. Looking fresh and crisp, it's set magnificently in a Gothic Dominican church. I sat with a dozen people, silently, as if at a symphony, as Schongauer's *Madonna* performed solo on center stage. Lit by 14th-century stained glass, its richness and tenderness cradled me in a Gothic sweetness that no textbook could explain. Even if you become so jaded that you "never want to see another Madonna and Child," give this one a chance.

*German or French? Colmar is both.*

The Unterlinden Museum, one of my favorite small museums, is housed in a 750-year-old convent next to the tourist office. It has the best collection anywhere of Alsatian folk art and art exhibits ranging from Neolithic and Gallo-Roman archaeological collections to works by Monet, Renoir, Braque, and Picasso. It's a medieval and Renaissance home show. You can lose yourself in a 17th-century Alsatian wine cellar complete with presses, barrels, tools, and aromas.

The highlight of the museum (and for me, the city) is Matthias Grünewald's gripping Isenheim altarpiece. This is actually a series of paintings on hinges that pivot like shutters. Designed to help people in a hospital suffer through their horrible skin diseases (long before the age of painkillers), it's one of the most powerful paintings ever. Stand petrified in front of it and let the agony and suffering of the Crucifixion drag its fingers down your face. Just as you're about to break down and sob with those in the painting, turn to the happy ending—a psychedelic explosion of Resurrection happiness. It's like jumping from the dentist's chair directly into a Jacuzzi. We know very little about Grünewald except that his work has played tetherball with human emotions for 500 years.

*Grünewald's gripping* Crucifixion

Colmar's tourist information office provides city maps, guides, and a room-finding service. They can also suggest side-trips around Alsace's wine road or into Germany's Black Forest and nearby Freiburg, or a tour of the Maginot Line.

For maximum local fun, remember that Colmar goes crazy during its 10-day wine fest in August. You'll enjoy plenty of revelry—feasting, dancing, music, and wine—Alsatian-style.

*For good-value accommodations in Colmar, try Hôtel le Rapp (1 rue Berthe Molly, tel. 03 89 41 62 10, fax 03 89 24 13 58, www.rapp-hotel.com) or the budget Maison Jund (12 rue de l'Ange, tel. 03 89 41 58 72, fax 03 89 23 15 83, www.martinjund.com). For more hotels, visit www.ricksteves.com/update, and for all the travel specifics, see this year's edition of* Rick Steves' France.

## 43. FROM FRANCE TO ITALY OVER MONT BLANC

Europe's ultimate mountain lift towers high above the tourist-choked French resort town of Chamonix. Ride the Aiguille du Midi *téléphérique* (gondola) to the dizzy 12,600-foot-high tip of a rock needle. As you get in, remind yourself that this thing has been going back and forth now since 1954; surely it'll make it one more time. Chamonix shrinks as trees fly by, soon replaced by whizzing rocks, ice, and snow, until you reach the top. Up there, even sunshine is cold. The air is thin. People are giddy. Fun things can happen if you're not too winded to join locals in the Halfway-to-Heaven tango.

*Dangle silently for 40 minutes as you glide over the glacier from France to Italy.*

The Alps spread out before you. In the distance is the bent little Matterhorn (called "Cervin" in French). You can almost reach out and pat the head of Mont Blanc, at 15,781 feet, the Alps' (and Europe's) highest point.

Next, for Europe's most exciting border crossing, get into the tiny red gondola and head south. Dangle silently for 40 minutes as you glide over the glacier to Italy. Squeeze out your porthole, exploring every corner of your view. You're sailing a new sea.

Cross into Italy at Helbronner Point (11,000 feet) and descend into the remote Italian Valle d'Aosta. It's a whole different world.

Your starting point for this adventure is Chamonix, a convenient overnight train ride from Paris or Nice. Chamonix is a resort town—

## Alpine Crossing from France to Italy

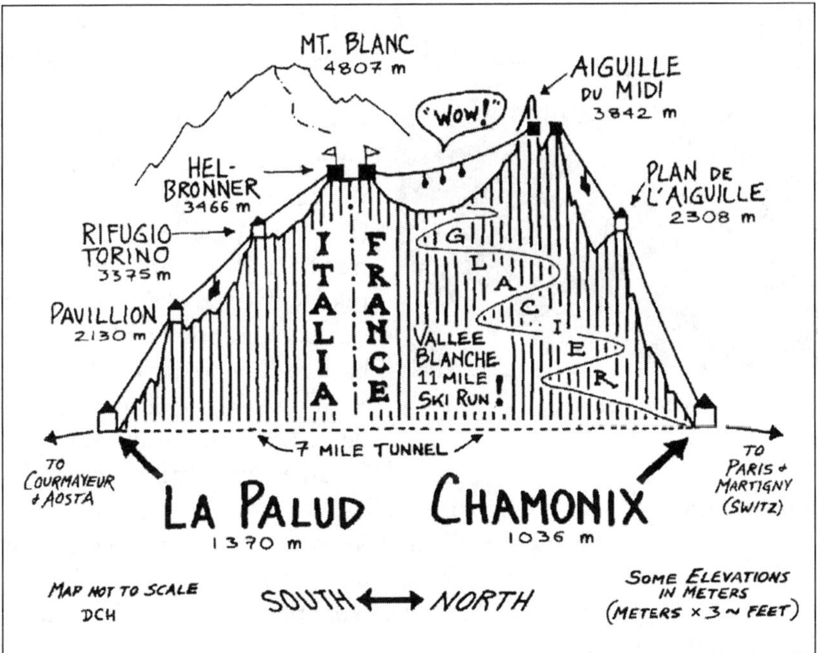


packed in August but surprisingly easy and affordable the rest of the year. Like Switzerland's Interlaken, it's a launchpad for mountain worshippers. The town has an efficient tourist information center and plenty of affordable accommodations.

From Chamonix, there are days of hikes and cable-car rides. The best hikes are opposite the most staggering peaks on the Gran Balcon Sud, a world of pristine lakes, great Mont Blanc range views, and hang gliders lunging off the cliff from the Brévent lift station. Watching these daredevils fill the valley like spaced-out butterflies is a thrilling spectator sport. Probably the best hike—two hours each way—is from the top of the Flégère lift to Lac Blanc. While demanding, the trail is well-signed and the views are breathtaking.

For the ultimate ride, take that *téléphérique* to the Aiguille du Midi. This lift ($45 round-trip from Chamonix, daily 6 a.m.–5 p.m. in the summer, shorter hours off-season, smart to reserve up to 10 days in advance) is Europe's highest and most spectacular. If the weather is good, forget your budget. Afternoons are most likely clouded and crowded. In August, ride very early to avoid miserable delays. If you plan to dillydally, ride directly to your farthest point and linger on your return.

To both save a little money and enjoy a hike, buy a ticket to the

*The Alps from atop the Aiguille du Midi, 12,600 feet up.*

top of the Aiguille du Midi, but only halfway back down. This gives you a chance to look down at the Alps and over at the summit of Mont Blanc from your lofty 12,600-foot lookout. Then you descend to the halfway point (Plan de l'Aiguille), where you're free to frolic in the glaciers and hike to Mer de Glace. Then you can catch a train at Montenvers back to Chamonix.

From the top of the Aiguille du Midi, you can continue (weather permitting) over the mountain to Italy. It's a long trip; the last departure is at about 2 p.m. The descent from Helbronner Point takes you into the remote Italian Valle d'Aosta, where a dash of France and a splash of Switzerland blend with the already rich Italian flavor and countless castles to give you an easy-to-like first taste of Italy.

The town of Aosta, your best valley home base, is a two-hour bus ride from the base of the lift in La Palud (hourly departures, change in Courmayeur). If a fellow cable-car passenger has a car parked in La Palud, charm a ride to Aosta.

"The Rome of the Alps," as Aosta is called, has many Roman ruins and offers a great introduction to the fine points of Italian life: cappuccino, gelato, and an obligatory evening stroll. An evening here is a fine way to ease into *la dolce vita*.

Chamonix, the Aiguille du Midi, and the Valle d'Aosta—surely a high point in anyone's European vacation.

*For good-value accommodations in Chamonix, try Hôtel de l'Arve (60 impasse des Anémones, tel. 04 50 53 02 31, fax 04 50 53 56 92, www.hotelarve-chamonix.com) or Hôtel Richemond (228 rue du Docteur Paccard, tel. 04 50 53 08 85, fax 04 50 55 91 69, www.richemond.fr, richemond@wanadoo.fr). For more hotels, visit www.ricksteves.com/update, and for all the travel specifics, see this year's edition of* Rick Steves' France.

# BELGIUM AND THE NETHERLANDS

## 44. BRUGES: PICKLED IN GOTHIC

With a smile, the shop owner handed me a pharaoh's head and two hedgehogs and said that her husband was busy downstairs finishing off another batch of chocolates. Happily sucking on a hedgehog, I walked out of the small chocolate shop with a $4, 100-gram assortment of Bruges' best pralines—filled-chocolate delights.

Bruggians are connoisseurs of chocolate. You'll be tempted by display windows all over town. Godiva is considered the best big factory brand, but for quality and service, drop by one of the many family-run shops. Pray for cool weather. They close down when it's hot.

With Renoir canals, pointy gilded architecture, and stay-awhile cafés, Bruges is a joy. Where else can you bike along a canal, munch mussels, drink fine monk-made beer, see a Michelangelo, and savor heavenly chocolate, all within 300 yards of a bell tower that rings out "Don't worry, be happy" jingles? And there's almost no language barrier.

The town is Bruges (broozh) in French and English, and Brugge (broo-gha) in Flemish. Before it was French or Flemish, the name was a Viking word for "wharf." Right from the start, Bruges was a trading center. By the 14th century, Bruges had a population of 35,000 (in a league with London) and the most important cloth market in northern Europe. By the 16th century, silt clogged the harbor and killed the economy.

Like so many small-town wonders, Bruges is well-pickled because its economy went sour. But rediscovered by modern-day tourists, Bruges thrives. This uniquely well-preserved Gothic city is no secret. But even with crowds, it's the kind of city where you don't mind being a tourist.

## Bruges

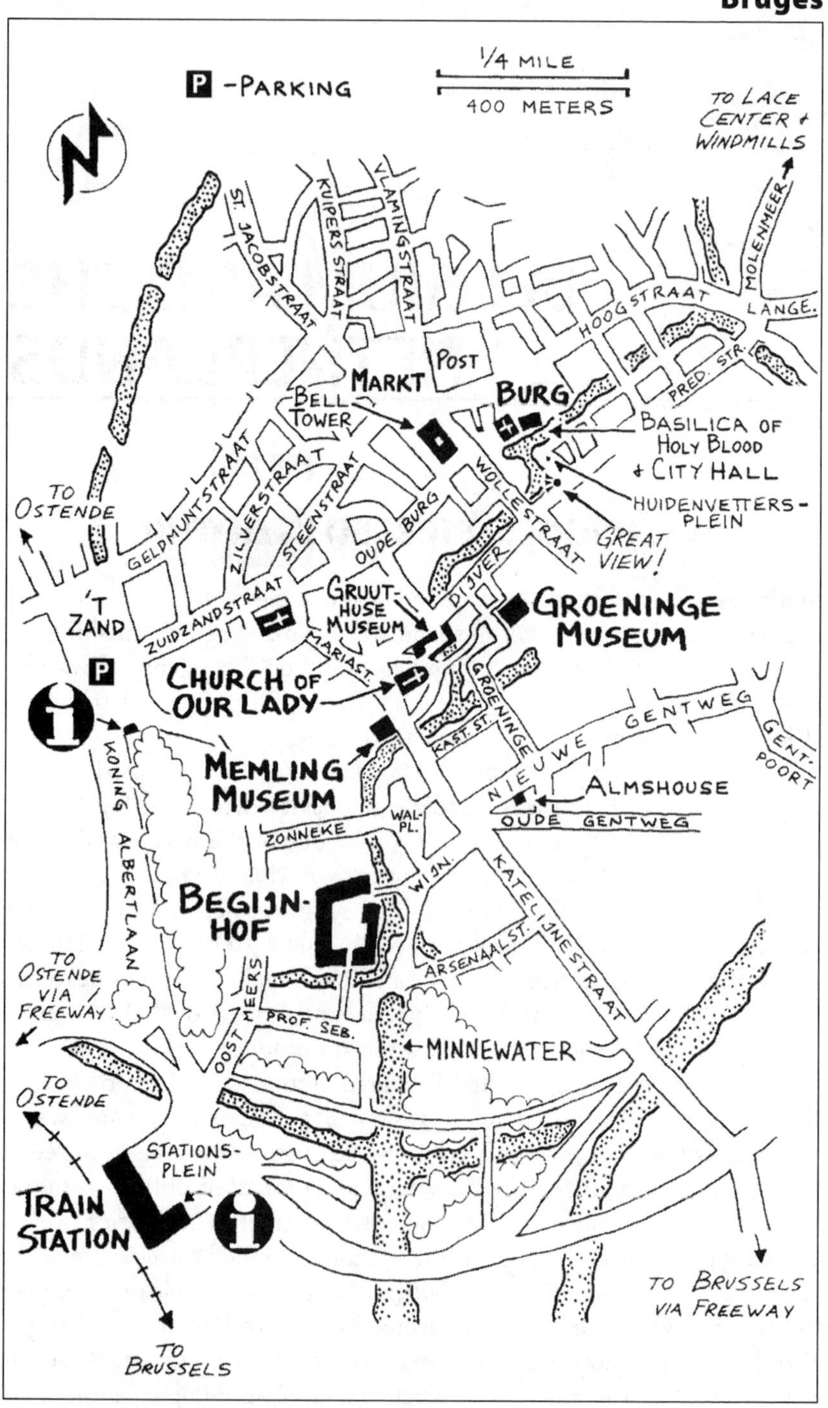

P -PARKING
1/4 MILE
400 METERS
TO LACE CENTER + WINDMILLS
ST. JACOBSSTRAAT
KUIPERS STRAAT
VLAMINGSTRAAT
MOLENMEER
HOOGSTRAAT
LANGE.
PRED. STR.
POST
MARKT
BELL TOWER
BURG
BASILICA OF HOLY BLOOD & CITY HALL
HUIDENVETTERS-PLEIN
GREAT VIEW!
WOLLESTRAAT
TO OSTENDE
GELDMUNTSTRAAT
ZILVERSTRAAT
STEENSTRAAT
OUDE BURG
DIJVER
'T ZAND
ZUIDZANDSTRAAT
GRUUTHUSE MUSEUM
GROENINGE MUSEUM
MARIAST.
CHURCH OF OUR LADY
GROENINGE
KAST. ST.
NIEUWE GENTWEG
GENT-POORT
MEMLING MUSEUM
KONING ALBERTLAAN
ALMSHOUSE
OUDE GENTWEG
ZONNEKE
WAL-PL.
WIJN.
KATELIJNESTRAAT
BEGIJN-HOF
ARSENAALST.
TO OSTENDE VIA FREEWAY
MEERS
OOST
PROF. SEB.
MINNEWATER
TO OSTENDE
STATIONS-PLEIN
TRAIN STATION
TO BRUSSELS VIA FREEWAY
TO BRUSSELS

*Bruges: canals, fine beer, a Michelangelo, and even leaning towers*

Bruges makes a fine first night on the Continent for travelers arriving from England: It's just 15 minutes by train from Ostende, where boats dock from Dover, and an hour from Brussels, where the Eurostar train arrives from London.

Bruges' Market Square, ringed by great old gabled buildings and crowned by the belfry, is the colorful heart of the city. Under the belfry are two great Belgian french-fry stands and a quadrilingual Braille description and model of the tower.

This bell tower has towered over Market Square since 1300. Climb 366 steps to survey the town. Just before the top, peek into the carillon room. On the quarter hour, the 47 bells are played mechanically with the giant barrel and movable tabs. For concerts, a carillonist plays the manual keyboard with fists and feet rather than fingers. Be there on the quarter hour when things ring. The *bellissimo* goes fortissimo at the top of the hour.

Within a block or three, you'll find a day's worth of sights. The Basilica of the Holy Blood is famous for its relic of the blood of Christ, which, according to tradition, was brought to Bruges in 1150 after the Second Crusade. The City Hall has the oldest and most sumptuous Gothic hall in the Low Countries. The Gruuthuse Museum, a wealthy brewer's home, is filled with a sprawling smattering of everything from medieval bedpans to a guillotine. The church of Our Lady, standing as a memorial to the power and wealth of Bruges in its heyday, has a delicate Madonna and Child by Michelangelo said to be the only statue of his to leave Italy in his lifetime (bought with money made from Bruges' lucrative cloth trade). The medieval St. Jans Hospital, now the Memling Museum, has six much-loved paintings by the greatest of the Flemish Primitives, Hans Memling.

Yadda, yadda, yadda...Michelangelo, the blood of Christ, leaning bell towers, and guillotines. You'd expect any medieval powerhouse to show off trinkets from its glory days. But Bruges has fun experiences, too.

The De Halve Maan brewery tour is a handy way to pay your respects to perhaps the favorite local beer. The happy gang at this working family brewery gives entertaining and informative 45-minute, four-language tours. At De Halve Maan ("The Half Moon"), they remind their drinkers: "The components of the beer are vitally necessary and contribute to a well-balanced life pattern. Nerves, muscles, visual sentience, and a healthy skin are stimulated by these in a positive manner. For longevity and lifelong equilibrium, drink De Halve Maan beer in moderation!"

Belgians are Europe's beer experts, and this country boasts more than 350 types of beer. Duvel ("Devil"), a potent local brew, is, even to a Bud Light kind of guy, obviously great beer. Trappist is the dark monk-made beer, and Dentergems is made with coriander and orange peel. Those who don't drink beer enjoy the cherry-flavored Kriek and strawberry-flavored Frambozen. Each beer is served in its own unique glass.

Walk off your beer buzz with a stroll through the *begijnhof* (buh-HINE-hof). For reasons of war and testosterone, there were more women than men in the medieval Low Countries. The order of Beguines offered women (often single or widowed) a dignified place to live and work. When the order died out, many *begijnhofs* were taken over by towns for subsidized housing, but some, like this one, became homes for nuns. You'll find *begijnhofs* all over Belgium and the Netherlands. Bruges' *begijnhof* almost makes you want to don a habit and fold your hands as you walk under its wispy trees and whisper past its frugal little homes.

For more peace, wander back in time to Bruges' four windmills, strung out along a pleasant, grassy canalside park. Joust with a windmill or just have a picnic.

Every once in a while as you travel, you stumble onto a town that somehow missed the 21st-century bus. Ironically, many of these wonderfully preserved towns are so full of Old World charm because, for various reasons, their economies failed. The towns became so poor that no one even bothered to tear them down to build more modern towns. England's Cotswolds lost their export market. Toledo was abandoned as Spain's capital. Stranded-in-the-past Dutch fishing towns were left high and dry as the sea around them was drained and the land reclaimed. And Bruges' harbor silted up.

Today, while some of these towns slumber on, many—like Bruges—enjoy a renewed prosperity as "tourist dreams come true."

*For good-value accommodations in Bruges, try Hotel Heritage (Niklaas Desparsstraat 11, tel. 050/444-444, fax 050/444-440, www.hotel-heritage.com)*

*or Koen and Annemie Dieltiens' B&B (Waalse Straat 40, tel. 050/334-294, fax 050/335-230, www.bedandbreakfastbruges.be). For more hotels, visit www.ricksteves.com/update, and for all the travel specifics, see this year's edition of* Rick Steves' Amsterdam, Bruges & Brussels.

## 45. AMSTERDAM'S COUNTER-CULTURE

Amsterdam is a laboratory of progressive living, bottled inside Europe's most 17th-century city. Like Venice, this city is a patchwork quilt of canal-bordered islands, anchored upon millions of wooden pilings. But unlike its dwelling-in-the-past cousin, Amsterdam sees itself as a city of the future, built on good living, cozy cafés, great art, street-corner jazz...and a spirit of live-and-let-live.

*Cruise by Amsterdam's stately 17th-century buildings.*

During its Golden Age in the 1600s, Amsterdam was the world's richest city, an international sea-trading port, and the cradle of capitalism. Wealthy, democratic burghers built a planned city of tree-shaded canals lined with town-houses topped with fancy gables. Immigrants, Jews, outcasts, and political rebels were drawn here by its tolerant atmosphere, and painters like young Rembrandt captured that atmosphere on canvas.

**Amsterdam Overview**

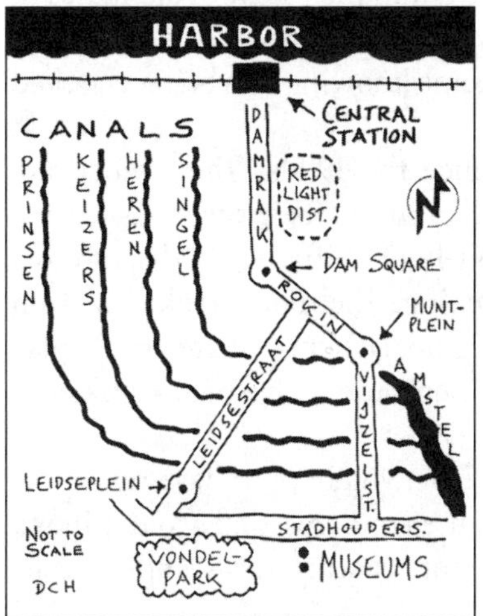



Rich as the city's history is, it's just one fine detail of today's colorful big picture. Many visitors find that it's best to approach the city not as a historian, but as an ethnologist observing a fascinating and unique culture. A stroll through any neighborhood is rewarded with things that are commonplace here but rarely found elsewhere. Carillons chime quaintly in neighborhoods selling

## Marijuana in Europe

Compared to the United States, many European countries have a liberal attitude toward marijuana users. They believe if "harm reduction" is the aim of a nation's drug policy, it makes more sense to treat marijuana as a health problem (and regulate it like alcohol) than as a criminal one. Simply put, many Europeans believe marijuana can be enjoyed responsibly by adults.

Still, drugs are not legal in Europe. The use, sale, and possession of any illegal drug can lead to stiff fines or a jail sentence. While laws against the use of drugs such as cocaine, heroin, LSD, and Ecstasy are still strictly enforced, more and more of Europe is reclassifying marijuana as a "soft drug" and tolerating recreational use in private or in certain bars.

Even in the most liberal countries, the sale of marijuana is permitted only in certain places. In Amsterdam and other Dutch cities, "coffeeshops"—often sporting red, green, and yellow Rastafarian flags—are allowed to sell small amounts for personal use to people over 18. In Copenhagen's "free city" of Christiania, the use of marijuana is generally tolerated (though the conservative government has been cracking down on sellers). Recently, Switzerland, Britain, and other countries have also been liberalizing their approach to marijuana.

Remember that you are subject to the laws of the country in which you travel when abroad, so be sensible and err on the side of caution.

sex, as young professionals smoke pot with impunity next to old ladies in bonnets selling flowers. Neighborhoods live by a quirky system of "social control," where a man feels safer in his home knowing he's being watched by the hookers next door.

Prostitution has been legal here since the 1980s. The women are often entrepreneurs, renting space and running their own businesses. Women usually rent their space for eight-hour shifts. A good spot costs $100 for a day shift and $200 for an evening. The rooms look tiny from the street ("Do they have to do it standing up?"), but most are just display windows, opening onto a room behind or upstairs with a bed, a sink, and little else.

Prostitutes are licensed. To get a license, you have to have no criminal record, keep your premises hygienic, use condoms, and avoid minors. Most prostitutes opposed legalization, not wanting taxes and bureaucratic regulations.

*Coffeeshops in Amsterdam offer a wide array of bongs.*

People who run coffeeshops warn that even a country that is "soft on soft drugs" needs to make a few marijuana arrests each year to maintain its "favorable trade status" with the United States (which wants European countries to maintain a harder stance on marijuana use).

Be warned that anywhere in Europe, especially in countries adjacent to countries famous for being easy on marijuana, border patrols can be particularly strict. And driving under the influence of any drug is a serious offense that can land you in jail.

For an overview and country-by-country summary of European drug laws, see the Web site of the National Organization for the Reform of Marijuana Laws (NORML) at www.norml.org. Americans interested in "going local" with marijuana in Europe may be interested in the vast and rapidly growing discussion on the Graffiti Wall at www.ricksteves.com.

Popular prostitutes charge $30–60 for a 20-minute visit and make about $650 a day. They fill out tax returns, and many belong to a loose union called the Red Thread. When a prostitute pushes her emergency button, the police, rather than a pimp, come to her rescue.

The Dutch people are unique. They may be the world's most handsome people—tall, healthy, and with good posture—and the most open, honest, and refreshingly blunt. As connoisseurs of world culture, they appreciate Rembrandt paintings, Indonesian food, and the latest French films, but with an un-snooty, blue-jeans attitude.

Un-snooty, but not un-sooty—about a third of the Dutch people smoke tobacco. Holland has a long tradition as a smoking culture, being among the first to import the tobacco plant from the New World. We Americans may not approve, but we should expect to find smoke in the air—in restaurants, bars, buses, almost everywhere. Smoking seems to be part of an overall diet and regimen that—no denying it—somehow makes the Dutch people among the healthiest in the world. Tanned-and-trim sixtysomething Dutch people sip their beer, take a drag, and ask me why Americans murder themselves with Big Macs. Strict no-smoking regulations implemented in the Netherlands in 2004 have not snuffed out the smoking culture.

If you can't avoid tobacco in Amsterdam, why not make it part of your sightseeing? At Rokin 92, the House of Hajenius is a temple of cigars—a "paradise for the connoisseur" showing "175 years of tradition and good taste." To enter this sumptuous Art Deco building with its painted leather ceilings is to step back into 1915. Visitors can sniff fine pipe tobacco from brown-capped canisters. The shop's "personal humidifiers" allow locals to call in an order and have their cigars waiting for them at just the right humidity.

Of course, smokers in Europe's counterculture mecca don't enjoy just tobacco. Throughout Amsterdam, you'll see "coffeeshops"—pubs selling marijuana—with menus that look like the inventory of a drug bust.

Most of downtown Amsterdam's coffeeshops feel grungy and foreboding to anyone over 30. The neighborhood places (and those in small towns around the countryside) are much more inviting to people who prefer James Taylor to Eminem.

Paradox is the most *gezellig* (pleasant) coffeeshop I found—a mellow, graceful place. The managers, Ludo and Jan, are patient with descriptions and are happy to walk you through all your options. This is a rare coffeeshop that serves light meals. The juice is fresh, the music is easy, and the neighborhood is charming. Colorful murals with bright blue skies are all over the walls, creating a fresh and open feeling (Eerste Bloemdwarsstraat 2, 2 blocks from Anne Frank House, tel. 020/623-5639, www.paradoxamsterdam.demon.nl).

Ludo explained to me that the Dutch think the concept of a "victimless crime" is a contradiction in terms. Although hard drugs are illegal, marijuana causes about as much excitement as a bottle of beer. If a tipsy tourist calls an ambulance after smoking too much pot, medics just say, "Drink something sweet and walk it off."

Amsterdam also has several "Smartshops"—bright, clean, fully professional retail outlets that sell a wide array of drugs, many of which are illegal in America. Their "natural" drugs include harmless nutrition boosters (royal jelly), harmful but familiar tobacco, organic versions of popular dance-club drugs (herbal Ecstasy), powerful psychoactive plants (psilocybin mushrooms), and joints made from an unpredictable mix of marijuana and other substances, sold under exotic names like "Herbal Love." The best-seller: marijuana seeds. Prices are clearly marked, with brief descriptions of the drugs, their ingredients, and effects.

The knowledgeable Smartshop salespeople enjoy talking about these "100-percent-natural products that play with the human senses." Still, my fellow Americans, *caveat emptor!* We've grown used to thinking, "If it's legal, it must be safe. If it's not, I'll sue." While legal in Amsterdam, some of these substances can cause powerful, often unpleasant reactions.

The Dutch also like plants you can't smoke, as I learned strolling through one of the oldest botanical gardens in the world. The De Hortus Botanical Garden dates from 1638, when medicinal herbs were grown here. The collection expanded in the 17th and 18th centuries as a wealth of flora were brought from faraway places by the Dutch East India Company. Today, its 6,000 different varieties of plants are spread throughout several greenhouses and a tropical palm house. No mobile phones are allowed because "our collection of plants is a precious community—treat it with respect." The "residents" are described thoughtfully: "A Dutch merchant snuck a coffee plant out of Ethiopia, which ended up in this garden in 1706. This first coffee plant in Europe was the literal granddaddy of the coffee cultures of Brazil—long the world's biggest coffee producer."

Amsterdam's tolerant culture has attracted some colorful residents. Nick Padalino is one cool cat who—with the help of ultraviolet lights—has found his niche in life. Nick's flowery window display at Tweede Leliedwarsstraat 5 hides a fluorescent wonderland: Electric Ladyland, a tiny, unique museum featuring black-light art. Nick lovingly demonstrates fluorescent minerals from all over the world and fluorescence in everyday objects (stamps, candy, and so on). He seems to get a bigger kick out of it than even his customers. Pulling out one of his prize artifacts, Nick says, "This is the historic first fluorescent crayon from San Francisco, from the 1950s. Wow. See the label? It says, 'Use with black light for church groups.' Wow."

*Electric Ladyland's Nick Padalino glows with pride as he adds more color to Amsterdam's colorful Jordaan district.*

Yes, Amsterdam is known for its tolerance of soft drugs—but the Dutch also think progressively about more mundane matters, like transportation. Amsterdam's 737,000 residents own an equal number of bikes.

Holland's 16 million people own 16 million bikes (many people own two: a long-distance racing bike and an in-city bike, often deliberately kept in poor maintenance so it's less enticing to the many bike thieves). The Dutch appreciate the efficiency of a self-propelled machine that travels five times faster than walking, without pollution, noise, parking problems, or high fuel costs. On a *fiets* (bicycle), a speedy local can traverse the historic center in 10 minutes. Pedestrians also enjoy the quiet of a people-friendly town where bikes outnumber cars.

Another way to see the city is by boat: Amsterdam has more canals than Venice. Amsterdam's canals tamed the flow of the Amstel River, creating pockets of dry land to build on. The city's 100 canals are about 10 feet deep, crossed by some 1,200 bridges, fringed with 100,000 Dutch elm and lime trees, and bedecked with 2,000 houseboats. A system of locks near the central train station controls the flow outward to (eventually) the North Sea, and the flow inward of the tides. The locks are opened periodically to flush out polluted water. Some of the boats in the canals look pretty funky by day, but Amsterdam is an unpretentious, anti-status city. When the sun goes down and the lights come on, people cruise the sparkling canals with an on-board hibachi grill and a bottle of wine, and, as my Dutch friends report, "even scows can become chick magnets."

Amsterdam, a bold experiment in freedom, may box your Puritan ears. Take it all in, then pause to watch the summer sunset—at 10 p.m.—and see the Dutch Golden Age reflected in a quiet canal.

*For good-value accommodations in Amsterdam, try Hotel Toren (Keizersgracht 164, tel. 020/622-6352, fax 020/626-9705, www.hoteltoren.nl) or Hotel Keizershof (Keizersgracht 618, where Keizers canal crosses Nieuwe Spiegelstraat, tel. 020/622-2855, fax 020/624-8412, www.hotelkeizershof.nl). For more hotels, visit www.ricksteves.com/update, and for all the travel specifics, see this year's edition of* Rick Steves' Amsterdam, Bruges & Brussels.

# GERMANY, AUSTRIA, AND SWITZERLAND

## 46. ROTHENBURG AND THE ROMANTIC ROAD: FROM THE RHINE TO BAVARIA THROUGH GERMANY'S MEDIEVAL HEARTLAND

Thirty years ago, I fell in love with a Rothenburg in the rough. At that time, the town still fed a few farm animals within its medieval walls. Today its barns are hotels, its livestock are tourists, and Rothenburg is well on its way to becoming a medieval theme park.

But Rothenburg is still Germany's best-preserved walled town. Countless travelers have searched for the elusive "untouristy Rothenburg." There are many contenders (such as Michelstadt, Miltenberg, Bamberg, Bad Windsheim, and Dinkelsbühl), but none holds a candle to the king of medieval German cuteness. Even with crowds, overpriced souvenirs, a Japanese-speaking night watchman, and, yes, even with *Schneeball*s, Rothenburg is best. Save time and mileage and be satisfied with the winner.

In the Middle Ages, when Frankfurt and Munich were just wide spots in the road, Rothenburg was Germany's second-largest city, with a whopping population of 6,000. Today, it's Europe's most exciting medieval town, enjoying tremendous tourist popularity.

To avoid the hordes of day-trippers, spend the night. In the deserted

moonlit streets, you'll risk hearing the sounds of the Thirty Years' War still echoing through turrets and clock towers.

A walking tour helps bring the ramparts alive. The tourist information office on the Market Square offers $7 tours in English led by a local historian—usually an intriguing character (April–Oct daily at 2 p.m., plus the more colorful Night Watchman's tour mid-March–Dec at 8 p.m.). A thousand years of history is packed between the cobbles.

For the best view of the town and surrounding countryside, climb the Town Hall tower. For more views, walk the wall that surrounds the old town. This 1.5-mile walk atop the wall is at its most medieval before breakfast or at sunset.

Rothenburg's fascinating Medieval Crime and Punishment Museum, all unusually well-explained in English, is full of legal bits and diabolical pieces, instruments of punishment and torture, and even an iron cage—complete with a metal nag gag. Some react with horror, others wish for a gift shop.

St. Jakob's Church contains the one must-see art treasure in Rothenburg: a glorious 500-year-old altarpiece by Riemenschneider, the Michelangelo of German woodcarvers. Pick up the brochure that explains the church's art treasures and climb the stairs behind the organ for Germany's greatest piece of woodcarving.

To hear the birds and smell the cows, take a walk through the Tauber Valley. The trail leads downhill from Rothenburg's idyllic castle gardens to a cute, skinny, 600-year-old castle, the summer home of the town's mayor in the 15th-century, Mayor Toppler. While called a castle, the floor plan is more like a four-story tree house. It's intimately furnished and well worth a look. On the top floor, notice the 1945 photo of a bombed-out Rothenburg. From here, walk past the covered bridge and trout-filled Tauber to the sleepy village of Detwang, which is actually older than Rothenburg and has a church with another impressive Riemenschneider altarpiece.

Warning: Rothenburg is one of Germany's best shopping towns. Do it here, mail it home, and be done with it. Lovely prints, carvings, wine glasses, Christmas-tree ornaments, and beer steins are popular.

The Käthe Wohlfahrt Christmas trinkets phenomenon is spreading across the half-timbered reaches of Europe. In Rothenburg, tourists flock to two Käthe Wohlfahrt Christmas Villages (just off Market Square). These Santa wonderlands are filled with enough twinkling lights to require a special electric hookup, instant Christmas mood music (best appreciated on a hot day in July), and American and Japanese tourists hungrily filling little woven shopping baskets with $6–10 goodies to hang on their trees. (OK, I admit it, my Christmas tree sports a few KW ornaments.) Prices have tour-guide kickbacks built into them. I prefer the friendlier Freise shop (on the northwest corner of Market Square), which offers cheaper prices, less glitter, and more variety.

At the English Conversation Club, held every Wednesday night at Mario's hotel, Altfränkische Weinstube, locals enjoy a weekly excuse to get together, drink, and practice their fanciest English on each other and on visiting tourists. Annaliese, who runs the Freise shop (see above) and is a regular at the Conversation Club, invites me to join her, so I meander into the pub through candlelit clouds of smoke and squeeze a three-legged stool up to a table already crowded with her and her family.

Annaliese pours me a glass of wine, then pulls a *Schneeball* (the local powdered-doughnut–like "snowball") from a bag. Raising a cloud of powdered sugar as she pokes at the name on the now empty bag, she says, "Friedel is the bakery I explained you about. They make the best *Schneeball*. I like it better than your American doughnut. Everyday I eat 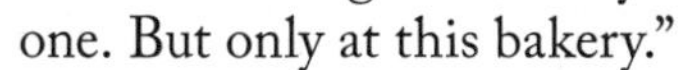one. But only at this bakery."

Shoving a big doughy ball my way, she says, "You like to eat this?"

I break off a little chunk, saying, "Only a teeny-weeny *bisschen*."

For years, Annaliese has playfully tried to get me to write good things about *Schneeball*s. I put *Schneeball*s (which originated in a hungrier age as a way to get more mileage out of leftover dough) in that category of penitential foods—like 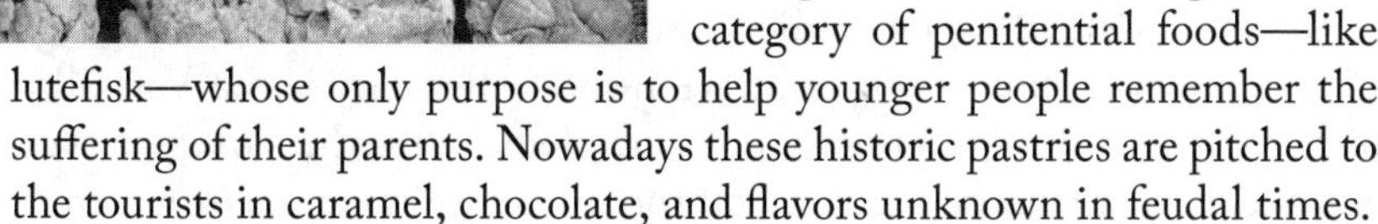lutefisk—whose only purpose is to help younger people remember the suffering of their parents. Nowadays these historic pastries are pitched to the tourists in caramel, chocolate, and flavors unknown in feudal times.

As Annaliese finishes the *Schneeball,* we share our favorite slang and tongue twisters. But medieval Rothenburg is waiting. I drain my glass of wine and bid a cheery, *"Tschüss!"*

In the night, I find myself alone with Rothenburg. The winds of history polish half-timbered gables. Following the grooves of centuries of horse carts, I head down to the castle garden. From a distance, the roars of laughter tumbling like waves out of *Biergartens* and over the ramparts sound as medieval as they do modern.

Sitting in a mossy niche in the town wall, I finger the medieval stonework. Nocking my imaginary crossbow, I aim an arrow into the dark forest that surrounds the city. Even now, it feels good to be within these protective walls.

On the ramparts after dark, I look over a choppy sea of red-tiled roofs to the murky and mysterious moat beyond the wall. The cannons are loaded. Torches illuminate the gory heads of bad guys on pikes that greet visitors at the city gates. With a dash of moonlight and a splash of wine, Rothenburg once again is a crossroads where modern-day travelers meet medieval wayfarers.

## Romantic Road

The Romantic Road, winding through the most beautiful towns and scenery of Germany's medieval heartland, is the best way to connect the dots between Frankfurt and Munich. Peppered with pretty towns today because it was such an important and prosperous trade route 600 years ago, the popular route is no secret. But even with its crowds, it's a must.

Along the Romantic Road (and especially just off it), visitors find the Germany most come to see. On the side roads, flower boxes decorate the unseen sides of barns and no unfamiliar car passes unnoticed. Church-steeple masts sail seas of rich, rolling farmland, and fragrant villages invite you to slow down. Stop wherever the cows look friendly or a town fountain beckons. At each village, ignore the signposts and ask an old woman for directions to the next town—just to hear her voice and enjoy the energy in her eyes. Thousands of tourists pass through. Few stop to chat.

After Rothenburg, consider these top stops along the Romantic Road: Dinkelsbühl, Rothenburg's well-preserved medieval sister city, comes with old walls, towers, gateways, and the peaceful green waters of the moat defending its medieval architecture from the 21st century. Würzburg has a fine Baroque prince bishop's Residenz—the Versailles of Franconia—and an oh-wow Baroque chapel. Another lovely carved altarpiece by Riemenschneider (and the unique thimble museum across the street) is just outside Rothenburg at Creglingen. To the south is the flamboyant church called the Wieskirche, near Oberammergau,

## Germany's Romantic Road

and "Mad" King Ludwig's Disney-esque Neuschwanstein Castle near Füssen.

The sections from Füssen to Landsberg and Rothenburg to Weikersheim are most characteristic. (If you're driving with limited time, drive these and then connect Rothenburg and Munich by autobahn.) Caution: The similarly promoted "Castle Road" (between Rothenburg and Mannheim) sounds intriguing but is much less interesting.

A car or bike gives you complete freedom—just follow the brown *Romantische Straße* signs. This is the best way to connect the castles of the Rhine and the lederhosen charm of Bavaria. Those without wheels can take the train or bus. The Deutsche Touring company runs buses daily between Frankfurt and Munich in each direction ($95–120, April–Oct, tel. 069/790-350, www.romantic-road-coach.de). I used to recommend this bus tour, but given its recent price spikes, increasingly inflexible schedule, and long travel times, it's no longer a good deal—take the train instead.

*For good-value accommodations in Rothenburg, try Gasthof zur Goldenen Rose (budget, Spitalgasse 28, tel. 09861/4638, fax 09861/86417, www.thegoldenrose.de) or Hotel Gerberhaus (classy, Spitalgasse 25, tel. 09861/94900, fax 09861/86555, www.gerberhaus.rothenburg.de). For more hotels, visit www.ricksteves.com/update, and for all the travel specifics, see this year's edition of* Rick Steves' Germany & Austria.

## 47. HALLSTATT, IN AUSTRIA'S COMMUNE-WITH-NATURE LAKE DISTRICT

With the longest life span and one of the shortest work weeks in Europe, Austrians spend their ample free time focusing on the fine points of life: music, a stroll, pastry, and a good cup of coffee. Austrians specialize in good living and *Gemütlichkeit.* A uniquely Austrian concept, and as difficult to translate as it is to pronounce, it means a warm, cozy, friendly, focus-on-the-moment feeling. Even tourists catch on in the Salzkammergut Lake District, where big-city Austrians go to relax.

Far from the urban rat race, though just two hours by train from Salzburg, this is the perfect place to commune with nature, Austrian-style. The Salzkammergut is a lushly forested playground dotted with cottages. Trains, buses, and boats lead the traveler through gentle mountains and shy lakes, winding from relaxed village to relaxed village.

*Hallstatt, in Austria's Salzkammergut Lake District*

The Salzkammergut's pride and joy is the town of Hallstatt. The minute it popped into view, I knew Hallstatt was my alpine Oz. It's just the right size (1,200 people), wonderfully remote, and almost traffic-free. A tiny ferry takes you from the nearest train station, across the

## Hallstatt

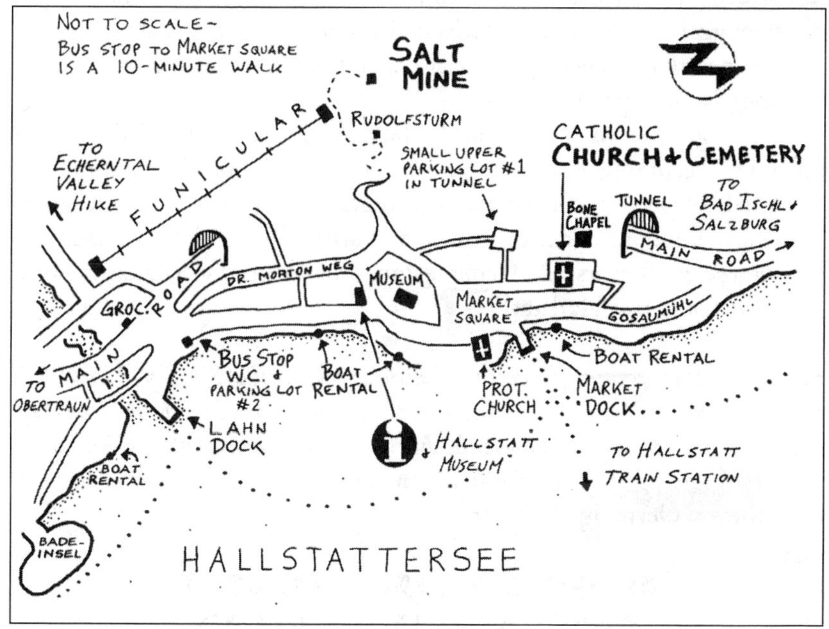


fjordlike lake, and drops you off on the town's storybook square.

Bullied onto its lakeside ledge by a selfish mountain, Hallstatt seems tinier than it is. Its pint-size square is surrounded by ivy-covered guest houses and cobbled lanes. It's a toy town. You can tour it on foot in about 10 minutes. Except in August, when tourist crowds trample most of Hallstatt's charm, there's no shortage of pleasant $25-per-person *Zimmers* (bed-and-breakfast places).

Three thousand years ago, this area was the salt-mining capital of Europe. An economic and cultural boom put it on the map back in Flintstone times. In fact, an entire 1,000-year chapter in the story of Europe is called "The Hallstatt Period." A humble museum next to the tourist office shows off Hallstatt's salty past. For a better look, you can tour the world's first salt mine, located a thrilling funicular ride above downtown Hallstatt. You'll dress up in an old miner's outfit, ride trains into the mountain where the salt was mined, cruise subterranean lakes, scream down long, sliver-free banisters, and read brief and dry English explanations while entertaining guides tell the fascinating story in German. You can return to Hallstatt by funicular, but the scenic 40-minute hike back into town is (with strong knees) a joy.

Hallstatt outgrew its little ledge, and many of its buildings climb the mountainside, with the street level on one side being three floors above the street level on the other. Land is limited—so limited that there's not enough room for the dead. Remains evicted from the cemetery are stacked neatly in an eerie chapel of decorated bones (see "Boning up on Europe's Relics," page 568).

Passing time in and around Hallstatt is easy. The little tourist office will recommend a hike—the 9,000-foot Mount Dachstein looms overhead—or a peaceful cruise in a rented canoe. Most people go to Hallstatt simply to relax, eat, shop, and stroll. To cloak yourself in the *Gemütlichkeit,* flowers, and cobblestones of Austria's Salzkammergut Lake District, visit Hallstatt.

*For good-value accommodations in Hallstatt, try Gasthof Simony (Markt 105, tel. & fax 06134/8231) or Gasthof Zauner (Marktplatz 51, tel. 06134/8246, fax 06134/82468, www.zauner.hallstatt.net). For more hotels, visit www.ricksteves.com/update, and for all the travel specifics, see this year's edition of* Rick Steves' Germany & Austria.

## 48. GIMMELWALD: FOR THE SWISS ALPS IN YOUR LAP

When told you're visiting Gimmelwald, Swiss people assume you mean the famous resort in the next valley, Grindelwald. When assured that Gimmelwald is your target, they lean forward, widen their eyes, and—with their sing-songy Swiss German accent—they ask, "Und how do you know about Gimmelvald?"

The traffic-free village of Gimmelwald hangs nonchalantly on the edge of a cliff high above Lauterbrunnen Valley, 30 minutes south of Interlaken by car or train. This sleepy village has more cow troughs than mailboxes. The songs of birds and brooks and the crunchy march of happy hikers constantly remind you why so many travelers say, "If Heaven isn't what it's cracked up to be, send me back to Gimmelwald."

*Downtown Gimmelwald*

Gimmelwald, an ignored station on the spectacular Schilthorn gondola, should be built to the hilt. But, led by a visionary schoolmaster, the farming community managed to reclassify its land as an "avalanche zone"—too dangerous for serious building

## Berner Oberland

projects. So while developers gnash their teeth, sturdy peasants continue to milk cows and make hay, thus surviving in a modern world only by the grace of a government that subsidizes such poor traditional industries.

Gimmelwald is a community in the rough. Take a walk—you can tour it in 15 minutes. Its two streets, a 700-year-old zig and zag, are decorated by drying laundry, hand-me-down tricycles, and hollowed stumps bursting proudly with geraniums. Little-boy cars are parked next to the tiny tank-tread cement mixers and mini-tractors necessary for taming this alpine environment. White-bearded elves smoke hand-carved pipes, and blond-braided children play "barn" instead of "house." Stones called *schindles* sit like heavy checkers on old rooftops, awaiting nature's next move. While these stones protect the slate from the violent winter winds, today it's so quiet you can hear the cows ripping tufts of grass.

Notice the traditional log-cabin architecture. The numbers on the buildings are not addresses, but fire insurance numbers. The cute little hut near the station is for storing and aging cheese, not hostelers. In Catholic Swiss towns, the biggest building is the church. In Protestant towns, it's the school. Gimmelwald's biggest building is the school (2 teachers share one job, 17 students, and a room that doubles as a chapel when the pastor makes his monthly visit).

There's nothing but air between Gimmelwald and the rock face of the Jungfrau a mile or two across. Small avalanches across the valley look and sound like distant waterfalls. Kick a soccer ball wrong and it ends up a mile below on the Lauterbrunnen Valley floor.

Gimmelwald has three families: von Allmen, Brunner, and Feuz. With the 130 townsfolk sharing three surnames, there are probably 10 Hans von Allmens and a wagonload of Maria Feuzes. To keep prescriptions and medical records straight, the doctor in nearby Lauterbrunnen goes by birth date first, then the patient's name.

The people of Gimmelwald systematically harvest the steep hillside. Entire families cut and gather every inch of hay the way children of the Depression polish their dinner plates. After harvesting what the scythe can reach, they pull hay from nooks and crannies by hand.

Half a day is spent on steep rocks harvesting what a machine can cut in two minutes on a flat field. It's tradition. It's like breathing. And there's one right way to do it.

To inhale the Alps and really hold it in, sleep high in Gimmelwald. Poor but pleasantly stuck in the past, the village has a creaky hotel, happy hostel, decent pension, and a couple of B&Bs.

Walter Mittler's Hotel Mittaghorn sits at the top end of Gimmelwald. The black-stained chalet has eight balconies and a few tables shaded by umbrellas on its tiny terrace. Everything comes with

*In a Back Door–style hotel, you get more by spending less. Here, the shower's down the hall, and the Alps are in your lap.*

huge views. Sitting as if anchored by pitons into the steep, grassy hillside, the hotel is disturbed only by the cheery chatter of hikers and the two-stroke clatter of passing tractors.

Evening fun in Gimmelwald is found in the hostel (with lots of young Alp-aholic hikers eager to share information on the surrounding mountains); on the Pension Gimmelwald terrace (with the best food in town); and, depending on Walter's mood, at Hotel Mittaghorn. If you're staying at Walter's, enjoy his simple supper and coffee schnapps. Then sit on the porch and watch the sun caress the mountaintops to sleep as the moon rises over the Jungfrau.

Starting early in the morning, the bright modern gondola swooshes by with 30 tourists gawking out the windows. In Gimmelwald, the modern world began in 1965 when it got the cable car. Before that, mothers ready to give birth had to hike an hour downhill to the valley floor for a ride into Interlaken. Many mothers didn't make it all the way to the hospital. Outside of Interlaken, a curve in the road is named for a Gimmelwald baby...born right there.

Today, the Schilthornbahn is the all-powerful lift that connects the valley floor with the mountain communities of Gimmelwald and Mürren on its way to the 10,000-foot Schilthorn summit. This artificial vein pumps life's essentials—mail, bread, skiers, hikers, school kids, coffins, hang gliders, and tourists—to and from each community.

From Gimmelwald, ride the gondola up the Schilthorn, a 10,000-foot peak capped by a revolving restaurant called Piz Gloria ($65 round-trip, discounts early and late). Lifts go twice hourly, involve two transfers, and take 30 minutes. Watch the altitude meter go up, up, up.

For the most memorable breakfast around, ride the early gondola to the summit, where you'll find the restaurant and a thrilling 360-degree view. Sip your coffee slowly to enjoy one complete circle. Drop into the theater to see clips from the James Bond movie *On Her Majesty's Secret Service,* in which the restaurant is blown up. Then go outside for the real thrills. Frolic on the ridge. Watch hang gliders methodically set up and jump into airborne ecstasy.

While you can hike down from the summit, the first station below the summit, Birg, is the best jumping-off point for high-country hikes.

Two minutes from the Birg station, I'm completely alone—surrounded by a harsh and unforgiving alpine world. Anything alive is here only by the grace of nature. A black ballet of rocks is accompanied by cow bells and a distant river. Wisps of clouds are exclamation points. The Alps put you close to God. A day like today has Lutherans raising their hands and holy rollers doing cartwheels.

*Thrill-seeking hang gliders are a common sight on alpine peaks. Here, an absent-minded hang glider prepares for his last takeoff.*

I make it to my target, a peak that stands dramatically high above Gimmelwald. After a steep descent, I step out of the forest at the top end of the village I call home. Walking over a pastel carpet of gold clover, bell flowers, milk kraut, and daisies, I'm surrounded by butterflies and cheered on by a vibrant chorus of grasshoppers, bees, and crickets.

The finish line is a bench that sits at the high end of Gimmelwald—one of my "savor Europe" depots. A great dimension of travel is finding the right spot and just sitting still. Crickets rattle congratulatory castanets, a river blurts out of a glacier, and Mürren crowns a bluff above me, keeping all the fancy tourists where they belong. An alpine farm that has intrigued me for years still sits high above the tree line, forever alone amid distant flecks of brown and white cows and goats.

Below me, the village schoolyard rumbles with children. Christian, the accordion player, who went up to the fields early this morning, chugs by on his mini-truck towing a wobbly wagonload of hay. His kids bounce like cartoons on top.

Enjoying this alone is fine. But share this bench with a new friend, the sun of a daylong hike stored in your smiling faces, and you too will sing, "If Heaven isn't what it's cracked up to be, send me back to Gimmelwald."

If you're interested in the alpine cream of Switzerland, it's best seen from nearby peaks and ridges (Jungfrau, Kleine Scheidegg, or the Schilthorn). If you're looking for Heidi and an orchestra of cowbells in a Switzerland that you thought existed only in storybooks—take off your boots in Gimmelwald.

## From Interlaken into the Jungfrau Region

When the 19th-century Romantics redefined mountains as something more than cold and troublesome obstacles, Interlaken became the original alpine resort. Ever since then, tourists have flocked to the Alps "because they're there." Interlaken's glory days are long gone, its elegant old hotels eclipsed by more jet-setting alpine resorts. Today, Interlaken's shops are filled with chocolate bars, Swiss Army knives, and sunburned backpackers.

I had always considered Interlaken overrated. Now I understand that Interlaken is only a springboard for alpine adventures. Stop in Interlaken for shopping, banking, post, and telephone chores, and to pick up information on the region. Then head south into the Berner Oberland.

You have several options (see the map in this chapter). Vagabonds who just dropped in on the overnight train (ideal from Paris) can do a loop trip, going down Grindelwald Valley, over the Kleine Scheidegg ridge, and then into Lauterbrunnen. From there you can head on out by returning to Interlaken, or settle into Gimmelwald for the alpine cuddle after the climax. Those with more time go directly to the village of Gimmelwald (skipping Grindelwald) and explore the region from that home base.

Loop-trippers should get an early start and catch the private train from the Interlaken East station to Grindelwald (discounted with a Eurailpass or Eurail Selectpass). Don't sleep in touristy Grindelwald, but take advantage of its well-informed tourist information office and buy a first-class mountain picnic at its Co-op grocery. Then ascend by train into a wonderland of white peaks to Kleine Scheidegg, or even higher by gondola to Männlichen (Eurail discounts for train and gondola). It's an easy one-hour walk from Männlichen down to Kleine Scheidegg.

Now you have successfully run the gauntlet of tourist traps and reached the ultimate. Before you towers Switzerland's mightiest mountain panorama. The Jungfrau, the Mönch, and the Eiger boldly proclaim that they are the greatest. You won't argue.

Like a saddle on the ridge, Kleine Scheidegg gives people something to hang onto. It has a lodge (with $40 dorm bunks) and an outdoor restaurant. People gather here to marvel at tiny rock climbers dangling from ropes halfway up the icy Eiger. You can splurge for the expensive ride from here to the towering Jungfraujoch ($82 round-trip from Kleine Scheidegg, discounts early and late)—expect crowds on sunny summer days, especially after a stretch of bad weather. The ride's impressive, but I couldn't have asked for more than the *Mona Lisa* of mountain views that I enjoyed from Kleine Scheidegg.

From Kleine Scheidegg, start your hike into the less-touristy Lauterbrunnen Valley. The hike is easy. My gear consisted only of shorts (watch the mountain sun), tennis shoes, a tourist brochure map, and a bib to catch the drool.

It's lunchtime as you hike into your own peaceful mountain world. Find a grassy perch, and your picnic will have an alpine ambience that no restaurant can match. Continuing downhill, you may well be all alone and singing to the rhythm of your happy footsteps. The gravelly walk gets steep in places, and you can abbreviate your hike by catching the train at one of two stations you'll pass along the way. As the scenery changes, new mountains replace the ones you've already seen. After two hours, you enter the car-free town of Wengen. Avoid the steep, dull hike from Wengen to Lauterbrunnen by taking the train down to the valley floor, where you can continue by bus and gondola (or funicular and train) to the village of Gimmelwald.

This is the scenic but very roundabout way to Gimmelwald. For a much more direct route, take the train from the Interlaken East station to Lauterbrunnen, transfer to the bus for Stechelberg, then ride the gondola up to Gimmelwald.

*For good-value accommodations in Gimmelwald, try Hotel Mittaghorn (tel. 033-855-1658, www.ricksteves.com/mittaghorn), Pension Restaurant Gimmelwald (tel. 033-855-1730, www.pensiongimmelwald.ch), or Maria and Olle Eggimann's B&B (tel. 033-855-3575, oeggimann@bluewin.ch). For more hotels, visit www.ricksteves.com/update, and for all the travel specifics, see this year's edition of* Rick Steves' Switzerland.

## 49. ALPINE ESCAPES

Even those who know a Rocky Mountain high find something special about the Alps. In the Alps, nature and civilization mix it up comfortably, as if man and mountain shared the same crib.

Imagine walking to the long, legato tones of an alpenhorn. Then, just when you need it most, there's a mechanical lift to whisk you silently and

## Alpine Escapes

effortlessly—if not cheaply—to the top of that staggering ridge or peak, where your partner can snap a photo of you looking ruggedly triumphant. You'll pass happy yodelers, sturdy grannies, and dirndl'd moms with apple-cheeked kids.

While the most famous corners are now solidly in the domain of tour groups, much of the best alpine charm is folded away in no-name valleys, often just over the ridge from the Holiday Inns and the slap-dancing stage shows.

Here are a few places that will make your alpine adventures more than a scenic hike.

**Log-cabin villages:** Both Switzerland and Austria have isolated log-cabin villages, smothered with alpine goodness, set in a flower-speckled world of serene slopes, lazy cows, and musical breezes. While both Taveyanne and Fallerschein are barely accessible by car, they're worth circling on the map if you suspect you may have been Kit Carson in a previous life.

*You can hike...or frolic... from France to Slovenia and never come out of the Alps.*

The village of Taveyanne is in the French-speaking part of Switzerland, two miles off the road from Col de la Croix to Villars (or take the footpath from Villars). It's just a jumble of log cabins and snoozing cows stranded all alone at 5,000 feet. The only business in town is the Refuge de Taveyanne, where the Siebenthal family serves hearty meals—great fondue and a delicious *croute au fromage avec oeuf*—in a prize-winning, rustic setting. Who needs electricity? There's a huge charred fireplace with a cannibal-size cauldron, a prehistoric cash register, low-beamed ceilings, and well-hung ornamental cowbells. For a memorable experience—and the only rentable beds in the village—rent one of five mattresses in their primitive loft (never full, accessible by a ladder outside, urinate with the cows, $10, open May–Oct, tel. 024-498-1947).

The similarly remote village of Fallerschein is in western Austria, south of Reutte. Thunderstorms roll down its valley as if it were God's bowling alley. But the blissfully simple pint-size church on the high ground seems to promise that this huddle of houses will remain standing. The people sitting on benches are Austrian vacationers or clandestine lovers who've rented cabins. Fallerschein is notorious as a hideaway for those having affairs. The town is 4,000 feet high at the end of a one-mile road near Namlos, on the Berwang road south of Reutte, in Austria's Tirol.

**Hinterhornalm over Gnadenwald:** The same mountains that put Innsbruck on the vacation map surround Hall. For a lazy look at life in the high Alps around these towns, drive up to 5,000-foot Hinterhornalm and walk to a remote working farm.

Begin your ascent in Gnadenwald, a chalet-filled village sandwiched between Hall and its Alps. Pay $6 at the toll hut, then wind your way upward, marveling at the crazy amount of energy put into this road, to the rustic Hinterhornalm Berg restaurant. This place serves hearty food with a cliff-hanger of a view (often closed, mobile 0664/211-2745). Hinterhornalm is a hang-gliding springboard. On sunny days, it's a butterfly nest of thrill-seekers ready to fly.

From there, it's a level 20-minute walk to Walderalm, a cluster of three dairy farms with 70 cows that share their meadow with the clouds. The cows—cameras dangling from their thick necks—ramble along ridge-top lanes surrounded by cut-glass peaks. The ladies of the farms serve soup, sandwiches, and drinks (very fresh milk in the afternoon) on rough plank tables. Below you spreads the Inn River Valley and, in the distance, tourist-filled Innsbruck.

*A firsthand look at fairy-tale alpine culture is just a hike away at Walderalm, near Gnadenwald.*

**Ebenalp in Appenzell:** Switzerland's Appenzell is a region whose forte is cow culture rather than staggering peaks. Its only famous peak, Säntis, is a modest 8,200 feet high. For a fun angle on alpine culture, go five miles south of Appenzell town to Wasserauen and ride the lift to the top of nearby Ebenalp ($20 round-trip). From its summit, enjoy a sweeping view of a major chunk of Switzerland. Then hike down about 15 minutes to a prehistoric cave home (its tiny museum is always open). Wander in and through until you reach a narrow, sunny ledge. Perched here is the Wildkirchli, a

*A Swiss cliff-hanger of a hideaway: Berggasthaus Aescher on Ebenalp*

400-year-old cave church that housed hermit monks from 1658 to 1853. Also clinging precariously to the cliffside is Berggasthaus Aescher. This rugged guest house, originally built to accommodate those who came here to pray with a hermit monk, now bunks hikers communing with nature.

Rather than sleep in the unmemorable town of Appenzell, stay in the Berggasthaus Aescher ($30 per dorm bed, includes breakfast and comforter, no sheets required or provided, Family Knechtle-Wyss, 12 min by steep trail below top of lift, open May–Oct, tel. 071-799-1142, www.aescher-ai.ch). This old house has only rainwater and no shower. The goats live inside a neighboring hut. The Berggasthaus is sometimes quiet and sometimes festive (locals party until the wee hours on weekends). While Saturdays can be packed with more hikers than mattresses, you'll normally get a small woody dorm to yourself.

The hut is actually built onto the cliffside; the back wall is the rock. Study this alpine architecture—and geology—from the toilet. Sip your coffee on the deck, behind a curtain of water dripping from the gnarled overhang a hundred yards above. Leave a note in the guest book, which goes back 60 years.

From this perch, cows look like dandruff littering meadows on the far side of the valley. In the distance, below Säntis, an hour's walk away, is the Seealpsee (alpine lake) and Wasserauen. Only the hang gliders, like neon jellyfish, tag your world as 21st century.

# EASTERN EUROPE

## 50. EASTERN EUROPE: FROM SURVIVING TO THRIVING

Two decades ago, my Polish friends were taking in their windshield wipers at night. (If stolen, they were impossible to replace.) Bomb craters appeared in front of Bulgarian train stations...and no one talked about it. People ran their kitchen faucets so neighbors in their flimsy apartment flats couldn't hear their conversations. Teenagers were allowed one rock concert a year—which happened to be scheduled the same time as Easter Mass. And train conductors checked my ticket before slipping secretively with me into the bathroom to change money at black-market rates.

*With the communist days sinking deeper into history, many of the countless statues of Lenin, Marx, and triumphant workers tossing off their chains are ending up in quirky parks, like Statue Park in suburban Budapest.*

Those days are long gone. Throughout Eastern Europe, it's a new morning—for locals and tourists alike.

It's amazing what a decade and a half of freedom can do. Rather than deadened with fear and frustration, Eastern European faces are lively with hope. Towns from Dresden to Dubrovnik are booming with small-

## Eastern Europe

business energy. Communism has become kitsch—you'll find stern Stalin-style statues dotting amusement parks and communist theme restaurants...serving dreary food from the '60s. A new generation of young English-speaking guides is eager to bring each city and village vividly to life for travelers. And, finally, competition and the free market are yielding some great hotel values.

For travelers, the rise of Eastern Europe means we all get a second chance to relive the good old days of European tourism—full of

*Eastern Europe feels peaceful and stable. The only security I encountered was at airports and at Jewish sights such as this, Budapest's Great Synagogue.*

color, surprise, and challenge. When you cross a border in the East, you'll learn all about strange new currencies: złotys, koruna, forints, kuna.... Exploring towns that spent decades in a communist cocoon, you'll encounter weathered locals, intellectual priests, rickety dirt-cheap trolleys, befuddling symbols for the men's and ladies' rooms, and new food adventures—from menus where the price doesn't matter. You can gulp the best beer in Europe for $0.50 a mug, munch a hearty plate of pierogi (Polish-style ravioli) for a buck, and enjoy classical music in palatial settings for $10.

While in Western Europe, hallucinogenic absinthe is illegal and mead (or honey wine) is served only in touristy castle banquets, both are basic brews in Bohemia. Scruffy children spin crude wooden tops, babushki bake doughnut-like breads, and Roma (Gypsies) dance with their bears on street corners. While in Kraków, I crossed paths with one of our tour groups. They griped, "You should have told us to bring more camera batteries!" That's my kind of tour complaint.

*Eastern European yuppies are embracing capitalism wholesale. The good-looking rich guys get the cute girls...and then ignore them to do business on their mobile phones. The result: Birthrates are way down. Young couples throughout Europe are more interested in buying cars and houses than paying for children.*

Despite the Old World romance, the efficiency is New World, with an English-speaking younger generation and Internet cafés on nearly every corner.

I traveled with one of our Eastern Europe tours recently. Rather than linger over another glass of the local Bull's Blood wine, I left the gang in search of an Internet café.

Strolling through the small Hungarian town of Eger, I passed Europe's northernmost minaret and stopped under a floodlit monument depicting warrior heroes. Looking into their intense eyes, I thought, "Hmm, they look as fierce as the Hungarian language sounds."

*These Hungarian school kids have no memory of communism.*

The Internet café was packed. Many kids here don't own computers—so it's standing room only at the neighborhood computer club. Writing my e-mail, I was surrounded by grade-schoolers playing the same games my teenager plays—a cacophony of explosions and chirpy computer-game tunes. While statues of raging Magyar warriors crushed 16th-century Turks out on the main square, their adolescent descendants battle space-age bad guys indoors. It's as if another group of villains—the Soviets—never existed.

Earlier that day, we lunched at a village school, and then enjoyed a Q&A session with the middle-schoolers. It took a while to dawn on our group of Cold War Baby Boomers—these kids have no memory of communism! To them, Hungary is a rapidly developing country, excited about their recent membership in the European Union. The shift from one generation to the next has been dramatic. While their grandparents may miss the cradle-to-grave "security" of the communist era, their parents seem enthusiastic about capitalism and thankful for the world of opportunity in their children's futures.

Throughout Eastern Europe, the new mixes it up with the old. The buxom babushki ladies are still collecting coins at the public toilets. But now they actually smile.

*For all the specifics, see this year's edition of* Rick Steves' Best of Eastern Europe.

## 51. CZECH OUT PRAGUE

Prague has always been historic. Now it's fun, too. No place in Europe has become so popular so quickly. And for good reason: The capital of

### EU Enlargement and the "New Europe"

The Czech Republic, Slovakia, Poland, Hungary, Slovenia, and five other countries joined the European Union in 2004. Though EU membership—and investment—should ultimately benefit everybody, old members and new members both have had their doubts.

For example, new EU member Poland survived the communist era without having to collectivize its small family farms. But now that they've joined the EU, collectivization is mandatory. Traditional Czech cuisine is also in jeopardy. EU hygiene standards dictate that cooked food can't be served more than two hours old. My Czech friend complained, "This makes many of our best dishes illegal." Czech specialties, often simmered, taste better the next day.

Even when the news is good, it's bad. Slovakia, one of the poorest new EU members, suffers from sky-high unemployment and a rusting armaments industry that was abandoned when the Soviets left. Foreign companies are taking advantage of Slovakia's prime location and cheap labor by building several new car factories—turning Slovakia into what *The New York Times* called "the European Detroit." It's a boost to the economy, sure—but as the poor Slovaks become the exploited workforce of wealthy Europe, is it truly good for Slovakia?

A wise Czech grandmother put it best. In her lifetime, she had lived in a country ruled from Vienna (Hapsburgs), Berlin (Nazis), and Moscow (communists). She said, "Now that we're finally ruled from Prague, why would we want to turn our power over to Brussels?"

For their part, longstanding EU members have been skeptical about taking on more countries. Wealthy nations have already spent huge fortunes to improve the floundering economies of poorer member countries (like Portugal, Greece, and Ireland). Most of the new members expect a similar financial-aid windfall. Also on the financial front, Westerners are fretting about an influx of cheap labor from the East.

the Czech Republic—the only Central European capital to escape the bombs of the last century's wars—is a people-friendly and entertaining showcase for Czech culture.

Prague is slinky with sumptuous Art Nouveau facades, offers tons of cheap Mozart and Vivaldi, and brews the best beer in Europe. It's an explosion of pent-up entrepreneurial energy jumping for joy after 40 years of communist rule. And its low prices will make your visit enjoyable and, with a few skills, nearly stress-free. Americans need no visa.

Finally, Western Europeans worry about their political power being diluted. When the 10 new nations joined the EU, the geographical center of Europe shifted from Brussels to Prague. In this "New Europe," Poland or the Czech Republic might emerge with a leading role. The East eagerly embraces the future, intent on distancing itself from its painful recent history, while the West tentatively clings to the past, when its power was at its peak (and French, not English, was the world's language).

*The new European Union: Austria, Belgium, Cyprus, Czech Republic, Denmark, Estonia, Finland, France, Germany, Great Britain, Greece, Hungary, Ireland, Italy, Latvia, Lithuania, Luxembourg, Malta, Netherlands, Poland, Portugal, Slovakia, Slovenia, Spain, and Sweden. Bulgaria and Romania join the club in 2007.*

As the "New Europe" takes shape, players on both sides will continue to define their new roles and seek compromise. So far, the general consensus in the East is that joining Europe was the right move. In 2007, Bulgaria and Romania hope to continue this trend by also becoming members. And in a few years, the Slovenes, Poles, Czechs, Bulgarians, and their neighbors will all be working harder than ever and enjoying more coins jangling in their pockets...and those coins will be euros.

Just flash your passport at the border. From Munich, Berlin, or Vienna, it's roughly a six-hour train ride (day or overnight) to Prague.

*Praha,* as locals call their town, is big, with 1.2 million people. For the quick visit, think of the town as small and focus on its historic core. Prague is charming, safe, and aggressive—welcoming you with big smiles, open cash registers, and plenty of scams.

Your Prague visit deserves at least two full days. With this much time, spend a morning seeing the castle and a morning in the Jewish

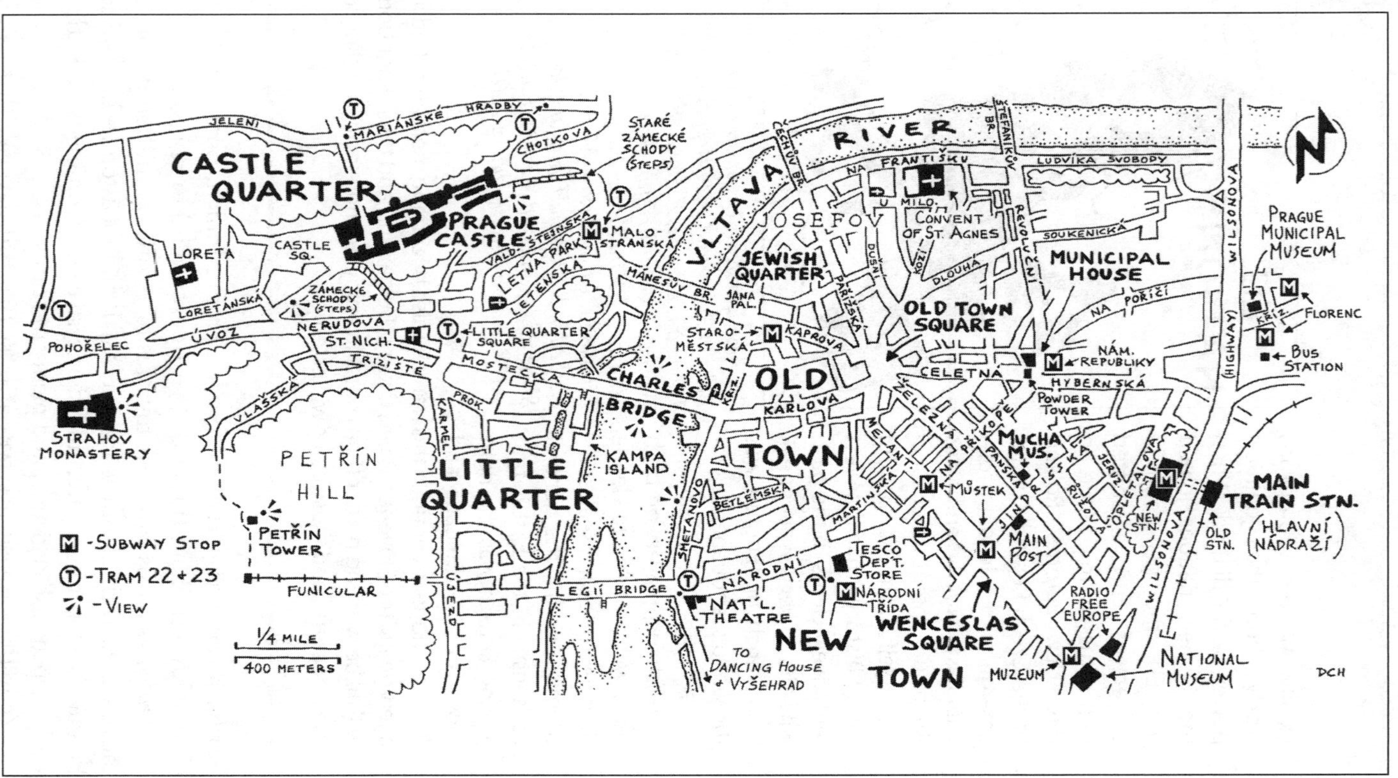
Prague
CASTLE QUARTER
PRAGUE CASTLE
CASTLE SQ.
LORETA
LORETÁNSKÁ
ÚVOZ
POHOŘELEC
STRAHOV MONASTERY
JELENÍ
MARIÁNSKÉ HRADBY
CHOTKOVA
STARÉ ZÁMECKÉ SCHODY (STEPS)
ZÁMECKÉ SCHODY (STEPS)
NERUDOVA
ST. NICH.
TRŽIŠTĚ
VLAŠSKÁ
PETŘÍN HILL
PETŘÍN TOWER
FUNICULAR
MALO-STRANSKÁ
VALD. PARK
VALDŠTEJNSKÁ
LETNÁ PARK
LETENSKÁ
LITTLE QUARTER SQUARE
MOSTECKÁ
KARMEL.
PROK.
LITTLE QUARTER
KAMPA ISLAND
CHARLES BRIDGE
LEGIÍ BRIDGE
ÚJEZD
MÁNESŮV BR.
VLTAVA RIVER
ČECHŮV BR.
ŠTEFÁNIKŮV BR.
STARO-MĚSTSKÁ
JANA PAL.
JEWISH QUARTER
JOSEFOV
KAPROVA
PAŘÍŽSKÁ
DUŠNÍ
NA FRANTIŠKU
U MILO.
CONVENT OF ST. AGNES
DLOUHÁ
KOZÍ
OLD TOWN SQUARE
OLD TOWN
KARLOVA
KŘIŽ.
CELETNÁ
ŽELEZNÁ
MELANT.
BETLÉMSKÁ
NÁRODNÍ
SMETANOVO
NAT'L. THEATRE
TO DANCING HOUSE + VYŠEHRAD
NEW TOWN
TESCO DEP'T. STORE
NÁRODNÍ TŘÍDA
MARTINSKÁ
NA PŘÍKOPĚ
MŮSTEK
WENCESLAS SQUARE
MAIN POST
MUCHA MUS.
PANSKÁ
JINDŘIŠSKÁ
RŮŽOVÁ
JERUZ.
POWDER TOWER
HYBERNSKÁ
NÁM. REPUBLIKY
MUNICIPAL HOUSE
REVOLUČNÍ
SOUKENICKÁ
LUDVÍKA SVOBODY
NA POŘÍČÍ
PRAGUE MUNICIPAL MUSEUM
KŘIŽ.
FLORENC
BUS STATION
WILSONOVA
(HIGHWAY)
MAIN TRAIN STN.
(HLAVNÍ NÁDRAŽÍ)
OLD STN.
NEW STN.
OPLETALOVA
RADIO FREE EUROPE
NATIONAL MUSEUM
MUZEUM
M -SUBWAY STOP
T -TRAM 22 + 23
-VIEW
1/4 MILE
400 METERS
DCH

*Prague, the golden city of a hundred spires*

Quarter—the only two chunks of sightseeing that demand any brainpower. Spend your afternoons strolling Charles Bridge and loitering around Old Town. Split your evenings between beer halls and classical concerts.

Prague Castle—which Czechs consider the biggest in Europe—has served as home to Czech rulers for more than a thousand years. The highlight is St. Vitus Cathedral, where locals go to remember Saint Wenceslas, patron saint of the Czechs. This "good king" of Christmas-carol fame was not a king at all, but a wise, benevolent Duke of Bohemia. After being assassinated in 935, Wenceslas became a symbol of Czech nationalism. His tomb sits in an extremely fancy chapel.

Apart from the underwhelming Royal Palace, there's little else of importance to see in Prague Castle. Its lower end is the sterile and gimmicky Golden Lane—once lined with goldsmith shops, now filled with boutiques, galleries, cafés, and gawking tourists.

While the Golden Lane is a tourist trap, the Toy and Barbie Museum (nearby, at the bottom

*A good local guide gives meaning to a great city like Prague.*

of the castle complex) is a treat. Its two entertaining floors of old toys and dolls are thoughtfully described in English. You'll see a century of teddy bears, 19th-century model train sets, and an incredible Barbie collection. Find the buxom 1959 first edition and you'll understand why these capitalistic sirens of material discontent weren't allowed here until 1989.

From the castle, the "King's Walk" leads into town. This ancient route of coronation processions, pedestrian-friendly and full of playful diversions, laces together most of Prague's essential sights. After being crowned in St. Vitus Cathedral, the king would walk through the historic town, cross Charles Bridge, and finish at the Old Town Square. If he hurried, he'd be done in 20 minutes. Like the main drag in Venice between St. Mark's and the Rialto Bridge, this walk mesmerizes tourists. Use it as a spine, but venture off it—especially to eat.

Kicking off the King's Walk, you leave the castle following steep and cobbled Nerudova Street towards the river. It's lined with old buildings still sporting the characteristic doorway signs that served as street addresses. In 1777, in order to more effectively collect taxes, Hapsburg empress Maria Theresa decreed that numbers be used instead of these quaint house names. The surviving signs are carefully restored and protected by law. Signs (you'll see a lion, 3 violinists, and golden suns) represent the family name, the occupation, or the various passions of the people who once inhabited the houses. This neighborhood's many old noble palaces are now generally used as foreign embassies.

The much-loved Charles Bridge is my vote for Europe's most pleasant quarter-mile stroll. Commissioned by the Holy Roman Emperor Charles IV in 1357, its chorus line of time-blackened Baroque statues mix it up with street vendors and musicians. Be on the bridge when the sun is low for the best light, people-watching, and photo opportunities.

After crossing the bridge, follow the shop-lined street to the Old Town Square. The focal point for most visits, this has been a market square since the 11th century. Today, old-time market stalls are replaced by cafés, touristy horse buggies, and souvenir hawkers.

The square's centerpiece, the Hus memorial—erected in 1915, 500 years after Jan Hus' burning—symbolizes the long struggle for Czech freedom. The statue of the Czech reformer stands tall, as he did against both Rome and the Hapsburgs. A mother with her children behind Hus represents the ultimate rebirth of the Czech nation.

A few blocks past the Old Town Square stretches the centerpiece of urban, modern Prague: Wenceslas Square. The most dramatic moments in modern Czech history were played out on this stage. The Czechoslovak state was proclaimed here in 1918. In 1969, Jan Palach set himself on fire

Prague's Wenceslas Square: When there's a revolution, this is where the action is.

here to protest the puppet Soviet government. And the massive demonstrations here 20 years after his death led to the overthrow of the communist government. Czechs still remember the night in 1989 when they gathered, hundreds of thousands strong, filling the square. Jangling their key chains at the presidential palace, they chanted, "It's time to go now." Their message was heard, and the next morning they woke up a free nation.

The great sights of Prague chronicle the struggle of the Czech people against the outside world. They also recall the struggles of the Jewish people within Czech society. I find Prague's Josefov the most interesting Jewish Quarter in Europe.

The Romans dispersed the Jews two thousand years ago. But "time was their sanctuary which no army could destroy," as their culture survived in enclaves throughout the Western world. The main intersection of Prague's Jewish Quarter was the meeting point of two medieval trade routes. Jewish traders settled here in the 13th century and built a synagogue.

When the pope declared that Jews and Christians should not live together, this Jewish Quarter was walled in and became a ghetto. In the 16th and 17th centuries, Prague's ghetto—with 11,000 inhabitants—was one of the biggest in Europe.

Pondering Jewish history

Europe's Jews relied mainly on profits from money lending (forbidden to Christians) and community solidarity to survive. While their money protected them, it was often also a curse. Throughout Europe, when times got tough and Christian debts to the Jewish community mounted, entire Jewish communities were evicted or killed.

In the 1780s, Emperor Joseph II eased much of the discrimination against Jews. In 1848, the walls were torn down, and the neighborhood—named Josefov in honor of the emperor, who was less anti-Semitic than the norm—was incorporated as a district of Prague.

In 1897, ramshackle Josefov was razed and replaced with a new modern town. This is what you'll see today: an attractive neighborhood of mostly Art Nouveau buildings, with a few surviving historic Jewish buildings.

Like any Jewish Quarter in Central Europe, Josefov was annihilated by Hitler. But, strangely, the museums of the Jewish Quarter are, in part, the work of Hitler. He preserved parts of Josefov to be his "museum of the exterminated race." Seven sites (six synagogues and a cemetery) scattered over a three-block area make the tourists' Jewish Quarter. Each has a fascinating exhibit, and one ticket includes admission to all but one.

The Pinkas Synagogue, a site of Jewish worship for 400 years, is a poignant memorial to the victims of the Nazis. Its walls are covered with the handwritten names of 77,297 Czech Jews who were sent from here to concentration-camp gas chambers. (You'll hear the somber reading of the names as you ponder this sad sight.) When the communists moved in, they closed the synagogue and erased everything. With freedom in 1989, the Pinkas Synagogue was reopened and all the names rewritten. The synagogue was closed briefly in 2002, as flood damage meant the names needed to be rewritten once again.

The Old Jewish Cemetery is the quarter's most photographed site. As you wander among 12,000 evocative tombstones, remember that until 1787, this was the only burial ground allowed for the Jews of Prague. Because space was severely limited, and because of the Jewish belief that the body should not be moved once buried, tombs were piled atop each other. With its many layers, the cemetery became a small plateau. And as things settled over time, the tombstones got crooked and mystically picturesque.

The "Old-New" Synagogue—"new" 700 years ago—has always been the most important synagogue and central building in Josefov. Standing like a bomb-hardened bunker, it feels like it's survived plenty of hard times. Stairs take you down to the street level of the 13th century and into the Gothic interior of this oldest synagogue in Central Europe.

Down the street from Josefov is the surreal sight of a giant metronome slowly ticking away. Locals know this marks the spot of a 100-foot-tall sculpture of Stalin—destroyed in 1962 after Khrushchev revealed the communist tyrant's crimes.

It's hard to imagine the gray and bleak Prague of the communist era. Before 1989, the city was a wistful jumble of possibility. Cobbled lanes were shadowed by sooty, crusty buildings. Thick, dark timbers bridging narrow streets kept decrepit buildings from crumbling. Consumer goods were plain and uniform, stacked like Legos on thin shelves in shops where customers waited in line for a beat-up cabbage, tin of ham, or bottle of ersatz Coke. The Charles Bridge was as sooty as its statues, with no commerce except for a few shady characters trying to change money. Hotels had two-tiered pricing: one for people of the Warsaw Pact nations and another (5–6 times as expensive) for capitalists. This made the run-down Soviet-style hotels as expensive as a fine Western one for most tourists. At the train station, frightened but desperate characters would meet arriving foreigners to rent them a room in their flat. They were scrambling to get enough hard Western cash to buy batteries or Levis at one of the hard-currency stores.

Prague's fascinating Museum of Communism traces the story of communism here: propaganda posters, busts of communist All-Stars (Marx, Lenin, Stalin), a photograph of that massive stone Stalin that overlooked Prague, and re-created slices of communist life—from a bland store counter to a typical classroom (with a poem on the chalkboard extolling the virtues of the tractor).

*Before the fall of communism, Czech freedom-lovers found inspiration at the graffiti-covered wall dedicated to John Lennon—an icon of Western freedom in the 1980s. Authorities whitewashed it countless times but the spirited graffiti kept coming back. Even today, after being independent since 1989, Czechs treasure their freedom and their Lennon wall.*

With capitalism came entrepreneurial con artists. Be on guard when changing money (even at banks) for bad arithmetic and inexplicable pauses while tellers count back your change. Understand the exact

*The communist era left Eastern Europe with some decent public transportation, but ugly train stations were erected, designed in the obligatory reds and grays of that era. The low ceilings still make the individual feel like staying in line.*

price before ordering at restaurants. Paying with cash rather than with credit cards is safer.

Taxis here are notorious rip-offs. Prague is walkable and also has fine public transportation, but if you prefer taxis, use only registered ones. These are marked by a roof lamp with the word "TAXI" in black on both sides, and the front doors sport a black-and-white checkered ribbon, the company name, license number, and rates. My rule of thumb: Know the approximate local rate. If overcharged, pay what you think is fair, and walk away.

With capitalism kicking into gear, a newly affluent Prague has spiffed up its fine architecture. Prague is the best Art Nouveau town in Europe, with fun-loving facades gracing streets all over town. Art Nouveau, born in Paris, is "nouveau" because it wasn't inspired by Rome. It's neo-nothing... a fresh answer to all the revival styles of the later 19th century and an organic response to the Eiffel Tower art of the Industrial Age. The streets of Josefov, the Mucha window in the St. Vitus Cathedral, and Hotel Evropa on Wenceslas Square are just a few Art Nouveau highlights.

If you like Art Nouveau, you'll love the Mucha Museum—one of Europe's most enjoyable little galleries. I find the art of Alfons Mucha (MOO-kah, 1860–1939) insistently likeable. This popular Czech artist's posters, filled with Czech symbols and expressing his people's ideals and aspirations, were patriotic banners arousing the national spirit. With the help of an abundant supply of slinky models, Mucha was a founding father of the Art Nouveau movement.

In the evening, Prague booms with live (and inexpensive) theater, opera, and classical, jazz, and pop music. You'll choose from half a dozen classical "tourist" concerts daily in Prague's ornate Old Town halls and churches. The music is crowd-pleasing: Vivaldi, best of Mozart, pop arias, and works by local boys Anton Dvořák and Bedřich Smetana. Leafleteers are everywhere, handing out their announcements of the evening's events.

Even if Mozart himself were performing, many visitors would rather spend the evening at a Prague beer hall. *Pivo* (beer) is a frothy hit with tourists. After all, the Czechs invented lager in nearby Plzeň. Ask for the famous Pilsner Urquell, a great lager available on tap everywhere. Budvar, another local beer, is the original Budweiser (no relation to the American brew). Czechs are the world's biggest beer drinkers, surpassing the runner-ups—Germans, Irish, and Belgians—with a per capita consumption of 80 gallons a year. In many Czech restaurants, a beer hits your table like a glass of water does in the United States. Be careful. *Pivo* for lunch has me sightseeing for the rest of the day on Czech knees. *Na Zdraví* is "cheers" in Czech. After a few *pivos,* fun-loving Czechs stumble on their own words, raising their mugs and bellowing *"Nádraží"* (which means "train station").

*Fifty years of communism left cities like Prague run-down and covered with grime. Today, as Eastern Europe looks West, cities like Prague are cleaning up their industries, giving elegant facades a face-lift, and replacing asphalt with charming cobbles and pedestrian zones. If you haven't been to Prague since 1989, you won't recognize it today.*

*For good-value accommodations in Prague, try Hotel Julian (Elišky Peškové 11, tel. 257-311-150, reception tel. 257-311-145, fax 257-311-149, www.julian.cz) or the Athos Travel room-booking service (tel. 241-440-571, fax 241-441-697, www.athos.cz). For more hotels, visit www.ricksteves.com/update, and for all the travel specifics, see this year's edition of* Rick Steves' Prague & the Czech Republic.

## 52. CHARMING KRAKÓW

The top stop in Poland is Kraków. Of all the Eastern European cities laying claim to the boast "the next Prague," Kraków is for real. And enjoying a drink on its marvelous main market square, you'll know why. The biggest square in medieval Europe remains one of Europe's most gasp-worthy public spaces.

Knowing this is one of Europe's least expensive countries, I choose the fanciest café on Kraków's fanciest piece of real estate and order without even considering the price. Sinking deep into my chair and sipping deep into my drink, I ponder the bustle of Poland, just a decade and a half after it won its freedom.

## Kraków

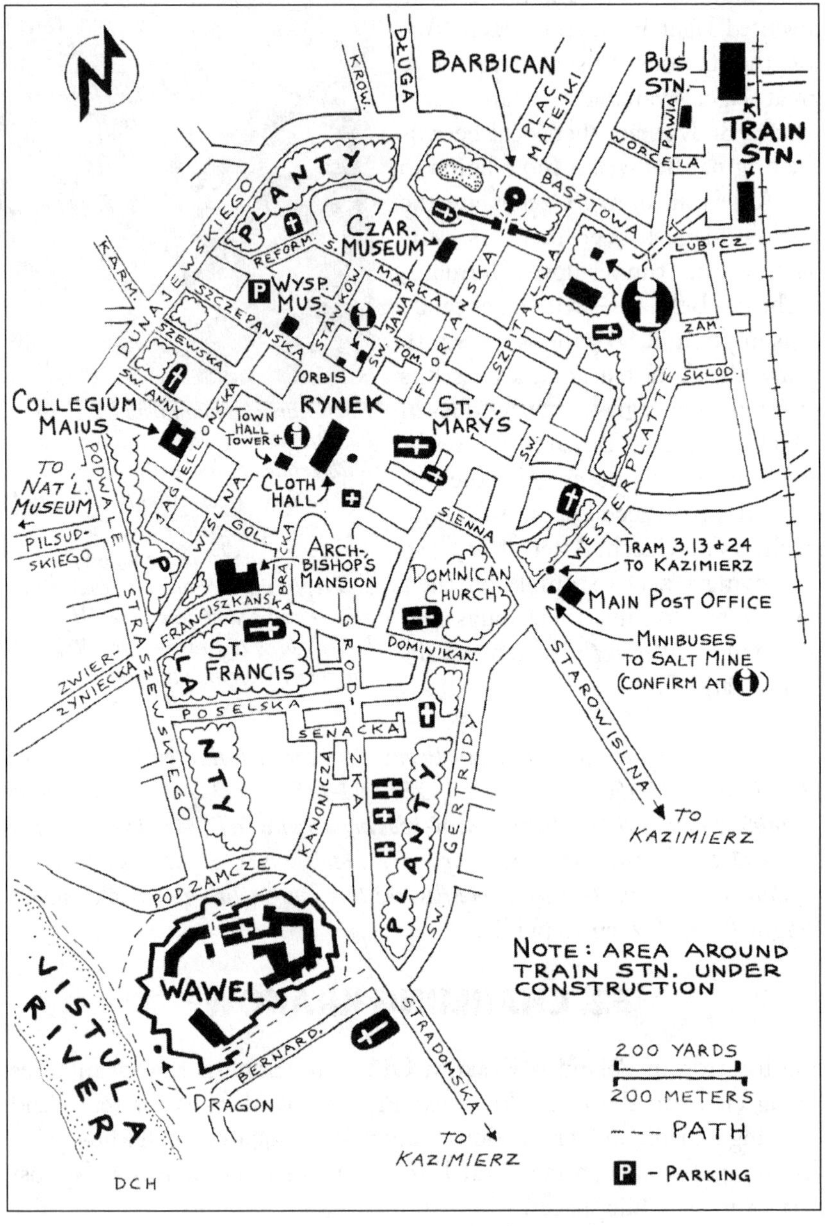
BARBICAN
BUS STN.
TRAIN STN.
PLANTY
CZAR. MUSEUM
WYSP. MUS.
COLLEGIUM MAIUS
RYNEK
ST. MARY'S
TOWN HALL TOWER
CLOTH HALL
TO NAT'L. MUSEUM
ARCH-BISHOP'S MANSION
DOMINICAN CHURCH
ST. FRANCIS
TRAM 3, 13 & 24 TO KAZIMIERZ
MAIN POST OFFICE
MINIBUSES TO SALT MINE (CONFIRM AT i)
TO KAZIMIERZ
WAWEL
VISTULA RIVER
DRAGON
NOTE: AREA AROUND TRAIN STN. UNDER CONSTRUCTION
200 YARDS
200 METERS
PATH
P - PARKING
DCH

Vast as it is, the square has a folksy intimacy. It bustles with street musicians, fragrant flower stalls, cotton-candy vendors, loitering teenagers, businesspeople commuting by bike, gawking tourists, and the lusty coos of pigeons. This square is where Kraków lives...and where visitors like me find themselves hanging out. To my left, activists protest Poland's EU membership. To my right, local teens practice break-dancing moves.

*Poland's top tourist attraction promises to be "the next Prague." Tourism has brought Kraków prosperity—great restaurants, comfy hotels, and plenty of welcoming sights.*

The folk band—swaggering in their colorful peasant costumes—give me a private little concert. Feeling flush, I tip them royally. (Perhaps too royally. Be warned: A big tip gets you "The Star-Spangled Banner.")

Kraków is the Boston of Poland: a captivating old-fashioned city buzzing with history, intriguing sights, colorful eateries, and college students. Even though the country's political capital moved from here to Warsaw 400 years ago, Kraków remains Poland's cultural and intellectual center.

Flat and easy to navigate, Kraków is made for walking. A greenbelt called the Planty rings the Old Town, where the 13th-century protective walls and moat once stood (a great place for a stroll or bike ride).

*Street musicians play "The Star-Spangled Banner" for big spenders.*

With its diverse sights, Kraków can keep a speedy tourist busy for three days. Most sights are inside the Planty park, except for the historic Wawel Castle grounds and the Jewish quarter in Kazimierz. You'll want to side-trip to the notorious Auschwitz Concentration Camp. And most visitors also visit Wieliczka Salt

Mine—my vote for the deepest art gallery in Europe.

Kraków grew wealthy from trade in the 12th century. Traders passing through were required to stop here for a few days and sell their wares cheap. Local merchants then sold those goods with big price hikes...and Kraków thrived. It became Poland's capital.

Tartars invaded in 1241, destroying the city. Krakovians took this opportunity to rebuild their streets in a near-perfect grid around the spectacular main market square. King Kazimierz the Great sparked Kraków's golden age in the 14th century. He established the university that still defines the city (and counts Copernicus and Pope John Paul II among its alumni).

But Kraków's power waned and the capital moved to Warsaw. Two centuries later, Poland was partitioned by neighboring powers. Warsaw ended up as a satellite of oppressive Moscow, and Kraków became a poor provincial backwater of Vienna. But despite Kraków's reduced prominence, Austria's comparatively liberal climate helped turn the city into a haven for intellectuals and progressives (including a young Russian revolutionary named Vladimir Lenin).

Kraków emerged from World War II virtually unscathed. But when the communists took over, they decided to give intellectual (and potentially dissident) Kraków an injection of good Soviet values—in the form of heavy industry. They built Nowa Huta, an enormous steelworks on the city's outskirts, dooming the city to decades of smog. Thankfully, Kraków is now much cleaner than 15 years ago.

Entering through the main gate of the Old Town wall, past an outdoor gallery for struggling art students, you walk down Floriańska Street, passing one McDonald's worth a visit. When renovating this building, they discovered a Gothic cellar. They excavated it and added seating. Today, you can super-size your ambience by dining on a Big Mac and fries under a medieval McVault.

*Got milk? Poland does. In milk bars, a throwback to the communist era, you can fill your tank cheaply.*

Even better, keep your eyes open for a *bar mleczny* ("milk bar"). In the communist era, the government subsidized the food at these cafeterias to provide working-class Poles with an affordable meal out.

The tradition continues, and today Poland still subsidizes your milk-bar meal. Prices are astoundingly low—soup for less than a złoty (about a quarter). And, while communist-era fare was gross, today's milk-bar cuisine is tastier. Just head to the counter, point to what you want, and get a quick and hearty meal for half the cost of McDonald's.

St. Mary's Church—overlooking the main square—marks the center of Kraków. From its taller tower (actually the city's watchtower), a bugler plays half a tune at the top of each hour. During the 1241 Tartar invasion, the story goes, a watchman in the tower saw the enemy approaching and sounded the alarm. Before he could finish the tune, an arrow pierced his throat—which is why even today, the music stops *subito* partway through. Today's buglers are firemen—serving as fire lookouts first...and musicians second.

*A glass of wine and a salad with a serenade on Kraków's floodlit main square caps one of the best days Europe has to offer.*

Wawel Hill (VAH-vehl) towers over old Kraków. This hill, with its castle, cathedral, and complex of sights, is a symbol of Polish royalty and independence. It's sacred ground to every Pole, and the country's leading tourist attraction. Crowds and a ridiculously complex admissions system for the hill's many historic sights can be exasperating. Thankfully, for most non-Polish visitors, a stroll through the cathedral and around the castle grounds covers the site adequately and requires no tickets. Wawel's many museums are mildly interesting but skippable.

Wawel Cathedral is Poland's national church—its Westminster Abbey. The national mausoleum, it holds the tombs of Poland's most important rulers and historical figures. The interior is slathered in Baroque memorials and tombs. Everyone visits the tomb of Kazimierz the Great. But even Kazimierz is outdone by a black crucifix marking the relics of St. Jadwiga, the 14th-century "Queen of Poland," who helped Christianize Lithuania and was sainted by John Paul II in 1997. All the candles flickering here indicate she's popular with Poles today.

Marshal Józef Piłsudski, the WWI hero who ruled Poland from 1926 to 1935, is buried downstairs in the crypt. His tomb was moved here so the soldiers who came to party on his grave wouldn't disturb the others. (It's interesting to note that Piłsudski encouraged Britain and France to preemptively attack Hitler in 1933. He was ignored, and Poland was devastated a decade later. Perhaps that is why Poles were predisposed to support America's preemptive war against Iraq.)

The Wawel Castle museums may be forgettable. But the complex has one "sight" which—while invisible—attracts travelers from around the world: chakra. Hindus believe the chakra is part of a powerful energy field that connects all living things. There are seven points on the surface of the earth where this chakra energy is most concentrated. These points include Jerusalem, Mecca, Rome...and Kraków's Wawel Hill. Look for peaceful people with their eyes closed. One thing's for sure: They're not thinking of Kazimierz the Great. The Wawel administration seems creeped out by all this. They've done what they can to discourage this ritual, but believers still gravitate from far and wide to hug the wall in the castle courtyard. (Just for fun, ask a Wawel tour guide about chakra and watch him squirm—they're forbidden to talk about it.)

A 20-minute walk beyond Wawel takes you to the historic center of Jewish Kraków, Kazimierz. After King Kazimierz the Great encouraged Jews to come to Poland in the 14th century, a large Jewish community settled in and around Kraków. According to legend, Kazimierz (the king) established Kazimierz (the village) for his favorite girlfriend—a Jewish woman named Ester—just outside the Kraków city walls. Kazimierz was an autonomous community, with its own town hall, market square, and city walls. By 1800, the walls came down, Kazimierz became part of Kraków, and the Jewish community flourished. By the start of World War II, 65,000 Jews lived in Kraków (mostly in Kazimierz), making up more than a quarter of the city's population. Only 6,000 Kraków Jews survived the war.

Today's Kraków has only about a hundred Jewish residents. Kazimierz still has an empty feeling, but the neighborhood has enjoyed a renaissance of Jewish culture lately following the popularity of *Schindler's List* (which was filmed partly in Kazimierz). The spirit of the Jewish tradition survives in the neighborhood's evocative synagogues, soulful cemeteries, and the lilting klezmer folk concerts put on by local restaurants.

Kazimierz has two Jewish cemeteries, both more undiscovered and powerful than the famous one in Prague. Locals shop at plac Nowy's market stalls, a gritty factory-workers-on-lunch-break contrast to Kraków's touristy main square. Fans of Spielberg's Holocaust movie—and the compassionate Kraków businessman who did his creative best to save the lives of his Jewish workers—can see Schindler's actual factory, currently the Telpod electronics manufacturing plant, across the river from Kazimierz.

Most of Kazimierz's Jews ended their lives at Auschwitz, a Nazi concentration camp in the Polish town of Oświęcim (a 70-min drive west of Kraków). This is one of Europe's most moving sights and certainly the most important of all the Holocaust memorials. (For more on Auschwitz, see page 589.)

*A bright and fun generation of new young guides (with or without cars) all across Eastern Europe are proud to share their cities and cultures, making your visit especially meaningful.*

Also near Kraków is the remarkable Wieliczka Salt Mine, which has been producing salt since 1250. Under Kazimierz the Great, one-third of Poland's income came from these precious deposits. Wieliczka miners spent much of their lives underground, rarely emerging into daylight. To pass the time, 19th-century miners began carving figures, chandeliers, and eventually even an entire chapel out of the salt.

The tour shows how the miners lived and worked (using horses who lived their whole lives underground, never seeing the light of day). It takes you through some impressive underground caverns, past subterranean lakes, and introduces you to some of the mine's many salt sculptures (including an army of salt elves and a life-size statue of this region's favorite son, Pope John Paul II). Your jaw will drop as you enter the enormous Chapel of the Blessed Kinga. Don't miss the extremely salty relief of the Last Supper.

Your walk finishes over 400 feet below the surface, from where a traditional miners' lift hoists you back up to a sunlit world which seems particularly bright.

*For good-value accommodations in Kraków, splurge at one of the Donimirski Boutique Hotels (3 swanky locations in or near the Old Town, www.donimirski.com), or sleep cheaper just off the main market square at Pensjonat Trecius (ulica Św. Tomasza 18, tel. 012/421-2521, www.trecius.krakow.pl). For all the travel specifics, see this year's edition of* Rick Steves' Best of Eastern Europe.

# GREAT BRITAIN AND IRELAND

## 53. LONDON: A WARM LOOK AT A COLD CITY

I've spent more time in London than in any other European city. It lacks the grandeur of Rome, the warmth of Munich, and the elegance of Paris, but its history, traditions, people, markets, museums, and entertainment keep drawing me back.

London has changed dramatically in recent years, and many visitors are surprised to find how "un-English" it is. Whites are now a minority in major parts of this city that once symbolized white imperialism. Arabs have nearly bought out the area north of Hyde Park. Chinese take-outs outnumber fish-and-chips shops. Many hotels are run by people with foreign accents (who hire English chambermaids). And outlying suburbs are home to huge communities of Indians and Pakistanis. London is learning—sometimes fitfully—to live as a microcosm of its formerly vast empire. With the English Channel Tunnel complete, many locals see even more foreign threats to the Britishness of Britain.

*The London Eye towers over Big Ben.*

London is a world in itself, a barrage on all the senses, an urban jungle sprawling over 600 square miles and teeming with nine million people. As a first stop for

## London

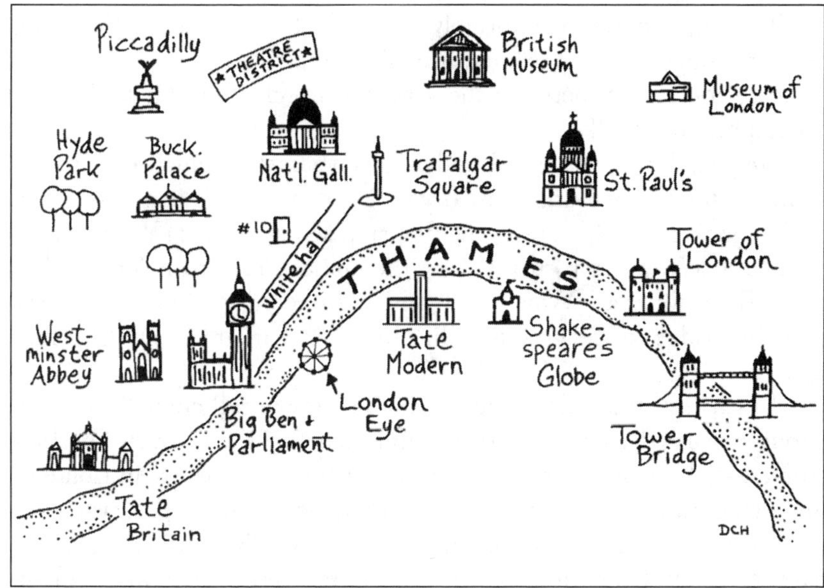


many travelers, this huge city can be overwhelming. On my first visit I felt like Oliver Twist asking for more soup. Here are a few ideas to soften and warm this hard and cold city.

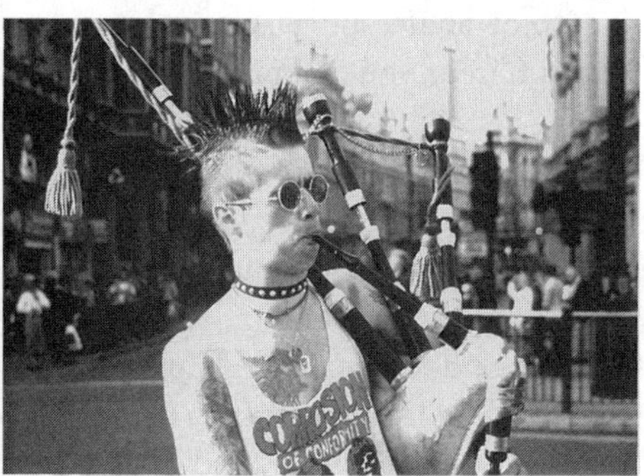

*Have you tried London lately?*

Have fun seeing the predictable biggies. Blow through the city on the open deck of a double-decker tour bus. Ogle the crown jewels in the Tower of London and see the Houses of Parliament in action. Hobnob with the tombstones in Westminster Abbey. Visit with Leonardo da Vinci, Botticelli, and Rembrandt in the National Gallery. Whisper across the dome of St. Paul's Cathedral and rummage through our civilization's attic at the British Museum. Take a spin on the towering London Eye observation wheel. You can enjoy some of Europe's best people-watching at Covent Garden and snap to at Buckingham Palace's Changing of the Guard.

Any guidebook recommends these worthwhile must-sees. But go beyond the big museums, churches, and castles. Take walks (self-guided and with a local guide), hit the offbeat museums, and seek out experiences that come without turnstiles.

To grasp London comfortably, see it as the old town without the modern, congested, and seemingly endless sprawl. After all, most of the visitors' London lies between the Tower of London and Hyde Park—a great three-mile walk.

On your first evening in London, give yourself a "pinch-me-I'm-in-London" floodlit walking tour. If you just flew in, this is an ideal way to fight jet lag. Catch a bus to the first stop across (east of) Westminster Bridge. Side-trip downstream along the Jubilee Promenade for a capital view. Then, for that "Wow, I'm really in London!" feeling, cross back over the bridge to view the floodlit Houses of Parliament and Big Ben up close.

To thrill your loved ones (or stoke their envy), call home from a pay phone near Big Ben at about three minutes before the hour. As Big Ben chimes, stick the receiver outside the booth and prove you're in London: ding dong ding dong...dong ding ding dong. It's an audio postcard.

Then cross Whitehall, noticing the Winston Churchill statue in the park. (He's electrified to avoid the pigeon problem that stains so many other great statues.) Walk up Whitehall toward Trafalgar Square. Stop at the barricaded and guarded little Downing Street to see #10, home of the British prime minister. Chat with the bored bobby. From Trafalgar, walk to hopping Leicester Square and continue to youth-on-the-rampage Piccadilly, through safely sleazy Soho (north of Shaftesbury Avenue) up to Oxford Street. From Piccadilly or Oxford Circus you can taxi, bus, or subway home.

To nibble on London one historic snack at a time, take any of the focused two-hour walking tours of the city. For about $10, local historians take small groups through the London story, one entertaining page at a time. Choose from London's Plague, Dickens' London, Roman Londinium, Legal London, the Beatles in London, Jack the Ripper's London (which is the most popular, even though guides admit it's a lousy walk), London and *The Da Vinci Code*, Harry Potter's London, and many more. Some walks focus on the various "villages" of London, such as trendy Chelsea and leafy Hampstead.

The South Bank of the River Thames, rapidly becoming gentrified, is a thriving arts and cultural center. From Westminster Bridge to the Tower Bridge, the slick Jubilee Promenade is a trendy jogging, yuppie pub-crawling walk—lined with fun and off-beat sights. The London Eye observation wheel, sponsored by British Airways, offers the city's highest public viewpoint (450 feet) and a chance to fly in British air without leaving London. Featuring modern art, the great Tate Modern on the South

Bank is connected with the sedate St. Paul's Cathedral on the North Bank by the pedestrian Millennium Bridge. Skip the South Bank's outrageously amateurish, heavily promoted, and overpriced "London Dungeon," but consider the Globe Theatre, the Bramah Tea and Coffee Museum, and the Imperial War Museum.

For megatons of things military, the impressive Imperial War Museum covers the wars of the last century. You'll see heavy weaponry, love notes from the front, Vargas Girl pin-ups, Monty's Africa-campaign tank, and Schwarzkopf's Desert Storm uniform. Trace the development of the machine gun, push a computer button to watch footage of the first tank battles, and hold your breath through the gruesome "WWI trench experience." You can even buy WWII-era toys. The museum doesn't glorify war, but chronicles the sweeping effects of humanity's most destructive century.

My favorite way to learn history is to stroll with a local guide, as if beachcombing. You pick up obscure shards of a neighborhood's distant past, unlocking unexpected stories. On a bright, brisk January morning, I joined a guide, David Tucker, who runs a tour company called The Original London Walks (www.walks.com).

From London Bridge, David pointed downriver past the Tower of London and said, "During the Second World War, Nazi bombers used the Thames as a guide on their nightly raids. When moonlit, they called it a 'silver ribbon of tin foil.' It led from the English Channel right to our mighty dockyards. Even with all the city lights carefully blacked out, those bombers easily found their targets. Neighborhoods on both banks of the river went up in flames. After the war, the business district on the North Bank was rebuilt, but the South Bank...it was long neglected."

Turning his back to St. Paul's Cathedral, he pointed to a vast complex of new buildings, displaying the recently restored, newly trendy South Bank, and continued, "Only now has the bombed-out South Bank been properly rebuilt. There's a real buzz in London about our South Bank."

We walked down to the beach. The Thames is a tidal river, and at low tide it's littered with history. Even today, many of the beaches are red with clay tiles from 500-year-old roofs. Picking up a chunky piece of tile worn oval by the centuries, with its telltale peg hole still clearly visible, the guide explained that these tiles were heavy, requiring hefty timbers for support. In the 16th century, when shipbuilding for the Royal Navy made these timbers more costly and rare, lighter slate tiles became the preferred roofing material. Over time, the heavy, red-clay tiles migrated from the rooftops to the riverbank...to the pockets of beachcombers like us.

Like kids on a scavenger hunt, we studied the pebbles. David picked up a chalky white tube to show me. It was the fragile stem of an 18th-century clay pipe. Back then, when tobacco was sold with disposable one-use pipes, used pipes were routinely tossed into the river. David tossed it down. Thinking, "King George may have sucked on this," I picked it up.

Climbing back to street level, we prowled through some fascinating relics of the South Bank neighborhood that survived both German bombs and urban renewal. Scaling steep stairs, we visited the Operating Theatre Museum, a crude surgical theater where amputations were performed in the early 1800s as medical students watched and learned. Down the street, the last surviving turret of the original London Bridge is the decorative centerpiece of an old hospital yard. We wandered through the still-bustling Borough Market to see farmers doing business with city shopkeepers.

Walking through this area put us through a time warp. David led us into a quiet courtyard, where we looked up at three sets of balconies climbing the front of an inn. He explained, "Courtyards like this provided struggling theater troupes—like young William Shakespeare's—with a captive audience."

Remember those roving troupes when you visit the Globe Theatre, a rebuilt version of the stage that eventually became their home. To see Shakespeare in an exact replica of the half-timbered, thatched theater for which he wrote his plays, attend a play at the Globe. This open-air, round theater does the plays as Shakespeare intended, with no amplification ($10 to stand, $25–55 to sit, May–Sept, usually nightly except Mon, www.shakespeares-globe.org). The $10 "groundling" or "yard" tickets—while open to rain—are most fun. Playing the part of a crude peasant theatergoer, you can walk around, munch a picnic dinner, lean your elbows on the stage, and even interact with the actors. I've never enjoyed Shakespeare as much as here, performed as the Bard intended it...in the "wooden O." The theater is open to tour when there are no plays; the Shakespeare exhibit is worthwhile (and open even during afternoon plays).

Cheap Globe Theatre tip: Plays are long. Many groundlings, who are allowed to come and go as they please, leave before the end. Peasants with culture hang out an hour before the finish and beg or buy a ticket off someone leaving early.

Shakespeare is just the first act here in the world's best theater city. Choose from top musicals, comedies, thrillers, sex farces, and more. Over the years I've enjoyed *Harvey,* starring James Stewart; *The King*

*and I,* with Yul Brynner; *My Fair Lady; A Chorus Line; Cats; Starlight Express; Les Misérables;* and *Chicago.* Performances are nightly except Sunday, usually with one matinee a week. Matinees are cheaper and rarely sell out. Tickets can be cheaper than in New York, ranging from about $20–80. Most theaters are marked on the tourist maps and cluster in the Piccadilly–Trafalgar area.

Unless you want this year's smash hit, getting a ticket is easy. The *Theatre Guide* (free at any hotel or tourist office) lists everything in town. Once you've decided on a show, call the theater directly, ask about seat availability and prices, and book a ticket using your credit card. Pick up your ticket 20 minutes before show time. You can even book tickets from the US before your trip. For this month's (and next month's) schedule, visit www.officiallondontheatre.co.uk or photocopy the schedule from the London newspaper at your library.

Ticket agencies, which charge a standard 20–25 percent booking fee, are scalpers with an address. Agencies are worthwhile only if a show you've just got to see is sold out at the box office. Many ticket agencies speculate, scarfing up hot tickets, in order to make a killing after the show is otherwise sold out. US booking agencies get their tickets from another agency, adding to your expense by involving yet another middleman. With the Internet, cheap international phone calls, and credit cards, there's no reason not to book direct.

Cheap theater tricks: Most theaters offer "concessions"—indicated by a "conc" or "s" in the listings—such as cheap returned tickets, standing room, matinee, and senior or student stand-by deals. Picking up a late return can get you a great seat at a cheap-seat price. Standing room can be very cheap. If a show is "sold out," there's usually a way to get a seat. Call and ask how. The famous half-price "tkts" booth in Leicester (pronounced "Lester") Square sells cheap tickets to shows on the push list the day of the show only (Mon–Sat 12 p.m.–7:00 p.m., Sun 12:00 p.m.–3:30 p.m., matinee tickets Tue–Sun from noon, cash only, lists of shows at www.tkts.co.uk). While theater box offices don't discount tickets, they may give you a better seat at a cheap-seat price on a slow day (if you ask).

I buy the second-cheapest tickets directly from the theater box office. Many theaters are so small that there's hardly a bad seat. After the lights go down, "scooting up" is less than a capital offense.

If your theatergoing puts you in a literary frame of mind, visit the British Library. While the library contains 180 miles of bookshelves filling London's deepest basement, one beautiful room filled with state-of-the-art glass display cases shows you the printed treasures of our civilization. You'll see ancient maps; early gospels on papyrus; illuminated manuscripts from the early Middle Ages; the Gutenberg Bible; the Magna Carta; pages from Leonardo's notebooks; original writing by the titans of English literature, from Chaucer and Shakespeare to Dickens and Wordsworth; and music manuscripts from Beethoven to the Beatles.

On Sunday, enjoy an hour of craziness at Speaker's Corner in Hyde Park. By noon, there are usually several soapbox speakers, screamers, singers, communists, or comics performing to the crowd of onlookers. "The grassroots of democracy" is actually a holdover from when the gallows stood here and the criminal was allowed to say just about anything he wanted to before he swung. I dare you to raise your voice and gather a crowd—it's easy to do. If you catch the London double-decker bus tour from Speaker's Corner Sunday at 10 a.m., you'll return at noon for the prime-time action.

The Kew Gardens are lively and open daily. Cruise the Thames or ride the Tube to London's favorite gardens for plants galore and a breezy respite from the city. While to most visitors the Royal Botanic Gardens of Kew are simply a delightful opportunity to wander among 33,000 different types of plants, they represent a hardworking organization committed to understanding and preserving the botanical diversity of our planet. Garden lovers could easily spend all day exploring Kew's 300 acres. For a quick visit, spend a fragrant hour wandering through three buildings. The famous Palm House, built of iron and glass in 1844–1848 and filled with exotic tropical plant life, is a veritable swing through the tropics. Nearby, there's a Waterlily House that Monet would swim for and the Temperate House—a modern greenhouse with many different climate zones growing countless cacti and bug-munching carnivorous plants.

Every morning you can find a thriving market. There are markets for fish, fruit, used cars, antiques, clothing, and on and on. Portobello Road (Mon–Wed and Fri–Sat 8 a.m.–6:30 p.m., Thu 8 a.m.–1 p.m., closed Sun) and Camden Lock (hip crafts and miscellany, daily 10 a.m.–6 p.m.) are just two of the many colorful markets that offer you great browsing.

But don't expect great prices. These days, the only people getting a steal at London's markets are the pickpockets.

Set your taste buds loose at London's trendy restaurants. I like several places in the throbbing Soho district, an easy stroll from the theater district: Belgo Centraal is a space-station world overrun with Trappist monks serving hearty Belgian specialties. The classy restaurant section requires reservations, but grabbing a bench in the boisterous beer hall is more fun. Belgians eat as well as the French and as hearty as the Germans. Specialties include mussels, great fries, and a stunning array of dark, blond, and fruity Belgian beers. Belgo actually makes Belgian things trendy–a formidable feat (near Covent Garden Tube station, 50 Earlham Street). Soho Spice Indian is where modern Britain meets Indian tradition—fine Indian cuisine in a trendy jewel-tone ambience (north of Piccadilly Circus at 124 Wardour Street). The Wagamama Noodle Bar is a mod, watch-it-boiled, pan-Asian slurpathon where a youthful crowd shares benches, and waiters take orders with walkie-talkies (10a Lexington Street and other locations). Yo! Sushi is a futuristic Japanese food extravaganza experience. With thumping rock, Japanese cable TV, a 195-foot-long conveyor-belt sushi bar, automated sushi machines, and a robotic drink trolley, just sipping a sake on a bar stool here is a trip (2 blocks south of Oxford Street at 52 Poland Street, as well as other locations).

Fun as the restaurants are, no visit to London is complete without enjoying a pint in a woody pub. Pubs are an integral part of English culture. You'll find all kinds, each with its own personality. Taste the different beers. If you don't know what to order, ask the bartender for a half pint of his or her favorite. Real ale, pumped by hand from the basement (look for the longest handles on the bar), is every connoisseur's choice. For a basic American-type beer, ask for a lager. Teetotalers can get lemon-lime soda pop by asking for a "lemonade." Children are welcome in most pubs but will not be served alcohol until they are 18. Order some pub grub and talk to the people: Enjoy a public house. By getting beyond the bobbies and beefeaters—by meeting the people—you see London take on a personality you can't capture on a postcard.

*For good-value accommodations in London's Victoria Station neighborhood, try Winchester Hotel (17 Belgrave Rd., tel. 020/7828-2972, fax 020/7828-5191, www.winchester-hotel.net). In South Kensington, stay at the Aster House Hotel (hotelesque splurge, 3 Sumner Place, tel. 020/7581-5888, fax 020/7584-4925, www.asterhouse.com). Near Kensington Palace, consider the Vicarage Private Hotel (10 Vicarage Gate, tel. 020/7229-4030, fax 020/7792-5989, www.londonvicaragehotel.com). For more hotels, visit www.ricksteves.com /update, and for all the travel specifics, see this year's edition of* Rick Steves' London, Rick Steves' England, *or* Rick Steves' Great Britain.

## 54. BATH: ENGLAND AT ITS ELEGANT AND FRIVOLOUS BEST

Two hundred years ago, this city of 80,000 was the Hollywood of Britain. Today, the former trendsetter of Georgian England invites you to take the 90-minute train ride from London and sample its aristocratic charms.

If ever a city enjoyed looking in the mirror, Bath's the one. It has more government-protected buildings per capita than any town in England. The entire city is built of a warm-tone limestone it calls "Bath stone." The use of normal bricks is forbidden, and Bath beams in its cover-girl complexion.

Bath is an architectural chorus line. It's a triumph of the Georgian style (British for "neoclassical"), with buildings as competitively elegant as the society they housed. If you look carefully, you'll see false windows built in the name of balance (but not used, in the name of tax avoidance) and classical columns that supported only Georgian egos. Two centuries ago, rich women wore feathered hats atop three-foot hairdos. The very rich stretched their doors and ground floors to accommodate this high fashion. And today many families have a tough time affording the cost

*Bath: Georgian on my mind*

## Bath

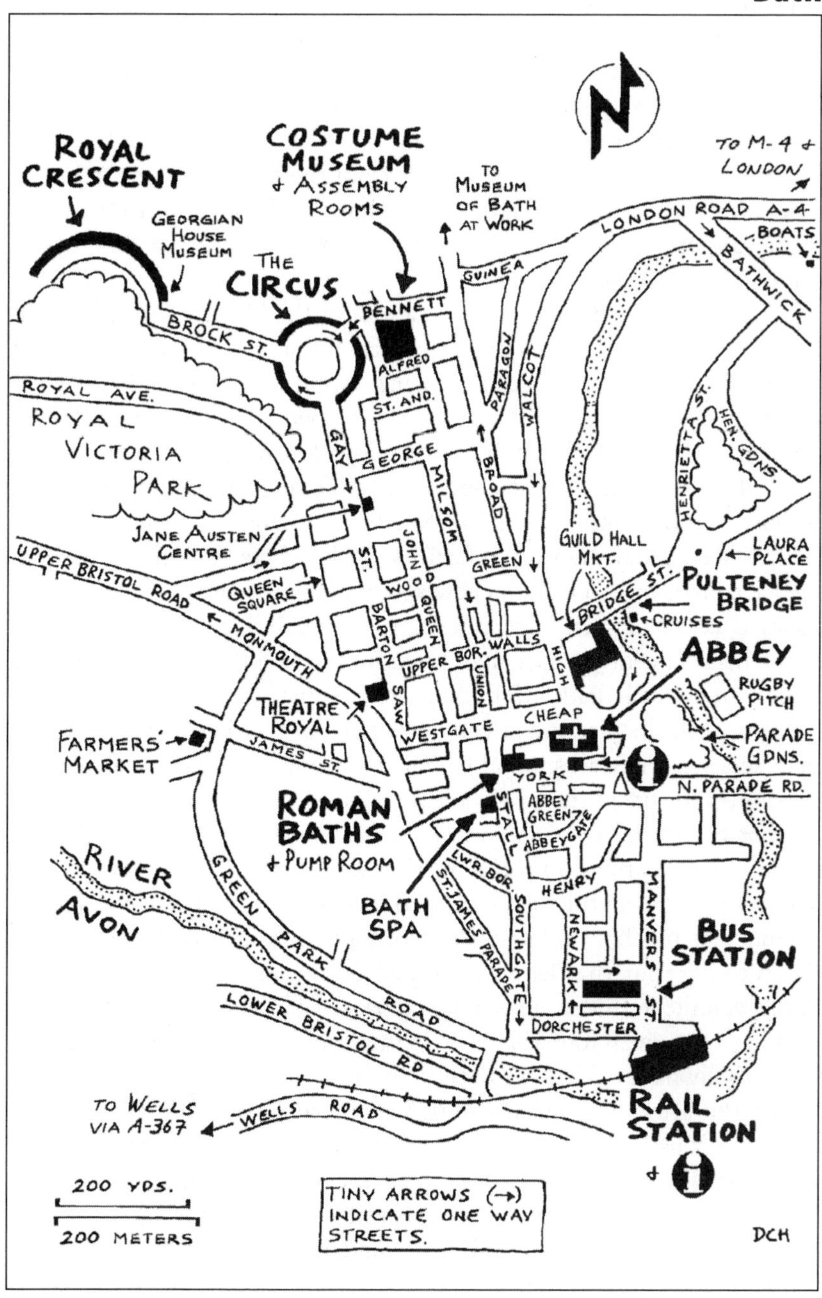
ROYAL CRESCENT
COSTUME MUSEUM & ASSEMBLY ROOMS
TO MUSEUM OF BATH AT WORK
TO M-4 & LONDON
GEORGIAN HOUSE MUSEUM
THE CIRCUS
LONDON ROAD A-4
BOATS
BATHWICK
GUINEA
BENNETT
BROCK ST.
ALFRED
PARAGON
WALCOT
ROYAL AVE.
ST. AND.
ROYAL VICTORIA PARK
GAY
GEORGE
MILSOM
BROAD
HENRIETTA ST.
HEN. GDNS.
JANE AUSTEN CENTRE
JOHN
GUILD HALL MKT.
LAURA PLACE
UPPER BRISTOL ROAD
GREEN
PULTENEY BRIDGE
QUEEN SQUARE
ST.
WOOD
BRIDGE ST.
CRUISES
MONMOUTH
BARTON
QUEEN
WALLS
ABBEY
UPPER BOR.
HIGH
RUGBY PITCH
THEATRE ROYAL
SAW
UNION
CHEAP
PARADE GDNS.
FARMERS' MARKET
JAMES ST.
WESTGATE
YORK
N. PARADE RD.
ROMAN BATHS & PUMP ROOM
STALL
ABBEY GREEN
ABBEYGATE
RIVER AVON
GREEN PARK ROAD
LWR. BOR.
HENRY
BATH SPA
ST. JAMES PARADE
SOUTHGATE
NEWARK
MANVERS ST.
BUS STATION
LOWER BRISTOL RD
DORCHESTER
RAIL STATION
TO WELLS VIA A-367
WELLS ROAD
200 YDS.
200 METERS
TINY ARROWS (→) INDICATE ONE WAY STREETS.
DCH

of peeling the soot of the last century from these tall walls.

Few towns combine beauty and hospitality as well as Bath. If you don't visit the tourist office, it'll visit you. In summer, a tourist-board crew, wearing red, white, and blue "visitor carer" T-shirts, roams the streets in search of tourists to help.

Bath's town square, a quick walk from the bus and train station, is a bouquet of tourist landmarks, including the Abbey, the Roman and medieval baths, the royal "Pump Room," and a Georgian flute player complete with powdered wig.

A good day in Bath starts with a tour of the historic baths. Even in Roman times, when the town was called Aquae Sulis, the hot mineral water attracted society's elite. The town's importance peaked in 973, when the first king of England, Edgar, was crowned in Bath's Anglo-Saxon abbey. Bath reached a low ebb in the mid-1600s, when the town was just a huddle of huts around the abbey and hot springs with 3,000 residents oblivious to the Roman ruins 18 feet below their dirt floors. Then, in 1687, Queen Mary, fighting infertility, bathed here. Within 10 months she gave birth to a son...and a new age of popularity for Bath. The town boomed as a spa resort. Ninety percent of the buildings you see today are from the 18th century. Local architect John Wood was inspired by the Italian architect Palladio to build a "new Rome." The town bloomed in the neoclassical style, and streets were lined with wide "parades" rather than scrawny sidewalks, upon which the women in their stylishly wide dresses could spread their fashionable tails.

For a taste of aristocracy, enjoy tea and scones with live classical music in the nearby Pump Room. For an authentic, if repulsive, finale, have a sip of the awfully curative Bath water from the elegant fountain. To make as much sense as possible of all this fanciness, catch the free city walking tour that leaves from just outside the Pump Room door. Bath's volunteer guides are as much a part of Bath as its architecture. A walking tour gives your visit a little more intimacy, and you'll feel like you actually have a friend in Bath.

In the afternoon, stroll through three centuries of fashion in the Costume Museum. Follow the evolution of clothing styles, one decade at a time, from the first Elizabeth in the 16th century to the second Elizabeth today. The guided tour is excellent—full of fun facts and fascinating trivia. Haven't you always wondered what the line, "Stuck a feather in his cap and called it macaroni," from "Yankee Doodle" means? You'll find the answer (and a lot more) in Bath—the town whose narcissism is justified.

*For good-value accommodations in Bath, try Brock's Guest House (32 Brock St., tel. 01225/338-374, fax 01225/334-245, www.brocksguesthouse.co.uk) or the simpler Woodville House (4 Marlborough Lane, tel. 01225/319-335, matoalster@freenet.co.uk). For more hotels, visit www.ricksteves.com/update, and for all the travel specifics, see this year's edition of* Rick Steves' England *or* Rick Steves' Great Britain.

## 55. YORK: VIKINGS TO DICKENS

Historians run around York like kids in a candy shop. But the city is so fascinating that even non-historians find themselves exploring the past with the same delight they'd give a fun-house hall of mirrors.

York is 200 miles north of London (just 2 hours by train). For a practical introduction to the city, start your visit by taking one of the free, entertaining, and informative guided walking tours (leaving morning, afternoon, and summer evenings from the tourist office). To keep the day open for museums and shopping and enjoy a quieter tour (with a splash of ghostly gore), take the evening walk. The excellent guides are likeably chatty and opinionated. By the end of the walk, you'll know the latest York city gossip, several ghost stories, and what architectural "monstrosity" the "insensitive" city planners are about to inflict on the public.

With this introductory tour under your belt, you're getting the hang of York and its history. Just as a Boy Scout counts the rings in a tree, you can count the ages of York by the different bricks in the city wall: Roman on the bottom, then Danish, Norman, and the "new" addition—from the 14th century.

*York's massive Minster*

The pride of the half-timbered town center is the medieval butchers' street called the Shambles, with its rusty old hooks hiding under the eaves. Six hundred years ago, bloody hunks of meat hung here, dripping into the gutter that still marks the middle of the lane. This slaughterhouse of commercial activity gave our language a new word. What was once a "shambles" is now ye olde tourist shopping mall.

York's four major sights—the York Castle Museum, the Jorvik Viking Centre, the best-in-Europe National Railway Museum, and the huge and historic York

## York

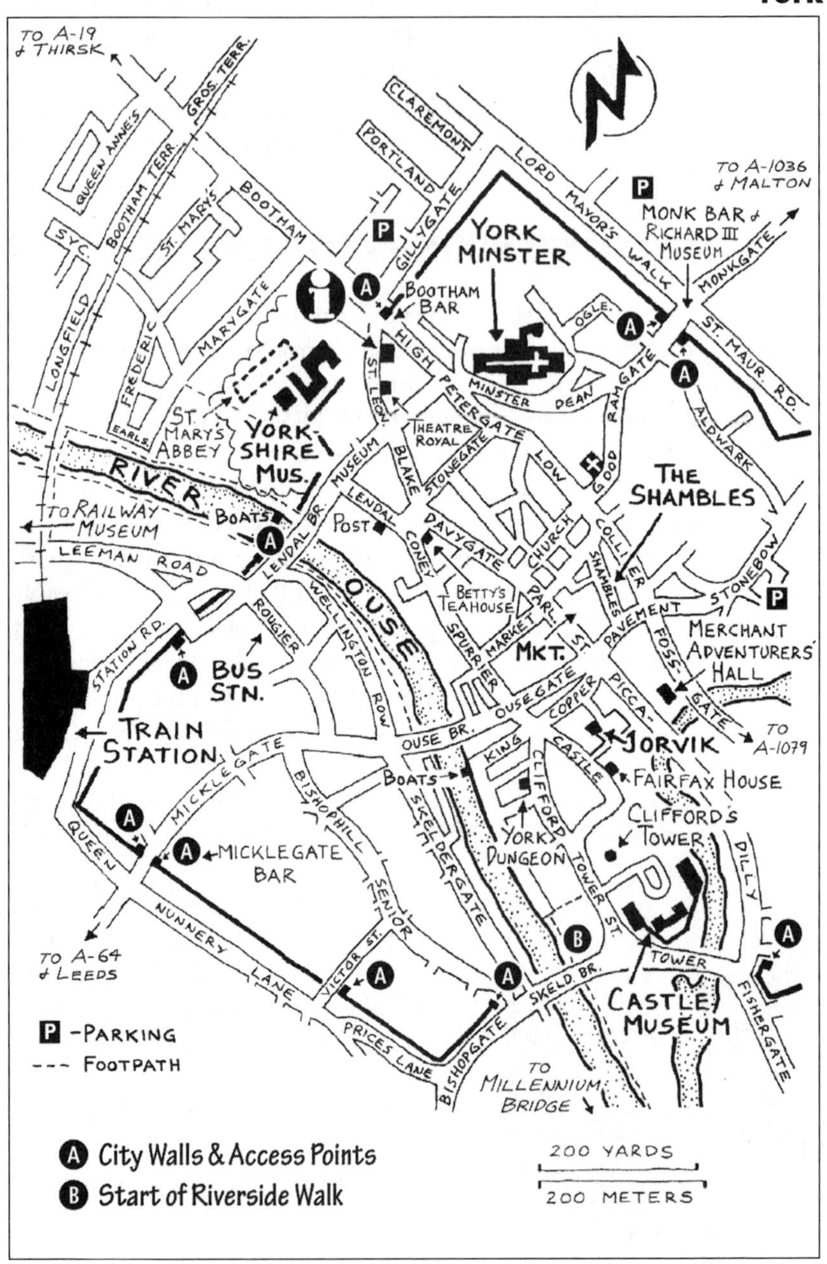

TO A-19 & THIRSK
TO A-1036 & MALTON
CLAREMONT
PORTLAND
GILLYGATE
LORD MAYOR'S WALK
YORK MINSTER
MONK BAR & RICHARD III MUSEUM
MONKGATE
QUEEN ANNE'S
GROS. TERR.
BOOTHAM TERR.
ST. MARY'S
BOOTHAM
SYC.
LONGFIELD
FREDERIC
MARYGATE
EARLS.
BOOTHAM BAR
HIGH PETERGATE
ST. LEON.
MINSTER
DEAN
OGLE.
RAMGATE
ST. MAUR RD.
ALDWARK
ST. MARY'S ABBEY
YORKSHIRE MUS.
THEATRE ROYAL
STONEGATE
BLAKE
MUSEUM
LOW
GOOD
THE SHAMBLES
RIVER
BOATS
TO RAILWAY MUSEUM
LEEMAN ROAD
LENDAL BR.
LENDAL
POST
DAVYGATE
CONEY
CHURCH
COLLIER
SHAMBLES
STONEBOW
BETTY'S TEAHOUSE
OUSE
WELLINGTON ROW
ROUGIER
SPURRIER
MARKET
PARL.
ST.
PAVEMENT
FOSS GATE
MERCHANT ADVENTURERS' HALL
STATION RD.
BUS STN.
MKT.
OUSEGATE
COPPER
PICCA-
TRAIN STATION
OUSE BR.
KING
CLIFFORD
CASTLE
JORVIK
TO A-1079
FAIRFAX HOUSE
MICKLEGATE
BISHOPHILL
BOATS
SKELDERGATE
YORK DUNGEON
TOWER ST.
CLIFFORD'S TOWER
DILLY
QUEEN
MICKLEGATE BAR
SENIOR
NUNNERY LANE
TO A-64 & LEEDS
VICTOR ST.
SKELD. BR.
TOWER
CASTLE MUSEUM
FISHERGATE
PRICES LANE
BISHOPGATE
TO MILLENNIUM BRIDGE
P -PARKING
--- FOOTPATH
A City Walls & Access Points
B Start of Riverside Walk
200 YARDS
200 METERS

Minster cathedral—can keep a speedy sightseer busy for two days.

At York's Castle Museum, Charles Dickens would feel at home. English memorabilia from the 18th and 19th centuries are cleverly displayed in a huge collection of craft shops, old stores, living rooms, and other intimate glimpses of those bygone days.

As towns were being modernized in the 1930s, the museum's founder, Dr. Kirk, collected entire shops and reassembled them here. On Kirkgate, the museum's most popular section, you can wander through a Lincolnshire butcher's shop, Bath bakery, coppersmith's shop, toy shop, and barbershop.

The shops are actually stocked with the merchandise of the day. Eavesdrop on English grannies as they reminisce their way through the museum's displays. The general store is loaded with groceries and candy, and the sports shop has everything you'd need for a game of 19th-century archery, cricket, skittles, or tennis. Anyone for "whiff-whaff" (Ping-Pong)? In the confectionery, Dr. Kirk beams you into a mouth-watering world of "spice pigs," "togo bullets," "hum bugs," and "conversation lozenges."

*Fiddling around old York*

In the period rooms, three centuries of Yorkshire living rooms and clothing fashions paint a cozy picture of life centered around the hearth. Ah, a peat fire warming a huge brass kettle while the aroma of freshly baked bread soaks into the heavy, open-beamed ceilings. After walking through the evolution of romantic valentines and unromantic billy clubs, you can trace the development of early home lighting—from simple waxy sticks to the age of electricity. An early electric heater has a small plaque explaining, "How to light an electric fire: Switch it on!"

Dr. Kirk's "memorable collection of bygones" is the closest thing in Europe to a time-tunnel experience, except perhaps for the Jorvik Viking Centre just down the street.

A thousand years ago, York was a thriving Viking settlement called Jorvik. While only traces are left of most Viking settlements, Jorvik is an archaeologist's bonanza, the best-preserved Viking city ever excavated.

Sail the "Pirates of the Caribbean" north and back in time 1,000 years, and you get Jorvik. More a ride than a museum, this exhibit drapes the abundant harvest of this dig in Disney cleverness.

You watch a brief movie showing two people going back in time.

Their clothes and the buildings in the background "morph" to fit the passing centuries, which flash by on the screen until...it's A.D. 975. You're in Jorvik.

You climb into a little car and slowly glide through the reconstructed village. Everything—sights, sounds, even smells—has been carefully recreated. You experience a Viking village.

Then your time-traveling train car rolls you into the excavation site, past the actual remains of the reconstructed village you just saw. Stubs of buildings, piles of charred wood, broken pottery—a time-crushed echo of a thriving town.

Your ride ends at the museum filled with artifacts from every aspect of Viking life: clothing, cooking, weapons, clever locks, jewelry, even children's games. The gift shop—the traditional finale of any English museum—capitalized nicely on my newly developed fascination with Vikings in England.

In summer Jorvik's midday lines are more than an hour long. Avoid the line by going very early or very late in the day, or by pre-booking (www.vikingjorvik.com, reservations tel. 01904/543-403). Jorvik's commercial success has spawned a series of similar historic rides that take you into Britain's burly, wax-peopled past. While innovative 20 years ago, Jorvik and its cousins seem tired and gimmicky today. For straightforward Viking artifacts, beautifully explained and set in historical context with no crowds at all, tour the nearby Yorkshire Museum.

York's thunderous National Railway Museum shows 150 fascinating years of British railroad history. Fanning out from a grand roundhouse is an array of historic cars and engines, including Queen Victoria's lavish royal car and the very first "stagecoaches on rails." Even spouses of train buffs will find the exhibits on dining cars, post cars, Pullman cars, and vintage train posters interesting.

York's Minster, or cathedral, is the largest Gothic church in Britain. Henry VIII, in his self-serving religious fervor, destroyed nearly everything that was Catholic—except the great York Minster. Henry needed a northern capital for his Anglican church.

The Minster is a brilliant example of how the High Middle Ages were far from dark. The east window, the largest medieval glass window in existence, is just one of the art treasures explained in the free hour-long tours given throughout the day. The church's undercroft gives you a chance to climb down, archaeologically and physically, through the centuries to see the roots of the much smaller but still huge Norman church (built in A.D. 1100) that stood on this spot and, below that, the Roman excavations. Constantine was proclaimed Roman emperor here in A.D. 306. The undercroft also gives you a look at the modern concrete and stainless steel save-the-church foundations.

To fully experience the cathedral, go for an evensong service (no offering plates, no sermon; Mon–Sat at 5:30 p.m., Sun at 4 p.m.). Arrive early and ask to be seated in the choir. You're in the middle of a spiritual Oz as 40 boys sing psalms—a red-and-white-robed pillow of praise, raised up by the powerful pipe organ. You feel as if you have elephant-size ears, as the beautifully carved choir stalls—functioning as giant sound scoops—magnify the thunderous, trumpeting pipes. If you're lucky, the organist will run a spiritual musical victory lap as the congregation breaks up. Thank God for York. Amen.

*For good-value accommodations in York, try Airden House (1 St. Mary's, tel. 01904/638-915, www.airdenhouse.co.uk) or The Sycamore (19 Sycamore Pl., tel. 01904/624-712, www.thesycamore.co.uk). For more hotels, visit www.ricksteves.com/update, and for all the travel specifics, see this year's edition of* Rick Steves' England *or* Rick Steves' Great Britain.

## 56. BLACKPOOL: BRITAIN'S CONEY ISLAND

Blackpool, England's tacky, glittering city of fun with a six-mile beach promenade, is ignored by American guidebooks. Located on the coast north of Liverpool, it's the private playground of North England's Flo and Andy Capps.

When I told Brits I was Blackpool-bound, their expressions soured and they asked, "Oh, God, why?" Because it's the ears-pierced-while-you-wait, tipsy-toupee place that local widows and workers go to year after year to escape. Tacky, yes. Lowbrow, OK. But it's as English as can be, and that's what I'm after. Give yourself a vacation from your sightseeing vacation. Spend a day just "muckin' about" in Blackpool.

*British people flock to Blackpool to soak up the seaside resort's atmosphere.*

Blackpool is dominated by the Blackpool Tower—a giant fun center that seems to grunt, "Have fun." You pay about $20 to get in, and after that the fun is free. Work your way up through layer after

## Blackpool

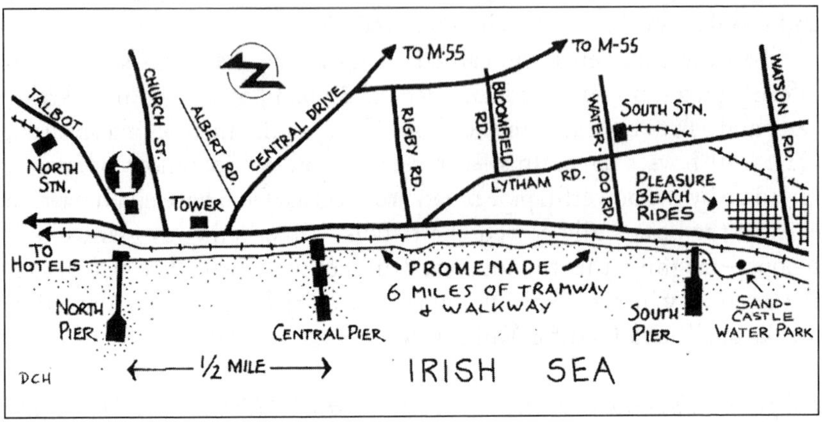


layer of noisy entertainment: circus, bug zone, space world, dinosaur center, aquarium, and the silly house of horrors. Have a coffee break in the elegant ballroom festooned with golden oldies barely dancing to barely live music. The finale at the tip of this 500-foot-tall symbol of Blackpool is a smashing view, especially at sunset. The Tower, a stubby version of its more famous Parisian cousin, was painted gold in 1994 to celebrate its 100th birthday.

Hop a vintage trolley car to survey Blackpool's beach promenade. The cars, which rattle constantly up and down the waterfront, are more fun than driving. Each of the three amusement piers has its own personality. Are you feeling sedate (north pier), young and frisky (central pier), or like a cowboy dragging a wagon full of children (south pier)?

Stroll the Promenade. A million greedy doors try every trick to get you inside. Huge arcade halls advertise free toilets and broadcast bingo numbers into the streets. The randy wind machine under a wax Marilyn Monroe blows at a steady gale, and the smell of fries, tobacco, and sugared popcorn billows everywhere. Milk comes in raspberry or banana in this land where people under incredibly bad wigs look normal. I was told that I mustn't leave without having my fortune told by a Gypsy spiritualist, but, at $5 per palm, I'll read them myself.

Don't miss an evening at an old-time variety show. Blackpool always has a few razzle-dazzle music, dancing-girl, racy-humor, magic, and tumbling shows ($15–30 tickets at the door). I enjoy the "old-time music hall" shows. The shows are corny—neither hip nor polished—but it's fascinating to be surrounded by hundreds of partying British seniors, swooning again and waving their hankies to the predictable beat. Busloads of happy widows come from all corners of North England to

## Liverpool's Magical Mystery Tour

About an hour south of Blackpool is Liverpool, with the gentrified Albert Dock harborfront featuring the city's top museums, a cheap hotel, vast parking, and plenty of Beatles lore.

Die-hard fans may want to pay homage at John and Paul's boyhood homes—both restored circa 1950s (must visit with a National Trust Tour, 2 hours, $20, reservations recommended, tel. 0151/708-8574). Or try the less in-depth Beatles "Magical Mystery" bus tour, which hits the lads' homes (exteriors only), Penny Lane, and so on. The tourist information office has specifics on the big bus that goes daily (also 2 hours). For something more extensive, fun, and intimate, consider a three-hour minibus Beatles tour with Phil Hughes. It's longer because it includes information on historic Liverpool as well as the Beatles stuff (www.tourliverpool.co.uk).

The "sights" each tour covers are basically houses where the Fab Four grew up, places they performed, and spots made famous by the lyrics of their hits ("Penny Lane," "Strawberry Fields," the Eleanor Rigby graveyard, etc.). While perfectly boring to non-fans, enthusiasts will enjoy the commentary and seeing the shelter in the middle of the roundabout, the fire station with the clean machine, and the barber who shaves another customer. It's still in my ears and in my eyes.

giggle at racy jokes. A perennial favorite is *Funny Girls*, a burlesque-in-drag show that delights footballers and grannies alike.

Blackpool's "Illuminations" light up the night every September and October. Blackpool (the first city in England to "go electric") stretches its season by illuminating its six-mile waterfront with countless blinking and twinkling lights. The American inside me kept saying, "I've seen bigger and I've seen better," but I filled his mouth with cotton candy and just had some simple fun like everyone else on my specially decorated tram.

For a fun forest of amusements, Blackpool Pleasure Beach is tops. These 42 acres of rides (more than 100, including "the best selection of white-knuckle rides in Europe"), ice-skating shows, cabarets, and amusements attract seven million people a year, making Pleasure Beach one of England's most popular attractions. Their roller coaster is among the world's highest (235 feet), fastest (85 mph), and least likely to have me on board.

For me, Blackpool's top sight is its people. You'll see England here

British people imagining sunshine at the beach in Blackpool

like nowhere else. Grab someone's hand and a big stick of candy floss (cotton candy) and stroll. Ponder the thought that legions of English actually dream of retiring here to spend their last years dog-paddling day after day through this urban cesspool of fun, wearing hats with built-in ponytails.

Blackpool is a scary thing to recommend. Maybe I overrate it. Many people (ignoring the "50 million flies can't all be wrong" logic) think I do. If you're not into kitsch and greasy spoons (especially if you're a nature lover and the weather happens to be good), skip Blackpool and spend more time in nearby North Wales or England's Lake District. But if you're traveling with kids—or still are one yourself—visit Blackpool, Britain's fun puddle where every Englishman goes, but none will admit it.

*For good-value accommodations in Blackpool, try Robin Hood Hotel (100 Queens Promenade, tel. 01253/351-599) or Beechcliffe Private Hotel (16 Shaftesbury Ave., tel. 01253/353-075). For more hotels, visit www.ricksteves.com/update, and for all the travel specifics, see this year's edition of* Rick Steves' England *or* Rick Steves' Great Britain.

## 57. THE COTSWOLD VILLAGES: INVENTORS OF QUAINT

The Cotswold region, a 25-by-50-mile chunk of Gloucestershire, is a sightseeing treat: crisscrossed with hedgerows, raisined with storybook villages, and sprinkled with sheep.

As with many fairy-tale regions of Europe, the present-day beauty of the Cotswolds was the result of an economic disaster. Wool was a huge industry in medieval England, and the Cotswold sheep grew it best. Wool money built lovely towns and palatial houses as the region prospered. Local "wool" churches are called "cathedrals" for their scale and wealth. A typical prayer etched into their stained glass reads, "I thank my God and ever shall, it is the sheep hath paid for all."

With the rise of cotton and the Industrial Revolution, the woolen industry collapsed, mothballing the Cotswold towns into a depressed

*It's hard to go wrong in the Cotswolds.*

time warp. Today visitors enjoy a harmonious blend of humanity and nature: the most pristine of English countrysides decorated with time-passed villages, gracefully dilapidated homes of an impoverished nobility, tell-me-a-story stone fences, and "kissing gates" you wouldn't want to experience alone. Appreciated by hordes of 21st-century romantics, and in spite of local moaning about "the recession," the Cotswolds are enjoying new prosperity.

The area is provincial. Chatty locals, while ever so polite, commonly rescue themselves from a gossipy tangent by saying, "It's all very... ummm...yyya." Rich people open their gardens to support their favorite charities, while the less couth fondly remember an outlawed sport called "badger baiting" (a gambling cousin of cockfighting where a badger, with its teeth and claws taken out, is mangled by dogs).

The north Cotswolds are best. Two of the region's coziest towns, Chipping Campden and Stow-on-the-Wold, are eight and four miles respectively from Moreton-in-Marsh, the only Cotswold town with a train station. Any of these—Chipping Campden, Stow, or Moreton—would make a fine home base for your exploration of the thatch-happiest of Cotswold villages and walks.

**Chipping Campden** is a working market town, home of some proudly thatched roofs and the richest Cotswold wool merchants. Both the great British historian Trevelyan and I call Chipping Campden's High Street the finest in England.

## The Cotswolds

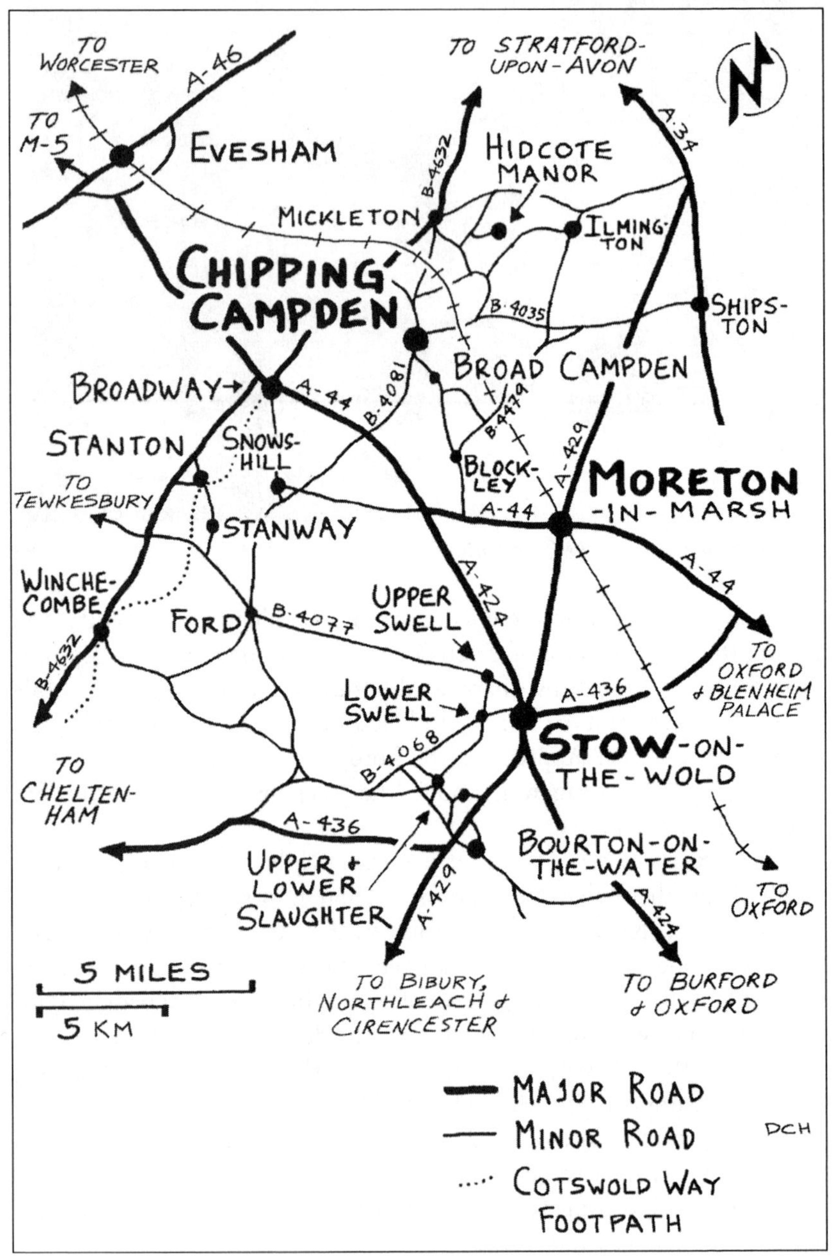

Walk the full length of High Street (like most market towns, wide enough for plenty of sheep business on market days). Near the south end, you'll find the best thatched homes. Walking north on High Street, you'll pass the Market Hall (1627), the wavy roof of the first great wool mansion, a fine and free memorial garden, and, finally, the town's famous 15th-century Gothic "wool" church.

*Imprisoned by the charm of the Cotswolds (and two teenyboppers)*

**Stow-on-the-Wold** has become a crowded tourist town, but most visitors are day-trippers, so even summer nights are lazy and quiet. The town has no real sights other than itself, some good pubs, cutesy shops, and art galleries draped seductively around a big town square. The tourist office sells a handy walking-tour brochure called "Town Trail." A visit to Stow is not complete until you've locked your partner in the stocks on the green.

**Moreton-in-Marsh,** an easy home base for those without a car, is a Stow or Chipping Campden without the touristic sugar. Rather than gift and antique stores, you'll find streets lined with real shops. Ironmongers sell cottage nameplates, and carpet shops are strewn with the remarkable patterns that decorate B&B floors. A traditional market filling High Street with 260 stalls gets the whole town shin-kicking each Tuesday. There is an economy outside of tourism in the Cotswolds, and you'll feel it in Moreton.

Stanway, Stanton, and Snowshill, between Stow and Chipping Campden, are my nominations for the cutest Cotswold villages. Like marshmallows in hot chocolate, they nestle side by side—awaiting your arrival.

**Stanway,** while not much of a village, is notable for its manor house. Lord Neidpath, whose family tree charts relatives back to 1202, occasionally opens his melancholy home to visitors ($11, $7.50 for gardens alone, includes 300-foot-tall fountain, July–Aug, Tue, Thu and Sat 2–5 p.m., June Tue and Thu only 2–5 p.m., tel. 01386/584-469). The 14th-century tithe barn predates the manor and was originally where monks, in the days before money, would accept one-tenth of whatever the peasants produced. Peek inside—this is a great hall for village hoedowns.

While the tithe barn is no longer used to greet motley peasants with their feudal "rents," the lord still collects rents from his vast landholdings. The place feels like a time warp even though the lord has recently remarried.

Ask the ticket-taker (inside) to demonstrate the spinning rent-collection table. In the great hall, marvel at the one-piece oak shuffleboard table and the 1780 Chippendale exercise chair (half an hour of bouncing on this was considered good for the liver).

*Lord Neidpath opens his quirky and fascinating manor house to the public and personally greets his guests.*

The manor dogs have their own cutely painted "family tree," but Lord Neidpath admits that his current dog, C.J., is "all character and no breeding." The place has a story to tell. And so do the docents stationed in each room—modern-day peasants who, even without family trees, probably have relatives going back just as far in this village. Really. Talk to these people. Probe. Learn what you can about this side of England.

Stanway and neighboring Stanton are separated by a great oak forest and grazing land with parallel waves actually echoing the furrows plowed by medieval farmers. Let someone else drive so you can hang out the window under a canopy of oaks as you pass stone walls and sheep.

In **Stanton,** flowers trumpet, door knockers shine, and slate shingles clap: a rooting section cheering visitors up the town's main street. The church, which dates back to the ninth century, betrays a pagan past. Stanton is at the intersection of two lines (called ley lines) connecting prehistoric sites. Churches such as Stanton's, built on a pagan holy ground, are dedicated to St. Michael. You'll see his well-worn figure above the door as you enter. Inside, above the capitals in the nave, find the pagan symbols for the moon and the sun. But it's Son worship that's long established, and the list of rectors goes back to 1269. Finger the back pew grooves, worn away by sheepdog leashes. A man's sheepdog accompanied him everywhere. The popular Mount Inn pub is just up the hill.

**Snowshill,** another nearly edible little bundle of cuteness, has a photogenic triangular square with a fine pub at its base. Snowshill Manor is a dark and mysterious old palace filled with the lifetime collection of the long-gone Charles Paget Wade. It's one big, musty celebration of craftsmanship, from finely carved spinning wheels to frightening samurai armor to tiny elaborate figurines carved by long-forgotten prisoners from the bones of meat served at dinner. Taking seriously his family motto, "Let Nothing Perish," he dedicated his life and fortune to preserving things finely crafted. The house (whose management made me promise not to promote it as an eccentric collector's pile of curiosities) really shows off Mr. Wade's ability to recognize and acquire fine examples of craftsmanship. It's all very...ummm...yyya.

*If you'd rather be riding, rent a horse.*

The Cotswolds are walker's country. The English love to walk the peaceful footpaths that shepherds walked back when "polyester" meant two girls. They vigorously defend their age-old right to free passage. Once a year, the Rambling Society organizes a "Mass Trespass," when each of England's 50,000 miles of public footpaths is walked. By assuring each path is used at least once a year, they frustrate fence-happy landlords. Most of the land is privately owned and fenced in, but you're welcome (and legally entitled) to pass through, using the various sheep-stopping steps, gates, and turnstiles provided at each stone wall.

After a well-planned visit, you'll remember everything about the Cotswolds—the walks, churches, pubs, B&Bs, thatched roofs, gates, tourist offices, and even the sheep—as quaint.

*For good-value accommodations in Chipping Campden, try Sandalwood House B&B (Back Ends, tel. & fax 01386/840-091); in Stow-on-the-Wold, West Deyne B&B (Lower Swell Rd., tel. 01451/831-011); and in Moreton-in-Marsh, Treetops B&B (London Road, tel. & fax 01608/651-036, www.treetopscotswolds.co.uk). For more hotels, visit www.ricksteves.com/update, and for all the travel specifics, see this year's edition of* Rick Steves' England *or* Rick Steves' Great Britain.

# 58. MYSTERIOUS BRITAIN

Stonehenge, Holy Grail, Avalon, Loch Ness...there's a mysterious side of Britain steeped in lies, legends, and at least a little truth. Haunted ghost walks and Nessie the Monster stories are profitable tourist gimmicks. But the cultural soil that gives us Beowulf, Shakespeare, and "God Save the Queen" is fertilized with a murky story that goes back to 3000 B.C., predating Egypt's first pyramids.

**Mysterious Britain**

As today's sightseers zip from castle to pub, they pass countless stone circles, forgotten tombs, man-made hills, and figures carved into hillsides whose stories will never be fully understood. Certain traveling druids skip the beefeater tours and zero right in on this side of Britain. But with a little background, even the skeptic can appreciate Britain's historic aura.

Britain is crisscrossed by lines connecting prehistoric Stonehenge-type sights. Apparently prehistoric tribes intentionally built sites along this huge network of "ley" lines, which some think may have functioned together as a cosmic relay or circuit.

**Glastonbury,** two hours west of London and located on England's most powerful ley line, gurgles with a thought-provoking mix of history and mystery. As you climb the Glastonbury Tor, notice the remains of the labyrinth that made the hill a challenge to climb 5,000 years ago.

In A.D. 37, Joseph of Arimathea—one of Jesus' disciples—brought vessels containing the blood and sweat of Jesus to Glastonbury, and with them, Christianity to England. While this is "proven" by fourth-century writings and accepted by the Church, the Holy Grail legend that sprang from this in the Middle Ages isn't.

In the 12th century, England needed a morale-boosting folk hero to inspire its people during a war with France. The ruins of a fifth-century Celtic timber fort at Glastonbury were considered proof of the greatness of that century's obscure warlord, Arthur. Glastonbury became linked with King Arthur and his knights after Arthur's supposed remains were found buried in the abbey. Arthur's search for the Holy Grail, the chalice used at the Last Supper, could be mere legend. But many people think the Grail trail ends at the bottom of the "Chalice Well," a natural spring at the base of Glastonbury Tor.

In the 16th century, Henry VIII, on his church-destroying rampage, wrecked the powerful Glastonbury Abbey. For emphasis, he hung and quartered the abbot, sending the parts of his body on four national tours...at the same time. While that was it for the abbot, two centuries later Glastonbury rebounded. In an 18th-century tourism campaign, thousands signed affidavits stating that water from the Chalice Well healed them, and once again Glastonbury was on the tourist map.

Today, Glastonbury and its tor are a center for searchers—too creepy for the mainstream church, but just right for those looking for a place to recharge their crystals. Since the society that built the labyrinth worshipped a mother goddess, the hill, or tor, is seen by many today as a Mother Goddess symbol.

After climbing the tor (great view, easy parking, always open), visit the Chalice Well at its base. Then tour the evocative ruins of the abbey, with its informative visitor's center and a model of the church before Henry got to it. Don't leave without a browse through the town. The Rainbow's End Café (2 min from the abbey at 17 High Street) is a fine place for salads and New Age people-watching. Read the notice board for the latest on midwives and male bonding.

From Glastonbury, as you drive across southern England, you'll see giant figures carved on hillsides. The white chalk cliffs of Dover stretch across the south of England, and almost anywhere you dig you hit chalk. While most of the giant figures are creations of 18th- and 19th-century humanists reacting against the coldness of the Industrial Age, three Celtic figures (the Long Man of Wilmington, the White Horse of Uffington, and the Cerne Abbas Giant) have, as far as history is concerned, always been there.

*Cerne Abbas Giant: "Maidens can still be seen leaping over his willy."*

The Cerne Abbas Giant is armed with a big club and an erection. For centuries, people fighting infertility would sleep on Cerne Abbas. And, as my English friend explained, "Maidens can still be seen leaping over his willy."

**Stonehenge,** England's most famous stone circle, is an hour's drive from Glastonbury. Built sometime between 3000 and 1000 B.C. with huge stones brought all

*Stonehenge is surrounded by a rope. This is as close as you'll get.*

the way from Wales or Ireland, it still functions as a remarkably accurate celestial calendar. A recent study of more than 300 similar circles in Britain found that each was designed to calculate the movement of the sun, moon, and stars, and even to predict eclipses in order to help these early societies know when to plant, harvest, and party. Even today, as the summer solstice sun sets in just the right slot at Stonehenge, pagans boogie. Modern-day tourists and druids are kept at a distance by a fence, but if you're driving, Stonehenge is just off the highway and worth a stop ($10). Even a free look from the road is impressive.

Why didn't the builders of Stonehenge use what seem like perfectly adequate stones nearby? There's no doubt that the particular "blue stones" used in parts of Stonehenge were found only in (and therefore brought from) Wales or Ireland. Think about the ley lines. Ponder the fact that many experts accept none of the explanations of how these giant stones were transported. Then imagine congregations gathering here 4,000 years ago, raising thought levels, creating a powerful life force transmitted along the ley lines. Maybe a particular kind of stone was essential for maximum energy transmission. Maybe the stones were levitated here. Maybe psychics really do create powerful vibes. Maybe not. It's as unbelievable as electricity used to be.

The nearby stone circle at **Avebury,** 16 times the size of Stonehenge, is one-sixteenth as touristy. You're free to wander among a hundred stones, ditches, mounds, and curious patterns from the past, as well as the village of Avebury, which grew up in the middle of this 1,400-foot-wide neolithic circle.

Spend some time at Avebury. Take the mile-long walk around the circle. Visit the fine little archaeology museum and pleasant Circle Restaurant next to the National Trust store. The Red Lion Pub (also within the circle) has good, inexpensive pub grub. As you leave, notice the pyramid-shaped Silbury Hill. This man-made mound, nearly 5,000 years old, is a reminder that you've only scratched the surface of Britain's fascinating prehistoric and religious landscape.

A fine way to mix neolithic wonders and nature is to explore one of England's many turnstile-free moors. You can get lost in these stark and sparsely populated time-passed commons, which have changed over the centuries about as much as the longhaired sheep that seem to gnaw on moss in their sleep. Directions are difficult to keep. It's cold and gloomy, as nature rises like a slow tide against human constructions. A crumpled castle loses itself in lush overgrowth. A church grows shorter as tall weeds eat at the stone crosses and tilted tombstones.

**Dartmoor** is the wildest moor—a wonderland of green and powerfully quiet rolling hills in the southwest, near the tourist centers of Devon and Cornwall. Crossed by only two or three main roads, most of the area is either unused or shared by its 30,000 villagers as a common grazing land—a tradition since feudal days. Dartmoor is best toured by car, but it can be explored by bike, rental horse, thumb, or foot. Bus service is meager. Several national park centers provide maps and information. Settle into a small-town B&B or hostel. This is one of England's most remote corners—and it feels that way.

Dartmoor, with more Bronze Age stone circles and huts than any other chunk of England, is perfect for those who dream of enjoying their own private Stonehenge sans barbed wire, police officers, parking lots, tourists, and port-a-loos. The local Ordnance Survey maps show the moor peppered with bits of England's mysterious past. Down Tor and Gidleigh are especially thought-provoking.

Word of the wonders lurking just a bit deeper into the moors tempted me away from my Gidleigh B&B. Venturing in, I sank into the powerful, mystical moorland. Climbing over a hill, surrounded by hateful but sleeping towers of ragged granite, I was swallowed up. Hills followed hills followed hills—green growing gray in the murk.

Where was that 4,000-year-old circle of stone? I wandered in a world of greenery, eerie wind, white rocks, and birds singing but unseen. Then the stones appeared, frozen in a forever game of statue-maker. For endless centuries they had waited patiently, still and silent, for me to come.

I sat on a fallen stone, holding the leash as my imagination ran wild, pondering the people who roamed England so long before written history documented their story. Grabbing the moment to write, I took out my journal. The moor, the distant town, the chill, this circle of stones. I dipped my pen into the cry of the birds and wrote.

*For good-value accommodations in Dartmoor, try St. Johns West B&B (in Murchington, near Chagford, tel. 01647/432-468, jwwest@ntlworld.com).*

## 59. THE AN DAINGEAN (DINGLE) PENINSULA: A GAELIC BIKE RIDE

Be forewarned, Ireland is seductive. In many areas, traditions are strong and stress is a foreign word. I fell in love with the friendliest land this side of Sicily. It all happened in a *Gaeltacht.*

*Gaeltachts* are national parks for the traditional culture, where the government protects the old Irish ways. Shaded green on many maps, these regions brighten the west coast of the Emerald Isle. *Gaeltacht* means a place where Irish (or Gaelic) is spoken. The Irish culture is more than just the old language. You'll find it tilling the rocky fields, singing in the pubs, and lingering in the pride of the small-town preschool that brags "all Irish." Signposts are in Irish only, with many in the old Irish lettering. If your map is in English...good luck. Irish yuppies report that the Irish language is cool and on the rise.

The An Daingean (Dingle) Peninsula—green, rugged, and untouched—is my favorite *Gaeltacht.* While the big tour buses clog the neighboring Ring of Kerry before heading east to kiss the Blarney Stone, in An Daingean it still feels like the fish and the farm actually matter. Fifty fishing boats sail from An Daingean. And a nostalgic whiff of peat continues to fill its nighttime streets, offering visitors an escape into pure Ireland. For more than 25 years, my Irish dreams have been set here, on this sparse but lush peninsula where locals are fond of saying, "The next parish is Boston."

*The Irish have all the time in the world to share* craic *(conversation) with you.*

Of the peninsula's 10,000 residents, 1,500 live in An Daingean (Dingle) town. Its few streets, lined with ramshackle but gaily painted shops and pubs, run up from a rainstung harbor. During the day, teenagers—already working on ruddy beer-glow cheeks—roll kegs up the streets and into the pubs in preparation for another tin-whistle night.

Fishing once dominated An Daingean, and the town's

only visitors were students of old Irish ways. Then, in 1970, the movie *Ryan's Daughter* introduced the world to An Daingean. The trickle of its fans has grown to a flood, as word has spread of its musical, historical, gastronomical, and scenic charms—not to mention Fungie the friendly dolphin, who hangs out in the harbor.

## The An Daingean Peninsula Circle—By Bike or Car

The An Daingean Peninsula is 10 miles wide and runs 40 miles, from Tralee to Ceann Sleibhe (Slea Head). The top of its mountainous spine is Mount Brandon—at 3,300 feet, the second-tallest mountain in Ireland. While only tiny villages lie west of An Daingean town, the peninsula is home to half a million sheep. The weather on this distant tip of Ireland is often misty, foggy, and rainy. Good and bad weather blow by in a steady meteorological parade. With stops, the 30-mile circuit (go with the traffic, clockwise) takes five hours by bike or three hours by car.

*Enjoy the Emerald Isle on two wheels.*

Leaving An Daingean town, it becomes clear that the peninsula is an open-air museum. It's littered with monuments reminding visitors that the town has been the choice of Bronze Age settlers, Dark Age monks, English landlords, and Hollywood directors. The Milestone B&B decorates its front yard not with a pink flamingo, but with a pillar stone—one of more than 2,000 stony pieces in the puzzle of prehistoric life here.

Across the bay, the manor house of Lord Ventry is surrounded by palms, magnolias, fuchsias, and fancy flora introduced to An Daingean by the Englishman who once owned the peninsula. His legacy—thanks only to the mild, Gulf Stream–protected weather–is the festival of fuchsias that lines the peninsula roads. And just down the street, locals point to the little blue house that once kept Tom Cruise and Nicole Kidman cozy during the filming of *Far and Away*.

Near a yellow schoolhouse, a street sign warns *Taisteal go mall*—slow down. Near the playground, students hide out in circular remains of a late Stone Age ring fort. In 500 B.C., it was a petty Celtic chieftain's headquarters—a stone-and-earth stockade filled with little stone houses. So many of these ring forts survived the centuries because of superstitious

## An Daingean (Dingle) Peninsula

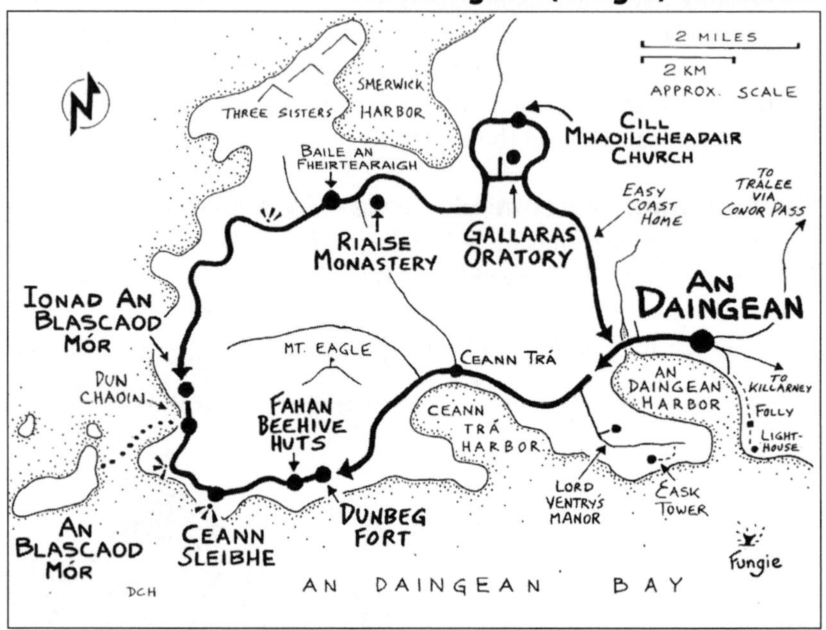


beliefs that they were "fairy forts."

In the little town of Ceann Tra' (Ventry in English), talk with the chatty Irish you'll meet along the roadside. I once met an elfish, black-clad old man here. When I asked if he was born here, he breathed deeply and said, "No, 'twas about six miles down the road." When I told him where I was from, a faraway smile filled his eyes as he looked out to sea and sighed, "Aye, the shores of Americay."

The wet sod of An Daingean is soaked with medieval history. In the darkest depths of the Dark Ages, when literate life almost died in Europe, peace-loving, bookwormish monks fled the chaos of the Continent and its barbarian raids. They sailed to this drizzly fringe of the known world and lived their monastic lives in lonely stone igloos or "beehive huts," which you'll see dotting the landscape.

Several groups of these mysterious huts, called *clochans*, line the road. Built without mortar by seventh-century monks, these huts take you back. Climb into one. You're all alone, surrounded by dank mist and the realization that it was these monks who kept literacy alive in Europe. To give you an idea of their importance, Charlemagne, who ruled much of Europe in the year 800, imported Irish monks to be his scribes.

It was from this peninsula that St. Brendan, the semi-mythical priest-explorer, is said to have set sail in the sixth century in search of a legendary

*Ireland's top attraction—the friendliest people in Europe*

western paradise. Some think he beat Columbus to North America...by almost a thousand years!

Rounding Ceann Sleibhe (Slea Head), the point in Europe closest to America, the rugged coastline offers smashing views of deadly black-rock cliffs and the distant Na Blascaodai (Blasket Islands). The crashing surf races in like white horses, while long-haired sheep—bored with the weather, distant boats, and the lush countryside—couldn't care less.

Just off the road you'll see the scant remains of the scant home that was burned by the movie-star equivalent of Lord Ventry as he evicted his potato-eating tenants in the movie *Far and Away*.

Even without Hollywood, this is a bleak and godforsaken place. Sand and seaweed heaped on the clay eventually became soil. The created land was marginal, just barely growing potatoes. Ragged patches of this reclaimed land climb the hillsides. Rocks were moved and piled into fences.

Stacks of history can be read into the stones. From the air, Ireland looks like alligator skin—a maze of stone fences. With unrivaled colonial finesse, the British required Irish families to divide their land among all heirs. This doomed even the largest estates to fragmentation, shrinking lots to sizes just large enough to starve a family. Ultimately, of course, the land ended up in the possession of British absentee landlords. The tiny rock-fenced lots that carve up the treeless landscape remind the farmers of the structural poverty that shaped their history. And weary farmers have never bothered with gates. Even today they take a hunk of wall down, let their sheep pass, and stack the rocks again.

Study the highest fields, untouched since the planting of 1845, when the potatoes never matured and rotted in the ground. You can still see the vertical ridges of the potato beds—a reminder of that year's Great Potato Famine, which, through starvation or emigration, nearly halved Ireland's population. Because its endearing people have endured so much, Ireland is called the Terrible Beauty.

Take your time at the Gallaras Oratory (c. A.D. 800)—the sightseeing highlight of your peninsula tour. One of Ireland's best-preserved early Christian churches, its shape is reminiscent of an upturned boat. Its watertight dry-stone walls have sheltered travelers and pilgrims for 1,200 years.

From the oratory, continue up the rugged one-lane road to the crest of the hill, then coast back into An Daingean—hungry, thirsty, and ready for...

*The enduring Gallarus Oratory*

## An Daingean Pubs

With 50 pubs for its 1,500 people, An Daingean is a pub-crawl waiting to happen. Even if you're not into pubs, give these a whirl. The town is renowned among traditional musicians as a place to get work ("€50 a day, tax-free, plus drink"). There's music every night and rarely a cover charge. The scene is a decent mix of locals, Americans, and Germans. While two pubs—the Small Bridge Bar (An Droichead Beag) and O'Flaherty's—are the most famous for their good beer and folk music, make a point to wander the town and follow your ear.

When you say "a beer, please" in an Irish pub, you'll get a pint of "the black beauty with a blonde head"—Guinness. If you want a small beer, ask for a half pint. Never rush your bartender when he's pouring a Guinness. It takes time—almost sacred time. If you don't like Guinness, try it in Ireland. It doesn't travel well and is better in its homeland. Murphy's is a very good Guinness-like stout, but a bit smoother and milder.

*On an An Daingean evening, follow your ear to a music-filled pub.*

The Irish government passed a law in 2004 making all pubs in the Republic smoke-free; Northern Ireland will follow in 2007. Smokers now take their pint outside, turning alleys into covered smoking patios. An incredulous Irishman responded to the new law by saying, "What will they do next? Ban drinking in pubs? We'll never get to heaven if we don't die."

In an Irish pub, you're a guest on

your first night; after that, you're a regular. Women traveling alone need not worry—you'll become part of the pub family in no time.

It's a tradition to buy your table a round, and then for each person to reciprocate. If an Irishman buys you a drink, thank him by saying, *"Go raibh maith agat"* (guh-rev-mah-a-gut). Offer him a toast in Irish—*"Slainte!"* (slahn-chuh). A good excuse for a conversation is to ask to be taught a few words of Irish. You've got a room full of native speakers who will remind you that every year, 10 languages go extinct. They'd love to teach you a few words of their favorite language.

*Craic* (crack) is the art of conversation—the sport that accompanies drinking in a pub. People are there to talk. Join in. Here's a goofy excuse for some *craic:* Ireland—small as it is—has many dialects. People from Cork (the big city of Ireland's south coast) are famous for talking very fast (and in a squeaky voice)...so fast that some even talk in letters alone. "ABCD fish?" (Anybody see the fish?) "DRO fish." (There are no fish.) "DR fish." (There are fish.) "CDBDI's?" (See the beady eyes?) "OIBJ DR fish." (Oh aye, be Jeeze, there are fish.) For a possibly more appropriate spin, replace "fish" with "bird" (girl). This is obscure, but your pub neighbor may understand and enjoy hearing it. If nothing else, you won't seem so intimidating to him anymore.

Also, you might ask if the people of one county are any smarter than the next. Kerry people are famous for being a bit out of it. It's said that when the stupidest man in county Cork moved to county Kerry, it raised the average IQ in each area.

## Traditional Irish Music

Traditional music is alive and popular in pubs throughout Ireland. "Sessions" (musical evenings) may be planned and advertised or impromptu. Traditionally, musicians just congregate and jam. There will generally be a fiddle, flute or tin whistle, guitar, *bodhrán* (goat-skin drum), and maybe an accordion. Things usually get going around 9:30 or 10 p.m. "Last call" (last chance to order a drink before closing) is around "half eleven" (11:30 p.m.).

The *bodhrán* is played with two hands: One wielding a small two-headed club and the other stretching the skin to change the tone and pitch. The wind and string instruments embellish melody lines with lots of improvised ornamentation. Occasionally the fast-paced music will stop, and one person will sing an a cappella lament. This is the one time when the entire pub will stop to listen, as sad lyrics fill the room. Stories—ranging from struggles against English rule to love songs—are always heartfelt. Spend a lament studying the faces in the crowd.

*Irish pubs—a blur of banjo pickin', flute tootin', great beer, and new friends.*

The music comes in sets of three songs. Whoever happens to be leading determines the next song, only as the song the group is playing is about to be finished. If he wants to pass on the decision, it's done with eye contact and a nod.

A session can be magic, or it may be lifeless. If the chemistry is right, it's one of the great Irish experiences. The music churns intensely while the group casually enjoys exploring each others' musical styles. The drummer dodges the fiddler's playful bow. Sipping their pints, they skillfully maintain a faint but steady buzz. The floor on the musicians' platform is stomped paint-free, and barmaids scurry artfully through the commotion, gathering towers of empty, cream-crusted glasses. With knees up and heads down, the music goes round and round. Make yourself right at home, "playing the boot" (tapping your foot) under the table in time with the music.

## An Blascoad Mór (Great Blasket Island)

An Blascoad Mór (Great Blasket in English), a rugged, uninhabited island off the tip of An Daingean Peninsula, seems particularly close to the soul of Ireland. Its population, once as many as 160 people, dwindled until the last handful of residents was moved by the government to the mainland in 1953. These people were the most traditional Irish community of the 20th century—the symbol of an antique culture. They had a special closeness to their island, combined with a knack for vivid storytelling. From this poor, primitive, but proud fishing and farming community came three writers of international repute whose work—basically tales of life on the island—is translated into many languages. In shops all over the peninsula, you'll find *Peig* (by Peig Sayers),

*Ghost town on An Blascoad Mór (Great Blasket Island)*

*Twenty Years A-Growing* (Maurice O'Sullivan), and *The Islandman* (Tomás O'Crohan).

Today, An Blascoad Mór is a grassy three-mile poem, overrun with memories. With fat rabbits, ruffled sheep, abandoned stone homes, and a handful of seals, it's ideal for windblown but thoughtful walks.

A ferry runs hourly, depending on weather and demand, from Dun Chaoin to An Blascoad Mór (April–Sept 10:00–17:00). Several boats depart from An Daingean town several times a day.

Before visiting the islands, stop at the state-of-the-art Ionad An Blascaod Mór (Great Blasket Centre, on An Daingean Peninsula facing the islands, tel. 066/915-6444). This center creatively gives visitors the best possible look at the heritage, language, literature, life, and times of Na Blascaodai's inhabitants. See the fine video, hear the sounds, read the poems, browse through old photos, and then gaze out the big windows at those rugged islands and imagine. Even if you never got past limericks, the poetry of these people—so pure and close to each other and nature—is an inspiration.

*For good-value accommodations in An Daingean, try Sraid Eoin B&B (John St., tel. 066/915-1409, fax 066/915-2156, sraideoinhouse@hotmail.com) or the simpler Corner House B&B (Dykegate St., tel. 066/915-1516). For more hotels, visit www.ricksteves.com/update, and for all the travel specifics, see this year's edition of* Rick Steves' Ireland.

## 60. NORTHERN IRELAND AND BELFAST

Ireland is a split island still struggling with questions left over from its stint as a British colony. While the island won its independence back in the 1920s, the predominantly Protestant northern section opted to stick with its Pope-ophobic partners in London. While somewhere between a headache and a tragedy for locals, this adds up to some fascinating travel opportunities for you and me. And lately there are some good, solid reasons to be hopeful.

With so many people working so hard to bring Ireland together, a browse through Belfast will give you more faith in people than despair over headlines. There's a guarded optimism as creative grassroots efforts to grow peace are taking hold.

Make your visit to Ireland complete by including Northern Ireland. This is a British-controlled six-county section of a nine-county area called Ulster. It offers the tourist a very different but still very Irish world. The British-ruled counties of Northern Ireland, long a secret enjoyed and toured mainly by its own inhabitants, are finally being recognized by international travelers.

Of course, people are being killed in Northern Ireland—but not as many as in any major American city. Car accidents kill more Northern Irish than do bombs or guns. With common sense, travel in this area is safe. No American has ever been injured by "the Troubles," and travelers give Northern Ireland rave reviews.

*With this Union Jack bulldog street mural, a Belfast Protestant neighborhood makes its Unionist feelings pit bull–clear.*

Include Belfast in your Irish travel plans. Here's an itinerary that will introduce you to a capital city of 400,000 and Ireland's best open-air folk museum. At the same time, you'll meet some of the friendliest people on earth and learn firsthand about their struggle.

## Belfast

Seventeenth-century Belfast was only a village. With the influx, or "plantation," of Scottish and English settlers, Belfast boomed, spurred by the success of the local linen, rope-making, and shipbuilding industries. The Industrial Revolution took root with a vengeance. While the rest of Ireland remained rural, Belfast earned its nickname, "Old Smoke," when many of the brick buildings you'll see today were built. The year 1888 marked the birth of modern Belfast. After Queen Victoria granted city status to this town of 300,000, citizens built its centerpiece, City Hall.

Belfast is the birthplace of the *Titanic*...and many ships that didn't sink. The two huge, mustard-colored cranes (the biggest in the world, nicknamed Samson and Goliath) rise like skyscrapers above the harbor, as if declaring this town's shipbuilding might. It feels like a new morning in Belfast. Security checks, once a tiresome daily routine, are now rare. What was the traffic-free security zone has shed its gray skin and become a bright and bustling pedestrian zone. On my last visit, the children dancing in the street were both Catholic and Protestant—part of a community summer-camp program giving kids from both communities reason to live together rather than apart.

Still, it's a fragile peace and a tenuous hope. The pointedly Protestant billboards and the helicopter that still hovers over the Catholic end of

## Belfast

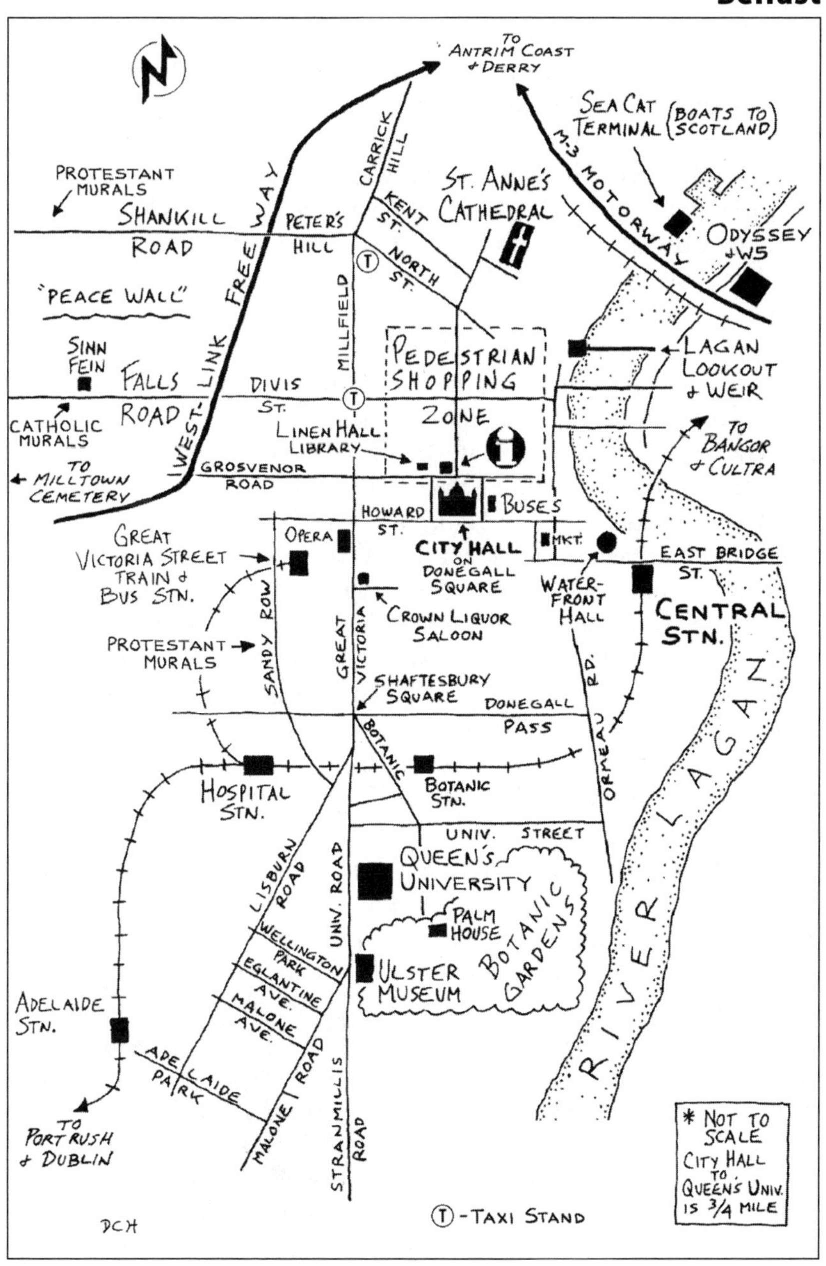

TO ANTRIM COAST & DERRY
SEA CAT TERMINAL (BOATS TO SCOTLAND)
M-3 MOTORWAY
PROTESTANT MURALS
SHANKILL ROAD
WEST-LINK FREEWAY
CARRICK HILL
PETER'S HILL
KENT ST.
NORTH ST.
ST. ANNE'S CATHEDRAL
ODYSSEY & W5
"PEACE WALL"
MILLFIELD
PEDESTRIAN SHOPPING ZONE
LAGAN LOOKOUT & WEIR
SINN FEIN
FALLS ROAD
DIVIS ST.
CATHOLIC MURALS
LINEN HALL LIBRARY
TO BANGOR & CULTRA
TO MILLTOWN CEMETERY
GROSVENOR ROAD
HOWARD ST.
BUSES
GREAT VICTORIA STREET TRAIN & BUS STN.
OPERA
CITY HALL ON DONEGALL SQUARE
MKT.
WATER-FRONT HALL
EAST BRIDGE ST.
CENTRAL STN.
CROWN LIQUOR SALOON
PROTESTANT MURALS
SANDY ROW
GREAT VICTORIA
SHAFTESBURY SQUARE
DONEGALL PASS
ORMEAU RD.
BOTANIC
BOTANIC STN.
HOSPITAL STN.
UNIV. STREET
QUEEN'S UNIVERSITY
LISBURN ROAD
UNIV. ROAD
PALM HOUSE
BOTANIC GARDENS
RIVER LAGAN
WELLINGTON PARK
EGLANTINE AVE.
ULSTER MUSEUM
MALONE AVE.
ADELAIDE STN.
ADELAIDE PARK
MALONE ROAD
STRANMILLIS ROAD
TO PORT RUSH & DUBLIN
* NOT TO SCALE
CITY HALL TO QUEEN'S UNIV. IS 3/4 MILE
DCH
(T) - TAXI STAND

town remain a reminder that the island is split...and 800,000 Protestant Unionists prefer it that way.

A visit to Belfast is actually easy from Dublin. Consider this plan for the most interesting Dublin day trip: With the handy two-hour Dublin–Belfast train ($45 "day-return" tickets except Fri and Sun), you can leave Dublin early and catch the Belfast City Hall tour at 11 a.m. After browsing through the pedestrian zone, ride a shared cab (see below) through the Falls Road neighborhood. At 3 p.m., head out to the Ulster Folk and Transport Museum in Cultra. Picnic on the evening train back to Dublin.

The well-organized day-tripper will get a taste of both Belfast's Industrial Age glory and the present (and related) Troubles. It will be a happy day when the sectarian neighborhoods of Belfast have nothing to be sectarian about. For a look at what was one of the home bases for the Troubles, explore the working-class-Catholic Falls Road neighborhood.

A few blocks from City Hall, just east of the intersection of Divis Street and Millfield Road, you'll find a parking garage filled with old black cabs—and the only Irish-language signs in downtown Belfast. These shared black cabs efficiently shuttle residents from outlying neighborhoods up and down the Falls Road and to the city center. All cabs go up the Falls Road to Milltown Cemetery, passing lots of murals and Sinn Fein (the Irish Republican Army's political wing) headquarters. Sit in front and talk to the cabbie. Easy-to-flag-down cabs run every minute or so in each direction on Falls Road. They do one-hour tours for about $50 (cheap for a small group of travelers).

At the Milltown Cemetery, you'll be directed past all the Gaelic crosses down to the IRA "Roll of Honor"—set apart from the thousands of other graves by little green railings. They are treated like fallen soldiers. You'll see a memorial to Bobby Sands and the nine other hunger strikers who starved themselves to death in the nearby Maze Prison in 1981 in support of a united Ireland.

*Murals reinforce political walls.*

The Sinn Fein headquarters is on the Falls Road (look for the protective boulders on the sidewalk and the Irish Republic flag on the roof). The adjacent bookstore is worth a look. Page through books featuring color photos of the political murals that decorate the local buildings. Money raised here

*Children march in a Protestant Orange parade: Political differences are taught at an early age.*

supports families of imprisoned IRA members.

A sad corrugated wall called the "Peace Line" runs a block or so north of the Falls Road (along Cupar Way), separating the Catholics from the Protestants in the Shankill Road area.

While you can ride a shared black cab up Shankill Road (catch one southeast of Peter's Hill and Millfield Roads), the easiest way to get a dose of the Unionist side is to walk Sandy Row—a working-class-Protestant street behind the Hotel Europa (said to be Europe's most-bombed hotel). You'll see a few murals filled with Unionist symbolism. The mural of William of Orange's victory over the Catholic King James II (Battle of the Boyne, 1690) stirs Unionist hearts.

Most of Ireland has grown disillusioned by the violence wrought by the IRA and the Protestants' Ulster Volunteer Force (UVF), which are now seen by many as rival groups of terrorists who actually work together, Mafia-style, to run free and wild in their established territories. Maybe the solution can be found in the mellowness of Ulster retirement homes, where old "Papishes" with their rosaries and old "Prods" with their prayer books sit side by side talking to the same heavenly father. But that kind of peace is elusive. An Ulster Protestant on holiday in England once told me with a weary sigh, "Tomorrow I go back to my tribe."

For a trip into a cozier age, take the eight-mile bus or train ride to the Ulster Folk and Transport Museum at Cultra. The Folk Museum is an open-air collection of 34 reconstructed buildings from all over the nine counties of Ulster, designed to showcase the region's traditional lifestyles. After wandering through the old town site (church, print shop, schoolhouse, humble Belfast row home, and so on), you'll head into the country to nip into cottages, farmhouses, and mills. Each house is warmed by a peat fire and a friendly attendant. The museum can be dull or vibrant, depending upon your ability to chat with the people staffing each building.

The adjacent Transport Museum traces the evolution of transportation from its beginning 7,500 years ago, when someone first decided to load an ox, and continues to the present, with an interesting exhibit on the sinking of the Belfast-made *Titanic.* In the next two buildings, you roll through the history of bikes, cars, and trains. The car section goes from the first car in Ireland (an 1898 Benz), through the "Cortina Culture" of the 1960s, to the local adventures of John DeLorean (with a 1981 model of his car).

Speeding on the train back to Dublin, gazing at the peaceful and lush Irish countryside while pondering DeLorean, the *Titanic,* and the Troubles, your delusions of a fairy-tale Europe have been muddled. Belfast is a bracing dose of reality.

*For good-value accommodations in Belfast, try Malone Guest House (79 Malone Road, tel. 028/9066-9565, fax 028/9037-5090, maloneguesthouse@btinternet.com) or Jurys Inn Belfast (Fisherwick Place, Great Victoria Street, tel. 028/9053-3500, fax 028/9053-3511, www.jurysdoyle.com). For more hotels, visit www.ricksteves.com/update, and for all the travel specifics, see this year's edition of* Rick Steves' Ireland.

# SCANDINAVIA

## 61. NORWAY IN A NUTSHELL: OSLO AND THE FJORDS

Oslo is the smallest and least earthshaking of the Nordic capitals, but this brisk little city is a scenic *smörgåsbord* of history, sights, art, and Nordic fun. Add on a "Norway in a Nutshell" excursion over the mountains and to the fjords, and this is potentially one of Europe's best three-day packages of sightseeing thrills.

On May 17, Norway's national holiday, Oslo bursts with flags, bands, parades, and pride. Blond toddlers are dressed up in colorful ribbons, traditional pewter buckles, and wool. But Oslo—surrounded by forests, near mountains, and on a fjord—has plenty to offer the visitor year-round.

In Oslo, sights of the Viking spirit tell an exciting story. From the city hall, hop the ferry for the 10-minute ride to Bygdøy. This cluster of sights reflects the Norwegian mastery of the sea. Some of Scandinavia's best-preserved Viking ships are on display here. Rape, pillage, and—ya sure you betcha—plunder were the rage

**Oslo**

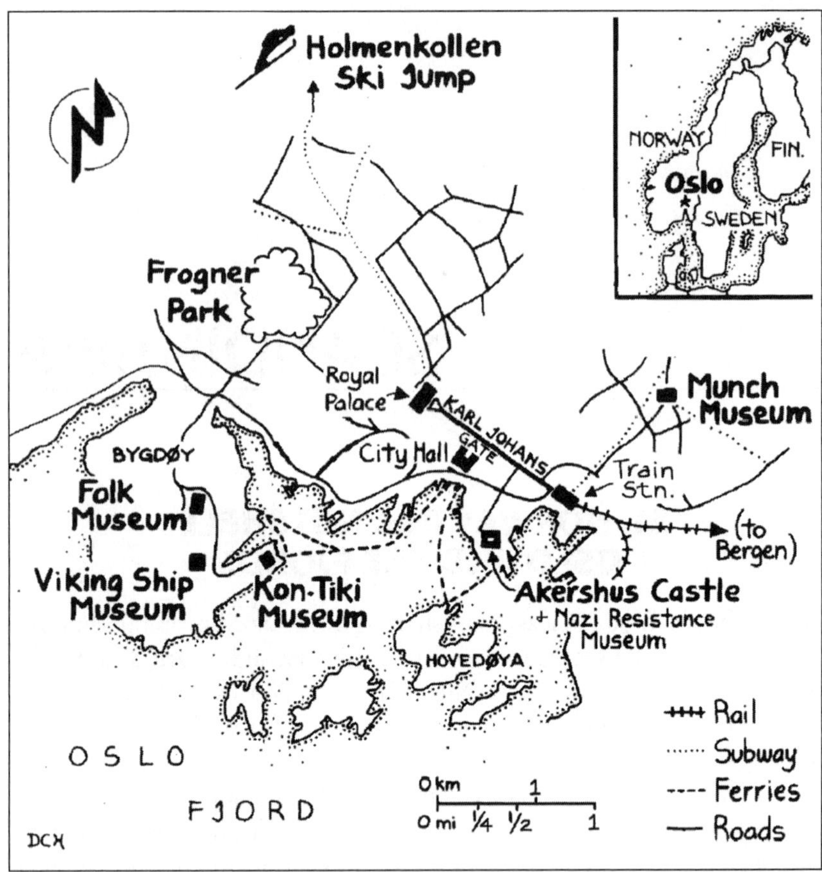


1,000 years ago in Norway. There was a time when much of a frightened Western Europe closed every prayer with, "And deliver us from the Vikings, amen." Gazing up at the prow of one of those sleek, time-stained vessels, you can almost hear the shrieks and smell the armpits of those redheads on the rampage.

Nearby, Thor Heyerdahl's balsa raft, *Kon-Tiki,* and the polar ship *Fram* illustrate Viking energy channeled in more productive directions. The *Fram,* serving both Nansen and Amundsen, ventured farther north and south than any other ship.

Just a harpoon toss away is Oslo's open-air folk museum. The Scandinavians were leaders in the development of these cultural parks that are now so popular around Europe. More than 150 historic log cabins and buildings from every corner of the country are gathered together in this huge folk museum. Inside each house, a person in local dress is happy to answer questions about traditional life in that part of Norway. Don't miss the 1,000-year-old wooden-stave church.

The place is lively only June through mid-August, when buildings are open and staffed. (Otherwise the indoor museum is fine, but the park is just a walk past lots of locked-up log cabins.) On summer Sundays, you'll enjoy folk dancing at 2 p.m. (mid-May–mid Sept only). If you don't take a tour, glean information from the $2 guidebook and the informative attendants ($14, or $11 off-season, daily mid-May–mid-Sept 10 a.m.–6 p.m., off-season daily 11 a.m.–3 p.m., www.norskfolke.museum.no).

Oslo's avant-garde city hall, built 40 years ago, was a communal effort of Norway's greatest artists and designers. Tour the interior. More than 2,000 square yards of bold, colorful murals are a journey through the collective mind of modern Norway. City halls, rather than churches, are the dominant buildings in the your-government-loves-you northern corner of Europe. The main hall of the city hall actually feels like a temple to good government—the altarlike mural celebrates "work, play, and civic administration." Each December, the Nobel Peace Prize is awarded in this room.

*Norwegian art in Oslo's Frogner Park*

Norway has given the world two outstanding modern artists: Edvard Munch (pronounced "monk") and Gustav Vigeland. Oslo's Frogner Park features 192 bronze and granite sculptures representing 30 years of Vigeland creativity. The centerpiece is the 46-foot-tall totem pole of tangled bodies known as the *Monolith of Life*. This, along with the neighboring Vigeland Museum, is a must on any list of Oslo sights.

Oslo's Munch Museum is a joy. It's small, displaying an impressive collection of one man's work, rather than numbing you with art by countless artists from countless periods. You leave the Munch Museum feeling like you've learned something about one artist, his culture, and his particular artistic "ism"—expressionism. You won't see his famous *Scream*, stolen from this museum in 2004 (but another version of it is in the National Gallery downtown).

You can also explore Oslo's 700-year-old Akershus Castle. Its fascinating Nazi-resistance museum shows how one country's spirit cannot be crushed, regardless of how thoroughly it's occupied by a foreign power. The castle itself is interesting only with a guided tour.

Language problems are few. The Norwegians speak better English than any other people on the Continent. My cousin, who attended the University of Oslo, had to specify British English or American English in her language studies. She learned American—and can slang me under the table.

Oslo has been called Europe's most expensive city. I'll buy that. Without local relatives, life on a budget is possible only if you have a good guidebook and take advantage of money-saving options. Budget tricks like picnicking and sleeping in private homes offer the most exciting savings in this most expensive city.

## One Day for the Fjords?

If you go to Oslo and don't get out to the fjords, you should have your passport revoked. Norway's greatest claim to scenic fame is its deep and lush fjords. Sognefjord, Norway's longest (120 miles) and deepest (more than a mile), is tops. Anything but Sognefjord is, at best, foreplay. This is it: the ultimate natural thrill Norway has to offer.

For the best one-day look at fjords, do "Norway in a Nutshell." This series of well-organized train, ferry, and bus connections lays this most beautiful fjord country spread-eagle on a scenic platter.

*Norway's Sognefjord*

Every morning, northern Europe's most spectacular train ride leaves Oslo at about 8 a.m. for Bergen. Cameras smoke as this train roars over Norway's mountainous spine. The barren, windswept heaths, glaciers, deep forests, countless lakes, and a few rugged ski resorts create a harsh beauty. The railroad is an amazing engineering feat. Completed in 1909, it's 300 miles long and peaks at 4,266 feet—which, at this Alaskan latitude, is far above the tree line. You'll go under 18 miles of snow sheds, over 300 bridges, and through 200 tunnels in just less than seven hours ($175, railpass-holders pay about $65, reservations required;

## Norway in a Nutshell

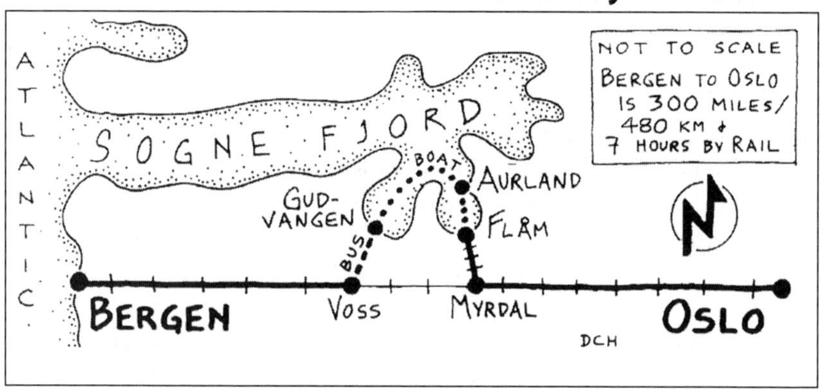


in peak season—July–mid-Aug—book several weeks in advance).

At Myrdal, a 12-mile spur line ($27, or $18 with a railpass) drops you 2,800 breathtaking feet in 50 minutes to the village of Flåm on Sognefjord. This is a party train. The engineer even stops the train for photographs at a particularly picturesque waterfall.

While most "Norway in a Nutshell" tourists zip immediately from the train onto the scenic fjord boat in Flåm, those with time enjoy an overnight stop on the fjord.

Flåm is a handy tourist depot with several simple hotels. Aurland, a few miles north of Flåm, is more of a town. It's famous for producing some of Norway's sweetest *geitost*—goat cheese. Aurland has as many goats as people (1,900). Nearly every train arriving in Flåm connects with a bus or boat to Aurland, also on Sognefjord. While nearby Bergen is famous for its rain—more than six feet a year—Sognefjord is a relative sun belt, with only two feet a year.

The train from Myrdal to Flåm is quite scenic, but the ride doesn't do the view justice. For the best single day's activity from Flåm, take the train to Berekvam (halfway back up to Myrdal), then hike or bike (rentable from the Flåm tourist office) the gravelly construction road back down to Flåm. Bring a picnic and extra camera batteries.

From Flåm, "Nutshellers" catch the most scenic of fjord cruises. Sightseeing boats leave throughout the day ($30, discounts with a student card or full-fare spouse). For 90 minutes, camera-clicking tourists scurry on the drool-stained deck like nervous roosters, scratching fitfully for a photo to catch the magic. Waterfalls turn the black-rock cliffs into a bridal fair. You can nearly reach out and touch the sheer, towering walls. The ride is one of those fine times, like being high on the tip of an Alp, when a warm camaraderie spontaneously combusts among the strangers who came together for the experience. The boat takes you up one narrow arm (Aurlandsfjord) and down the next (Nærøyfjord) to the nothing-to-stop-for town of Gudvangen, where waiting buses ($13) shuttle you back to the main train line at Voss. From Voss, return to Oslo or carry on into Bergen for a short evening visit.

Bergen, Norway's second city and historic capital, is an entertaining place. You can finish the day there by browsing the touristy but fun wharf area, or zipping up the funicular to the top of 1,000-foot-tall "Mount" Fløyen for city and fjord views, before catching the overnight train back to Oslo.

Back in Oslo's station, as you yawn and stretch and rummage around for a cup of morning coffee, it'll hit you: You were gone for 24 hours, experienced the fjord wonder of Europe, and saw Bergen to boot.

*For good-value accommodations in Oslo, try Thon Hotel Astoria (Dronningens Gate 21, tel. 24 14 55 50, fax 22 42 57 65, www.thonhotels.no/astoria) or City Hotel (Skippergaten 19, tel. 22 41 36 10, fax 22 42 24 29, www.cityhotel.no). Sleep cozy near the palace at Ellingsen's Pensjonat (Holtegata 25, tel. 22 60 03 59, ep@tiscali.no), or cheap in the trendy Grünerløkka neighborhood at Arve Naess' rooms (Toftesgate 45, tel. 98 83 68 36). For more hotels, visit www.ricksteves.com/update, and for all the travel specifics, see this year's edition of* Rick Steves' Scandinavia.

## 62. ÆRØ: DENMARK'S SHIP-IN-A-BOTTLE ISLAND

Few visitors to Scandinavia even notice Ærø, a sleepy, 6-by-22-mile island on the south edge of Denmark. Ærø has a salty charm. Its tombstones are carved with such sentiments as: "Here lies Christian Hansen at anchor with his wife. He'll not weigh until he stands before God." It's a peaceful and homey island, where baskets of new potatoes sit in front of farmhouses—for sale on the honor system.

*Main Street, Ærøskøbing*

Ærø's capital, Ærøskøbing, makes a fine home base. Temple Fielding said it's "one of five places in the world that you must see." Many Danes agree, washing up the cobbled main drag in waves with the landing of each ferry. In fact, this is the only town in Denmark that is entirely protected and preserved by law.

Ærøskøbing is a town-in-a-bottle kind of place. Wander down lanes right out of the 1680s, when the town was the wealthy home port to more than 100 windjammers. The post office dates to 1749, and cast-iron gaslights still shine each evening. Windjammers gone, the harbor now caters to German and Danish holiday yachts. On midnight low tides, you can almost hear the crabs playing cards.

*A warm and traditional welcome awaits you at an old-fashioned Danish country inn.*

The Hammerich House, full of old junk, is a 1900s garage sale open daily in summer. The "Bottle Peter" museum on Smedegade is a fascinating house with a fleet of 750 different bottled ships. Old Peter Jacobsen died in 1960 (and is probably buried in a glass bottle), leaving a lifetime of his tedious little creations for visitors to squint and marvel at.

Touring Ærø by car is like sampling chocolates with a snow shovel. Enjoy a breezy 18-mile tour of Ærø's subtle charms by bike. Borrow a bike from your hotel or rent one from the Energi Station at the top of town. On Ærø, there are no deposits and no locks. If you start in the morning, you'll be home in time for a hearty lunch.

Ready? Leave Ærøskøbing west on the road to Vrå past many U-shaped farms, typical of this island. The three sides block the wind and are used for storing cows, hay, and people. *"Gaard"* (meaning "farm") shows up in many local names. Bike along the coast in the protection of the dike, which turned the once-salty swampland to your left into farmable land. Pedal past a sleek modern windmill and Borgnæs, a pleasant cluster of mostly modern summer cottages. (At this point, bikers with one-speeds can shortcut directly to Vindeballe.)

After passing a secluded beach, climb uphill over the island's summit to Bregninge. Unless you're tired of thatched and half-timbered cottages, turn right and roll through Denmark's "second longest village" to the church. Peek inside. Then roll back through Bregninge, head a mile down the main road to Vindeballe, and take the Vodrup turnoff to the right.

## Denmark'sÆro Island Bike Ride

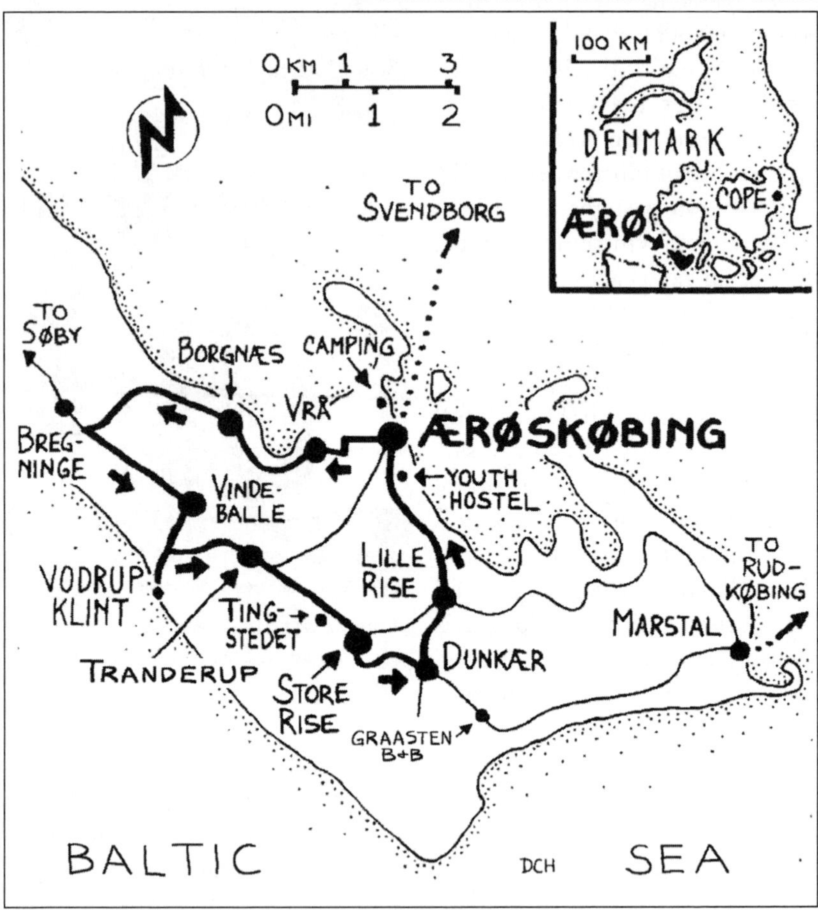


A road leads downhill to an ancient site on a rugged bluff called Vodrup Klint. If I were a pagan, I'd stop here to worship. Savor the sea, the wind, and the chilling view.

Pedal to Tranderup, past a lovely farm and a potato stand. At the old town of Olde, you'll hit the main road. Turn right toward Store Rise—marked by its church spire in the distance. Just behind the church is a 6,000-year-old neolithic burial place, the Langdysse (Long Dolmen) Tingstedet. Hunker down. Ærø had more than 200 of these. Only 13 survive.

Inside the Store Rise church, notice the little ships hanging in the nave, the fine 12th-century altarpiece, and Martin Luther in the stern making sure everything's theologically shipshape.

Continue down the main road, with the hopeful forest of modern windmills whirring on your right, until you get to Dunkær.

For the homestretch, take the small road past the topless windmill. Except for "Lille Rise," it's all downhill as you coast home past great sea views to Ærøskøbing.

After a power tour of big-city Scandinavia, Ærø offers a perfect time-passed island on which to wind down, enjoy the seagulls, and pedal a bike into the essence of Denmark. After a break in this cobbled world you may understand the sailors who, after the invention of steam-driven boat propellers, decided that building ships in bottles was more their style.

*For good-value accommodations in Ærø, try Pension Vestergade (Vestergade 44, tel. & fax 62 52 22 98, www.pension-vestergade44.dk) or Det Lille Hotel (Smedegade 33, tel. & fax 62 52 23 00). For more hotels, visit www.ricksteves.com/update, and for all the travel specifics—including a more thorough description of the bike ride—see this year's edition of* Rick Steves' Scandinavia.

# THROUGHOUT EUROPE

## 63. OFFBEAT EUROPE

No one planning a trip to Europe needs to be reminded to see Big Ben and the Leaning Tower. But did you know that you can spelunk the sewers of Paris, quaff homebrews with German monks, or ski in Scotland in summer? It's those unexpected experiences that are often the most memorable part of a trip. Here are a few that I've especially enjoyed writing home about.

**Salzburg's Super-Soaker Prince:** Salzburg's 17th-century Hellbrunn Castle entertains with a garden full of trick fountains and tour guides sadistically soaking tourists. At the touch of a button, paths (and pedestrians) get doused and benches turn into fountains. It's silly fun, especially with kids on a sunny day ($10, closed Nov–March, www.hellbrunn.at).

*Belgium's little squirt*

**Belgium's Little Squirt:** For more dribbling diversions, stop by Brussels' *Manneken-Pis,* a statue of a young boy urinating, and the irreverent mascot of this great Belgian city. You'll find this little squirt three blocks off the main square, La Grand Place. He'll probably be aiming through some clever outfit. By tradition, costumes for the lad are sent to Brussels from around the world. Go figure. Cases displaying scores of these colorful get-ups are on display in Brussels' City Museum.

## Offbeat Europe

**TV and the Downfall of Tea:** London's Bramah Tea and Coffee Museum is a hit with aficionados of the brown brews. This small museum passionately tells the story of each drink ($7.50, www.bramahmuseum.co.uk). The owner, Edward Bramah, who comes from a big tea family, wants the world to know how the advent of commercial television—with breaks too short to brew a proper pot of tea—required a faster hot drink. In came the horrible English instant coffee. The tea industry countered with minced leaves in tea bags, and it's gone downhill ever since.

**Frankfurt's Red Light Towers:** Near Frankfurt's central station, people killing time between trains can visit one of 20 "Eros Towers"—each a five-story brothel filled with hookers. Frankfurt's prostitutes, who are legal and taxed, note that business varies with the theme of the trade show at the nearby convention center. While Frankfurt's annual auto show is boom time, hookers complain that the world's largest annual book fair is a complete bust. (No, I'm not a customer. Beware—drug addicts and pushy barkers make this neighborhood feel unsafe after dark.)

**Europe's Skinniest Park:** Paris' skinny, two-mile-long Promenade Plantée Park is a narrow garden walk on a viaduct once used for train tracks. The elevated park, which cuts through lots of modern condos, gives a fun peek into the workaday lives of Parisians today. Staircases lead to the street level, where artsy, offbeat shops (whose rent is subsidized by the city government) fill the viaduct's arches. The park runs from place de la Bastille, along avenue Daumesnil to Saint-Mandé.

*A sliver of a park slices through downtown Paris.*

**Skiing in Edinburgh:** If you'd rather be skiing, the Midlothian Ski Centre, just outside Edinburgh, has

## Boning Up on Europe's Relics

Centuries ago, relics were an important focus of worship. These holy relics, often bones, were the "ruby slippers" of the medieval age. They gave you power—got your prayers answered and helped you win wars—and ultimately helped you get back to your eternal Kansas.

*The Cappuccin monks have a thought-provoking habit of hanging their dead brothers out to dry for all to see...for ever and ever, amen.*

The bones of monks were venerated, and sometimes even artistically arranged in crypts and chapels. In **Rome's** Cappuccin Crypt, hundreds of skeletons decorate the walls to the delight—or disgust—of the always wide-eyed visitor. The crypt offers unusual ideas in home decorating, as well as a chance to pick up a few of Rome's most interesting postcards. A similar Cappuccin Crypt is a highlight of many visits to **Palermo** in Sicily. In **Évora,** Portugal, osteophiles make a pilgrimage to the macabre "House of Bones" chapel at the Church of St. Francis, lined with the bones of thousands of monks.

*Head to Hallstatt's Bone Chapel.*

Overcrowding in cemeteries has prompted unusual solutions. Austria's tiny town of **Hallstatt** is crammed between a mountain and a lake. Space is so limited that bones get only 12 peaceful buried years in the church cemetery before making way

a brush-skiing hill with a chairlift, two slopes, a jump slope, and rentable skis, boots, and poles (http://ski.midlothian.gov.uk). While you're actually skiing over what seems like a million toothbrushes, it feels like snow skiing on a slushy day. It's open nearly year round (probably closed when it snows). Beware: Local doctors are used to treating an ailment called "Hillend Thumb"—digits dislocated when people fall and get tangled in the brush.

**The Tide Went Out and Never Came Back:** Holland is twice as big today as it was 300 years ago. How? By "reclaiming" land from the sea using dikes and windmill-powered pumps. During the process, for the newly dead. The result is a fascinating chapel of bones in the cemetery. Each skull is lovingly named, dated, and decorated, with the men getting ivy, and the women, roses. Hallstatt stopped this practice in the 1960s, about the same time the Catholic Church began permitting cremation.

**Kutná Hora's** ossuary, an hour by train from Prague, is decorated with the bones of 40,000 people, many of them plague victims. The monks who stacked these bones 400 years ago wanted viewers to remember that the earthly church is a community of both the living and the dead. Later bone-stackers were more into design than theology—creating, for instance, a chandelier made with every bone in the human body.

*Kutná Hora's ossuary, decorated Early Ghoulish.*

Some cities such as Paris and Rome have catacombs. Many cities opened up a little extra space by de-boning graveyards, which used to surround medieval churches. During the French Revolution, **Paris** experienced a great church cemetery land grab. Skeletons of countless Parisians were dug up and carefully stacked along miles of tunnels beneath the city.

Seekers of the macabre can bone up on Europe's more obscure ossuaries, but any tourist will stumble onto bones and relics. Whether in a church, chapel, or underground tunnel in Europe, you might be surprised by who's looking at you, kid.

many tiny islands—home to traditional fishing villages—were stranded high and dry in the middle of Dutch farmland. The fishing village of Schotlan, once on an island in the Zuider Zee, is one such village. The village has a now-useless lighthouse, and you can walk right up to a buoy that once bobbed in the harbor. A bent and rusty propeller from a WWII English bomber ornaments the village square...a reminder that when farmers first tilled their new soil, they uncovered more than just muck and mollusks.

**Roman Pyramid:** You don't need to go to Egypt to see an ancient pyramid. Standing 90 feet tall, Rome's pyramid was built in 12 B.C.

*Pyramid power in Rome*

as a tomb for the Roman Gaius Cestius, after the Cleopatra and Mark Antony scandal brought exotic Egyptian styles into vogue. Later the pyramid was incorporated into Rome's city wall.

**Rome's Fake Dome:** Rome's St. Ignazio church (near the Pantheon) is a riot of Baroque illusions. As you walk into the church, admire the dome. Keeping your eyes on the dome, walk under and past it. It's false. When the church was built, a nearby monastery didn't want its light blocked by a huge dome, so the flat roof was instead skillfully painted to look like a dome.

**The Original Ice Man:** The South Tirol Museum of Archaeology in Bolzano, Italy, is an excellent museum featuring "Ötzi the Ice Man," a 5,000-year-old body found frozen with his gear in a glacier by some German tourists in 1991. With the help of informative displays and a great audioguide, you'll learn about life in this prehistoric period way before ATM machines. You'll see a convincing reconstruction of Ötzi, and yes, you actually get to see the man himself—lying peacefully inside a specially built freezer ($10, www.iceman.it).

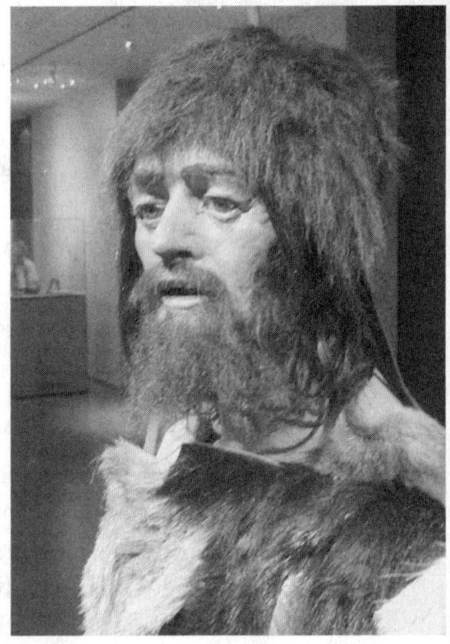
*Tourists get a chilly reception from Bolzano's Ötzi the Ice Man.*

**Choco-sightseeing:** Along with its rich culture, Europe is loved for its delicious chocolate. All day long, rivers of molten chocolate work their way through factories into small foil packages. While chocolate factories generally give tours only to clients or groups, many have museums, showrooms, video presentations, and free tasting rooms where visitors are welcome. Chocoholics love the Imhoff-Stollwerck Chocolate Museum in Köln. Their self-proclaimed "Mmmuseum" takes you on a well-described-in-English tour from the origin of the cocoa bean to the finished product. You can see displays on the culture of chocolate and watch treats trundle down the conveyor belt in the functioning chocolate factory, the museum's highlight. The top floor's exhibit of chocolate advertising is fun. Sample sweets from the chocolate fountain, or take some home from the fragrant choc-full gift shop ($8, www.schokoladenmuseum.de).

**Skinny-Dipping in Downtown Munich:** Munich's Central Park, the Englischer Garten, offers a variety of offbeat things to explore. Up to 300,000 locals commune with nature here on a hot summer day...many of them buck naked. Nudism, denoted by the code letters "F.K.K.," is perfectly legal and widely practiced here—quite a spectacle to most Americans (they're the ones riding their bikes into the river and trees).

*Munich's English Garden offers more than nude sunbathing. Surfers "hang ten" in the rapids of the city's little river.*

**Monk Brewers:** Imagine a fine Bavarian Baroque church at a monastery that serves hearty food and Germany's best beer in a carnival setting full of partying locals. That's the Andechs monastery, crouching happily between two lakes at the foot of the Alps, just south of Munich. Come ready to eat tender chunks of pork, huge soft pretzels, spiraled white radishes, savory sauerkraut, and Andecher monk-made beer that would almost make celibacy tolerable. Everything is served in medieval portions; two people can split a meal. Andechs has a fine picnic center offering first-class views and second-class prices (tel. 08152/3760). From Munich without a car, take the S-5 train to Herrsching and catch a sporadic shuttle bus, taxi, or hike three miles. Don't leave before strolling up to see the church.

**A Swiss Urban River Promenade:** In Bern, join the local merchants, students, and carp in a lunchtime float down the Aare River. The Bernese, proud of their health and clean river, have a wet tradition. On hot summer days, they hike upstream and float back down to the excellent (and free) riverside baths and pools (Aarebad) just below the Parliament building. While the locals make it look easy, this can be dangerous—the

*If you miss the last pole, you're history.*

current is swift. If you miss the last pole, you're history. If the river is a bit much, you're welcome to enjoy just the pools, and watch this fast-flowing fun from the sidelines.

**Paris' Historic Sewers:** In Paris, the Sewer Tour takes you along a few hundred yards of an underground water tunnel, lined with interesting displays, well-described in English, explaining the evolution of the world's longest sewer system. Flush hard: If you lined up Paris' sewers end to end, they would reach beyond Istanbul ($5, closed Thu–Fri, located where pont de l'Alma greets the Left Bank).

**Swiss Military Readiness:** Travelers marvel at how Swiss engineers have conquered their Alps with the world's most-expensive-per-mile road system. But no one designs a Swiss bridge or tunnel without designing its destruction. Each comes with built-in explosives so, in the event of an invasion, the entire country can be blasted into a mountain fortress. When driving, notice ranks of tank barriers lined up like giant Tic-Tacs along strategic roadsides. As you approach each summit, look for the explosive patches ominously checkering the roads.

But the Swiss are realizing that the cost of maintaining their strategic defense initiative is no longer justified. In fact, many of the country's 15,000 secret underground military installations are being decommissioned, and some are being opened to the public as museums.

*In Switzerland, fake barns hide guns and underground shelters.*

The Fortress Fürigen Museum of War History offers a rare glimpse into Swiss military preparedness. This little country dug some 20,000 bunkers into the sides of the Alps—and the Festung Fürigen, built during World War II, is one of the few open to the public. Tour the kitchen, hospital, dorms, and machine-gun nests ($4, April–Oct open to public on weekends, tel. 041-618-7522). It's in Stansstad on Lake Luzern, a 15-minute train ride from Luzern.

**Ride the Luge:** The *Sommerrodelbahn* is one of the most exhilarating alpine experiences. Local speed demons spend entire summer days riding chairlifts up in order to "luge" down the concrete bobsled courses on oversize skateboards. You sit with a brake stick between your legs. Push to go fast. Pull to stop. Luge courses are normally open daily in the summer 9 a.m.–5 p.m. and each ride costs $3–10. The course banks on the corners, and even a first-timer can go very, very fast. Most are careful on their first run and really rip on their second. To avoid a slow-healing souvenir, keep both hands on your stick. You'll rumble, windblown and smile-creased, across the finish line with one thought on your mind—"Do it again!"

*There's more than one way to get down an Alp.*

You've got several luge options. In the French mountain resort of Chamonix at the base of Mount Blanc, two concrete courses run side by side (the slow one marked by a tortoise and the fast one marked by a hare). In Austria, south of Salzburg on the road to Hallstatt, you'll pass two metal courses: one near Wolfgangsee (scenic with grand lake views) and one at Fuschlsee (half as long and cheaper).

In Germany and Austria, near "Mad" King Ludwig's Neuschwanstein Castle, you'll find three courses. Two are in Austria on the Lermoos–Reutte road: Bichlbach (4 miles past Reutte's castle ruins) is steep and short. Just beyond Biberwier (under Zugspitze, Germany's tallest mountain), the Biberwier Sommerrodelbahn is the longest in Austria at 4,000 feet. And just a mile from Neuschwanstein is Germany's Tegelberg course—because it's metal rather than concrete, it's often open when the other courses have closed at the least sprinkle of rain.

Head for the hills, or go underground. Anywhere in Europe, the offbeat sights are a fun way to get some distance from the crowds and lighten up a heavy-duty museum itinerary.

# 64. THE FLAVORS OF EUROPE

In my quest to experience Europe as the locals do—intimately and on all fronts—I make a point to eat well. In a given year, I'm lectured by a Belgian woman who tells me that the guts are the absolute best part of a crab. I crunch into the cartilage of a prized plate of pigs' ears on a back street in Madrid. And I pay a ransom for barnacles, gathered at great risk by teams of divers off the coast of Galicia in northwest Spain. (How do you eat barnacles? With a simple twist, rip, and bite). Eating well wherever I go, I find my budget survives and my trip is always the better for it. While each country vies for my favor, France and Italy contribute most to my noticeably expanding waistline.

To fully enjoy the art of eating in France, my wife Anne, my daughter Jackie, and I decide to take an all-day class with a renowned Parisian cook. We prowl through the market with her, gather the needed ingredients, cook it all up in her kitchen, and (of course) devour the delicious fruits of our labor... all spiced with lots of tips, philosophy, and attitude.

When it comes to cuisine, there's no false modesty among French chefs. Our chef cooks with strong principles: "In France, we love fat because fat is where the flavor is...never cook with a wine you wouldn't drink...in America, you just don't have a great leek culture...it's always a good thing to let your meat rest, you know...water is the friend of the enemy...pat your pears."

Wandering with her from shop to shop and through a bustling market, we learn plenty: Baking and pastry are separate arts; a chef can't do both well. (Go to a *boulangerie* for bread, and a *patisserie* for pastry.) Fish shops need to indicate how the fish was caught: *pêché en* means fished rather than farmed; *élevé en* is "raised" on a fish farm. Poultry sold with the head attached is a sign of freshness.

My favorite discovery: a bottle of Fleur de Sel, the top crust of hand-harvested sea salt (generally from Brittany). This grappa of salt—which you sprinkle by the pinch—is $10 very well spent.

After Anne and Jackie fly home, I continue my dogged quest for great-yet-affordable taste treats on the road—this time by working on the restaurant listings in my Paris guidebook.

Restaurateurs dazzle me with their cooking: gizzard salads, made of fresh greens with rich kidneys and gizzards; crêpes, where something magic happens to the Emmentaler cheese when it's cooked in all that butter; escargot, with a hot plate to keep the sauce steamy for dipping the crunchy bread into the garlic.

I experience high-class eating with Dominique—as fragile and elegant as her petite restaurant—who gives me empathy for those force-fed geese by force-feeding *me* the foie gras. And I enjoy quality food at budget prices at a Greek restaurant with plastic tables. I ask, "Do you have yogurt with honey?" They say, "Sure, we're Greek," and bring me a bowl that takes me straight to Santorini.

In Paris, you can't escape the desserts: the ritual cracking of the caramelized crust of a crème brûlée...the tangy peach sorbet drenched in liqueur that you lap up like a thirsty puppy...and plates of pastel mini-macaroons (pistachio, rose, mint, or raspberry) served with tea at the palatial Laudrée café on the Champs-Elysées.

I'm not a food sophisticate, but I love people—especially cooks—who love their work. Monsieur Isaac, the self-proclaimed "ace of falafels" in the Jewish Quarter, brags, "I've got the biggest pita on the street...and I fill it up!"

When I head south to Italy, it seems the entire country is singing, *"Mangia, mangia."* In the rugged Riviera villages of the Cinque Terre, people are famously passionate about their food. In Vernazza, Giovanni makes pasta. "I like the pasta too much," he says, holding a belly far bigger than mine.

Alessandro has clearly found his niche. Rolling his cart into Vernazza for the weekly market as he has for 22 years of Tuesdays, he sells porcini mushrooms, dried cod, and sturdy parmesan cheese to Vernazzan shoppers who've proudly never set foot in a big city mall.

Valerio, a waiter in my favorite Riviera restaurant, is evangelical about the beauties of anchovies. Knowing I want to teach Americans the wonders of Italian anchovies, he brings me a plate with the little fish prepared four ways and says, "It's not harsh and cured in salt like yours in America. I know, people in America say, 'Pizza—but hold the anchovies.' Our anchovies were swimming yesterday—they are fresh. Taste this."

Further south and far from the sea, the Tuscan landscape is dotted with *agriturismos*. These traditional family farms rent out spare rooms to make ends meet—and to show off Italy's knack for fine country living. Signora Gori, who runs a noble old farm, takes me on a walk through her estate. As a horrendous chorus of squeals comes from a rustic slaughterhouse on the horizon, she says, "This is our little Beirut." But the view is lush, pristine, and tranquil.

Taking me into a room dominated by a stainless steel table piled with red sides of pork, she declares, "And here we make the prosciutto." Burly men in aprons squeeze the blood out of hunks of meat the size of dancing partners. Then they cake the hamhocks in salt to begin a curing process that takes months. While the salt helps cure the meat, a coating of pepper seals it. In spooky but great-smelling rooms, racks of hanging hamhocks age. A man, dressed and acting like a veterinarian, tests each ham by sticking it with a horse-bone needle and giving it a sniff.

Passing a sty dominated by a giant pig nicknamed Pastenetto ("the little pastry"), Signora Gori escorts me into the next barn, where fluffy white lambs jump to wobbly attention in their hay. Backlit, it's a dreamy, almost biblical scene. Picking up a baby lamb, she explains, "We use unpasteurized milk in making the pecorino cheese. This is allowed but only with strict health safeguards. I must really know our sheep."

This close-to-the-land-and-animals food production is part of Italy's Slow Food movement (www.slowfood.it). Advocates believe there's more to life than increasing its speed. They produce and serve food in the time-honored way. It may be more labor-intensive and expensive, but it's tastier and—just as important—connects consumers more directly with their food. They know who made it and how.

On the far side of the farm, the son empties his last bucket of purple grapes into the dump truck, and it—in turn—unloads into a grinder that munches through the bunches. The machine spits stems one way and juice (with mangled grapes) the other. Following that promising little river into the cellar, we're surrounded by tall vats of aging grape juice. My guide jokes that while making wine is labor-intensive, right now the grapes are doing all the work. And as they ferment, we head home to dinner.

Around a long, rustic table polished by many decades of feasting, the entire Gori family—three generations surrounded by heirlooms from many more—gathers and welcomes their American guest. It's a classic Tuscan table: simplicity, a sense of harmony, no hurry, and a glass of fine red wine.

A key word for your Tuscan travels is *corposo*—full-bodied. Lifting the elegant glass to my lips, I sip, while enjoying the pride in the eyes of a family so comfortably and happily rooted in their heritage and cultural soil. Entirely satisfied, I say, "*Corposo.*" They say, "*Si, bravo.*"

As I dip my bread in extra-virgin olive oil and savor a slice of their prosciutto, my friends explain that great wine goes best with simple food. With each bite and every sip, I better understand the art of Tuscan living—and why I'll always hunger to return to Europe.

# 65. DUNGEONS AND DRAGONS: EUROPE'S NINE MOST MEDIEVAL CASTLE EXPERIENCES

Castles excite Americans. Medieval fortresses are rotting away on hilltops from Ireland to Israel, from Sweden to Spain, lining the Loire and guarding harbors throughout the Mediterranean. From the west coast of Portugal to the crusader city of Rhodes, you'll find castle thrills lurking in every direction.

Most of Europe's castles have been discovered, but some are forgotten, unblemished by entrance fees, postcard racks, and coffee shops, and ignored by guidebooks. Since they're free, nobody promotes them. The aggressive traveler finds them by tapping local sources, such as the town tourist office and the friendly manager of your hotel or pension.

Stroll inside the ramparts to see what life was really like in those places your bedtime fairy tales reserved for fairy princesses and Prince Charmings. Life in the Middle Ages was actually a lot like the people: nasty, brutish, and short. In cities, there was some measure of safety and security, but the countryside was the domain of outlaw bands of "merry men," who invaded farms and villages to fill their pockets and satisfy their thirst for violence. In those days, the difference between robbers and armies was only a matter of "how big."

Most countryside castles began not as palaces for princes, but as armored bunkers to protect landowners, their harvest, hired hands, and the foolhardy traveler who might pass through (some castles also "protected" key roads and rivers, extorting tolls from all who trespassed).

A real castle had all the romance of a fallout shelter. Sure, it had a lofty tower or two, but only to spot trespassers and to give attackers second thoughts. When the bad guys came knocking, a negotiated ransom was the typical outcome—not a swashbuckling battle.

In the 17th and 18th centuries, large-scale European wars made these castles handy tactical tools. But for the most part, they became obsolete against ever-growing armies and cannons (and between wars, better law enforcement made the countryside safer). Most castles fell into ruin, used as quarries to build more practical things.

Suddenly, in the late 19th century, everything changed. Under the Prussian leadership of Bismarck, the Germanic cluster of mini-states quickly came together as a single powerful nation. There was a great surge in German nationalism, and a popular obsession with "roots," both real and Romantic. Wagner's fairy-tale operas and King Ludwig II's recreated castles epitomized the new German "pop history," which was rewritten to express the ideal spirit of German-ness instead of its grim

## Europe's Best Castles

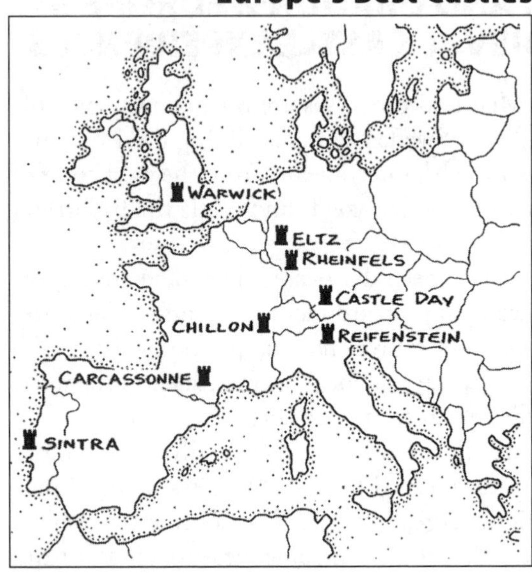


reality. Modern tourism took root during this same time. So there was not only a patriotic spirit, but also an economic incentive behind the "reinterpreting" of castles in a Romantic style. A few short decades later, Walt Disney made the fairy-tale castle his trademark, and ("authentic" or not) the rest is history.

What travelers see today is a muddle of Middle Age bunker mentality and 150-year-old Romantic renovation...which also happens to be real. While confusing, this weird mix makes for great sightseeing.

Visiting Europe can overwhelm you with too many castles to tour in too little time. To help you prioritize, here are my favorites: nine medieval castles—some forgotten, some discovered—where the winds of the past really howl.

### Carcassonne, France

Before me lies Carcassonne, the perfect medieval city. Like a fish that everyone thought was extinct, Europe's greatest Romanesque fortress-city somehow survives.

*Best stormed early or late*

Medieval Carcassonne is a 13th-century world of towers, turrets, and cobblestone alleys. It's a walled city and Camelot's castle rolled into one, frosted with too many day-tripping tourists. At 10 a.m., the salespeople stand at the doors of their main-street shops, their gauntlet of tacky temptations poised and ready for their daily ration of customers. But an empty Carcassonne rattles in the early morning or late-afternoon breeze.

*Carcassonne: walls within walls topped by turrets.*

Enjoy the town early or late. Spend the night.

I was supposed to be gone yesterday, but it's sundown and here I sit—imprisoned by choice—curled in a cranny on top of the wall. The moat is one foot over and 100 feet down. Happy little weeds and moss upholster my throne. The wind blows away many of the sounds of today, and my imagination "medievals" me.

Twelve hundred years ago, Charlemagne stood below with his troops, besieging the town for several years. As the legend goes, just as food was running out, a cunning townswoman had a great idea. She fed the town's last bits of grain to the last pig and tossed him over the wall. Splat. Charlemagne's restless forces, amazed that the town still had enough food to throw fat party pigs over the wall, decided they'd never succeed in starving the people out. They ended the siege, and the city was saved. Today, the walls that stopped Charlemagne open wide for visitors.

## Warwick Castle, England

From Land's End to John O'Groats, I searched for the best castle in Britain. I found it. With a lush, green, grassy moat and fairy-tale fortifications, Warwick Castle will entertain you from dungeon to lookout (www.warwick-castle.co.uk). Standing inside the castle gate, you can see the mound where the original Norman castle of 1068 stood. Under this mound (or motte), the wooden stockade (bailey) defined the courtyard as the castle walls do today. The castle is a 14th- and 15th-century fortified shell holding an 18th- and 19th-century royal residence surrounded by dandy gardens, landscaped by Lancelot "Capability" Brown in the 1750s.

There's something for every taste—an educational armory, a terrible torture chamber, a knight in shining armor on a horse that rotates with

*Warwick Castle—for kings and queens of any age*

a merry band of musical jesters, a Madame Tussaud re-creation of a royal weekend party with an 1898 game of statue-maker, a queenly garden, and a peacock-patrolled, picnic-perfect park. The great hall and staterooms are the sumptuous highlights. The "King Maker" exhibit (it's 1471 and the townsfolk are getting ready for battle...) is highly promoted but not quite as good as a Disney ride. Be warned: The tower is a one-way, no-backing-out, 250-step climb offering a view not worth a heart attack. Even with its crowds of modern-day barbarians and its robber-baron entry fee ($25–30, most expensive late July–Aug), Warwick's worthwhile.

## Eltz Castle, Germany

Burg Eltz is my favorite castle in all of Europe. Lurking in a mysterious forest, it's been left intact for 700 years and is furnished throughout as it was 500 years ago. Thanks to smart diplomacy and clever marriages, Burg Eltz was never destroyed. It's been in the Eltz family for nearly 850 years.

The first *burg* on the *Eltz* (castle on the stream) appeared in the 12th century to protect a trade route. By 1472, the castle looked like it does today: the homes of three big landlord families gathered around a tiny courtyard within one formidable fortification. Today, the excellent 45-minute tours wind you through two of those homes, while the third remains the fortified quarters of the Eltz family. The elderly Countess of Eltz traces her family back 33 generations here (you'll see a photo of her family). She enjoys flowers, and each week for 40 years she's adorned the castle's public rooms with grand bouquets.

*Eltz Castle, near Cochem, on Germany's Mosel River*

It was a comfortable castle for its day: 80 rooms made cozy by 40 fireplaces and wall-hanging tapestries. Its 20 toilets were automatically flushed by a rain drain. The delightful chapel is on a lower floor. Because "no one lives above God," this was problematic. But because the chapel fills a bay window—which floods the delicate Gothic space with light—its position was acceptable. The three families met—working out common problems as if sharing a condo—in the large conference room. There, a carved jester ("fool's freedom") and a rose ("rose of silence") look down on the big table, reminding those who gather that they are free to discuss anything, but nothing discussed leaves this room.

Burg Eltz is between Koblenz and Cochem, about an hour's drive from the Rhine River. The only way to see the inside of the castle is with a 45-minute tour (in English, included with $7.50 admission ticket, www.burg-eltz.de).

## Rheinfels Castle, Germany's Rhineland

Sitting like a dead pit bull above St. Goar, this mightiest of Rhine castles rumbles with ghosts from its hard-fought past. Burg Rheinfels (built in 1245) withstood a siege of 28,000 French troops in 1692. But in 1797, the French Revolutionary army destroyed it.

Rheinfels was huge. Once the biggest castle on the Rhine, it spent the 19th century as a quarry. So today, while still mighty, it's only a small fraction of its original size. This hollow but interesting shell offers your single best hands-on ruined-castle experience on the river.

A highlight of your Rheinfels experience may be meeting Günther—"the last knight of Rheinfels"—who greets visitors at the turnstile and is a wealth of information.

The massive Rheinfels was the only Rhineland castle to withstand Louis XIV's assault during the 17th century. For centuries, the place was self-sufficient and ready for a siege. Circling the central courtyard, you'd find a bakery, pharmacy, herb garden, animals, brewery, well, and livestock. During peacetime, about 500 people lived here; during a siege, there could be more than 4,000.

Any proper castle was prepared to survive a six-month siege. With 4,000 people, that's a lot of provisions. The count owned the surrounding farmland. Farmers—in return for the lord's protection—got to keep 20 percent of their production. Later, in more liberal feudal times, the nobility let them keep 40 percent. (Today, the German government leaves workers with 60 percent after taxes...and provides a few more services.)

Hike around the castle perimeter. Notice the smartly placed crossbow-arrow slit. Thoop...you're dead. While you're lying there, notice the

*Even in ruins, Rheinfels is mighty.*

fine stonework and the chutes high above. Uh-oh...boiling oil...now you're toast.

To protect their castle, the Rheinfellas cleverly booby-trapped the land just outside their walls by building tunnels topped by thin slate roofs and packed with explosives. By detonating the explosives when under attack, they could kill hundreds of approaching invaders. In 1626, a handful of underground Protestant Germans blew 300 Catholic Spaniards to (they assumed) hell.

You're welcome to wander through a set of never-blown-up tunnels. But be warned: It's completely black, unmarked, and with confusing dead-ends. The ground is generally muddy. Assuming you make no wrong turns, it's a 200-yard-long adventure, never letting you walk taller than a deep crouch. It cannot be done without a light (bring a flashlight or candles, available from Günther at the turnstile).

A door blasted through the castle wall takes you to the small, barren prison. You walk through a door prisoners only dreamed of 400 years ago. (They came and went through the little square hole in the ceiling.) The holes in the walls supported timbers that thoughtfully gave as many as 15 miserable residents something to sit on to keep them out of the filthy slop that gathered on the floor. Twice a day, they were given bread and water. Some prisoners actually survived for more than two years in this dark hole. While the town could torture and execute, the castle had permission only to imprison criminals in these dungeons. According to town records, the two men who spent the most time down here—2.5 years each—died within three weeks of regaining their freedom. Perhaps after a diet of bread and water, feasting on meat and wine was just too much.

Germany's Rhine River is filled with castle-crowned hills. These can be enjoyed conveniently by train, car, or boat. The best 50-mile stretch is between Koblenz and Mainz. The best one-hour cruise is from St. Goar to Bacharach.

## Château de Chillon, Switzerland

Set romantically at the edge of Lake Geneva near Montreux, this wonderfully preserved 13th-century castle is worth a side-trip from anywhere in southwest Switzerland. Château de Chillon (shee-yon) has never been damaged or destroyed—it's always been inhabited and maintained. Its oldest fortifications dating to the 11th century, the castle was expanded by the Savoy family in the 13th century, when this was a prime location—at a crossroads of a major trade route between England and France and Rome. It was the Savoys' fortress and residence, with four big halls (a major status symbol) and impractically large lakeview windows (their powerful navy could defend against possible attack by sea).

*Shimmering Château de Chillon*

When the Bernese invaded in 1536, the castle was conquered in just two days, and the new governor made Château de Chillon his residence (and a Counter-Reformation prison). Inspired by the Revolution in Paris, the French-speaking people on Lake Geneva finally kicked out their German-speaking Bernese oppressors in 1798. The castle became—and remains—property of the Canton of Vaud. It has been used as an armory, a warehouse, a prison, a hospital, and a tourist attraction. Rousseau's writings first drew attention to the castle, inspiring visits by Romantics such as Lord Byron and Victor Hugo, plus other notables including Dickens, Goethe, and Hemingway.

Follow the English brochure, which takes you on a self-guided tour through fascinatingly furnished rooms (www.chillon.ch). The dank dungeon, mean weapons, and 700-year-old toilets will excite even the dullest travel partner. Attack or escape the castle by ferry (free with your railpass).

## Reifenstein Castle, Italy

For an incredibly medieval kick in the pants, get off the autobahn one hour south of Innsbruck at the Italian town of Vipiteno (called "Sterzing" by residents who prefer German). With her time-pocked sister just opposite, Reifenstein bottled up this strategic valley leading to the easiest way to cross the Alps.

Reifenstein offers castle connoisseurs the best-preserved medieval-castle interior I've ever seen. The lady who calls the castle home, Frau Blanc, takes groups through in Italian, German, and *un poco di inglese* (open Easter–Oct, 4 tours daily Sat–Thu, closed Fri, tel. 0472-765-879). You'll discover the mossy past as she explains how the cistern collected water, how drunken lords managed to get their keys into the keyholes, and how prisoners were left to rot in the dungeon (you'll look down the typical only-way-out hole in the ceiling). In the only surviving original knights' sleeping quarters (rough-hewn plank boxes lined with hay), you'll see how knights spent their nights. Lancelot would cry a lot.

*Rugged Reifenstein Castle*

## Moorish Ruins of Sintra, Portugal

The desolate ruins of an 800-year-old Moorish castle overlook the sea and the town of Sintra, just west of Lisbon. Ignored by most of the tourists who flock to the glitzy Pena Palace (capping a neighboring hilltop), the ruins of Sintra offer a reminder of the centuries-long struggle between Muslim Moorish forces and Christian European forces for the control of Iberia. From 711 until 1492, major parts of Iberia (Spain and Portugal) were occupied by the Moors. Contrary to the significance that Americans place on the year 1492, a European remembers the date as the year the Moors were finally booted back into Africa. For most, these ruins are simply a medieval funtasia of scramble-up-and-down-the-ramparts delights and atmospheric picnic perches with vast Atlantic views in an enchanted forest. With a little imagination, it's 800 years ago, and you're under attack.

*Run with the winds of the past in Europe's countless ruined castles. Here, with a little imagination, you're under attack a thousand years ago in Portugal.*

## Castle Day: Neuschwanstein (Bavaria) and the Ehrenberg Ruins (Reutte in Tirol)

Three of my favorite castles—two famous, one unknown—can be seen in one busy day. "Castle Day" takes you to Germany's Disneylike Neuschwanstein Castle, the more stately Hohenschwangau Castle at its foot, and the much older Ehrenberg Ruins across the Austrian border in Reutte.

**Castle Day**

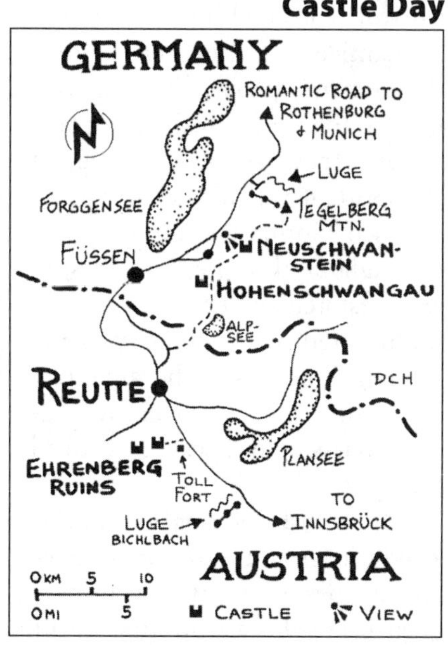


Make the Austrian town of Reutte your home base. (It's just over the German border, 3 Alp-happy hours by train west of Innsbruck.)

From Reutte, catch the early bus across the border to touristy Füssen, the German town nearest Neuschwanstein. (Planning ahead, note the times buses return to Reutte.) From Füssen, you can walk, pedal a rented bike, or ride a local bus a couple of miles to Neuschwanstein.

Neuschwanstein is the greatest of King Ludwig II's fairy-tale castles. His extravagance and Romanticism earned this Bavarian king the title "Mad" King Ludwig...and an early death. His castle is one of Europe's most popular attractions.

*Some of Europe's most popular attractions, such as "Mad" Ludwig's castles, sell tickets with entry times. Arrive early to get tour appointments or risk not getting in at all.*

Arrive by 8 a.m. to buy a ticket ($12 for one castle, $22 for both, plus $2 extra if reserved ahead) and you'll likely be touring soon after. Your ticket lists appointed times for you to visit Ludwig's boyhood home, Hohenschwangau Castle, and then the neighboring Neuschwanstein on the hill. If you arrive late, you'll spend a couple of hours in the ticket line and may find all tours booked. (Consider reserving a minimum of 24 hours in advance at tel. 08362/930-830 or www.hohenschwangau.de.)

Hohenschwangau Castle, where Ludwig grew up, offers a good look at his life. Like its more famous neighbor, it takes about an hour to tour. Afterward, head up the hill to Ludwig's castle in the air.

Neuschwanstein Castle, which is about as old as the Eiffel Tower, is a textbook example of 19th-century Romanticism. After the Middle Ages ended, people disparagingly named that era "Gothic," or barbarian. Then, all of a sudden, in the 1800s it was hip to be square, and neo-Gothic became the rage. Throughout Europe, old castles were restored and new ones built—wallpapered with chivalry. King Ludwig II put his medieval fantasy on the hilltop not for defensive reasons, but simply because he liked the view.

*"Mad" King Ludwig's Neuschwanstein Castle*

The lavish interior, covered with damsels in distress, dragons, and knights in gleaming armor, is enchanting. (A little knowledge of Wagner's operas goes a long way in bringing these stories to life.) Ludwig had great taste—for a mad king. Read up on this political misfit—a poetic hippie king in the realpolitik age of Bismarck. After Bavarians complained about the money Ludwig spent on castles, the 40-year-old king was found dead in a lake under suspicious circumstances, never to enjoy his medieval fantasy-come-true. After the tour, climb farther up the hill to Mary's Bridge for the best view of this crazy yet elegant castle.

This is a busy day. By lunchtime, catch the bus back to Reutte and get ready for a completely different castle experience.

Pack a picnic and your camera, and with the help of some local directions, walk 30 minutes out of town to the brooding Ehrenberg Ruins. You'll see a small hill crowned by a ruined castle.

The Kleine Schloss ("small castle") is really ruined but wonderfully free of anything from the 21st century—except for a fine view of Reutte sleeping peacefully in the valley below.

Standing like a conqueror on a broken piece of wall, imagine how proud Count Meinrad II of Tirol (who built the castle in 1290) would be to know that his castle repelled 16,000 Swedish soldiers in the defense of Catholicism in 1632. When cloaked in a cloud shroud, you can peer into the spooky mist and almost see medieval knights in distress and damsels in shining armor. Grab a sword fern, shake your hair free, and unfetter that imagination.

Recently the ruins have been the focus of an exciting project, spearheaded by Armin Walch and funded in part by the European Union. Walch—the Indiana Jones of Tirolean archaeologists—is excavating an "ensemble" of four castles. Once the largest complex in the region, its purpose was to defend Tirol against Bavaria and northern Europe.

*The brooding Ehrenberg Ruins*

The "toll fort" on the valley floor—which levied duties along the ancient Via Claudia in Roman times—is flanked by Ehrenberg and a sister castle (Fort Claudia) on the opposite side. After locals rained cannon balls on Ehrenberg from the bluff above it, a much bigger castle was built higher up. Over the centuries it became completely overgrown and concealed. Today, the trees have been shaved away, the ruin has been excavated, and it's once again visible.

This is part of a huge project to create a European Castle Museum, showing off 500 years of military architecture in one sweep. A sound-and-light show at the base of the hill is already up and running, and more exhibits are planned over the next few years (www.ehrenberg.at). The European Union has stepped in to help fund the project because it promotes the heritage of a region (Tirol) rather than a nation. The EU's vision for Europe's future is to help create a continent of "regions" rather than nations.

Until then, you will find Ehrenberg's castle reconstructed on Reutte's restaurant walls. Ask at your hotel where you can find a folk evening full of slap-dancing and yodel foolery. A hot, hearty dinner and an evening of local Tirolean entertainment is a fitting way to raise the drawbridge on your memorable "Castle Day."

*For good-value accommodations in* ***Carcassonne****, try Hôtel des Remparts (5 place de Grands-Puits, contact through Hôtel le Donjon, tel. 04 68 11 23 00, fax 04 68 25 06 60, www.hotel-donjon.fr); in* ***St. Goar****, Hotel am Markt (Am Markt 1, tel. 06741/1689, fax 06741/1721, www.hotel-am-markt-sankt-goar.de);*

*in **Reutte,** Moserhof Hotel (Planseestrasse 44, in nearby Breitenwang, tel. 05672/62020, www.hotel-moserhof.at); and in **Füssen**, Altstadthotel zum Hechten (Ritterstrasse 6, tel. 08362/91600, www.hotel-hechten.com). For more hotels, visit www.ricksteves.com/update, and for all the travel specifics, see this year's editions of the pertinent Rick Steves' country guides.*

# 66. SOBERING SITES OF NAZI EUROPE

Fondue, nutcrackers, Monet, Big Ben...gas chambers. A trip to once-upon-a-time Europe can be a fairy tale. It can also help tell the story of Europe's 20th-century fascist nightmare. While few travelers go to Europe to dwell on the horrors of Nazism, most people value visiting the memorials of fascism's reign of terror and honoring the wish of its survivors—"Forgive, but never forget." These sites are committed to making the point that intolerance and fascism are still alive and strong. Their message: Fascism can emerge from its loony fringe if we get complacent and think the horrors of Hitler could never happen again.

Why are these sites worth a bit of your vacation? Because we can learn from them. Even today, the destiny of great nations can be hijacked by Machiavellian politicians who artfully manipulate fear, patriotism, and mass media to accomplish their aggressive agenda.

*Memorial at the Dachau concentration camp*

## Concentration Camps

The most sobering of all Nazi sites are concentration camps. Of the many concentration-camp memorials in Europe, the most moving is Auschwitz-Birkenau (near Kraków, Poland). Three others are also evocative and convenient to visit: Dachau (just outside of Munich), Mauthausen (between Vienna and Salzburg), and Terezín (near Prague).

No sight in all of Europe is as powerful as **Auschwitz-Birkenau** (www.auschwitz.org.pl). This Nazi concentration camp in the Polish town of Oświęcim (a 70-min drive west of Kraków) was the site of the systematic murder of more than a million innocent people.

Auschwitz was the biggest, most notorious concentration camp in the Nazi system...strategically located in the heart of Jewish Europe. Since the Middle Ages, Poland was known for its tolerance of Jews. By the beginning of World War II, Poland had Europe's largest concentration of Jews: 3.5 million. Throughout the Holocaust, the Nazis murdered 4.5 million Jews in Poland (many brought in from other countries). Today, fewer than 2,000 Jews live in all of Poland.

*"Work sets you free"*

A visit to Auschwitz is obligatory for Polish students. You'll often see Israeli high school groups walking through the grounds waving their Star of David flags. Many people, including Germans, leave flowers and messages. One of the messages reads: "Nations who forget their own history are sentenced to live it again."

There are two camps: Auschwitz I and Auschwitz II (better known as Birkenau). Most visitors begin at Auschwitz I. After seeing a grippingly graphic video, you cross under the notorious gate with the cruel message *Arbeit Macht Frei* ("Work sets you free") and into the rows of barracks—each containing an exhibit.

People being transported here, thinking they were going to a new homeland, were encouraged to bring luggage. After they were killed, everything of value was plundered by the Nazis. In these barracks, room after room is literally full to the ceiling of prisoners' personal effects: eyeglasses; fine Jewish prayer shawls; crutches and prosthetic limbs; shoes;

suitcases; and even human hair.

The "Death Block," from which nobody ever left alive, is particularly evocative. The Starvation Cell held prisoners selected to starve to death when a fellow prisoner escaped. The Dark Cell, where 30 people at a time were crammed, had only a small window for ventilation. If it became covered with snow, the prisoners suffocated.

Seven hundred people at a time could be gassed in the Auschwitz crematorium. This wasn't efficient enough for the Nazis, so they built a far bigger death camp two miles away. From Auschwitz, a shuttle bus takes visitors to part two of their visit: Birkenau.

At first sight, it's clear: Birkenau is all about the efficient mass production of death. It held 100,000 prisoners and could cremate 16,000 a day. From the top of the guard tower, survey the staggering scope of Birkenau: a few wooden barracks housing exhibits, and a vast field of chimneys—all that remains of the other barracks—stretching nearly as far as the eye can see.

The train tracks lead through the middle of the camp to the dividing platform, where a Nazi doctor would evaluate each prisoner. If he pointed right, the prisoner was sentenced to death, and trudged—unknowingly—to the gas chamber. If he pointed left, the person would be registered and generally worked to death. It was here that families from all over Europe were torn apart forever.

Beyond the dividing platform, the tracks arrive at the finale of this wrenching visit: the ruins of the gas chambers and crematoria. As they entered the undressing rooms, people were given numbered lockers, conned into thinking they were coming back. (The Nazis didn't want a panic.) Then they piled into the "shower room," where they were murdered and cremated. Finally, their ashes were dumped into a ghostly lake.

*Birkenau: Remembering the Holocaust's mass production of death*

The Auschwitz crematoria were destroyed by the Nazis as the Soviet army approached, leaving today's haunting ruins. The Soviets arrived on January 27, 1945, and the

## Nazi Sites

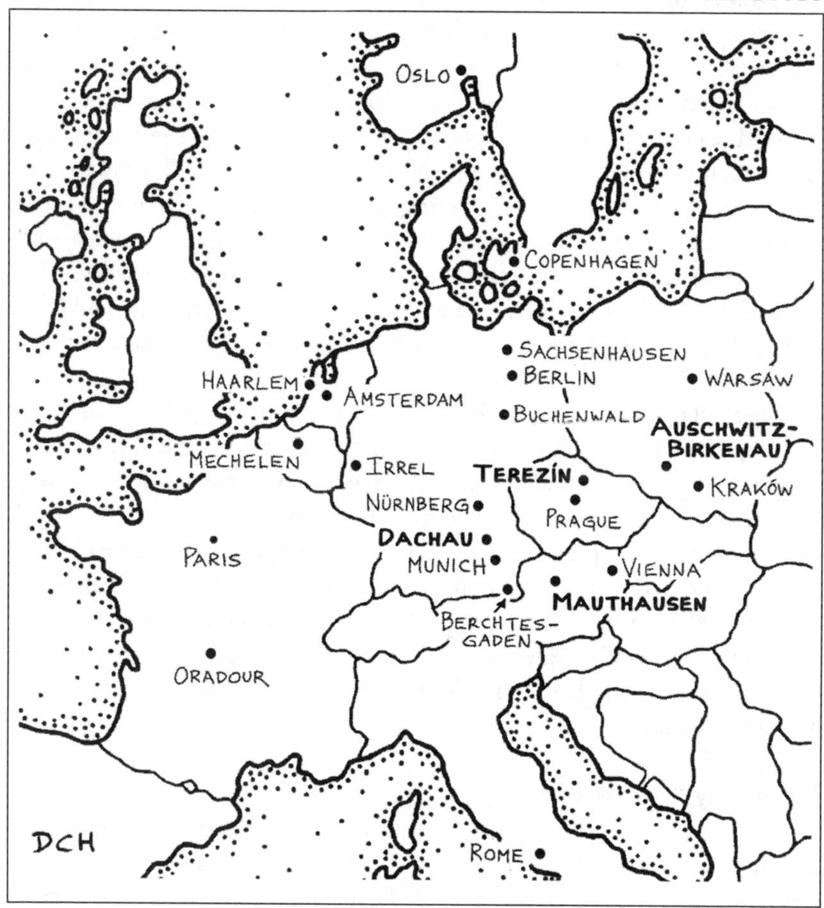


nightmare of Auschwitz was over. The Polish parliament quickly voted to turn these grounds into a museum, so that the world would understand, and never forget, the horror of what happened here.

**Dachau,** near Munich, is a much tamer concentration-camp experience (closed Mon, www.kz-gedenkstaette-dachau.de). While some visitors complain that Dachau is too "prettied-up," it gives a powerful look at how these camps worked. Built in 1933, this first Nazi concentration camp offers a compelling voice from our recent, grisly past, warning and pleading "Never Again"—the memorial's theme. On arrival, pick up the mini-guide and check when the next documentary film in English will be shown. The museum, the movie, the chilling camp-inspired art, the reconstructed barracks, the gas chambers, the cremation ovens, and the memorial shrines will chisel into you the hidden meaning of fascism.

**Mauthausen** town sits cute and prim on the romantic Danube at the start of the very scenic trip downstream to Vienna. But nearby, atop a now-still quarry, linger the memories of a horrible slave-labor camp. Mauthausen is a solemn place of meditation and continuous mourning. Fresh flowers adorn yellowed photos of lost loved ones. The home country of each victim has erected a gripping monument. You'll find yourself in an artistic gallery of grief, resting on a foundation of Never Forget. Retrace the steep and treacherous steps of the camp's inmates—the "stairway of death" *(Todesstiege)*—to and from the quarry where they worked themselves to death. Mauthausen offers an English booklet, a free audioguide, an English movie, and a painful but necessary museum (www.mauthausen-memorial.at).

Just outside of Prague is **Terezín** concentration camp (Theresienstadt in German, www.pamatnik-terezin.cz). This particularly insidious place was dolled up as a model camp for Red Cross inspection purposes. Inmates had their own newspaper, and the children put on cute plays. But after the camp passed its inspection, life returned to slave labor and death. Ponder the touching collection of Jewish children's art, also on display in the Pinkas Synagogue in Prague's Jewish Quarter.

You can also visit **Sachsenhausen** near Berlin (www.gedenkstaette-sachsenhausen.de), **Buchenwald** near Weimar (www.buchenwald.de), and many others.

## Germany and Austria

Since destruction and death are fascist fortes, only relatively insignificant bits and pieces of Hitler's Germany survive. But as time passes, today's Germans are increasingly aware of the need to remember the horrors that began in their country.

Hitler got his start—and had his strongest support—in the beer halls of **Munich.** The **Munich City Museum** (Münchner Stadtmuseum) traces the origin and development of Nazism. To uncover Nazi sites in Munich, take the **Hitler and the Third Reich walking tour** by Radius Tours (www.radiusmunich.com). Ironically, we have the Nazis to thank for the accuracy of Munich's postwar reconstruction. When Allied bombings were imminent, Nazi photographers documented Munich's great architecture—allowing it to be rebuilt exactly as it was after the war.

Berlin, now that its Wall is history, is giving its Nazi chapter a little more attention. Most original Nazi sites are hidden. To help you find them, take the **Infamous Third Reich Sites walking tour** by Berlin Walks (www.berlinwalks.com). But don't even bother looking for

"Hitler's Bunker"—it's long gone.

Berlin has several new Nazi-related museums and memorials. The **Topography of Terror** exhibit illustrates SS tactics (in the ruins of the former SS/Gestapo headquarters, near what was Checkpoint Charlie; due to be converted into a museum in the near future). The adjacent four small "mountains" are made from the rubble of the bombed-out city. The chilling **Book Burning Monument** commemorates the 20,000 books that were burned on Berlin's Bebelplatz at the order of the Nazis. Glance into the glass floor in the middle of the square (on Unter den Linden) to see a huge underground room with empty shelves. The gripping **Käthe Kollwitz Museum** is filled with art inspired by the horrors of Berlin's Nazi experience. **Berlin's New Synagogue** was burned on Kristallnacht in 1938, but has since been restored. The excellent **Jewish Museum Berlin,** which focuses on Jewish culture, was designed by the American architect Daniel Libeskind. The zigzag shape of the zinc-walled building is pierced by voids, symbolic of the irreplaceable cultural loss caused by the Holocaust (www.juedisches-museum-berlin.de). In nearby **Wannsee** (near Potsdam), you can tour the house where Hitler's cronies came up with the "Final Solution" of the Holocaust (www.ghwk.de).

There was strong resistance to Hitler even in Berlin. In front of the glass-domed **Reichstag** is a row of slate slabs imbedded in the ground memorializing the 96 politicians who were murdered and persecuted because their politics didn't agree with Chancellor Hitler's. Near the Kulturforum museums is a former military headquarters (Bendlerblock) where conspirators plotted an ill-fated attempt to assassinate Hitler—and where they were also shot for the crime. It's now the site of the **German Resistance Memorial** (Gedenkstätte Deutscher Widerstand, free audioguide available). Just outside of the city is the **Plötzensee Prison,** where Nazi enemies were imprisoned and executed (www.gedenkstaette-ploetzensee.de).

*As he consolidated his power in the 1930s, Hitler arrested 96 members of the German Parliament who opposed him. He sent them to concentration camps, where most perished. This monument, outside the renovated Reichstag where they once worked, is their memorial.*

Berlin's newest Nazi site is the **Memorial to the Murdered Jews of Europe**. This monument, consisting of 2,711 gravestone-like pillars and completed in 2005,

*Berlin's new Memorial to the Murdered Jews of Europe is a moving monument to one of history's greatest tragedies.*

is the first formal German government-sponsored Holocaust memorial. It's controversial for the focus—just Jews. The government promises to make memorials to the other groups targeted by Hitler. The pillars are made of hollow concrete, each chemically coated for easy removal of graffiti. The number of pillars, symbolic of nothing, is simply how many fit on the provided land. Is it a labyrinth...symbolic cemetery...intentionally disorienting? The meaning is entirely up to the visitor. Its location—where the Berlin Wall once stood—is coincidental. It's just a place where lots of people will experience it. The bunker of Nazi propagandist Joseph Goebbels was discovered during the work and left buried (under the northeast corner of the memorial). Hitler's bunker is just 200 yards away, under a nondescript parking lot. Such Nazi sites are intentionally left hidden to discourage neo-Nazi elements from creating a shrine (www.stiftung-denkmal.de).

In Nürnberg, the ghosts of Hitler's showy propaganda rallies still rustle in the **Rally Grounds** (now Dutzendteich Park), down the Great Road, and through the Congress Hall. The north wing of the hall houses the Nazi Documentation Center, with a "Fascination and Terror" exhibit that examines the causes and consequences of the Nazi phenomenon (www.museen.nuernberg.de). Across town, you can also tour the **Nürnberg Trials Courtroom**—where high-ranking Nazi officers answered to an international tribunal after the war ended.

The town of **Berchtesgaden,** near the Austrian border, is any German's choice for a great mountain hideaway—including Hitler's. The remains of Hitler's Obersalzberg headquarters, with its extensive tunnel system and Nazi Documentation Center, will interest WWII buffs (www.obersalzberg.de).

Just north of Trier in the town of Irrel is the **Westwall Museum,** with tourable bunkers that made up part of the Nazis' supposedly impenetrable western fortification (closed in winter, www.westwall-museum.de).

On Vienna's Judenplatz, you'll find the **Austrian Holocaust Memorial**—a library turned inside-out to remind visitors that each victim had a story. Nearby is the **Judenplatz Museum,** displaying the ruins of a forgotten 14th-century synagogue unearthed during the memorial's construction.

## The Netherlands and Scandinavia

In Amsterdam, **Anne Frank's House** gives the cold, mind-boggling statistics of fascism the all-important intimacy of a young girl who lived through it and died from it. Even bah-humbug types, who are dragged in because it's raining and their spouses read the diary, find themselves caught up in Anne's story (www.annefrank.org).

The small town of Haarlem, 20 minutes by train from Amsterdam, has its own Anne Frank–type story. Touring a cozy apartment above a clock shop just off the busy market square, you'll see **Corrie Ten Boom's "Hiding Place."** The sight was popularized by an inspirational book and movie about this woman and her family's experience hiding Jews from Nazis. Tipped off by an informant, Nazis raided their house but didn't find the Jews, who were hiding behind a wall in Corrie's bedroom. Because the Nazis found a suspiciously large number of ration coupons, they sent the Ten Boom family to a concentration camp. Only Corrie survived (www.corrietenboom.com).

Amsterdam's **Dutch Theater,** which was used as an assembly hall for local Jews destined for Nazi concentration camps, is a powerful memorial. On the wall, 6,700 family names represent the 104,000 Dutch Jews deported and killed by the Nazis. The nearby **Jewish History Museum**—four historic synagogues joined together by steel and glass to make one modern complex—tells the story and struggles of Judaism through the ages (www.jhm.nl).

While Hitler controlled Europe, each country had a courageous, if small, resistance movement. All over Europe you'll find streets and squares named after the martyrs of the resistance. Any history buff or champion of the underdog will be inspired by the patriotism documented in Europe's Nazi-resistance museums—the most extensive is Amsterdam's **Dutch Resistance Museum.** You'll see propaganda movie clips, study a forged ID card under a magnifying glass, and read of ingenious, daring efforts to hide local Jews from the Germans (www.verzetsmuseum.org).

The **Museum of Deportation and the Resistance** in Mechelen, Belgium, is fascinating (www.cicb.be), as are resistance museums in **Oslo** (www.mil.no/felles/nhm) and **Copenhagen** (www.frihedsmuseet.dk).

## Poland

Poland was hit harder by World War II than any other country—more than six million Poles died, half of them Jews. But the Poles—Jewish or not—did not go quietly. Monuments around the capital city remember their valiant—though eventually unsuccessful—uprisings. In 1940 and 1941, a million and a half Jews were moved into a ghetto in Warsaw. By 1943, only a tenth of the ghetto's Jews survived—the rest had died from disease or been shipped to concentration camps. The survivors staged the **Ghetto Uprising** against their Nazi oppressors, but almost all of them were eventually killed in the fighting, captured and executed, or sent to concentration camps. A year later, as the Soviet army approached, a Polish resistance army staged the **1944 Warsaw Uprising** against the Nazis, which resulted in the deaths of nearly a quarter of a million Warsaw civilians. Both of these events are depicted in the Oscar-winning 2002 film *The Pianist.* Today, you can still visit the neighborhoods and landmarks where these brave uprisings began. A new high-tech museum about the 1944 Uprising tells the story eloquently (www.1944.pl).

The real Oskar Schindler—hero of the film ***Schindler's List***—lived and worked in the Polish city of Kraków. Fans of the film can visit Schindler's factory, currently the Telpod electronics factory (near the Kraków–Zabłocie train station). The Jarden Bookshop, located in Kraków's Jewish Quarter, offers *Schindler's List* tours.

## The Czech Republic

After completing his "final solution," Hitler had hoped to build a grand museum of the "decadent" Jewish culture in Prague. Today, the museums and synagogues of **Prague's Jewish Quarter** (Josefov), containing artifacts the Nazis assembled from that city's once-thriving Jewish community, stand together as a persistently unforgettable memorial (see Chapter 51).

## France

Paris commemorates the 200,000 French victims of Hitler's camps with the **Memorial de la Déportation.** Walking through this evocative park, on the tip of the Ile de la Cité just behind Notre-Dame, is like entering a work of art. Walk down the claustrophobic stairs into a world of concrete, iron bars, water, and sky. Inside the structure, the eternal flame, triangular niches containing soil from various concentration camps, and powerful quotes will etch the message into your mind. Then gaze at the 200,000 crystals—one for each person who perished.

Rivaling Auschwitz as the most moving sight of all is the martyred village of **Oradour-sur-Glane,** in central France. This town, 15 miles northwest of Limoges, was machine-gunned and burned in 1944 by Nazi SS troops. Seeking revenge for the killing of one of their officers, they left 642 townspeople dead in a blackened crust of a town under a silent blanket of ashes. The poignant ruins of Oradour-sur-Glane—scorched sewing machines, pots, pans, bikes, and cars—have been preserved as an eternal reminder of the reality of war. When you visit, you'll see the simple sign that greets every pilgrim who enters: *Souviens-toi...* remember.

# EAST MEDITERRANEAN

## 67. PELOPONNESIAN HIGHLIGHTS: OVERLOOKED GREECE

The Peloponnesian Peninsula stretches south from Athens. Studded with antiquities, this land of ancient Olympia, Corinth, and Sparta offers plenty of fun in the eternal Greek sun, with pleasant fishing villages, sandy beaches, bathtub-warm water, and none of the tourist crowds that plague the much-scrambled-after Greek Isles.

The Peloponnesian port town of Nafplion, two hours southwest of Athens by car or bus, is small, cozy, and strollable. It's a welcome relief after the black-hanky intensity of smoggy Athens. Not only is Nafplion itself fun, but it's a handy home base for exploring two of Greece's greatest ancient sights—Epidavros and Mycenae.

Nafplion's harbor is guarded by two castles, one on a small island and the other capping the hill above the town. Both are wonderfully floodlit at night. Just looking from the town up to its castle makes you need a tall iced tea.

But this old Venetian outpost, built in the days when Venice was the economic ruler of Europe, is the best-preserved castle of its kind in Greece and well worth the 999-step climb. From the highest ramparts, you'll see several Aegean islands (great day trips by boat from Nafplion) and look deep into the mountainous interior of the Peloponnesian Peninsula. Below you lies an enticing beach.

Nafplion has plenty of hotels, and its harbor is lined with restaurants specializing in fresh seafood. An octopus dinner cost me $8—succulent!

## The Peloponnesian Peninsula

The infamous resin-flavored *retsina* wine is a drink you'll want to experience—once. Maybe with octopus. The first glass is like drinking wood. The third glass is dangerous: It starts to taste good. If you drink any more, you'll smell like it the entire next day.

On another night, I left Nafplion's popular waterfront district and had a memorable meal in a hole-in-the-wall joint. There was no menu—just an entertaining local crowd and a nearsighted man who, in a relaxed frenzy, ran the whole show. He scurried about, greeting eaters, slicing, dicing, laughing, singing to himself, cooking, serving, and billing. Potato stew, meatballs, a plate of about 30 tiny fried fish with lime, and unlimited wine cost $20 for two—and could have fed four.

Epidavros, 18 miles northeast of Nafplion, is the best-preserved ancient Greek theater. It was built 2,500 years ago to seat 14,000. Today, it's kept busy reviving the greatest plays of antiquity. You can catch performances of ancient Greek comedies and tragedies on weekends from mid-June through September. Try to see Epidavros either early or late in the day. The theater's marvelous acoustics are best enjoyed in near-solitude. Sitting in the most distant seat as your partner stands on the stage, you can practically hear the *retsina* rumbling in her stomach.

*Epidavros' state-of-the-art acoustics*

Thirty minutes in the other direction from Nafplion are the ruins of Mycenae. This was the capital of the Mycenaeans, who won the Trojan War and dominated Greece 1,000 years before Socrates.

As you tour this fascinating fortified citadel, remember that these people were as awesome to the ancient Greeks of Socrates' day as those Greeks are to us. The classical Greeks marveled at the huge stones and workmanship of the Mycenaean ruins. They figured that only a race of giants (cyclopes) could build with such colossal rocks...and called it "cyclopean" architecture.

Visitors today can gape at the Lion's Gate, climb deep into a cool, ancient cistern, and explore the giant *tholos* tombs. The tombs, built in 1500 B.C., stand like huge stone igloos, with smooth subterranean domes 40 feet wide and 40 feet tall. The most important Mycenaean artifacts, like the golden "Mask of Agamemnon," are in the National Museum in Athens.

## Finikoundas

The prize-winning Peloponnesian hideaway is the remote village of Finikoundas. Located on the southwest tip of the peninsula between the twin Venetian fortress towns of Koroni and Methoni (two hours by public bus from Kalamata), Finikoundas is big enough to have a good selection of restaurants, pensions, and a few shops, but it's small enough to escape the typical resort traffic, crowds, and noise. It's just right for a sleepy Greek sabbatical.

Finikoundas has plenty of private rooms, or *dhomatia,* for rent. Plan to spend about $30 for a simple double a few steps from the beach. The little bay just east of the rock breakwater was the best beach I found, and the swimming was fine—even in October.

After a little Apollo worshiping, I wandered through town in search of Dionysus at just the right waterfront restaurant. The place I found

*You can be a guest of honor at a Greek wedding festival.*

couldn't have been more "waterfront." Since the fishing village had no dock, its Lilliputian fishing boats were actually anchored to the restaurant. I settled my chair comfortably into the sand and the salty atmosphere, as weak wavelets licked my table's legs. I dined amid rusty four-hook anchors, honorably retired old ropes, and peeling dinghies. A naked 20-watt bulb dangled from the straw roof, which rotted unnoticed by Greeks and a few perpetually off-season Germans who seemed to be regulars.

Cuisine in a village like this is predictable. I enjoyed fresh seafood, Greek salad, and local wine. After a few days in Greece, you become a connoisseur of the salad, appreciating the wonderful tomatoes, rich feta cheese, and even the olive-oil drenching.

Almost within splashing distance of my table, young Greek men in swimsuits not much bigger than a rat's hammock gathered around a bucketful of just-caught octopi. They were tenderizing the poor things to death by whipping them like wet rags over and over on a big flat rock. They'd be featured momentarily on someone's dinner plate—someone else's.

Evening is a pleasant routine of strolling and socializing. Dice clatter on dozens of backgammon boards, entrepreneurial dogs and soccer goal–oriented children busy themselves, and a tethered goat chews on something inedible in its low-profile corner. From the other end of town comes the happy music of a christening party. Dancing women fill the building, while their children mimic them in the street. Farther down, two elderly, black-clad women sit like tired dogs on the curb.

Succumbing to the lure of the pastry shop, I sat down for my day-end ritual: honey-soaked baklava. I told the cook I was American. "Oh," he said, shaking his head with sadness and pity, "you work too hard."

I answered, "Right. But not today."

*For good-value accommodations in Finikoundas, try Korakakis Beach Hotel (tel. 2723/071-221, korakaki@otenet.gr) or Dhomatia Anastasios Tomaras (private rooms, tel. 2723/071-378).*

# 68. TURKEY'S HOT

Turkey is a proud new country. It was born in 1923, when Kemal Atatürk, the father of modern Turkey, rescued it from the buffet line of European colonialism. He divided church and state, liberated women (at least on paper), replaced the Arabic script with Europe's alphabet, and gave the battle-torn, corrupt, and demoralized remnants of the Ottoman Empire the foundation of a modern nation. Because of Atatürk, today's 66 million Turks have a flag—and reason to wave it. For a generation, many young Turkish women actually worried that they'd never be able to really love a man because of their love for the father of their country.

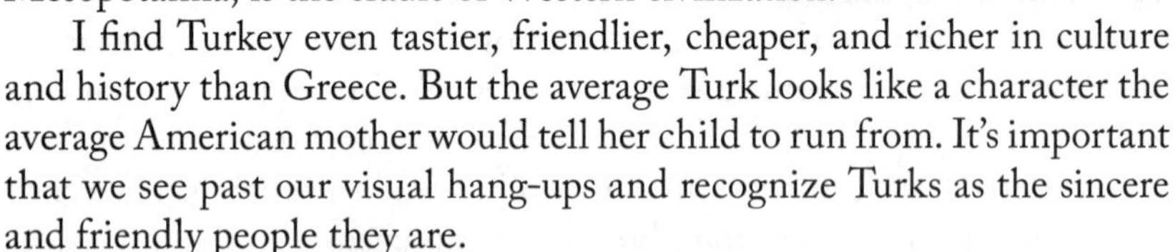

At the same time, Turkey is a musty archaeological attic, with dusty civilization stacked upon civilization. The more they dig, the more they learn that Turkey, not Mesopotamia, is the cradle of Western civilization.

I find Turkey even tastier, friendlier, cheaper, and richer in culture and history than Greece. But the average Turk looks like a character the average American mother would tell her child to run from. It's important that we see past our visual hang-ups and recognize Turks as the sincere and friendly people they are.

Those who haven't been to Turkey wonder why anyone would choose to go there. Those who have been there dream of returning. Turkey is being discovered. Tourists are learning that the image of the terrible Turk is false, created to a great degree by its unfriendly neighbors. Turks are quick to remind visitors that, surrounded by Syria, Iraq, Iran, Georgia, Bulgaria, and Greece, they're not living in Mr. Rogers' neighborhood.

Many visitors are put off by Turkey's "rifles on every corner" image. Turkey is not a police state. Its NATO commitment is to maintain nearly a million-man army. Except far to the east, where this million-man army is dealing with the Kurds and Iraq, these soldiers have little to do but "patrol" and "guard"—basically, loiter in uniform.

Today's Turkey is on the move. It's looking West and getting there. You can travel throughout the country on Turkey's great bus system. Telephones work. Hotels have e-mail. I had a forgotten plane ticket express-mailed across the country in 24 hours for $5. Fifty percent of

Turkey's 42,000 villages had electricity in 1980. Now all do. Does all this modernization threaten the beautiful things that make Turkish culture so Turkish? An old village woman assured me, "We can survive TV and tourism because we have deep and strong cultural roots."

English is more widely spoken, and tourism is booming. Even the Turkish lira has recently been reborn. On January 1, 2005, the New Turkish Lira (Yeni Türk Lirası, or YTL) entered into circulation, trimming off six zeroes and sporting a fresh new look. Now $1 is worth about 1.30 YTL...and tourists can leave their calculators at home.

Travel in Turkey is cheap. Good, comfortable double rooms with private showers cost $30. Vagabonds order high on menus. And buses, which offer none of the romantic chaos of earlier years, take travelers anywhere in the country nearly any time for about $2 an hour.

Turkey knows it's on the fence between the rising wealth and power of an ever-more-united Europe and a forever-fragile-and-messy Middle East. Turks know the threat of the rising tide of Islamic fundamentalism and, while the country is 99.8 percent Muslim, they want nothing of the Khomeini-style rule that steadily blows the dust of religious discontent over their border. But fundamentalists are making inroads. As they walk by, veiled women in tow, modern-minded Turks grumble—a bit nervously.

Two months after the first Gulf War, I enjoyed my ninth trip through Turkey, this time with 22 travel partners and a Turkish co-guide. We had a life-changing 15 days together, enjoyed a level-headed look at Islam, took a peek at a hardworking, developing country with its act impressively together, and learned how our mass media can wrongly shape America's assessment of faraway lands. No survey was necessary to know that we all brought home a better understanding of our world. But a survey did show that 14 people bought carpets (mostly less than $1,000, one for $3,000), eight people had diarrhea (seven for less than two days, one for six days), and nine of us learned to play backgammon well enough to challenge a Turk in a smoky teahouse. For the price of a Big Mac, you can buy tea for 20 new friends, play backgammon until the smoke doesn't bother you, and rock to the pulse of Turkey. Oh, those tiny handmade dice...cockeyed dots in a land where time is not money.

Turkey reshuffles your cards. A beautiful girl is called a pistachio. A person with a beautiful heart but an ugly face is called a Maltese plum—the ugliest fruit you'll ever enjoy. Industrious boys break large chocolate bars into small pieces to sell for a profit. For $2, a trained bear will do a show called "your mother-in-law dancing in a Turkish bath."

Much of Turkey is scrambling into the modern Western world, but the Turkish way of life is painted onto this land with an indelible cultural ink. If you're able to put your guidebook aside and follow your wanderlust, you'll still find sleepy goats playing Bambi on rocks overlooking a nomad's black tent. High above on the hillside, the lone but happy song of the goatherd's flute plays golden oldies. The mother bakes bread and minds the children, knowing her man is near.

Riding the waves of Turkey is like abstract art, a riveting movie without a plot, a melody of people, culture, and landscape that you just can't seem to stop whistling.

## Güzelyurt—Cappadocia without Tourists

Cappadocia is rightly famous as the most bizarre and fascinating bit of central Turkey that accepts credit cards. The most exciting discovery I made on my last trip was a town on the edge of Cappadocia called Güzelyurt.

Güzelyurt means "beautiful land." It's best known in Turkey as the town where historic enemies—Greeks, Turks, Kurds, and Bulgarians—live in peace. The town is a harmony of cultures, history, architecture, and religions. Walk down streets that residents from 3,000 years ago might recognize, past homes carved into the rocks, enjoying friendly greetings of *merhaba*. Scowling sheepdogs, caged behind 10-foot-high troglodyte rookeries, give the scene just enough tension.

Walk to a viewpoint at the far side of town (above the Sivisli church), toward the snowy slopes of the Fuji-like volcano that rules the horizon. Before you is a lush and living gorge. The cliff rising from the gorge is stacked with building styles: Upon the 1,600-year-old church sit troglodyte caves, Selcuk arches, and Ottoman facades. And on the horizon gleams the tin dome of the 20th-century mosque, with its twin minarets giving you a constant visual call to prayer. The honey that holds this architectural baklava together is people.

Put your camera away, shut your mouth, and sit silently in the sounds of 1000 B.C. Children play, birds chirp, roosters crow, shepherds chase goats, and mothers cackle. (Ignore that distant motorbike.)

Below you, sleeping in the greens and browns of this land of simple living, is the church of St. Gregorius. Built in 385, it's thought by Gregorian fans to be the birthplace of church music, specifically the Gregorian chant. Its single minaret indicates that it's preserved as a mosque today in a valley where people call god Allah.

Who needs three-star sights and tourist information offices? In Güzelyurt, we dropped by the city hall. The mayor scampered across town to arrange a lunch for us in his home. He welcomed us Christians, explaining, "We believe in the four books"—the local way of saying, "It doesn't matter what you call Him, as long as you call Him." He showed us the names of his Greek Christian friends, kept as safe and sacred as good friends could be in his most precious and holy possession, the family Quran bag.

*Traditional lifestyles survive in Turkey.*

The lady of the house made tea. Overlapping carpets gave the place a cozy bug-in-a-rug feeling. As the lady cranked up the music, we all began to dance like charmed snakes until our fingers could snap no more. A small girl showed me a handful of almonds and said, "Buy dem." *Badam* is Turkish for almond, and this was her gift to me. Enjoying her munchies, I reciprocated with a handful of Pop Rocks. As the tiny candies exploded in her mouth, her surprised eyes became even more beautiful.

The town's name is spelled proudly across its volcanic backdrop. The black bust of Atatürk seems to loom just as high over the small modern market square. The streets are alive with the relaxed click of victorious *tavla* (backgammon) pieces. The men of the town, who seem to be enjoying one eternal cigarette break, proudly make a point not to stare at the stare-worthy American visitors searching for postcards in a town with no tourism.

Güzelyurt, in central Turkey, is a short bus ride from Aksaray. It's near the Peristrema Valley, famous for its seven-mile hike through a lush valley of poplar groves, eagles, vultures, and early Christian churches.

Belisirma, a village near Güzelyurt, is even more remote. With a population of "100 homes," Belisirma zigzags down to its river, which rushes through a poplar forest past the tiny Belisirma Walley Wellkome Camping (one bungalow). A group of bangled women in lush purple wash their laundry in the river under the watchful eyes of men who seem to have only a ceremonial function. Children on donkeys offer to show off the troglodyte church carved into the hill just past the long, narrow farm plots. A lady, face framed in the dangling jewelry of her shawl, her net worth hanging in gold around her neck, points to my postcard, a picture of a little girl holding a baby sheep. The girl is her niece. They call the card "Two Lambs."

## 14 Days in Turkey

Turkey offers the most enjoyable culture shock within striking distance of Europe. But it's a rich brew, and, for most, two weeks is enough. Here's my recommendation for the best two-week look at Turkey. (This plan is tried and tested, as it's the route our guided Turkey tours follow.)

Flying to Istanbul is about as tough as flying to Paris. For instance, if you fly SAS, both are about a two-hour flight from your Copenhagen hub. When planning your trip, remember that flying "open jaw" into Istanbul and home from Athens is usually a little cheaper than flying in and out of Istanbul...and makes for a more diverse and efficient itinerary.

Spend your first two days in Istanbul. Take a taxi from the airport to the Hippodrome, near the Blue Mosque in the Sultanahmet district, where you'll find several decent small hotels and pensions.

For an easygoing first evening, walk over to the Blue Mosque and enjoy the free sound-and-light show in the park. Spend the next day doing the historic biggies: Topkapi Palace, Blue Mosque, and the Aya Sofya (Hagia Sophia) church. The latter was completed in 537, when Istanbul was called Constantinople and was the leading city in Christendom. It was the largest domed building in Europe until Brunelleschi built Florence's great dome in the Renaissance, almost a thousand years later.

Bone up on Anatolian folk life in the Islamic Arts Center (just off the old Roman racetrack called the Hippodrome), then taxi to the modern center of bustling Istanbul for dinner in the "Flower Passage" restaurant arcade, where Istanbul's beautiful people and tourists alike enjoy the funky elegance. If you like baklava, stroll the city's main drag, Istiklal Street, in search of a pastry shop. From the heartbeat of modern Istanbul, Taksim Square, catch a cab home. Less touristy dinner options include Kumkapi, a fishermen's wharf district teeming with seafood restaurants and happy locals (a pleasant walk from the Hippodrome), and the more romantic Ortakoy district (in the shadow of the Bosporus bridge).

The next morning, browse the bizarre Grand Bazaar and Egyptian Spice Market. After lunch take an intercontinental cruise up the Bosporus. If you disembark in "Asian" Istanbul (everything east of the Bosphorus), you can taxi quickly to the station to catch your overnight train to Ankara.

This, the only reliable train in Asian Turkey, gets you to the country's capital by 8 a.m. As you munch feta cheese, olives, tomatoes, and cucumbers for breakfast in the dining car, it dawns on you that you're far from home.

## 14 Days in Turkey

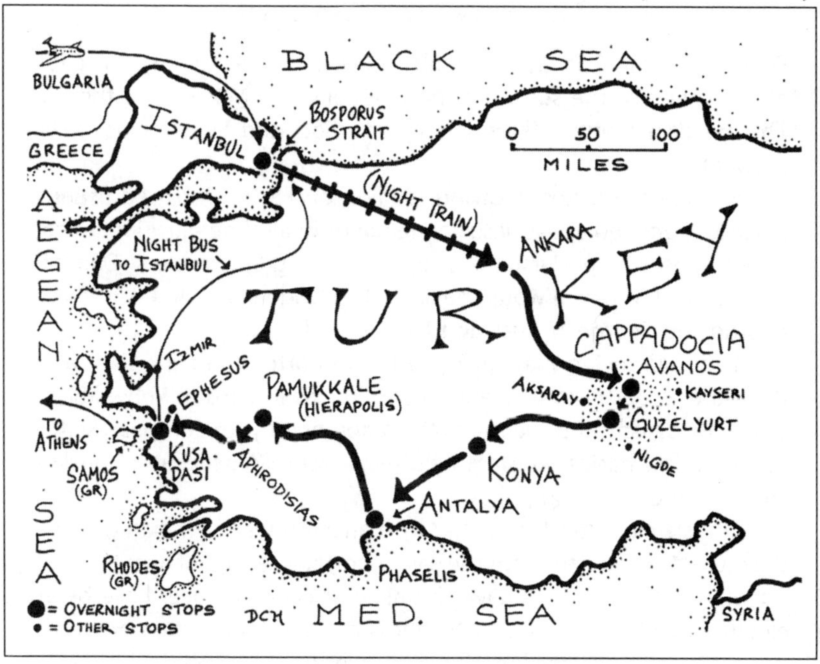

Ankara has two blockbuster sights. The Museum of Anatolian Civilizations is a prerequisite for meaningful explorations of the ancient ruins that litter the Turkish countryside. The Atatürk Mausoleum shines a light on the recent and dramatic birth of modern Turkey and gives you an appreciation of that country's love of its George Washington. For a happening scene, a great view, and a look at modern Turkey, ride to the top of the Ankara tower.

From Ankara, it's a four-hour bus ride to exotic and evocative Cappadocia, an eroded wonderland of cave dwellings that go back to the early Christian days, when the faithful fled persecution by hiding in Cappadocian caves. Cappadocia gives you a time-tunnel experience, with its horse carts, strangely eroded mini-Matterhorns called "fairy chimneys," traditional crafts, and labyrinthine underground cities. Don't miss the Back Door town of Güzelyurt (see page 604).

From mysterious Cappadocia, cross the Anatolian Plateau to Konya, the most conservative and orthodox Muslim city in Turkey, home of the Mevlana order and the whirling dervishes. The dance of the dervish connects a giving god with our world. One hand is gracefully raised, and the other is a loving spout as he whirls faster and faster in a trance the modern American attention span would be hard-pressed to understand.

## Islam in a Pistachio Shell

Five times a day, God enjoys a global wave as the call to prayer sweeps at the speed of the sun from the Philippines to Morocco to the US. The muezzin chants, "There is only one God, and Muhammad is His prophet."

Islam is the fastest-growing religion on Earth. Unbiased listings place Muhammad above Jesus on rankings of all-time most influential people. For us to understand Islam by studying Muammar al-Qaddafi and Osama bin Laden would be like a Turk understanding Christianity by studying George W. Bush and Jerry Falwell.

Your journeying may give you the opportunity to travel in, and therefore to better understand, Islam. Just as it helps to know about spires, feudalism, and the saints to comprehend your European sightseeing, a few basics on Islam help make your sightseeing in Muslim countries more meaningful.

The Islamic equivalent of the Christian bell tower is a minaret, which the muezzin climbs to chant the call to prayer. In a kind of architectural Darwinism, the minarets have shrunken as calls to prayer have been electronically amplified; their height is no longer necessary or worth the expense. Many small modern mosques have one tin mini-minaret about as awesome as your little toe.

Worshipers pray toward Mecca, which, from Turkey, is about in the same direction as Jerusalem but not quite. In Istanbul, Aya Sofya was built 1,400 years ago as a church, its altar niche facing Jerusalem. Since it became an out-of-sync-with-Mecca mosque, the Muslim focus-of-prayers niche is to the side of what was the altar.

A mosque is a shoes-off place. Westerners are welcome to drop in. The small stairway that seems to go nowhere is symbolic of the growth of Islam. Muhammad had to stand higher and higher to talk to his growing following. Today every mosque has one of these as a kind of pulpit. No priest ever stands on the top stair. That is symbolically reserved for Muhammad.

The "five pillars" of Islam are basic to an understanding of a religious force that is bound to fill our headlines for years to come. Followers of Islam should:

1. Say and believe, "There is only one God, and Muhammad is His prophet."

2. Pray five times a day. Modern Muslims explain that it's important to wash, exercise, stretch, and think of God. The ritual of Muslim prayer works this into every day—five times.

3. Give to the poor (one-fortieth of your wealth, if you are not in debt).

4. Fast during daylight hours through the month of Ramadan. Fasting is a great social equalizer and helps everyone to feel the hunger of the poor.

5. Visit Mecca. This is interpreted by some Muslims as a command to travel. Muhammad said, "Don't tell me how educated you are, tell me how much you've traveled."

You'll notice women worship in back of the mosque. For the same reason I find it hard to concentrate on God at aerobics classes, Muslim men decided prayer would go better without the enjoyable but problematic distraction of bent-over women between them and Mecca.

How Muslims can have more than one wife is a bigamistery to many. While polygamy is illegal in Turkey, Islam does allow a man to have as many wives (up to 4) as he can love and care for equally. This originated as Muhammad's pragmatic answer to the problem of too many unattached women caused by the deaths of so many men in the frequent wars of his day. Religious wars have been as common in Islam as they have been in Christendom.

*Muslims in modern-day Turkey—a mix of East and West*

These basics are a simplistic but honest attempt by a non-Muslim to help travelers from the Christian West understand a very rich but often misunderstood culture worthy of our respect. These days, religious extremists can polarize entire populations. And those who profit from the related strife—either from arms sales or by turning news into entertainment to sell more advertisements—are clever at riding the bloody coattails of any religious conflict. Therefore, we need all the understanding we can muster.

*Exotic terrain, ornery transport...Cappadocia*

Then follow the steps of St. Paul over the Taurus Mountains to the Mediterranean resort of Antalya. You can hire a *gulet* (a Turkish yacht) to sail the Mediterranean coast to your choice of several beachside ruins. After a free day on the beach, travel inland to explore the ruins of Aphrodisias and its excellent museum.

Nearby is Pamukkale, a touristy village and Turkey's premier mineral spa. Soak among broken ancient columns in a mineral spring atop the white cliff, terraced with acres and acres of steamy mineral pools. Watch frisky sparrows hop through a kaleidoscope of white birdbaths.

For the final leg of your two-week swing through Turkey, head west to the coastal resort of Kusadasi. Nearby is my favorite ancient site, the ruins of Ephesus. For a relaxing finale, take a Turkish *hamam* (bath with massage) in Kusadasi before flying back to Istanbul from nearby Izmir or catching the daily boat to the entertaining island of Sámos in Greece (see below). Boats and planes take travelers from Sámos to other Greek islands and on to Athens.

## Some Hints to Make Turkey Easier

Good information is rare here, especially in the East. Bring a good guidebook from home. Take advantage of Lonely Planet's guidebook to Turkey (9th edition published in 2005). Maps are easy to get in Turkey and useful to have.

Eat carefully. Find a cafeteria-style restaurant and point. Choose your food personally by tasting and pointing to what you like. Joke around with the cooks. They'll love you for it. The bottled water, soft drinks, *chai* (tea), and coffee are cheap and generally safe. Watermelons are a great source of safe liquid. If you order a glass of tea, your waiter will be happy to "process" your melon, giving it to you peeled and in little chunks on a big plate.

Learn to play backgammon before you visit Turkey. Backgammon, the local pastime, is played by all the men in this part of the world. Join in. It's a great way to instantly become a contributing member of the local teahouse scene.

Really get away from it all. Catch a *dolmuş* (shared taxi) into the middle of nowhere. Get off at a small village. If the bus driver thinks you must be mistaken or lost to be getting off there, you've found the right place. Explore the town, befriend the children, trade national dance lessons. Act like an old friend returning after a 10-year absence, and you'll be treated like one.

You'll be stared at all day long. Preserve your sanity with a sense of humor. Joke with the Turks. Talk to them, even if there's no hope of communication. One afternoon, in the town of Ercis, I was waiting for a bus and writing in my journal. A dozen people gathered around me, staring with intense curiosity. I felt that they needed entertainment. I sang the Hoagy Carmichael classic, "Huggin' and Chalkin'." When the bus came, my friend and I danced our way on board, waving good-bye to the cheering fans. From then on, my singing entertained most of eastern Turkey.

Make invitations happen and accept them boldly. While exploring villages with no tourism, I loiter near the property of a large family. Very often the patriarch, proud to have a foreign visitor, will invite me to join him cross-legged on his large, bright carpet in the shade. The women of

*Greek and Turkish travel agencies are more helpful than they look.*

**The Greek Islands and Southwest Turkey**

the household bring tea, then peer at us from around a distant corner. Shake hands, jabber away in English, play show and tell, pass around photos from home, take photos of the family, and get their addresses so you can mail them copies. They'll always remember your visit. And so will you.

## The Best Way from Athens to Turkey

See what's important in Athens (Acropolis, Agora, Plaka, and National Archaeological Museum), then go to Turkey! Catch a boat or plane to Sámos, Rhodes, or Kos. Each of these islands is connected daily by boat to Turkey. This short boat ride gives you more of a cultural change than the flight from the US to Athens.

Leaving Greece via Sámos offers a look at one of my favorite Greek islands and drops you in Kusadasi, a pleasant place to enter Turkey and a 20-minute drive from Ephesus.

Sámos—green, mountainous, diverse, and friendly—has tourist crowds, but not as bad as other Greek islands. Bus transportation on the island is fine. And it's cheap to crisscross Sámos on your own moped. Pounding over potholes, dodging trucks, stopping to dream across the sea at the hills of Turkey, and being spanked happily by the prickly wind and Greek sun, you will find that a moped ride around Sámos is exhilarating.

The tourist map shows plenty of obscure sights on Sámos. Gambling that the Spiliani monastery was worth the detour, I traded potholes for gravel and wound up the hill. The road ended at a tiny church overlooking the sunburnt island.

Behind the church was the mouth of a cave, with whitewashed columns carved like teeth into the rock. I wandered into the drippy, dank darkness, cool and quiet as another world. Sitting still, I could almost hear the drip-by-drip growth of the stalagmites and the purr of my brain. The only motion was the slight flicker of slender candles. I was ready to venture out of Christendom and into Islam.

*For good-value accommodations in Güzelyurt, try Hotel Karballa (tel. 382/451-2103, fax 382/451-2107, www.kirkit.com, karballa@hotmail.com). In Kusadasi, consider the Anzac Golden Bed Pansiyon (Ugurlu I. Cikmazi 4, tel. & fax 256/614-8708, www.kusadasihotels.com/goldenbed, anzacgoldenbed@yahoo.com) or Özhan Pansiyon (Dag Mah. Kibris Caddesi 5, tel. 256/614-2932, www.ozhanpansiyon.com, info@ozhanpansiyon.com). In Sámos (Greece), try Hotel Sámos (11 The. Sofouli, tel. 22730-283-778, fax 22730-237-71, www.samoshotel.gr, hotsamos@otenet.gr).*

## 69. EASTERN TURKEY

Istanbul and the western Turkish coast—while still fascinating, cheap, and eager to please—are moving toward European-style mainstream tourism. For the most cultural thrills, head east. Tour inland Anatolia with abandon, using Ankara as a springboard. From here, buses transport you to the region, culture, and era of your choice.

Find a town that has yet to master the business of tourism, like Kastamonu (5 hours northeast of Ankara). The business hotel where I stayed was cheap ($20 doubles) and comfortable, but not slick. I handed a postcard to the boy at the desk, hoping he could mail it for me. He looked it over a couple of times on both sides, complimented me, and politely handed it back. As I left, he raised his right hand like a cigar-store Indian and said, "Hello." While changing money, I was spotted by the bank manager, who invited me into his office for tea. Since I was his first American customer, he wanted to celebrate.

Outside, a gaggle of men wearing grays, blacks, and browns were shuffling quietly down the street. A casket floated over them as each

**Eastern Turkey**

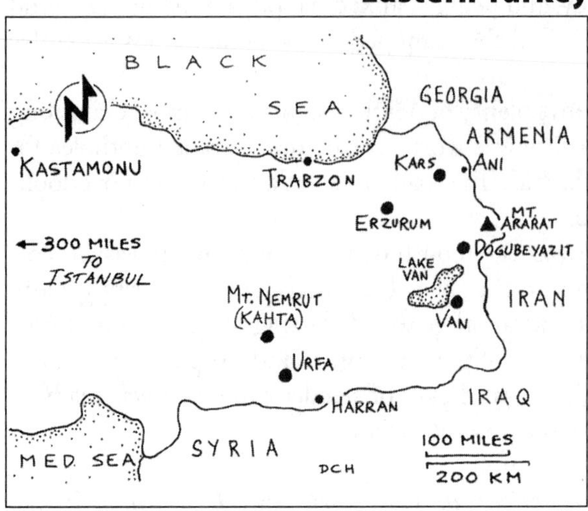


man jostled to the front to pay his respects by "giving it a shoulder."

Turkey is a land of ceremonies. Rather than relying on a list of festivals, travel with sharp eyes, flexibility, and some knowledge of the folk culture. Local life here is punctuated with colorful, meaningful events. As the dust from the funeral procession clears, you may see a proud eight-year-old boy dressed like a prince or a sultan. The boy is celebrating his circumcision, a rite of passage that some claim is an echo from the days of matriarchal Amazon rule, when entry into the priesthood required c-c-c-castration. This is a great day for the boy and his family. Turks call it the "happiest wedding"—because there are no in-laws.

Having an interpreter helps you explore and mingle with meaning, but it's not required. Many older Turks speak German. The friendliness of Turkey is legendary among those who have traveled beyond the cruise ports. While relatively few small-town Turks speak English, their eagerness to help makes the language barrier an often enjoyable headache.

Enjoy jabbering with the people you meet. If Turkish sounds tough to you, remember, it's the same in reverse. Certain sounds, like our "th," are tricky. My friend Ruth was entertained by the tortured attempts Turks made at pronouncing her name: "Woooott." Any English-speaking Turk can remember spending long hours looking into the mirror, slowly enunciating: "This and these are hard to say. I think about them every day. My mouth and my teeth, I think you see, help me say them easily."

Throughout Turkey, travelers cringe at the sight of ugly, unfinished construction that scars nearly every town with rusty tangles of steel rebar waiting to reinforce future concrete walls. But in Turkey, unfinished buildings are family savings accounts. Inflation here is ruinous. Any local in need of a hedge against inflation keeps a building under construction. Whenever there's a little extra cash, rather than watch it evaporate in

*In Turkey, you don't need museums—they're living in the streets.*

the bank, Ahmed will invest in the next stage of construction. It's the goal of any Turkish parent to provide each child with a house or apartment with which to start adult life. A popular saying is, "Rebar holds the family together."

If you're looking for a rain forest in Turkey, go to the northeast, along the Black Sea coast, where it rains 320 days a year. This is the world's top hazelnut-producing region and home of the Laz people. A highlight of one tour (which I led through Eastern Turkey with 22 American travelers and a Turkish co-guide) was spending an evening and a night with a Laz family. Actually the families of three brothers, they all lived in one large three-layered house provided to them by their elderly parents.

The people in our group were the first Americans that the 16 people who lived there had ever seen. We were treated to a feast. In Turkey, it's next to impossible to turn down this kind of hospitality. As we praised the stuffed peppers, members of our group discreetly passed Pepto-Bismol tablets around under the table. (The pouring tea didn't quite mask the sound of ripping cellophane.)

After dinner, we paid our respects to the grandma. Looking like a veiled angel in white, she and her family knew she would soon succumb to her cancer. But for now, she was overjoyed to see such a happy evening filling her family's home.

When we wondered about having an extended family under one roof, one of the sons said, "If a day goes by when we don't see each other, we are very sad." To assure harmony in the family, the three brothers married three sisters from another family. They also assured us that entertaining our group of 22 was no problem. If we weren't there, they'd have had as many of their neighbors in.

No Turkish gathering is complete without dancing, and anyone who can snap fingers and swing a hula hoop can be comfortable on the living-room dance floor of new Turkish friends. Two aunts, deaf and mute from meningitis, brought the house down with their shoulders fluttering like butterflies. We danced and talked with four generations until after midnight.

Stepping into the late-night breeze, I noticed what had seemed to be a forested hillside was now a spangled banner of lights shining through windows, each representing a "Third World" home filled with as many "family values" as the one we were a part of that night. So much for my stereotypical image of fanatical Muslim hordes. Before we left the next morning, our friends tossed a gunnysack of hazelnuts into our bus.

For decades, this eastern end of Turkey's Black Sea coast was a dead end, butting up against the closed border of Soviet Georgia. But today the former USSR is ringed by sprawling "Russian markets" rather than foreboding guard posts.

From Finland to Turkey, we found boxy Lada automobiles overloaded with the lowest class of garage-sale junk, careening toward the nearest border on a desperate mission to scrape together a little hard cash. In the Turkish coastal town of Trabzon, 300 yards of motley tarps and blankets displayed grandpa's tools, pink and yellow "champagnski," Caspian caviar (the blue lid is best), battered samovars, fur hats, and nightmarish Rube Goldbergian electrical gadgetry. A Georgian babushka lady with a linebacker's build, caked-on makeup, and bleached blonde hair offered us a wide selection of Soviet pins, garish plastic flowers, and practically worthless ruble coins.

To satisfy my group's strange appetite for godforsaken border crossings, we drove out to the Georgian border. No one knew if we could cross or not. As far as the Turkish official was concerned, "No problem." We were escorted through the mud, past pushcarts bound for flea markets and huge trucks mired in red tape. In this strange economic no-man's-land, the relative prosperity of Muslim Turkey was clear. Just a prayer call away from Georgia, a sharp little Turkish mosque with an exclamation-point minaret seemed to holler, "You sorry losers, let us help you onto our boat." Young Georgian soldiers with hardly a button on their uniforms checked identity cards, as those who qualified squeezed past the barbed wire and through the barely open gate. A soldier told us we couldn't pass. In search of a second opinion, we fetched an officer who said, "Visa no, problem"—a negative that, for a second, I misinterpreted as a positive.

Driving inland from the Black Sea under 10,000-foot peaks, our bus crawled up onto the burnt, barren, 5,000-foot-high Anatolian plateau to Erzurum, the main city of Eastern Turkey (24 hours by bus from Istanbul). Life is hard here. Blood feuds, a holdover from feudal justice under the Ottomans, are a leading cause of imprisonment. Winters are below-zero killers. Villages spread out onto the plateau like brown weeds, each with the same economy: ducks, dung, and hay.

But Allah has given this land some pleasant surprises. The parched plain hides lush valleys where rooftops sport colorful patches of sun-dried apricots, where shepherd children still play the eagle-bone flute, and where teenage boys prefer girls who dress modestly. And you can crack the sweet, thin-skinned hazelnuts with your teeth.

Entering a village, we passed under a banner announcing, "No love is better than the love for your land and your nation." Another ducks, dung, and hay town, it took us warmly into its callused hands. Each house wore a tall hat of hay—food for the cattle and insulation for the winter. Mountains of cow pies were neatly stacked and promised warmth and cooking fuel for six months of snowed-in winter that was on its way. A man with a donkey cart wheeled us through town. Veiled mothers strained to look through our video camera's viewfinder to see their children's mugging faces. The town's annually elected policeman bragged that he keeps the place safe from terrorists. Children scampered around women beating raw wool with sticks—a rainbow of browns that would one day be woven into a carpet to soften a stone sofa, warm up a mud-brick wall, or serve as a daughter's dowry.

Driving east from Erzurum, we set our sights on 17,000-foot Mount Ararat. Villages growing between ancient rivers of lava expertly milk the land for a subsistence living. After a quick reread of the flood story in Genesis, I realized this powerful, sun-drenched, windswept land had changed little since Noah docked.

Turkey is in the middle of a small war in the east. Forty thousand Kurdish guerrillas ("terrorists" or "freedom fighters," depending on your politics) are "in the mountains," while 10 million Turkish Kurds, leading more normal lives, help provide their base of support. On a ridge high above our bus, I could make out the figure of a lone man silhouetted against a bright blue sky waving at us.

When I got up early the next morning to see the sunrise over Mount Ararat, I could make out a long convoy of Turkish army vehicles. It reminded me that these days it takes more than 40 days of rain to fix things. Our world is a complicated place in which the nightly news is just a shadow play of reality. To give it depth, you need to travel.

*For the entire script of my Eastern Turkey public television program, check out www.ricksteves.com/tvr/eastturkrse110_scr.htm.*

# 70. THE TREASURES OF LUXOR, EGYPT

With my travel spirit flapping happily in the breeze, I pedal through Luxor on my rented one-speed, catching the cool shade and leaving the stifling heat with the pesky *baksheesh*—beggar kids in the dusty distance.

Choosing the "local ferry" over the "tourist ferry," I'm surrounded by farmers rather than sightseers. As the sun rises, reddening the tomb-filled mountains, I pedal south along the West Bank of the Nile. The noisy crush of tourists is gone. The strip of riverbank hotels back in Luxor is faint and silent. I'm alone in Egypt: a lush brown-and-green world of reeds, sugarcane, date palms, mud huts, and a village world amazingly apart from what the average tourist sees.

An irrigation ditch leads me into the village of Elbairat. Here, I am truly big news on two wheels. People scurry, grabbing their families to see the American who chose them over King Tut. I'm sure somewhere in the Egyptian babble were the words, "My house is your house." They would have given me the Key to the Village, but there were no locks.

Elbairat is a poor village with a thriving but extremely simple farm economy. A little girl balances a headful of grass—heading home with a salad for the family water buffalo. A proud woman takes me on a tour of her mud-brick home, complete with a no-fly pantry filled with chickens and pigeons.

This is the real Egypt...how the majority of Egypt's 70 million people live. So close to all the tourists, yet rarely seen.

Start your Egyptian experience in the urban jungle of Cairo. It has a chaotic charm. With each visit, I stay at the Windsor Hotel (www.windsorcairo.com). Stepping into the ramshackle elevator most recently, I asked the boy who ran it if he spoke English. He said, "Up and down." I said, "Up." He babied the collapsing door to close it, turned the brass crank to send us up, and expertly stopped us within an inch of the well-worn second-floor lobby where even people who don't write feel like writers. I kept looking for the English Patient.

*One of the more interesting ways to see Egypt*

Across the street, the neighborhood gang sat in robes sucking

## Luxor

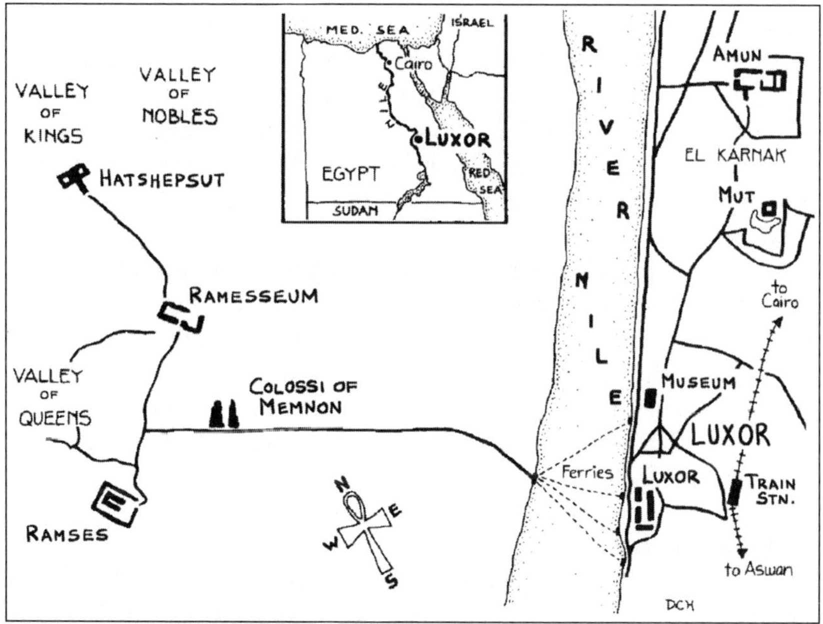


lazy water-pipes called *shishas* (a.k.a. hookahs or hubbly-bubblies). With everyone wearing what looked like hospital robes, playing backgammon and dominoes with pipes stuck in their mouths like oxygen tubes, and clearly going nowhere in a hurry, it seemed like some strange outdoor hospital game room. For about 25 cents, the smoke boy brought me one of the big free-standing pipes and fired up some apple-flavored tobacco.

For a sensuous immersion in this cultural blast furnace, hire a taxi and cruise through the teeming poor neighborhood called "old Cairo." Roll down the windows, crank up the Egyptian pop on the radio, lean out, and give pedestrians high fives as you glide by.

Then head for Luxor. The overnight train ride from Cairo to Luxor is posh and scenic, a fun experience itself. A second-class, air-conditioned sleeping car provides comfortable two-bed compartments, fresh linen, a wash basin, dinner, and a wake-up service.

I spent more time in and around Luxor than in any European small town, and I could have stayed longer. On top of the "village-by-bike" thrills, there are tremendous ancient ruins. The East Bank offers two famous sites: Karnak (with the Temples of Amun, Mut, and Khonsu, one mile north of Luxor) and the Temple of Luxor, which dominates Luxor town.

To the ancient Egyptian, the world was a lush green ribbon cutting north and south through the desert. It was only logical to live on the East Bank, where the sun rises, and bury your dead on the West Bank, where the sun is buried each evening. Therefore, all the tombs, pyramids, and funerary art in Egypt are on the West Bank.

Directly across the Nile from Luxor is the Temple of Queen Hatshepsut, Deir el-Medina, Ramesseum, Colossi of Memnon, and the Valleys of the Kings, Queens, and Nobles. Be selective. You'll become jaded sooner than you think.

Luxor town itself has plenty to offer. Explore the market. You can get an inexpensive custom-made caftan with your name sewn on in arty Arabic. I found the merchants who pester the tourists at the tombs across the Nile had the best prices on handicrafts and instant antiques. A trip out to the camel market is always fun—and you can pick up a camel for half the US price. For me, five days in a small town is asking for boredom. But Luxor fills five days like no town its size.

## Five Days in Luxor

**Day 1.** Your overnight train from Cairo arrives around 5 a.m. If it's too early to check in, leave your bags at a hotel, telling them you'll return later to inspect the room. Hop a horse carriage to be at the temples at Karnak when they open, while it's still cool. These comfortable early hours should never be wasted. Check into a hotel by midmorning. Explore Luxor town. Enjoy a felucca ride on the Nile at sunset.

**Day 2.** Cross the Nile and rent a taxi for the day. It's easy to gather other tourists and split the transportation costs. If you're selective and start early, you'll be able to see the best sites and finish by noon. That's a lot of work, and you'll enjoy a quiet afternoon back in Luxor.

**Day 3.** Through your hotel, arrange an all-day minibus trip to visit Aswan, the Aswan Dam, and the important temples (especially Edfu) south of Luxor. With six or eight tourists filling the minibus, this day should cost no more per person than a fancy dinner back home.

**Day 4.** Rent bikes and explore the time-passed villages on the west side of the Nile. Bring water, your camera, and a bold spirit of adventure. This was my best Egyptian day.

**Day 5.** Tour the excellent Luxor museum. Enjoy Luxor town and take advantage of the great shopping opportunities. Catch the quick flight or overnight train back to Cairo.

Egypt seems distant and, to many, frightening. The constant hustle ruins the experience for some softer tourists. But once you learn the local ropes, that's less of a problem, and there's a reasonable chance you'll survive and even enjoy your visit.

In the cool months (peak season), it's wise to make hotel reservations. Off-season, in the sweltering summer heat, plenty of rooms lie vacant. Air-conditioning is found in moderately priced hotels. Budget hotels with a private shower, fan, and balcony offer doubles for about $20. A cot in the youth hostel costs $3. But Egypt is not a place where you should save money at the expense of comfort and health. For $100, you'll get a double room with a buffet breakfast in a First World resort–type hotel with an elitist pool and a pharaoh's complement of servants. (Consider the riverside Sofitel New Winter Palace Hotel; the new section is less atmospheric but half the price of the historic old palace; from the US, dial 011-20-952/380-422, www.sofitel.com, h1661@accor.com.)

*Lounging on a felucca as the sun sets on the Nile*

Eat well and carefully. With the terrible heat, your body requires lots of liquid. Bottled water is cheap and plentiful, as are soft drinks. Watermelons are thirst quenching. Cool your melon in your hotel's refrigerator. Choose a clean restaurant. Hotels generally have restaurants comparable to their class and price range.

To survive the summer heat, limit your sightseeing day to 5 a.m. until noon. The summer heat, which they say can melt car tires to the asphalt, is unbearable and dangerous after noon. Those early hours are prime time: The temperature is comfortable, the light is crisp and fresh, and the Egyptian tourist hustlers are still sleeping. Spend afternoons in the shade. Carry water and wear a white hat (on sale there). An Egypt guidebook (I'd use one by Lonely Planet or Rough Guide) is a shield that shows unwanted human guides that you need no help.

Stay on the budgetary defense. No tip will ever be enough. Tip what you believe is fair by local standards and ignore the inevitable plea for more. Unfortunately, if you ever leave them satisfied, you were ripped off. Consider carrying candies or little gifts for the myriad children constantly screaming *"Baksheesh!"* ("Give me a gift!") Hoard small change in a special pocket so you'll have tip money readily available. Getting change back from your large bill is tough.

Transportation in and around Luxor is a treat. The local taxis are horse-drawn carriages. These are a delight, but drive a hard bargain and settle on a price before departing. The locals' ferry crosses the Nile from dawn until late at night and costs only pennies.

Travel on the West Bank by donkey, bike, or automobile taxi. You can rent donkeys for the romantic approach to the tombs and temples of West Thebes. Sun melts the romance fast. Bikes work for the cheap and hardy. A taxi is the quickest and most comfortable way to explore. When split among four, a taxi for the "day" (6–noon) is reasonable. Save money by assembling a tour group at your hotel. You'll enjoy the quick meet-you-at-the-ferry-landing service and adequately cover Luxor's West Bank sights.

Cruise on the Nile in a felucca, the traditional sailboat, for just a few dollars an hour. Lounging like Cleopatra in the cool beauty of a Nile sunset is a romantic way to end the day and start the night.

## See Europe with Rick Steves—on TV

Rick Steves' travel shows air on public television stations across the United States. We've done four seasons of our current series, *Rick Steves' Europe* (54 episodes total, produced 1999–2006). Rick's first 52 programs (the original *Travels in Europe* series produced in the 1990s) have been reworked: redundant, out-of-date episodes have been retired, and we've spiffed up the 16 still-timely, non-overlapping episodes. This means we've got a cohesive family of 70 episodes that take you to Rick's favorite Back Doors—covering Europe from top to bottom.

*Producer/director Simon Griffith, cameraman Karel Bauer, writer/host Rick Steves, and* David*—working together to bring the best of Europe home to you on public television.*

Other recent developments: In late 2005, public television stations begin broadcasting *Rick Steves' Europe* in glorious high definition. And for Christmas 2005, Rick released his *Rick Steves' European Christmas* special on public television (in which we drop in on intimate, traditional family celebrations in 7 different cultures).

Production of *Rick Steves' Europe* is made possible through the generous support of American Airlines (www.aa.com). For all the scripts, shooting news, streaming video bloopers, and to order DVDs, see www.ricksteves.com/tv.

# How Was Your Trip?

If you enjoyed a successful trip with the help of this book and would like to share your discoveries, please fill out the survey at www.ricksteves.com/feedback. I personally read and value all feedback. Thanks in advance—it helps a lot. We're all in the same traveler's school of hard knocks...and it's OK to compare notes. Your feedback helps us improve this book for future travelers!

For our latest travel tips, tap into our information-packed Web site: www.ricksteves.com. For any updates to this book, check www.ricksteves.com/update.

**Europe Through the Back Door is more than Rick Steves. All 70 of us are pooling our travel experience and working hard to help you enjoy the trip of a lifetime!**

# APPENDIX

*Rick's readers—his Road Scholars—have a wealth of travel information to share. For thousands of great hot-out-of-the-rucksack tips on more than 100 different travel topics, visit www.ricksteves.com/graffiti. Here are just a few travelers' tips from the packing, flying, scams, communicating, and chocoholic sections of the Graffiti Wall.*

*Thanks to all our Road Scholars who take the time to share their travel intelligence. For piles more tips on everything from jet lag and tourist scams to ATM tricks and best beaches, visit our Graffiti Wall at www.ricksteves.com/graffiti.*

## Packing: Creative Extras

■ Xerox copies of the mug-shot page of my passport for when a hotel or bank needs to have my passport.

■ Sarong: A large piece of lightweight material, it can be used as a quick-drying towel, blanket, pillow, etc.

■ Extra pair of insoles: For when shoes get wet. Overnight, I pulled the insoles out of the pair I wore and let the shoes and insoles air out. A second pair of insoles is much lighter than a second pair of shoes.

■ Disposable cameras: Once shot, break them apart, toss away all but the film, and put the film in a plastic baggie.

■ Inflatable hangers: Clothes dry faster ($5 at AAA, light and tiny).

■ The two most useful medicines: Tylenol is a general analgesic and helps reduce fatigue. Benadryl is a great sedative and sleep aid.

■ Small suction cups with hooks: To hang a toiletry bag from the mirror in small bathrooms and to dangle money belt from the youth-hostel shower wall.

■ Ladies—two words: Fem Wipes. Towelettes by Summer's Eve, individually wrapped like Handi-Wipes...great for freshening up and pigeon doo.

■ Half a tennis ball works as a stopper in any sink!

■ Earplugs for the night the hostel gets rowdy!

■ Small plastic baggie: To save theater stubs, train tickets, subway tickets, and all kinds of other tiny souvenirs.

■ Dental floss or fishing line: Strong, versatile, waterproof, nearly weightless. Tied backpack together when it broke, doubled as a shoelace, etc.

■ "Freshette," a feminine standup

urinary aide, made by Sani-Fem company, tel. 800-542-5580.

■ Sleep machine/alarm clock: In noisy hotel rooms, the sleep machine (which emits various soothing sounds) is a true godsend.

■ Local cassette tapes: We rented a car, and in each country we visited we bought cassette tapes of traditional music. We'd be driving down German side roads, passing maypoles, and listening to tubas.

■ Comfy slippers: If your feet aren't happy, YOU aren't happy. Pamper them!

■ A combination alarm clock/flashlight/motion-sensor ($30 from Brookstone): Attach to the hotel door or window. If someone moves the door or window, the motion sensor emits a high-pitched sound similar to a fire alarm.

■ If you have a fancy camera, a little black electrician's tape across the brand name discourages thieves. What appears to be a generic camera is almost worthless to those who regularly "hunt" Canon, Leica, Nikon, and so on.

■ I "cinch-tied" the opening of my backpack to make it less accessible for would-be thieves (punched holes in the band at the top of the bag and ran an extendable cable lock through the holes, pulled it tight, and locked it).

■ Fake hair: My thin, sweaty hair looks fabulous with Revlon's fake hair (Spare Hair, $7–35). Of many styles, my favorite is the Twist, a "scrunchie" of curled hair on an elastic band. I pull my hair back in a modified pony tail with some hair sticking up out of the elastic band like a bun, bobby pin the loose end of the pony tail around this, then use the Spare Hair scrunchie around the bun twice, and it looks like I've spent hours curling my hair. It takes about 15 minutes to do. I can go days with only washing my bangs.

■ A headlight instead of a flashlight. Better for reading in bed. Frees your hands if needed.

■ Post-It notes to flag guidebooks.

■ Women, pack some yeast infection cream or Monistat one-day suppositories—difficult to find in some countries.

■ Body Shop's "Refreshing Foot Spray" and "Peppermint Foot Lotion" in small, travel-size bottles: Soothe tired, aching feet.

■ Tiny musical instrument: If you can play a harmonica, the spoons, the bones, or another tiny instrument, bring it. Playing music can break the ice, start friendships, and even earn you a free meal!

■ Pillowcase: To put your backpack/travel bag in while you sleep on it on an overnight train. It's another obstacle thieves must overcome. Also, set up the Coke-can warning system on your compartment door (a few pennies in an empty can).

■ Put your extra camera lenses in a thick ankle sock. You can toss them in your day pack without worrying about damage and they take up less room than bulky lens cases.
■ Pack a picture of your home town and a small map to locate it.
■ Tie something distinctive, like a ribbon, to your luggage handle for quick spotting at airport carousels.
■ Mailing tubes: To collect prints and posters, also handy for small items and breakables. A very thin placemat from a favorite Paris restaurant made it home safely this way and is now framed and hanging in my home.
■ Walkman: for listening to local radio stations.
■ Ziploc bags: to store the second half of that huge café sandwich.
■ Digital tape recorder: a great way to catch the waves, traffic, sounds in the cafés, and more. I send audio files to friends via the Internet, with digital photos.
■ Combo journal/scrapbook: Buy a fancy (lightweight) journal and take colored pens and a glue stick. As you write each day, add creative touches by sketching in color, paste in museum tickets, or even cut/paste local brochures, etc.
■ Vitamin B6: Makes your blood undesirable to mosquitoes. You have to take it for a few days before it works. Also, a couple of years ago I bought a neat little gadget at Babies-R-Us that keeps mosquitoes away. It's designed for babies (who are too young for bug-spray), but works for anyone! This magical red, plastic ladybug clips onto your clothing...or diapers.

### Shoes: Walking Softly

■ My Ecco Gore-Tex hiking shoes scrambled thru Scottish highlands and County Kerry, muddy bogs, wet grass, and muck, not to mention cobbled medieval rambles. Excellent grip. It's not a heavy shoe. The waterproofing is a good idea.
■ Last year I took a pair of Merrell men's walking shoes to Italy. The best part is they are an oxford-type lace-up shoe, but with a cross-training-type sole. We used them for light jogging before breakfast, all-day sightseeing, and for dining out in dressy evening restaurants. They're great shoes if you only want to bring one pair.
■ I've had great luck with any shoes made by Montrail. The soles are specifically designed to handle the added weight of, say, a backpack. You can find them at most outdoor stores.
■ I've loved my Dr. Martens since my punk-rock years in the early '80s and have yet to find a more comfortable walking shoe. However, these shoes have about a two-week breaking-in period, during which they're pretty darn stiff and uncomfortable.

■ I picked up a pair of Campers about a month before going to Rome, and I was very pleased. They are light, comfortable, and stylish. In fact, many an Italian foot was shod exactly like mine.

■ I took one pair of Rockport Pro Walkers to Europe for two weeks, and they were wonderful. Comfortable and stylish, they went with everything. With only one pair of shoes, I was careful to shake a little foot powder into them every night to keep them from smelling too bad.

■ Hush Puppies work for me. A cloudburst in Siena soaked me and my shoes. They dried out and looked as good as new. Mine are roomy enough for thick socks, which helps for long walks. The smooth black leather looks great with a little touching up. I wear orthotics and they fit fine in the shoes. I carry a lightweight pair of flip-flops for showering and wearing around my hotels or B&Bs.

■ I bought a pair of Ecco shoes three and a half years ago. They kept me comfortable and dry during a three-month European backpacking trip—not easy in the Swiss Alps! I am now a tour guide, and for two years these shoes have been the only ones I've used to pound the cobblestones.

■ I purchased a pair of Mephisto Diva boots (workboot styling) for $67 at the Jezebel shoe store on the rue Cler in Paris (back here in the States they cost $295!). My feet really like these boots! I got great shoes, and a great souvenir from France that I can wear anytime.

■ I have tried several different brands, but always come back to Dansko. I have traveled to Europe on several occasions and have worn the sandals and/or the clogs without any problems. Recently, Dansko has come out with a new sport clog. You can purchase "slightly imperfect" Dansko footwear for 30 percent less at www.danskooutlet.com.

■ I traveled Europe for six weeks this spring with an 18-pound backpack and one pair of shoes: Teva Hydro Rodiums. They were great for everything—walking, hiking, whatever. They're light, breathable, and dry very quickly. No socks necessary, either, unless it's cold.

■ I've worn Arizona Birkenstocks for years. They have a new Arizona with a padded sole that is really comfortable for standing and walking. They have microfiber straps, and the Birk clerk said the shoes were originally designed for diabetics. Translation: No blisters. Bonus with Birks: They slip off easily to allow a few minutes of barefooted bliss.

■ I've been searching for the perfect travel shoes. For me, they must meet four criteria: 1) won't look too goofy with khakis; 2) won't look too goofy with shorts;

3) provide enough comfort and support to walk all day; and 4) preferably waterproof. I finally found a shoe to meet all four requirements: Rockports. Mine are nubuck leather, Gore-Tex, and comfortable. And I don't feel like a dork when wearing shorts.

■ As a doctor who treats foot and ankle problems, here are a few tips: Buy quality, break them in first, get used to walking before you go (maybe you'll discover that foot problem before you leave and have it treated here), take along some Advil or other pain reliever, and consider the use of prescription orthotics. They will make your foot do what you hope the "right" shoe will do—but often doesn't.

■ I find that a good pair of hiking shoes (low-cut, lightweight boots) can be more supportive than most shoes. A hiking shoe with a nylon shank (sole stiffener) and some ankle support can take most of the load off your feet when you're walking on cobblestones or hard pavement.

■ As a physical therapist, I would recommend taking two pairs of shoes with good socks. If you are on your feet a lot, simply changing shoes every eight hours prevents foot discomfort.

■ I just came back from 10 days in London and Paris. I saw bowling shoes everywhere, on both men and women. And the matching handbags look like bowling-ball bags. Who'd have thought that if I'd brought my ugly bowling shoes I'd be trendy while walking in Trafalgar Square or strolling the Champs-Elysées?

■ I travel frequently to London and Paris, often in winter. I wear Ecco shoes and couldn't be happier. Even though they're rubber-soled, I always pack a pair of Tingely Moccasin Stretch Storm Rubbers in case it rains. They look like shoes and really keep a rainy day from becoming soggy.

■ If your feet still hurt after a long day tramping around, regardless of your shoes, try this: Put about four inches of cold water in the tub, sit on the side, and put your bare feet in the water. The cold water will numb your aching feet and help reduce swelling. You could also stick your bare feet in any other cold water, like a stream.

■ If you're prone to blisters, try this: Use your underarm antiperspirant on your feet. I'll use it on my heel, arch, toes, and on the top of my foot. Blisters come from heat, heat comes from friction, and the body's response is sweat. Antiperspirant saves your socks and your feet. Remember to use antiperspirant, not deodorant. If you use deodorant, you'll just have nice-smelling blisters.

■ After two trips to Europe that were uncomfortable for my feet, I've finally found a solution. I switched to more technical socks. Good socks are as important as good walking shoes. Use a pair of light running socks that are blended (not 100 percent cotton) and designed to wick away moisture.

■ SmartWool makes a great sock. They keep your feet relatively dry and odor free.

■ What does Rick wear? Mephistos are comfy for my Stateside needs. But for all the walking I do in Europe, I need something sturdier. For many years I wore Rockport Walkers, but now I'm really into the warmth and solid support of my Eccos.

## Flying Smart

■ You can save hundreds of dollars booking flights on the Web, but always call the airline after you book to confirm that you actually have the reservation.

■ Can't get enough frequent-flyer miles to take your whole family to Europe? Use your US award to get your family to a busy airport such as Newark/New York, Washington D.C., or Miami where there are cheap departures. Using half the frequent-flyer miles we'd need to get to Europe, we got free flights to Newark, where our $300 round-trip tickets to London were less than half of what we'd pay from Colorado. Extra bonus: We got a long layover on the East Coast and spent a week with family there on the way to Europe.

■ With earplugs known as Earplanes, I overcame my problems with ear air-pressure equalization during flights.

■ For the flight over, take earplugs, ski socks, and a large bottle of water. Once the plane takes off, remove your shoes and put on the warm socks. Rather than constantly bugging flight attendants for water, you'll have your own supply. For the kids, bring Benadryl, so they'll sleep (just don't tell Grandma).

■ On long flights with small kids, bring a tiny flashlight. The light will quiet a crying toddler.

## Tourist Scams

■ If you see someone playing the shell game or three-card monty, be careful. No matter how easy it looks, only the "plants" in the crowd will win. These guys operate in teams of several people. If any native is playing, then he or she is a plant. My friend and I fell victim to the shell game on one of the alleys leading up to the Sacré-Coeur church in Paris. Yeah, we were stupid, but our initial intention was only to watch. Of course, it all looked so easy. We lost about $70.

■ In the Paris Métro or similar places, if you want to determine who the thieves are, then simply watch what others are watching. Thieves look to see what others are carrying. On the Métro, thieves love to walk up and down the aisles until just before the doors close. They time their grab with the closing of the door and quickly jump through as it shuts.

■ I met a wonderfully friendly young man in Istanbul who suggested we stop by a bar close to my hotel for some beer. Inside, we were having a beer when a girl sat next to me. My new friend ordered her a drink. At that point it clicked in my head...this is that scam I read about. Sure enough, there was no one in the bar other than the big guy standing by the door and the mean-looking bartender. The bill was $80 for my beer and the girl's drink. I had no choice but to pay.

■ My wife and I were ready to leave Rome after a great 10-day visit. We were picked up at our hotel by a cab and asked to be taken to the train station. The cab driver asked if we were leaving to fly home, and we said yes. He then proceeded to tell us that there were major problems with the train to Fiumicino Airport, the line was down, etc....but he would be glad to take us to the airport for €80! Thank God I had built enough time into our schedule so that I could investigate the train situation myself. I told him no thanks and asked him to take us to the train station anyway. There was no problem with the train and we made it home sans difficulty.

■ While in Paris, the only problem with pickpockets we encountered was on a very crowded elevator to the top of the Eiffel Tower. A group of young men was horsing around a bit. One of the men pushed one of his friends, causing him to bump into my husband and allowing him to stick his hand into the pocket where he expected to find a wallet. Fortunately for us, the day wallet was deep in his front pocket, and most of our money and cards were in his money belt.

■ On my last trip, two men claimed they were police and flashed IDs (and quickly put them away), then asked for my identification with the casual afterthought, "Passport is okay." I said, "Hold up your ID so I can read it carefully." The men looked shocked, then became abusive. I said, "I am now going to scream at the top of my lungs for a real policeman. Would you like to wait and talk to him?" They ran away. This type of scam always takes place away from crowds and out of sight of uniformed policemen. Never be afraid to scream loudly for assistance. I did that once on a bus (yes, #64 in Roma). I screamed *"Aiuto! Ladro!"* ("Help! Thief!") and the Italians on the bus almost killed the poor thief, shoving her off the bus.

■ Beware of fast-talking, fast-moving taxi drivers! I got into a taxi at the Spanish Steps in

Rome, only to have the driver turn around and begin talking loudly in broken English, asking for "yellow euro" while patting the bags my purchases were in, waving frantically, and generally being distracting. I pulled out the remainder of my cash for the day in frustration to prove that I had money for the cab ride. He reached over for the €50 bill (which is yellow), reassured me that that was what he needed to see, and handed it back to me (or so I thought). He then said that his cab was not allowed to go to the church that was my destination. (Later I realized it was only two blocks away.) He advised me to take a "radio taxi." After I got out, he sped away, and only then did I realize he had replaced my €50 note with a blank piece of paper in a fast sleight-of-hand move.

■ In Madrid, be careful of strangers who approach you and ask to see what euros and US dollars look like. They will try to take the cash right out of your hand. Trust no one who approaches you in public with a strange request.

■ I have lived in Europe for nearly eight years. I've loved every second of it. I have been accosted many times, but never with success. Although I wouldn't recommend this tactic to everyone, here's my secret: If you are forced to walk somewhere dodgy, such as the Albayzin or Sacromonte areas of Granada in Spain (tiny thousand-year-old streets, a labyrinth where masked thieves—usually little punk kids—like to prey), one thing I've found that works is putting on the "Oh man, what have I done?!" face. This is the kind of face one may have as they are thinking to themselves: "Oh man, I shouldn't have hit that last person so hard...I wonder if they're dead?" Imagine it. It's the face of a person who has absolutely cracked, gone off the deep end, and just killed someone. This may sound really weird, but trust me, if you wear that face, and you round a corner and catch the eye of some shady punk, he will jump out of your way. Being a tough guy will invite a challenge. Being a sheep will get you eaten. But being a total psycho... NOBODY wants to play punchy punchy with Hannibal Lecter. With all my years here, I still don't look like a local, but that face really works.

■ Budapest is a wonderful gem of a city, surprisingly cosmopolitan with very warm, attractive people eager to practice their English and help you with Hungarian in return. That said, young, single men should beware of women, usually walking in pairs, who approach them on the Váci Utca pedestrian drag. They may invite you to have a drink at a "private restaurant," usually run by the Mafia. If you don't have the $200 to pay the large bill you find yourself saddled with, you may be in trouble.

■ I made a solo trip to London a few years ago and spent an evening visiting the pubs in the Soho area. A woman called me over to one, and being the naive Midwesterner, I stopped. She described the place as being a strip joint. I thought to myself, "what the hey." Once inside, I realized it wasn't a strip joint at all, and that I was in serious trouble. I excused myself to visit the WC and decided I was going to calmly walk out. I made it across the room when I was confronted by one of the girls. She yelled "Security!" as I breezed past her. I was about 15 feet from the stairs and freedom when a huge guy burst through a fake wall and tried to tackle me as I rounded the corner and headed up the stairs. He went low but couldn't hold on. I dog-paddled my way up the stairs before getting my feet under me. I saw a silhouette of a man blocking the door. I hit him low and shot into the street like a bullet. He was another punter and must have been shocked when I took his legs out from under him. Once in the street, I turned on the burners, and he gave up somewhere along Regent Street. It's hard for a bodybuilder to chase down a scrawny little track athlete like myself.

■ My husband and I arrived at Paris' Gare du Nord train station in the early evening, and proceeded to read the map to find out how to get to our hotel via the Métro. One guy came up and advised us to buy tickets from the ticket machine. When we were at the machine trying to read the French, another guy came out and "helped" us to buy tickets. Later, what was supposed to be a three-day ticket turned out to be a one-way, single-use ticket. We paid him €48, the price shown on the ticket machine, but he must have cancelled the transaction and bought us the single-trip ticket instead.

■ I spent some time working in Egypt and noticed that when tourists paid to ride camels (especially at the pyramids), they would always get stuck having to pay twice for their rides. The owners of the camels would kindly ask for the fee before the tourist got up on the camel, and then, when the ride was done, would not let the tourist off until they paid the fee again. It's a big, difficult jump down from a camel!

■ Be careful if you are parking at the Tronchetto garage in Venice and want to take a vaporetto into the city. Men surrounded us, told us where to walk, and directed us to private taxi boats. They refused to allow us to go to the vaporetto. They raised their voices at us and insisted that we take their private taxis. I pulled out my Rick Steves book and showed them I wanted the vaporetto, but they yelled at me and made us walk to the taxi boats. When we arrived at the taxi, the man asked for more money than we were told it would cost. When I questioned him, he yelled, "Get out!" As we walked back to the parking garage, we saw signs pointing to the vaporetto and found it easily. We later realized that the men kept positioning us so that we could not see those signs when we originally entered the parking garage.

■ Pickpockets on the Lisbon subway were very active. They didn't get anything from me because the money was in my money belt, but my purse was opened twice in the same day! And I thought I was alert!

■ On the overnight train from Paris to Florence, we shared a *couchette* with a younger Spanish couple who seemed very nice. The only time my husband and I left the *couchette* was for about 15 minutes to allow the other couple to prepare for sleeping. In the morning we got ready to leave the train. I went to retrieve my tote bag from under my bunk and it was nowhere to be found! I woke the other couple and they swore that they had never left the room while we were out. We had only been gone 15 minutes, I was awake all night, and the door never opened. So who took the tote? Luckily all of my real valuables were on my body throughout the night. We have gone over this many times, and the other couple either robbed us and threw the bag out within the 15 minutes or they put it in one of their larger suitcases. Do not trust anyone with your belongings for a minute.

■ I have only heard of this happening in Spain on the Costa del Sol, but it could happen anywhere. This scam depends on you paying a restaurant/bar bill in cash, usually with a €50 note. The waiter will take your payment, then return shortly after, apologetically telling you that the note is a fake and that you need to pay again. He will return the "fake" bill to you, and any change you're due. Of course, you gave him a REAL note, he gave you a FAKE note, and you gave him a second real note, so you paid €100 for a €50 meal. What I do now is write unobtrusively on all large notes I get, so I can challenge them if it happens to me.

■ In Paris, at a boutique across the street from the Louvre, the shop owner presented me with a receipt for €25 for my two T-shirts, but gave me a receipt for €250 to sign for the credit-card purchase. When I called him on it, he claimed it was a mistake. I have no doubt that it was intentional, so consider yourself warned, keep track of your decimals, and watch what you sign.

■ We went into a small bar in Rome near St. Peter's, even though our tour guide told us not to. We ordered two cokes and a sandwich. We paid €20 for the cokes and €13 for the sandwich. The next day we met the guide again and told him, and he said you should always ask how much it will cost before you sit down or take the goods into your hands.

■ When we visited France—mainly in Paris—we as Americans started wondering why we were getting quarters in our pockets from change. We finally figured it out when we realized that the €1 coin is the same size as the American quarter. I finally caught on after we bought tickets at a Métro station and realized that the cashier had made this exchange. What a bundle she must be making!

■ While riding in the RER (Paris Métro) a man came through the car and dropped a package containing a notepad and pen beside each of the four of us. I immediately told my traveling companions not to touch it, and they didn't. A short while later, the man came through and took the packages back, but those passengers in the car who had picked them up found themselves on the receiving end of a demand for payment. The lesson: Don't allow ANYONE to give you something you may not want; you'll have a battle giving it back.

■ When arriving in Rome for the first time, we made the mistake of taking a cab from the train station to our hotel. The driver charged us what seemed to be a huge amount. We argued with the driver outside the hotel, and when he appeared to get agitated we just gave in. We asked the hotel manager what the cab should have cost, and we did indeed get ripped off. The advice the manager gave us was that if you feel the driver is scamming you, politely say to him that the best way to resolve the dispute is to go into the hotel and ask them what the fare should be. Then do it! According to the manager, the cab driver will immediately admit he may have made a mistake.

■ While we were in the Milan train station seated in a first-class compartment, four well-dressed Italian men joined us. One announced, "These seats are taken!" We said no—we had checked the slip posted outside—but my husband stood up. Immediately, the other three guys entered the compartment and started a sort of Marx Brothers shuffling around. My husband got manipulated all the way outside to the hallway with one guy facing him. He later said the man was surely looking for the right pocket to pick. (My husband was wearing a safari-type jacket with multiple pockets!) Being in the train station, they were on and off the car in minutes without any danger of police. Never get up if this happens...tell them to find the conductor, just hold your ground, or lean out the window and yell!

■ Be warned when buying from street artists. A lot of the "original" artwork (mostly the watercolors) is actually just printed by computer on watercolor paper.

■ In Prague, our baggage was being taken off the bus when a gentleman offered to help a woman in our group. He removed her bag from the luggage hold. She thought that he was from the hotel and laid her purse down next to her carry-on bag. By the time the suitcase was out of the luggage hold and she got her bearings, her purse was gone. Be especially vigilant right after your transatlantic flight; you are tired and it's easy to let your guard down.

■ In London, only the familiar "black" cabs can be hailed from the street. If any other kind of car stops for you, tell them to get lost, no matter how insistent they may be.

■ At a hotel in Paris, I handed over a wad of €50 bills and told the clerk that there was €600 there. She counted the bills and said, "This is only €550." I had no way to prove that it was really €600 since I didn't count it in front of her. (I had counted it earlier.) We both searched around and didn't find the missing €50. I gave her another €50, figuring it was the only thing I could do. I learned that it would have been better to have counted out the money to her rather than just handing over the cash. I still don't know what happened; it is possible that I dropped a bill someplace. It's also possible that she palmed it. The irony is that I was paying cash, rather than using a credit card, in order to save a few euros!

■ I had just arrived at one of the big train stations in Paris and was looking at the Métro map to figure out how to get to my hotel when a friendly French guy came over and asked me where I was going. After showing me the best route to take, he offered to help me buy a ticket at the ticket machine. He asked me how many days I would be in Paris for, and I said seven. He selected a seven-day Métro pass for me—or that's what he told me it was, but how would I know if I can't read French? It cost €77 (which I saw on the screen), and I put my credit card in the machine to purchase. When it didn't work he touched a few buttons and quickly put in his credit card. The ticket came out and he had me give him the cash. I knew something was wrong, but it happened so fast that I didn't walk away like

I should have. As I discovered later when I tried to use it on my second trip on the Métro, it was a €1 single-journey ticket.

■ Beware of letting your round-trip tickets out of sight on the overnight train from Kraków to Prague (or any other Eastern European routes, for that matter). The "conductor" took my round-trip ticket as I got into the *couchette* and assured me that I'd get it back in the morning. Come morning, he said he gave it to me, then later said he said he put it in my *couchette*. Then he went through the motions of looking in his pockets, but I was screwed. My roundtrip ticket was gone and he'd likely sell it for the 25 bucks it was worth. If possible, get a round-trip ticket that is physically two separate pieces of paper, and then only give the conductor the one necessary for that leg of the trip.

■ On a Sunday in Barcelona, I was going from the Picasso Museum to the Palau de la Música Catalana. In order to get there as quickly as possible I headed through one of the side streets—a big mistake! I vaguely noticed three young men standing off to the side. Everything happened very fast. One came in front of me, snatched my travel purse—which I carry across one shoulder and round my neck—with enough force to break the tough strap. He took off down an alley. Fortunately, I lost little of real value because I wear a money belt. The incident made me more conscious of keeping to the more frequented streets.

■ While driving a rental car from Granada to Seville, motorcyclists punctured our tire. After we yanked out the luggage and jacked up the car to change the tire, a "good Samaritan" came along to say, "There's a mechanic over here, look, over here" to my wife. While she was looking, another thief tried to steal her purse from our car. Luckily, I stood up just in time to see the thief in the car with the purse (with our credit cards and passports inside) in his hands. He let go and ran. I nearly clobbered him with the tire iron.

■ When traveling, use ATMs only when the bank is open. An ATM machine ate our card, and when we went back to the bank in the morning, we found out that it was missing. There were charges already made before we could cancel the card. Train stations and airports often have the best ATMs, with lots of people around to help.

■ While driving through Naples to get to Sorrento, we noticed boys on mopeds pass us in the opposite direction. Shortly after, we stopped for a train crossing. My husband happened to catch sight of the kids approaching from behind and immediately hit the power door locks the

INSTANT that two boys jumped off the bikes (they were passengers) and tried to pull the side door and rear hatch open. They would have had my sister-in-law's bag from her lap with everything in it and my camera and camcorder from the back. The kids were checking us out as they passed, and then returned when we were stopped with nowhere to go. Lock your doors!

## Communication: Connecting With Locals

■ Sincere admiration opens doors. Admiring a local's dog/cat/flowers/motorcycle/garden/whatever is a great way to start a conversation.

■ Meet friendly locals in the Czech Republic by attending a hockey game. I am a 26-year-old woman who turned loneliness into lots of fun this way. I'm planning my second solo trip for October, and the hockey arena will be my first stop!

■ When you're on a train, make conversation. Many Europeans want to practice English as much as you may want to practice their native language.

■ One night in Paris, we noticed a hundred or so people on the Pont Neuf, so we checked it out. Locals our age were just hanging out drinking beer, wine, Coke—even smoking pot. Everyone was simply relaxing. My wife and I found a nice spot to sit (Notre-Dame ahead, Eiffel Tower behind), bought a few beers from a vendor, and hung out until well past 1 a.m. No police and no trouble, just a lot of fun.

■ If you're traveling with a skateboard-loving kid, take skateboard/surfer-type stickers for them to give to new friends.

■ Make eye contact. After a week in Rome, I hadn't really met a soul. So I thought about it—and I realized that I hadn't actually looked at anyone! Being a big-city dweller, I was in the habit of avoiding eye contact with people on the streets. That evening, I made plenty of eye contact, and within an hour I was having the time of my life with new friends at a nearby trattoria!

■ Irish nightlife centers around the pubs. To meet locals, arrive a bit early to snag a big table with several extra chairs. As the night gets busier, people always ask to share the table. Every time I've tried this, I've met a fun montage of great people.

■ A couple of tips: Eat by yourself in busy restaurants. You may be seated at a table of locals with an empty chair, or they may come and sit by you. And fake ignorance. Even if you know the answer, just ask that cute German girl a question. It could lead to a long conversation.

■ When I'm taking local transportation, I like to engage people by asking simple questions (like making sure I'm on the right train, or where to get off), which signals to locals that I'm a traveler looking to connect.

■ The easiest way to meet locals is to be where they are. Locals are not watching the 10:10 a.m. bell-ringing festival or prowling through souvenir shops. They're living their normal lives: the guy at the car wash, people at the local town pool. Visitors are always welcome for a buck or two. Just wander the shopping area of any little town and strike up conversations.

■ Don't be so stuck on your schedule that you miss out on once-in-a-lifetime opportunities. We had just parked our car in a small German town, and a kindly gentleman walking by made a comment about the tight squeeze and how lucky we were to find a place. In chatting with him, we learned that he had served with Rommel in North Africa. Our schedule was suffering, so we said our good-byes. Later it dawned on me that I had missed the chance to discuss real history with a participant. I was too concerned with my plans to take the time to buy the guy a beer, so I missed out on an experience I can never recapture.

■ Pictures of grandchildren are great icebreakers!

■ If you belong to a service club like Kiwanis or Rotary, check the Internet for local club meetings.

■ Just as you want to meet local folks when abroad, look kindly on foreign travelers in the United States. They just might be looking for the same kind of experience.

■ Everywhere I've traveled a polite, genuine smile is the best icebreaker.

■ Attending church services can be a great way to meet locals. Neighborhood churches (rather than famous cathedrals and huge "downtown" churches) are the best, since visitors are less common there, and people go out of their way to make you feel welcome. Many have a welcoming coffee-and-cookies time after Mass.

■ Try second-class seating on trains. You'll find lively locals instead of stuffy businessmen and American tourists.

■ Track down your European roots! The highlight of my recent European adventure was visiting my Italian relatives—a truly priceless experience. Four months before I left for Europe, I sent my relatives a brief letter. I introduced myself, let them know when I would be in Italy, and told them I would be interested in meeting them. They quickly responded, offering me a ride from the nearest train station and a place to stay. They met me at the station in Trento and brought me to their small village north of the city. I was the only tourist in town, and all 500 inhabitants of the village (many of them my relatives) seemed as excited to meet me as I was honored to meet them.

■ While in Germany, be sure to visit one of the many thermal baths that are found in just about any large town. These places are only frequented by Germans. If you have the courage, pay a bit extra and visit the saunas. Clothing inside a sauna is not optional—it's forbidden! And in most places, men and women sauna together. How's that for an icebreaker?

■ I have just returned from St. Petersburg, Russia. This was my first-ever trip out of the country. I handed out pencils (with pictures of American dollar bills) and candy to the local children. I was the talk of the town. I found the people to be very appreciative of me, the dorky American tourist from a small farm town, thanks to candy and funny-looking pencils.

■ Don't know anyone in your destination? You might just make contact over the Internet. Last fall I visited Croatia. Before going I posted to an Internet travel bulletin board while doing research for my trip. A Croatian journalist responded to several of my posts. He gave me lots of good ideas, and when I asked about getting to some of the more remote places in Istria, he responded that he would love to show me his country. I was a little wary about meeting him—but I knew the minute I met him that everything was okay. My new online pal drove me around Istria and showed me things few tourists see.

■ I collect little pins from places I've been and display them on my favorite travel hat. When I'm on the road, the hat gets piles of attention. People comment, want to look at it closely, and ask which pin was from my home city. I bring a few pins from my home, which I give as gifts to new friends.

■ I volunteer for my local sheriff's office, and I've recently started collecting police-uniform patches. On my last trip I took several patches from home to swap with local law-enforcement agencies. Everywhere I went, I visited the police, who were glad to swap patches. I built my collection and I made a lot of new friends!

■ Try to speak their language. After a seemingly futile attempt to communicate in French, many of the locals would laugh and switch to English and we were fine. The French appreciated our efforts (and we learned as we went).

■ We made personal business cards on our computer and passed these out to people we met as we traveled. Today we still receive e-mail from folks we met. It's great to be remembered and to still keep in touch.

■ Find a good international pen-pal website (I used Penpal International at http://ppi.searchy.net) and meet people from all over the world. Now I have places to go and people to see next time I'm in Europe.

■ Rick's 3-in-1 German, Italian, and French phrase book was my best friend during a recent three-month adventure throughout Europe. I quickly learned that one of the most important phrases was, "Which is your favorite dish/cheese/wine/etc.?" By asking this in restaurants and open-air markets, it shows an interest in the local menu and respect for the waiter or vendor and his opinion. The usual result: a great dish, and friendly conversation to boot.

■ Join a club, seek out weekend soccer teams, go to town meetings, visit public swimming pools, shop in small markets, attend school concerts and sporting events, go to nightclubs, attend personal appearances and book-signings in bookstores, track down travel slide shows, go to church, use public transportation, use local barbers/hairdressers, buy from small vintners—there are many low-key ways to meet locals. Be courteous, inquisitive, and willing to participate when appropriate. Show people you are interested in them and their lives, not just the tourist traps, and your trip suddenly becomes more meaningful.

■ One of the best ways to meet locals is to bring children with you! We took our two kids for two months around Europe. We did something we would never do in the States, and it worked like a charm: We bribed them. We told them if someone told us how well-behaved or polite they were, they would get the equivalent of $3. We didn't realize how great our kids could be! They discovered right away that saying "please" and "thank you" in the local language, smiling, and saying "good day," earned them a smile and a pat on the head. The money actually became a secondary reward, and they worked harder at learning how to say foreign words and make connections with locals than we did.

■ Before a trip overseas, go to your local chamber of commerce/hospitality association/ tourist board, and they will usually give you small flags or lapel pins of your state to give away to friends you make in your travels.

■ I break barriers by complimenting people and stating (in the local language) when I like something. In a restaurant in Croatia, I saw the cook and said, "Dobro"—Croatian for "good." Soon the entire staff was smiling at me, and when I left an hour later I felt more like a friend than just another tourist.

■ The best thing I did to strike up conversation with locals was to sew my state flag's patch to my pack. So many people of all nationalities asked me what it was.

■ Along with "please" and "thank you" it is really useful to learn to say, in the local language, "You have a beautiful country. We are having a wonderful time." Say it over and over. You will be happy and so will everyone else.

■ I notice that whenever I attempt a few words of the local language, the people I'm speaking to are always more open and willing to share great "insider" information with me.

■ Food is truly universal, so if possible, I ask questions about what I'm eating, how it's made, if it's a personal favorite, and so on. Locals appreciate my genuine interest in their food and cultures and seem delighted to explain the "special ingredient" that makes their dish so good. A great souvenir is bringing the recipe of a favorite place home.

■ In Germany, I shared a bench along the river with an older German lady. We sat in silence for a few minutes until three very good-looking men jogged past on the path. I looked at her, looked at the guys, raised my eyebrows, and said, "Yummm." She laughed, nodded her head, and the ice was broken. We had a fun chat and agreed to meet again the next day. When I showed up, she had brought a German dessert to share with me.

■ Wherever you go, do something local—like a flea market. This is a great way to mingle with the locals (and see what they shop for).

■ Before a recent trip to Paris, I accidentally stuck a picture of my dog in the book I was reading. When we got to our hotel, the picture fell out, and I instantly learned I had a great conversation starter. For the rest of the trip, I was showing off my dog like a proud parent. Love of animals is an international language!

■ Here's one good way to meet the locals in England: Ask to photograph their dogs! All last summer in England I was on a self-appointed mission to photograph as many Jack Russell terriers as I could. Dog owners love to show off their dogs, demonstrate their best tricks, and tell stories.

■ With four of us traveling together, we knew we were at a disadvantage when it came to "mingling with the locals." To make sure that we did get to have stories to relate over dinner, we separated several times during the day.

■ Remember, the locals you meet are individuals, not tourist attractions who cease to exist when you put away your camera.

## Chocoholics Unite

■ Cadbury chocolate bars are awesome. The Dairy Milk, Crunchie, and Wispa bars are fantastic. Also, when in London, try the hot chocolate—tastes just like a liquid Dairy Milk bar.

■ After many years of Swiss-chocolate adoration, I now bow to the Belgians. They are the masters.

■ The best chocolate is in Germany. I lived in Germany for 12 years and couldn't get enough of their chocolate. Milka and Ritter Sport are great! The Kinder Überaschung (Kid's Surprise) eggs are very popular. Also, during Christmas they come out with Advent calendars that have chocolate hidden behind the flip-open door for each day. Eating those made the wait bearable. In London, visit Charbonnel et Walker, 28 Old Bond Street, near Kensington, for the best chocolates anywhere.

■ My favorite European chocolate: Ritter Sport. It's German, but it's sold all over Europe. Ritter Sport is a square bar that comes in a million varieties. My favorite is praline (dark blue wrapper).

■ Near Zürich, tour the Lindt factory in Kilchberg. Tours are free (Wed–Fri, catch S-1 or S-8 from Zürich Hauptbahnhof to Kilchberg, walk three min).

■ One word: Sprungli, Zürich, Bahnhofstrasse...OK, that was three words, but when in Zürich, go to the Sprungli shop on Bahnhofstrasse and enjoy... mmmm...makes my mouth water just thinking about it.

■ We did the equivalent of a pub crawl in Bruges and sampled truffles at all the small chocolate shops. By noon we were on a major sugar buzz. The best was at Depla's.

■ Once I met a man on a plane who told me he was the chocolate taster for Hershey's and his job was to travel the world tasting chocolate. His favorite? Belgian.

■ Did you know they put the equivalent of 1.5 cups of milk into every huge Cadbury Dairy Milk bar? At last, a palatable solution to the specter of osteoporosis!

■ A good friend from Brussels explained that "Mary's" had the best chocolate in Brussels (and thus the world). He noted that there are two stores of every type, which are appointed by the King. One is a large, commercial place (Godiva in this case) and one is a small place, where the King actually buys his goods. Mary's is that place.

■ If you are a chocoholic, then you must tour the Cadbury factory (train to Birmingham, then local train to Bournville, then a 10-min walk). Upon entering, you're greeted with the most heavenly smell, a lively tour, and an entire chocolate bar! As you munch, you walk through the history of chocolate.

■ Try the hot chocolate in Paris to truly experience it the way it was meant to be. The best place is Angelina near the Louvre, across from the Tuileries on rue de Rivoli. Order the Africain, a pot of liquid pleasure. We loved Angelina so much that we named our cat after it.

■ After two trips to Paris, walking everywhere and tasting along the way, we've found our favorite chocolatier. It's Puyricard (on avenue Rapp in the seventh arrondissement).

■ The chocolate factory alone is reason enough to visit Köln, Germany. They offer tours with a history of chocolate-making and a great look at all the machines in action.

## How Europe Compares to North America

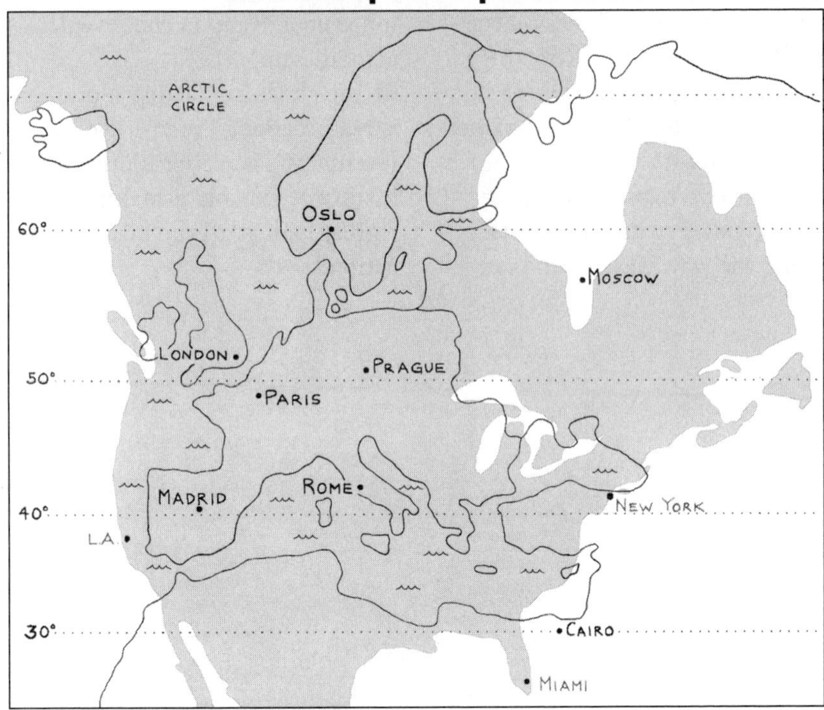


*Wondering what clothes to pack? Europe and North America share the same latitudes and a similar climate. This map shows Europe superimposed over North America (shaded) with latitude lines. Use the map as a general weather guide. For example, London and Canada's Vancouver have a similar latitude and are both near the sea, so you can assume their climates are nearly the same. But you can't go by latitude alone. Rome and New York City should have similar weather, but Rome is hotter because it's surrounded by the warm Mediterranean. Inland areas have colder winters, so Prague can get as chilly as Minneapolis. Elevation affects climate as well. For more info, see the climate charts below and www.weatherbase.com. Bon voyage!*

## European Weather

Here is a climate chart. This can be helpful in planning your itinerary, but I have never found European weather to be particularly predictable. The first line shows the average daily low, the second line is the average daily high, and the third line shows the average number of days without rain.

| | J | F | M | A | M | J | J | A | S | O | N | D |
|---|---|---|---|---|---|---|---|---|---|---|---|---|
| **AUSTRIA • Vienna** | | | | | | | | | | | | |
| | 25° | 28° | 30° | 42° | 50° | 56° | 60° | 59° | 53° | 44° | 37° | 30° |
| | 34° | 38° | 47° | 58° | 67° | 73° | 76° | 75° | 68° | 56° | 45° | 37° |
| | 16 | 17 | 18 | 17 | 18 | 16 | 18 | 18 | 20 | 18 | 16 | 16 |

| | J | F | M | A | M | J | J | A | S | O | N | D |
|---|---|---|---|---|---|---|---|---|---|---|---|---|
| **BELGIUM • Brussels** | | | | | | | | | | | | |
| | 30° | 32° | 36° | 41° | 46° | 52° | 54° | 54° | 51° | 45° | 38° | 32° |
| | 40° | 44° | 51° | 58° | 65° | 72° | 73° | 72° | 69° | 60° | 48° | 42° |
| | 10 | 11 | 14 | 12 | 15 | 15 | 14 | 13 | 17 | 14 | 10 | 12 |
| **CROATIA • Dubrovnik** | | | | | | | | | | | | |
| | 42° | 43° | 57° | 52° | 58° | 65° | 69° | 69° | 64° | 57° | 51° | 46° |
| | 53° | 55° | 58° | 63° | 70° | 78° | 83° | 82° | 77° | 69° | 62° | 56° |
| | 13 | 13 | 11 | 10 | 10 | 6 | 4 | 3 | 7 | 11 | 16 | 15 |
| **CZECH REPUBLIC • Prague** | | | | | | | | | | | | |
| | 23° | 24° | 30° | 38° | 46° | 52° | 55° | 55° | 49° | 41° | 33° | 27° |
| | 31° | 34° | 44° | 54° | 64° | 70° | 73° | 72° | 65° | 53° | 42° | 34° |
| | 18 | 17 | 21 | 19 | 18 | 18 | 18 | 19 | 20 | 18 | 18 | 18 |
| **DENMARK • Copenhagen** | | | | | | | | | | | | |
| | 29° | 28° | 31° | 37° | 45° | 51° | 56° | 56° | 51° | 44° | 38° | 33° |
| | 37° | 37° | 42° | 51° | 60° | 66° | 70° | 69° | 64° | 55° | 46° | 41° |
| | 14 | 15 | 19 | 18 | 20 | 18 | 17 | 16 | 14 | 14 | 11 | 12 |
| **EGYPT • Cairo** | | | | | | | | | | | | |
| | 47° | 48° | 52° | 57° | 63° | 68° | 70° | 71° | 68° | 65° | 58° | 50° |
| | 65° | 69° | 75° | 83° | 91° | 95° | 96° | 95° | 90° | 86° | 78° | 68° |
| | 30 | 27 | 30 | 30 | 31 | 30 | 31 | 31 | 30 | 31 | 29 | 30 |
| **FINLAND • Helsinki** | | | | | | | | | | | | |
| | 17° | 15° | 20° | 30° | 40° | 49° | 55° | 53° | 46° | 37° | 30° | 23° |
| | 26° | 25° | 32° | 44° | 56° | 66° | 71° | 68° | 59° | 47° | 37° | 31° |
| | 11 | 10 | 17 | 17 | 19 | 17 | 17 | 16 | 16 | 13 | 11 | 11 |
| **FRANCE • Paris** | | | | | | | | | | | | |
| | 34° | 34° | 39° | 43° | 49° | 55° | 58° | 58° | 53° | 46° | 40° | 36° |
| | 43° | 45° | 54° | 60° | 68° | 73° | 76° | 75° | 70° | 60° | 50° | 44° |
| | 14 | 14 | 19 | 17 | 19 | 18 | 19 | 18 | 17 | 18 | 15 | 15 |
| **FRANCE • Nice** | | | | | | | | | | | | |
| | 35° | 36° | 41° | 46° | 52° | 58° | 63° | 63° | 58° | 51° | 43° | 37° |
| | 50° | 53° | 59° | 64° | 71° | 79° | 84° | 83° | 77° | 68° | 58° | 52° |
| | 23 | 22 | 24 | 23 | 23 | 26 | 29 | 26 | 24 | 23 | 21 | 21 |
| **GERMANY • Munich** | | | | | | | | | | | | |
| | 23° | 23° | 30° | 38° | 45° | 51° | 55° | 54° | 48° | 40° | 33° | 26° |
| | 35° | 38° | 48° | 56° | 64° | 70° | 74° | 73° | 67° | 56° | 44° | 36° |
| | 15 | 12 | 18 | 15 | 16 | 13 | 15 | 15 | 17 | 18 | 15 | 16 |
| **GREAT BRITAIN • London** | | | | | | | | | | | | |
| | 36° | 36° | 38° | 42° | 47° | 53° | 56° | 56° | 52° | 46° | 42° | 38° |
| | 43° | 44° | 50° | 56° | 62° | 69° | 71° | 71° | 65° | 58° | 50° | 45° |
| | 16 | 15 | 20 | 18 | 19 | 19 | 19 | 20 | 17 | 18 | 15 | 16 |

| | J | F | M | A | M | J | J | A | S | O | N | D |
|---|---|---|---|---|---|---|---|---|---|---|---|---|
| **GREECE • Athens** | | | | | | | | | | | | |
| | 44° | 44° | 46° | 52° | 61° | 68° | 73° | 73° | 67° | 60° | 53° | 47° |
| | 55° | 57° | 60° | 68° | 77° | 86° | 92° | 92° | 84° | 75° | 66° | 58° |
| | 15 | 17 | 20 | 21 | 23 | 26 | 29 | 28 | 26 | 23 | 18 | 16 |
| **HUNGARY • Budapest** | | | | | | | | | | | | |
| | 25° | 28° | 35° | 44° | 52° | 58° | 62° | 60° | 53° | 44° | 38° | 30° |
| | 34° | 39° | 50° | 62° | 71° | 78° | 82° | 81° | 74° | 61° | 47° | 39° |
| | 13 | 12 | 11 | 11 | 13 | 13 | 10 | 9 | 7 | 10 | 14 | 13 |
| **IRELAND • Dublin** | | | | | | | | | | | | |
| | 34° | 35° | 37° | 39° | 43° | 48° | 52° | 51° | 48° | 43° | 39° | 37° |
| | 46° | 47° | 51° | 55° | 60° | 65° | 67° | 67° | 63° | 57° | 51° | 47° |
| | 18 | 18 | 21 | 19 | 21 | 19 | 18 | 19 | 18 | 20 | 18 | 17 |
| **ITALY • Rome** | | | | | | | | | | | | |
| | 40° | 42° | 45° | 50° | 56° | 63° | 67° | 67° | 62° | 55° | 49° | 44° |
| | 52° | 55° | 59° | 66° | 74° | 82° | 87° | 86° | 79° | 71° | 61° | 55° |
| | 13 | 19 | 23 | 24 | 26 | 26 | 30 | 29 | 25 | 23 | 19 | 21 |
| **ITALY • Palermo, Sicily** | | | | | | | | | | | | |
| | 46° | 47° | 48° | 52° | 58° | 64° | 69° | 70° | 66° | 60° | 54° | 49° |
| | 60° | 62° | 63° | 68° | 74° | 81° | 85° | 86° | 83° | 77° | 71° | 64° |
| | 19 | 20 | 23 | 24 | 28 | 28 | 31 | 29 | 26 | 23 | 22 | 21 |
| **MOROCCO • Marrakech** | | | | | | | | | | | | |
| | 40° | 43° | 48° | 52° | 57° | 62° | 67° | 68° | 63° | 57° | 49° | 42° |
| | 65° | 68° | 74° | 79° | 84° | 92° | 101° | 100° | 92° | 83° | 73° | 66° |
| | 24 | 23 | 25 | 24 | 29 | 29 | 30 | 30 | 27 | 27 | 27 | 24 |
| **NETHERLANDS • Amsterdam** | | | | | | | | | | | | |
| | 31° | 31° | 34° | 40° | 46° | 51° | 55° | 55° | 50° | 44° | 38° | 33° |
| | 40° | 42° | 49° | 56° | 64° | 70° | 72° | 71° | 67° | 57° | 48° | 42° |
| | 9 | 9 | 15 | 14 | 17 | 16 | 14 | 13 | 11 | 11 | 9 | 10 |
| **NORWAY • Oslo** | | | | | | | | | | | | |
| | 19° | 19° | 25° | 34° | 43° | 50° | 55° | 53° | 46° | 38° | 31° | 25° |
| | 28° | 30° | 39° | 50° | 61° | 68° | 72° | 70° | 60° | 48° | 38° | 32° |
| | 16 | 16 | 22 | 19 | 21 | 17 | 16 | 17 | 16 | 17 | 14 | 14 |
| **POLAND • Kraków** | | | | | | | | | | | | |
| | 22° | 22° | 30° | 38° | 48° | 54° | 58° | 56° | 49° | 42° | 33° | 28° |
| | 32° | 34° | 45° | 55° | 67° | 72° | 76° | 73° | 66° | 56° | 44° | 37° |
| | 16 | 15 | 12 | 15 | 12 | 15 | 16 | 15 | 12 | 14 | 15 | 16 |
| **PORTUGAL • Lisbon** | | | | | | | | | | | | |
| | 46° | 47° | 50° | 53° | 55° | 60° | 63° | 63° | 62° | 58° | 52° | 47° |
| | 57° | 59° | 63° | 67° | 71° | 77° | 81° | 82° | 79° | 72° | 63° | 58° |
| | 16 | 16 | 17 | 20 | 21 | 25 | 29 | 29 | 24 | 22 | 17 | 16 |

| | J | F | M | A | M | J | J | A | S | O | N | D |
|---|---|---|---|---|---|---|---|---|---|---|---|---|
| **PORTUGAL • Faro (Algarve)** | | | | | | | | | | | | |
| | 48° | 49° | 52° | 55° | 58° | 64° | 67° | 68° | 65° | 60° | 55° | 50° |
| | 60° | 61° | 64° | 67° | 71° | 77° | 83° | 83° | 78° | 72° | 66° | 61° |
| | 22 | 21 | 21 | 24 | 27 | 29 | 31 | 31 | 29 | 25 | 22 | 22 |
| **SLOVENIA • Ljubljana** | | | | | | | | | | | | |
| | 25° | 25° | 32° | 40° | 48° | 54° | 57° | 57° | 51° | 43° | 36° | 30° |
| | 36° | 41° | 50° | 60° | 68° | 75° | 80° | 78° | 71° | 59° | 47° | 39° |
| | 13 | 11 | 11 | 13 | 16 | 16 | 12 | 12 | 10 | 14 | 15 | 15 |
| **SPAIN • Madrid** | | | | | | | | | | | | |
| | 35° | 36° | 41° | 45° | 50° | 58° | 63° | 63° | 57° | 49° | 42° | 36° |
| | 47° | 52° | 59° | 65° | 70° | 80° | 87° | 85° | 77° | 65° | 55° | 48° |
| | 23 | 21 | 21 | 21 | 21 | 25 | 29 | 28 | 24 | 23 | 21 | 21 |
| **SPAIN • Almería (Costa del Sol)** | | | | | | | | | | | | |
| | 46° | 47° | 51° | 55° | 59° | 65° | 70° | 71° | 68° | 60° | 54° | 49° |
| | 60° | 61° | 64° | 68° | 72° | 78° | 83° | 84° | 81° | 73° | 67° | 62° |
| | 25 | 24 | 26 | 25 | 28 | 29 | 31 | 30 | 27 | 26 | 26 | 26 |
| **SWEDEN • Stockholm** | | | | | | | | | | | | |
| | 26° | 25° | 29° | 37° | 45° | 53° | 57° | 56° | 50° | 43° | 37° | 32° |
| | 30° | 30° | 37° | 47° | 58° | 67° | 71° | 68° | 60° | 49° | 40° | 35° |
| | 15 | 14 | 21 | 19 | 20 | 17 | 18 | 17 | 16 | 16 | 14 | 14 |
| **SWITZERLAND • Geneva** | | | | | | | | | | | | |
| | 29° | 30° | 36° | 42° | 49° | 55° | 58° | 58° | 53° | 44° | 37° | 31° |
| | 38° | 42° | 51° | 59° | 66° | 73° | 77° | 76° | 69° | 58° | 47° | 40° |
| | 20 | 19 | 22 | 21 | 20 | 19 | 22 | 20 | 20 | 21 | 19 | 21 |
| **TURKEY • Istanbul** | | | | | | | | | | | | |
| | 37° | 36° | 38° | 45° | 53° | 60° | 65° | 66° | 61° | 55° | 48° | 41° |
| | 46° | 47° | 51° | 60° | 69° | 77° | 82° | 82° | 76° | 68° | 59° | 51° |
| | 13 | 14 | 17 | 21 | 23 | 24 | 27 | 27 | 23 | 20 | 16 | 13 |

## Metric Conversion

| | | | | | |
|---|---|---|---|---|---|
| 1 inch | = | 25 millimeters | 1 ounce | = | 28 grams |
| 1 foot | = | 0.3 meter | 1 pound | = | 0.45 kilogram |
| 1 yard | = | 0.9 meter | Temp. (°F) | = | 9/5 °C + 32 |
| 1 mile | = | 1.6 kilometers | 1 kilogram | = | 2.2 pounds |
| 1 sq. yd. | = | 0.8 square meter | 1 kilometer | = | 0.62 mile |
| 1 acre | = | 0.4 hectare | 1 centimeter | = | 0.4 inch |
| 1 quart | = | 0.95 liter | 1 meter | = | 39.4 inches |

# INDEX

# *Start your trip at*
# ***www.ricksteves.com***

**Rick Steves' web site is packed with over 3,000 pages of timely travel information. It's also your gateway to getting FREE monthly travel news from Rick—and more!**

### Free Monthly European Travel News
Fresh articles on Europe's most interesting destinations and happenings. Rick will even send you an e-mail every month (often direct from Europe) with his latest discoveries!

### Timely Travel Tips
Rick Steves' best money-and-stress-saving tips on trip planning, packing, transportation, hotels, health, safety, finances, hurdling the language barrier. . . and more.

### Travelers' Graffiti Wall
Candid advice and opinions from thousands of travelers on everything listed above, plus whatever topics are hot at the moment (discount flights, packing tips, scams. . . you name it).

### Rick's Annual Guide to European Railpasses
The clearest, most comprehensive guide to the confusing array of railpass options out there, and how to choo-choose the railpass that best fits your itinerary and budget. Then you can order your railpass (and get a bunch of great freebies) online from us!

### Great Gear at the Rick Steves Travel Store
Enjoy bargains on Rick's guidebooks, planning maps and TV series DVDs, and on his custom-designed carry-on bags, roll-aboard bags, day packs and light-packing accessories.

### Rick Steves Tours
This year more than 10,000 lucky travelers will explore Europe on a Rick Steves tour. Learn more about our 25 different one-to-three-week itineraries, read uncensored feedback from our tour alums, and sign up for your dream trip online!

### Rick on Radio and TV
Download free podcasts of our weekly "Travel with Rick Steves" public radio show; read the scripts from public television's "Rick Steves' Europe".

### Respect for Your Privacy
Ordering online from us is secure. When you buy something from us, join a tour, or subscribe to Rick's free monthly travel news e-mails, we promise to never share your name, information, or e-mail address with anyone else. You won't be spammed!

**Have fun raising your Travel I.Q. at**
**www.ricksteves.com**

**For a complete list of Rick Steves' guidebooks, see page 15.**

Avalon Travel Publishing
1400 65th Street, Suite 250
Emeryville, CA 94608

AVALON
publishing group incorporated

Avalon Travel Publishing
An Imprint of Avalon Publishing Group, Inc.



Printed in the USA by Worzalla.
First printing August 2006

For the latest on Rick's lectures, guidebooks, tours, and public television series, contact Europe Through the Back Door, Box 2009, Edmonds, WA 98020, tel. 425/771-8303, fax 425/771-0833, www.ricksteves.com, rick@ricksteves.com.

ISBN (10) 1-56691-808-1
ISBN (13) 978-1-56691-808-4
ISSN 1096-794X

**Europe Through the Back Door Senior Editor:** Cameron Hewitt
**ETBD Researchers:** Cameron Hewitt, Lauren Mills
**ETBD Managing Editor:** Risa Laib
**Avalon Travel Publishing Editor and Series Manager:** Madhu Prasher
**Avalon Travel Publishing Project Editor:** Patrick Collins
**Copy Editor:** Matthew Reed Baker
**Proofreader:** Pamela Vevea
**Indexer:** Stephen Callahan
**Production and Typesetting:** Holly McGuire, Patrick David Barber
**Cover Design:** Kari Gim, Laura Mazer
**Maps & Graphics:** David C. Hoerlein, Laura VanDeventer, Lauren Mills, Barb Geisler, Mike Morgenfeld
**Cover Photos:** Front: Kardamyli, Greece © Laura VanDeventer; back: Venus de Milo, Louvre Museum, Paris, France © Vanni / Art Resource, NY
**Front Matter Color Photos:** p.i, Linderhof, Germany © Dominic Bonuccelli; p.iv, Arnhem Open-Air Museum in the Netherlands © Dominic Bonuccelli
**Photography:** Rick Steves (unless otherwise credited)